ORAL HISTORY COLLECTIONS

Compiled and edited by
Alan M. Meckler and Ruth McMullin

R. R. BOWKER COMPANY
A Xerox Education Company
New York & London 1975

Published by R. R. Bowker Co. (A Xerox Education Company)
1180 Avenue of the Americas, New York, N.Y. 10036

Copyright © 1975 by Xerox Corporation

Library of Congress Cataloging in Publication Data

Meckler, Alan M 1945-
    Oral history collections.

    Includes index.
    1. Indexes.   I. McMullin, Ruth, joint author.
II. Title.
A13.M4   026.9098'025   74-32128
ISBN 0-8352-0603-3

Foreword

As this volume is being prepared for publication, the oral history movement has been in existence for a quarter of a century. Twenty-five years of growth and development, some of it slow and much of it unanticipated, has followed the first oral history interviews arranged by Allan Nevins in 1948. The next most important event in the oral history movement probably took place in 1967, when the Oral History Association was organized at Columbia University's conference center, Arden House. This organizational meeting was attended by 145 people representing most areas of the United States. During the six years that the Association has been in existence, it has experienced a growth of membership unusual for a professional society. An increase of several hundred percent has brought the total membership to more than one thousand, and all indications are that this trend will continue.

The most noticeable characteristic of the oral history movement, therefore, has been explosively rapid growth, both in the number of collectors of material and in the volume of the data collected. Thus oral history's most acute problem is that its dynamic expansion has outpaced the dissemination of necessary information about the discipline.

The manifest nature of this problem has caused the directors of many oral history projects to prepare their own guides for their individual collections. Probably, almost all of the several hundred such project administrators in the United States have some sort of reference guide to supply information about their collection. And, although these guides may be generously supplied on request, it is obvious that this is not an adequate method for securing needed information about specific topics of study or about oral history holdings in general.

Some of these guides to individual collections, however, are works of high quality and considerable usefulness. An excellent example is the catalog entitled *The Oral History Collection of Columbia University,* edited by Elizabeth B. Mason and Louis M. Starr in 1973. This 460-page publication is a guide to 360,000 pages of transcripts from interviews with approximately 2,700 persons. This collection, which has expanded substantially after the publication of the guide, continues to grow steadily. It was, in fact, out of date before it was distributed.

And even if it were up-to-date, its very excellence would illustrate the inadequacy of guides to single projects to supply the general need for information about oral history.

There were 230 research programs listed in the Oral History Association's *Directory* which was published in 1971. A substantial majority of these have been established within a few years prior to that date. All later indications are that the rate at which oral history programs are being started has not declined. It may well have increased. This growth illustrates the rapid obsolescence of such reference sources as the Oral History Association's *Directory* and the need for this new guide. For even if each of these programs published directories of the highest quality, the use of several hundred sources to locate needed information is manifestly difficult.

The proposal of the R. R. Bowker Company to publish a current and comprehensive international directory of oral history projects and holdings was therefore welcomed by those involved in the oral history movement. The *Directory* of the Oral History Association, although an excellent publication, was already in need of replacement. Likewise, the valuable effort of the Library of Congress in listing oral history manuscripts in its *National Union Catalogue of Manuscript Collections* and of the *New York Times,* in cooperation with the Microfilming Corporation of America, in filming oral history material and making it available to users had not filled the need for a comprehensive directory. *Oral History Collections,* prepared under the experienced direction of the Bowker Company, presented an opportunity to move toward closing the gap between the development of oral history and the information available about it.

The methodology relied on for the preparation of this volume has involved direct contact by the Bowker Company with those known to be engaged in oral history research. This initial solicitation was implemented in 1973 by a request to all members on the Oral History Association mailing list to supply information on a standard format to be used in the directory. Collated with other material, the replies to these questionnaires have been used to provide a basic collection of material used in *Oral History Collections.* Consequently, in this book is a comprehensive annotated listing of oral history collections located in libraries, oral history centers, and archives. The names of those whose memoirs are included comprises a list of the people most active in recent and contemporary history.

Since this is the first edition of *Oral History Collections*, it does not claim a permanent or definitive source. Future revisions will undoubtedly be needed to keep pace with continuing expansion of the oral history movement. It is to be hoped also that improvements will take place in the reporting of holdings by collectors of oral history material. Any imbalance of representation in this collection was caused in part by the failure of project directors to respond to the Bowker questionnaire. Some of the forms were returned with a plethora of information, others were partially completed, while several were not re-

turned. The consequent variations in listings may be expected to be corrected as the importance of this directory becomes more widely known. Continuing development of oral history research outside the United States will also require additional attention in future revisions of this work.

All of those who are interested in either the collection or the use of oral history material owe much to Alan Meckler and Ruth McMullin for their valuable service in editing the most complete directory in print on this important subject.

CHARLES W. CRAWFORD
Memphis State University
Past President, 1973-1974
Oral History Association

Preface

Prior to the availability of *Oral History Collections*, researchers were dependent upon guesswork and intuition in locating oral history materials in a desired field. The publication of *Oral History Collections* eliminates this research difficulty by providing a comprehensive index to the thousands of interviews located at several hundred oral history centers in the United States and in selected foreign countries.

Questionnaires were sent to over 5000 libraries and institutions in an effort to include every oral history center in existence. However, the difficulties inherent in collecting data for the first edition of a reference book required our employing a cutoff date of January 1974 for accepting information. Consequently, certain interviews and recently established oral history centers have not been included in this first edition. They will certainly be included in the next edition. In some cases, varying degrees of completeness will be noticed for entries in both the name and subject index and in the section pertaining to the oral history centers. The reason for such unevenness was due in part to varying interpretations of the questionnaire, suggesting that plans for future editions shall start with a refinement of the questionnaire itself. There were some oral history centers that, for one reason or another, did not answer our requests for information. To make this book as useful as possible, we have included information about these centers if it was available from another source.

We would like to thank the many people associated with oral history centers who took a great deal of time in supplying us with the information that follows. Our special thanks goes to Louis M. Starr, Director of the Oral History Research Office at Columbia University for his help in the initial stages of this undertaking, and to Charles W. Crawford, President of the Oral History Association for his cooperation and generous advice.

ALAN M. MECKLER
RUTH McMULLIN

How to Use This Book

Oral History Collections has been arranged in two parts: a name and subject index, and a center section consisting of U.S. and foreign oral history centers. Information that applies to all of the interviews in a collection is contained in the section on the oral history centers. Information that applies to a single interview is contained in the name and subject index for that interview. These two sections of the book complement each other and must be used together if the full value of the book is to be realized.

The use of this book will depend greatly upon individual interest. A scholar interested in researching a particular subject will want to know what oral history materials are available, where they are located, and what restrictions might apply. The researcher should be sure to refer to *both* sections of this book in connection with each interview in a field. Because the method of compilation and reporting makes the name part of the index the most complete, the user should be careful to look at listings for all persons involved in a subject as well as at listings for subject categories. While the entries in the name and subject index contain much useful information, one should always check the material about the center itself, since information that applies to every interview at a center will appear there and not in the listings for each interview.

We have tried to include as much information as was available for each name and subject entry. It is wise, however, to contact the center itself because more material may be available now than at the time of compilation and also because the material may have been reevaluated and restrictions removed. New material may be available or existing material may have become indexed since the oral history center answered our questionnaires.

EXCLUSIONS

We have listed as many names and subjects as possible, but have tried to limit the name entries to those which will be valuable to researchers. Since it is unlikely that a researcher will survey the index for names of persons whose names are unknown, we have limited the entries for such interviews to a sub-ject entry only. This occurs most frequently with local history, social and cultural history subjects, and with "anonymous" interviews.

There are several oral history repositories which do not appear in the center section under their respective states, but have still been cited in the name and subject index for the researcher's benefit. These include: Berkeley Baptist Divinity School, California; Brookings Institution, District of Columbia; Carnegie Endowment for International Peace, New York, and Geneva, Switzerland; Delaware State Historical Society; Occidental College, California; Rockefeller Foundation Archives, New York; Syracuse University, New York and University of the Air, Maxwell Air Force Base, Alabama. Information concerning these institutions was unavailable.

ARRANGEMENT

The Name and Subject Index headings are filed alphabetically according to the American Library Association rules for filing. Subject headings are based on the *Sears List*, though not without adaptation. Where it was necessary to yield to a more specialized term, Library of Congress headings were consulted. Where neither *Sears* nor *LC* subject headings were applicable, a more appropriate head was devised. Within subjects, oral history materials are filed alphabetically by the *oral history center* which appears in italic, and then by the *project title*, if necessary.

The U.S. Oral History Centers section and the Foreign Oral History Centers section are organized alphabetically by state or country, and then within each state or country arranged alphabetically by the center.

See references and *See also* references have been included in both sections for the researcher's convenience.

The samples that follow are of entries in the name and subject index and indicate the type of information that is included if it was available to us. Some centers were unable to supply detailed information on each interview in their collection but will be able to answer specific questions from readers about particular interviews.

BISSELL, RICHARD MERVIN, JR. (1909–)

A ——— Economist; Deputy director, Central Intelligence Agency

Eisenhower administration project (1967, 48 pages, permission required to cite or quote, also at *Dwight D. Eisenhower Library KS*) ——— G

Columbia University NY ——— D

B ——— (51 pages, permission of interviewee required) *John F. Kennedy Library MA*

C ——— Dulles oral history collection (1966, 57 pages, open) *Princeton University NJ*

D ——— open) *Princeton University NJ*

BITAN, MOSHE

Deputy general, Israel Foreign Ministry (Jerusalem)

WORLD WAR II: THE HOLOCAUST—RESISTANCE AND RESCUE: (6) Rescue of Jewish children (Hebrew, 17 pages, open) *Hebrew University, Israel* ——— C

CARDON, PHILIP VINCENT (1889–1965)

Agriculturist

(1952, 806 pages, also microfiche, permission required to cite or quote) *Columbia University NY* ——— H

CARDOZO, BENJAMIN

Discussed in Columbia University interviews with Frederic Rene Coudert; James McCauley Landis; John Lord O'Brian ——— I

CAREY, MARGARET CHASE

Smith alumna, class of 1966; Community and college service volunteer

F ——— (1973, 2 hours, 40 pages) *Smith College MA* ——— J

A. Identification by title or position of person.

B. Number of pages if interview has been transcribed.

C. Name of the collection in which this interview took place, if any. Some names of collections may be quite detailed, as is the case with the Hebrew University. This detailed information will help the reader locate the particular collection and subcollections of which this interview is a part.

D. Conditions under which the interview may be available for use. Listed here are restrictions, if any, that are special to this interview and differ from those described in connection with all material at a particular oral history center. Information contained within parentheses refers to the center in italic outside the parentheses. The institution which follows the words "also at" within the parentheses is another center where the material is on deposit. Readers are urged to contact centers regarding any restrictions placed on material they wish to use.

E. Language in which the interview took place (if not English).

F. Number of hours of tape.

G. Date of interview. If the material is from several interviews, the date listed will be the date of the most recent interview. *In process* indicates that the oral material is being prepared for a particular center's archives. The interview may not have been completed, it may not have been completely transcribed, or may be still *in process* for another reason. Readers are urged to contact the center itself to discover the current status of any material they would like to use.

H. Name of oral history center. When either tapes or transcripts are on deposit at more than one center, all such centers are listed.

I. Reference to another interview in which this person or subject was discussed in some detail. This information was available only occasionally and no indication that the subject is discussed in another interview means only that the authors were not informed of any, not that none exists.

J. State or country in which the center is located. This information will enable the reader quickly to locate information about the center itself in the center section.

ABBREVIATIONS

The names of the centers in the name and subject index, wherever not apparent, are followed by the two-letter abbreviations used by the U.S. Post Office for the various states. A list of such abbreviations follows for anyone who may be unfamiliar with them.

Alabama	AL	Hawaii	HI	Missouri	MO
Alaska	AK	Idaho	ID	Montana	MT
Arizona	AZ	Illinois	IL	Nebraska	NE
Arkansas	AR	Indiana	IN	Nevada	NV
California	CA	Iowa	IA	New Hampshire	NH
Canal Zone	CZ	Kansas	KS	New Jersey	NJ
Colorado	CO	Kentucky	KY	New Mexico	NM
Connecticut	CT	Louisiana	LA	New York	NY
Delaware	DE	Maine	ME	North Carolina	NC
District of Columbia	DC	Maryland	MD	North Dakota	ND
Florida	FL	Massachusetts	MA	Ohio	OH
Georgia	GA	Michigan	MI	Oklahoma	OK
Guam	GU	Minnesota	MN	Oregon	OR
		Mississippi	MS	Pennsylvania	PA

Puerto Rico	PR
Rhode Island	RI
South Carolina	SC
South Dakota	SD
Tennessee	TN
Texas	TX
Utah	UT
Vermont	VT
Virgin Islands	VI
Virginia	VA
Washington	WA
West Virginia	WV
Wisconsin	WI
Wyoming	WY

Name and Subject Index

Thomas D. White, 47; Noel Wien, 68; A. S. Wilcockson, 24; Harold B. Willis, 75; Gill Robb Wilson, 89; Charles Yeager, 34 (5264 pages, permission of interviewee required to cite or quote, except as otherwise noted, also at *United States Air Force Academy CO* and *University of the Air, Maxwell Air Force Base AL*) *Columbia University NY*

Long Beach Public Library CA

Oral history project, National Air and Space Museum *Smithsonian Institution DC*

Naval aviation collection *U.S. Naval Institute MD*

Mortimer Wyndham interview *University of California, Los Angeles*

Aeronautical history collection (20 hours, open) *University of Southern California Library*

AEROSPACE INDUSTRIES
Oral history project, National Air and Space Museum *Smithsonian Insitition DC*

AFRICA
Fisk University TN

AFRICA, SOUTH
Charles Eric Lincoln tape *Fisk University TN*

Howard University DC

St. John's University NY

AFRO-AMERICAN STUDIES *see* Black Studies

AFRO-AMERICANS *see* Blacks

AGAMI, CHAYA
YOUTH MOVEMENTS: (2) Netzach in Latvia (Hebrew, 28 pages, open) *Hebrew University, Israel*

YOUTH MOVEMENTS: (2) Netzach in Latvia (Hebrew, 13 pages; Hebrew, 26 pages; open) *Hebrew University, Israel*

AGAMI (AVERBUCH), MOSHE
ANTECEDENTS TO THE STATE OF ISRAEL: (2) "Brichah" (organized escape) (Hebrew, 66 pages, open) *Hebrew University, Israel*

YOUTH MOVEMENTS: (2) Netzach in Latvia (Hebrew, 13 pages; Hebrew, 26 pages; open) *Hebrew University, Israel*

AGHNIDES, THANASSOS (1899–)
Greek diplomat

League of Nations (1966, 506 pages, permission required) *Columbia University NY*

AGING AND AGED
Shirley Camper Soman Collection NY
Washington School of Psychiatry DC

AGOSTINI, PETER (1913–)
Sculptor

(1968, 99 pages) *Archives of American Art—Smithsonian Institution NY*

AGREE, PETER
Challenges to governance by students project (1969, 65 pages, permission required to cite or quote) *Cornell University NY*

AGRICULTURE
Agricultural leaders project *Cornell University NY*
Participants: Morton Adams; Richard Bradfield; Barton W. Bull; Daniel J. Carey; Wm. A. Chandler; James C. Corwith; Harold Cowles; Verne A. Fogg; Edward S. Foster; Donald F. Green, Sr.; Arthur J. Heinicke; Raymond G. Hitchings; Maurice W. Johnson; Halsey B. Knapp; George Lamb; Lawrence MacDaniels; Thomas E. Milliman; William I. Myers; Edgar Raish; Seymour K. Rodenhurst; Paul Smith; Harold Soner; William Stempfle; Philip G. Wakeley; William Waldorf

Sangamon State University IL

Man-land confrontation in the southwest (110 hours, 2000 pages, open) *Texas Tech University*

South Dakota experience, South Dakota Oral History Project *University of South Dakota*

University of Wisconsin, River Falls

Walla Walla College WA

Agricultural transition in the twentieth century *Western Michigan University*

AHARONSON FAMILY
JEWISH COMMUNITIES: (10) Jewish life in Iraq (Hebrew, translated from Arabic, 6 pages, open) *Hebrew University, Israel*

AIKEN, GEORGE DAVID (1892–)
U.S. senator (Vermont)

Eisenhower administration project (1967, 31 pages, open, also at *Dwight D. Eisenhower Library KS*) *Columbia University NY*

(42 pages, open) *John F. Kennedy Library MA*

Dulles oral history collection (1966, 13 pages, open) *Princeton University NJ*

AIMONE, PARNELL M. (1927–)
Chairman, UTU local LC 9

United Transportation Union project (1970, 38 pages, open transcript, permission required to use tape) *Cornell University NY*

AIR FORCE ACADEMY *see* U.S. Air Force

AIRCRAFT PRODUCTION *see* Aerospace Industries

AISO, JOHN FUJIO
Biographical collection (open) *University of California, Los Angeles*

AITCHISON, A. E.
Weyerhaeuser Timber Company (85 pages, permission required) *Columbia University NY*

AKERMAN, HINDA
WORLD WAR II: THE HOLOCAUST—RESISTANCE AND RESCUE: (13) Underground activities of the Lithuanian Jews (Hebrew, 7 pages, open) *Hebrew University, Israel*

AKIN, MORRIS (1911–)
Organizer and district director, Oil, Chemical and Atomic Workers International Union

(46 pages, open) *University of Texas, Arlington*

AKINS, ZOE
Discussed in Columbia University interview with John Hall Wheelock

AKZIN, BINYAMIN
Professor of political science, Hebrew University

HISTORY OF THE YISHUV (PALESTINIAN JEWRY): (7) Etzel and Lehi organizations (Hebrew, 49 pages, open) *Hebrew University, Israel*

ALABAMA—POLITICS AND GOVERNMENT
Alabama Congressmen *Auburn University AL*

ALAMPRESE, MICHAEL R. (1931–)
Chairman, UTU Local 825

United Transportation Union project (1971, 36 pages, permission required to cite or quote transcript, permission required to use tape) *Cornell University NY*

ALAN, CHARLES (1908–)
Art dealer

(1970, 40 pages) *Archives of American Art—Smithsonian Institution NY*

ALASKA
Alaska Historical Library

Alaskan pioneers project. Participants and pages: Jack Brooks, 7; Nat Browne, 33; Edward Crawford, 57; George Gasser, 23; Bobby Sheldon, 36; William R. Sherwin, 40; Sam White, 39; Oscar Winchell, 159 (1959–1962, 394 pages, open) *Columbia University NY*

Tanana-Yukon Historical Society AK

Tongass Historical Society AK

ALAZRAKI, SAMY
Holon orthopedic doctor

JEWISH COMMUNITIES: (8) Izmir community (Hebrew, 33 pages, open) *Hebrew University, Israel*

ALBEE, EDWARD (1928–)
Theatre on film and tape *New York Public Library*

ALBEE, EDWARD
with Alan Schneider
Popular arts collection (86 pages, permission required) *Columbia University NY*

ALLEN, GEORGE VENABLE (1903–1970)
U.S. diplomat

(1962, 77 pages, permission required) *Columbia University NY*

Eisenhower administration project (1967, 136 pages, permission required, also at *Dwight D. Eisenhower Library KS) Columbia University NY*

Dulles oral history collection (1965, 1966, 83 pages, permission required to cite or quote) *Princeton University NJ*

ALLEN, JAMES E., JR.
Educator

(1966, 55 pages, permission required) *Columbia University NY*

ALLEN, JESSIE

South Dakota experience (1962), South Dakota Oral History Project *University of South Dakota*

ALLEN, LEWIS (1908–) with Dorothy Allen (1908–)
Fine printers

(1968, 61 pages) *University of California, Berkeley*

ALLEN, NETTA POWELL (1890–)

China missionaries collection (83 pages, open, also at *Columbia University NY) Claremont Graduate School CA*

ALLEN, ROBERT L.
Author and associate editor, *Black Scholar;* Vice president, Black World Foundation

Fisk University TN

ALLEN, ROGER
Architect

Ferris State College MI

ALLEN, ROY (1921–)
Army Air Corps veteran

Prisoner-of-war project (1970, 88 pages, open) *North Texas State University Oral History Collection*

ALLEN, SALLY VANCE
Smith alumna, class of 1962

(1973, 2 hours, 35 pages) *Smith College MA*

ALLEN, WILLIAM HARVEY (1874–1963)
Civic worker

(1950, 532 pages, also microfiche, permission required to cite or quote) *Columbia University NY*

ALLEN FAMILY, CHURCHILL COUNTY, NEVADA

Discussed in Cecyl Allen Johnson interview *University of Nevada, Reno*

ALLEN MEMORIAL PLANETARIUM
Vigo County Public Library IN

ALLIANCE COLLEGE
Alliance College PA

ALLISON, JOHN

U.S. Air Force Academy project (83 pages, consult center for restriction, also at *United States Air Force Academy CO) Columbia University NY*

ALLISON, JOHN M.

International negotiations project (23 pages, permission required) *Columbia University NY*

ALLRED, DAVID (1936–)
Journalist; Member, Texas House of Representatives (Wichita Falls)

Legislative project (1967, 103 pages; 1968, 66 pages; closed until interviewee's death) *North Texas State University Oral History Collection*

ALLRED, MRS. JAMES V. (1905–)
Wife of former Governor James V. Allred

Ex-governors project (1967–1968, 40 pages, open) *North Texas State University Oral History Collection*

ALLRED, RENNE (1901–)
Attorney for the Receiver (State Insurance Board)

(1968, 328 pages, open upon notification as defined by written agreement) *North Texas State University Oral History Collection*

ALMARZA, CAMILO (1904–)
Labor leader

Argentina in the 1930s (1971, Spanish, 160 pages, open) *Columbia University NY*

ALMELEH, JACOB
University of Washington Libraries

ALMOG (KOPPELEVITZ), YEHUDA
Museum director (Masada)

HISTORY OF THE YISHUV (PALESTINIAN JEWRY): (5) Gedud Ha-Avoda (Labor Brigade) (Hebrew, 21 pages; Hebrew, 87 pages; open) *Hebrew University, Israel*

JEWISH COMMUNITIES: (4) Zionist movement in U.S.S.R. (1917–1935) (Hebrew, 11 pages, open) *Hebrew University, Israel*

ALMOND, EDWARD

Discussed in Columbia University interview with Oliver Prince Smith

ALMOND, J. LINDSAY
Governor (Virginia)

(25 pages, open) *John F. Kennedy Library MA*

ALON, MENACHEM

WORLD WAR II: THE HOLOCAUST—RESISTANCE AND RESCUE: (6) Rescue of Jewish children (Hebrew, 7 pages, open) *Hebrew University, Israel*

ALPHAND, HERVE
French ambassador to United States

(11 pages, permission of interviewee required) *John F. Kennedy Library MA*

ALPINE LAKES PROTECTION SOCIETY
University of Washington Libraries

ALSBERG, HENRY G.

Discussed in Columbia University interview with William Terry Couch

ALSOP, JOSEPH WRIGHT (1910–)
Journalist

Eisenhower administration project (18 pages, permission required to cite or quote, also at *Dwight D. Eisenhower Library KS) Columbia University NY*

Dulles oral history collection (1966, 25 pages, permission required to cite or quote) *Princeton University NJ*

ALSOP, STEWART (1914–1974)
Journalist

Dulles oral history collection (1966, 30 pages, open) *Princeton University NJ*

ALSTON, CHARLES (1907–)
Painter

(1968, 26 pages) *Archives of American Art—Smithsonian Institution NY*

ALTER, GERALD (1919–), HAROLD LARSEN, AND JOHN DE WILDE

World Bank (32 pages, permission of contributor required to cite or quote, also at *Brookings Institution DC) Columbia University NY*

ALTMAN, ARIE, DR.

THE HISTORY OF THE YISHUV (PALESTINIAN JEWRY): (7) Etzel and Lehi organizations (Hebrew, 279 pages, open) *Hebrew University, Israel*

ALTMEYER, ARTHUR JOSEPH (1891–1972)
Administrator

Social Security collection (231 pages, permission required to cite or quote, also at *Social Security Administration MD) Columbia University NY*

Discussed in Columbia University interviews with Barbara Armstrong; A. Henry Aronson; Frank Bane; Bernice Bernstein; Eveline Mabel Burns; Ewan Clague; Isidore Sydney Falk; Maurine Mulliner; Paul and Elizabeth (Mrs. Paul) Raushenbush; Herman Miles Somers; Jack Bernard; Russell Gordon Wagenet

ALTOSE, SOPHIE
University of Washington Libraries

ALTSCHUL, HELEN (MRS. FRANK) (1887–)

Herbert Henry Lehman project (13 pages, permission required to cite or quote) *Columbia University NY*

ALUMNI MAGAZINES

Alumni News project. John Marcham interview *Cornell University NY*

ANDERSON, MAXWELL (1888–1959)
Author; Playwright

(1956, 34 pages, also microfiche, permission required to cite or quote) *Columbia University NY*

ANDERSON, ORVIL A. (1895–)

Aviation collection (51 pages, permission of interviewee required to cite or quote, also at *United States Air Force Academy CO* and *University of the Air, Maxwell Air Force Base AL*) *Columbia University NY*

Henry H. Arnold project (1959, 113 pages, permission required, also at *United States Air Force Academy CO*) *Columbia University NY*

ANDERSON, PALMER

South Dakota experience (1971), South Dakota Oral History Project *University of South Dakota*

ANDERSON, PEARL C.
Philanthropist, Dallas TX

Fisk University TN

ANDERSON, RALPH *see Abe Ruckdaschel*

ANDERSON, ROBERT B.

Discussed in Columbia University interview with Clarence Douglas Dillon

ANDERSON, RUSSELL

McGraw-Hill, Inc. (47 pages, permission required) *Columbia University NY*

ANDERSON, SHERWOOD

Discussed in Columbia University interviews with Mildred Gilman; Ben W. Huebsch

ANDERSON, WALTER STRATTON
Naval officer

Naval history collection (1962, 290 pages, also microfiche, permission required to cite or quote, also at *Division of Naval History DC*) *Columbia University NY*

ANDERSON, MR. AND MRS. WARWICK

Adlai E. Stevenson project (35 pages, permission required) *Columbia University NY*

ANDERSON, WILLIAM HAMILTON (1874–1959)
Prohibitionist

(1950, 148 pages plus papers, open) *Columbia University NY*

ANDERVONT, HOWARD B.
National Institutes of Health MD

ANDREW, GEOFFREY C.

Carnegie Corporation collection (64 pages, permission required) *Columbia University NY*

ANDREWS, BENNY (1930–)
Painter

(1968, 30 pages) *Archives of American Art—Smithsonian Institution NY*

ANDREWS, DANA (1909–)
Popular arts collection (50 pages, open) *Columbia University NY*

ANDREWS, FRANK
Discussed in Columbia University interview with Ira C. Eaker

ANDREWS, FREDERICK N.
Educator, Purdue University

(1970, 51 pages) *Purdue University Archives IN*

ANDREWS, JOHN B.
Discussed in Columbia University Social Security collection

ANDREWS, JUSTIN M.
National Institutes of Health MD

ANDREWS, R. L.
Trainer of pilots for revolutions in Mexico

(1968, 30 minutes, 7 pages, open) *University of Texas, El Paso*

ANESTHETICS

(50 interviews) *Wood Library—Museum of Anesthesiology IL*

ANGELL, JAMES R.
Discussed in Columbia University Carnegie Corporation collection

ANGELL, SIR NORMAN (1872–1967)
Author

(1951, 278 pages, also microfiche, permission required to cite or quote) *Columbia University NY*

ANGELL, ROBERT C.
University of Michigan

ANGELOU, MAYA
Author; Actress; Screenwriter; Playwright; Poet

Fisk University TN

ANGLE, PAUL
Discussed in Sangamon State University IL George W. Bunn interview

ANHALT, EDWARD
Screenwriter

An oral history of the motion picture in America (open) *University of California, Los Angeles*

ANI, ELIAHU (–1963)

JEWISH COMMUNITIES: (10) Jewish life in Iraq (Hebrew, translated from Arabic, 7 pages, open) *Hebrew University, Israel*

ANI, ROSE
with Violet Gabbay

JEWISH COMMUNITIES: (10) Jewish life in Iraq (Hebrew, 5 pages, open) *Hebrew University, Israel*

ANN, DORIS
(1 reel) *Broadcast Pioneers Library DC*

ANN ARBOR, MICHIGAN
University of Michigan

ANNAN, ROBERT

Mining Engineers (24 pages, permission required to cite or quote) *Columbia University NY*

ANNETT, FRED A. (1879–1959)

McGraw-Hill, Inc. (65 pages, permission required) *Columbia University NY*

ANNIS, EDWARD ROLAND (1913–)
Physician

(1967, 84 pages, closed during interviewee's lifetime) *Columbia University NY*

ANSBACHER, YEHUDA
Tel-Aviv rabbi

WORLD WAR II: THE HOLOCAUST—RESISTANCE AND RESCUE: (2) Rescue of Jews via Spain and Portugal (Hebrew, 23 pages, open) *Hebrew University, Israel*

ANSORGE, MARTIN CHARLES (1882–1967)
Lawyer; Congressman

(1949, 74 pages, also microfiche, permission required to cite or quote) *Columbia University NY*

ANTHAL, ROBERT
Accountant, Warburg and Company (New York)

WORLD WAR II: THE HOLOCAUST—RESISTANCE AND RESCUE: (1) The Joint (American Jewish Joint Distribution Committee) (English, 2 pages, closed, written interview) *Hebrew University, Israel*

ANTONINUS, BROTHER (1912–)
Poet; Handpress printer

(1966, 97 pages) *University of California, Berkeley*

ANTOVIL, SHRAGA

JEWISH COMMUNITIES: (3) Lithuanian Jewry between the two world wars (Hebrew, 34 pages, open) *Hebrew University, Israel*

ANUNDSON, JOHN

South Dakota experience (1970), South Dakota Oral History Project *University of South Dakota*

APACHE INDIANS (WESTERN)

Doris Duke American Indian Oral History Project *Arizona State Museum*

APENCELER, URI

Formerly active in the American Jewish Joint Distribution Committee (Nice)

WORLD WAR II: THE HOLOCAUST—RESISTANCE AND RESCUE: (3) Jewish underground movement in wartime France (Hebrew, 47 pages, open) *Hebrew University, Israel*

APLIN, CHARLES W. (1877-1971)
Painter; Carpenter
(1968, 87 pages, open) *University of Nevada, Reno*

APPALACHIAN REGION
Appalachian oral history project *Alice Lloyd College KY*
Appalachian State University NC
East Tennessee State University
Emory & Henry College VA
Madison College VA

APPLEBY, PAUL HENSON (1891-1963)
Political scientist
(1952, 360 pages, also microfiche, permission required to cite or quote) *Columbia University NY*

APPLEMAN, ROY E.
Historic preservation *Charles B. Hosmer, Jr. Collection IL*
Independence National Historical Park (27 pages, permission required) *Columbia University NY*

APOLLINAIRE, GUILLAUME
Discussed in Columbia University interview with Jacques Barzun

ARAPAHO INDIANS
State Historical Society of Colorado

ARAM, JOHN LORENZO (1912-)
Weyerhaeuser Timber Company (98 pages, permission required) *Columbia University NY*

ARARAT, ZALMAN
YOUTH MOVEMENTS: (3) He-Halutz movement (Hebrew, 11 pages, open) *Hebrew University, Israel*

ARATA, LARRY
White House upholsterer (6 pages, open) *John F. Kennedy Library MA*

ARCHBOLD, JOHN
Discussed in Columbia University interview with Michael Late; and in Benedum and the oil industry collection

ARCHER, WILLIAM ANDREW
Hunt Institute for Botanical Documentation

ARCHIBALD, DAVID W.
Ricks College ID

ARCHIBALD, DOUGLAS N.
Challenges to governance by students project (1970, 78 pages, permission required to cite or quote) *Cornell University NY*

ARCHIBALD, LILLY S.
Ricks College ID

ARCHITECTURE—CALIFORNIA
Robert Field interview, Fine arts collection *University of California, Los Angeles*

ARCHITECTURE—CONSERVATION AND RESTORATION
Charles B. Hosmer, Jr. Collection IL
Independence National Historical Park *Columbia University NY*
Historic preservation in Nantucket *Cornell University NY*

ARCHITECTURE—INDIANA
Vigo County Public Library IN

ARCHITECTURE—TERRE HAUTE, INDIANA
Vigo County Public Library IN

ARCHITECTURE—WORCESTER, MASSACHUSETTS
Worcester Historical Society MA

ARENDS, LESLIE CORNELIUS (1895-)
Robert A. Taft project (21 pages, permission required) *Columbia University NY*

AREST, AVRAHAM
JEWISH COMMUNITIES: (4) Zionist movement in U.S.S.R. (1917-1935) (Hebrew, 11 pages, open) *Hebrew University, Israel*

ARENSBERG, ROSE
University of Washington Libraries

ARGENTINA
Argentina in the 1930s. Participants and pages: Diego Abad de Santillan, 20; Camilo Almarza, 160; Cecilio Benitez de Castro, 13; Lucio Bonilla, 103; Andres Cabona, 116; Guido Clutterbuck, 20; Luis Danussi, 87; Jorge del Rio, 41; Jose Domenech, 192 (*certain pages closed*); Hector Duarte, 40; Carlos Emery, 33; Jesus Fernandez, 31; Alfredo Fidanza, 21; Manuel Fossa, 39; Mateo Fossa, 77; Luis F. Gay, 107; Americo Ghioldi, 50; Rafael Ginocchio, 67; Roberto Giusti, 59; Ricardo Guardo, 62; Roberto Habiague, 147; Carlos Ibarguren, 48; Julio Irazusta, 51; Ernesto Janin, 57; Arturo Juaretche, 221; Emilio Jofre, 40; Julio A. Lagos, 31; Roberto Lobos, 55; Juan Maggi, 123; Ernesto Malacorto, 64 (*closed until 1980*); Luciano F. Molinas, 25; Alberto Morello, 30; Francisco Muro de Nadal, 59; Maria Rosa Oliver, 57; Jose Luis Pena, 74; Francisco Perez Leiros, 180 (*permission required to cite or quote*); Jorge Walter Perkins, 3; Federico Pinedo, 84 (*permission required to cite or quote*); Pedro Pistarini, 46; Jose Luis Portos, 47; Luis Ramicone, 43; Juan Rodriguez, 70; Luis Maria Rodriguez, 21; Julian Sancerni Gimenez, 7; Silvano Santander, 81; Dario Sarachaga, 21; Fernando Sola, 50; Diogenes Taboada, 25; Mariano Tedesco, 78; Adolfo Vicchi, 173 (1971, continuing project, Spanish, 3349 pages, open except as noted) *Columbia University NY*
JEWISH COMMUNITIES: (7) Jewish life in Latin America *Hebrew University, Israel*

ARGOV, LEVI
ANTECEDENTS TO THE STATE OF ISRAEL: (2) (organized escape) (Hebrew, 42 pages, open) *Hebrew University, Israel*

ARGUEDAS
Discussed in University of Texas, El Paso, Chester Christian interview (two tapes)

ARIEL, ALEXANDER
Member, Kibbutz Mishmarot
JEWISH COMMUNITIES: (4) Zionist movement in U.S.S.R. (1917-1935) (Hebrew, 12 pages, open) *Hebrew University, Israel*

ARIEL (FISCHER), JOSEPH
Central figure, French Jewry during World War II
WORLD WAR II: THE HOLOCAUST—RESISTANCE AND RESCUE: (2) Rescue of Jews via Spain and Portugal (Hebrew, 9 pages, open) *Hebrew University, Israel*

ARIEL, TOVA
YOUTH MOVEMENTS: (2) Netzach in Latvia (Hebrew, 46 pages, open) *Hebrew University, Israel*

ARIELI, MOSHE
YOUTH MOVEMENTS: (2) Netzach in Latvia (Hebrew, 21 pages, open) *Hebrew University, Israel*

ARIKARA INDIANS
American Indian research project *University of South Dakota*

ARIZONA
Arizona State University

ARKANSAS
State College of Arkansas

ARKHURST, JOYCE COOPER
Librarian; Author
Fisk University TN

ARLIN, HAROLD
First full-time radio announcer
(1971, 1 reel) *Broadcast Pioneers Library DC*

ARMAN (ARMAN, PIERRE FERNANDEZ) (1928-)
Sculptor
(1968, 25 pages) *Archives of American Art—Smithsonian Institution NY*

ARMOUR, CLAUDE
Edward Hull Crump and his regime *Memphis Public Library and Information Center TN*

ARMSTRONG, BARBARA (1890-)
Lawyer
Social Security collection (1965, 317 pages, permission required, also at Social Security Administration MD) *Columbia University NY*
Discussed in Columbia University interview with James Douglas Brown

ARMSTRONG, CALVIN
University of Washington Libraries WA

ARMSTRONG, CHARLES
National Institutes of Health MD

ARMSTRONG, HENRY
Black St. Louis leaders collection *University of Missouri, St. Louis*

ARMSTRONG, JAMES SINCLAIR (1915–)
Eisenhower administration project (94 pages, closed during interviewee's lifetime, also at *Dwight D. Eisenhower Library KS) Columbia University NY*

ARMSTRONG, LOUIS
Tulane University LA

Jazzmen on the Mississippi *University of Missouri, St. Louis*

Discussed in Columbia University interview with Max Gissen

ARMSTRONG, ROY
Communications Workers of America collection *University of Iowa Libraries*

ARMSTRONG, W. PARK, JR. (1907–)
Foreign Service officer

Dulles oral history collection (1965, 45 pages, permission required to cite, quote, or copy) *Princeton University NJ*

ARMY *see U.S. Army*

ARNASON, H. HARVARD (1909–)
Art administrator; Art historian

(1970, 45 pages) *Archives of American Art— Smithsonian Institution NY*

ARNER, FRED
Social Security collection (47 pages, closed during interviewee's lifetime, also at *Social Security Administration MD) Columbia University NY*

ARNESON, ART
South Dakota experience (1971), South Dakota Oral History Project *University of South Dakota*

ARNEY, CECIL
Special Forces technical sergeant, Vietnam War

Jennings County Public Library IN

ARNHEIM, RUDOLPH (1904–)
Psychologist

(1965, 10 pages) *Archives of American Art— Smithsonian Institution NY*

ARNOLD, ELEANOR (MRS. HENRY H.)
Henry H. Arnold project (1959, 108 pages, permission required, also at *United States Air Force Academy CO) Columbia University NY*

ARNOLD, FRANCIS A., JR.
National Institutes of Health MD

ARNOLD, FRANK ATKINSON (1867– 1958)
Radio pioneers collection (1951, 101 pages, open) *Columbia University NY*

ARNOLD, LESLIE PHILIP (1894–)
Aviation collection (25 pages, permission of interviewee required to cite or quote, also at *United States Air Force Academy CO and University of the Air, Maxwell Air Force Base AL) Columbia University NY*

ARNOLD, HENRY H. (1886–1950)
General; First Commander of Army Air Forces

Henry H. Arnold project. Participants and pages: Orvil A. Anderson, 113; Eleanor Pool (Mrs. Henry H.) Arnold, 108; John Leland Atwood, 26; Eugene Beebe, 80; James Henry Burns, 26; Charles P. Cabell, 59; Benjamin Castle, 78; Frederick Warren Conant, 28; Donald Wills Douglas, 137; Ira C. Eaker, 184; Grandison Gardner, 54; Robert Ellsworth Gross, 29; W. Averell Harriman, 60; Sir Arthur Harris, 85; James Howard Kindelberger, 57; Frank P. Lahm, 31; Robert Abercrombie Lovett, 69; Leroy Lutes, 32; Thomas D. Milling, 100; A. C. Peterson, 31; Elwood Quesada, 18; Arthur Emmons Raymond, 24; Sir Henry Self, 56; Sir John Slessor, 38; Carl Spaatz, 81; Henry Wyman Strangman, 38; Hayden Wagner, 35; Kenneth B. Wolfe, 49 (1959–1960, 1726 pages, permission required, also *United States Air Force Academy CO) Columbia University NY*

Discussed in Columbia University interviews with John Richardson Alison and Lawrence Dale Bell

ARNOLD, HENRY J.
Hartwick College NY

ARNOLD, THURMAN WESLEY (1891– 1970)
Lawyer

(1962, 46 pages, permission required) *Columbia University NY*

James Lawrence Fly project (16 pages, closed until January 1, 1982) *Columbia University NY*

Discussed in Columbia University interview with Gordon Evans Dean

ARNOLD, WILLIAM W. (1878–1957)
Benedum and the oil industry (15 pages, open) *Columbia University NY*

ARNST, JOHN *see Arthur Ashem*

ARNSTEIN, FLORA JACOBI
Teacher

(1964, 35 pages) *University of California, Berkeley*

ARNSTEIN, LAWRENCE (1880–)
Public servant

(1964, 292 pages) *University of California, Berkeley*

ARNSTEIN, MARGARET
Smith alumna, class of 1925; Dean, Yale Nursing School

(1973, 2 hours, 36 pages) *Smith College MA*

ARONSON, A. HENRY
Director of personnel, Social Security Board

Social Security collection (1965, 173 pages, closed during interviewee's lifetime, also at *Social Security Administration MD) Columbia University NY*

ARROWSMITH, WILLIAM (1924–) with Roger Shattuck
American cultural leaders project (16 pages, closed pending publication of a study) *Columbia University NY*

ART, AFRO-AMERICAN
Fisk University TN

ART, AMERICAN
(1200 interviews) *Archives of American Art— Smithsonian Institution NY*

ART—CALIFORNIA
Conrad Buff interview, Fine arts collection *University of California, Los Angeles*

Caroline Liebig interview, Fine arts collection *University of California, Los Angeles*

ART—COLLECTORS AND COLLECTING
Archives of American Art—Smithsonian Institution NY

ART, LATIN AMERICAN
Hispanic Society of America NY

ART—OHIO
Arts in Columbus (1960–1970) collection *Ohio Historical Society*

ART—STUDY AND TEACHING
Temple University PA

ART CRITICISM
Archives of American Art—Smithsonian Institution NY

ART CURATORS
Archives of American Art—Smithsonian Institution NY

ART DEALERS
Archives of American Art—Smithsonian Institution NY

ARTHUR, GEORGE K. (1899–)
Popular arts collection (22 pages, open) *Columbia University NY*

ARTHUR ANDERSEN AND COMPANY
see E. L. Wehner

ATWELL, ROSS
Labor leader, United Steelworkers of America

(1968, 23 pages) *Pennsylvania State University*

ATWOOD, JOHN LELAND (1904–)
Henry H. Arnold project (26 pages, permission required, also at *United States Air Force Academy CO*) *Columbia University NY*

Oral history project, National Air and Space Museum *Smithsonian Institution DC*

AUB, JOSEPH CHARLES (1890–)
Physician

(1957, 481 pages, permission required to cite or quote) *Columbia University NY*

AUBURN UNIVERSITY
Auburn University AL

AUDEMARS, EDMOND
Aviation collection (8 pages, permission of interviewee required to cite or quote, also at *United States Air Force Academy CO* and *University of the Air, Maxwell Air Force Base AL*) *Columbia University NY*

AUDUBON SOCIETIES
The National Audubon Society *Vigo County Public Library IN*

AULTMAN, LELA MAY
(1970) *State Historical Society of Colorado*

AUNG, U HTIN (1909–)
Burmese educator

(1965, 128 pages, permission required) *Columbia University NY*

AURAND, EVAN PETER (1917–)
U.S. Naval officer; Naval aide to President Eisenhower (1957–1961)

Eisenhower administration project (1967, 138 pages, permission required to cite or quote, also at *Dwight D. Eisenhower Library KS*) *Columbia University NY*

AURAND, HENRY S. (1894–)
Army officer

Eisenhower administration project (1968, 34 pages, permission required to cite or quote, also at *Dwight D. Eisenhower Library KS*) *Columbia University NY*

AUSCHWITZ AND BIRKENAU CAMPS
WORLD WAR II: THE HOLOCAUST—RESISTANCE AND RESCUE: (8) Theresienstadt ghetto; (9) Resistance to the "final solution" in Auschwitz *Hebrew University, Israel*

AUSLANDER, JOAN *see* Electric Power Failures

AUSMUS, DELBERT
Colonel

Biographical collection *University of California, Los Angeles*

AUSTIN, LOUIE T., M.D.
Mayo Clinic Foundation MN

AUSTIN, WARREN
Discussed in Columbia University interview with James William Barco

AUSTRAL ISLANDS, SOUTH PACIFIC
The Genealogical Society of the Church of Jesus Christ of Latter-Day Saints UT

AUTHORS
Writers and authors collection. Participants: Aldous Huxley; William Inge; Christopher Isherwood; Lawrence Lipton; Kyle Palmer; Dorothy Parker; Ramon Sender (20 hours, 75 pages, open) *University of Southern California Library*

AUTHORS, AMERICAN
Interviews with southern writers *Memphis State University TN*

Montgomery County—Norristown Public Library PA

Samuel Guy Endore interview Biographical collection *University of California, Los Angeles*

Alfred E. Van Vogt interview *University of California, Los Angeles*

AUTHORS, EXPATRIATE
Southern Illinois University

AUTOMOBILE INDUSTRY AND TRADE
Flint Public Library MI

Ford Archives MI

General Motors Corporation MI

Wyndham Mortimer interview *University of California, Los Angeles*

Reed Scott interview *University of California, Los Angeles*

AVENOL, JOSEPH
Discussed in Columbia University interviews with Thanassos Aghnides; Pablo de Azcarate y Florez; Branko Lukac

AVERY, ISAAC
White House carpenter

(22 pages, open) *John F. Kennedy Library MA*

AVERY, OSWALD T.
Discussed in Columbia University interview with René Jules Dubos

AVERY, SALLY
(1973, 48 pages, permission required to use) *Cornell University NY*

AVERY, TEX
Animator and director

An oral history of the motion picture in American (open) *University of California, Los Angeles*

AVIATION *see* Aeronautics

AVIGDORI, BELLA
YOUTH MOVEMENTS: (2) Netzach in Latvia (Hebrew, 40 pages, open) *Hebrew University, Israel*

AVNER (HIRSCH), GERSHON
Former official, Jewish Agency (London); Israeli foreign service

ANTECEDENTS TO THE STATE OF ISRAEL: (1) Jewish Agency (Hebrew, 16 pages, open) *Hebrew University, Israel*

AVRAHAMI, ELIEZER
JEWISH COMMUNITIES: (11) Jewish community of Iran (Hebrew, 62 pages, open) *Hebrew University, Israel*

AVRIEL, EHUD
Chairman, Zionist General Council

ANTECEDENTS TO THE STATE OF ISRAEL: (3) "Ha 'apalah" (illegal immigration) (Hebrew, 38 pages, open) *Hebrew University, Israel*

WORLD WAR II: THE HOLOCAUST—RESISTANCE AND RESCUE: (6) Rescue of Jewish children (Hebrew, 11 pages, open) *Hebrew University, Israel*

AVRUTIS, WILLIAM J. (1901–)
National Labor Relations Board project (1970, 33 pages, open) *Cornell University NY*

AYCOCK, A. LEWIS
Wake Forest University NC

AYMAN, SVEN
Dag Hammarskjold project (11 pages, permission required to cite or quote) *Columbia University NY*

AYRES, HOMER
South Dakota experience (1971), South Dakota Oral History Project *University of South Dakota*

AZARIA, MALKA
WORLD WAR II: THE HOLOCAUST—RESISTANCE AND RESCUE: (2) Rescue of Jews via Spain and Portugal (Hebrew, 25 pages, open) *Hebrew University, Israel*

AZARIA (HELFGOTT), ZVI
Rabbi

ANTECEDENTS TO THE STATE OF ISRAEL: (2) "Brichah" (organized escape) (Hebrew, 46 pages, open) *Hebrew University, Israel*

AZCARATE FLOREZ, PABLO DE (1890–)
Diplomat

League of Nations (1966, 80 pages, permission required to cite or quote) *Columbia University NY*

League of Nations (joint interview with Edouard de Haller and W. Van Asch Van Wijck, 1965, 156 pages, permission required to cite or quote) *Columbia University NY*

B

BAKER, NEWTON D.
Discussed in Columbia University interviews with Stanley Myer Isaacs; James Wolcott Wadsworth

BAKER, ROY
(1972) *Wabash Carnegie Public Library IN*

BAKER, SARAH
Saranac Valley history (1 cassette, open) *Plattsburgh State University College NY*

BAKER, WALTER RANSOM GAIL (1892-1960)
Radio pioneers collection (20 pages, open) *Columbia University NY*

BAKHMETEFF, BORIS ALEXANDER (1880-1951)
Diplomat
(1950, 568 pages, permission required) *Columbia University NY*
Discussed in Columbia University interview with Frederic René Coudert

BAKKE, MARIE
South Dakota experience (1971), South Dakota Oral History Project *University of South Dakota*

BAKSHI, HAIM
Jerusalem dentist
CULTURE AND EDUCATION: (2) Higher education among Iraqi Jews (Hebrew, 6 pages, open) *Hebrew University, Israel*

BALABAN, EDITH
Widow of Nathan Harry Miller (deputy district attorney, Alameda County)
(1971, 10 pages) *University of California, Berkeley*

BALANCHINE, GEORGE
Discussed in Columbia University interview with Richard Rodgers

BALDWIN, CALVIN BENHAM (1902-)
Executive
(1951, 37 pages, closed during lifetime) *Columbia University NY*
Discussed in Columbia University interview with Will Winton Alexander

BALDWIN, CHARLES
U.S. ambassador to Malaysia
(78 pages, open) *John F. Kennedy Library MA*

BALDWIN, HANSON
Journalism lectures (17 pages, permission required to cite or quote) *Columbia University NY*

BALDWIN, JOHN E. (1894-)
Sales representative
(1964, 131 pages, permission required to cite or quote) *Cornell University NY*

BALDWIN, JOSEPH CLARK (1897-1957)
U.S. congressman
(1950, 73 pages plus papers, also microfiche, permission required to cite or quote) *Columbia University NY*

BALDWIN, MILDRED
James B. Duke project (49 pages, permission required, also at *Duke University NC*) *Columbia University NY*

BALDWIN, RAYMOND E.
University of Connecticut

BALDWIN, ROGER NASH (1884-)
Political reformer
(1954, 666 pages; 1963, 183 pages; 1965, 30 pages; also microfiche, permission required to cite or quote) *Columbia University NY*
Occupation of Japan (1961, 116 pages, permission required to cite or quote) *Columbia University NY*

BALDWIN, VIRA MAY THOMPSON
Ricks College ID

BALER, DONALD MARTIN
Ricks College ID

BALEWA, ALHAJI SIR ABUBAKER TRAFAWA
Prime minister, Federal Republic of Nigeria
(4 pages, open) *John F. Kennedy Library MA*

BALFOUR, ARTHUR
Discussed in Columbia University interview with Sir Robert Alexander Watson-Watt

BALINT, MICHAEL
Psychoanalytic movement collection (1965, 78 pages, permission required to cite or quote) *Columbia University NY*

BALL, EVE
Author; Authority on American Indians
(1969, 30 minutes, 18 pages, open) *University of Texas, El Paso*

BALL, GEORGE WILDMAN (1909-)
Adlai E. Stevenson project (29 pages, permission required) *Columbia University NY*
Discussed in Columbia University interview with Marietta (Mrs. Ronald) Tree

BALL, LUCILLE
Actress
Hollywood Center for the Audio-Visual Arts CA

BALL, ROBERT M. (1914-)
Social Security collection (84 pages, permission required, also at *Social Security Administration MD*) *Columbia University NY*

BALLADS *see* Folk Songs

BALLANTINE, JOSEPH (1888-1973)
Consular officer
Occupation of Japan (1961, 271 pages, also microfiche, permission required to cite or quote) *Columbia University NY*

BALLANTINE, NORMAN S.
(1964) *State Historical Society of Colorado*

BALLANTINE, JOHN JENNINGS (1896-1970)
Naval officer
Naval history collection (1964, 758 pages, also microfiche, permission required to cite or quote) *Columbia University NY*

BALLEW, SMITH
"Big Band" era (open) *Texas Tech University*

BALOGH, FRANK D.
Hungarian history *University of Southern California Library*

BALTIMORE, MARYLAND
Maryland Historical Society

BAMBLE, MRS. J. O.
South Dakota experience (1970), South Dakota Oral History Project *University of South Dakota*

BAMBLE, TOM
South Dakota experience (1971), South Dakota Oral History Project *University of South Dakota*

BANCROFT, MRS. NORTON, AND CAROLINE BANCROFT
(1958) *State Historical Society of Colorado*

BANCROFT, PHILIP (1881-)
Farmer
Interviews on agriculture, water resources, and land use (1962, 508 pages) *University of California, Berkeley*
Recollections of Hubert Howe Bancroft (1971, 41 pages) *University of California, Berkeley*

BANE, FRANK (1893-)
Public administrator; Government official
(1965, 281 pages, permission required to cite or quote, also at *Columbia University NY*) *University of California, Berkeley*
Social Security collection (1965, 121 pages, open, also at *Social Security Administration MD*) *Columbia University NY*
Discussed in Columbia University interviews with Ewan Clague; Lavinia Engle

BANGS, EVA HALL
South Dakota experience (1970), South Dakota Oral History Project *University of South Dakota*

BANKS, CHARLES LOUIS (1914-)
Brigadier general, U.S. Marine Corps (service: 1936-1959)

BARKIN, SOLOMON (1907–   )
Economist
(1960, 141 pages, closed during interviewee's lifetime) *Columbia University NY*

BARKLE, CHARLES
South Dakota experience (1971), South Dakota Oral History Project *University of South Dakota*

BARLAS, HAIM
Former director, Jewish Agency Immigration Department; Wartime representative, Jewish Agency (Istanbul)
WORLD WAR II: THE HOLOCAUST—RESISTANCE AND RESCUE: (15) Contacts between the Yishuv (Palestinian Jewry) and the U.S.S.R. during W.W. II. (Hebrew, 33 pages, open) *Hebrew University, Israel*

BARLOW, HOWARD (1892–1972)
Orchestra conductor
Radio pioneers collection (1951, 213 pages, open) *Columbia University NY*

BARLOW, MARK, JR.
Challenges to governance by students project (1970, 111 pages, permission to use for next 5 years; 1970, 28 pages, open) *Cornell University NY*

BARNABY, LOUIS
Former William H. Miner employee
(Open) *Plattsburgh State University College NY*

BARNARD, B. W.
University of North Carolina, Charlotte

BARNARD, ROLLIN (1922–   )
Assistant postmaster general (1959–1961)
Eisenhower administration project (1967, 60 pages, permission required, also at *Dwight D. Eisenhower Library KS*) *Columbia University NY*

BARNEA, DOV
Director, Municipal Education Department (Beer-Sheva)
WORLD WAR II: THE HOLOCAUST—RESISTANCE AND RESCUE: (8) Theresienstadt ghetto (Hebrew, 44 pages, open) *Hebrew University, Israel*

BARNES, BEN (1937–   )
Former speaker, Texas House of Representatives (1964–1968)
Legislative project (1968, 37 pages, open; 1970, 19 pages, open) *North Texas State University Oral History Collection*

BARNES, BRUCE A.
South Dakota experience (1971), South Dakota Oral History Project *University of South Dakota*

BARNES, DONALD
Presidential interpreter, Department of State
(108 pages, permission of interviewee required) *John F. Kennedy Library MA*

BARNES, ESTELLA
Appalachian State University NC

BARNES, HENRY L.
South Dakota experience (1971), South Dakota Oral History Project *University of South Dakota*

BARNES, JOSEPH (1907–1970)
Newspaperman
(1953, 300 pages, closed until February 28, 1975) *Columbia University NY*

BARNES, OTHO
University of Southern Mississippi

BARNES, PATRICK HENRY (–1969)
Radio pioneers collection (35 pages, open) *Columbia University NY*

BARNES, ROSWELL P. (1901–   )
Clergyman
Dulles oral history collection (1964, 42 pages, permission required to cite or quote) *Princeton University NJ*

BARNES, STANLEY N.
Southern California leader in the formation of the California Republican Assembly
Earl Warren oral history project (in process) *University of California, Berkeley*

BARNES, WILLIAM
Discussed in Columbia University interview with John Lord O'Brian

BARNET, WILL (1911–   )
Painter
(1964, 120 pages; 1968, 78 pages) *Archives of American Art—Smithsonian Institution NY*

BARNETT, JOSEPH M.
Radio pioneers collection (30 pages, open) *Columbia University NY*

BARNETT, POWELL
University of Washington Libraries

BARNETT, ROSS
Mississippi governor
Journalism lectures (23 pages, permission required to cite or quote) *Columbia University NY*
(24 pages, open) *John F. Kennedy Library MA*
University of Southern Mississippi

BARNHARDT, W. H.
University of North Carolina, Charlotte

BAROSS, GABOR
Hungarian history *University of Southern California Library*

BARR, DAVID PRESWICK (1889–   )
Physician
(1957, 130 pages, permission required) *Columbia University NY*

BARRAZA, MACLOVIO
Labor leader
(1969, 54 pages) *Pennsylvania State University*

BARRETT, EDWARD W.
Discussed in Columbia University International negotiations collection

BARRETT, WILLIAM (1888–   )
Farm manager
(1964, 66 pages, open) *Cornell University NY*

BARRIERE, JOHN E.
Member, 1948 Democratic national committee
Harry S. Truman Library MO

BARRON, WILLIAM
Attorney general: West Virginia governor
(14 pages, open) *John F. Kennedy Library MA*

BARSHOP, IRVING
Socialist movement project (27 pages, permission required to cite or quote) *Columbia University NY*

BART, ZEEV
Wartime leader, Slovakian Betar movement; Editor, Yedioth Chadashoth (Tel-Aviv)
WORLD WAR II: THE HOLOCAUST—RESISTANCE AND RESCUE: (11) Jewish resistance in Slovakia (Hebrew, 12 pages, open) *Hebrew University, Israel*

BARTEMEIER, LEO, M.D.
Former president, American Psychiatric Association
American Psychiatric Association DC

BARTHELMESS, WES
Robert F. Kennedy's press secretary
(171 pages, permission of interviewee required, no quoting permitted) *John F. Kennedy Library MA*

BARTHELMESS, RICHARD (1897–1963)
Popular arts collection (45 pages, open) *Columbia University NY*

BARTHOLOMEW, HARLAND
Civil engineer; Planner
American Society of Civil Engineers NY

BARTLETT, DAVID
Weyerhaeuser Timber Company (59 pages, permission required) *Columbia University NY*

BARTLETT, COLONEL LELAND D. (1899–   )
Retired Army colonel; Survivor of the Siege of Corregidor
Prisoner-of-war project (1972, 126 pages, open) *North Texas State University Oral History Collection*

BAXTER, PROF. HUBERT E.
(1969, 32 pages, open) *Cornell University NY*

BAXTER, LEONE
Cofounder, Whitaker & Baxter, Inc., early political public relations firm involved in Earl Warren's 1942 campaign

Earl Warren oral history project (in process) *University of California, Berkeley*

BAYLESS, JAMES
Rauscher-Pierce, Oral business history project *University of Texas, Austin*

BAYLEY, EDWIN
Wisconsin Governor Gaylord Nelson's press secretary, Peace Corps and AID administrator

(121 pages, permission of interviewee required) *John F. Kennedy Library MA*

BAYLOR UNIVERSITY
Baylor project *Baylor University TX*

BAYNE-JONES, STANHOPE (1888-1971)
Robert A. Taft project (62 pages, permission required) *Columbia University NY*

BAZELON, DAVID
Chief judge, U.S. Court of Appeals, District of Columbia Circuit; chairman, Task Force on law and public awareness; member, President's panel on mental retardation

(22 pages, open) *John F. Kennedy Library MA*

BEACH, EDWARD LATIMER (1918-)
Military officer; Naval aide to President Eisenhower (1953-1957)

Eisenhower administration project (1967, 470 pages, permission required, also at *Dwight D. Eisenhower Library KS*) *Columbia University NY*

BEACH, SPENCER AMBROSE
Hunt Institute for Botanical Documentation PA

BEACHEY, HILARY
Aviation collection (25 pages, permission of interviewee required to cite or quote, also at *United States Air Force Academy CO* and *University of the Air, Maxwell Air Force Base AL*) *Columbia University NY*

BEACHEY, LINCOLN
Discussed in Columbia University interview with Lawrence Dale Bell

BEADLE, GEORGE WELLS (1903-)
Nobel Laureates collection (46 pages, permission required) *Columbia University NY*

Discussed in Columbia University interview with Warren Weaver

BEAL, JACK (1931-)
Painter

(1968, 35 pages) *Archives of American Art—Smithsonian Institution NY*

BEAL, JOHN R.
Journalist; Author

Dulles oral history collection (1965, 30 pages, permission required to cite or quote) *Princeton University NJ*

BEAL, MERRILL DEE
Ricks College ID

BEALE, ELIZABETH
Adlai E. Stevenson project (36 pages, permission required) *Columbia University NY*

BEALE, SIR HOWARD (1898-)
Former Australian ambassador to the United States

(21 pages, open) *John F. Kennedy Library MA*

Dulles oral history collection (1964, 23 pages, open) *Princeton University NJ*

BEAM, KENNETH S.
Community organization executive

(1972, 35 pages,) *University of California, Berkeley*

BEAMS, ROBERT W.
Dallas Indian urbanization project *Baylor University TX*

BEAN, LILLIAN
Allan Nevins project (47 pages, closed until March 5, 1976) *Columbia University NY*

BEAN, LOUIS H. (1896-)
Economist

(1953, 303 pages, also microfiche, permission required to cite or quote) *Columbia University NY*

BEAN, LUTHER
(1958) *State Historical Society of Colorado*

BEAN, WOODROW W.
Former member, Texas legislature

(1968, 9 pages, open) *University of Texas, El Paso*

BEANS, FRED DALE (1906-)
Brigadier general, U.S. Marine Corps (service: 1930-1948)

(1971, 119 pages, permission required, also at *Columbia University NY* and *U.S. Naval Institute MD*) *United States Marine Corps DC*

BEARD, CHARLES A.
Discussed in Columbia University interview with Alfred A. Knopf

BEARD, ROBERT L. (1896-1965)
McGraw-Hill, Inc. (38 pages, permission required) *Columbia University NY*

BEARD, WILLIAM KELLY, JR. (1898-)
McGraw-Hill, Inc. (35 pages, permission required) *Columbia University NY*

BEARDEN, ROMARE (1914-)
Painter

(1968, 28 pages) *Archives of American Art—Smithsonian Institution NY*

BEASLEY, D. OTIS
Administrative assistant secretary, Department of the Interior

(24 pages, open) *John F. Kennedy Library MA*

BEATTIE, DONALD S. (1921-)
Executive secretary, Congress of Railway Unions

United Transportation Union project (1971, 65 pages, open, transcript, permission required to reproduce tape) *Cornell University NY*

BEATTY, MORGAN
(1968, 1 reel, 27 pages) *Broadcast Pioneers Library DC*

BEAVER, FARRELL
Communications Workers of America collection *University of Iowa Libraries*

BEBRING, DR. GRETE
Student of Freud
Brandeis University MA

BECHARD, EUGENE
Reminiscences of Mr. and Mrs. William H. Miner (1 cassette, open) *Plattsburgh State University College NY*

BECKER, CARL
Discussed in Columbia University interview with Allan Nevins

BECKER, EUGENE
Son of John Becker

Ives project (1971) *Yale University School of Music CT*

BECKER, HARRY J. (1909-)
Social Security collection (40 pages, closed during lifetime, also at *Social Security Administration MD*) *Columbia University NY*

BECKER, J. BILL
Eisenhower administration project (33 pages, permission required to cite or quote, also at *Dwight D. Eisenhower Library KS*) *Columbia University NY*

BECKER, LOFTUS E. (1911-)
Legal adviser, U.S. State Department

Dulles oral history collection (1964, 38 pages, open) *Princeton University NJ*

BECKERSTAFF, THOMAS A.
Mill Valley Public Library CA

BEDFORD, LEWIS ARTHUR
Municipal Court judge (Dallas, Texas)
Fisk University TN

BEDONI, SIDNEY
(13 pages, permission required, also at Columbia University, NY and U.S. Naval Institute MD) United States Marine Corps DC

BEDORD, FRED (1910-)
Food processor
(1964, 99 pages, permission required to cite or quote) Cornell University NY

BEEBE, EUGENE
Henry H. Arnold project (80 pages, permission required, also at United States Air Force Academy CO) Columbia University NY

BEEBY, CLARENCE EDWARD (1902-)
Carnegie corporation collection (1968, 89 pages, permission required) Columbia University NY

BEECHER, HENRY
Discussed in Columbia University interview with Edward Delos Churchill

BEEDE, VIRGINIA STEARNS
Smith alumna, class of 1927; Community worker
(1973, 30 minutes, 10 pages) Smith College MA

BEER-MONTI, FEDERICA
Art dealer
(1967, 15 pages) Archives of American Art—Smithsonian Institution NY

BEESMAN, GEORGE with Freeman Steel, Sr., et al.
South Dakota experience (1952), South Dakota Oral History Project University of South Dakota

BEETS AND BEET SUGAR
Sugar Beet industry in New York State Cornell University NY
Participants: Nyle C. Brady; Church; John Debrueque; Charles Dickens; Beverly Easton; Harold Giles; D. Leo Hayes; Ralph Hemminger; Nathan R. Herendeen; George Humphreys; W. Keith Kennedy; Floyd Klipple; Harold Kludt; Paul Lattimore; Joseph F. Metz, Jr.; Charles C. Miller; Michael L. Peduto; Horace C. Reynolds; Paul and William Rockefeller; Keith Rowan; Thomas W. Scott; Harvey Smith; James B. Smith; John Sodoma; Henry Stack; Dr. Dewey Stewart; Benjamin Swayze; Dale Thompson; Frank Turek

BEGAB, MICHAEL
Kennedy administration consultant on mental retardation
(25 pages, open) John F. Kennedy Library MA

BEHAVIORAL SCIENCES
American Psychiatric Association DC

BEHR, KARL HOWELL (1885-)
Theodore Roosevelt Association (19 pages, permission required to cite or quote) Columbia University NY

BEHRENS, EARL C. (1892-)
Newspaperman; Political editor, San Francisco Chronicle
Eisenhower administration project (1967, 44 pages, permission required, also at Dwight D. Eisenhower Library KS) Columbia University NY

BEILBY, MANRY
Associate librarian
Collective bargaining at SUNY project (1973, 54 minutes, 22 pages) Cornell University NY

BEIN, WILLIAM
WORLD WAR II: THE HOLOCAUST—RESISTANCE AND RESCUE: (1) The Joint (American Jewish Joint Distribution Committee) (English, 73 pages, open) Hebrew University, Israel

BEIRNE, JOSEPH ANTHONY (1911-)
President, Communications Workers of America
(1957, 66 pages, permission required) Columbia University NY
Communications Workers of America collection University of Iowa Libraries

BEIT-ARIE, DAVID
Former member, Jewish Agency Executive
WORLD WAR II: THE HOLOCAUST—RESISTANCE AND RESCUE: (6) Rescue of Jewish children (Hebrew, 7 pages, open) Hebrew University, Israel

BEIT-OR (LICHTAUSE), BARUCH
HISTORY OF THE YISHUV (PALESTINIAN JEWRY): (5) Gedud Ha-Avoda (Labor Brigade) (Hebrew, 3 pages, written interview, open) Hebrew University, Israel

BEIT-ZVI, SHABTAI
Tel-Aviv teacher
JEWISH COMMUNITIES: (4) Zionist movement in U.S.S.R. (1917-1935) (Hebrew, 46 pages, open) Hebrew University, Israel

BELDEN ASSOCIATES
Texas economic history project Baylor University TX

BELDING, MILO
Discussed in Columbia University Association for the Aid of Crippled Children collection

BELKIN, MORRIS
National Institute of Health MD

BELKIND, EYTAN
Rishon Le-Zion businessman
HISTORY OF THE YISHUV (PALESTINIAN JEWRY): (2) Jewish private sector in Palestine (Hebrew, 24 pages, open) Hebrew University, Israel

BELKNAP, CHAUNCEY (1891-)
Robert P. Patterson project (51 pages, closed until January 1, 1980) Columbia University NY
(1954, 526 pages, closed until October 3, 1996) Columbia University NY

BELL, ASAEL E.
Ricks College ID

BELL, DANIEL (1919-)
Richard Hofstadter project (42 pages, permission required to cite or quote) Columbia University NY
Socialist movement project (49 pages, permission required to cite or quote) Columbia University NY
(169 pages, permission of interviewee required to cite, quote, or paraphrase) John F. Kennedy Library MA

BELL, DANIEL WAFENA (1891-1971)
Banker
Dulles oral history collection (1964, 34 pages, permission required to cite or quote) Princeton University NJ

BELL, DAVID
Director, Bureau of the Budget; Administrator, AID

BELL, DICKSON
Dental history (in process) University of California, Berkeley

BELL, ELLIOT V. (1902-)
Editor; Publisher

BELL, GRACE KETZEBACK
South Dakota experience (1971), South Dakota Oral History Project University of South Dakota

BELL, H. O.
One of the first northwestern auto dealers University of Montana

BELL, JACK L. (1904-)
Newspaperman
Eisenhower administration project (31 pages, permission required to cite or quote, also at Dwight D. Eisenhower Library KS) Columbia University NY
Robert A. Taft project (1969, 22 pages, permission required to cite or quote) Columbia University NY
(71 pages, open) John F. Kennedy Library MA

BELL, KATHLEEN
Smith alumna, class of 1944; State Department employee
(1973, 2 hours, 37 pages) Smith College MA

BELL, LAWRENCE DALE (1894-1956)
Corporation executive
Aviation collection (1955, 288 pages, open, also at United States Air Force Academy

CO and University of the Air, Maxwell Air Force Base AL) Columbia University NY

BELL, MARY
Singer
Ives project (1970) Yale University School of Music CT

BELLAMY, FREDERICA LE FEVRE
(1958) State Historical Society of Colorado

BELLAMY, RALPH (1904–   )
Popular arts collection (31 pages, open) Columbia University NY

BELLARD, EMORY
Athletic boom in West Texas (open) Texas Tech University

BELMONT, AUGUST
Discussed in Columbia University interviews with John T. Hettrick; Morris Lincoln Strauss

BELVISO, THOMAS H.
Copyright expert; Pioneer member, NBC music department
(1966, 2 reels, 35 pages) Broadcast Pioneers Library DC

BEN-AMMI, OVED
Netanya mayor

BEN-ARI, YEHUDA
Director, Jabotinsky Institute (Tel-Aviv)
HISTORY OF THE YISHUV (PALESTINIAN JEWRY): (8) Revisionist "Ha'apalah" (illegal immigration) (Hebrew, 10 pages, open) Hebrew University, Israel

BEN-BARUKH, LEVI
JEWISH COMMUNITIES: (12) Jews of Bukhara (1900–1935) (Hebrew, 11 pages, open) Hebrew University, Israel

BEN-DAOV, AKIVA
Director, Histadarut (Haifa)
HISTORY OF THE YISHUV (PALESTINIAN JEWRY): (5) Gedud Ha-Avoda (Labor Brigade) (Hebrew, 16 pages, open) Hebrew University, Israel

BEN-DAVID, GERSHON
WORLD WAR II: THE HOLOCAUST—RESISTANCE AND RESCUE: (17) Forced labor camps under Nazi occupation in Tunisia (Hebrew, 50 pages, open) Hebrew University, Israel

BEN-DAVID, MOSHE
ANTECEDENTS TO THE STATE OF ISRAEL: (2) "Brichah" (organized escape) (Hebrew, 30 pages, open) Hebrew University, Israel

BEN-EZRA, AVRAHAM AND TOVA
JEWISH COMMUNITIES: (11) Jewish community of Iran (Hebrew, 3 pages, open) Hebrew University, Israel

BEN-GAL, MICHAEL
Director, Jerusalem district office, Israel Land Authority
ANTECEDENTS TO THE STATE OF ISRAEL: (2) "Brichah" (organized escape) (Hebrew, 79 pages, open) Hebrew University, Israel

BEN-GURION, DAVID
Brandeis University MA
JEWISH COMMUNITIES: (4) Zionist movement in the U.S.S.R. (1917–1935) (Hebrew, 2 pages, written interview, open) Hebrew University, Israel

BEN-HORIN, DAVID
ANTECEDENTS TO THE STATE OF ISRAEL: (3) "Ha'apalah" (illegal immigration) (tape only, open) Hebrew University, Israel

BEN-HUR, ELIAHU
Tel-Aviv insurance engineer
ANTECEDENTS TO THE STATE OF ISRAEL: (3) "Ha'apalah" (illegal immigration) (Hebrew, 97 pages, open) Hebrew University, Israel

BEN-NAHUM, EPHRAIM
Central Committee, Ha-Poel Ha-Mizrachi (Tel-Aviv)
JEWISH COMMUNITIES: (10) Jewish life in Iraq (Hebrew, 18 pages, open) Hebrew University, Israel

BEN-NATAN, ASHER
Former Israeli ambassador to West Germany
ANTECEDENTS TO THE STATE OF ISRAEL: (2) "Brichah" (organized escape) (Hebrew, 38 pages, open) Hebrew University, Israel

BEN-UZIEL, NISSIM
Jerusalem rabbinic lawyer
JEWISH COMMUNITIES: (10) Jewish life in Iraq (Hebrew, 16 pages, open) Hebrew University, Israel

BEN-YAAKOV, BARUCH
YOUTH MOVEMENTS: (2) Netzach in Latvia (Hebrew, 21 pages, open) Hebrew University, Israel

BEN-YEHUDA, YAACOV
Director, Timna copper company
ANTECEDENTS TO THE STATE OF ISRAEL: (2) "Brichah" (organized escape) (Hebrew, 21 pages, open) Hebrew University, Israel

BEN-ZVI, GEDALIAH
WORLD WAR II: THE HOLOCAUST—RESISTANCE AND RESCUE: (8) Theresienstadt ghetto (German, 66 pages, open) Hebrew University, Israel

BENALLY, JOHN
(32 pages, permission required, also at Columbia University NY and U.S. Naval Institute MD) United States Marine Corps DC

BENCHLEY, ROBERT
Discussed in Columbia University interview with Mildred Gilman

BENDER, MORRIS P.
Mount Sinai Hospital Investitures (24 pages, permission required, also at Mount Sinai Medical Center NY) Columbia University NY

BENDER, RAY (1905–   )
County agricultural agent
(1964, 112 pages, open) Cornell University NY

BENDIX CORPORATION
Discussed in Reed Scott interview, Biographical collection University of California, Los Angeles

BENEDICT, STEPHEN (1927–   )
Consultant
Eisenhower administration project (1968, 137 pages, closed during interviewee's lifetime, also at Dwight D. Eisenhower Library KS) Columbia University NY

BENEDUM, DARWIN (1902–   )
Benedum and the oil industry (6 pages, open) Columbia University NY

BENEDUM, JAMES CLAXTON (1909–   )
Benedum and the oil industry (16 pages, open) Columbia University NY

BENEDUM, MICHAEL LATE (1869–1959)
Oil executive
Benedum and the oil industry (144 pages, open) Columbia University NY

BENEDUM, PAUL (1902–   )
Oil executive
Benedum and the oil industry (87 pages, open) Columbia University NY

BENEDUM, PEARL
Benedum and the oil industry (30 pages, open) Columbia University NY

BENEDUM, SOPHIE
Benedum and the oil industry (30 pages, open) Columbia University NY

BENES, EDUARD
Discussed in Columbia University interview with Jan Papanek

BENEWAY, FRANK (1884–   )
Farmer
(172 pages, open) Cornell University NY

BENITEZ DE CASTRO, CECILIO
Argentina in the 1930s (Spanish, 13 pages, open) Columbia University NY

BENJAMIN, CURTIS G. (1901–)
Publisher (McGraw-Hill)
McGraw-Hill, Inc. (1953, 78 pages, permission required) *Columbia University NY*

BENJAMIN, EARL W. (1889–)
Agricultural businessman
Agricultural leaders project (1964, 72 pages, open) *Cornell University NY*

BENJAMIN, ROBERT S. (1909–)
Adlai E. Stevenson project (39 pages, permission required) *Columbia University NY*

BENNER, CHARLES N. (1941–)
United Transportation Union project (1970, 85 pages, permission required to cite or quote transcript, permission required to use tape) *Cornell University NY*

BENNETT, WILLIAM STILES (1870–1962)
Lawyer, Congressman
(1951, 216 pages, also microfiche, permission required to cite or quote) *Columbia University NY*

BENNETT, CHARLES EDWARD (1910–)
Democratic congressman from Florida
Eisenhower administration project (18 pages, permission required to cite or quote, also at *Dwight D. Eisenhower Library KS*) *Columbia University NY*

BENNETT, JAMES V.
Law Enforcement Assistance Administration project (1971, 53 pages, 1½ hours) *Cornell University NY*

BENNETT, JOHN
Socialist movement project (30 pages, permission required to cite or quote) *Columbia University NY*

BENNETT, JOHN COLEMAN (1902–)
Theologian
Dulles oral history collection (1965, 38 pages, open) *Princeton University NJ*

BENNETT, PAUL R. (1919–)
United Transportation Union project (1971, 50 pages, permission required to cite or quote transcript, permission required to use tape) *Cornell University NY*

BENSON, ELMER A.
Minnesota Historical Society

BENSON, EZRA TAFT (1899–)
Secretary of Agriculture (1953–1961)
Eisenhower administration project (1968, 12 pages, permission required to cite or quote, also at *Dwight D. Eisenhower Library KS*)
Discussed in Columbia University interviews with Earl Lauer Butz; Don Paarlberg; Edward J. Thye; Milton R. Young

BENSON, LUCY WILSON
President, League of Women Voters
Smith alumna, class of 1949; (1973, 3 hours, 80 pages) *Smith College MA*

BENSON, MARGUERITE
Wisconsin political figure
(21 pages, open) *John F. Kennedy Library MA*

BENSON, MRS. G. M.
(1969, 8 pages, open) *University of Texas, El Paso*

BENSON, MRS. LE GRACE
(1972, 76 pages, permission required to cite or quote) *Cornell University NY*

BENSON, OTIS (1902–)
Aviation collection (38 pages, permission required to cite or quote, also at *United States Air Force Academy CO* and *University of the Air, Maxwell Air Force Base AL*) *Columbia University NY*

BENSON, RICHARD K.
Airplane pilot
Dulles oral history collection (1965, 34 pages, open) *Princeton University NJ*

BENSON, VIRGINIA (ca. 1890–)
Farmer's wife
(1969, 22 pages, open) *North Texas State University Oral History Collection*

BENTLEY, RICHARD (1894–)
Adlai E. Stevenson project (35 pages, permission required) *Columbia University NY*

BENTON, THOMAS HART
Artist
Harry S. Truman Library MO

BENTON, WILLIAM (1900–)
U.S. senator (Connecticut); Chairman of the board, *Encyclopaedia Britannica*; U.S. ambassador
(1968, 224 pages, open except for specified pages) *Columbia University NY*
Adlai E. Stevenson project (40 pages, permission required) *Columbia University NY*
(78 pages, portions closed) *John F. Kennedy Library MA*
Discussed in Columbia University interviews with Chester Bowles; Dorothy Stebbins Bowles; Robert Maynard Hutchins

BENTWICH, NORMAN
Former attorney general (Mandatory Palestine); Professor emeritus of international relations, Hebrew University
HISTORY OF THE YISHUV: (8) Revisionist "Ha'apalah" (English, 12 pages, open) *Hebrew University, Israel*

BENYAMIN, YIGAL (KURT)
WORLD WAR II: THE HOLOCAUST—RESISTANCE AND RESCUE: (2) Rescue of Jews via Spain and Portugal (Hebrew, 20 pages, open) *Hebrew University, Israel*

BERDING, ANDREW H. (1902–)
Journalist; Deputy director, U.S. Information Agency (1953–1957); Assistant Secretary of State for public affairs (1957–1961)
Eisenhower administration project (1967, 38 pages, open, also at *Dwight D. Eisenhower Library KS*) *Columbia University NY*

BERELSON, BERNARD R. (1912–)
Educator
Carnegie Corporation collection (1967, 119 pages, permission required) *Columbia University NY*
Dulles oral history collection (1964, 25 pages, open) *Princeton University NJ*

BERENDSEN, SIR CARL
New Zealand ambassador to the United States
Dulles oral history collection (1965, 46 pages, open) *Princeton University NJ*

BERENSON, BERNARD
Discussed in Columbia University interview with Thomas Cassin Kinkaid

BERENSON, MOSHE
Holon industrialist
WORLD WAR II: THE HOLOCAUST—RESISTANCE AND RESCUE: (3) Jewish underground movement in wartime France (Hebrew, 25 pages, open) *Hebrew University, Israel*

BERGAZZI, MICHAEL
Central California coast collection (1964, 207 pages) *University of California, Santa Cruz*

BERGER, ARTHUR
Composer
Ives project (1970) *Yale University School of Music CT*

BERGER, LAWRENCE
Columbia crisis of 1968 (43 pages, permission required) *Columbia University NY*

BERGER, VICTOR
Discussed in Columbia University interview with John Spargo

BERGER, MRS. WILLIAM B.
(1960) *State Historical Society of Colorado*

BERGSON, HENRI
Discussed in Columbia University interview with Rene Frederic Coudert

BERIO, LUCIANO
Composer
American music project (1971) *Yale University School of Music CT*

BERKELEY, JAMES PHILLIPS (1907–)
Lieutenant general, U.S. Marine Corps (service: 1927–1965)

(1969, 481 pages, open, also at *Columbia University NY* and *U.S. Naval Institute MD*) *United States Marine Corps DC*

BERKI, SYLVESTER
(60 pages) *Cornell University NY*

BERKMAN, ANTON with John Waller
(1969, 24 pages, open) *University of Texas, El Paso*

BERKNER, LLOYD VIEL (1905–1967)
Physicist
(1959, 60 pages, also microfiche, permission required to cite or quote) *Columbia University NY*

BERKOVICH, M.
Hicem official during World War II (Lisbon)
WORLD WAR II: THE HOLOCAUST—RESISTANCE AND RESCUE: (2) Rescue of Jews via Spain and Portugal (German, 17 pages, open) *Hebrew University, Israel*

BERKOVITZ, YITZHAK DOV (–1967)
Author
CULTURE AND EDUCATION: (1) Authors and their work (Hebrew, 12 pages, open) *Hebrew University, Israel*

BERLE, ADOLF AUGUSTUS (1895–1971)
Attorney
(1969, 36 pages; 1970, 190 pages plus papers; permission required) *Columbia University NY*
Journalism lectures, Basic issues in the news—economics (29 pages, permission required) *Columbia University NY*

BERLIN, SIR ISAIAH
Kennedy associate; Professor of social and political theory, Oxford University
(24 pages, permission of interviewee required) *John F. Kennedy Library MA*

BERMAN, IDA
YOUTH MOVEMENTS: (2) Netzach in Latvia (Hebrew, 27 pages, open) *Hebrew University, Israel*

BERMAN, MENDEL
YOUTH MOVEMENTS: (2) Netzach in Latvia (Hebrew, 26 pages, open) *Hebrew University, Israel*

BERMAN, MORTON M.
Karen Ha-Yesod (Jerusalem)
JEWISH COMMUNITIES: (5) Jewish nationalism and the Reform movement in the United States (English, 12 pages, open) *Hebrew University, Israel*

BERMAN, PANDRO S.
American Film Institute CA

BERMAN, YAAKOV
Director, Seminary for Religious Teachers in Secondary Schools (Rehovot)

BIOGRAPHICAL INTERVIEWS (Hebrew, 129 pages, open) *Hebrew University, Israel*

BERMAN, YITZHAK
Tel-Aviv lawyer
HISTORY OF THE YISHUV (PALESTINIAN JEWRY): (7) Etzel and Lehi organizations (Hebrew, 95 pages, open) *Hebrew University, Israel*

BERNARIS, ANTHONY
Secretary-general to Greek Ministry of National Economy
Harry S. Truman Library MO

BERNAYS, EDWARD L. (1891–   )
Public relations counselor
(1971, 403 pages, closed during interviewee's lifetime) *Columbia University NY*

BERNER, MOSHE
Jerusalem physician
CULTURE AND EDUCATION: (4) Jewish schools in Transylvania (Hungarian, 23 pages, open) *Hebrew University, Israel*

BERNERI, MRS. SAMUEL
Secretary, Ives & Myrick
Ives project (1972) *Yale University School of Music CT*

BERNHARD, PRINCE OF THE NETHERLANDS
(4 pages, open) *John F. Kennedy Library MA*

BERNHARDT, SARAH
Discussed in Columbia University interview with Eddie Dowling

BERNSTEIN, ADOLPHINE
WORLD WAR II: THE HOLOCAUST—RESISTANCE AND RESCUE: (6) Rescue of Jewish children (English, 12 pages, open) *Hebrew University, Israel*

BERNSTEIN, ALVIN H.
Challenges to governance by students project (1970, 33 pages, open) *Cornell University NY*

BERNSTEIN, BERNICE
Lawyer
Social Security collection (1965, 125 pages, open; also at *Social Security Administration MD*) *Columbia University NY*

BERNSTEIN, LEO
Director, World Jewish Congress (Israel)
WORLD WAR II: THE HOLOCAUST—RESISTANCE AND RESCUE: (13) Underground activities of the Lithuanian Jews (Hebrew, 30 pages, open) *Hebrew University, Israel*

BERNSTEIN, LEONARD
Composer, Conductor, New York Philharmonic
(15 pages, permission of interviewee required to cite, quote, or paraphrase) *John F. Kennedy Library MA*

BERNSTEIN, LOUIS (1878–1962)
Popular arts collection (22 pages, open) *Columbia University NY*

BERNSTEIN, OSCAR
New York political studies collection, Brooklyn politics (1930–1950) (79 pages, permission required) *Columbia University NY*

BERNSTEIN, PERETZ
Former minister of commerce (Israel); Member, Knesset
HISTORY OF THE YISHUV (PALESTINIAN JEWS): (2) Jewish private sector in Palestine (Hebrew, 3 pages, written, open) *Hebrew University, Israel*

BERNSTEIN (SHEINBAUM), PESSIA
Polish Immigrants Association (Tel-Aviv)
WORLD WAR II: THE HOLOCAUST—RESISTANCE AND RESCUE: (13) Underground activities of the Lithuanian Jews (Hebrew, 30 pages, open) *Hebrew University, Israel*

BERNSTEIN, PHILIP S.
Rabbi (Rochester NY)
ANTECEDENTS TO THE STATE OF ISRAEL: (2) "Brichah" (organized escape) (English, 20 pages, open) *Hebrew University, Israel*

BERNSTEIN, YESHAYAHU
Director, Education and Culture Department, World Mizrachi Center (Jerusalem)
HISTORY OF THE YISHUV (PALESTINIAN JEWRY): (6) Ha-Poel Ha-Mizrachi movement (Hebrew, 107 pages, open) *Hebrew University, Israel*

BERRIGAN, DANIEL
Jesuit; Anti-war activist leader
Daniel Berrigan weekend project *Cornell University NY*
Participants: Alvin H. Bernstein; Stuart M. Brown, Jr.; Mark J. Barlow; Jackson O. Hall; Alfred E. Kahn; Steven Muller
Challenges to governance by students project: Student activism (1969, 32 pages; 7 pages since; most open) *Cornell University NY*

BERRY, BRIAN
Geographer
(1971, 10 minutes) *Plymouth State College NH*

BERRY, FRANK BROWN (1892–   )
Physician
(In process) *Columbia University NY*

BERRY, WATSON
Journalism lectures (25 pages, permission required to cite or quote) *Columbia University NY*

BERRYMAN, JOE
University of Southern Mississippi

BERS, MELVIN
Communications Workers of America collection *University of Iowa Libraries*

BLANCHFIELD, COL. FLORENCE
Nursing Archive *Boston University MA*

BLANCK, AGNES LOUISE
(1963) *State Historical Society of Colorado*

BLANCK, JASON
WORLD WAR II: THE HOLOCAUST—RESISTANCE AND RESCUE: (6) Rescue of Jewish children (English, 7 pages, open) *Hebrew University, Israel*

BLAND, LEON
Pioneer river man
Fisk University TN

BLANDING, SARAH GIBSON (1898–)
College president

BLANEY, HARRY FRENCH
Water resources collection (open) *University of California, Los Angeles*

BLANFORD, CHARLES J. (1909–)
Public administrator
(1965, 497 pages, permission required to cite or quote) *Cornell University NY*

BLANKE, HENRY
Motion picture producer
An oral history of the motion picture in America (open) *University of California, Los Angeles*

BLANKENHORN, HEBER (1884–1956)
Labor researcher
(1955, 564 pages, permission required to cite or quote) *Columbia University NY*

BLANKENSHIP, BEN
Communications Workers of America collection *University of Iowa Libraries*

BLANTON, JACK (1921–)
Businessman; Member, Texas House of Representatives (Dallas)
Legislative project (1970, 58 pages; 1971, 80 pages; open) *North Texas State University Oral History Collection*

BLATCHFORD, PAUL
(27 pages, permission required, also at Columbia University and U.S. Naval Institute MD) *United States Marine Corps DC*

BLATNIK, JOHN
U.S. representative (Minnesota)
(34 pages, open) *John F. Kennedy Library MA*

BLAU, YEHUDA
HISTORY OF THE YISHUV (PALESTINIAN JEWRY): (4) Extreme Orthodox Jewry in Palestine (Hebrew, 24 pages, open) *Hebrew University, Israel*

BLAUSCHIELD, GAMLIEL
YOUTH MOVEMENTS: (2) NETZACH IN LATVIA (Hebrew, 16 pages; Hebrew, 31 pages; Hebrew, 39 pages; open) *Hebrew University, Israel*

BLAYLOCK, TOM (1918–)
Army Air Corps veteran; Bataan Death March survivor
Prisoner-of-War project (1971, 101 pages, open) *North Texas State University Oral History Collection*

BLAZIN, GEORGE P. (1919–)
Vice Chairman, UTU Local 1469
United Transportation Union project (1972, 39 pages, open, transcript permission required to use tape) *Cornell University NY*

BLEDSOE, SAMUEL B. (1898–)
Agriculturist
(1954, 689 pages, also microfiche, permission required to cite or quote) *Columbia University NY*

BLEEKER, HIRAM
Associate professor of physics
Collective bargaining at SUNY project (1972, 52 minutes, 29 pages) *Cornell University NY*

BLERIOT, LOUIS
Discussed in Columbia University interview with Ross Browne

BLIGHTON, FRANK
Discussed in Columbia University interview with James Thomas Williams, Jr.

BLISS, C. PRESBY (1900–)
McGraw-Hill, Inc. (43 pages, permission required) *Columbia University NY*

BLIVEN, BRUCE ORMSBY (1889–)
Editor
(1964, 60 pages, permission required) *Columbia University NY*
Dorothy Straight Elmhirst biography (75 pages) *Cornell University NY*

BLOCH, ERNEST
Discussed in Columbia University interview with Roger Huntington Sessions

BLOCH, FELIX (1905–)
Nobel Laureates collection (24 pages, permission required) *Columbia University NY*

BLOCK, AUGUSTA HAUCK
State Historical Society of Colorado

BLOCK, HARRY
Labor leader
(1967, 59 pages) *Pennsylvania State University*

BLOCK, HERBERT
Journalism lectures (34 pages, permission required to cite or quote) *Columbia University NY*

BLOCK, RALPH
Staff member, Office of War Information; State Department employee
Harry S. Truman Library MO

BLOCKER, DAN
Discussed in Biographical collection *Texas Tech University*

BLOOM, ANDREW
Discussed in Columbia University interview with William L. Maxwell

BLOOMER, STEVEN
Challenges to governance by students project: Pentagon March (1967) (1968, 32 pages, open) *Cornell University NY*

BLOSSOM, VIRGIL
Discussed in Columbia University interview with Orval Eugene Faubus

BLOUNT, JOHN H. (1934–)
Chairman, UTU Local 1596
United Transportation Union project (1972, 39 pages, open) *Cornell University NY*

BLOUNT, KEN
Communications Workers of America collection *University of Iowa Libraries*

BLUES (SONGS, ETC.)
Memphis Public Library and Information Center TN

BLUHM, NORMAN (1920–)
Painter
(1969, 70 pages) *Archives of American Art—Smithsonian Institution NY*

BLUMENFELD, DR. KURT (–1963)
BIOGRAPHICAL INTERVIEWS (German, 306 pages, open) *Hebrew University, Israel*

BLUMENSON, LEO
WORLD WAR II: THE HOLOCAUST—RESISTANCE AND RESCUE: (8) Theresienstadt ghetto (Hebrew and German, 83 pages; report, German, 91 pages; summary, German, 14 pages, open) *Hebrew University, Israel*

BLUMENTHAL, HELEN B.
University of Washington Libraries WA

BLUMER, LOUIS
South Dakota experience, South Dakota Oral History Project *University of South Dakota*

BLUNT, JEFFREY M.
Challenges to governance by students project (1969, 20 pages, open) *Cornell University NY*

BLUNTZER, ROBERT (1897–)
Land speculation, settlement, and development of the Coastal Bend area of South Texas, 1900–1925 (1969, 33 pages, open), Miscellaneous collection *North Texas State University Oral History Collection*

BOLSA CHICA GUN CLUB
Claremont Graduate School CA

BOLT, RICHARD
Ranching collection *Texas Tech University*

BOLTE, CHARLES L.
General, U.S. Army
United States Army Military Research Collection PA

BOLTON, FRANCES P.
Peggy Lamson collection *Arthur and Elizabeth Schlesinger Library MA*

BONAPARTE, MARIE
Discussed in Columbia University interview with Rudolph Maurice Loewenstein

BOND, DR. CLAUDE C.
Assistant superintendent of education, Chattanooga
(1971) *Fisk University TN*

BOND, JULIAN
Fisk University TN

BOND, NELSON L. (1903–   )
McGraw-Hill, Inc. (26 pages, permission required) *Columbia University NY*

BOND, DR. SARA A.
Careers of New England women in medicine *Arthur and Elizabeth Schlesinger Library MA*

BONDI (BASHAN), RUTH
Tel-Aviv journalist
WORLD WAR II: THE HOLOCAUST—RESISTANCE AND RESCUE: (8) Theresienstadt ghetto (Hebrew, 20 pages, open) *Hebrew University, Israel*

BONDURANT, WILLIAM R.
Mining in the Coeur d'Alenes *Idaho Bicentennial Commission*

BONESTEEL, CHARLES H., III
General, U.S. Army
United States Army Military Research Collection PA

BONILLA, LUCIO
Labor leader
Argentina in the 1930s (Spanish, 103 pages, open) *Columbia University NY*

BONN, LOUIS A.
Popular arts collection (33 pages, open) *Columbia University NY*

BONNET TAIL, CHIEF
University of Utah

BONTEMPS, DR. ARNA W.
Author; Poet; Librarian
(1972) *Fisk University TN*

BOOHER, EDWARD E. (1911–   )
McGraw-Hill, Inc. (84 pages, permission required) *Columbia University NY*

BOOK-OF-THE-MONTH-CLUB
Book-of-the-Month Club collection. Participants and pages: Henry Seidel Canby, 45; Harry Dale, 22; Clifton Fadiman, 45; Helen R. Feil, 16; Dorothy Canfield Fisher, 129; George Gallup, 32; Robert K. Haas, 31; Gilbert Highet, 18; Gordon Hyle, 24; Edwina Kohlman, 18; Amy Loveman, 17; Warren Lynch, 28; John Marquand, 30; Oscar Ogg, 25; Axel Rosin, 45; Maxwell Sackheim, 17; Harry Scherman, 371; Ralph Thompson, 28; Lester Troob, 26; Edith Walker, 40; Meredith Wood, 117 (1955, 1124 pages, open) *Columbia University NY*

BOOKBINDER, HYMAN
Special assistant to the Secretary of Commerce
(35 pages, open) *John F. Kennedy Library MA*

BOOKER, SIMEON
Journalist
(39 pages, portions closed) *John F. Kennedy Library MA*

BOOKMAN, MAX
Water resources collection (quotations not permitted, interviewee has sole and exclusive right and license to publish until 1989 or during his lifetime) *University of California, Los Angeles*

BOOLE, ELLA ALEXANDER (MRS. WILLIAM H.) (1858–1952)
Church and temperance worker
(1950, 28 pages, open) *Columbia University NY*

BOONE, PHILIP
Arts and the community (in process) *University of California, Berkeley*

BOONE, RICHARD ALLEN (1917–   )
Popular arts collection (36 pages, open) *Columbia University NY*

BOOTHBY, WALTER
Discussed in Columbia University interview with Frank Brown Berry

BOOTON, JOSEPH
Historic preservation *Charles B. Hosmer, Jr. Collection IL*

BOR, NORMAN LOFTUS
Hunt Institute for Botanical Documentation PA

BORAH, WILLIAM E.
Discussed in Columbia University interviews with James Aloysius Farley; Burton Kendall Wheeler

BORGENICHT, GRACE (1915–   )
Art dealer

(1963, 7 pages) *Archives of American Art—Smithsonian Institution NY*

BORIE, LYSBETH BOYD

BORING, MR. AND MRS. DAVID E.
(1968) *State Historical Society of Colorado*

BORLENGHI, ANGEL
Discussed in Columbia University interview with Ernesto Janin

BOROBIK, DASHA
YOUTH MOVEMENTS: (2) Netzach in Latvia (Hebrew, 46 pages, open) *Hebrew University, Israel*

BOROUGH, REUBEN WARRINGER
Government and politics collection *University of California, Los Angeles*

BORTON, HUGH (1903–   )
State Department official
(1956, 52 pages, permission required to cite or quote) *Columbia University NY*

BOSCH, JOHN
Farm Holiday Association collection (56 pages, open) *Columbia University NY*

BOSCH, JUAN
President of the Dominican Republic
(23 pages, open) *John F. Kennedy Library MA*

BOSCH, RICHARD
Farm Holiday Association collection (27 pages, open) *Columbia University NY*

BOSLER, GUSTAVE A.
Radio pioneers collection (21 pages, open) *Columbia University NY*

BOSTICK, JACK
Officer, Texas State Association of Fire Fighters and International Association of Fire Fighters
(34 pages, open) *University of Texas, Arlington*

BOSTON
Boston Public Library MA

BOSTWICK, HELEN
Mill Valley Public Library CA

BOTANY
Hunt Institute for Botanical Documentation PA

BOTT, GEORGE J. (1910–   )
National Labor Relations Board (1969, 72 pages, permission required to cite or quote) *Cornell University NY*

BRACHFIELD, SALOMON
Diamond merchant; Journalist (Belgium)

WORLD WAR II: THE HOLOCAUST—RESISTANCE AND RESCUE: (5) Hiding children in Belgium (French, 3 pages, open) *Hebrew University, Israel*

BRACKETT, CHARLES (1892–)
Popular arts collection (25 pages, open) *Columbia University NY*

BRADBURY, RAY DOUGLAS
Author

Biographical collection (open) *University of California, Los Angeles*

BRADEMAS, JOHN

Adlai E. Stevenson project (23 pages, permission required) *Columbia University NY*

BRADEN, AMY STEINHART (1879–)
Public welfare official and volunteer

(1965, 263 pages) *University of California, Berkeley*

BRADEN, ANNE (MRS. CARL) (1924–)
Journalist; Civil rights activist

(in process) *Columbia University NY*

BRADEN, SPRUILLE (1894–)
Diplomat; Mining engineer

(1956, 3188 pages, permission required) *Columbia University NY*

BRADFIELD, RICHARD (1896–)

Agricultural leaders project (1965, 39 pages, permission required to cite or quote) *Cornell University NY*

BRADLEY, CARTER

Social Security collection (27 pages, open, also at *Social Security Administration MD*) *Columbia University NY*

BRADLEY, CHESTER (1884–)
Entomologist

Agricultural leaders project (1964, 58 pages, open) *Cornell University NY*

BRADLEY, DON
California political figure

(27 pages, open) *John F. Kennedy Library MA*

BRADLEY, J. ROBERT
Singer; Music promoter

(1972) *Fisk University TN*

BRADLEY, MICHAEL JOSPEH (1897–)

Independence National Historical Park (27 pages, permission required) *Columbia University NY*

BRADLEY, OMAR NELSON (1893–)
U.S. Army officer

Eisenhower administration project (1965, 23 pages, permission required to cite or quote,

also at *Dwight D. Eisenhower Library KS*) *Columbia University NY*

Discussed in Columbia University interviews with Edward Latimer Beach; John Lesslie Hall, Jr.

BRADLEY, PRESTON
Pioneer religious broadcaster

(1964, 1 reel, 22 pages) *Broadcast Pioneers Library DC*

BRADLEY, R. L. (1894–)

Law Enforcement Assistance Administration project (1971, 1 ½ hours, 55 pages) *Cornell University NY*

BRADY, NYLE C.

Sugar beet industry in New York State (1967, 31 pages, open) *Cornell University NY*

BRADY, T. P.
Judge

University of Southern Mississippi

BRAGDON, EVERETT L.
Pioneer radio editor, *New York Sun*; *Popular Science Monthly* writer; Public relations executive, RCA

(1950, 20 pages; 1965, 1 reel, 26 pages) *Broadcast Pioneers Library DC*

Radio pioneers collection (1950, 20 pages, open, also at *Broadcast Pioneers Library*) *Columbia University NY*

BRAGINSKI, YEHUDA
Former member, Jewish Agency

ANTECEDENTS TO THE STATE OF ISRAEL: (3) "Ha'apalah" (illegal immigration) (Hebrew, 14 pages, open) *Hebrew University, Israel*

BRAITHWAITE, WILLIAM STANLEY BEAUMONT (1878–1962)
Author

(1956, 233 pages, open) *Columbia University NY*

BRAMS, SOFUS

South Dakota experience (1971), South Dakota Oral History Project *University of South Dakota*

BRAN, JAMIE, AND ALFREDO PLA

(1967, 1 reel) *Broadcast Pioneers Library DC*

BRANCH, HILARION NOEL (1880–1966)
Lawyer

(1966, 182 pages, also microfiche, permission required to cite or quote) *Columbia University NY*

BRAND, SHLOMO
Ramat-Gan merchant

WORLD WAR II: THE HOLOCAUST—RESISTANCE AND RESCUE: (13) Underground activities of the Lithuanian Jews (Hebrew, 30 pages; Yiddish, 63 pages; open) *Hebrew University, Israel*

BRANDEIS, LOUIS D.

Discussed in Columbia University interviews with Adolf Augustus Berle; Learned Hand; Gardner Jackson; James McCauley Landis; John Lord O'Brian; Paul and Elizabeth Raushenbush; Bernard G. Richards

BRANDES, NACHUM

HISTORY OF THE YISHUV (PALESTINIAN JEWRY): (8) Revisionist "Ha'apalah" (illegal immigration) (Hebrew, 32 pages, open) *Hebrew University, Israel*

BRANDEWIEDE, GREGORY J. (1899–)

Aviation collection (66 pages, permission of contributor required to cite or quote, also at *United States Air Force Academy CO* and *University of the Air, Maxwell Air Force Base AL*) *Columbia University NY*

BRANDNER, GEORGE
National Institutes of Health MD

BRANDON, HENRY
Journalist and editor, *The Sunday Times of London*

(22 pages, open) *John F. Kennedy Library MA*

BRANDT, CARL AMANDUS (1906–)

Aviation collection (34 pages, permission of contributor required to cite or quote, also at *United States Air Force Academy CO* and *University of the Air, Maxwell Air Force Base AL*) *Columbia University NY*

BRANDT, DAVID M. (1945–)
President, executive committee of Cornell's student government

Challenges to governance by students project: Pentagon March (1967) (1967, 155 pages, permission required to cite or quote transcript, tape open) *Cornell University NY*

BRANDT, HARRY (1897–)

Popular arts collection (67 pages, open) *Columbia University NY*

BRANDT, KARL (1899–)

Eisenhower administration project (69 pages, closed during interviewee's lifetime, also at *Dwight D. Eisenhower Library KS*) *Columbia University NJ*

BRANDT, WILLY (1913–)
Former West Berlin mayor

Dulles oral history collection (1964, 19 pages, open) *Princeton University NJ*

BRANHAM, JOHN
Agricultural extension agent, Tennessee

(1972) *Fisk University TN*

BRANNAN, CHARLES FRANKLIN (1903–)
Former Secretary of Agriculture

(1953, 183 pages, closed during interviewee's lifetime) *Columbia University NY*

United States Air Force Academy CO and University of the Air, Maxwell Air Force Base AL) Columbia University NY

BRIGGS, PAUL W.
Cleveland State University Library OH

BRIGGS, ROBERT P.
University of Michigan

BRIGHAM YOUNG UNIVERSITY
Brigham Young University UT

BRIGHTMAN, SAMUEL
Deputy chairman, Democratic national committee
Harry S. Truman Library MO

BRIGHTON, WILLIAM
Mayor
Vigo County Public Library IN

BRILL, A. A.
Discussed in Columbia University interview with Abram Kardiner

BRINCKLE, GERTRUDE (1885–   )
Secretary to Howard Pyle
(1966, 10 pages) *Archives of American Art—Smithsonian Institution NY*

BRINDLE, JAMES
with Martin Cohen
Social Security collection (35 pages, open, also at *Social Security Administration MD) Columbia University NY*

BRISCOE, ROBERT
Journalism lectures (24 pages, permission required to cite or quote) *Columbia University NY*

BRISTOL, ARTHUR
Discussed in Columbia University interview with Robert Bostwick Carney

BRITO, FRANK
Last of the Rough Riders
(one tape, open) *University of Texas, El Paso*

BRITTAIN, SIR HARRY E.

BRITTON, MASON (1890–   )
McGraw-Hill, Inc. (56 pages, permission required) *Columbia University NY*

BROCK, HENRY
Ranching in New Mexico, Pioneers Foundation (also at *University of Arizona) University of New Mexico*

BROCK, HORACE
Labor leader
(1968, 61 pages) *Pennsylvania State University*

BROCKWAY, LORD (A. FENNER) (1888–   )
Law Enforcement Assistance Administration project (1971, 90 minutes, 33 pages) *Cornell University NY*

BRODE, WALLACE REED (1900–   )
Eisenhower administration project (51 pages, closed during interviewee's lifetime, also at *Dwight D. Eisenhower Library KS) Columbia University NY*

BRODERICK, THOMAS
Massachusetts political figure
(72 pages, open) *John F. Kennedy Library MA*

BRODIE, ISRAEL
Chief Rabbi, United Hebrew Congregations of the British Commonwealth (1948–1965)
JEWISH COMMUNITIES: (13) Jews in the Far East (English, 16 pages, open) *Hebrew University, Israel*

BRODNER, YITZHAK
JEWISH COMMUNITIES: (4) Zionist movement in U.S.S.R. (1917–1935) (Hebrew, 10 pages, open) *Hebrew University, Israel*

BRODY, GANDY (1924–   )
Painter
(1965, 15 pages) *Archives of American Art—Smithsonian Institution NY*

BROE, BERNICE MARY
South Dakota experience (1971, South Dakota Oral History Project *University of South Dakota*

BROEK, JAN
Geographer
(1970, 10 minutes) *Plymouth State College NH*

BRONSON, LEWIS H.
Member of Yale Quartet
Ives project (1969) *Yale University School of Music CT*

BROOKE, BRYAN
Mount Sinai Hospital (46 pages, permission required, also at *Mount Sinai Medical Center NY) Columbia University NY*

BROOKLYN COLLEGE
Brooklyn College NY

BROOKLYN, NEW YORK
Brooklyn College NY

New York political studies collection, Brooklyn politics (1930–1950) (1960–1962, 2723 pages, permission required) *Columbia University NY*

BROOKS, JACK
Alaskan pioneers project (7 pages, open) *Columbia University NY*

BROOKS, JOHN
Lear Siegler, Inc., Oral business history project *University of Texas, Austin*

BROOKS, LOUISE McNAMARA
(1960) *State Historical Society of Colorado*

BROOKS, ROZANNE
Collective bargaining at SUNY project (1973, 54 minutes, 42 pages) *Cornell University NY*

BROOKS, VAN WYCK
Discussed in Columbia University interview with John Hall Wheelock

BROOKSHIRE, STANFORD
University of North Carolina, Charlotte

BROOKWOOD LABOR SCHOOL
Black St. Louis leaders collection *University of Missouri, St. Louis*

BROPHY, JOHN (1883–1963)
Labor union official
(1955, 1036 pages, also microfiche, permission required to cite or quote) *Columbia University NY*

BROSIO, MANLIO
International negotiations project (24 pages, permission required) *Columbia University NY*

BROTEN, LOUIS J.
United Transportation Union project (1971, 138 pages, permission required) *Cornell University NY*

BROTHERHOOD OF SLEEPING CAR PORTERS
Black St. Louis leaders collection *University of Missouri, St. Louis*

BROTMAN, ADOLF (–1970) AND FANNY
Former education adviser, Baghdad Jewish community; Headmaster, Shammash Boys' School
JEWISH COMMUNITIES: (10) Jewish life in Iraq (English, 33 pages, open) *Hebrew University, Israel*

BROTT, YEHUDA
Pharmacy division chief, Jerusalem Ministry of Health
WORLD WAR II: THE HOLOCAUST—RESISTANCE AND RESCUE: (6) Rescue of Jewish children (Hebrew, 2 pages, written, open) *Hebrew University, Israel*

BROUN, HEYWOOD
Discussed in Columbia University interviews with Mildred Gilman; Dan Golenpaul

BROWNE, VIVIAN (1929–   )
Painter
(1968, 20 pages) *Archives of American Art—Smithsonian Institution NY*

BROWNELL, HERBERT (1904–   )
Lawyer; Politician; Former U.S. attorney general
Eisenhower administration project (1967, 347 pages, permission required to cite or quote, also at *Dwight D. Eisenhower Library KS) Columbia University NY*
Dulles oral history collection (1965, 45 pages, permission required to cite or quote) *Princeton University NJ*
Discussed in Columbia University interview with Sherman Adams

BROWNELL, SAMUEL MILLER (1900–   )
Educator; U.S. commissioner of education (1953–1956)
Eisenhower administration project (1967, 83 pages, permission required to cite or quote, also at *Dwight D. Eisenhower Library KS) Columbia University NY*
University of Connecticut

BROWNELL, STANLEY (1893–   )
Extension specialist
Agricultural leaders project (1964, 74 pages, permission required to cite or quote) *Cornell University NY*

BROWNELL, WILLARD "BILL"
Peace Corps project (1969, 48 pages, open) *Cornell University NY*

BROWNLEE, JOHN
Labor leader
(1968, 37 pages) *Pennsylvania State University*

BROWNLOW, LOUIS
Discussed in Columbia University interview with Charles Ascher

BRUBACH, HOWARD F.
National Institutes of Health MD

BRUCE, DAVID (1898–   )
U.S. ambassador to Great Britain; Diplomat
(4 pages, open) *John F. Kennedy Library MA*
Dulles oral history collection (1964, 21 pages, permission required to quote or cite) *Princeton University NJ*

BRUCE, JOHN
Newspaper editor and reporter; Author

Earl Warren oral history project (1972, 13 pages) *University of California, Berkeley*

BRUCE, MARIE
Communications Workers of America collection *University of Iowa Libraries*

BRUCE, PRESTON
White House doorman
(21 pages, open) *John F. Kennedy Library MA*

BRUCHEY, STUART (1917–   )
American historians collection (92 pages, permission required to cite or quote) *Columbia University NY*

BRUCHONI, SHLOMO
HISTORY OF THE YISHUV (PALESTINIAN JEWRY) (6) Ha-Poel Ha-Mizrachi movement in Palestine (Hebrew, 8 pages, open) *Hebrew University, Israel*

BRUCKER, WILBER
University of Michigan

BRUERE, HENRY (1882–1958)
Civic worker; Financier
(1949, 170 pages, also microfiche, permission required to cite or quote) *Columbia University NY*

BRUMLEY, JIM
South Dakota experience (1971), South Dakota Oral History Project *University of South Dakota*

BRUNDAGE, AUGUSTUS
University of Connecticut

BRUNDAGE, PERCIVAL FLACK (1892–   )
Bureau of the Budget director (1956–1958)
Eisenhower administration project (1967, 52 pages, permission required to cite or quote, also at *Dwight D. Eisenhower Library KS) Columbia University NY*
Dulles oral history collection (1966, 30 pages, open) *Princeton University NJ*

BRUNNER-ORNE, DR. MARTHA
Careers of New England women in medicine *Arthur and Elizabeth Schlesinger Library MA*

BRUNO, HARRY A. (1893–   )
Public relations counsel
Aviation collection (1960, 118 pages, closed until May 1, 1985, also at *United States Air Force Academy CO* and *University of the Air, Maxwell Air Force Base AL) Columbia University NY*

BRUNS, EUGENIA M. (1876–1970)
Educator
(1965–1966, 37 pages, open) *University of Nevada, Reno*

BRUSKA, WALTER G.
Ithaca Festival (Center for the Arts at Ithaca) project (1967, 113 pages, permission re-

quired to cite or quote) *Cornell University NY*

BRUSTEIN, ROBERT
American cultural leaders collection (17 pages, closed pending publication of a study) *Columbia University NY*

BRYAN, JOHN
Historic preservation *Charles B. Hosmer, Jr. Collection IL*

BRYAN, WILLIAM RAY
Health science collection (82 pages, permission required, also at *National Library of Medicine MD) Columbia University NY*
National Institutes of Health MD

BRYANT, HAROLD C. (1876–1968) with Newton B. Drury
Nature interpreter; Educator
Development of the Naturalist Program in the National Park Service (1964, 49 pages) *University of California, Berkeley*

BRYANT, JAY CLARK
National Institutes of Health MD

BRYANT, TRAPHES
White House electrician
(17 pages, open) *John F. Kennedy Library MA*

BRYANT, W. D.
Mayor of Wabash
(1972) *Wabash Carnegie Public Library IN*

BRYANT, WILLIAM CULLEN, II
Allan Nevins project (21 pages, closed until March 5, 1976) *Columbia University NY*

BRYN MAWR COLLEGE
Bryn Mawr College Alumnae Association PA

BRYSON, LYMAN LLOYD (1888–1959)
Educator
Radio pioneers collection (254 pages, open) *Columbia University NY*

BUCHANAN, A. A.
Benedum and the oil industry (14 pages, open) *Columbia University NY*

BUCHANAN, CLARENCE E.
James B. Duke project (31 pages, permission required, also at *Duke University NC) Columbia University NY*

BUCHANAN, FATHER
(3 tapes, open) *University of Texas, El Paso*

BUCHANAN, R. E.
Iowa State University of Science and Technology

BUCHANAN, DR. RUSSELL A.
Campus history *University of California, Santa Barbara*

BURCHFIELD, CHARLES (1893–1967)
Painter

(1959, 54 pages) *Archives of American Art—Smithsonian Institution NY*

BURCKHARDT, FREDERICK H. (1912–   )
Educator

Carnegie Corporation collection (1968, 84 pages, permission required) *Columbia University NY*

BURDEN, WILLIAM ARMISTEAD MOALE (1906–   )
U.S. diplomat; Member, National Aeronautics and Space Council (1958–1959)

Eisenhower administration project (1968, 81 pages, closed during interviewee's lifetime, also at *Dwight D. Eisenhower Library KS*) *Columbia University NY*

BURGE, JOHN R. (1913–   )

United Transportation Union project (1971, 31 pages, permission required to cite or quote) *Cornell University NY*

BURGER, JOSEPH CHARLES (1902–   )
Lieutenant general, U.S. Marine Corps (service: 1925–1961)

(1969, 377 pages, permission required, also at *Columbia University NY* and *U.S. Naval Institute MD*) *United States Marine Corps DC*

BURGER, MR.

WORLD WAR II: THE HOLOCAUST—RESISTANCE AND RESCUE: (17) Forced labor camps under Nazi occupation in Tunisia (German, 56 pages, open) *Hebrew University, Israel*

BURGESS, CARTER L. (1916–   )
Secretary to general staff of SHAEF; State Department official; Assistant defense secretary for manpower (1954–1957); Corporation executive

Eisenhower administration project (1967, 40 pages, open, also at *Dwight D. Eisenhower Library KS*) *Columbia University NY*

BURGESS, GELETT

Discussed in Columbia University interview with Ben W. Huebsch

BURGESS, WARREN RANDOLPH (1889–   )
U.S. government official; Former U.S. representative to NATO

Carnegie Corporation collection (1967, 50 pages, permission required) *Columbia University NY*

Interviewed with Mrs. Burgess, Dulles oral history collection (1965, 48 pages, open) *Princeton University NJ*

BURGIN, YEHIEL
Ramat-Gan clerk

WORLD WAR II: THE HOLOCAUST—RESISTANCE AND RESCUE: (13) Underground activities of the Lithuanian Jews (Yiddish, 49 pages, open) *Hebrew University, Israel*

BURGOIN, ALICE (1902–   )
College teacher

(1964, 90 pages, permission required to cite or quote) *Cornell University NY*

BURGOON, BEATRICE M.
Director, Office of Labor Management Relations Services

United Transportation Union project (1972, 63 pages, permission required to use) *Cornell University NY*

BURK, DEAN
National Institutes of Health MD

BURK, LINDA

Challenges to governance by students project: School of the Ozarks (1969, 24 pages, most open) *Cornell University NY*

BURK, VOLNIE S. (1917–   )
Army veteran; Survivor of the siege on Fort Hughes near Corregidor

Prisoner-of-war project (1972, 91 pages, open) *North Texas State University Oral History Collection*

BURKAN, AVRAHAM
Deputy director, Mashav construction company (Tel-Aviv)

HISTORY OF THE YISHUV (PALESTINIAN JEWRY): (8) Revisionist "Ha 'apalah" (illegal immigration) (Hebrew, 63 pages, open) *Hebrew University, Israel*

BURKART, ARTURO ERHARDO

Hunt Institute for Botanical Documentation PA

BURKE, AGNES
Educator

(1967, 50 pages, open) *Columbia University NY*

Discussed in Columbia University interview with Charlotte Garrison

BURKE, ARLEIGH ANDREW (1901–   )
Admiral; Chief, U.S. naval operations

Eisenhower administration project (249 pages, permission required to cite or quote, also at *Dwight D. Eisenhower Library KS*) *Columbia University NY*

(39 pages, permission of interviewee required) *John F. Kennedy Library MA*

Dulles oral history collection (1966, 57 pages, permission required to cite or quote) *Princeton University NJ*

BURKE, GRACE
Secretary, John F. Kennedy's Boston office

(23 pages, open) *John F. Kennedy Library MA*

BURKE, JAMES D. (1907–   )
Extension specialist

Agricultural leaders project *Cornell University NY*

See also George W. Tailby

BURKE, JAMES VINCENT, JR. (1911–   )

Eisenhower administration project (52 pages, permission required to cite or quote, also at *Dwight D. Eisenhower Library KS*) *Columbia University NY*

BURKE, JOHN P. (1902–   )

McGraw-Hill, Inc. (27 pages, permission required) *Columbia University NY*

BURKE, KENNETH
White House policeman

(8 pages, open) *John F. Kennedy Library MA*

BURKE, LEO

South Dakota experience (1971), South Dakota Oral History Project *University of South Dakota*

BURKE, WALTER
Secretary-treasurer, United Steelworkers of America

(In process) *Pennsylvania State University*

BURKE, WALTER H. with Curtis B. Mateer

South Dakota experience (1970), South Dakota Oral History Project *University of South Dakota*

BURKHARDT, ROBERT
New Jersey political figure; Director, 1960 national voters' registration drive; Assistant postmaster general

(8 pages, open) *John F. Kennedy Library MA*

BURLA, YEHUDA (–1969)

CULTURE AND EDUCATION: (1) Authors and their work (Hebrew, 55 pages, open) *Hebrew University, Israel*

BURLAGE, GEORGE (1918–   )
Public affairs officer, Federal Aviation Administration; Marine Corps veteran; Siege of Corregidor survivor

Prisoner-of-war project (1970, 114 pages, open) *North Texas State University Oral History Collection*

BURLIN, PAUL (1886–1969)
Painter

(1962, 40 pages) *Archives of American Art—Smithsonian Institution NY*

BURLINGHAM, CHARLES CULP (1858–1959)
Lawyer

(1949, 45 pages, also microfiche, permission required to cite or quote) *Columbia University NY*

BURNETT, MRS. T. R.

(Not transcribed) *University of Texas, El Paso*

BURNEY, LEROY E. (1906–   )

Health science collection (46 pages, permission required, also at *National Library of Medicine MD*) *Columbia University NY*

BUTTON, ROBERT

(1967, 1 reel, 22 pages) *Broadcast Pioneers Library DC*

BUTTON, RON

Southern California attorney; Republican convention leader (1952); California national committee

Earl Warren oral history project (in process) *University of California, Berkeley*

BUTTS, ORILLA (1904–   )

College extension leader

(1964, 127 pages, permission required to cite or quote) *Cornell University NY*

BUTZ, EARL LAUER (1909–   )

Educator, Purdue University; Official, U.S. Department of Agriculture

Eisenhower administration project (1968, 51 pages, open, also at *Dwight D. Eisenhower Library KS*) *Columbia University NY*

(1970, 45 pages) *Purdue University Archives IN*

BUTZIN, YAAKOV

Agricultural director (Galilee)

HISTORY OF THE YISHUV (PALESTINIAN JEWRY): (8) Revisionist "Ha 'apalah" (illegal immigration) (Hebrew, 63 pages, open) *Hebrew University, Israel*

BUXMAN, WILLIAM (1884–1954)

McGraw-Hill, Inc. (70 pages, permission required) *Columbia University NY*

BUXTON, DARRELL C.

Ricks College ID

BUXTON, WARNER

Challenges to governance by students project: Student activism—Jackson State College (1972, 31 pages; 1971, 45 minutes; permission required to use) *Cornell University NY*

BYERS, JOSEPH AND FRANCES

South Dakota experience (1970), South Dakota Oral History Project *University of South Dakota*

BYNUM, BEN

Texas Legislator (representative)

Legislative project *North Texas State University Oral History Collection*

BYRD, RICHARD

Discussed in Columbia University interview with Richard Blackburn Black

BYRNE, CLARISSA YOUNG

Mill Valley Public Library CA

BYRNE, EDWIN

Ricks College ID

BYRNE, GARRETT

Massachusetts political figure

(46 pages, open) *John F. Kennedy Library MA*

BYRNES, JAMES F. (1879–   )

Former U.S. Secretary of State

Dulles oral history collection (1965, 9 pages, open) *Princeton University NY*

Discussed in Columbia University interviews with William Benton; Chester Bowles; William Lockhart Clayton; William Hammatt Davis; Marvin Jones

BYRNES, JOHN W. (1913–   )

Social Security collection (51 pages, open, also at *Social Security Administration MD*) *Columbia University NY*

C

CABELL, CHARLES F. (1903–   )

Former Deputy Director, Central Intelligence Agency

Dulles oral history collection (1965, 22 pages, open) *Princeton University NJ*

CABELL, CHARLES PEARRE (1903–1971)

Henry H. Arnold project (59 pages, permission required, also at *United States Air Force Academy CO*) *Columbia University NY*

U.S. Air Force Academy project (joint interview with Haywood S. Hansell, 133 pages, consult center for restriction, also at *United States Air Force Academy CO*) *Columbia University NY*

CABONA, ANDRES (1899–   )

Labor leader

Argentine in the 1930s (1970, Spanish, 116 pages, open) *Columbia University NY*

CABOT, JOHN M. (1901–   )

U.S. diplomat

Dulles oral history collection (1965, 26 pages, permission required to cite or quote) *Princeton University NJ*

CADY, LEE D.

Physician, World War II, General Hospital 21, North Africa, Italy, France

Washington University School of Medicine MO

CAESAR, IRVING 1895–   )

Popular arts collection (32 pages, open) *Columbia University NY*

CAGNEY, JAMES (1904–   )

Popular arts collection (56 pages, open) *Columbia University NY*

CAHILL, HOLGER (1893–1960)

Writer; Art director

(1957, 622 pages, permission required) *Columbia University NY*

CAHILL, ROBBINS E. (1905–   )

Nevada trade association executive

(1971–1972, in process) *University of Nevada, Reno*

CAHLAN, JOHN F. (1902–   )

Journalist; Developer

(1968, 320 pages, open) *University of Nevada, Reno*

CAHOON, FRANK K. (1934–   )

Geologist; Independent oil operator; Former state legislator from Midland; Republican

Legislative project (1967, 72 pages, open) *North Texas State University Oral History Collection*

CAIN, MRS. ALVIE, AND MRS. NELSON IRWIN

South Dakota experience (1971), South Dakota Oral History Project *University of South Dakota*

CAIRNS, MARY LYONS

(1958) *State Historical Society of Colorado*

CAKE, RALPH HARLAN (1891–   )

Executive

Eisenhower administration project (1969, 78 pages, permission required to cite or quote, also at *Dwight D. Eisenhower Library KS*) *Columbia University NY*

CALAMITY JANE

Discussed in University of South Dakota South Dakota Oral History Project interviews with Joe Hilton and Pauline Pearson and Freeman Steel, Sr., *et al.*

CALDERONE, MARY

Discussed in Columbia University interview with Charles Ascher

CALDWELL, CYRIL C.

Aviation collection (39 pages, permission required of interviewee required to cite or quote, also at *United States Air Force Academy CO* and *University of the Air, Maxwell Air Force Base AL*) *Columbia University NY*

CALDWELL, ERSKINE

University of Southern Mississippi

CALDWELL, ORESTES HAMPTON (1888–1967)

Radio pioneers collection (28 pages, open) *Columbia University NY*

CALDWELL, WILLIAM VAN DAVIS

U.S. Air Force veteran of Vietnam War

(1972) *Fisk University TN*

CALHOUN, REV. AND MRS. ROBERT L.

Personal friends of Hindemith

Hindemith project (1973) *Yale University School of Music CT*

CAMPBELL, WILL
Centenarian, Nashville TN
(1973) *Fisk University TN*

CAMPBELL, REV. WILL D.
Author; White civil rights participant
(1972) *Fisk University TN*

CAMPOS, PEDRO ALBIZU
Discussed in Columbia University interview with Roger Nash Baldwin

CAMPOS, ROBERTO DE OLIVEIRA
Brazilian ambassador to the United States
(56 pages, open) *John F. Kennedy Library MA*

CANBY, HENRY SEIDEL (1878-1961)
Book-of-the-Month Club (45 pages, open) *Columbia University NY*

CANDELL, VICTOR (1903–   )
Painter
(1965, 22 pages) *Archives of American Art—Smithsonian Institution NY*

CANDIDO, ANTHONY (1924–   )
Painter; Architect
(1970, 32 pages) *Archives of American Art—Smithsonian Institution NY*

CANE, MELVILLE HENRY (1879–   )
Lawyer; Poet
(1956, 83 pages, also microfiche, permission required to cite or quote) *Columbia University NY*

CANFIELD, CASS (1897–   )
Publisher
(1966, 417 pages, also microfiche, permission to cite or quote) *Columbia University NY*

CANNADY, CHARISSE A.
Challenges to governance by students project (1969, 46 pages, permission required to cite or quote) *Cornell University NY*

CANNON, CHARLES A.
James B. Duke project (45 pages, permission required; also at *Duke University NC*) *Columbia University NY*

CANNON, JOHN D.
Columbia crisis of 1968 (86 pages, permission required) *Columbia University NY*

CANNON, ROBERT
Retired lieutenant general, U.S. Army; Chief, U.S. military advisory group in the Philippines (1953)
(2 hours, 40 pages) *United States Naval War College RI*

CANNON, WALTER
Discussed in Columbia University interview with Joseph Charles Aub

CANON, R. T., M.D.
One of Franklin D. Roosevelt's White House physicians
(Open) *Texas Tech University*

CANTONI, RAFFAELE
ANTECEDENTS TO THE STATE OF ISRAEL: (3) "Ha'apalah" (illegal immigration) (Hebrew, translated from Italian, 11 pages, open) *Hebrew University, Israel*

CANTRIL, HADLEY
Discussed in Columbia University interview with Paul Felix Lazarsfeld

CANTY, WALTER H. (1914–   )
General Chairman, UTU conductors
United Transportation Union project (1971, 92 pages, permission required to cite or quote) *Cornell University NY*

CAPE VERDE ISLANDS
Rhode Island Department of State Library Services

CAPEHART, ADRIAN
Chairman, Frederick Douglass Prison Movement
(1972) *Fisk University TN*

CAPENER, HAROLD R.
Challenges to governance by students project (1969, 27 pages, permission required to cite or quote) *Cornell University NY*

CAPERS, ROBERTA
Specialist in the fine arts
Carnegie Corporation collection (1967, 124 pages, permission required) *Columbia University NY*

CAPONE, AL
Discussed in Columbia University interview with Edwin A. Lahey

CAPPA, JOSEPH D.
Discussed in Columbia University interviews with Samson Raphaelson; Albert Edward Sutherland

CAPRA, FRANK (1897–   )
Popular arts collection (73 pages, open) *Columbia University NY*

CARALEY, DEMETRIOS
New York political studies collection, Citizens Budget Commission (41 pages, permission required) *Columbia University NY*

CARAWAY, PAUL W.
Lieutenant general, U.S. Army
United States Army Military Research Collection PA

CARBON, CON (1871-1907)
King's College PA

CARCELLA, HUGH
United Steelworkers of America labor leader
(1967, 51 pages) *Pennsylvania State University*

CARDIFF, GEORGE H.
Central California coast collection (1964, 395 pages) *University of California, Santa Cruz*

CARDON, PHILIP VINCENT (1889–1965)
Agriculturist
(1952, 806 pages, also microfiche, permission required to cite or quote) *Columbia University NY*

CARDOZO, BENJAMIN
Discussed in Columbia University interviews with Frederic René Coudert; James McCauley Landis; John Lord O'Brian

CAREW, VIRGINIA B.
UCLA fiftieth anniversary interviews, University history collection *University of California, Los Angeles*

CAREY, DANIEL J. (1897–   )
Farm organization official
(1968, 410 pages, permission required to cite or quote) *Cornell University NY*

CAREY, JAMES BARRON (1911–   )
President, International Brotherhood of Electrical Workers
(1958, 352 pages, closed during interviewee's lifetime) *Columbia University NY*
(19 pages, open) *John F. Kennedy Library MA*
Discussed in Columbia University interviews with Edwin A. Lahey; Lee Pressman

CAREY, MARGARET CHASE
Smith alumna, class of 1966; Community and college service volunteer
(1973, 2 hours, 40 pages) *Smith College MA*

CAREY, RAYMOND G.
(1961) *State Historical Society of Colorado*

CARIBBEAN AREA
Willard Van der Veer interview, Motion picture and television collection (open) *University of California, Los Angeles*

CARLE, C. E. "TEET"
Motion picture publicist
An oral history of the motion picture in America *University of California, Los Angeles*

CARLETON, ALICIA SKINNER
Smith alumna, class of 1932; Home, family, and community service volunteer
(1973, 1 hour, 28 pages) *Smith College MA*

CARLIN, PHILLIPS (1894-1971)
Radio pioneers collection (27 pages, open) *Columbia University NY*

CARROLL, JOHN
Communications Workers of America collection *University of Iowa Libraries*

CARROTHERS, GEORGE EZRA (1880–1966)
Teacher, Philippine Islands, 1909–1913
University of Michigan

CARSON, CLARENCE
Discussed in Columbia University interview with William Terry Couch

CARSON, JOHN
Discussed in Columbia University interview with Maurine Mulliner

CARSON, MRS. JOSEPH
Independence National Historical Park (22 pages, permission required) *Columbia University NY*

CARSON, KIT
Discussed in State Historical Society of Colorado William T. Carson interview

CARSON, WILLIAM T.
(1962) *State Historical Society of Colorado*

CARSTENSEN, CORINA *see* Jack Trople

CARSTENSEN, EMIL *see* Jack Trople

CARSTENSEN, NELS
South Dakota experience (1971), South Dakota Oral History Project *University of South Dakota*

CARSTENSON, BLUE
Social Security collection (1966, 227 pages, plus papers, open, also at *Social Security Administration MD*) *Columbia University NY*

CARTER, BENNIE LESTER
Musician; Composer
(1972) *Fisk University TN*

CARTER, ELLIOTT
Composer
Ives project (1969) *Yale University School of Music CT*

CARTER, GEORGE
Geographer
(1970, 10 minutes) *Plymouth State College NH*

CARTER, HODDING (1907–1972)
Journalism lectures, Forum II (permission required to cite or quote) *Columbia University NY*

CARTER, JESSE W. (1888–1959)
Justice, California Supreme Court
(1959, 546 pages) *University of California. Berkeley*

CARTER, JOHN FRANKLIN
Journalist (Jay Franklin, pseud.)
Harry S. Truman Library MO

CARTER, KATE B.
Ricks College ID

CARTER, JUDGE OLIVER
Assemblyman who carried Warren's legislation
Earl Warren oral history project (in process) *University of California. Berkeley*

CARTER, UELL (1922–)
Army veteran; Former member, "Lost Battalion"
Prisoner-of-war project (1970, 110 pages, open) *North Texas State University Oral History Collection*

CARTER, W. HARRISON, JR.
University of Connecticut

CARTWRIGHT, HANLEY
Musician
Jennings County Public Library IN

CARTWRIGHT, MORSE ADAMS (1890–)
Educational administrator
Carnegie Corporation collection (1967, 242 pages, permission required) *Columbia University NY*
Discussed in Columbia University interviews with Roberta Capers; Trevor Lloyd; John McFarlane Russell

CARTY, ED
Personal friend of Warren; Member, State Fish and Game Commission
Earl Warren oral history project (in process) *University of California. Berkeley*

CARUTHERS, EDWARD
Centenarian, Franklin TN
(1972) *Fisk University TN*

CARVER, GEORGE WASHINGTON
Discussed in History of Iowa State University collection Iowa State University of Science and Technology

CARY, WILLIAM
Chairman, U.S. Securities and Exchange Commission
(187 pages with other members of Regulatory Agencies Panel, portions closed) *John F. Kennedy Library MA*

CASE, JAMES G.
Food processor
(1964, 22 pages, permission required to cite or quote) *Cornell University NY*

CASEY, JOSEPH
Massachusetts political figure
(25 pages, open) *John F. Kennedy Library MA*

CASEY, RICHARD G., LORD OF BERWICK (1890–)
Former Australian minister for external affairs
Dulles oral history collection (1964, 32 pages, permission required to cite or quote) *Princeton University NJ*

CASHIN, DR. JOHN
(1970) *Fisk University TN*

CASHMORE, JOHN
Discussed in Columbia University New York political studies collection

CASPARI, CLAUS
Hunt Institute for Botanical Documentation PA

CASPI, JOSEPH
YOUTH MOVEMENTS: (3) He-Halutz movement (Hebrew, 7 pages, open) *Hebrew University, Israel*

CASSAVETES, JOHN (1929–)
Popular arts collection (28 pages, open) *Columbia University NY*

CASSIDY, BUTCH
Outlaw
University of Utah

CASSIDY, ROSALIND FRANCES
University history collection (portions closed) *University of California, Los Angeles*

CASSIDY, MRS. T. J.
(1960) *State Historical Society of Colorado*

CASTELLANOS
Latin author
Discussed in University of Texas, El Paso, Chester Christian interview (two tapes)

CASTELLI, LEO (1907–)
Art dealer
(1969, 95 pages) *Archives of American Art—Smithsonian Institution NY*

CASTERLINE, L. E. (1919–)
Businessman
Observations on the development of the seafood industry in the Coastal Bend area of South Texas 1925–1971 (1971, 37 pages, open) *North Texas State University Oral History Collection*

United States Air Air Force Academy CO and University of the Air, Maxwell Air Force Base AL) Columbia University NY

CHAMBERLAIN, EDWIN J.
Member, Michigan State Dental Board (1913-1917)
University of Michigan

CHAMBERLAIN, OWEN (1920-)
Nobel Laureates on scientific research (44 pages, permission required) *Columbia University NY*

CHAMBERLAIN, RICHARD H. (1894-)
Superior Court judge, retired
(1972, 37 pages) *University of California, Berkeley*

CHAMBERLAIN, THOMAS GASSNER (1892-)
Lawyer
(1951, 181 pages, closed until 5 years after death) *Columbia University NY*

CHAMBERLAIN, WALDO (1905-)
Historian
(1952, 112 pages, also microfiche, permission required to cite or quote) *Columbia University NY*

CHAMBERS, REED
Aviation collection (84 pages, permission required to cite or quote, also at *United States Air Force Academy CO and University of the Air, Maxwell Air Force Base AL)* Columbia University NY

CHAMBERS, WHITTAKER
Discussed in Columbia University interview with Max Gissen

CHAMOUN, CAMILLE (1900-)
Former president of Lebanon
Dulles oral history collection (1964, 50 pages, open) *Princeton University NJ*

CHAMPION, GEORGE
(1962) *State Historical Society of Colorado*

CHANDLER, GEORGE FLETCHER (1872-1964)
Surgeon; Penologist
(1950, 113 pages, open) *Columbia University NY*

CHANDLER, HARRY
Discussed in Columbia University interview with Donald Wills Douglas

CHANDLER, JAMES
Proprietor, Chandler Construction Co., Nashville
(1973) *Fisk University TN*

CHANDLER, WILLIAM HENRY
University history collection (open) *University of California, Los Angeles*

CHANEY, RALPH WORKS (1890-1971)
Paleobotanist; Conservationist
(1960, 277 pages) *University of California, Berkeley*

CHANG, FA-K'UEI
Chinese oral history (in process) *Columbia University NY*

CHANG MYUN (1899-)
Former Korean prime minister
Dulles oral history collection (1964, 27 pages, permission required to cite or quote) *Princeton University NJ*

CHAPIN, ARTHUR
Democratic national committee staff member; Government employee
(52 pages, open) *John F. Kennedy Library MA*

CHAPIN, EMERSON
International negotiations project (1970, 25 pages, permission required) *Columbia University NY*

CHAPLIN, CHARLIE
Discussed in Columbia University interview with Albert Edward Sutherland

CHAPLIN, W.W.
(1965, 1 reel) *Broadcast Pioneers Library DC*

CHAPMAN, ALFRED
West Virginia political figure
(29 pages, open) *John F. Kennedy Library MA*

CHAPMAN, ALGER BALDWIN (1904-)
Lawyer
(1949, 76 pages, closed during interviewee's lifetime) *Columbia University NY*

New York political studies (14 pages, permission required to cite or quote) *Columbia University NY*

CHAPMAN, HARRY (1891-)
Food processor
Agricultural leader, project (1964, 26 pages, permission required to cite or quote) *Cornell University NY*

CHAPMAN, PAUL J. (1900-)
Entomologist
Regional history collection (1965, 189 pages, permission required to cite or quote) *Cornell University NY*

CHAPPELLE, EDNA JAMES (MRS. DELOS)
(1964) *State Historical Society of Colorado*

CHARBONEAU AND JIM BRIDGER
University of Utah

CHARITIES
Field Enterprises IL

CHARLESTON, SOUTH CAROLINA
Historic preservation *Charles B. Hosmer, Jr. Collection IL*

CHARLESTON, WEST VIRGINIA
Kanawha County Public Library WV

CHARLOT, JEAN (1898-)
Painter
(1961, 21 pages) *Archives of American Art—Smithsonian Institution NY*

CHARLTON, LILLIAN
McGraw-Hill, Inc. (25 pages, permission required) *Columbia University NY*

CHARMATZ, JOSEPH
Director, O.R.T. (Israel)
WORLD WAR II: THE HOLOCAUST—RESISTANCE AND RESCUE: (13) Underground activities of the Lithuanian Jews (Hebrew, 41 pages, open) *Hebrew University, Israel*

CHARTERS, W. W.
Discussed in Columbia University interview with William Harold Cowley

CHASE, HARRY WOODBURN
Discussed in Columbia University interview with William Terry Couch

CHASE, ISAAC H.
South Dakota experience (1970), South Dakota Oral History Project *University of South Dakota*

CHASE, PEARL
Santa Barbara conservationist and community development activist
University of California, Santa Barbara

CHASE, WILLIAM
Discussed in Columbia University interview with Edwin Walter Dickinson

CHASINS, ABRAM (1903-)
Radio pioneers collection (89 pages, open) *Columbia University NY*

CHASSEL, DR. J. L.
South Dakota experience (1971), South Dakota Oral History Project *University of South Dakota*

CHATELAIN, NICOLAS (1913-)
Journalist
(1961, 55 pages, open) *Columbia University NY*

CHATELAIN, VERNE
Historic preservation *Charles B. Hosmer, Jr. Collection IL*

CHATMAN, MARION
U.S. Army veteran
Fisk University TN

CHATTANOOGA, TENNESSEE
Chattanooga Area Historical Association TN

CHINESE LANGUAGE
Chinese Culture Foundation of San Francisco CA

CHING, CYRUS (1876–1967)
Industrial relations expert; Chairman, Wage Stabilization Board (1951)

(1965, 721 pages, permission required to cite or quote, also at *Columbia University NY*) *Cornell University NY*

CHISHOLM, DOUGLAS
Communications Workers of America collection *University of Iowa Libraries*

CHISHOLM, ELIZABETH WISNER
Smith alumna, class of 1924; Patron of arts

(1973, 2 hours, 35 pages) *Smith College MA*

CHISHOLM, LOUIS C. (1918–)
General Chairman, UTU

United Transportation Union project (1971, 101 pages, permission required to cite or quote transcript, permission required to use tape) *Cornell University NY*

CHISHOLM, SHIRLEY
U.S. Congresswoman

(1972) *Fisk University TN*

CHISM, JOHN
Discussed in University of Texas, El Paso, George Adlai Feather interview

CHOATE, JOSEPH
Discussed in Columbia University interview with Allen Wardwell

CHOPE, CHESTER
Former city editor, *El Paso Times*

(1968, 35 pages, open) *University of Texas, El Paso*

CHOREY, JOHN
United Steelworkers of America labor leader

(1966, 23 pages) *Pennsylvania State University*

CHORLEY, KENNETH (1893–)
Conservationist

Jackson Hole Preserve (1966, 160 pages, permission required) *Columbia University NY*

CHOY, JUN-KE
Chinese oral history (in process) *Columbia University NY*

CHRIST-JANER, ALBERT (1910–)
Painter; Writer

(1964, 7 pages) *Archives of American Art— Smithsonian Institution NY*

CHRISTENSEN, CHARLES ELMER
Ricks College ID

CHRISTENSEN, FRED
(1962) *State Historical Society of Colorado*

CHRISTENSEN, LAURA
Ricks College ID

CHRISTENSEN, NEPHI
Ricks College ID

CHRISTIAN, CHESTER
Contemporary Latin authors (15 tapes, open) *University of Texas, El Paso*

CHRISTIAN, GEORGE (1927–)
Journalist; Public relations executive; Former press secretary to President Lyndon B. Johnson

(1968, 86 pages, open) *North Texas State University Oral History Collection*

CHRISTIAN, J. O.
University of Connecticut

CHRISTIAN SCIENCE
Ruth St. Denis interview, Fine arts collection *University of California, Los Angeles*

CHRISTIANSON, MRS. *see* Mrs. Thomas Gillespie

CHRISTIE, SIDNEY
West Virginia political figure

(8 pages, open) *John F. Kennedy Library MA*

CHRYSLER, WALTER P., JR.
Art collector

(1964, 6 pages) *Archives of American Art— Smithsonian Institution NY*

CHRYSSA, V. (1933–)
Sculptor

(1967, 20 pages) *Archives of American Art— Smithsonian Institution NY*

CHUNG IL KWON
Former Korean prime minister

Dulles oral history collection (1964, Korean and English, 43 pages, open) *Princeton University NJ*

CHURCH, ARTHUR B.
(1966, 1 reel, 27 pages) *Broadcast Pioneers Library DC*

CHURCH, DOUGLAS
Sugar beet industry in New York State (1968, 36 pages, open) *Cornell University NY*

CHURCH, ELLEN
Aviation collection (22 pages, permission required to cite or quote, also at *United States Air Force Academy CO* and *University of the Air, Maxwell Air Force Base AL*) *Columbia University NY*

CHURCH, J. M.
(1958) *State Historical Society of Colorado*

CHURCH OF JESUS CHRIST OF LATTER-DAY SAINTS *see* Mormons and Mormonism

CHURCH OF THE NAZARENE
Trevecca Nazarene College TN

CHURCHILL, DR. ANNA
Careers of New England women in medicine *Arthur and Elizabeth Schlesinger Library MA*

CHURCHILL, EDWARD DELOS (1895–1972)
Surgeon

(1957, 691 pages, plus papers, permission required to cite or quote) *Columbia University NY*

Discussed in Columbia University interview with Joseph Charles Aub

CHURCHILL, SIR WINSTON
Discussed in Columbia University interviews with Richard Austen Butler; Ira C. Eaker; William Morrow Fechteler; James C. Hagerty; Livingston Tallmadge Merchant; Sir Muhammed Zafrulla Khah

CHURCHILL-DAVIDSON, HARRY CUNNINGHAM, M.D.
Anesthesiologist

Wood Library—Museum of Anesthesiology IL

CIANO, GALEAZZO
Discussed in Columbia University interview with Thomas Cassin Kinkaid

CIDOR, HANAN
Former Israeli ambassador to Netherlands

WORLD WAR II: THE HOLOCAUST—RESISTANCE AND RESCUE: (6) Rescue of Jewish children (Hebrew, 2 pages, open) *Hebrew University, Israel*

CIKUTH, LUKE P.
The Pajaro Valley apple industry (1890–1930) (1967, 210 pages), Central California coast collection *University of California, Santa Cruz*

CINEMA *see* Moving Pictures

CITRUS FRUIT
Claremont Graduate School CA

CITY PLANNING
University of Baltimore MD

South Dakota experience, South Dakota Oral History Project *University of South Dakota*

CIVIL ENGINEERING
American Society of Civil Engineers NY

CIVIL RIGHTS
State Historical Society of Wisconsin

See also Blacks—Civil Rights; Woman—Civil Rights

CIVIL RIGHTS DEMONSTRATIONS *see* Blacks—Civil Rights

CIVIL WAR—U.S. *see* U.S.—History—Civil War

CLEAVER, KATHLEEN (MRS. ELDRIDGE)

(1971) *Fisk University TN*

CLELAND, RALPH ERSKINE

Hunt Institute for Botanical Documentation PA

CLEM, ONNIE (1919–   )

Marine Corps veteran; Survivor of the Bataan Campaign

Prisoner-of-war project (1972, 101 pages, open) *North Texas State University Oral History Collection*

CLEM, SAM

(1961) *State Historical Society of Colorado*

CLEMENS, PAUL

(1959) *State Historical Society of Colorado*

CLEMENS, SAMUEL LANGHORNE (1835–1910)

American Author

Henry James Forman interview, Biographical collection *University of California, Los Angeles*

Discussed in Chemung County Historical Center NY Dr. Ida Langdon interview

CLEMENT, FRANK C.

Discussed in Memphis Public Library and Information Center TN Gordon R. Browning memoir

CLEMENT, THOMAS

Socialist movement project (39 pages, permission required to cite or quote) *Columbia University NY*

CLEPPER, HENRY (1901–   )

Executive secretary, Society of American Foresters

(1968, 36 pages) *University of California, Berkeley*

CLEVELAND, DONALD

Challenges to governance by students project: Student activism—Jackson State College (1971, permission required to cite or quote) *Cornell University NY*

CLEVELAND, GROVER

Discussed in Columbia University interviews with William Stiles Bennet; Charles Warren

CLEVELAND, RICHARD FOLSOM

Son of President (Stephen) Grover Cleveland; Whittaker Chambers's lawyer

Maryland Historical Society

CLICKMAN, WALTER

(1968, 25 pages, open) *Cornell University NY*

CLIFFE, EDWARD

Chief, U.S. Forest Service

(17 pages, open) *John F. Kennedy Library MA*

CLIFFORD, CORNELIUS

Discussed in Columbia University interview with Frederic René Coudert

CLIFFORD, JOHN G.

Plattsburgh Idea, businessmen's camp of 1915 (1½ cassettes, open) *Plattsburgh State University College NY*

CLIFTON, FLORENCE

Democratic Party political leader (southern California; Campaign leader against Warren

Earl Warren oral history project (in process) *University of California, Berkeley*

CLIFTON, ROBERT

Superior Court judge

Earl Warren oral history project (in process) *University of California, Berkeley*

CLINE, JOHN W. (1898–   )

Physician

California Medical Association (1971, 38 pages) *University of California, Berkeley*

CLINICAL BIOCHEMISTRY see Biochemistry, Clinical

CLINTON, ANN L.

University of Michigan

CLINTON, HELEN

Mill Valley Public Library CA

CLOBY, MRS. CHARLES (MARY)

Geographer

(1972, 10 minutes) *Plymouth State College NH*

CLOONEY, ROSEMARY

Popular singer

Hollywood Center for the Audio-Visual Arts CA

CLOUD, GEORGE HARLON (1904–   )

Major general, U.S. Marine Corps (service: 1927–1964)

(115 pages, open, also at Columbia University NY and U.S. Naval Institute MD) *United States Marine Corps DC*

CLUTE, R. V.

Weyerhaeuser Timber Company (65 pages, permission required) *Columbia University NY*

CLUTTERBUCK, HAROLDO RODOLFO GUIDO (1907–   )

Corporation executive

Argentina in the 1930s (Spanish, 1971, 61 pages, open) *Columbia University NY*

COAKLEY, FRANK

Assistant district attorney; district attorney

Earl Warren oral history project (in process) *University of California, Berkeley*

COASH, CARL (1905–   )

McGraw-Hill, Inc. (51 pages, permission required) *Columbia University NY*

COATNEY, GEORGE ROBERT (1902–   )

Health science collection (90 pages, permission required, also at *National Library of Medicine MD*) Columbia University NY

National Institutes of Health MD

COBB, CANDLER (1887–1955)

Lawyer

(1951, 175 pages, also microfiche, permission required to cite or quote) *Columbia University NY*

COBB, MR. AND MRS. CLARENCE

(1962) *State Historical Society of Colorado*

COBB, CULLY ALTON (1884–   )

Agricultural publisher

Cotton section of the Agricultural Adjustment Administration (1933–1937) (1968, 242 pages, also at *Columbia University NY*) *University of California, Berkeley*

COBB, JERRIE

Aviation collection (8 pages, permission required to cite or quote, also at *United States Air Force Academy CO* and *University of the Air, Maxwell Air Force Base AL*) Columbia University NY

COBB, MONTAGUE

Anatomist; Physical anthropologist

(1973) *Fisk University TN*

COBHAM, ALAN

Aviation collection (39 pages, permission required to cite or quote, also at *United States Air Force Academy Co* and *University of the Air, Maxwell Air Force Base AL*) Columbia University NY

COBURN, JUDITH

Smith alumna, class of 1965; Writer; Civil rights activist

(1973, 2 hours, 69 pages) *Smith College MA*

COCHRAN, JACQUELINE (MRS. FLOYD B. ODLUM)

Aviation collection (1960, 105 pages, open, also at *United States Air Force Academy* and *University of the Air, Maxwell Air Force Base AL*) Columbia University NY

COCHRANE, WILLARD

Director, Agricultural Economics, U.S. Department of Agriculture

(30 pages, open) *John F. Kennedy Library MA*

COCKCROFT, JOHN

Discussed in Columbia University interview with Warren Weaver

COCKE, NORMAN ATWATER (1884-)
Lawyer
James B. Duke project (1964, 204 pages, permission required, also at *Duke University NC*) *Columbia University NY*

COCOPA INDIANS
Doris Duke American Indian oral history project *Arizona State Museum*

COCTEAU, JEAN
Discussed in Columbia University interview with Jacques Barzun

COEUR D'ALENE, IDAHO
Idaho Bicentennial Commission

COFFEY, A. L. (1907-)
Secretary to August Vollmer (1931-1933); Bureau chief, Berkeley Police Department
(1972, 8 pages) *University of California, Berkeley*

COFFIN, CHARLES CLARK (1899-)
Historic preservation in Nantucket (1968, 61 pages, open) *Cornell University NY*

COFFIN, FRANK
Deputy administrator, AID
(30 pages, open) *John F. Kennedy Library MA*

COFFIN, HENRY SLOANE
Discussed in Columbia University interview with Willard Earl Givens

COFFMAN, JOHN D. (1882-1973)
Chief forester, National Park Service, retired
(1973, 126 pages) *University of California, Berkeley*

COFFYN, FRANK T. (-1960)
Aviation collection (43 pages, permission required to cite or quote, also at *United States Air Force Academy CO* and *University of the Air, Maxwell Air Force Base AL*) *Columbia University NY*

COGGESHALL, L. T.
Health science collection (52 pages, permission required, also at *National Library of Medicine MD*) *Columbia University NY*

COGGINS, HERBERT L. (1881-)
Businessman: Author
(1957, 172 pages) *University of California, Berkeley*

COGGS, ISAAC
Wisconsin political figure
(14 pages, open) *John F. Kennedy Library MA*

COGLEY, JOHN
Contributing editor, *Commonweal*
(55 pages, open) *John F. Kennedy Library MA*

COHEN (BARTERER), ADI
YOUTH MOVEMENTS: (11) Jewish community of Iran (Hebrew, 21 pages, open) *University, Israel*

COHEN, AHARON
Member, kibbutz Alonim

COHEN, AVRANHAM, AND YEHEZKIEL COHEN
Ramat-Gan, workmen
JEWISH COMMUNITIES: (10) Jewish life in Iraq written interview, (Hebrew, 3 pages, open) *Hebrew University, Israel*

COHEN, BEZALEL, with Skop Koppel
YOUTH MOVEMENTS: (2) Netzach in Latvia (Hebrew, 31 pages, open) *Hebrew University, Israel*

COHEN, DAVID
Member, Kibbutz Ein-Harod (Ihud)
JEWISH COMMUNITIES: (4) Zionist movement in U.S.S.R. (1917-1935) (Hebrew, 74 pages, open) *Hebrew University, Israel*

COHEN, DAVID A.
JEWISH COMMUNITIES: (10) Jewish life in Iraq (Hebrew, translated from Arabic, 19 pages, open) *Hebrew University, Israel*

COHEN, EDITH
JEWISH COMMUNITIES: (9) Jewish community in Egypt (French, 81 pages, open) *Hebrew University, Israel*

COHEN, GEORGE (1913-)
Painter
(1965, 12 pages) *Archives of American Art—Smithsonian Institution NY*

COHEN, HENRY
New York political studies collection, Citizens Budget Commission (36 pages, permission required) *Columbia University NY*

COHEN (KIRCHNER), HANAN
Instructor, Ruppin Training College
YOUTH MOVEMENTS: (1) Jewish youth movements in Czechoslovakia (Hebrew, 18 pages, open) *Hebrew University, Israel*

COHEN, JOSEPH
University of Washington Libraries WA

COHEN, JOSEPH N.

COHEN, JOSEPH
JEWISH COMMUNITIES: (10) Jewish life in Iraq (Hebrew, written interview, 5 pages, open) *Hebrew University, Israel*

COHEN, LUDI, AND MRS. LUDI COHEN
WORLD WAR II: THE HOLOCAUST—RESISTANCE AND RESCUE: (2) Rescue of Jews via Spain and Portugal (Hebrew, 4 pages, open) *Hebrew University, Israel*

COHEN, MARTIN with James Brindle
Social Security collection (35 pages, open, also at *Social Security Administration MD*) *Columbia University NY*

COHEN, MILAN
YOUTH MOVEMENTS: (1) Jewish youth movements in Czechoslovakia (German, 6 pages, open) *Hebrew University, Israel*

COHEN, MORDECHAI
Manager, Lapidot Company (Tel-Aviv)
YOUTH MOVEMENTS: (2) Netzach in Latvia (Hebrew, 40 pages, open) *Hebrew University, Israel*

COHEN, MORRIS RAPHAEL
Discussed in Columbia University interview with Joseph J. Klein

COHEN, MOSHE J.
JEWISH COMMUNITIES: (10) Jewish life in Iraq (Hebrew, 7 pages written interview, open) *Hebrew University, Israel*

COHEN, NATHAN with Yerucham Efrati
Treasurer, Solel Boneh (Tel-Aviv)

COHEN, SALMAN
JEWISH COMMUNITIES: (10) Jewish life in Iraq (Hebrew, written interview, 2 pages, open) *Hebrew University, Israel*

COHEN, WALLACE M. (1908-)
National Labor Relations Board (1969, 28 pages, open) *Cornell University NY*

COHEN, WILBUR JOSEPH
U.S. Secretary of Health, Education and Welfare
Social Security collection (57 pages, open, also at *Social Security Administration MD*) *Columbia University NY*

COHEN, YAAKOV
Former activist, French O.S.E.
WORLD WAR II: THE HOLOCAUST—RESISTANCE AND RESCUE: (6) Rescue of Jewish children (French, 17 pages, open) *Hebrew University, Israel*

COHEN, YAAKOV, AND MRS. YAAKOV COHEN
WORLD WAR II: THE HOLOCAUST—RESISTANCE AND RESCUE: (2) Rescue of Jews via

Spain and Portugal (Hebrew, 15 pages, open) *Hebrew University, Israel*

COHEN, YONA
Jerusalem journalist

ANTECEDENTS TO THE STATE OF ISRAEL: (2) "Brichah" (organized escape) (Hebrew, 18 pages, open) *Hebrew University, Israel*

COHN, BENNO
Director, Central European Immigrants Association

JEWISH COMMUNITIES: (1) German Jewry (1933–1935) (German, 48 pages) *Hebrew University, Israel*

COHN, EDWIN
Discussed in Columbia University interview with Edward Delos Churchill

COHN, HARRY
Discussed in Columbia University interview with Samson Raphaelson

COHN, MARCUS
James Lawrence Fly project (39 pages, closed until January 1, 1982) *Columbia University NY*

COIT, JOHN ELIOT
University history collection (open) *University of California, Los Angeles*

COIT, MARGARET
Author-in-residence, Fairleigh Dickinson University

(40 pages, permission of interviewee required) *John F. Kennedy Library MA*

COIT AGRICULTURAL SERVICE
John Eliot Coit interview, University history collection *University of California, Los Angeles*

COLAHAN, THOMAS S.
Columbia crisis of 1968 (49 pages, permission required) *Columbia University NY*

COLBERT, MARY
Massachusetts political figure

(11 pages, open) *John F. Kennedy Library MA*

COLBY, BAINBRIDGE
Discussed in Columbia University interview with William Ambrose Prendergast

COLBY, WILLIAM E. (1875–1964)
Attorney; Conservationist

(1954, 145 pages) *University of California, Berkeley*

COLE, CHARLES
U.S. ambassador to Chile

(77 pages, portions closed) *John F. Kennedy Library MA*

COLE, STEPHEN A.
Peace Corps project (1970, 61 pages, open transcript, permission required to use or reproduce tape) *Cornell University NY*

COLE, WILLIAM M.
Harvard University Graduate School of Business MA

COLEMAN, HENRY S.
Columbia crisis of 1968 (46 pages, permission required) *Columbia University NY*

COLER, BIRD S.
Discussed in Columbia University interview with John A. Heffernan

COLES, LILY GANGE
Ricks College ID

COLGAN, RICHARD A. (1891–   )
Private forester

Forestry in the California pine region (1968, 50 pages) *University of California, Berkeley*

COLIN, RALPH (1900–   )
Lawyer; Art collector

(1969, 24 pages) *Archives of American Art—Smithsonian Institution NY*

COLLADO, EMILIO GABRIEL (1910–   )
Marshall Plan (14 pages, permission required to cite or quote) *Columbia University NY*

COLLBOHM, FRANKLIN RUDOLF (1907–   )
Aviation collection (21 pages, permission required to cite or quote, also at *United States Air Force Academy CO* and *University of the Air, Maxwell Air Force Base AL*) *Columbia University NY*

COLLEGE ATHLETICS *see* Athletics

COLLEGES AND UNIVERSITIES *see* names of individual institutions

COLLIDGE, CHARLES A.
Special assistant to the Secretary of Defense (1955–1958); Director, Joint State Department—Defense Disarmament Study (1959)

(36 pages) *Dwight D. Eisenhower Library KS*

COLLIER, JOHN
University of Utah

COLLIER, MRS. ROBERT
(1961) *State Historical Society of Colorado*

COLLIER, W. A.
Nashville businessman

(1973) *Fisk University TN*

COLLIER'S

COLLIN STREET BAKERY
Texas economic history project (46 hours, 1072 pages) *Baylor University TX*

COLLINS, J. LAWTON (1896–   )
General, U.S. Army

Dulles oral history collection (1966, 28 pages, open) *Princeton University NJ*

United States Army Military Research Collection PA

COLLINS, JOHN F.
United Transportation Union project (1970, 73 pages, permission required to cite or quote transcript, permission required to use tape) *Cornell University NY*

COLLINS, JOSEPH (1886–1950)
Neurologist; Writer

(1949, 62 pages plus papers, also microfiche, permission required to cite or quote) *Columbia University NY*

COLLINS, LEROY
Florida governor; President, National Association of Broadcasters; Under-secretary of Commerce

(56 pages, open) *John F. Kennedy Library MA*

COLONIAL WILLIAMSBURG FOUNDATION
Colonial Williamsburg Foundation VA

COLORADO
Denver Public Library CO

Metropolitan State College CO

Pikes Peak Regional Library District CO

State Historical Society of Colorado

COLORADO CITY, TEXAS
Oil industry collection *Texas Tech University*

COLORADO SPRINGS ADAMAN CLUB
Margaretta M. Boas Colorado and western history collection *Pikes Peak Regional Library District CO*

COLP, RALPH
Mount Sinai Hospital (22 pages, permission required, also at *Mount Sinai Medical Center NY*) *Columbia University NY*

COLTON, WILLIAM
(1968, 33 pages, mostly open) *Cornell University NY*

COLUMBIA UNIVERSITY
Columbia crisis of 1968. Participants and pages: Jacques Barzun, 17; Lawrence Berger, 43; Bureau of Applied Social Research Study, 46; John D. Cannon, 86; Thomas S. Colahan, 49; Henry S. Coleman, 46; Columbia Concerned Parents meeting, 72; Cathleen Cook, 45; William Cumming, 58; Herbert A. Deane, 34; William T. de Bary, 29; Jay Facciolo, 59; Mark Flanigan, 95; Robert Fogelson, 44; Joel Frader, 48; James Goldman, 24; James Grossman, 38; Marvin

CONKLING, HAROLD

Water resources collection (open) *University of California, Los Angeles*

CONLON, WILLARD

Public figure

(2 hours, 20 pages, open) *Sangamon State University IL*

CONNECTICUT

University of Connecticut

CONNALLY, GOLFREY M.

Special projects *Baylor University TX*

CONNELL, DAVID

Children's Television Workshop (33 pages, open) *Columbia University NY*

CONNELLY, KARIN

Mill Valley Public Library CA

CONNELLY, MARC (MARCUS COOK) (1890–)

Popular arts collection (43 pages, open) *Columbia University NY*

CONNELLY, MATTHEW J.

Secretary to the President (1945–1953)

Harry S. Truman Library MO

CONNER, DUDLEY

University of Southern Mississippi

CONNOBLE, ALFRED B.

University of Michigan

CONNOR, REV. DAVID W.

Challenges to governance by students project (1969, 50 pages, open) *Cornell University NY*

CONNOR, FRANK

University of Connecticut

CONNORS, WILLIAM

Regional manager, Veterans Administration, Boston MA

(22 pages, open) *John F. Kennedy Library MA*

CONNORTON, JOHN V.

New York political studies collection; Citizens Budget Commission (34 pages, permission required) *Columbia University NY*

CONOLLY, RICHARD L. (1892–1962)

Naval officer

Naval history collection (1959, 411 pages, open, also at *Division of Naval History DC*) *Columbia University NY*

CONRAD, FRANK

Discussed in Columbia University interview with Donald G. Little

CONSCIENTIOUS OBJECTORS

Schowalter collection on conscientious objection during World War I (250 hours) *Bethel College KS*

Government and politics collection *University of California, Los Angeles*

Socialists of St. Louis and Missouri collection *University of Missouri, St. Louis*

CONSEDINE, WILLIAM R. (1910–)

National Labor Relations Board (1969, 48 pages, open) *Cornell University NY*

CONSERVATION OF BUILDINGS *see* Architecture—Conservation and Restoration

CONSERVATION OF NATURAL RESOURCES

Denver Public Library—Conservation Library CO

Forest History Society CA

National Park Service Archives WV

University of Wisconsin, River Falls

CONWELL, RUSSELL H.

Founder and first president, Temple University

Temple University PA

COOK, ALICE M.

Professor; Democratic delegate pledged to McCarthy

Challenges to governance by students project *Cornell University NY*

Eugene McCarthy project (1968, 139 pages, most open, permission required to use pages 105–139) *Cornell University NY*

COOK, CATHLEEN

Columbia crisis of 1968 (45 pages, permission required) *Columbia University NY*

COOK, CHARLES D. (1924–)

Lawyer

Eisenhower administration project (1964, 658 pages, closed until 1979, also at *Dwight D. Eisenhower Library KS*) *Columbia University NY*

COOK, EVERETT R.

Brigadier general, U.S. Army

Brigadier General Everett R. Cook memoir *Memphis Public Library and Information Center TN*

COOK, HOWARD ALEXANDER (1915–)

Former chief, U.S. Department of State, public services division

Eisenhower administration project (16 pages, permission required to cite or quote, also at *Dwight D. Eisenhower Library KS*) *Columbia University NY*

Dulles oral history collection (1966, 40 pages, open) *Princeton University NJ*

COOK, NILEY

Appalachian State University NC

COOK, DR. R. C.

University of Southern Mississippi

COOK ISLANDS, NEW ZEALAND

The Genealogical Society of the Church of Jesus Christ of Latter-day Saints UT

COOKE, JESSE

Discussed in Columbia University interview with Omar Titus Pfeiffer

COOKE, ROBERT

Member, Medical Advisory Board, Joseph P. Kennedy, Jr. Foundation

(46 pages, portion closed) *John F. Kennedy Library MA*

COOLEY, ALBERT DUSTIN (1900–)

Lieutenant general, U.S. Marine Corps (service: 1921–1954)

(32 pages, open, also at *Columbia University NY*) *United States Marine Corps DC*

COOLEY, JANET

Historic preservation *Charles B. Hosmer, Jr. Collection IL*

COOLIDGE, CALVIN

State Historical Society of Colorado

Discussed in Columbia University interviews with Horace Marden Albright; Guy Emerson; Claude Moore Fuess; Hans V. Kaltenborn; Eugene Meyer; James Thomas Williams, Jr.

COOLIDGE, CHARLES ALLERTON (1894–)

Lawyer

Eisenhower administration project (1967, 35 pages, permission required, also at *Dwight D. Eisenhower Library KS*) *Columbia University NY*

COON, MARTHA SUTHERLAND

South Dakota experience (1971) South Dakota Oral History Project *University of South Dakota*

COONEY, JOAN GANZ

Children's Television Workshop (24 pages, open) *Columbia University NY*

COONEY, MABEL

Communications Workers of America collection *University of Iowa Libraries*

COONS, DR. ARTHUR

Anaheim Public Library CA

COOPER, CHESTER

Central Intelligence Agency liaison officer with National Security Staff; Staff assistant to Ambassador Harriman, Geneva Conference on Laos, 1961–1962

(59 pages, permission of interviewee required) *John F. Kennedy Library MA*

Reeve Parker; F. Dana Payne; Norman Penney; James W. Pewett; George R. Pfann; Frank Rosenblatt; Clinton Rossiter; Mark Sharefkin; Peter J. Sharfman; Joel Silbey; Allan P. Sindler; Walter Slatoff; Rev. John Lee Smith; Arthur Spitzer; William L. Stallworth; S. Cushing Strout, Jr.; Steven W. Telsey; Raymond G. Thorpe; Sheila Tobias; Thomas Tobin; William G. Tomlinson; O. M. Ungers; Stephen Wallenstein; Burton Weiss; John W. Wikins; Robin H. Williams; Herman J. Wilson; Michael J. Wright; Madeleine H. Zelin; James L. Zwingle

Challenges to governance by students project: Open House Ithaca *Cornell University NY* Participants: Barbara F. Hanna, Kristina Miller, David V. W. Stringham, Jeffrey Weiss

Challenges to governance by students project: Pentagon March (1967) *Cornell University NY* Participants: Peter Bates; Sandra Birnbaum; Stephen Bloomer; David M. Brandt; Myra Coopersmith; Bruce Dancis; Douglas F. Dowd; Jeanne Dowd; Harriet Edwards; Sheryl Epton; Peter Lang; Malcolm Odell; Robert Pearlman; Lawrence Ravlin; Jay Schulman; Alan M. Snitow; Burton Weiss

Challenges to governance by students project: Student activism *Cornell University NY* Participants: Daniel Berrigan; David M. Brandt; Jane (Cowan) Brown; Jerald Brown; C. Michael Curtis; Mrs. Winston Dancis; Paul Goodman

Challenges to governance by students project: *Trojan Horse* incident *Cornell University NY* Participants: James M. Herson; John Marcham; Elizabeth Reed

Cornell University Libraries project *Cornell University NY* Participants: David Kaser; Stephen A. McCarthy; J. Gormly Miller

CORNER, EDRED JOHN HENRY
Hunt Institute for Botanical Documentation PA

CORRENTI, RICHARD
Associate Director for Student Affairs, SUNY Cortland

Collective bargaining at SUNY project (1973, 46 minutes, 19 pages) *Cornell University NY*

CORSI, EDWARD (1896–1965)
Specialist in migration and refugee problems

Dulles oral history collection (1965, 45 pages, open) *Princeton University NJ*

CORSO, GREGORY NUNZIO (1930–   )
Poets on their poetry (131 pages, permission required) *Columbia University NY*

CORT, WILLIAM WALTER (1887–1971)
Parasitologist

(1966, 31 pages, open) *Columbia University NY*

CORWIN, NORMAN (1910–   )
Writer; Director; Producer

James Lawrence Fly project (49 pages, closed until January 1, 1982) *Columbia University NY*

Radio pioneers collection (100 pages, closed during interviewee's lifetime) *Columbia University NY*

CORWITH, DORIS

(1964, 2 reels, 18 pages) *Broadcast Pioneers Library DC*

CORWITH, JAMES C. (1895–1966)

(1965, 99 pages, open) *Cornell University NY*

CORYELL, CHARLES DUBOIS (1912–1971)
Chemist

(1960, 441 pages, open) *Columbia University NY*

COSBY, ULYSSES

Special projects *Baylor University TX*

COSGRAVE, LIAM
Irish political figure

(5 pages, open) *John F. Kennedy Library MA*

COSGROVE, DELOS M., JR.
Personal friend of John Foster Dulles

Dulles oral history collection (1965, 22 pages) *Princeton University NJ*

COSIO VILLEGAS, DANIEL (1898–   )
Lawyer; Educator

(1963, 297 pages, permission required to cite or quote) *Columbia University NY*

COSTAIN, FLORENCE

South Dakota experience (1971), South Dakota Oral History Project *University of South Dakota*

COSTAIN, GEORGE

South Dakota experience (1971), South Dakota Oral History Project *University of South Dakota*

COSTELLO, JERRY, AND JOHN VIVIAN

Flying Tigers (12 pages, permission required to cite or quote) *Columbia University NY*

COSTELLO, JOHN D. (1894–   )
Lawyer; Clerk for Senator James D. Phelan

Reminiscences of John D. Costello (1960, 73 pages) *University of California, Berkeley*

COSTIKYAN, EDWARD (1924–   )
Politician

(1966, 677 pages; 1970, 76 pages; permission required) *Columbia University NY*

Discussed in Columbia University interview with Justin N. Feldman

COTT, TED (1917–   )
Radio and television executive

(1961, 297 pages, closed during interviewee's lifetime) *Columbia University NY*

Journalism lectures (36 pages, permission required to cite or quote) *Columbia University NY*

COTTAM, KENNETH
Vigo County School Corporation Superintendent

Vigo County Public Library IN

COTTEN, JAMES (1920–   )
Attorney; State legislator

Legislative project (1964, 150 pages, closed until death of five men) *North Texas State University Oral History Collection*

COTTERILL, MURRAY
Public relations director, Toronto

(1967, 37 pages) *Pennsylvania State University*

COTTINGAME, DONALD
Venture capitalist

Oral business history project *University of Texas, Austin*

COTTINGHAM, MRS. T. L.
University of Southern Mississippi

COTTON, THOMAS (–1964)

Flying Tigers (31 pages, permission required to cite or quote) *Columbia University NY*

COTTON CARNIVAL, MEMPHIS, TENNESSEE

Brigadier General Everett R. Cook memoir *Memphis Public Library and Information Center TN*

COTTON MANUFACTURE AND TRADE

History of cotton in east Texas *East Texas State University*

Millsaps College MS

Cotton industry collection *Texas Tech University*

COTTONE, BENEDICT PETER (1909–   )

James Lawrence Fly project (24 pages, closed until January 1, 1982) *Columbia University NY*

COUCH, WILLIAM TERRY (1901–   )
Publisher

Southern Intellectual leaders (1970, 571 pages plus papers, closed pending publication of a study) *Columbia University NY*

Discussed in Columbia University interview with Rupert B. Vance

COUDERT, FREDERIC RENE (1871–1955)
Lawyer

(1950, 170 pages, also microfiche, permission required to cite or quote) *Columbia University NY*

Discussed in Columbia University interview with Boris Alexander Bakhmeteff

CRAIG, ROBERT (1920–)
McGraw-Hill, Inc. (24 pages, permission required) *Columbia University NY*

CRAIG, WALTER

CRAIGIE, LAURENCE C. (1902–)
Aviation collection (53 pages, permission required to cite or quote, also at *United States Air Force Academy CO* and *University of the Air, Maxwell Air Force Base AL*) *Columbia University NY*

U.S. Air Force Academy project (81 pages, consult center for restriction, also at *United States Air Force Academy CO*) *Columbia University NY*

CRAMER, GUS
Communications Workers of America collection *University of Iowa Libraries*

CRAMPTON, LOUIS
National Park Service Archives WV

CRANE, BURTON (–1963)
Occupation of Japan (74 pages, permission required to cite or quote) *Columbia University NY*

CRANE, ESTHER
Occupation of Japan (58 pages, permission required to cite or quote) *Columbia University NY*

CRANE, H. RICHARD
American Institute of Physics NY

CRANE, HART
Hart Crane project. Participants and pages: Mrs. Margaret Babcock, 50; Waldo Frank, 53; Fredrica Crane Lewis, 17; Samuel A. Loveman, 46; Allen Tate, 35 *(closed during interviewee's lifetime)* (1963, 201 pages, permission required) *Columbia University NY*

CRANFORD, NEW JERSEY
Cranford Historical Society NJ

CRANMER, GEORGE
(1958) *State Historical Society of Colorado*

CRANMER, JEAN CHAPPELL (MRS. GEORGE)
(1959) *State Historical Society of Colorado*

CRANSTON, EARL (1885–1970)
China missionaries collection (130 pages, also at *Columbia University NY*) *Claremont Graduate School CA*

CRARY, ALBERT P. (1911–)
Geophysicist; Oceanographer
(1962, 87 pages, also microfiche, permission required to cite or quote) *Columbia University NY*

CRARY, HAROLD
Aeronautical history collection *University of Southern California Library*

CRAWFORD, EDWARD
Alaskan pioneers project (57 pages, open) *Columbia University NY*

CRAWFORD, KENNETH GALE (1902–)
Journalist
Eisenhower administration project (1967, 26 pages, permission required to cite or quote, also at *Dwight D. Eisenhower Library KS*) *Columbia University NY*

CREAL, HAROLD (1896–)
Farmer
Agricultural leaders project (1964, 101 pages, permission required to cite or quote) *Cornell University NY*

CREATH, CHARLIE
Jazzmen on the Mississippi *University of Missouri, St. Louis*

CREMIN, LAWRENCE ARTHUR (1925–)
Educator
Carnegie Corporation collection (1968, 107 pages, permission required) *Columbia University NY*

CRENA DE IONGH, DANIEL
World Bank (47 pages, permission of interviewee required to cite or quote, also at *Brookings Institution DC*) *Columbia University NY*

CREW, LESLIE AND JESSE
South Dakota experience (1969), South Dakota Oral History Project *University of South Dakota*

CREWS, T. G. (1917–)
Law endorcement officer; Marine Corps veteran
Prisoner-of-war project (1972, 84 pages, open) *North Texas State University Oral History Collection*

CRICHLOW, ERNEST (1914–)
Painter
(1968, 25 pages) *Archives of American Art—Smithsonian Institution NY*

CRILEY, ELIZABETH
(1957) *State Historical Society of Colorado*

CRIME AND CRIMINALS
Texas crime collection (26 hours, 26 pages, open) *Texas Tech University*

CRIPPS, STAFFORD
Discussed in Columbia University interview with Sir Robert Alexander Watson-Watt

CRISWELL, DR. W. A.
Religion and culture project *Baylor University TX*

CRITCHFIELD, BURKE H. (1888–1970)
Agricultural economist
California wine industry interviews (1972, 79 pages,) *University of California, Berkeley*

CRITES, MRS. F. A.
Wife of pioneer leader, Chadron NE
Chadron State College NE

CROFT, FRANK CORNELIUS (1903–)
Major general, U.S. Marine Corps (service: 1928–1959)
(1970, in process) *United States Marine Corps DC*

CROFUT, ANDREW D. (1889–)
Rancher; Retailer
(1969, 835 pages, open) *University of Nevada. Reno*

CROLY, HERBERT
Discussed in Columbia University interview with Alvin Johnson

CROMWELL, JOHN (1888–)
Popular arts collection (45 pages, open) *Columbia University NY*

CRONIN, EUGENE R. (1917–)
Salesman; Former Army Air Corps officer
Prisoner-of-war project (1972, 92 pages, open) *North Texas State University Oral History Collection*

CROPP, COLONEL RICHARD
South Dakota experience (1971), South Dakota Oral History Project *University of South Dakota*

CROSBY, WILLIAM S.
Crosby tapes (15 hours, closed) *Pikes Peak Regional Library District CO*

CROSS, BURNET
On the electronic experiments of Percy Grainger, American music project (1972) *Yale University School of Music CT*

CROSS, EPHRAIM
Professor, City College of New York
Alumni Association of the City College CUNY

CROSS, IRA BROWN (1880–)
Professor of economics
(1967, 128 pages) *University of California, Berkeley*

CROSS, ROBERT DOUGHERTY (1924–)
American historians collection (122 pages, permission required to cite or quote) *Columbia University NY*

CROSS, ROWLAND McLEAN (1888–)
China missionaries collection (200 pages, certain pages closed, also at *Columbia University NY*) *Claremont Graduate School CA*
Planned interview *Lakewood Branch Dallas Public Library TX*

(1961, 215 pages) *University of California, Berkeley*

CUNNINGHAM, JOHN
University of Connecticut

CUNNINGHAM, PRISCILLA
Smith alumna, class of 1958; Community service volunteer, especially with autistic children
(1973, 3 hours, 61 pages) *Smith College MA*

CUNNINGHAM, THOMAS
Ran Southern California campaign in 1946
Earl Warren oral history project (in process) *University of California, Berkeley*

CUNNINGHAM, WILLIAM J.
Harvard University Graduate School of Business MA

CUPP, RODERICK B.
Radio pioneers collection (1963, 13 pages, also at *Broadcast Pioneers Library DC*) *Columbia University NY*

CURLEY, JAMES MICHAEL
Boston Public Library MA

CURLEY, MICHAEL
Discussed in Columbia University interview with Eddie Dowling

CURRAN, JOSEPH (1906–)
Labor union executive
(1964, 193 pages, closed during interviewee's lifetime) *Columbia University NY*
Discussed in Columbia University interview with M. Hedley Stone

CURRAN, PHILIP
Pennsylvania Bureau of Mediation member
(1968, 21 pages) *Pennsylvania State University*

CURRIER, DONALD
Pianist; Hindemith student at Yale
Hindemith project (1973) *Yale University School of Music CT*

CURRY, CHARLES F.
Friend of Harry S. Truman
Harry S. Truman Library MO

CURTI, MERLE
University of Wisconsin, Madison

CURTIS, ALBERT B. (1903–)
Chief fire warden, Weyerhaeuser Timber Company
(1956, 103 pages, permission required) *Columbia University NY*

CURTIS, C. MICHAEL
Challenges to governance by students project: Student activism (1968, 64 pages, written permission required) *Cornell University NY*

CURTIS, DONALD (1896–)
Brigadier general, U.S. Marine Corps (service: 1917–1949)
(1970, 117 pages, open, also at *Columbia University NY* and *U.S. Naval Institute MD*) *United States Marine Corps DC*

CURTIS, JAMES FREEMAN (1878–1952)
Lawyer
(1951, 334 pages, also microfiche, permission required to cite or quote) *University of Columbia NY*

CURTIS, KEN "FESTUS"
Biographical collection (open) *Texas Tech University*

CURTIS, REV. PURVIS
University of Southern Mississippi

CURTIS, THOMAS B. (1911–)
Eisenhower administration project (40 pages, permission required to cite or quote, also at *Dwight D. Eisenhower Library KS*) *Columbia University NY*

CURTIS, VERN
United Steelworkers of America labor leader
(1969, 27 pages) *Pennsylvania State University*

CURTISS, MINA KIRSTEIN
Smith alumna, class of 1918; Professor of English; Writer
(1973, 2 hours, 38 pages) *Smith College MA*

CUSHING, HARVEY
Discussed in Columbia University interview with Edward Delos Churchill

CUSHING, RICHARD CARDINAL
Former Archbishop of Boston
(22 pages, open) *John F. Kennedy Library MA*

CUSHMAN, BERNARD (1911–)
National Labor Relations Board (1969, 45 pages, permission required to cite or quote) *Cornell University NY*

CUSHMAN, THOMAS JACKSON (1895–1972)
Lieutenant general, U.S. Marine Corps (service: 1917–1954)
(31 pages, open, also at *Columbia University NY* and *U.S. Naval Institute MD*) *United States Marine Corps DC*

CUSTER, BENJAMIN SCOTT (1905–)
Naval officer
Naval history collection (1965, 1022 pages, permission required, also at *Division of Naval History DC*) *Columbia University NY*

CUSTER, GEORGE A.
Monroe County Library System MI

CUTLER, ELLIOTT
Discussed in Columbia University interview with Edward Delos Churchill

CUTLER, LLOYD
Lawyer involved in Cuban prisoner exchange; Counsel, Pharmaceutical Manufacturers Association
(23 pages, open) *John F. Kennedy Library MA*

CUTTER, DAVID
Cutter Laboratories (in process) *University of California, Berkeley*

CUTTER, ROBERT
Cutter Laboratories (in process) *University of California, Berkeley*

CUYLER, OTTO W. (1897–)
Food machinery dealer
(1964, 78 pages, open) *Cornell University NY*

CYGELMAN, RENEE
Member, Dror movement; Jerusalem Ministry of Social Welfare employee
WORLD WAR II: THE HOLOCAUST—RESISTANCE AND RESCUE: (4) Jews in the underground in Belgium (French, 18 pages, open) *Hebrew University, Israel*

CZERNIAK, AVRAHAM
Jerusalem architect
JEWISH COMMUNITIES: (4) Zionist movement in U.S.S.R. (1917–1935) (Hebrew, 15 pages, open) *Hebrew University, Israel*

CZERNIAK, TZIPPORAH
JEWISH COMMUNITIES: (4) Zionist movement in U.S.S.R. (1917–1935) (Hebrew, 5 pages, open) *Hebrew University, Israel*

CZYZEWSKI, FRANCIS
Northern Indiana Historical Society

D

DABBI, YEHEZKIEL
Ramat-Gan physician
CULTURE AND EDUCATION: (2) Higher education among Iraqi Jews (Hebrew, 16 pages, open) *Hebrew University, Israel*

DACE, CATHERINE EGBERT
State and local history collection (open) *University of California, Los Angeles*

DaCOSTA, MORTON
Popular arts collection (43 pages, open) *Columbia University NY*

DAHLBERG, ARTHUR C. (1896–1964)
Diary chemist
Agricultural leaders project (1964, 40 pages, open) *Cornell University NY*

DAILEY, GRACE
(1959) *State Historical Society of Colorado*

DAILEY, W. O.
South Dakota experience (1963), South Dakota Oral History Project *University of South Dakota*

Harry S. Truman Library MO

University of North Carolina, Charlotte

Discussed in Columbia University interview with William Terry Couch

DANIELS, JOSEPHUS

Discussed in Columbia University interviews with Walter Stratton Anderson; Jonathan Worth Daniels; James Thomas Williams, Jr.

DANIELS, MRS. L. A.

South Dakota experience (1970), South Dakota Oral History Project *University of South Dakota*

DANIELS, WILBUR

Missouri political figure

(10 pages, open) *John F. Kennedy Library MA*

DANIELS, WOODIE E.

Milk drivers' union in San Francisco East Bay (1957, 105 pages) *University of California Institute of Industrial Relations*

DANNON, YEHUDA

JEWISH COMMUNITIES: (8) Izmir community (Hebrew, 50 pages, open) *Hebrew University, Israel*

DANTAS, SANTIAGO

Brazilian minister of foreign affairs; Minister of Finance

(7 pages, open) *John F. Kennedy Library MA*

DANUSSI, LUIS (1913–   )

Labor leader

Argentina in the 1930s (1971, Spanish, 87 pages, open) *Columbia University NY*

DAPHNIS, NASSOS (1914–   )

Painter

(1964, 12 pages; 1968, 26 pages) *Archives of American Art—Smithsonian Institution NY*

DAR, JOSEPH

ANTECEDENTS TO THE STATE OF ISRAEL: (3) "Ha 'apalah" (illegal immigration) (Hebrew, 62 pages, open) *Hebrew University, Israel*

DAR, ZVI (LEDERER, FRANZ)   –1969)

YOUTH MOVEMENTS: (1) Jewish youth movements in Czechoslovakia (Hebrew, 13 pages, open) *Hebrew University, Israel*

DARBY, HARRY (1895–   )

U.S. senator (Kansas; 1949–1950); Member, Republican national committee (1940–1964); Chairman, Eisenhower Library Commission

Eisenhower administration project (1967, 73 pages, permission required, also at *Dwight D. Eisenhower Library KS*) *Columbia University NY*

DARCY, SAM ADAMS

Former official, San Francisco Communist party

(In process) *Pennsylvania State University*

DARLEY, MRS. WARD

(1959) *State Historical Society of Colorado*

DARLING, RUTH

Challenges to governance by students project (1969, 119 pages, permission required) *Cornell University NY*

DARR, EVERETT

University of Washington Libraries

DARROW, CLARENCE

Ossian Sweet murder trial in Detroit *University of Michigan*

DARWISH, SHALOM

Former secretary, Jewish Schools Education Committee, Iraq; Haifa lawyer

JEWISH COMMUNITIES: (10) Jewish life in Iraq (Hebrew, 50 pages, open) *Hebrew University, Israel*

DAUMAN, MRS. WALTER C.

South Dakota experience (1971), South Dakota Oral History Project *University of South Dakota*

DAURAT, DIDIER

Aviation collection (18 pages, permission of interviewee required to cite or quote, also at *United States Air Force Academy CO* and *University of the Air, Maxwell Air Force Base AL*) *Columbia University NY*

DAVENPORT, FREDERICK MORGAN (1866–1956)

Politician

(1952, 101 pages, open) *Columbia University NY*

DAVENS, EDWARD

Member, President's panel on mental retardation

(38 pages, open) *John F. Kennedy Library MA*

DAVES, DELMAR LAWRENCE (1904–   )

Popular arts collection (66 pages, open) *Columbia University NY*

DAVID, ALVIN

Social Security collection (27 pages, closed during interviewee's lifetime, also at *Social Security Administration MD*) *Columbia University NY*

DAVIDOWV, BRACHA

JEWISH COMMUNITIES: (12) Jews of Bukhara (1900–1935) (Hebrew, 18 pages, open) *Hebrew University, Israel*

DAVIDSON, BEN (1900–   )

Representative, New York City Teachers Union progressive group during the 1930s

(1968, 52 pages, permission required to cite or quote) *Cornell University NY*

DAVIDSON, HOWARD CALHOUN

U.S. Air Force Academy project (35 pages, consult center for restriction, also at *United States Air Force Academy CO*) *Columbia University NY*

DAVIDSON, MARY BLOSSOM (1884–1968)

Dean of women, University of California, Berkeley

(1967, 79 pages) *University of California, Berkeley*

DAVIDSON, MEIR

ANTECEDENTS TO THE STATE OF ISRAEL: (3) "Ha 'alpalah" (illegal immigration) (Hebrew, 177 pages, open) *Hebrew University, Israel*

DAVIDSON, ROBERT

Children's Television Workshop (36 pages, open) *Columbia University NY*

DAVIDSON, SHIRLEY (1930–   )

Perception of change in Ithaca school district project (1973, 93 minutes) *Cornell University NY*

DAVIDSON COUNTY, TENNESSEE

Race Relations Information Center Library TN

DAVIE, EUGENIE MARY (1885–   )

Civic and political leader

Robert A. Taft project (69 pages, permission required) *Columbia University NY*

Dulles oral history collection (1965, 47 pages, permission required to cite or quote) *Princeton University NJ*

DAVIES, ARTHUR

Discussed in Columbia University interview with Max Weber

DAVIES, EDWARD A., AND JAMES TISDALE

The WIP-Philadelphia story (1964, 1 reel, 22 pages) *Broadcast Pioneers Library DC*

DAVIS, ANGELA

Black revolutionary

(1972) *Fisk University TN*

DAVIS, B. A.

University of Southern Mississippi

DAVIS, BENJAMIN

Discussed in Columbia University interview with George Samuel Schuyler

DAVIS, BENJAMIN O., JR.

Cleveland State University Library, OH

DAY, KARL SCHMOLSMIRE (1896–1973)
Lieutenant general, U.S. Marine Corps (service: 1917–1957)

(86 pages, permission required, also at Columbia University NY and U.S. Naval Institute MD) United States Marine Corps DC

DAY, RUFUS, JR.
Cleveland State University Library OH

DAY, RUTH (1897–)
College extension teacher

(1964, 125 pages, permission required to cite or quote) Cornell University NY

DEAKIN, HAROLD OSBORNE (1913–)
Brigadier general, U.S. Marine Corps (service: 1934–1957)

(1968, 101 pages, permission required to cite or quote, also at Columbia University NY and U.S. Naval Institute MD) United States Marine Corps DC

DEAN, ARTHUR (1898–)
Partner, Sullivan & Cromwell

Dulles oral history collection (1964, 97 pages, written permission required to read) Princeton University NJ

DEAN, GORDON EVANS (1905–1958)
Lawyer

(1954, 146 pages, also microfiche, permission required to cite or quote) Columbia University NY

DEAN, JIMMY
Discussed in Texas Tech University Biographical collection (open)

DEAN, MALLETTE (1907–)
Artist; Printer

(1970, 105 pages) University of California, Berkeley

DEAN, WILLIAM (1899–)
Major general, U.S. Army

Vollmer's influence on the career of an army general (1972, 11 pages), August Vollmer collection University of California, Berkeley

DEANE, HERBERT A.
Columbia crisis of 1968 (34 pages, permission required) Columbia University NY

DEANE, MARTHA BLANCHARD
University history collection (open) University of California, Los Angeles

DE ANGELI, MARGUERITE
Author of children's books

Montgomery County—Norristown Public Library PA

DEARING, WARREN PALMER (1905–)
Health science collection (95 pages, permission required, also at National Library of Medicine MD) Columbia University NY

DEARY, WILLIAM
Discussed in Columbia University William L. Maxwell interview and in Weyerhaeuser Timber Company collection

DEAS, ALSTON
Historic preservation Charles B. Hosmer, Jr. Collection IL

DEASON, JAMES R.
State and local history collection (open) University of California, Los Angeles

DEATON, MRS. D. A.
Early Watauga County Appalachian State University NC

DeBAKEY, MICHAEL
Surgeon

Discussed in Columbia University interview with Edward Delos Churchill

DE BALOGH, FRANK
Hungarian history University of Southern California Library

DE BARY, WILLIAM THEODORE
Columbia crisis of 1968 (29 pages, permission required) Columbia University NY

DE BLIEUX, J. D.
Louisiana political figure

(22 pages, open) John F. Kennedy Library MA

DE BLIJ, HARM J.
Geographer

(1972, 10 minutes) Plymouth State College NH

DeBOER, S. R.
(1963) State Historical Society of Colorado

DEBRUEQUE, JOHN, SR.
Sugar beet industry in New York State (1968, 25 pages, open) Cornell University NY

DEBS, EUGENE V.
Discussed in Columbia University interviews with Asa Philip Randolph; Max Shachtman; John Spargo; and in Socialist movement collection

DEBUS, KURT
Director, Launch Operations Center; Director, John F. Kennedy Space Center, NASA

(11 pages, open) John F. Kennedy Library MA

DEBYE, PETER J. W. (1884–1966)
Nobel prize winner, chemistry

(1967, 178 pages, open) Cornell University NY

DECKER, GEORGE
General and chief of staff, U.S. Army

(45 pages, no direct quoting permitted) John F. Kennedy Library MA

United States Army Military Research Collection PA

DE FORD, MIRIAM ALLEN
Suffragists (in process) University of California, Berkeley

DE FOREST, CHARLOTTE
Smith alumna, class of 1901; Missionary and educator in Japan

(1973, 1 hour, 25 pages) Smith College MA

DE FOREST, LEE (1873–1961)
Radio pioneers collection (9 pages, open) Columbia University NY

DE GAULLE, CHARLES
Discussed in Columbia University interviews with Joseph Clark Baldwin; Michel Gordey; James C. Hagerty; Amory Houghton

DEGENAAR, BILL
South Dakota experience (1971), South Dakota Oral History Project University of South Dakota

DEGNAN, GLADYS
South Dakota experience (1971), South Dakota Oral History Project University of South Dakota

DE GRUBEN, HERVE
Director of political affairs (1945–1953), Belgium

Harry S. Truman Library MO

DEHN, ADOLPH (1895–1968)
Painter

(1964, 50 pages) Archives of American Art—Smithsonian Institution NY

DEHNER, DOROTHY (1908–   )
Sculptor

(1966, 19 pages) Archives of American Art—Smithsonian Institution NY

DE HUFF, WILMER ARTHUR (1888–
Educator; Principal, Baltimore Polytechnic Institute (1921–1958); University of Baltimore faculty member (1958–1971); Engineer

(1972, 2 hours) Maryland Historical Society

DEKIEWIET, CORNELIS WILLEM (1902–   )
Historian

Carnegie Corporation collection (1968, 117 pages, permission required) Columbia University NY

DE KNIGHT, AVEL (1926–   )
Painter

(22 pages) Archives of American Art—Smithsonian Institution NY

DE LA CHAPELLE, CLARENCE E. (1897–   )
Physician

(1962, 461 pages, permission required) Columbia University NY

DE LA CHAPELLE, CLARENCE E. (cont.)
New York political studies collection, Brooklyn politics (1930–1950) (56 pages, permission required) *Columbia University NY*

DE LA COLINA, RAFAEL (1898–)
Mexican diplomat
Dulles oral history collection (1966, 35 pages, permission required to cite or quote) *Columbia University NY*

DELACORTE, ALFRED
Popular arts collection (57 pages, open) *Columbia University NY*

DELANEY, MATTHEW
(90 minutes, open) *Plattsburgh State University College NY*

DELANO, WILLIAM ADAMS (1874–1960)
Architect
(1950, 94 pages, also microfiche, permission required to cite or quote) *Columbia University NY*

DELAWARE
Hagley Museum DE

DeLEON, DANIEL
Discussed in Columbia University interview with John Spargo

DELLUMS, C. L. (1900–)
International president, Brotherhood of Sleeping Car Porters; Civil rights leader
(1973, 151 pages) *University of California, Berkeley*

DELONG, EDMUND (1900–)
Journalist
(1962, 198 pages, also microfiche, permission required to cite or quote) *Columbia University NY*

DEL RIO, JORGE
Lawyer
Argentina in the 1930s (1971, Spanish, 41 pages, open) *Columbia University NY*

DEL VALLE, PEDRO AUGUSTO (1893–)
Lieutenant general, U.S. (service: 1915–1948)
(1966, 245 pages, permission required to cite or quote, also at *Columbia University NY* and *U.S. Naval Institute MD*) *United States Marine Corps DC*

DE MAIO, ERNEST
District director, United Electrical, Radio, and Machine Workers of America, Chicago
(1970–1971, 4 hours, 131 pages) *Roosevelt University IL*

DeMARCO, WILLIAM
Massachusetts political figure
(14 pages, open) *John F. Kennedy Library MA*

DEMAREST, WILLIAM (1892–)
Popular arts collection (62 pages, open) *Columbia University NY*

DEMEREE, GEORGE (1934–), and NANCY DEMEREE (1936–)
President, Herkimer County NY chapter, National Farmers Organization
(1967, 190 pages, permission required to cite or quote) National Farmers Organization project *Cornell University NY*

DE MILLE, CECIL BLOUNT (1881–1959)
Popular arts collection (24 pages, open) *Columbia University NY*

DEMMON, ELWOOD LEONARD
Forester
University of Michigan

DEMOCRATIC PARTY
Paul Ziffren interview, Government and politics collection *University of California, Los Angeles*

DEMPSEY, FRANK
South Dakota experience (1970), South Dakota Oral History Project *University of South Dakota*

DEMPSEY, JOHN
Lieutenant, Massachusetts state police
(16 pages, permission of interviewee required) *John F. Kennedy Library MA*

DEMUTH, RICHARD HOLZMANN (1910–)
International official
World Bank (1961, 91 pages, permission required to cite or quote, also at *Brookings Institution DC*) *Columbia University NY*

DENFELD, LOUIS
Discussed in Columbia University interview with James Lemuel Holloway, Jr.

DENHAM, REGINALD
Popular arts collection (64 pages, open) *Columbia University NY*

DENIG, ROBERT LIVINGSTON (1884–)
Brigadier general, U.S. Marine Corps (service: 1905–1945)
(1967, in process *United States Marine Corps DC*

DENNES, WILLIAM (1898–)
Philosopher; Educator
Philosophy and the university since 1915 (1970, 162 pages) *University of California, Berkeley*

DENNIS, EDNA WEATHERS
Director, Katherine Gibbs School; Managing editor, *Bride's Magazine*; Smith alumna, class of 1948
(1973, 1 hour, 32 pages) *Smith College MA*

DENNIS, LAWRENCE (1893–)
Writer; Banker
(1967, 90 pages, permission required to cite or quote) *Columbia University NY*

DENNY, CHARLES RUTHVEN (1912–)
James Lawrence Fly project (28 pages, closed until January 1, 1982) *Columbia University NY*

DENNY, REGINALD LEIGH (1891–1967)
Popular arts collection (34 pages, open) *Columbia University NY*

DENTON, LANE
Special projects *Baylor University TX*

DENVER, COLORADO
Denver Public Library CO
Metropolitan State College CO

DePATIE, EDMUND
Motion picture and television collection (open) *University of California, Los Angeles*

DePEW, CHAUNCEY
Discussed in Columbia University interview with Beverly Randolph Robinson

DEPRESSIONS
Alice Lloyd College KY
The Great Depression in east Texas *Texas State University*
Depression in western Kansas *Fort Hays Kansas State College*
Everyday life in the Southwest during the 1930s *Fort Worth Public Library TX*
Moorhead State College MN
Southwest Minnesota State College
Cattle shoot of 1934–1935 (27 hours, 810 pages, open) *Texas Tech University*
Man–land confrontation in the southwest (110 hours, 2000 pages, open) *Texas Tech University*
University of Delaware
Institute of Labor and Industrial Relations *University of Michigan*
South Dakota experience, South Dakota Oral History Project *University of South Dakota*
University of Texas, Arlington
University of Wisconsin, La Crosse
Effects of Great Depression on agriculture *Walla Walla College WA*

DE RIVERA, JOSÉ (1904–)
Sculptor
(1968, 30 pages) *Archives of American Art—Smithsonian Institution NY*

DERMATOLOGY
Dermatology Foundation of Miami FL

DOAN, RICHARD K.

Radio pioneers collection (26 pages, open) *Columbia University NY*

DOANE, D. HOWARD (1883–)

Agricultural businessman

Agricultural leaders project (1963, 278 pages, permission required to cite or quote) *Cornell University NY*

DOBIE, FRANK

Friend of President John F. Kennedy

(12 pages, open) *John F. Kennedy Library MA*

DOBIE, J(AMES) FRANK

Author

Artists in depth (2 tapes, not transcribed, open) *University of Texas, El Paso*

DOBKIN, ELIAHU

WORLD WAR II: THE HOLOCAUST—RESISTANCE AND RESCUE: (2) Rescue of Jews via Spain and Portugal (Hebrew, 4 pages, open) *Hebrew University, Israel*

DOBZHANSKY, THEODOSIUS (1900–)

Geneticist

(1962, 637 pages, permission required) *Columbia University NY*

Discussed in Columbia University interview with Leslie Clarence Dunn

DOCHEZ, ALPHONSE RAYMOND (1882–1964)

Physician

(1955, 165 pages, open) *Columbia University NY*

DOCKING, ROBERT

Kansas political figure; Chairman, Small Business Administration advisory board

(13 pages, open) *John F. Kennedy Library MA*

DODDS, HAROLD W. (1889–)

Princeton University president

(1966, 292 pages, permission required) *Columbia University NY*

Carnegie Corporation collection (70 pages, permission required) *Columbia University NY*

Discussed in Columbia University interview with William Harold Cowley

DODGE, ARTHUR (1923–)

Business executive; Army veteran

(1971, 120 pages, open) *North Texas State University Oral History Collection*

DODGE, BERNARD OGILVIE

Hunt Institute for Botanical Documentation PA

DODGE, CHEE

University of Utah

DODGE, CLEVELAND E. (1888–)

Mining engineers (25 pages, permission required to cite or quote) *Columbia University NY*

DODGE, GRACE

Discussed in Columbia University interview with Charlotte Garrison

DODGE, HOMER LEVI (1887–)

American Association of Physics Teachers (47 pages, permission required to cite or quote, also at *American Institute of Physics NY*) *Columbia University NY*

DODGE, RICKLEY SMITH

Smith alumna, class of 1963; Social worker; Associate political director, Zero Population Growth

(1973, 1 hour, 31 pages) *Smith College MA*

DODGSON, JAMES

Aviation collection (34 pages, permission of interviewee required to cite or quote, also at *United States Air Force Academy CO* and *University of the Air, Maxwell Air Force Base AL*) *Columbia University NY*

DODSON, JAMES E.

Director, U.S. Department of Labor, Office of Budget and Management (1942–1952)

Harry S. Truman Library MO

DODSON, OWEN VINCENT

Poet; Playwright; Director; Novelist

(1972) *Fisk University TN*

DODSWORTH, DON

Ohio Historical Society

DOFT, FLOYD S. (DAFT)

National Institutes of Health MD

DOHENY, EDWARD L.

Discussed in Columbia University interviews with Michael Late Benedum; Hilarion Noel Branch; and in Benedum and the oil industry collection

DOHERTY, WILLIAM CHARLES (1902–)

Union official

(1956, 57 pages, open) *Columbia University NY*

DOISY, EDWARD ADELBERT (1893–)

Nobel Laureates collection (30 pages, permission required) *Columbia University NY*

DOLAN, CHARLES

U.S. Air Force Academy project (25 pages, consult center for restriction, also at *United*

States Air Force Academy CO) *Columbia University NY*

DOLAN HENRY P.

New York political studies collection, Brooklyn politics (1930–1950) (76 pages, permission required) *Columbia University NY*

DOLAN, JOSEPH

Assistant deputy attorney general involved in Cuban prisoner exchange

(16 pages; 120 pages; open) *John F. Kennedy Library MA*

DOLBERG, GLENN

Radio pioneers collection (1963, 9 pages, open, also at *Broadcast Pioneers Library DC*) *Columbia University NY*

DOLGOFF, SAM, AND ESTHER DOLGOFF

Socialists; Industrial Workers of the World organizers

(1972, 1 hour, 28 pages) *Roosevelt University IL*

D'OLIVE, CHARLES

U.S. Air Force Academy project (58 pages, consult center for restriction, also at *United States Air Force Academy CO*) *Columbia University NY*

DOLLARD, CHARLES (1907–)

Foundation executive, Carnegie Corporation

Association for the Aid of Crippled Children (30 pages, permission required) *Columbia University NY*

Carnegie Corporation collection (1966, 329 pages, permission required) *Columbia University NY*

Discussed in Columbia University interviews with Florence Anderson; Cornelis Willem deKiewiet; Caryl Parker Haskins; Gunnar Karl Myrdal; Frederick Osborn; John McFarlane Russell; Stephen Stackpole

DOLLFUSS, CHARLES

Aviation collection (31 pages, permission of interviewee required to cite or quote, also at *United States Air Force Academy CO* and *University of the Air, Maxwell Air Force Base AL*) *Columbia University NY*

DOLMETSCH, CARL

Musician

Miscellaneous collection *University of Southern California Library*

DOMENECH, JOSE

Labor leader

Argentina in the 1930s (1970, Spanish, 192 pages, open except for specified pages) *Columbia University NY*

Discussed in Columbia University interviews with Ernesto Janin; Juan Rodriguez

DOMINGUEZ, LAURA

Anaheim Public Library CA

Eisenhower administration project (24 pages, permission required) *Columbia University NY*

Marshall Plan (2 pages, permission required to cite or quote) *Columbia University NY*

DOUGLAS, MANSFIELD
Nashville councilman; Former president, Nashville NAACP

(1972) *Fisk University TN*

DOUGLAS, MELVYN (1901–)
Popular arts collection (29 pages, open) *Columbia University NY*

DOUGLAS, PAUL HOWARD (1892–)
U.S. senator (Illinois)

Herbert H. Lehman project (22 pages, permission to cite or quote) *Columbia University NY*

(33 pages, open) *John F. Kennedy Library MA*

Discussed in Columbia University interview with Lawrence Irvin

DOUGLAS, WILLIAM
Associate justice, U.S. Supreme Court

(39 pages, open) *John F. Kennedy Library MA*

DOUGLAS-HOME, SIR ALEC
British minister of state for foreign affairs; British prime minister

(7 pages, open) *John F. Kennedy Library MA*

DOUGLAS-HOME, WILLIAM
Kennedy associate, Great Britain

(22 pages, open) *John F. Kennedy Library MA*

DOUGLAS OF KIRTLESIDE, LORD (WILLIAM SHOLTO DOUGLAS) (1893–)

Aviation collection (28 pages, permission of interviewee required to cite or quote, also at *United States Air Force Academy CO* and *University of the Air, Maxwell Air Force Base AL*) *Columbia University NY*

DOUTHIT, GEORGE

Eisenhower administration project (48 pages, permission required to cite or quote, also at *Dwight D. Eisenhower Library KS*) *Columbia University NY*

DOUIEB, YEHOSHUA
Official, Jerusalem Ministry of Health

WORLD WAR II: THE HOLOCAUST—RESISTANCE AND RESCUE: (17) Forced labor camps under Nazi occupation in Tunisia (Hebrew, 29 pages, open) *Hebrew University, Israel*

DOW, ARTHUR
Discussed in Columbia University interview with Max Weber

DOWD, JEANNE (MRS. JEANNE ORMOND)

Challenges to governance by students project: Pentagon March (1967) (1968, 30 pages, open) *Cornell University NY*

DOWD, MARGARET
Mill Valley Public Library CA

DOWE, O. C.
Customs inspector at Terlingua (1907)

(1968, 10 pages, open) *University of Texas, El Paso*

DOWLING, EDDIE (1894–)
Actor; Producer; Director

(1963, 838 pages, open) *Columbia University NY*

DOWNEY, STEPHEN W. (1886–1958)
Attorney

(1957, 316 pages) *University of California, Berkeley*

DOWNS, STEVEN F., AND WILL R. DOWNS

Peace Corps project (1969, 79 pages, open) *John F. Kennedy Library MA*

DOWS, SUTHERLAND (1891–1969)

History of Cedar Rapids and Iowa City Railway, Railroad in Iowa collection *University of Iowa Libraries*

DOXIADIS, CONSTANTINOS A.
Greek minister of housing and reconstruction (1945–1948)

Harry S. Truman Library MO

DOYLE, JAMES
Wisconsin political figure

(21 pages, open) *John F. Kennedy Library MA*

DOYLE, LAWRENCE
Folk-poet

University of Maine

DOYLE, PATRICK
Deputy special assistant to the President for mental retardation

(39 pages, open) *John F. Kennedy Library MA*

DRAKE, LANDERS
Centenarian

(1972) *Fisk University TN*

DRAPER, JUSTICE MURRAY
Head of Northern California gubernatorial campaign for Earl Warren

Earl Warren oral history project (in process) *University of California, Berkeley*

DRAPER, WARREN FALES (1883–)

Health science collection (77 pages, permission required, also at *National Library of Medicine MD*) *Columbia University NY*

DRAPER, WILLIAM H.

Eisenhower administration project (18 pages, permission required to cite or quote, also at *Dwight D. Eisenhower Library KS*) *Columbia University NY*

DRIER, JOHN C. (1906–)
Former director, Office of Regional American Political Affairs

Dulles oral history collection (1965, 25 pages, permission required to cite or quote) *Princeton University NJ*

DREIFUS, BETTY
University of Washington Libraries

DREISER, THEODORE

Discussed in Columbia University interviews with Ellen Coyne (Mrs. Edgar Lee) Masters; Carl Van Vechten

Discussed in Vigo County Public Library IN interview with Vera Dreiser

DREISER, VERA
Vigo County Public Library IN

DRESSLER, DAVID (1907–)
Social worker; Writer

(1961, 185 pages, also microfiche, permission required to cite or quote) *Columbia University NY*

DRESSLER, JOHN (1916–1970)
Washo Indian leader

(1970, 156 pages, open) *University of Nevada, Reno*

DRIEGERT, MRS. ROBERT
University of Southern Mississippi

DRIGGS, BYRON D.
Ricks College ID

DRINKER, CECIL

Discussed in Columbia University interview with Edward Delos Churchill

DRINKWATER, EVERETT

Aeronautical history collection *University of Southern California Library*

DRISCOLL, JOHN
University of Connecticut

DRISCOLL, MRS. THOMAS A.

San Francisco earthquake of 1906, Santa Barbara *University of California, Santa Barbara*

DRISKELL, DAVID C.
Art department chairman, Fisk University

(1972) *Fisk University TN*

DRIVER, THOMAS W.
(1967) *State Historical Society of Colorado*

DROKER, HOWARD
with Gary Gayton
University of Washington Libraries

Journalism lectures (27 pages, permission required to cite or quote) *Columbia University NY*

Dulles oral history collection (1965, 84 pages, written permission required to read or copy in any form) *Princeton University NJ*

Discussed in Columbia University interviews with Eleanor Lansing Dulles; Frederick P. Jessup

DULLES, AVERY
John Foster Dulles's youngest son

Dulles oral history collection (1966, 41 pages, permission required to quote or cite) *Princeton University NJ*

DULLES, ELEANOR LANSING (1895–   )
Economist; U.S. diplomat

Eisenhower administration project (1967, 973 pages, permission required, also at *Dwight D. Eisenhower Library KS) Columbia University NY*

Dulles oral history collection (145 pages, written permission required to read until August 23, 1976) *Princeton University NJ*

DULLES, JOHN FOSTER (1888–1959)

New York political studies collection, New York election of 1949 (13 pages, permission required to cite or quote) *Columbia University NY*

Dulles oral history collection *Princeton University NJ*

Dulles oral history collection advisory committee conference (1964, 75 pages, closed until July 17, 1984) *Princeton University NJ*

Discussed in Columbia University interviews with Elie Abel; Sherman Adams; Hugh Meade Alcorn, Jr.; George Venable Allen; Dillon Anderson; James William Barco; Robert Richardson Bowie; Prescott Bush; Charles D. Cook; William Wilson Cumberland; Clarence Douglas Dillon; Roscoe Drummond; Eleanor Lansing Dulles; Milton Stover Eisenhower; Ernest A. Gross; John Murmann Hightower; Amory Houghton; Walter H. Judd; Clare Boothe (Mrs. Henry R.) Luce; Carl Wesley McCardle; Livingston Tallmadge Merchant; Flora Macdonald Rhind; Chalmers McGeagh Roberts; Walter Spencer Robertson; James Robinson Shepley

DUMONT, DONALD A. (1911–   )
Eisenhower administration project (75 pages, in process, also at *Dwight D. Eisenhower Library KS) Columbia University NY*

DUMONT, PAUL
Pioneer radio performer, announcer, and producer, NBC

(1965, 1 reel, 41 pages) *Broadcast Pioneers Library DC*

DUNBAR, LLOYD T.

South Dakota experience (1971), South Dakota Oral History Project *University of South Dakota*

DUNBAR, PAUL LAWRENCE
Poet

James A. Emanuel tape *Fisk University TN*

DUNCAN, DONALD (1896–   )
Naval officer

Naval history collection (1964, 981 pages, closed until 5 years after interviewee's death, also at *Division of Naval History DC) Columbia University NY*

DUNCAN, TODD
Actor; Concert artist

(1972) *Fisk University TN*

DUNGAN, RALPH
Staff assistant to Senator John F. Kennedy; Staff member, Senate committee on labor and public welfare

(125 pages, unedited transcript available with interviewee's permission; permission of interviewee required to cite, quote, or paraphrase) *John F. Kennedy Library MA*

DUNHAM, EDWIN L.
Retired manager, NBC music service

(4 reels, 67 pages) *Broadcast Pioneers Library DC*

DUNHAM, ELLEN ANN (1911–   )
Businesswoman

(1964, 55 pages, permission required to cite or quote) *Cornell University NY*

DUNLAVY, MAY WHITESCARVER

(1971) *State Historical Society of Colorado*

DUNLOP, JOHN
Economic stabilization program project *Cost of Living Council DC*

DUNN, LESLIE CLARENCE (1893–   )
Geneticist

(1960, 1086 pages, permission required) *Columbia University NY*

DUNN, LOULA FRIEND

Social Security collection (73 pages, open, also at *Social Security Administration MD) Columbia University NY*

Discussed in Columbia University interview with Charles Irwin Schottland

DUNN, WILLIAM
CBS war correspondent

(1966, 1 reel, 39 pages) *Broadcast Pioneers Library DC*

Communications Workers of America collection *University of Iowa Libraries*

DUNNE, JOE

Communications Workers of America collection *University of Iowa Libraries*

DUNNING, HAROLD

(1959) *State Historical Society of Colorado*

DUNNING, JOHN R. (1907–   )
Journalism lectures, Basic issues in the news: Nuclear energy (104 pages, permission required) *Columbia University NY*

DUNSHEE, BERTRAM K.
Water company official; Conservationist

(1965, 53 pages) *University of California, Berkeley*

DUPREE, DAVID

Challenges to governance by students project (1969, 22 pages, permission required to cite or quote) *Cornell University NY*

DUPREY, WILLIAM
William H. Miner employee (1907–   )

(open) *Plattsburgh State University College NY*

DURANDETTO, OSCAR
Labor leader

(1968, 142 pages) *Pennsylvania State University*

DURBROW, WILLIAM (1876–1958)
Irrigation district manager

(1958, 213 pages) *University of California, Berkeley*

DURDEN, DENNIS

Federated Department Stores project (44 pages, permission required) *Columbia University NY*

DURDIN, FRANK TILLMAN (1907–   )
International negotiations project (20 pages, permission required) *Columbia University NY*

DURMENT, T. S.

Weyerhaeuser Timber Company (45 pages, permission required) *Columbia University NY*

DURNFORD, DELOVA

Tacoma Public Library WA

DURR, CHARLES

Thomas Alva Edison project (20 pages, permission required pending completion of project) *Columbia University NY*

DURR, CLIFFORD JUDKINS (1899–   )

James Lawrence Fly project (32 pages, closed until January 1, 1982) *Columbia University NY*

DURR, VIRGINIA FOSTER (MRS. CLIFFORD)
Civil rights worker

(1970, 96 pages, permission required) *Columbia University NY*

DURSTINE, ROY SARLES (1886–1962)
Advertising man

(1949, 49 pages, open) *Columbia University NY*

EATON, CLEMENT (1898–)

American historians collection (89 pages, permission required to cite or quote) *Columbia University NY*

EBAN, ABBA (1915–)

Former Israeli ambassador to the United States

Dulles oral history collection (1964, 47 pages, permission required to quote or cite) *Princeton University NJ*

EBBINGHOUSE, JAMES

(1972) *Wabash Carnegie Public Library IN*

EBERHART, RILLA

Northern Indiana Historical Society

EBERSTADT, FERDINAND (1890–1969)

Investment banker

Robert P. Patterson project (27 pages, closed until January 1, 1980) *Columbia University NY*

Dulles oral history collection (1965, 41 pages, open) *Princeton University NJ*

EBERT, FREDERICK J.

O'Brien interview *State Historical Society of Colorado*

EBRIGHT, CARROLL "KY" (1894–)

Crew coach, University of California and the Olympics

(1968, 66 pages) *University of California, Berkeley*

EBRIGHT, HUGH

South Dakota experience (1971), South Dakota Oral History Project *University of South Dakota*

ECKARDT, FELIX VON (1903–)

Former press chief, Federal German Republic

Dulles oral history collection (1964, German, 38 pages, open) *Princeton University NJ*

ECONOMIC DEPRESSIONS *see* Depressions

ECONOMICS

Texas economic history project *Baylor University TX*

See also Business

EDDY, BERNICE ELAINE

National Institutes of Health MD

EDDY, NATHAN B.

National Institutes of Health MD

ECONOMIC ASSISTANCE

Marshall plan memoirs. Participants and pages: Dean Acheson, 5; Will Clayton, 32; Emilio G. Collado, 14; Lewis W. Douglas, 2; Livingston Merchant, 3; Norman Ness, 5; Paul Nitze, 8; Arthur Stevens, 4; James Stillwell, 5; Leroy Stinebower, 6; Ivan White, 19 (1947–1961, 103 pages, permission required to cite or quote) *Columbia University NY*

EDELMAN, JOHN W. (1893–1971)

Labor representative

(1957, 247 pages, permission required) *Columbia University NY*

Social Security collection (99 pages, open, also at *Social Security Administration MD*) *Columbia University NY*

EDELSTEIN, JULIUS

Herbert H. Lehman project (45 pages, permission required to cite or quote) *Columbia University NY*

New York political studies collection, Citizens Budget Commission (24 pages, permission required) *Columbia University NY*

EDELSTEIN, LEONARD

Ithaca Festival (Center for the Arts at Ithaca) project (105 pages, permission required) *Cornell University NY*

EDEN, ANTHONY

Discussed in Columbia University interviews with James Fife; Livingston Tallmadge Merchant

EDER, PHANOR JAMES (1880–1971)

Lawyer

(1965, 110 pages, also microfiche, permission required to cite or quote) *Columbia University NY*

EDGERTON, GLEN

Civil and military engineer

American Society of Civil Engineers NY

EDISON, CHARLES (1890–1969)

Industrialist

(1953, 294 pages, open) *Columbia University NY*

Discussed in Columbia University interviews with Francis Anthony Jamieson; Henry Williams

EDISON, THEODORE M.

Thomas Alva Edison project (26 pages, permission required pending completion of project) *Columbia University NY*

EDISON, THOMAS ALVA

Thomas Alva Edison project. Participants and pages: Edward Daly, 38; Charles Durr, 20; Theodore M. Edison, 26; Madeleine Edison Sloane, 35 (1972, 119 pages, permission required pending completion of project) *Columbia University NY*

Discussed in Columbia University interviews with Thomas H. Cowan; Charles Edison

EDLEFSEN, JESSE A.

Ricks College ID

EDMONDS, HARRY (1883–)

Founder, International House movement

(1971, 221 pages) *University of California, Berkeley*

EDSALL, DAVID

Discussed in Columbia University interviews with Joseph Charles Aub; Edward Delos Churchill

EDUCATION

Alumni Association of the City College, *CUNY*

Brooklyn College NY

Claremont Graduate School CA

Danforth Foundation Lectures on relationships between religion, the social sciences and education. Participants and pages: Bernard Barber, 40; Will Herberg, 60; Robert Lekachman, 48; Eugen Rosenstock-Huessy, 87 (1961–1962, 235 pages, permission required) *Columbia University NY*

Collective bargaining at SUNY project (1973, 22 hours) *Cornell University NY*

Perception of change in Ithaca school district project (1973, 13 interviews, 28 hours) *Cornell University NY*

Model school controversy in Montgomery County, Maryland (30 hours, 460 pages, open) *George Washington University, DC*

Higher education among Iraqi Jews *Hebrew University, Israel*

One room schools (8 hours, 44 pages, open) *Sangamon State University IL*

Temple University PA

Education collection (99 hours, 2526 pages, open) *University of California, Los Angeles*

St. Louis Teachers' Strike (15 hours, 213 pages, on-going) *University of Missouri, St. Louis*

South Dakota experience, South Dakota Oral History Project *University of South Dakota*

Growth of a regional university *Western Michigan University*

See also Culture; Physical Education and Training; Religions education

EDUCATION, ART *see* Art—Study and Teaching

EDUCATION, MEDICAL *see* Medicine— Study and Teaching

EDUCATION OF WOMEN

Development of the Continuing Education for Women program *George Washington University DC*

EDUCATIONAL TELEVISION *see* Television in Education

EDUCATORS

University of Delaware

EDWARDS, DR. DONALD

Physicist; Educator

(1972) *Fisk University TN*

M. Lambie, 49; Alvin H. Lane, 39; Sigurd Larmon, 41; William H. Lawrence, 37; J. Bracken Lee, 70; Barry Leithead, 52; R. A. Lile, 31; John D. Lodge, 195; Edward A. McCabe, 165 (open); Kevin McCann, 158; Carl W. McCardle, 48; John J. McCloy, 55; John McCone, 16; E. P. McGuire, 97; Theodore R. McKeldin, 78; Sidney S. McMath, 31; Henry R. McPhee, Jr., 58; Livingston T. Merchant, 86; Henry L. Miller, 59; L. Arthur Minnich, 34; William Mitchell, 84 (open); E. Frederick Morrow, 175; Robert D. Murphy, 45; Ancher Nelsen, 34; Arthur Nevins, 87; Dennis O'Rourke, 41; Bradley H. Patterson, Jr., 65; John S. Patterson, 54; Charles H. Percy, 33; Howard C. Petersen, 68; Richard M. Pittenger, 40; Terrell Powell, 34; Elwood R. Quesada, 89; Ogden R. Reid, 22; Ralph Reid, 51; Chalmers Roberts, 36; Richard Rovere, 44; Stanley M. Rumbough, Jr., 43 (open); Harrison Salisbury, 23; Irving Salomon, 39; Leverett Saltonstall, 151; Irene Samuel, 48; Howland Sargeant, 26; Raymond J. Saulnier, 71 (open); Leonard A. Scheele, 44 (open); Raymond L. Scherer, 54 (open); Gerard David Schine, 24; Fred C. Scribner, 83; Dudley Sharp, 67; Joseph S. Sheldon, 28; William T. Shelton, 35; James R. Shepley, 39; Robert Sherrod, 53; Allan Shivers, 58; David M. Shoup, 29; Ellis Slater, 38; Bromley Smith, 36; Howard K. Smith, 44; William J. Smith, 90; Murray Snyder, 67; Mansfield Sprague, 57; Elmer Staats, 59; Robert Storey, 63; Theodore Streibert, 35; Robert H. Thayer, 44; Walter N. Thayer, 52; Edward J. Thye, 76; Webster B. Todd, 88; Wayne Upton, 64; James J. Wadsworth, 248; David W. Wainhouse, 33; Arthur V. Watkins, 98; Anne W. Wheaton, 178; Francis O. Wilcox, 63; E. Grainger Williams, 65; Charles F. Willis, Jr., 50; Henry Wriston, 51; Charles R. Yates, 34. (12,430 pages)

Permission required: George V. Allen, 213; Allen V. Astin, 57; Rollin D. Barnard, 60; Edward L. Beach, 470; Earl C. Behrens, 44; Mark W. Clark, 91; Charles A. Coolidge, 35; John A. Danaher, 58; Harry Darby, 73; Clarence A. Davis, 106; Thomas E. Dewey, 43; Douglas Dillon, 94; Robert J. Donovan, 51; Eleanor Lansing Dulles, 973; John S. D. Eisenhower, 144; Robert H. Finch, 69; James M. Gavin, 36; Gordon Gray, 338; James C. Hagerty, 569; Robert E. Hampton, 57; Raymond Hare, 114; Karl G. Harr, Jr., 41; Brooks Hays, 165; Robert C. Hill, 105; Eric Hodgins, 162; Katherine Howard, 600; Frederick P. Jessup, 105; Walter H. Judd, 149; David W. Kendall, 85; Goodwin Knight, 94; Mary Pillsbury Lord, 428; Robert A. Lovett, 21; John Luter, 79; Neil H. McElroy, 88; Thomas Clifton Mann, 60; Robert Merriam, 209; True D. Morse, 144; Robert D. Murphy, 21; Herschel D. Newsom, 108; Roderick O'Connor, 144; Don Paarlberg, 164; Wilton Persons, 161; Maxwell Rabb, 38; Walter S. Robertson, 194; Ilene Slater, 58; Merriman Smith, 79; Arthur Summerfield, 93; Everett Tucker, Jr., 62; Sinclair Weeks, 172. (7524 pages)

Closed during lifetime except as noted: Dale Alford, 115; J. Sinclair Armstrong, 94; James W. Barco, 1061 (*until January 1, 1984*); Stephen G. Benedict, 137; Douglas M. Black, 53; Ellis O. Briggs, 134 (*until 1978*); Karl Brandt, 69; Wiley Branton, 61; John W. Bricker, 40; W. R. Brode, 51; W. T. Buchanan, 178 (*until 1993*); William A. M. Burden, 81; C. Conger, 25; Charles D. Cook, 658 (*until 1979*); Donald A. Dumont, 75; Ed Edwin, 47 (*until 1990*); Dwight D. Eisenhower, 114 (*until August 21, 1987*); Edgar Eisenhower, 117 (*until 1980*); J. Clifford Folger, 43 (*until January 1, 1977*); Barry M. Goldwater, 85 (*until April 12, 1974*); Alfred Gruenther, 97; Leonard Hall, 59; D. B. Hardeman, 146; Bryce N. Harlow, 144; Luther H. Hodges, 39; Leo A. Hoegh, 95; Amory Houghton, 96; James Karam, 29; James R. Killian, 375 (*until 1985*); Herbert G. Klein, 39; Lyman Lemnitzer, 26; J. E. Lever, 62; Clare Booth Luce, 108; James McCrory, 19; Earl Mazo, 52; James B. Mintener, 65; Malcolm Moos, 41; Edward P. Morgan, 53; Gerald D. Morgan, 133; Kenneth D. Nichols, 100; Hugh B. Patterson, Jr., 85; Homa Jack Porter, 47; Wesley Pruden, 33; Howard Pyle (with Charles Masterson), 134; William P. Rogers, 51 (*until 1977*); Charles Roberts, 35; Clifford Roberts, 878 (*until 20 years after death*); Nelson A. Rockefeller, 40 (*until 1997 or death, whichever is later*); Robert Roosa, 98; R. Richard Rubottom, 95; Robert L. Schulz, 165 (*until 1993*); Stephen A. Shadeg, 30; Maurice H. Stans, 83; Harold Stassen, 68 (*until 1985*); John R. Steelman, 89 (*until 1990*); Thomas E. Stephens, 98; Lewis L. Strauss, 177 (*until 1985*); Joseph M. Swing, 76; Jessie W. Thornton, 41; Elbert P. Tuttle, 113; Nathan Twining, 250; Abbott Washburn, 91; W. Walter Williams, 103; Milton R. Young, 30. (7926 pages)

(1962–1972, 27,800 pages; also at *Dwight D. Eisenhower Library KS*) *Columbia University NY*

(28 pages, interview conducted by Dr. Forrest C. Pogue, also at *Dwight D. Eisenhower Library KS*) *George C. Marshall Research Library VA*

(35 pages, interview conducted by Raymond Henle, also at *Dwight D. Eisenhower Library KS*) *Herbert Hoover Oral History Program DC*

John C. Stennis collection *Mississippi State University*

Dulles oral history collection (1964, 57 pages, open, also at *Dwight D. Eisenhower Library KS*) *Princeton University NJ*

James A. Farley collection *Scott E. Webber Collection NY*

Discussed in Columbia University interviews with Barry Bingham; Robert Richardson Bowie; Leo Cherne; Ewan Clague; Frank Diehl Fackenthal; William Morrow Fechteler; John Earl Fetzer; John Lesslie Hall, Jr.; Roswell Burchard Perkins, Kenneth Claiborne Royall; Charles Irwin Schottland; William Sullivan; Lloyd Taft

Discussed in *Dwight D. Eisenhower Library KS collection*

EISENHOWER, EDGAR N. (1889–1971)
Brother of President Eisenhower; Lawyer

Eisenhower administration project (1967, 117 pages, closed until 1980, also at *Dwight D. Eisenhower Library KS*) *Columbia University NY*

EISENHOWER, JOHN SHELDON DAVID (1922–   )
U.S. Army officer

Eisenhower administration project (144 pages, permission required, also at *Dwight D. Eisenhower Library KS*) *Columbia University NY*

EISENHOWER, MILTON STOVER (1899–   )
Government official; Educator; President's brother

Eisenhower administration project (115 pages, permission required to cite or quote, also at *Dwight D. Eisenhower Library KS*) *Columbia University NY*

Discussed in Columbia University interview with John Clifford Folger

Kansas State University

(1972, 45 pages, 1 1/2 hours, open) *Maryland Historical Society*

Dulles oral history collection (1965, 33 pages, permission required to quote or cite) *Princeton University NJ*

EISENMENGER, JACOB
Lawyer

South Dakota experience (1971), South Dakota Oral History Project *University of South Dakota*

ELAM, DOROTHY CONLEY
Fisk University TN

ELDAD, DOV
YOUTH MOVEMENTS: (2) Netzach in Latvia (Hebrew, 28 pages, open) *Hebrew University, Israel*

ELDRED, ROY
Idaho Bicentennial Commission

ELDREDGE, INMAN F.
(12 pages, permission required to cite or quote, also at *Columbia University NY*) *Forest History Society CA*

ELDRIDGE, ARTHUR
Crew member of the *Menemsha*

Dulles oral history collection (1965, 47 pages, permission required to quote or cite) *Princeton University NJ*

ELDRIDGE, MRS. JANER O. (1919–   )
Perception of change in Ithaca school district project (1967, 121 pages, open) *Cornell University NY*

ELECTIONS
New York political studies collection, New York election of 1949 (1949, 292 pages, permission required to cite or quote) *Columbia University NY*

McCarthy historical project *Georgetown University DC*

The model school controversy in Montgomery County, Maryland (open) *George Washington University DC*

ELSON, EDWARD LEE ROY (1906–   )
Pastor, National Presbyterian Church, Washington, DC

Eisenhower administration project (1969, 293 pages, permission required to cite or quote, also at *Dwight D. Eisenhower Library KS*) *Columbia University NY*

ELSTON, CLARE
University of Connecticut

EMANUEL, JAMES A.
Poet; Professor of English

(1972) *Fisk University TN*

EMENS, DR. JOHN
Ferris State College MI

EMENY, BROOKS (1901–   )
Author; Lecturer

Dulles oral history collection (1966, 35 pages, permission required to quote or cite) *Princeton University NJ*

EMERSON, GUY (1886–1969)
Lawyer; Banker

(1951, 249 pages, also microfiche, permission required to cite or quote) *Columbia University NY*

EMERSON, GUY LAVERNE
(1970) *State Historical Society of Colorado*

EMERSON, HAVEN (1874–1957)
Physician

(1950, 103 pages, also microfiche, permission required to cite or quote) *Columbia University NY*

EMERSON, MARY

Discussed in Columbia University interview with Richard Gordon

EMERSON, THOMAS IRWIN (1907–   )
Attorney; Professor

(1953, 2227 pages; 1955, 279 pages; permission required) *Columbia University NY*

National Labor Relations Board project (1970, 115 pages, open) *Cornell University NY*

EMERY, CARLOS

Argentina in the 1930s (Spanish, 33 pages, open) *Columbia University NY*

EMIGRATION *see* Immigration and Emigration

EMMERICH, HERBERT

Discussed in Columbia University interview with Charles Ascher

EMMERICH, J. O.
University of Southern Mississippi

EMMERSON, LOUIS LINCOLN (1863–1941)
Illinois governor

Discussed in Sangamon State University IL Mining and John L. Lewis collection

EMMET, JESSIE (MRS. RICHARD)

Association for the Aid of Crippled Children (45 pages, permission required) *Columbia University NY*

EMMONS, CHESTER W.
National Institutes of Health MD

EMMONS, DELOS CARLETON (1888–1965)

Aviation collection (21 pages, permission required to cite or quote, also at *United States Air Force Academy CO* and *University of the Air, Maxwell Air Force Base AL*) *Columbia University NY*

EMORE, ANNIE

(1962) *State Historical Society of Colorado*

EMPLOYMENT OF WOMEN *see* Woman—Employment

EMSPAK, JULIUS (1904–1962)
Union official

(1960, 363 pages, also microfiche, permission required to cite or quote) *Columbia University NY*

ENARSON, HAROLD L.
Cleveland State University Library OH

ENBUTSU, SUMIKO FUJIWARA
Smith alumna, class of 1960; Translator and interpreter

(1973, 2 hours, 35 pages) *Smith College MA*

ENDICOTT, KENNETH M. (1916–   )

Health science collection (45 pages, permission required, also at *National Library of Medicine MD*) *Columbia University NY*

ENDORE, SAMUEL GUY

Biographical collection (open) *University of California, Los Angeles*

ENDRESS, ROBERT P.
University of Michigan

ENGEL, GENERAL GERHARD

German military opposition to Hitler *Harold C. Deutsch Collection DC*

ENGEL, LEHMAN
Composer; Conductor

Ives project (1969) *Yale University School of Music CT*

ENGLAND, ELYSE

Smith alumna, class of 1962; Director of advertising/public relations; Real estate agent

(1973, 2 hours, 43 pages) *Smith College MA*

ENGLE, LAVINIA
Government official

Social Security collection (1967, 184 pages, open, also at *Social Security Administration MD*) *Columbia University NY*

ENGLEMAN, FINIS
University of Connecticut

ENGLISH LANGUAGE—DIALECTS
University of Southern Mississippi

ENGLUND, CONSTENTINE EVERET
Ricks College ID

ENGLUND, WILLIAM S.

South Dakota experience (1971), South Dakota Oral History Project *University of South Dakota*

ENGRAVERS

Archives of American Art—Smithsonian Institution NY

ENGSTROM, HAROLD
School board member, Little Rock AR (1957)

Eisenhower administration project (61 pages, permission required to cite or quote, also at *Dwight D. Eisenhower Library KS*) *Columbia University NY*

ENNIS, EDWARD

Assistant U.S. attorney general in charge of Enemy Alien Control Unit

Earl Warren oral history project (in process) *University of California, Berkeley*

ENNIS, JOHN
State legislator

Vigo County Public Library IN

ENNIS, THOMAS GATES (1904–   )
Major general, U.S. Marine Corps (service: 1928–1962)

(141 pages, permission required, also at *Columbia University NY* and *U.S. Naval Institute MD*) *United States Marine Corps DC*

ENO, MR.
with Simon Rifkind

ANTECEDENTS TO THE STATE OF ISRAEL: (2) "Brichah" (organized escape) (English, 8 pages, open) *Hebrew University, Israel*

ENOCH, PAUL
Lecturer, Haifa Technion

WORLD WAR II: THE HOLOCAUST—RESISTANCE AND RESCUE: (4) Jews in the underground in Belgium (French, 10 pages, open) *Hebrew University, Israel*

ENZIE, WALTER D. (1904–   )
Horticulturist

(1965, 25 pages, permission required to cite or quote) *Cornell University NY*

EPIC MOVEMENT

Reuben Warringer Borough interview, Government and politics collection *University of California, Los Angeles*

FAGLEY, RICHARD M. (cont.)
Dulles oral history collection (1964, 46 pages, permission required to cite or quote) *Princeton University NJ*

FAHY, CHARLES (1892-)
Lawyer; Judge
(1958, 451 pages, permission required) *Columbia University NY*

FAILING, JEAN (1913-)
College administrator
(1965, 161 pages, permission required to cite or quote) *Cornell University NY*
National Labor Relations Board (1968, 63 pages, open) *Cornell University NY*
Challenges to governance by students project (1969, 32 pages, open) *Cornell University NY*

FAIR, CLINTON (1909-)
Social Security collection (75 pages, closed during interviewee's lifetime, also at *Social Security Administration MD*) *Columbia University NY*

FAIRBANK, JOHN (1907-)
International negotiations project (25 pages, permission required) *Columbia University NY*

FAIRBANKS, DOUGLAS, SR.
Discussed in Columbia University interview with Albert Edward Sutherland and in Popular arts collection

FAIRCHILD, WILMA
Geographer
(1971, 10 minutes) *Plymouth State College NH*

FAIRFIELD, LESLIE AND MARY
China missionaries collection (75 pages, open, also at *Columbia University NY*) *Claremont Graduate School CA*

FAKTOR, GERSHON
Rehovot physician
JEWISH COMMUNITIES: (3) Lithuanian Jewry between the two world wars (Hebrew, 33 pages, open) *Hebrew University, Israel*

FALES, CHARLES
South Dakota experience (1959), South Dakota Oral History Project *University of South Dakota*

FALK, ADRIEN, J. (1884-1971)
President, S & W Fine Foods, Inc.
(1955, 180 pages) *University of California, Berkeley*

FALK, ISIDORE SYDNEY (1899-)
Public health specialist; Medical economist
Health science collection (79 pages, permission required, also at *National Library of Medicine MD*) *Columbia University NY*

FALL, ALBERT B.
Discussed in Columbia University interviews with Arthur Joseph Altmeyer; William Reidy

FAMILY
Discussed in Columbia University interview with Horace Marden Albright
Shirley Camper-Soman Collection NY

FANNING, HERMAN
State legislator
Vigo County Public Library IN

THE FAR EAST SOCIETY
JEWISH COMMUNITIES: (13) Jews in the Far East *Hebrew University, Israel*

FARBER, RIVKA
ANTECEDENTS TO THE STATE OF ISRAEL: (2) "Brichah" (organized escape) (Hebrew, 28 pages, open) *Hebrew University, Israel*

FARBER, FISHL
ANTECEDENTS TO THE STATE OF ISRAEL: (2) "Brichah" (organized escape) (Hebrew, 24 pages, open) *Hebrew University, Israel*

FARIES, McINTYRE
Judge; Republican national committee member; Southern California political leader
Earl Warren oral history project (in process) *University of California, Berkeley*

FARLEY, EDWARD PHILIP (1886-1956)
Shipping executive
(1949, 44 pages, open) *Columbia University NY*

FARLEY, JAMES ALOYSIUS (1888-)
Politician
(1958, 400 pages, closed until 2 years after interviewee's death) *Columbia University NY*
Social Security collection (1968, 289 pages, open, also at *Social Security Administration MD*) *Columbia University NY*
Herbert H. Lehman project (44 pages, permission required to cite or quote) *Columbia University NY*
Discussed in Columbia University interviews with Edward Costikyan; Joseph Christopher O'Mahoney
Scott E. Webber Collection NY

FARLEY, MORGAN
Cinema collection
University of Southern California Library

FARLEY, PHILIP
U.S. government official
(18 pages, open) *John F. Kennedy Library MA*

FARM HOLIDAY ASSOCIATION
Participants and pages: John Bosch, 56; Richard Bosch, 27; Homer Hush, 56; Dale Kramer, 23; Donald Ridgway Murphy, 32 (1960-1961), 194 pages, open) *Columbia University NY*
Southwest Minnesota State College
Nebraska State Historical Society

FARM LIFE
Farm families project. Twenty families interviewed at 2-year intervals in a study of decision-making process on New York farms *Cornell University NY*

FARM TENANCY
Mary Holmes College MS

FARMAN, MAURICE (-1964)
Aviation collection (17 pages, permission required to cite or quote, also at *United States Air Force Academy CO* and *University of the Air, Maxwell Air Force Base AL*) *Columbia University NY*

FARMER, JAMES
National director, CORE
(29 pages, permission of interviewee required) *John F. Kennedy Library MA*

FARMERS MUSEUM
Charles B. Hosmer, Jr. Collection IL

FARMING *see* Agriculture; National Farmer's Organization

FARQUHAR, FRANCIS P. (1887-)
Certified public accountant
(1960, 376 pages; 1968, 22 pages) *University of California, Berkeley*

FARR, BARCLAY H.
Theodore Roosevelt Association (33 pages, permission required to cite or quote) *Columbia University NY*

FARR, DR. CHARLES
Ives project (1970) *Yale University School of Music CT*

FARR, RUBEN
Labor leader
(1968, 52 pages) *Pennsylvania State University*

FARRAKHAN, LOUIS
(1971) *Fisk University TN*

FARRAR, STUART K. (1890-)
Food processor
(1964, 29 pages, open) *Cornell University NY*

FARRELL, FRANCIS DAVID
Kansas State University president
Kansas State University

FARRELL, GLENDA (1904–)
Popular arts collection (61 pages, open) *Columbia University NY*

FARRELL, JAMES
Harvard sports equipment man

(8 pages, open) *John F. Kennedy Library MA*

FARRELL, MARIE
Nursing Archive *Boston University MA*

FARRELL, WALTER GREATSINGER (1897–)
Major general, U.S. Marine Corps (service: 1917–1946)

(1970, in process) *United States Marine Corps DC*

FARWELL, MARGARET M. (MRS. JOHN V. FARWELL, III)
Adlai E. Stevenson project (31 pages, permission required) *Columbia University NY*

FAST, LOUISA KIMBALL
League of Women Voters organizer and director; American Association of University Women director; Smith alumna, class of 1898

(1973, 1 hour, 22 pages) *Smith College MA*

FAUBER, EVERETTE
Historic preservation *Charles B. Hosmer, Jr. Collection IL*

FAUBUS, ORVAL EUGENE (1910–)
Arkansas governor

Eisenhower administration project (1971, 135 pages, permission required to cite or quote, also at *Dwight D. Eisenhower Library KS*) *Columbia University NY*

Discussed in Columbia University interview with Brooks Hays

FAULKNER, WILLIAM
Discussed in Columbia University interviews with Dorothy Berliner Commins; Donald Simon Klopfer

FAURI, FEDELE FREDERICK (1909–)
Social Security collection (59 pages, open, also at *Social Security Administration MD*) *Columbia University NY*

FAVERMAN, GERALD A.
University of Michigan

FAYNE, JAMES
Joseph P. Kennedy's associations with Herbert Hoover and Hoover commission (no more than 2 pages may be copied, also at *Herbert Hoover Oral History Program DC*) *John F. Kennedy Library MA*

FEATHER, GEORGE ADLAI
(1968, 18 pages, open) *University of Texas, El Paso*

FECHTELER, WILLIAM MORROW (1896–1967)
Naval officer

Naval history collection (1962, 266 pages, permission required, also at *Division of Naval History DC) Columbia University NY*

FEDER, TED
Director, American Jewish Joint Distribution Committee (Geneva)

WORLD WAR II: THE HOLOCAUST—RESISTANCE AND RESCUE: (1) The Joint (American Jewish Joint Distribution Committee) (English, 20 pages, open) *Hebrew University, Israel*

FEDERATED DEPARTMENT STORES
Participants and pages: Edward Coughlin, 33; Alfred H. Daniels, 46; Dennis Durden, 44; Abe Fortas, 9; Robert Fuoss, 58; Alfred Gruenther, 38; George Hammond, 38; George C. Hayward, 58; Walter Heymann, 22; Harold D. Hodgkinson, 27; Gray Hussey, 18; Mrs. Gray Hussey, 10; Joseph Kasper, 45; Bernard S. Klayf, 42; Herbert Landsman, 81; Celia R. Lazarus, 99; Charles Lazarus, 21; Eleanor and Margaret Lazarus, 47; Fred Lazarus, Jr., 1,039; Fred Lazarus III, 42; Irma M. Lazarus, 40; Jeffrey Lazarus, 32; Maurice Lazarus, 59; Ralph Lazarus, 54; Mrs. Ralph Lazarus, 22; Robert Lazarus, 32; Simon Lazarus, 44; John F. Lebor, 56; Robert Lenhart, 28; Paul M. Mazur, 59; Leonard Minster, 26; Alfred Neal, 38; Mrs. Jesse Evans Ross, 34; Lewis Saille, 28; Oral Scheaf, 40; Ann Lazarus Schloss, 47; Trent Sickles, 37; Myron Silbert, 99; William T. Snaith, 46; Sydney Solomon, 42; Herbert Stein, 29; J. Paul Sticht, 55; Frank Sulzburger, 20; Ann Visconti, 51; George Whitten, 42; Charles Wiedemer, 12; John C. Wilson, 22 (1965, 2911 pages, permission required) *Columbia University NY*

FEDERMAN, SHMUEL
WORLD WAR II: THE HOLOCAUST—RESISTANCE AND RESCUE: (2) Rescue of Jews via Spain and Portugal (Hebrew, 2 pages, open) *Hebrew University, Israel*

FEDOULENKO, VALENTIN V. (1894–)
Russian émigré, Shanghai

(1967, 171 pages) *University of California, Berkeley*

FEEDING AND FEEDS
Man-land confrontation in the Southwest (110 hours, 2000 pages, open) *Texas Tech University*

FEENBERG, EUGENE
American Institute of Physics NY

FEENEY, JOSEPH G.
Administrative assistant to the president (1952–1953)

Harry S. Truman Library MO

FEES, BURT
South Dakota experience (1969), South Dakota Oral History Project *University of South Dakota*

FEIGENBAUM, B. J.
Office partner of Steinhart (deceased); Political advisor to Warren; Fund raiser

Earl Warren oral history project (in process) *University of California, Berkeley*

FEIGENBAUM, JOEL
Active in McCarthy project in New Hampshire, 1968

Eugene McCarthy project (1968, 97 pages, written permission required) *Cornell University NY*

FEIGHTNER, HAROLD
Newspaperman (1920s)

Indiana State Library IN

FEIKER, FREDERICK MORRIS (1881–1967)
McGraw-Hill, Inc. (45 pages, permission required) *Columbia University NY*

FEIL, HELEN R.
Book-of-the-Month Club collection (16 pages, open) *Columbia University NY*

FEIN, FREIDA
YOUTH MOVEMENTS: (2) Netzach in Latvia (Hebrew, 28 pages, open) *Hebrew University, Israel*

FEINBERG, JACOB
Pike Place Market *University of Washington Libraries WA*

FEINBERG, NATHAN
Emeritus professor of international law, Hebrew University

JEWISH COMMUNITIES: (1) German Jewry 1933–1935 (Hebrew, 15 pages, open) *Hebrew University, Israel*

JEWISH COMMUNITIES: (3) Lithuanian Jewry between the two world wars (Hebrew, 13 pages, open) *Hebrew University, Israel*

FEINBLOOM, DEBORAH HELLER
Smith alumna, class of 1961; Sociologist; Teacher

(1973, 2 hours, 40 pages) *Smith College MA*

FEJOS, PAUL (1897–1963)
Anthropologist

(1962, 244 pages plus papers, permission required) *Columbia University NY*

Discussed in Columbia University interview with Albert Anthony Giesecke

FELDMAN, GITTA
WORLD WAR II: THE HOLOCAUST—RESISTANCE AND RESCUE: (4) Jews in the underground in Belgium (Yiddish, 33 pages, open) *Hebrew University, Israel*

FELDMAN, JUSTIN N. (1919–)
Lawyer; Politician

(1968, 330 pages, closed during interviewee's lifetime) *Columbia University NY*

FIELD ENTERPRISES, INC.
Field Enterprises IL

FIELDS, DOROTHY (1905–)
Popular arts collection (40 pages, open) *Columbia University NY*

FIELDS, GRACIE (1898–)
Popular arts collection (49 pages, open) *Columbia University NY*

FIELDS, MRS. JAMES
(1971) *State Historical Society of Colorado*

FIELDS, LEWIS JEFFERSON (1909–)
Lieutenant general, U.S. (service: 1932–1970)

(1971, 267 pages, permission required, also at *Columbia University NY* and *U.S. Naval Institute MD*) *United States Marine Corps DC*

FIELDS, MARSHALL (1919–)
Marine Corps veteran

Prisoner-of-war project (1972, 64 pages, open) *North Texas State University Oral History Collection*

FIELDS, OGDEN W. (1910–)
National Labor Relations Board (1969, 66 pages, open) *Cornell University NY*

FIELDS, W. C.
Discussed in Columbia University interview with Albert Edward Sutherland and in Popular arts collection

FIFE, JAMES (1897–)
Naval officer

Naval history collection (1962, 617 pages, also microfiche, permission required to cite or quote, also at *Division of Naval History DC*) *Columbia University NY*

FINBERG, BARBARA
Children's Television Workshop (11 pages, open) *Columbia University NY*

FINCH, EDWARD R.
Discussed in Columbia University interview with Hokan Bjornstrom Steffanson

FINCH, GLENN E. (1891–)
Food processor

(1964, 40 pages, permission required to cite or quote) *Cornell University NY*

FINCH, JAMES K.
Civil engineer; Educator
American Society of Civil Engineers NY

FINCH, ROBERT HUTCHINSON (1925–)
Government official

Eisenhower administration project (1967, 69 pages, permission required, also at *Dwight D. Eisenhower Library KS* and *Occidental College, Los Angeles*) *Columbia University NY*

FINE, BENJAMIN (1905–)
Journalism lectures (25 pages, permission required to cite or quote) *Columbia University NY*

FINE, PERLE (1908–)
Painter

(1963, 6 pages; 1968, 30 pages) *Archives of American Art—Smithsonian Institution NY*

FINE, PHIL
Kennedy Boston associate; Former deputy administrator, Small Business Administration

(14 pages, open) *John F. Kennedy Library MA*

FINE ARTS *see* The Arts

FINEGAN, W. ROBERT
Challenges to governance by students project (1969, 38 pages, open) *Cornell University NY*

FINK, WILLIAM
Former manager of mines in Mexico

(1968, 8 pages, open) *University of Texas, El Paso*

FINLETTER, THOMAS K. (1893–)
Former U.S. Secretary of the Air Force; U.S. ambassador to NATO

Adlai E. Stevenson project (62 pages, permission required) *Columbia University NY*

(13 pages, portion closed) *John F. Kennedy Library MA*

FINLEY, JOHN H.
Discussed in Columbia University interview with Charles Henry Tuttle

FINNEY, BURNHAM (1899–)
McGraw-Hill, Inc. (23 pages, permission required) *Columbia University NY*

FINNEY, THOMAS
Adlai E. Stevenson project (33 pages, permission required) *Columbia University NY*

FINUCANE, PETER
Robert P. Patterson project (21 pages, closed until January 1, 1980) *Columbia University NY*

FIORELLO, ALBERT
Joseph M. Proskauer project (20 pages, permission required) *Columbia University NY*

FIRESTONE, LEONARD
Industrialist

Eisenhower administration project (15 pages, open, also at *Dwight D. Eisenhower Library KS*) *Columbia University NY*

FISCHER, FRANK
West Virginia political figure

(16 pages, open) *John F. Kennedy Library MA*

FISCHER, JOHN
Discussed in Columbia University interview with Will Winton Alexander

FISCHER, MAURICE AND SYLVIE
Doctor, Assaf Ha-Rofe Hospital, Sarafand

WORLD WAR II: THE HOLOCAUST—RESISTANCE AND RESCUE: (4) Jews in the underground in Belgium (Hebrew, 27 pages, open) *Hebrew University, Israel*

FISHEL, CHANKA

WORLD WAR II: THE HOLOCAUST—RESISTANCE AND RESCUE: (8) Theresienstadt ghetto (German, 46 pages, open) *Hebrew University, Israel*

FISHER, ADRIAN
Deputy director, U.S. Arms Control and Disarmament Agency

(28 pages, open) *John F. Kennedy Library MA*

FISHER, ARTHUR A.
(1964) *State Historical Society of Colorado*

FISHER, DOROTHY CANFIELD (1879–1958)
Author

Book-of-the-Month Club collection (1955, 129 pages, also microfiche, permission required to cite or quote) *Columbia University NY*

FISHER, EDWIN SHELTON (1911–)
McGraw-Hill, Inc. (45 pages, permission required) *Columbia University NY*

FISHER, OLIVER DAVID (1875–)
Weyerhaeuser Timber Company (73 pages, permission required) *Columbia University NY*

FISHER, PAUL
Hunt Institute for Botanical Documentation PA

FISHER, WALTER TAYLOR (1892–)
Adlai E. Stevenson project (27 pages, permission required) *Columbia University NY*

FISHING
Fishing and lobstering *University of Maine*

FIGARI, WILLIAM (1886–)
Sea captain

(1969, 169 pages) *University of California, Berkeley*

FIKE, STANLEY
Executive director, Symington presidential campaign, 1960; Symington's administrative assistant

(91 pages, permission of interviewee required) *John F. Kennedy Library MA*

FITCH, LYLE C. (1913–)
New York political studies collection, Citizens Budget Commission (28 pages, permission required) Columbia University NY

FITCH, WILLIAM KOUNTZ (1889–)
Government official
Social Security collection (1966, 100 pages, open, also at Social Security Administration MD) Columbia University NY

FITTS, WILLIAM COCHRAN, JR. (1905–)
James Lawrence Fly project (52 pages, closed until January 1, 1982) Columbia University NY

FITZGERALD, ALBERT
President, United Electrical, Radio & Machine Workers of America
(1968, 31 pages) Pennsylvania State University

FITZGERALD, ALICE (MRS. WILLIAM)
Association for the Aid of Crippled Children (78 pages, permission required) Columbia University NY

FITZGERALD, F. SCOTT
Discussed in Columbia University interview with Carl Van Vechten

FITZGERALD, GERALDINE
Theatre on film and tape New York Public Library at Lincoln Center

FITZGERALD, RAY
South Dakota political figure; Deputy administrator, Agricultural Stabilization and Conservation Services
(15 pages, open) John F. Kennedy Library MA

FITZPATRICK, JAMES A.
History and activities of W. H. Miner Foundation (20 minutes, open) Plattsburgh State University College NY

FITZGERALD, THOMAS
Employee of W. H. Miner for 50 years
(open) Plattsburgh State University College NY

FITZSIMMONS, EMMA S.
(1955) State Historical Society of Colorado

FIVEY, THOMAS
United Steelworkers of America leader
(1967, 5 pages) Pennsylvania State University

FLAMM, RUSSELL
Ricks College ID

FLANIGAN, LON
Food processor
(1964, 76 pages, permission required) Cornell University NY

FLANAGAN, ARTHUR B.
Health science collection (42 pages, permission required, also at National Library of Medicine MD) Columbia University NY

FLEISHHACKER, MORTIMER, JR.
Northern California Jewish Community series (permission required to quote, also at the University of California, Berkeley CA) Western Jewish History Center CA

FLEISCHMAN, LAWRENCE (1925–)
Art dealer; collector
(1970, 45 pages) Archives of American Art—Smithsonian Institution NY

FLEISCHMAN, HARRY
Socialist movement project (38 pages, permission required to cite or quote) Columbia University NY

FLEISCHER, EHUD
WORLD WAR II: THE HOLOCAUST—RESISTANCE AND RESCUE: (2) Rescue of Jews via Spain and Portugal (Hebrew, 9 pages; French, 7 pages; open) Hebrew University, Israel

FLEISCHER, DAVE
Director and producer, motion picture cartoons
An oral history of the motion picture in America (open) University of California, Los Angeles

FLEET, REUBEN
Oral history project, National Air and Space Museum Smithsonian Institution DC

FLEET, JAMES VAN
Discussed in Columbia University interview with Kenneth Claiborne Royall

FLEENOR, HOWARD D. (1915–)
Chairman, UTU local 492
United Transportation Union project (1971, 46 pages, open transcript, permission required to use tape) Cornell University NY

FLATO, EDWIN F. (ca. 1885–)
Retired businessman
(1970, 46 pages, open) North Texas State University Oral History Collection

FLATH, AUGUST WILLIAM (1898–1969)
Police inspector
(1959, 91 pages, open) Columbia University NY

FLANDERS, RALPH EDWARD (1880–1969)
U.S. senator (Vermont, 1946–1958)
Eisenhower administration project (1967, 51 pages, permission required to cite or quote, also at Dwight D. Eisenhower Library KS) Columbia University NY

FLANIGAN, MARK
Communications Workers of America collection (permission required) Columbia University NY

FLEMING, W. C.
Dental history (in process) University of California, Berkeley

FLETCHER, CURTIS
Communications Workers of America collection University of Iowa Libraries

FLETCHER, FRANK
Owner since 1914 of Acme Laundry, El Paso
(1968, 4 pages, open) University of Texas, El Paso

FLETCHER, SYLVIA
Challenges to governance by students project: School of the Ozarks (1971, 27 pages, special permission required) Cornell University

FLEXNER, ABRAHAM (1866–1959)
Educator
(1954, 36 pages, also microfiche, permission required to cite or quote) Columbia University NY

FLEXNER, CAROLIN A.
Herbert H. Lehman project (67 pages, permission required to cite or quote) Columbia University NY

FLEXNER, JAMES
Historian
Ives project (1970, restricted) Yale University School of Music CT

FLEXNER, SIMON
Discussed in Columbia University interviews with Frederic René Coudert; Abraham Flexner

FLINT, MICHIGAN
Flint Public Library MI

FLOODS
Black Hills Flood of 1972 (1972–1973, 200 interviews, 150 hours, 4000 pages, permission required) University of South Dakota

FLORES, ALONSO
Doris Duke American Indian Oral History Project Arizona State Museum

FLOREZ, LUIS DE
Aviation collection (39 pages, permission of interviewee required to cite or quote, also at United States Air Force Academy CO and University of the Air, Maxwell Air Force Base AL) Columbia University NY

FLORIDA
University of Florida
University of West Florida

FLOYD, EVAN BURBANK
Ricks College ID

FLY, JAMES LAWRENCE (1898–1966)
Chairman, Federal Communications Commission (1939–1944)

James Lawrence Fly project. Participants and pages: Thurman W. Arnold, 16; Edward Brecher, 35; Marcus Cohn, 39; Thomas Corcoran, 29; Norman Corwin, 49; Benedict Peter Cottone, 24; Charles R. Denny, 28; Clifford J. Durr, 32; William C. Fitts, Jr., 52; Abe Fortas, 11; Fred W. Friendly, 14; Lucien Hilmer, 16; Rosel H. Hyde, 19; Leonard H. Marks, 25; Neville Miller, 33; Charles S. Murphy, 13; John Lord O'Brian, 14; Harry Plotkin, 36; Paul A. Porter, 30; Joseph Rauh, 35; James Rowe, 9; Pete Shuebruk, 36; Telford Taylor, 60 (1967, 655 pages, closed until January 1, 1982) Columbia University NY

"FLYING TIGERS"
Participants and pages: Mrs. Anna Chennault and Thomas Corcoran, 4; Thomas Corcundale, 16; Jerry Costello and John Vivian, 12; Tom Cotton, 31; Doreen Davis, 47; Tex Hill, 23; Joe Jordan, 38; Gayle McAlister, 13; Robert Neale, 60; Charley Older, 38; Bob Prescott, 43; Doc Richardson and Bob Blyer, 21; Don Rodewald and Wilfred Schaper, 40; Don Rodewald, Harvey Wirta, and Wilfred Schaper, 57; Robert James Smith and Tom Trumble, 78; John Vivian, 24 (1962, 583 pages, permission required to cite or quote) Columbia University NY

FLYNN, EDWARD JOSEPH (1892–1953)
Politician
(1950, 24 pages, also microfiche, permission required to cite or quote, also at John F. Kennedy Library MA) Columbia University NY

Discussed in Columbia University interview with Willaim O'Dwyer

FLYNN, F. E. (1877–   )
Food processor
(1964, 82 pages, permission required to cite or quote) Cornell University NY

FLYNN, KEN BENSON
(30 minutes, not transcribed, open) University of Texas, El Paso

FLYNT, HENRY AND HELEN
Historic preservation Charles B. Hosmer, Jr. Collection IL

FOARD, F. MILLARD (1898–   )
Language instructor, City College (1920–1959); Alumni Relations correspondent; Law instructor, Director, Asian Cultural Exchange Foundation
(37 pages, 2 hours, open) Maryland Historical Society

FOGARTY, JOHN
U.S. representative (Rhode Island)
(12 pages, open) John F. Kennedy Library MA

FOGELSON, ROBERT
Columbia crisis of 1968 (44 pages, permission required) Columbia University NY

FOGG, VERNE A. (1897–   )
Agricultural businessman

Agricultural leaders project (1965, 261 pages, permission required to cite or quote) Cornell University NY

FOHL, THEODORE
Discussed in Columbia University interview with Albert B. Curtis

FOLDES, FRANCIS FERENC
Anesthesiologist
Wood Library—Museum of Anesthesiology IL

FOLEY, GEORGE
State Historical Society of Colorado

FOLEY, WILLIAM (1880–1964)
Food processor
(1964, 20 pages, open) Cornell University NY

FOLEY'S OF HOUSTON see Max Levine

FOLGER, JOHN CLIFFORD (1896–   )
Investment banker
Eisenhower administration project (1968, 43 pages, closed until 1977, also at Dwight D. Eisenhower Library KS) Columbia University NY

FOLK SONGS, INDIAN
Doris Duke American Indian Oral History Project Arizona State Museum

FOLK SONGS—U.S.
Alice Lloyd College KY
Cary Library ME
East Tennessee State University
King's College PA
State Historical Society of Colorado
University of Maine
West Virginia University

FOLKLORE, AFRICAN
Fisk University TN

FOLKLORE, INDIAN
Doris Duke American Indian Oral History Project Arizona State Museum

FOLKLORE—U.S.
Alaska Historical Library
Alice Lloyd College KY
Appalachian State University NC
East Tennessee State University
King's College PA
Madison College VA
Folk culture of the central Ozarks Memphis State University TN
Southern Highlands Literary Fund, Inc. GA
Mormon Church collection Southern Utah State College Library
South Texas oral history and folklore collection Texas A & I University

Western Kentucky folklore and folklife collection Western Kentucky University

FOLKS, HOMER (1867–1963)
Social worker
(1949, 98 pages, also microfiche, permission required to cite or quote) Columbia University NY

FOLLIARD, EDWARD THOMAS (1899–   )
Washington Post journalist
Eisenhower administration project (1967, 72 pages, permission required to cite or quote, also at Dwight D. Eisenhower Library KS) Columbia University NY

(34 pages, permission of interviewee required to cite, quote, or paraphrase) John F. Kennedy Library MA

FOLLIS, ED
Communications Workers of America collection University of Iowa Libraries

FOLSOM, MARION BAYARD (1893–   )
Executive; Government official
Eisenhower administration project (1968, 163 pages, permission required to cite or quote, also at Dwight D. Eisenhower Library KS) Columbia University NY

Social Security collection (1965, 207 pages, permission required to cite or quote, also at Social Security Administration MD) Columbia University NY

Discussed in Columbia University interview with Charles Irwin Schottland

FONDA, HENRY (1905–   )
Popular arts collection (62 pages, open) Columbia University NY

FONDILLER, WILLIAM (1885–   )
Engineer
(1970, 18 pages, permission) Columbia University NY

FONER, ERIC
Richard Hofstadter project (21 pages, permission required to cite or quote) Columbia University NY

FONTAINE, MRS. JULES
Historic preservation Charles B. Hosmer, Jr. Collection IL

FONTAINE, WILLIAM E.
Educator; Herrick professor of mechanical engineering, Purdue University
(1970, in preparation) Purdue University Archives IN

FONTANA, BERNARD L.
Ethnologist
Doris Duke American Indian Oral History Project Arizona State Museum

FOOD, FROZEN
Walla Walla College WA

FOOD AND DRUG REGULATION see
Drugs—Laws and Regulations

FOOD INDUSTRY AND TRADE
Food processing project Cornell University
NY
Participants: Morton Adams; John E. Bald-
win; Fred W. Bedford, Jr.; Mark E. Buck-
man; Laurence V. Burton; James G. Case;
Harry Chapman; Richard W. Comstock;
Martin H. Corcoran; Howard T. Cumming;
Otto W. Cuyler; Bernard Dawe; Walter D.
Enzie; Stuart K. Farrar; Glenn E. Finch;
Lon P. Flanigan; F. E. Flynn; William
Foley; Edgar J. Heber; John C. Hem-
ingway; George J. Hucker; Kenneth M. In-
gison; Warren D. Kennell; Harry T. King;
Gertrude Leckinger; Stanley Macklem;
George J. Olney; Max H. Olney; Nahum B.
Pratt; John Rees; James L. Rothwell; Caleb
C. Schutt; Karl W. Seiter; Garth A. Shoe-
maker; J. R. Shoemaker; Clarence W.
Smith; Harold Soper; R. Miller Stanton;
Edward C. Steele; John M. Stroup; Harden
F. Taylor; Frank Tormey; Donald Tressler;
Winfield D. Tyler; Gordon Van Eenwyk; M.
Martin Wahl; Norton A. Waterman; John
F. Welch; Roy E. Wheeler; Jerome Young

FOOTBALL
Athletic boom in West Texas (open) Texas
Tech University

FOOTE, EMERSON
Advertising executive
(1968, 2 reels, 20 pages) Broadcast Pioneers
Library DC

FORAND, AIME JOSEPH (1895–1972)
Social Security collection (77 pages, open, also
at Social Security Administration MD) Columbia University NY

FORBES, HOWARD JEFF
Pioneer broadcasting executive
(1965, 1 reel, 32 pages) Broadcast Pioneers Library DC

FORBES, JOHN F. (1876–1965)
Certified public accountant
(1959, 15 pages) University of California,
Berkeley

FORBUSH, ELLIE CLAYTON
Ricks College ID

FORBUSH, HAROLD S.
Ricks College ID

FORBUSH, JEANINE
Ricks College ID

FORCE, ALBERT W. (1897–1970)
(1970, 99 pages, open) Cornell University NY

FORD, GEORGE BARRY (1885–)
Priest; Student counselor
(1956, 126 pages, also microfiche, permission
required to cite or quote) Columbia University NY

FORD, GUY STANTON (1873–1962)
Historian
(1955, 963 pages, also microfiche, permission
required to cite or quote) Columbia University NY

FORD, HENRY
Ford Archives MI

FORD, JOHN
Discussed in Columbia University interviews
with Elmer Holmes Davis; Clarence Bud-
ington Kelland

FORD, JOHN ANSON
Government and politics collection (open)
University of California, Los Angeles

FORD, KATHERINE
Carnegie Corporation collection (61 pages,
permission required) Columbia University
NY

FORD, MARY (1907–)
Psychologist
(1964, 153 pages, permission required to cite
or quote) Cornell University NY

FORD, O'NEILL
Historic preservation Charles B. Hosmer, Jr.
Collection IL

FORD, WILBUR
Wabash industrialist
(1972) Wabash Carnegie Public Library IN

FORD MOTOR COMPANY
Ford Archives MI

FORDYCE, ALICE (1905–)
Foundation officer
(1964, 108 pages, permission required) Columbia University NY

FOREIGN AID PROGRAM see Economic
Assistance

FOREIGN RELATIONS see International
Relations

FOREMAN, CARL (1914–)
Popular arts collection (44 pages, open) Columbia University NY

FORESTS AND FORESTRY
Denver Public Library—Conservation Li-
brary CO
Forest History Society CA

FORMAN, CLARK
Discussed in Columbia University interview
with Virginia Foster Durr

FORMAN, HENRY JAMES
Biographical collection (open) University of
California, Los Angeles

FORNEY, ABRAM
Boyhood friend of Eisenhower in Abilene
(18 pages) Dwight D. Eisenhower Library KS

FORREST, J. T.
Lindneaux interview State Historical Society
of Colorado

FORRESTAL, EMMET P.
Vice admiral, U.S. Navy (Ret.); Biographer of
Spruance
(2 hours, 42 pages) United States Naval War
College RI

FORRESTAL, JAMES V.
Discussed in Columbia University interviews
with Joseph James Clark; Thomas Charles
Hart; James Lemuel Loway, Jr.; Kenneth
Claiborne Royall; Eugene Edward Wilson

FORT, HANK (MRS. WILLIAM
MCAULIFFE)
Pioneer songwriter; Performer
(1966, 1 reel, 40 pages) Broadcast Pioneers Library DC

FORT BLISS, TEXAS
Discussed in University of Texas, El Paso,
Chester Chope interview

FORT HARRISON, INDIANA
Vigo County Public Library IN

FORT HAYS KANSAS STATE COLLEGE
Fort Hays Kansas State College

FORT ROBINSON, NEBRASKA
Nebraska State Historical Society

FORTAS, ABE (1910–)
Federated Department Stores project (9
pages, permission required) Columbia University NY
James Lawrence Fly project (11 pages, closed
until January 1, 1982) Columbia University
NY

FOSDICK, HARRY EMERSON
Discussed in Columbia University interview
with Willard Earl Givens

FOSDICK, RAYMOND B. (1883–)
Former president, Rockefeller Foundation
Dulles oral history collection (1965, 18 pages,
open) Princeton University NJ

FOSHEE, JANE CAROL
University of Southern Mississippi

FOSHEIM, OSCAR
South Dakota experience (1970), South Dakota Oral History Project *University of South Dakota*

FOSSA, MANUEL
Argentina in the 1930s (Spanish, 39 pages, open) *Columbia University NY*

FOSSA, MATEO (1897–)
Labor leader

Argentina in the 1930s (1970, Spanish, 77 pages, open) *Columbia University NY*

FOSTER, EDWARD A. (1901–)
Farm organization official

Agricultural leaders project (1964, 233 pages, written permission required) *Cornell University NY*

FOSTER, GEORGE WILLIAM (1920–)
Professor

Joseph McCarthy project (1968, 260 pages, special permission required to cite or quote) *Cornell University NY*

FOSTER, HERBERT B. (1885–1968)
University of California engineer

(1960, 134 pages) *University of California, Berkeley*

FOSTER, J. FAGG (ca. 1922–)

Involvement in Rainey controversy (1967, 31 pages, open), Miscellaneous collection *North Texas State University Oral History Collection*

FOSTER, MICHAEL M.
Challenges to governance by students project: School of the Ozarks (1969, 22 pages, open) *Cornell University NY*

FOSTER, PAUL F. (1889–1972)
U.S. naval officer

Naval history collection (1966, 373 pages, permission required, also at *Division of Naval History DC*) *Columbia University NY*

FOSTER, WILLIAM C. (1897–)
Director, U.S. Arms Control and Disarmament Agency: Former Deputy Secretary of Defense

(40 pages, access in accordance with the regulations of the Arms Control and Disarmament Agency) *John F. Kennedy Library MA*

Dulles oral history collection (1966, 10 pages, permission required to cite or quote) *Princeton University NJ*

FOSTER, WILLIAM Z.
Discussed in Columbia University interview with John Brophy

FOULKE, WILLIAM B.
Resident of Patapsco Neck and site of the Battle of North Point (September 12, 1814)

(1970, 60 pages, 2 hours, open) *Maryland Historical Society*

FOULOIS, BENJAMIN D. (1879–1967)
Aviation collection (81 pages, permission required to cite or quote, also at the *United States Air Force Academy CO* and *University of the Air, Maxwell Air Force Base AL*) *Columbia University NY*

FOUNDATION FOR CHILD DEVELOPMENT *see* Association for the Aid of Crippled Children

FOUNTAIN, ARMAND
University of Southern Mississippi

FOUR SIXES RANCH
See 6666 Ranch

FOWLER, DONALD
World Bank (44 pages, permission required to cite or quote, also at *Brookings Institution DC*) *Columbia University NY*

FOWLER, WICK (1909–1972)
Journalist

(1968, 62 pages, open) *North Texas State University Oral History Collection*

FOWLER, WILLIAM A.
American Institute of Physics NY

FOWLES, EDWARD
Art dealer

(1959, 18 pages) *Archives of American Art—Smithsonian Institution NY*

FOX, CHRIS
Executive, State National Bank, El Paso

(1972, not transcribed open) *University of Texas, El Paso*

FOX, J. C.
(1 tape, open) *University of Texas, El Paso*

FOX, JOHN
James B. Duke project (68 pages, permission required, also at *Duke University NC*) *Columbia University NY*

FOX, JOSEPH A.
White House correspondent, *Washington Evening Star* (1943–1954) *Harry S. Truman Library MO*

FOX, WILLIAM T. R. (1912–)
Carnegie Corporation collection (97 pages, permission required) *Columbia University NY*

United Nations Conference, San Francisco, 1945 (1951, 77 pages, open) *Columbia University NY*

FOXFIRE MAGAZINE
Southern Highlands Literary Fund, Inc. GA

FRADER, JOEL
Columbia crisis of 1968 (48 pages, permission required) *Columbia University NY*

FRAENKEL, ALFRED
WORLD WAR II: THE HOLOCAUST—RESISTANCE AND RESCUE: (2) Rescue of Jews via Spain and Portugal (Hebrew, 31 pages, open) *Hebrew University, Israel*

FRALEIGH, WILLIAM
Political affairs counselor, U.S. embassies (Madrid, Rome)

(19 pages, open) *John F. Kennedy Library MA*

FRANCE
WORLD WAR II: THE HOLOCAUST—RESISTANCE AND RESCUE: (3) Jewish underground movement in wartime France *Hebrew University, Israel*

FRANCIS, CLARENCE (1888–)
Corporation executive

Eisenhower administration project (1967, 37 pages, permission required to cite or quote, also at *Dwight D. Eisenhower Library KS*) *Columbia University NY*

FRANCO, FRANCISCO
Discussed in Columbia University interview with John Davis Lodge

FRANK, ALFRED
Haifa lawyer

WORLD WAR II: THE HOLOCAUST—RESISTANCE AND RESCUE: (2) Rescue of Jews via Spain and Portugal (Hebrew, 14 pages, open) *Hebrew University, Israel*

FRANK, ED *see* John Badten

FRANK, EPHRAIM
ANTECEDENTS TO THE STATE OF ISRAEL: (2) "Brichah" (organized escape) (Hebrew, 39 pages, open) *Hebrew University, Israel*

FRANK, JEROME NEW (1889–1957)
Judge

(1952, 194 pages, permission required) *Columbia University NY*

Discussed in Columbia University interviews with Cully Alton Cobb; Gardner Jackson

FRANK, WALDO (1889–1967)
Hart Crane project (53 pages, permission required) *Columbia University NY*

FRANKE, WILLIAM BIRRELL (1894–)
Eisenhower administration project (50 pages, permission required to cite or quote, also at *Dwight D. Eisenhower Library KS*) *Columbia University NY*

FRANKEL, CHARLES (1917–)
Journalism lectures, Forum I (permission required to cite or quote) *Columbia University NY*

FRANKENTHALER, HELEN (1928–)
Painter

(1965, 10 pages; 1968, 33 pages) *Archives of American Art—Smithsonian Institution NY*

FRANKFURTER, ESTELLE (1895–) National Labor Relations Board (1970, 113 pages, open, reproduction restricted) *Cornell University NY*

FRANKFURTER, FELIX (1882–1965) U.S. Supreme Court justice (1955, 337 pages, also microfiche, permission required to cite or quote, also at John F. Kennedy Library MA) *Columbia University*

(75 pages, open) *John F. Kennedy Library MA*

Discussed in Columbia University interviews with Marquis William Childs; Edward Samuel Greenbaum; Learned Hand; Gardner Jackson; James McCauley Landis; David A. Morse

FRANKLIN, GEORGE S., JR. (1913–) Executive director, Council on Foreign Relations Dulles oral history collection (1965, 44 pages, permission required to cite or quote) *Princeton University NJ*

FRANKLIN, JAY (Pen name of John Franklin Carter) Journalist *Harry S. Truman Library MO*

FRANKLIN, (DR.) JOHN HOPE Author; Historian (1972) *Fisk University TN*

FRANKLIN, (DR.) WILLIAM (1971) *Fisk University TN*

FRANKLIN COUNTY, INDIANA *Franklin County Centennial Committee IN*

FRANKS, NANCY Communications Workers of America collection *University of Iowa Libraries*

FRANKS, SIR OLIVER SHEWELL (1905–) Former British ambassador to the United States Dulles oral history collection (1965, 18 pages, permission required to cite or quote) *Harry S. Truman Library MO*

FRANKS, ROBERT Discussed in Columbia University Carnegie Corporation collection

FRANTZ, ALISON Smith alumna, class of 1924; Archeologist; Writer (1973, 1 hour, 29 pages) *Smith College MA*

FRASCONI, ANTONIO (1919–) Printmaker (1971, 30 pages) *Archives of American Art—Smithsonian Institution NY*

FRASER, CLARA *University of Washington Libraries WA*

FRASER, HUGH British government official Discussed in Columbia University interviews with George Horace Gallup; Broadus Mitchell

FRASER, JOSEPH (1898–) Museum director (1970, 43 pages) *Archives of American Art—Smithsonian Institution NY*

FRASER, PETER M. Insurance executive Ives project (1969) *Yale University School of Music NY*

FRASER, PHYLLIS Discussed in Columbia University interview with Bennett Alfred Cerf

FRECCERO, YVONNE (1929–) (1966, 21 pages, open) *Cornell University NY*

FREDERICKSON, A. N. Weyerhaeuser Timber Company (71 pages, permission required) *Columbia University NY*

FREDERICKSON, HANSEN A. (Closed until interviewee's death; interviewee's permission required to use for research), University history collection *University of California, Los Angeles*

FREED, ARTHUR (1894–) Popular arts collection (16 pages, open) *Columbia University NY*

FREEBORN, MALCOLM (1907–) (1965, 173 pages, permission required to cite or quote) *Cornell University NY*

FREEBORN, SIDNEY M. (1885–) Observations concerning the development of the Coastal Bend area of South Texas, 1920–1970 (1972, 61 pages, open), Miscellaneous collection *North Texas State University Oral History Collection*

FREEDMAN, MAX Journalism lectures (29 pages, permission required to cite or quote) *Columbia University NY*

FREEHAFER, LYTLE J. Purdue University administrator (1970, 43 pages) *Purdue University Archives IN*

FREEHOF, SOLOMON B. Rabbi emeritus, Rodeph Shalom Congregation (Pittsburg); Honorary president, World Union for Progressive Judaism JEWISH COMMUNITIES: (5) Jewish nationalism and the Reform movement in the United States (English, 16 pages, open) *Hebrew University, Israel*

FREEMAN, DOUGLAS SOUTHALL Discussed in Columbia University interviews with George Horace Gallup; Broadus Mitchell

FREEMAN, EDWARD M. Discussed in Columbia University interview with J. George Harrar

FREEMAN, HARRY L. Discussed in Yale University School of Music CT Valdo Freeman interview

FREEMAN, HOWARD U.S. Army veteran *Fisk University TN*

FREEMAN, VALDO Son of Harry L. Freeman, composer American music project (1971) *Yale University School of Music CT*

FREEMAN, VERNE C. Educator; Associate dean of agriculture, Purdue University (1970, 108 pages) *Purdue University Archives IN*

FREERS, EDWARD L. (1911–) Foreign Service officer Dulles oral history collection (1966, 28 pages, permission required to cite or quote) *Princeton University NJ*

FREIDEL, FRANK (1916–) Richard Hofstadter project (22 pages, permission required to cite or quote) *Columbia University NY*

FREIDMAN, H. New York City blackout (1965) *Cornell University NY*

FREIER, SHALHEVET Deputy director, Weizmann Institute (Rehovot) ANTECEDENTS TO THE STATE OF ISRAEL: (3) "Ha 'apalah" (illegal immigration) (Hebrew, 53 pages, open; tape only, open) *Hebrew University, Israel*

FREIGHT AND FREIGHTAGE *University of California Institute of Industrial Relations*

FRELENG, FRITZ Animator and director, Warner Brothers cartoons An oral history of the motion picture in America (open) *University of California, Los Angeles*

FRENCH, ADELAIDE (1969) *State Historical Society of Colorado*

FRENCH, ENOCH PERCIVAL (1882–1970) with Newton B. Drury Timber evaluation expert (1963, 86 pages) *University of California, Berkeley*

FRENCH, ORVAL C.
Challenges to governance by students project (1969, 36 pages, permission required to cite or quote) *Cornell University NY*

FRERICKS, ANDREW G. (1890–   )
Technologist
California wine industry during the Depression *University of California, Berkeley*

FREUD, ANNA
Discussed in Columbia University interviews with Willi Hoffer, Joseph Sandler

FREUD, RALPH
University history collection (open) *University of California, Los Angeles*

FREUD, SIGMUND
Discussed in Columbia University interviews with Edward L. Bernays; Edward Glover; Willi Hoffer, Abram Kardiner; Theodor Reik; and in Psychoanalytic movement collection

FREUND, PAUL
Discussed in Columbia University interview with David A. Morse

FREY, JOHN PHILIP (1871–1957)
Union official
(1955, 762 pages, open) *Columbia University NY*

FRIDAY, DR. WILLIAM C.
University of North Carolina, Charlotte

FRIDMANN, NAPHTALI
Zim Company employee (Tel-Aviv)
ANTECEDENTS TO THE STATE OF ISRAEL: (2) "Brichah" (organized escape) (Hebrew, 13 pages, open) *Hebrew University, Israel*

FRIEDAN, BETTY
Smith alumna, class of 1942; Writer; Feminist; Teacher; Founder of NOW
(1973, 2 hours, 41 pages) *Smith College MA*

FRIEDLANDER, HAROLD
National Institutes of Health MD

FRIEDLICH, HERBERT AARON (1893–   )
Robert P. Patterson project (30 pages, closed until January 1, 1980) *Columbia University NY*

FRIEDMAN, HARRY J.
University of Washington Libraries WA

FRIEDMAN, JANE
Challenges to governance by students project (1969, 10 pages, permission required) *Cornell University NY*

FRIEDMAN, MARTIN L.
Special assistant in the White House (1950–1953)
Harry S. Truman Library MO

FRIEDMAN, SAMUEL
Socialist movement project (54 pages, permission required to cite or quote) *Columbia University NY*

FRIENDLY, FRED W. (1915–   )
James Lawrence Fly project (14 pages, closed until January 1, 1982) *Columbia University NY*
Radio Pioneers collection (50 pages, open) *Columbia University NY*
Discussed in Columbia University interview with Frank Stanton

FRIENDLY, HENRY JACOB (1903–   )
Aviation collection (24 pages, permission of interviewee required to cite or quote, also at *United States Air Force Academy CO* and *University of the Air, Maxwell Air Force Base AL*) *Columbia University NY*

FRIENDS, MR. *see* Fred Peetz

FRIENDS, SOCIETY OF
Guilford College Library NC
Haverford College PA

FRIENDS OF THE COLUMBIA LIBRARIES
Participants and pages: Robert Halsband, 19; Rockwell Kent, 20; Helmut Lehman-Haupt, 36; Ogden Nash, 20 (95 pages, permission required to cite or quote) *Columbia University NY*

FRILLMAN, PAUL W. (1912–1972)
Missionary
(1962, 416 pages, also microfiche, permission required to cite or quote) *Columbia University NY*

FRINK, W. H.
Discussed in Columbia University interview with Abram Kardiner

FRISBEE, DR. GERTRUDE
Careers of New England women in medicine *Arthur and Elizabeth Schlesinger Library MA*

FRISBY, HERBERT (1900–   )
Second Black to go to North Pole (1956); Chairman, Matthew A. Henson Memorial Projects; Retired teacher
(1971, 25 pages, 5 hours, open) *Maryland Historical Society*

FRISCH (NEE MOSES), RUBY
Secretary to James N. Rosenberg, American Jewish Joint Distribution Committee
WORLD WAR II: THE HOLOCAUST—RESISTANCE AND RESCUE: (1) The Joint (American Jewish Joint Distribution Committee) (English, 4 pages, written interview) *Hebrew University, Israel*

FRITCHEY, CLAYTON
Adlai E. Stevenson project (26 pages, permission required) *Columbia University NY*

FRITZ, EMANUEL (1886–   )
Professor of forestry
(1972, 336 pages) *University of California, Berkeley*

FRODING, OSKAR
Discussed in Columbia University interview with Hokan Bjornstrom Steffanson

FROELICHER, HANS, JR.
Headmaster, Park School
(1971–1972, 5 hours, restricted) *Maryland Historical Society*

FRONTIER AND PIONEER LIFE
Alaska Historical Library
Changing patterns on the lingering frontier (1880–1966) collection (100 hours, open) *Augustana College SD*
Carnegie-Bookmobile ND
Cassia County Historical Society and Museum ID
Nebraska State Historical Society
New Mexico State Library
Pend Oreille County Historical Society WA
State Historical Society of Colorado
Tanana-Yukon Historical Society AK
Man–land confrontation in the Southwest (110 hours, 2000 pages, open) *Texas Tech University*
Tulsa County Historical Society OK
South Dakota experience, South Dakota Oral History Project *University of South Dakota*
University of Wisconsin, La Crosse
University of Wisconsin, River Falls
Victor Valley College CA

FROST, ROBERT
Discussed in Columbia University interviews with Dorothy Baker; William Stanley Beaumont Braithwaite

FROZEN FOOD *see* Food, Frozen

FRUMKIN, ALLAN (1926–   )
Art dealer
(1970, 35 pages) *Archives of American Art—Smithsonian Institution NY*

FRY, GUY S.
John Robert Gregg project (46 pages, permission required) *Columbia University NY*

FRY, LUTHER
Discussed in Columbia University interview with Paul Felix Lazarsfeld

FRYE, HELENE
McGraw-Hill, Inc. (24 pages, permission required) *Columbia University NY*

FRYE, PETER
Theater and film director (Tel-Aviv)
JEWISH COMMUNITIES: (2) Jews in the Spanish Civil War (Hebrew, 30 pages, open) *Hebrew University, Israel*

FUCHS, HERBERT (1905-)
National Labor Relations Board (1969, 54 pages, permission required) *Cornell University, NY*

FUCHS, LAWRENCE
Associate of Eleanor Roosevelt; Dean of faculty, Brandeis University; Peace Corps director in the Philippines
(57 pages, open) *John F. Kennedy Library, MA*

FUENTES
Latin author
Discussed in University of Texas, El Paso, Chester Christian interview (one tape)

FUESS, CLAUDE MOORE (1885-1963)
Educator
(1962, 285 pages, also microfiche, permission required to cite or quote) *Columbia University, NY*

FUGUA, HATTIE
Widow of Charles Fugua, founding member of "The Inkspots"
Fisk University, TN

FUJITA, FRANK (1921-)
Artist; Army veteran; Former member of the Prisoner-of-war project (246 pages, permission of interviewee required, 1970, 132 pages, open) *North Texas State University Oral History Collection*

FUJIYAMA, AIICHIRO (1894-)
Former foreign minister of Japan
Dulles oral history collection (1964, Japanese and English, 30 pages, open) *Princeton University, NJ*

FUKS, JOSEPH
Government official (Tel-Aviv)
WORLD WAR II: THE HOLOCAUST—RESISTANCE AND RESCUE: (3) Jewish underground movement in wartime France (Hebrew, 17 pages, open) *Hebrew University, Israel*

FUKS, MIRIAM
ANTECEDENTS TO THE STATE OF ISRAEL: (2) "Brichah" (organized escape) (Hebrew, 17 pages, open) *Hebrew University, Israel*

FULBRIGHT, JAMES WILLIAM (1905-)
U.S. senator
(1957, 176 pages, closed until 5 years after interviewee's death) *Columbia University, NY*
Dulles oral history collection (1966, 27 pages, permission required) *Princeton University, NJ*

FULLER, HOWARD
Director, Malcolm X Liberation University
(1972) *Fisk University, TN*

FULLER, HOYT
Author; Editor
(1972) *Fisk University, TN*

FULLER, ROBERT
Retired BMI executive
Radio pioneers collection (1963, 13 pages, also at *Broadcast Pioneers Library, DC) Columbia University, NY*

FULLER, WAYNE
Professor of history
(1969, 13 pages, open) *University of Texas, El Paso*

FULLINGTON, WAYLAND
Field representative, BMI
Radio pioneers collection (1963, 24 pages, also at *Broadcast Pioneers Library, DC) Columbia University, NY*

FULMER, MR. AND MRS. CHARLES
Ricks College, ID

FULTON, JAMES G. (1903-)
U.S. congressman
Dulles oral history collection (1966, 14 pages, open) *Princeton University, NJ*

FULTZ, JAMES
(1973) *Wabash Carnegie Public Library, IN*

FULWEILER, MRS. HOWARD WELLS with Virgil Boyle
South Dakota experience (1968), South Dakota Oral History Project *University of South Dakota*

FUNK, HOWARD
Boyhood friend of Eisenhower in Abilene KS (12 pages) *Dwight D. Eisenhower Library, KS*

FUOSS, ROBERT (1912-)
Federated Department Stores project (58 pages, permission required) *Columbia University, NY*

FUREY, MOST REV. FRANCIS
Religion and culture project *Baylor University, TX*

FURST, OSCAR (-1968)
CULTURE AND EDUCATION: (4) Jewish schools in Transylvania (Hebrew, 18 pages, open) *Hebrew University, Israel*

G

GABBAY, JOSEPH
Jerusalem physician
WORLD WAR II: THE HOLOCAUST—RESISTANCE AND RESCUE: (2) Rescue of Jews via Spain and Portugal (Hebrew, 11 pages, open) *Hebrew University, Israel*
JEWISH COMMUNITIES: (10) Jewish Life in Iraq (Hebrew, 2 pages, open) *Hebrew University, Israel*

GABBAY, VIOLET with Rose Ani
JEWISH COMMUNITIES: (10) Jewish life in Iraq (Hebrew, 5 pages, open) *Hebrew University, Israel*

GABBAY, SHLOMO SALIH see Sima Gabbay

GABBAY, SIMA
Ramat-Gan teacher

GABL, JOSEPH

GABLE, CLARK
Actor
Hollywood Center for the Audio-Visual Arts, CA

GABLER, MILTON
Popular arts collection (69 pages, open) *Columbia University, NY*

GABRIEL, QUINTON C. (1913-)
UTU vice-president
United Transportation Union project (1971, 56 pages, open) *Cornell University, NY*

GABRIEL, VICTOR
West Virginia political figure
(35 pages, permission of interviewee required) *John F. Kennedy Library, MA*

GAGE, MATILDA
South Dakota experience (1970) South Dakota Oral History Project *University of South Dakota*

GAL (GLAZER, SHKLAR), ISRAEL
ANTECEDENTS TO THE STATE OF ISRAEL: (2) "Brichah" (organized escape) (Hebrew, 43 pages; Hebrew, 34 pages; open) *Hebrew University, Israel*

GALEZER, ELIAHU
Tel-Aviv optician

GALILI, ELAZAR
Brigadier-colonel (Res.) Galili; Formerly director "Maarachot" Publishing House
JEWISH COMMUNITIES: (4) Zionist movement in the U.S.S.R. (1917-1935) (Hebrew, 138 pages, open) *Hebrew University, Israel*

GALILI, MOSHE
HISTORY OF THE YISHUV (PALESTINIAN JEWRY): (8) Revisionist "Ha 'apalah" (illegal immigration) (Hebrew, 9 pages, open) *Hebrew University, Israel*
YOUTH MOVEMENTS: (2) Netzach in Latvia (Hebrew, 69 pages, open) *Hebrew University, Israel*
(1934-1939) (Hebrew, 116 pages, open) *Hebrew University, Israel*

GALLAGHER, BUELL

Discussed in Columbia University interview with Charles Henry Tuttle

GALLAGHER, CHARLES D. (1884–   )

Photographer

(1965, 160 pages, open) *University of Nevada, Reno*

GALLAGHER, EDWARD

Kennedy family friend

(31 pages, open) *John F. Kennedy Library MA*

GALLAGHER, JAMES

United Steelworkers of America labor leader

(1967, 16 pages) *Pennsylvania State University*

GALLAGHER, MARGUERITE

Legal secretary

Administrative procedures in Earl Warren's office (1938–1953) Earl Warren oral history project (1973, 28 pages) *University of California, Berkeley*

GALLAGHER, MARY (1883–1965)

Industrial Workers of the World sympathizer

(1955, 121 pages) *University of California, Berkeley*

GALLAHER, EDDIE

Pioneer announcer; WTOP (WA) personality

(1967, 1 reel, 13 pages) *Broadcast Pioneers Library DC*

GALLANT, PAUL J.

Former NBC master control engineer

(1965, 1 reel, 21 pages) *Broadcast Pioneers Library DC*

GALLO, ERNEST (1909–   )

Winemaker; E. & J. Gallo Winery

(152 pages, permission required) *University of California, Berkeley*

GALLUCIO, ANTHONY

Massachusetts political figure

(15 pages, permission of interviewee required) *John F. Kennedy Library MA*

GALLUP, GEORGE HORACE (1901–   )

Public opinion statistician

(1962, 158 pages, permission required to cite or quote) *Columbia University NY*

Book-of-the-Month Club collection (32 pages, open) *Columbia University NY*

GALMI, HAIM (GRUNHUT, ERWIN)

YOUTH MOVEMENTS: (1) Jewish youth movements in Czechoslovakia (Hebrew, 26 pages, open) *Hebrew University, Israel*

GALPIN, PERRIN COMSTOCK (1889–   )

Educator

(1956, 40 pages, also microfiche, permission required to cite or quote) *Columbia University NY*

GALVIN, HOYT

University of North Carolina, Charlotte

GAMBLING, JOHN B. SR.

Radio personality, WOR (then Bamberger's, Newark NJ, 1925)

(1969, 1 reel, 9 pages) *Broadcast Pioneers Library DC*

GAMBRELL, DR. HERBERT

Planned interview *Lakewood Branch Dallas Public Library TX*

GAMMONS, EARL

Former manager, WCCO (Minneapolis); Retired vice-president, CBS (Washington)

(1964, 5 reels, 63 pages) *Broadcast Pioneers Library DC*

GAMZON, ROBERT (–1961) AND MRS. GAMZON

Former leaders of E.I.F.

WORLD WAR II: THE HOLOCAUST—RESISTANCE AND RESCUE: (2) Rescue of Jews via Spain and Portugal (Hebrew, 14 pages, open) *Hebrew University, Israel*

GANDHI, MOHANDAS KARAMCHAND (MAHATMA) (1869–1948)

Centre of Asian Studies UK

Discussed in Columbia University interviews with Frank W. Rounds, Jr.; Sir Muhammed Zafrulla Khan

GANDY, EVELYN

University of Southern Mississippi

GANNETT, LEWIS

Discussed in Columbia University interview with Arthur B. Spingarn

GANS, HIRAM SELIG (1905–   )

New York political studies, New York election of 1949 (68 pages, permission required to cite or quote) *Columbia University NY*

GANT, CHARLES GREEN

Government and politics collection (open) *University of California, Los Angeles*

GARABEDIAN, CHARLES

Massachusetts political figure

(19 pages, open) *John F. Kennedy Library MA*

GARBO, GRETA

Discussed in Columbia University interview with Rouben Mamoulian

GARCIA, CARLOS P. (1896–   )

Former president of the Philippines

Dulles oral history collection (1964, 53 pages, open) *Princeton University NJ*

GARCIA, GILBERT (ca. 1920–   )

Businessman

(1969, 38 pages, open) *North Texas State University Oral History Collection*

GARDELLA, LOUIE A. (1908–   )

Agricultural extension agent; Real estate operator

(1973) *University of Nevada, Reno*

GARDENING see Horticulture

GARDI (GRODZINSKI), NATHAN

Director, Cultural department Ha-Poel Ha-Mizrachi Union, Moshavim

HISTORY OF THE YISHUV (PALESTINIAN JEWRY): (6) Ha-Poel Ha-Mizrachi movements in Palestine (Hebrew, 263 pages, open) *Hebrew University, Israel*

GARDINER, DR. CHARLES FOX

Magaretta M. Boas Colorado and western history collection *Pikes Peak Regional Library District CO*

GARDNER, GRACE BROWN

(1968, 36 pages, open) Historic preservation in Nantucket *Cornell University NY*

GARDNER, GRANDISON

Henry H. Arnold project (54 pages, permission required, also at *United States Air Force Academy CO) Columbia University NY*

GARDNER, JOHN WILLIAM (1912–   )

Foundation executive

Carnegie Corporation collection (1969, 221 pages, permission required) *Columbia University NY*

Discussed in Columbia University interviews with Florence Anderson; Cornelis Willem deKiewiet; Charles Dollard; Caryl Parker Haskins; Frederick Herbert Jackson; Earl James McGrath; Alan Pifer; Arthur Singer; Stephen Stackpole

GARDNER, ROY

with W. B. Lane

Benedum and the oil industry (44 pages, open) *Columbia University NY*

GAREL, GEORGES

Leader of O.S.E. during World War II

WORLD WAR II: THE HOLOCAUST—RESISTANCE AND RESCUE: (3) Jewish underground in wartime France (French, 26 pages, open) *Hebrew University, Israel*

15

GELBARD, HAIM

ANTECEDENTS TO THE STATE OF ISRAEL: (3) Ha 'apalah (illegal immigration) (Hebrew, 33 pages, open) *Hebrew University, Israel*

GELBER, BRUCE A.

Challenges to governance by students project (1969, 52 pages, open) *Cornell University NY*

GELBER, MICHAEL

Rabbi; Dean, Academy of Jewish Religion, (New York)

ANTECEDENTS TO THE STATE OF ISRAEL: (2) "Brichah" (organized escape) (English, 45 pages, open) *Hebrew University, Israel*

GELDERS, JOSEPH

Discussed in Columbia University interview with Virginia Foster Durr

GELDZAHLER, HENRY (1935–   )

Curator

(1970, 75 pages) *Archives of American Art—Smithsonian Institution NY*

GELLER, LUBA

Employee, Prime Minister's office (Jerusalem)

ANTECEDENTS TO THE STATE OF ISRAEL: (2) "Brichah" (organized escape) (Hebrew, 9 pages, open) *Hebrew University, Israel*

GELLER, SHMUEL

WORLD WAR II: THE HOLOCAUST—RESISTANCE AND RESCUE: (10) Belorussian Jewry (Yiddish, 39 pages, open) *Hebrew University, Israel*

GELLER, ZEEV

Kfar-Saba mayor

ANTECEDENTS TO THE STATE OF ISRAEL: (2) "Brichah" (organized escape) (Hebrew, 10 pages, open) *Hebrew University, Isarel*

GELLES, GERRY

Socialist movement project (50 pages, permission required to cite or quote) *Columbia University NY*

GELLHORN, EDNA (MRS. GEORGE)

(1959, 17 pages, open) *Columbia University NY*

GELLHORN, WALTER (1906–   )

Lawyer

(1955, 590 pages, closed until 5 years after interviewee's death) *Columbia University NY*

GELLING, HOWARD P. *see* John Badten

GENAUER, BEN

University of Washington Libraries WA

GENEALOGY

Alice Lloyd College KY

The Genealogical Society of the Church of Jesus Christ of Latter-Day Saints UT

GENERAL DYNAMICS *see* Frank W. Davis

GENERAL MOTORS CORPORATION

General Motors Corporation MI

GENIZARO INDIANS

Doris Duke American Indian Oral History Project *Arizona State Museum*

GENNS, WHITNEY T.

University of California, Santa Barbara

GENT, JIM

Keelan interview *Pennsylvania State University*

GENUNG, ALBERT B. (1890–1963)

Agricultural economist

Agricultural leaders project (1963, 59 pages, open) *Cornell University NY*

GENUNG, MRS. ALBERT B. (1891–1967)

George Junior Republic project (1965, 49 pages) *Cornell University NY*

GEOGRAPHY

(9 hours) *Plymouth State College NH*

GEORGE, HAROLD L., AND HAYWOOD HANSELL

U.S. Air Force Academy project (60 pages, consult center for restriction, also at *United States Air Force Academy CO) Columbia University NY*

GEORGE, WALTER F.

Discussed in University of California, Berkeley interview with Cully Alton Cobb

GEORGE, DR. ZELMA WATSON

Sociologist; Educator; Diplomat; Musician

Fisk University TN

GEORGE WASHINGTON UNIVERSITY

(15 hours, 40 pages, open) *George Washington University DC*

GEORGETOWN UNIVERSITY

Georgetown University DC

GEORGIA

Claudia White Harreld memoirs *Arthur and Elizabeth Schlesinger Library MA*

Southern Highlands Literary Fund, Inc. GA

GERARD, JAMES WATSON (1867–1951)

Lawyer; Diplomat

(1950, 96 pages, also microfiche, permission required to cite or quote) *Columbia University NY*

GERATY, EDWARD, JR. (1926–   ) AND DOROTHY (1929–   )

New York State NFO field representative

National Farmers Organization project (1968, 301 pages, permission required to cite or quote) *Cornell University NY*

GERDES, MRS. DICK (ca. 1910–   )

Housewife

(1969, 29 pages, open) *North Texas State University Oral History Collection*

GERING, JOHN JAY

South Dakota experience (1970), South Dakota Oral History Project *University of South Dakota*

GERING, LEON

South Dakota experience (1970), South Dakota Oral History Project *University of South Dakota*

GERMANS IN THE U.S.

German Americans (3 hours, open) *Sangamon State University IL*

GERMANY

German military opposition to Hitler *Harold C. Deutsch Collection DC*

ANTECEDENTS TO THE STATE OF ISRAEL: (2) "Brichah" (organized escape) *Hebrew University, Israel*

JEWISH COMMUNITIES: (1) German Jewry (1933–1935) *Hebrew University, Israel*

WORLD WAR II: THE HOLOCAUST—RESISTANCE AND RESCUE: (6) Rescue of Jewish children *Hebrew University, Israel*

GERONIMO

University of Utah

GERONTOLOGY *see* Aging and Aged

GERSHONI, A. A.

JEWISH COMMUNITIES: (4) Zionist movement in U.S.S.R. (1917–1935) (Hebrew, 15 pages, open) *Hebrew University, Israel*

GERSHWIN, GEORGE

Discussed in Columbia University interview with Max Weber and in Popular Arts collection

GERSTER, JOHN CARL ARPAD (1881–   )

Mount Sinai Hospital (21 pages, permission required, also at *Mount Sinai Medical Center NY) Columbia University NY*

GERSON (DeLEEUW), MIRIAM

WORLD WAR II: THE HOLOCAUST—RESISTANCE AND RESCUE: (6) Rescue of Jewish children (Dutch, 41 pages, open) *Hebrew University, Israel*

GESHURI, MEIR SHIMON

Director, Religious music department, Hechal-Shlomo (Jerusalem)

HISTORY OF THE YISHUV (PALESTINIAN JEWRY): (6) Ha-Poel Ha-Mizrachi movement in Palestine (Hebrew, 184 pages, open) *Hebrew University, Israel*

GETZ WOLD, KNUT

Chief, Marshall Plan division, Ministry of Commerce (1948–1958). Norway

Harry S. Truman Library MO

GEVIRTZ, YITZHAK

Mukhtar, Shefayim (1945); Director, Department for Regional Councils, Ministry of the Interior (Jerusalem)

GILLIGAN, JOHN J.
Cleveland State University Library OH

GILLIS, DON
Pioneer broadcast musician; Conductor; Teacher

(1966, 1 reel, 8 pages) *Broadcast Pioneers Library DC*

GILLUM, RICHARD P.
Vigo County Public Library IN

GILMAN, ELIZABETH
Discussed in Columbia University interview with Broadus Mitchell

GILMAN, MILDRED (MRS. ROBERT WOHLFORTH)

(1969, 82 pages, also microfiche, permission required to cite or quote) *Columbia University NY*

GILMOUR, JOHN SCOTT LENNOX
Hunt Institute for Botanical Documentation PA

GILOTZ, MANAHEM
Tel-Aviv founder

HISTORY OF THE YISHUV (PALESTINIAN JEWRY): (2) Jewish private sector in Palestine (Hebrew, 44 pages, open) *Hebrew University, Israel*

GILRUTH, ROBERT
Director, NASA Manned Spacecraft Center

(11 pages, open) *National Aeronautics and Space Administration DC*

GINAT, EYTAN
Tel-Aviv industrialist

WORLD WAR II: THE HOLOCAUST—RESISTANCE AND RESCUE: (3) Jewish underground movement in wartime France (Hebrew, 86 pages, open) *Hebrew University, Israel*

GINAT, EYTAN
with Eliahu Mitelman

WORLD WAR II: THE HOLOCAUST—RESISTANCE AND RESCUE: (3) Jewish underground movement in wartime France (Hebrew, 49 pages, open) *Hebrew University, Israel*

GINAT, YOHANAN

WORLD WAR II: THE HOLOCAUST—RESISTANCE AND RESCUE: (6) Rescue of Jewish children (Hebrew, 58 pages, open) *Hebrew University, Israel*

GINGELL, GEORGE
News director, WRBL, Columbus GA

(1963, 14 pages, also at *Columbia University NY) Broadcast Pioneers Library DC*

GINOCCHIO, RAFAEL
Argentina in the 1930s (Spanish, 67 pages, open) *Columbia University NY*

GINSBURG, NORTON
Geographer

(1971, 10 minutes) *Plymouth State College NH*

GINZBERG, LEON
Mount Sinai Hospital (31 pages, permission required, also at *Mount Sinai Medical Center NY) Columbia University NY*

GISEVIUS, HANS BERND
German military opposition to Hitler *Harold C. Deutsch Collection DC*

GISSEN, MAX
Journalist

(1963, 298 pages, closed during interviewee's lifetime) *Columbia University NY*

GIUSTI, ROBERTO F.
Editor; Legislator

Argentina in the 1930s (1971, Spanish, 59 pages, open) *Columbia University NY*

GIVENS, Willard Earl (1886–   )
Educator

(1968, 64 pages, permission required to cite or quote) *Columbia University NY*

GIVONI (BERGMANN), YEHUDA ARIE
Aycor Company employee

YOUTH MOVEMENTS: (1) Jewish youth movements in Czechoslovakia (Hebrew, 42 pages, open) *Hebrew University, Israel*

GLADIEUX, BERNARD LOUIS (1907–   )
Government official; Management consultant

(1951, 744 pages, permission required) *Columbia University NY*

GLASER, HERBERT (1907–   )
National Labor Relations Board (1969, 72 pages, open) *Cornell University NY*

GLASMANN, THEODORE A.

(1961) *State Historical Society of Colorado*

GLASS, ALTON E. (1893–1966)
Banker

(1965, 95 pages, open) *University of Nevada, Reno*

GLASSEN, MARY (MRS. WILLIAM H.)
James B. Duke project (33 pages, permission required, also at *Duke University NC) Columbia University NY*

GLASSFORD, PELHAM
Discussed in Columbia University interview with Frances Perkins

GLAVINOVICH, ROSE
Journalist

(1972, 8 pages) *University of California, Berkeley*

GLAZER, ISRAEL

YOUTH MOVEMENTS: (3) He-Halutz movement (Hebrew, 6 pages, open) *Hebrew University Israel*

GLENN, JOHN
Astronaut, Project Mercury

Cleveland State University Library OH

(32 pages, open) *John F. Kennedy Library MA*

GLIKIN, MOSHE
BIOGRAPHICAL INTERVIEWS (Hebrew, 22 pages, open) *Hebrew University, Israel*

GLOVER, EDWARD (–1972)
Psychoanalyst

Psychoanalytic movement collection (1965, 108 pages, permission required) *Columbia University NY*

GLOVER, L. F.
South Dakota experience (1971), South Dakota Oral History Project *University of South Dakota*

GLOVER, LILLIE MAY
Memphis Public Library and Information Center TN

GLOVER, VIRGINIA DOUGHERTY
Smith alumna, class of 1943; Singer

(1973, 1 hour, 35 pages) *Smith College MA*

GODBEY, ERMA D. (1905–   )
Nevada housewife

(1966, 129 pages, open) *University of Nevada, Reno*

GODBOLD, BRYGHTE D. (1914–   )
Retired Marine Corps brigadier general

Prisoner-of-war project (1972, 86 pages, open) *North Texas State University Oral History Collection*

GODDARD, ESTHER C. (MRS. ROBERT H.)
Aviation collection (85 pages, closed until 5 years after interviewee's death, also at *United States Air Force Academy CO and University of the Air, Maxwell Air Force Base AL) Columbia University NY*

GODDARD, GUY
South Dakota experience (1971), South Dakota Oral History Project *University of South Dakota*

GODFREY, ARTHUR
Thomas A. Dooley collection *University of Missouri, St. Louis*

GODOWSKY, LEOPOLD, II
Son of pianist Leopold Godowsky

American music project (1970) *Yale University School of Music CT*

GOLDSTEIN, ISRAEL

Former president, Zionist Organization of America and other American Jewish bodies

ANTECEDENTS TO THE STATE OF ISRAEL: (1) Jewish Agency (English, 13 pages; English, 3 pages; open) *Hebrew University, Israel*

GOLDSTEIN, JONAH J. (1886–1967)

Judge; A.J.D.C. member

(1966, 686 pages, open) *Columbia University NY*

GOLDSTEIN, SIDNEY

Author

Montgomery County—Norristown Public Library PA

GOLDWATER, BARRY MORRIS (1909–)

U.S. senator (Arizona)

Eisenhower administration project (1967, 85 pages, open, also at *Dwight D. Eisenhower Library KS*) *Columbia University NY*

(27 pages, permission of interviewee required) *John F. Kennedy Library MA*

Discussed in Columbia University interviews with Hugh Meade Alcorn, Jr.; Stephen Shadegg; F. Clifton White

GOLENPAUL, DAN (1900–)

Radio producer

(1964, 205 pages, permission required to cite or quote) *Columbia University NY*

GOLUB, LEON (1922–)

Painter

(1965, 10 pages; 1968, 105 pages) *Archives of American Art—Smithsonian Institution NY*

GOMBOS, GYULA

Hungarian history *University of Southern California Library*

GOMEZ, MODESTO

(1968, 3 pages, open) *University of Texas, El Paso*

GOMPERS, SAMUEL

Discussed in Columbia University interviews with John Brophy; John Philip Frey; Florence Calvert Thorne; Eva MacDonald Valesh; and in Socialist movement collection

GONZALEZ, ANGEL

Mexican American project *Baylor University TX*

GONZALEZ, LUIS (1916–)

Assistant chairman, General Committee, UTU

United Transportation Union project (1971, 32 pages, open, permission required to reproduce tape) *Cornell University NY*

GOOD, CLARENCE

Communications Workers of America collection *University of Iowa Libraries*

GOOD, GEORGE FRANKLIN, JR. (1901–)

Lieutenant general, U.S. Marine Corps (service: 1923–1968)

(141 pages, permission required, also at *Columbia University NY*) *United States Marine Corps DC*

GOOD, ROBERT M.

Challenges to governance by students project: School of the Ozarks (1969, 61 pages most open, tape open) *Cornell University NY*

GOODHARTZ, ABRAHAM S.

Dean emeritus, Brooklyn College

Brooklyn College NY

GOODLANDER, SHERMAN

(1971, 9 pages) *Wabash Carnegie Public Library IN*

GOODMAN, BENNY (1909–)

Popular arts collection (16 pages, open) *Columbia University NY*

GOODMAN, CLARA BROWNING (1886–)

Housewife

(1964, 52 pages, permission required to cite or quote) *Cornell University NY*

GOODMAN, HARRY

Pioneer Chicago broadcasting musician

Radio pioneers collection (1963, 8 pages, open, also at *Broadcast Pioneers Library DC*) *Columbia University NY*

GOODMAN, PAUL (1911–1972)

Challenges to governance by students project: Student activism (20 pages in 1968, 72 pages in 1969, most open) *Cornell University NY*

GOODPASTER, ANDREW JACKSON (1915–)

U.S. Army officer; Presidential staff assistant

Eisenhower administration project (1967, 137 pages, permission required to cite or quote, also at *Dwight D. Eisenhower Library KS*) *Columbia University NY*

Dulles oral history collection (1966, 44 pages, open) *Princeton University NJ*

GOODRICH, LAWRENCE KEITH (1906–1968)

McGraw-Hill, Inc. (22 pages, permission required) *Columbia University NY*

GOODRICH, LELAND MATTHEW (1899–)

Professor of international relations

(1967, 151 pages, open) *Columbia University NY*

United Nations Conference, San Francisco, 1945 (1951, 77 pages, open) *Columbia University NY*

GOODRICH, LLOYD (1897–)

Writer; Curator; Art historian

(1962, 1963, 511 pages) *Archives of American Art—Smithsonian Institution NY*

American cultural leaders collection (1967, 86 pages, closed pending publication of a study) *Columbia University NY*

GOODRICH, LUTHER CARRINGTON (1894–)

Sinologist

(1959, 159 pages, also microfiche, permission required to cite or quote) *Columbia University NY*

GOODWICH, DR. ANDREW

Musician

Fisk University TN

GOODWIN, KATHRYN

Social Security collection (80 pages, open, also at *Social Security Administration MD*) *Columbia University NY*

GOODWIN, ROBERT

Administrator, Bureau of Employment Security

(30 pages, permission of interviewee required) *John F. Kennedy Library MA*

GOODWIN, TERENZ

University of Washington Libraries WA

GOODWYN, LAWRENCE

Fisk University TN

GOOSHAY, STELLA

Nursing Archive *Boston University MA*

GORDER, JACOB E.

South Dakota experience (1970), South Dakota Oral History Project *University of South Dakota*

GORDEY, MICHEL (1913–)

Journalist

(1962, 106 pages, permission required) *Columbia University NY*

GORDON, D. K.

Communications Workers of America collection *University of Iowa Libraries*

GORDON, DOROTHY (1893–)

Radio pioneers collection (1951, 168 pages, open; 1965, 2 reels, 28 pages, also at *Broadcast Pioneers Library DC*) *Columbia University NY*

GORDON, DOUGLAS HUNTLEY

(1971, 38 pages) *Maryland Historical Society*

GORDON, HAIM

JEWISH COMMUNITIES: (3) Lithuanian Jewry between the two world wars (Yiddish, 32 pages, open) *Hebrew University, Israel*

GORDON, JOSEPH

Occupation of Japan (31 pages, permission required to cite or quote) *Columbia University NY*

GORDON, LINCOLN
U.S. ambassador to Brazil
(144 pages, portion closed) *John F. Kennedy Library MA*

GORDON, MYRA
Challenges to governance by students project (1969, 70 pages, permission required) *Cornell University NY*

GORDON, RICHARD (1882-1956)
Actor
(1951, 203 pages, open) *Columbia University NY*

GORDON, WALTER A.
Former chairman, Adult Authority; Past president, Alameda County NAACP; Close friend of Earl Warren
Earl Warren oral history project (in process) *University of California, Berkeley*

GORDON, YITZHAK AND RIVKA
Jewish Communities: (3) Lithuanian Jewry between the two world wars (Yiddish, 50 pages, open) *Hebrew University, Israel*

GORE, ALBERT
U.S. senator (Tennessee)
(13 pages, open) *John F. Kennedy Library MA*

GORE, DR. GEORGE W.
Journalist; Educator
(1972) *Fisk University TN*

GORMAN, CARL
(3 pages, permission required, also at Columbia University NY and U.S. Naval Institute MD) *United States Marine Corps DC*

GORMAN, CHARLES
University of Nevada executive
Harold S. Gorman interview *University of Nevada, Reno*

GORMAN, HAROLD S. (1903-   )
Banker
(1973, in process) *University of Nevada, Reno*

GORNEY, JAY
Popular arts collection (42 pages, open) *Columbia University NY*

GORODETZKY, RABBI
Antecedents to the State of Israel: (4) "Brichah" (organized escape) (English, 2 pages, written interview, open) *Hebrew University, Israel*

GOSHANSKI, NISSAN
Member, Kibbutz Yagur
Jewish Communities: (4) Zionist movement in U.S.S.R. (1917-1935) (Hebrew, 28 pages, open) *Hebrew University, Israel*

GOSSARD, MRS. RALPH
Victor Valley College CA

GOSSETT, ED (1902-   )
Attorney; Former U.S. congressman (Wichita Falls, 1938-1951); Judge
(1969, 46 pages, open) *North Texas State University Oral History Collection*

GOSSETT, LARRY
University of Washington Libraries WA

GOTTLIEB, ADOLPH (1903-   )
Painter
(1965, 10 pages; 1967, 27 pages) *Archives of American Art—Smithsonian Institution*

GOTTLIEB, CHAVA
Official, Israeli Foreign Ministry (Jerusalem)
World War II: The Holocaust—Resistance and Rescue: (2) Rescue of Jews via Spain and Portugal (Hebrew, 15 pages, open) *Hebrew University, Israel*

GOULD, PETER
Geographer
(1971, 10 minutes) *Plymouth State College NH*

GOULD, ARTHUR
Education collection (open) *University of California, Los Angeles*

GOVAN, ALFRED M.
South Dakota experience (1971), South Dakota Oral History Project *University of South Dakota*

GOVERNMENT *see* Political Science; and names of countries, cities, states with the subdivision Politics and Government, e.g. U.S.—Politics and Government

GRABHORN, EDWIN (1889-1968)
Fine printer
(1968, 90 pages) *University of California, Berkeley*

GRABHORN, JANE (1911-   )
Book publisher; Fine printer, Colt Press
(1966, 43 pages) *University of California, Berkeley*

GRABHORN, ROBERT (1900-   )
Fine printer
(1968, 129 pages) *University of California, Berkeley*

GRABSCHEID, JOSEPH
Youth Movements: (1) Jewish youth movements in Czechoslovakia (German, 25 pages, open) *Hebrew University, Israel*

GRACE, ALONZO
University of Connecticut

GRACE DE MONACO
Princess of Monaco
(10 pages, open) *John F. Kennedy Library MA*

GRADY, CHRISTOPHER V. (1921-   )
United Transportation Union project (1970, 19 pages, open transcript, permission required to use, cite, or quote tape) *Cornell University NY*

GRAEBEL, RICHARD
Adlai E. Stevenson project (39 pages, permission required) *Columbia University NY*

GRAFF, HENRY F. (1921-   )
Richard Hofstadter project (35 pages, permission required to cite or quote) *Columbia University NY*

GRAGG, WILLIAM L. (1915-   )
Perception of change in Ithaca school district project (1967, 238 pages, open) *Cornell University NY*

GRAHAM, EDWARD K.
Director, Office of institutional research
(1968, 47 pages, special permission required) *Cornell University NY*

GRAHAM, EVARTS
Discussed in Columbia University interview with Edward Delos Churchill

GRAHAM, FRANK PORTER (1886-1972)
University of North Carolina president (1930-   )
(1961, 38 pages, permission required to cite or quote) *Columbia University NY*
Social Security collection (24 pages, open, also at Social Security Administration MD) *Columbia University NY*
Discussed in Columbia University interviews with William Terry Couch; Jonathan Worth Daniels; Arthur Franklin Raper; Rupert B. Vance
University of North Carolina, Chapel Hill

GRAHAM, GERTRUDE
(1960) *State Historical Society of Colorado*

GRAHAM, HELEN TREDWAY, M.D. with Oliver H. Lowry, M.D.
Washington University School of Medicine MO

GRAHAM, SHEILAH
Popular arts collection (21 pages, open) *Columbia University NY*

GRAINGER, PERCY
Discussed in Yale University School of Music CT interviews with Burnet Cross; Mrs. Percy Grainger

GRAINGER, MRS. PERCY
American music project (1972) *Yale University School of Music CT*

GRAJCIAR, JOHN N.
United Steelworkers of America labor leader

GRILLO, JOHN (1917–)
Painter
(1964, 58 pages) *Archives of American Art—Smithsonian Institution NY*

GRIMES, LEOLA, AND EDITH CHAPMAN
University of Washington Libraries WA

GRIMLEY, OLIVER
Artist
Montgomery County—Norristown Public Library PA

GRIMM, PETER (1886–)
Real estate executive
(1972, 181 pages, permission required) *Columbia University NY*
Eisenhower administration project (32 pages, permission required to cite or quote, also at *Dwight D. Eisenhower Library KS) Columbia University NY*

GRIMSHAW, MARY ALICE
Anaheim Public Library CA

GRINGROSS, SHENIA
ANTECEDENTS TO THE STATE OF ISRAEL: (2) "Brichah" (organized escape) (Hebrew, 17 pages, open) *Hebrew University, Israel*

GRISCOM, CLEMENT
Discussed in Columbia University interview with Lloyd Carpenter Griscom

GRISCOM, LLOYD CARPENTER (1872–1959)
U.S. diplomat
(1951, 123 pages, also microfiche, permission required to cite or quote) *Columbia University NY*

GRISWOLD, NAT R.
Eisenhower administration project (84 pages, permission required to cite or quote, also at *Dwight D. Eisenhower Library KS) Columbia University NY*

GROAG, TRUDI
Kiryat-Tivon artist
WORLD WAR II: THE HOLOCAUST—RESISTANCE AND RESCUE: (8) Theresienstadt ghetto (German, 106 pages, open) *Hebrew University, Israel*

GROAG, WILLY
WORLD WAR II: THE HOLOCAUST—RESISTANCE AND RESCUE: (8) Theresienstadt ghetto (German, 121 pages, open) *Hebrew University, Israel*

GROAH, ROBERT W. (1925–)
Local chairman, UTU local 1597
United Transportation Union project (1972, 122 pages, special permission required) *Cornell University NY*

GROAT, WILLIAM B.
Judge

Industrial and labor relations project (1967, 58 pages, special permission required) *Cornell University NY*

GROCERY CLERKS UNION
University of California Institute of Industrial Relations

GROFF, ELLIS
U.S. deputy chief of budget (1929–1949); University of California budget officer (1949–1971)
Earl Warren oral history project (in process) *University of California, Berkeley*

GROGAN, THOMAS (1922–)
McGraw-Hill, Inc. (39 pages, permission required) *Columbia University NY*

GROMYKO, ANDREI
Discussed in Columbia University interview with Andrew Wellington Cordier

GROOMES, KATHERINE
University of Michigan

GROPPER, WILLIAM (1897–)
Painter
(1965, 20 pages) *Archives of American Art—Smithsonian Institution NY*

GROSS, BARUCH
Official, Herut cooperative (Jerusalem)
YOUTH MOVEMENTS: (1) Jewish youth movements in Czechoslovakia (Hebrew, 27 pages, open) *Hebrew University, Israel*

GROSS, CALVIN
Discussed in Columbia University interview with Frederick Charles McLaughlin

GROSS, CHAIM (1904–)
Sculptor
(1964, 15 pages) *Archives of American Art—Smithsonian Institution NY*

GROSS, ERNEST A. (1906–)
Lawyer; U.S. delegate to the United Nations
Dag Hammarskjold project (100 pages, permission required to cite or quote) *Columbia University NY*
Eisenhower administration project (1968, 984 pages, permission required to cite or quote, also at *Dwight D. Eisenhower Library KS) Columbia University NY*
National Labor Relations Board (1970, 95 pages, open) *Cornell University NY*
Dulles oral history collection (1964, 56 pages, permission required to cite or quote) *Princeton University NJ*

GROSS (NEE ROTH), MALKA
School nurse
YOUTH MOVEMENTS: (1) Jewish youth movements in Czechoslovakia (Hebrew, 61 pages, open) *Hebrew University, Israel*

GROSS, ROBERT ELLSWORTH (1897–1961)
Henry H. Arnold project (29 pages, permission required, also at *United States Air Force Academy CO) Columbia University NY*

GROSS, YITZHAK
HISTORY OF THE YISHUV (PALESTINIAN JEWRY): (4) Extreme Orthodox Jewry in Palestine (Hebrew, 17 pages, open) *Hebrew University, Israel*

GROSSMAN, AUBREY
A defense attorney in King, Ramsay, Conner case
Earl Warren oral history project (in process) *University of California, Berkeley*

GROSSMAN, IRVING
Challenges to governance by students project (1969, 21 pages, open) *Cornell University NY*

GROSSMAN, JAMES
Columbia crisis of 1968 (1968, 38 pages, permission required) *Columbia University NY*

GROSSMAN, TATYANA
Printer; Teacher
(1970, 25 pages) *Archives of American Art—Smithsonian Institution NY*

GROSVENOR, VERTA MAE
Author; Actress; Designer; Columnist
(1972) *Fisk University TN*

GROVER, SHERWOOD (1910–), AND KATHARINE GROVER (1911–)
Fine printers, Grabhorn Press and Grace Hoper Press
(1972, 94 pages) *University of California, Berkeley*

GROVES, GEORGE
Motion picture and television collection (open) *University of California, Los Angeles*

GROVES, HAROLD
Discussed in Columbia University interview with Paul and Elizabeth (Mrs. Paul) Raushenbush

GROVES, LESLIE A. (1896–1970)
Robert P. Patterson project (51 pages, closed until January 1, 1980) *Columbia University NY*
Discussed in Columbia University interview with Norman Ramsey

GRUBER, YITZSHAK
JEWISH COMMUNITIES: (2) Jews in the Spanish Civil War (Hebrew, 19 pages, open) *Hebrew University, Israel*

GRUENBAUM, YITZHAK
Former member, Jewish Agency Executive; Minister of interior, Israeli provisional government (1948–1949)

GUTIERREZ, JOSE ANGEL (1944–)

Chicano leader

Baylor University TX

(75 pages, open) *University of Texas, Arlington*

GUY, RAY W. (1913–)

Chairman, General Committee, UTU

United Transportation Union project (1971, 25 pages, permission required to cite or quote) *Cornell University NY*

GUY, RAYMOND FREDERICK (1899–)

(1965, 1 reel, 23 pages) *Broadcast Pioneers Library DC*

Radio pioneers collection (78 pages, open) *Columbia University NY*

GUYLAY, L. RICHARD (1913–)

Eisenhower administration project (1967, 90 pages, permission required to cite or quote, also at *Dwight D. Eisenhower Library KS*) *Columbia University NY*

Robert A. Taft project (136 pages, permission required) *Columbia University NY*

GWATHMEY, ROBERT (1903–)

Painter

(1968, 72 pages) *Archives of American Art—Smithsonian Institution NY*

GWIN, CLAUDE

Communications Workers of America collection *University of Iowa Libraries*

H

HAAKON COUNTY PEOPLE

Pioneer memories

South Dakota experience (1957), South Dakota Oral History Project *University of South Dakota*

HAAS, CAROLYN BUHAI

Smith alumna, class of 1947; Lecturer; Editor

(1973, 1 hour, 25 pages) *Smith College MA*

HAAS, ELISE

Jewish history (in process) *University of California, Berkeley*

HAAS, IRENE

University of Southern Mississippi

HAAS, PAUL R.

Investor

Oral business history project *University of Texas, Austin*

HAAS, PETER

Levi Strauss & Company collection (in process) *University of California, Berkeley*

HAAS, ROBERT K. (1890–)

Book-of-the-Month Club collection (31 pages, open) *Columbia University NY*

HAAS, VICTOR (1924–)

Health science collection (137 pages, permission required, also at *National Library of Medicine MD*) *Columbia University NY*

HAAS, WALTER, SR.

Levi Strauss & Company collection (in process) *University of California, Berkeley*

HAAS, WALTER, JR.

Levi Strauss & Company collection (in process) *University of California, Berkeley*

HAAS, WALTER, AND ELISE (MRS. WALTER) HAAS

Northern California Jewish Community series (permission required to quote, also at *University of California, Berkeley*) *Western Jewish History Center CA*

HABER, SAMUEL L.

American Jewish Joint Distribution Committee, director-general (Germany)

WORLD WAR II: THE HOLOCAUST—RESISTANCE AND RESCUE: (1) The Joint (American Jewish Joint Distribution Committee) (English, 44 pages, open) *Hebrew University, Israel*

HABER, WILLIAM (1899–)

Social Security collection (78 pages, closed during interviewee's lifetime, also at *Social Security Administration MD*) *Columbia University NY*

HABIAGUE, ESTEBAN

Argentina in the 1930s (Spanish, 1971, 147 pages, open) *Columbia University NY*

HACKETT, ALBERT (1900–)

Popular arts collection (37 pages, open) *Columbia University NY*

HACKETT, DAVID

Member, John F. Kennedy and Robert F. Kennedy presidential campaign staffs (interviewed as part of a special Robert F. Kennedy oral history program)

(115 pages, unedited transcript, permission of interviewee required to read, cite, quote, or paraphrase) *John F. Kennedy Library MA*

HACKETT, FRANCIS

Discussed in Columbia University interview with Ben W. Huebsch

HACKLER, RICHARD

Communications Workers of America collection *University of Iowa Libraries*

HADARI (POMERANZ), ZEEV

ANTECEDENTS TO THE STATE OF ISRAEL: (2) "Brichah" (organized escape) (Hebrew, 44 pages, open) *Hebrew University, Israel*

HADASH, MORDECHAI

ANTECEDENTS TO THE STATE OF ISRAEL: (2) "Brichah" (organized escape) (Hebrew, 33 pages, open) *Hebrew University, Israel*

HADDAD, EZRA

Former headmaster, Al Watania Boys' School; Member, Histadrut Executive (Tel-Aviv)

JEWISH COMMUNITIES: (10) Jewish life in Iraq (Hebrew, 17 pages, open) *Hebrew University, Israel*

HADLEY, MORRIS (1894–)

Carnegie Corporation collection (84 pages, permission required) *Columbia University NY*

Discussed in Columbia University interview with Frederick Osborn

HAEFFNER, JOSEPH ANTHONY (1907–)

Radio pioneers collection (30 pages, open) *Columbia University NY*

HAEKKERUP, PER

Journalist; Member of Danish Parliament (1950)

Harry S. Truman Library MO

HAFZADI, NAHUM (–1968)

JEWISH COMMUNITIES: (10) Jewish life in Iraq (Hebrew, 22 pages, open) *Hebrew University, Israel*

HAGAR, ELLA BARROWS

(In process) *University of California, Berkeley*

HAGEMEYER, JOHAN (1884-1962)

Photographer

(1956, 107 pages) *University of California, Berkeley*

HAGER, KOLIN

Radio pioneers collection (36 pages, open) *Columbia University NY*

HAGERTY, JAMES C. (1909–)

Journalist; Press secretary to the President (1953-1961)

Eisenhower administration project (1968, 569 pages, permission required, also at *Dwight D. Eisenhower Library KS*) *Columbia University NY*

Dulles oral history collection (1950, 50 pages, open) *Princeton University NJ*

HAGGERTY, CORNELIUS J.

Head of California Federation of Labor in period under study

Earl Warren oral history project (in process) *University of California, Berkeley*

HAGINS, JOHN W.

United Steelworkers of America labor leader

(1966, 6 pages) *Pennsylvania State University*

HAGUE, MRS. ARTHUR

Wife of Arthur Hague, Yale faculty colleague of Paul Hindemith

Hindemith project (1973) *Yale University School of Music CT*

HALL-PATCH, SIR EDMUND
Executive committee chairman, Organization of European Economic Cooperation, Great Britain

Harry S. Truman Library MO

HALLANAN, WALTER SIMMS (1890–1962)
Bendum and the oil industry (63 pages, open) *Columbia University NY*

HALLE, KAY
Author; Kennedy family friend

(25 pages, open) *John F. Kennedy Library MA*

HALLECK, CHARLES A. (1900–   )
U.S. congressman (Indiana)

Eisenhower administration project (1967, 35 pages, permission required to cite or quote, also at *Carnegie Endowment for International Peace NY* and *Geneva, Switzerland*) *Columbia University NY*

(39 pages, open) *John F. Kennedy Library MA*

Dulles oral history collection (1966, 26 pages, open) *Princeton University NJ*

HALLER, EDOUARD de
with Pablo de Azcarate y Florez and W. Van Asch Van Wijck

League of Nations (1965, French, 156 pages, permission of interviewees required to cite or quote, copies of memoirs also at *Carnegie Endowment for International Peace NY* and *Geneva, Switzerland*) *Columbia University NY*

HALLEY, RUDOLPH
Discussed in Columbia University New York political studies collection

HALLSTEIN, WALTER (1901–   )
Former Secretary of State, German foreign office

Dulles oral history collection (1964, 34 pages, permission required to cite or quote) *Princeton University NJ*

HALPER, NATHAN
Art dealer

(1963, 10 pages) *Archives of American Art—Smithsonian Institution NY*

HALPERIN, HAIM
Director, Agricultural Bank (Tel-Aviv)

JEWISH COMMUNITIES: (4) Zionist movement in U.S.S.R. (1917–1935) (Hebrew, 38 pages, open) *Hebrew University, Israel*

HALPERIN, LEA
JEWISH COMMUNITIES: (4) Zionist movement in U.S.S.R. (1917–1935) (Hebrew, 4 pages, open) *Hebrew University, Israel*

HALPERIN, PEARL
Union leader

Yivo Institute for Jewish Research, Inc. NY

HALSBAND, ROBERT
Friends of the Columbia Libraries (19 pages, permission required to cite or quote) *Columbia University NY*

HALSEY, WILLIAM
Discussed in Columbia University interview with Felix Budwell Stump; Robert Bostwick Carney; DeWitt Pack; Frank W. Rounds, Jr.

HALSTED, WILLIAM
Discussed in Columbia University interview with Abraham Flexner

HALVORSON, H. H.
Friend of Harry S. Truman

Harry S. Truman Library MO

HAMER, FANNIE LOU
Civil rights activist

(1972) *Fisk University TN*

University of Southern Mississippi

HAMIL, MARY CONVERSE (MRS. J. C.)
(1961) *State Historical Society of Colorado*

HAMILTON, ANDREW JACKSON
University history collection (open) *University of California, Los Angeles*

HAMILTON, BRUTUS (1900–   )
Track coach

(1967, 50 pages) *University of California, Berkeley*

HAMILTON, CARL (1914–   )
Agricultural journalist

(1953, 735 pages, closed until 5 years after interviewee's death) *Columbia University NY*

HAMILTON, GENE
Pioneer NBC announcer

(1966) *Broadcast Pioneers Library DC*

HAMILTON, LUCIUS C. (1919–   )
Chairman, UTU local 1515

United Transportation Union project (1971, 25 pages, permission required to cite or quote) *Cornell University NY*

HAMILTON, RAY V.
President and sole owner, Hamilton, Landis Associates

(1964, 1 reel, 13 pages) *Broadcast Pioneers Library DC*

HAMILTON, ROBERT W.
Texas judicial systems project *Baylor University TX*

HAMILTON, THOMAS F.
Discussed in Columbia University interview with Eugene Edward Wilson

HAMILTON, WILLIAM A.
Mill Valley Public Library CA

HAMLIN, HILDA EDWARDS
Smith alumna, class of 1912;

(1973, 1 hour, 22 pages) *Smith College MA*

HAMLIN, JAMES D.
Judge

Biographical collection (open) *Texas Tech University*

HAMLIN, OLIVER D.
Federal circuit court judge, retired

(1972, 16 pages) *University of California, Berkeley*

HAMMARSKJOLD, DAG
Dag Hammarskjold project. Participants and pages: Sven Ayman, 11; Andrew W. Cordier, 22; Ernest A. Gross, 100; C. V. Narasimhan, 48 (1962, 181 pages, permission required to cite or quote) *Columbia University NY*

Discussed in Columbia University interviews with Thanassos Aghnides; James William Barco; Andrew Wellington Cordier; Luther Harris Evans

HAMMEL, SHIMON
Wartime leader, E.I.F.

WORLD WAR II: THE HOLOCAUST—RESISTANCE AND RESCUE: (2) Rescue of Jews via Spain and Portugal (Hebrew, 7 pages, written interview, open) *Hebrew University, Israel*

HAMMERSTEIN, OSCAR, II (1895–1960)
Popular arts collection (34 pages, open) *Columbia University NY*

Discussed in Columbia University interview with Richard Rodgers

HAMMO, JOSEPH (–1965)
JEWISH COMMUNITIES: (10) Jewish life in Iraq (Hebrew, based on an Arabic conversation, 2 pages, open) *Hebrew University Israel*

HAMMOCK, CHARLES P.
Executive director, National Black Lay Catholic Caucus

(1971) *Fisk University TN*

HAMMOND, GEORGE
Federated Department Stores project (38 pages, permission required) *Columbia University NY*

HAMMOND, JAMES EDWARD (1895–   )
Certified public accountant

(1959, 23 pages) *University of California, Berkeley*

HAMMOND, JOHN, JR.
Producer, Columbia Records; Discoverer of jazz musicians

American music project (1972) *Yale University School of Music CT*

HARDMAN, GEORGE (1890–   )
Soil conservationist

(1967, 95 pages, open) *University of Nevada. Reno*

HARDMAN, J. B. S. (1882–1968)
Labor leader

(1962, 83 pages, open) *Columbia University NY*

HARDY, DR. HARRIET
Careers of New England women in medicine *Arthur and Elizabeth Schlesinger Library MA*

HARDY, ROYCE ALLER (1886–   )
Mining engineer

(1965, 41 pages, open) *University of Nevada, Reno*

HARE, DAVID (1917–   )
Sculptor

(1968, 77 pages) *Archives of American Art—Smithsonian Institution NY*

HARE, RAYMOND ARTHUR (1901–   )
Diplomat

Eisenhower administration project (114 pages, permission required, also at *Dwight D. Eisenhower Library KS*) *Columbia University NY*

Dulles oral history collection (1966, 34 pages, permission required to cite or quote) *Princeton University NJ*

HARE, RICHARD W. (1936–   )
Local chairman and secretary, UTU local 292

United Transportation Union project (1972, 91 pages, special permission required) *Cornell University NY*

HARKAVI, ZVI
Jerusalem rabbi

JEWISH COMMUNITIES: (4) Zionist movement in U.S.S.R. (1917–1935) (Hebrew, 17 pages, open) *Hebrew University, Israel*

HARKNESS, RICHARD (1907–   )
News commentator; Journalist

Dulles oral history collection (1966, 72 pages, permission required to cite or quote) *Princeton University NJ*

HARKNESS, WILLIAM E. (1873–   )
Radio pioneers collection (1951, 99 pages open) *Columbia University NY*

HARLAN, JOHN MARSHALL (1899–1972)
Adlai E. Stevenson project (23 pages, permission required) *Columbia University NY*

HARLLEE, JOHN
Kennedy associate; Chairman, Federal Marine Commission

(17 pages, open) *John F. Kennedy Library MA*

HARLOW, BRYCE NATHANIEL (1916–   )
U.S. government official

Eisenhower administration project (1967, 144 pages, closed during interviewee's lifetime, also at *Dwight D. Eisenhower Library KS*) *Columbia University NY*

Dulles oral history collection (1966, 33 pages, permission required to cite or quote) *Princeton University NJ*

HARLOW, MYRTLE
Richmond Public Library CA

HARMON, AVRAHAM
Cleveland State University Library OH

HAROLD, JOHN
Occupation of Japan (54 pages, permission required to cite or quote) *Columbia University NY*

HARPER, CLARENCE
Former county clerk, El Paso

(1968, 10 pages, open) *University of Texas. El Paso*

HARPER, FOWLER
Discussed in Columbia University interview with Jack Bernard Tate

HARPSICHORD
Alice Ehlers interview, Fine arts collection (open) *University of California, Los Angeles*

HARR, KARL GOTTLIEB, JR. (1922–   )
Lawyer; U.S. government official

Eisenhower administration project (1967, 41 pages, permission required, also at *Dwight D. Eisenhower Library KS*) *Columbia University NY*

Dulles oral history collection (1966, 54 pages, permission required to cite or quote) *Princeton University NJ*

HARRAR, J. GEORGE (1906–   )
Foundation executive

(In process, *also at Rockefeller Foundation Archives NY*) *Columbia University NY*

Discussed in Columbia University interview with Flora Macdonald Rhind

HARRELD, CLAUDIA WHITE
Recollections of her mother, a former slave, Claudia White Harreld memoirs *Arthur and Elizabeth Schlesinger Library MA*

HARRELL, BEN
General, U.S. Army

United States Army Military Research Collection PA

HARRIMAN, FLORENCE JAFFRAY (MRS. J. BORDEN) (1870–1967)
Politician; Diplomat

(1950, 40 pages, also microfiche, permission required to cite or quote) *Columbia University NY*

HARRIMAN, W. AVERELL (1891–   )
Former New York governor

Henry H. Arnold project (60 pages, permission required, also at *United States Air Force Academy CO*) *Columbia University NY*

International negotiations project (1969, 353 pages, permission required to cite or quote) *Columbia University NY*

Dulles oral history collection (1966, 36 pages, permission required to cite or quote) *Princeton University NJ*

Discussed in Columbia University interviews with Prescott Bush; Edward Costikyan; Justin N. Feldman; Arthur Joseph Goldberg

HARRINGTON, J. C.
Historic preservation *Charles B. Hosmer, Jr. Collection IL*

HARRINGTON, MICHAEL
U.S. government poverty policy (May 1971) (open) *Plattsburgh State University College NY*

HARRIS, SIR ARTHUR
Henry H. Arnold project (85 pages, permission required, also at *United States Air Force Academy CO*) *Columbia University NY*

HARRIS, BENNIE
Municipal judge, Chattanooga

(1972) *Fisk University TN*

HARRIS, CARROLL T.
Books and printing (in process) *University of California, Berkeley*

HARRIS, CHAUNCY
Geographer

(1971, 10 minutes) *Plymouth State College NH*

HARRIS, CULLEN N., JR.
Special projects *Baylor University TX*

HARRIS, EMORY (1910–   )
Chairman, UTU local 1670

United Transportation Union project (1971, 43 pages, open) *Cornell University NY*

HARRIS, ETHEL
Historic preservation *Charles B. Hosmer, Jr. Collection IL*

HARRIS, EVERETT WHITE (1903–   )
Professor of mechanical engineering

(1967, 95 pages, open) *University of Nevada. Reno*

HARRIS, HUGH P.
U.S. Army general; President of The Citadel

The Citadel Archives-Museum SC

HARRIS, IKE
Texas legislator (senator)

Legislative project *North Texas State University Oral History Project*

HARRIS, JENNIE
(1960) *State Historical Society of Colorado*

HARRIS, JOSEPH
Social Security collection (44 pages, open, also at *Social Security Administration MD*) *Columbia University NY*

HARRIS, JULIE (1925–)
Popular arts collection (31 pages, open) *Columbia University NY*

HARRIS, LUCIEN
Former Jewish Agency official (London)
ANTECEDENTS TO THE STATE OF ISRAEL: (1) Jewish Agency (English, 32 pages, open) *Hebrew University, Israel*

HARRIS, MAL
Fisk University TN

HARRIS, MARVIN
Columbia crisis of 1968 (50 pages, permission required) *Columbia University NY*
Columbia television lectures (74 pages, open) *Columbia University NY*

HARRIS, MYRON
Defense attorney
Earl Warren oral history project (in process) *University of California, Berkeley*

HARRIS, O. H. (1932–)
Attorney; Texas state senator (Dallas); Republican
Legislative project (1969, 39 pages; 1971, 53 pages; open) *North Texas State University Oral History Collection*

HARRIS, OREN
U.S. representative (Arkansas)
(66 pages, open) *John F. Kennedy Library MA*

HARRIS, SEYMOUR
Economic advisor to Senator John Kennedy; Senior consultant to the Secretary of the Treasury
(84 pages, open) *John F. Kennedy Library MA*

HARRISON, SIR GEOFFREY
International negotiations project (34 pages, permission required) *Columbia University NY*

HARRISON, GILBERT
Editor and publisher, *New Republic*
(18 pages, open) *John F. Kennedy Library MA*

HARRISON, GUY B.
Baylor project *Baylor University TX*

HARRISON, LOU
Composer
Ives project (1970) *Yale University School of Music CT*

HARSCH, JOSEPH C. (1905–)
Journalist
Dulles oral history collection (1966, 29 pages, permission required to cite or quote) *Princeton University NJ*

HARSH, ELMER L.
(1959) *State Historical Society of Colorado*

HART, FRED J.
with Ira D. Smith
Radio pioneers collection (82 pages, open) *Columbia University NY*

HART, HERSCHELL
Radio pioneers collection (21 pages, open) *Columbia University NY*

HART, JAMES D. (1911–)
Professor of English; Amateur printer
(1969, 86 pages) *University of California, Berkeley*

HART, JOHN FRASER
Geographer
(1972, 11 minutes) *Plymouth State College NH*

HART, JOHN NEELY (1902–1970)
Major general, U.S. Marine Corps (service; 1925–1955)
(192 pages, open, also at Columbia University NY and U.S. Naval Institute MD) *United States Marine Corps DC*

HART, LARRY
Discussed in Columbia University interviews with Henry Myers

HART, LORENZ
Discussed at Columbia University interview with Richard Rodgers

HART, PHILIP A.
Cleveland State University Library OH

HART, ROBERT F., JR.
Business associate and sailing companion of John Foster Dulles
Dulles oral history collection (1965, 92 pages, open) *Princeton University NJ*

HART, THOMAS CHARLES (1877–1971)
U.S. naval officer
Naval history collection (1962, 284 pages, permission required to cite or quote, also at *Division of Naval History DC*) *Columbia University NY*
Discussed in Columbia University interviews with James Fife; Paul F. Foster; John Leslie Hall, Jr.

HART, VAN B. (1894–)
Agricultural economist Agricultural leaders project (1964, 91 pages, permission required to cite or quote) *Cornell University NY*

HART, WALTER
West Virginia political figure
(22 pages, open) *John F. Kennedy Library MA*

HART, WELDON (1909–)
Public relations man; Executive director, Texas Good Roads Association
(1966, 1967, 150 pages, open) *North Texas State University Oral History Collection*

HART, WILLIAM
Steck-Warlick, Oral business history project (37 pages, open) *University of Texas, Austin*

HARTE, BRET
University of Utah

HARTE, HOUSTON (1893–1971)
Benedum and the oil industry (37 pages, open) *Columbia University NY*

HARTELL, JOHN A.
(1969, 66 pages open) *Cornell University NY*

HARTFORD, HUNTINGTON (1911–)
Collector
(1970, 14 pages) *Archives of American Art—Smithsonian Institution NY*

HARTIGAN, WILLIAM
Massachusetts political figure; White House staff member; Assistant postmaster general
(29 pages, open) *John F. Kennedy Library MA*

HARTING, HERBERT B. (1898–1967)
(1965, 74 pages, open) *Cornell University NY*

HARTMANN, HEINZ (1894–1970)
Psychoanalyst
Psychoanalytic movement collection (1963, 145 pages, open except for specified pages, open portion also at *New York Psychoanalytic Institute*) *Columbia University NY*
Discussed in Columbia University interview with Rudolph Maurice Loewenstein

HARTSHORNE, RICHARD
Geographer
(1972, 30 minutes) *Plymouth State College NH*

HARTZOG, GEORGE B. (1920–)
Director, National Park Service
(1973, 90 pages) *University of California, Berkeley*

HARTWICK COLLEGE
Hartwick College NY

HARTWICK SEMINARY
Hartwick College NY

HARUSSI, EMANUEL
Herzliyya poet
JEWISH COMMUNITIES: (4) Zionist movement in U.S.S.R. (1917–1935) (Hebrew, 35 pages, open) *Hebrew University, Israel*

HEATH, HORTON
Former RCA and NBC public relations staff member

(1966, 1 reel, 16 pages) *Broadcast Pioneers Library DC*

HEATON, LEONARD D. (1902–)
Commanding general, Walter Reed Army Medical Center

Dulles oral history collection (1966, 19 pages, open) *Princeton University NY*

HEBRAICA
Hebrew University, Israel

Yivo Institute for Jewish Research, NY

HECHT, BEN (1894–1964)
Popular arts collection (64 pages, open) *Columbia University NY*

HECKENDORF, PERCY C.
Santa Barbara district attorney; Judge

Earl Warren oral history project (in process) *University of California, Berkeley*

HECKER, GEORGE S.
Washington University School of Medicine MD

HECKLER, MARGARET
Peggy Lamson collection *Arthur and Elizabeth Schlesinger Library MA*

HECKSCHER, AUGUST (1913–)
Arts administrator

(1970, 30 pages) *Archives of American Art— Smithsonian Institution NY*

(1973, 29 pages) *University of California, Berkeley*

HEDGER, HAROLD EVERETT

Water resources collection (open) *University of California, Los Angeles*

HEDGES, WILLIAM SAXBY (1895–)
Radio executive

(1959, 90 pages; 1969, 1 reel, 12 pages) *Broadcast Pioneers Library DC*

Radio pioneers collection (1951, 123 pages, open; also at *Broadcast Pioneers Library DC*) *Columbia University NY*

HEDIAN, HELENE
Teacher of costume design and illustration, Maryland Institute of Art

(1971, 2 hours, open) *Maryland Historical Society*

HEDLUND, GLENN W. (1909–)
Agricultural economist

Agricultural leaders project (1964, 15 pages, open) *Cornell University NY*

HEDMAN, GOTFRED
South Dakota experience (1971), South Dakota Oral History Project *University of South Dakota*

HEDRICK, ULYSSES PRENTISS
Hunt Institute for Botanical Documentation PA

HEENEY, A. D. P. (1902–)
Former Canadian ambassador to the United States

Dulles oral history collection (1965, 48 pages, permission required to cite or quote, may not be copied in any form) *Princeton University NJ*

HEFFERNAN, JOHN A. (1871–1952)
Newspaperman

(1950, 87 pages, open) *Columbia University NY*

HEFNER, ROBERT A.
Oklahoma Christian College

HEGNA, HERBERT *see* Abe Ruckdaschel, Ralph Anderson, and Joe Cooper

HEHER, EDGAR J. (1898–)
Food processor

Agricultural leaders project (1964, 116 pages, permission required to cite or quote) *Cornell University NY*

HEIDE, PAUL (1909–)
ILWU business agent

(1970, 20 pages) *University of California, Berkeley*

HEILBRONER, ROBERT (1919–)
American historians collection (86 pages, permission required to cite or quote) *Columbia University NY*

HEIN, MARJORIE
Robert A. Taft project (27 pages, permission required) *Columbia University NY*

HEIN, MRS. PEARL
South Dakota experience (1971), South Dakota Oral History Project *University of South Dakota*

HEINEMANN, JOSEPH
Hebrew University lecturer

WORLD WAR II: THE HOLOCAUST—RESISTANCE AND RESCUE: (6) Rescue of Jewish children (Hebrew, 4 pages, open) *Hebrew University, Israel*

HEINICKE, ARTHUR J. (1892–1971)
Pomologist

(1964, 138 pages, in process) *Cornell University NY*

HEINRICH, CARL
South Dakota experience (1968), South Dakota Oral History Project *University of South Dakota*

HEINRICHS, BEVERLY R. (1908–)
Legal secretary

(1972, 26 pages) *University of California, Berkeley*

HEINSOHN, EDMUND
Religion and culture project *Baylor University TX*

HEISER, VICTOR
Discussed in Columbia University interview with John B. Grant

HEISKELL, MARIAN (MRS. ANDREW) (1918–)
Adlai E. Stevenson project (27 pages, permission required) *Columbia University NY*

HEISLER, EDWARD T. (1942–)
National secretary, UTU Right to Vote Committee

United Transportation Union project (1972, 169 pages, permission required) *Cornell University NY*

HEITMANN, FRANK R.
Former chief electrician, NBC (New York)

(1965, 1 reel, 18 pages) *Broadcast Pioneers Library DC*

HELBURN, NICHOLAS F.
Geographer

(1972, 10 minutes) *Plymouth State College NH*

HELD, ADOLPH
Labor leader

Socialist movement project (28 pages, permission required to cite or quote) *Columbia University NY*

Yivo Institute for Jewish Research, Inc. NY

HELDENFELS, JAMES R. (1914–)
Businessman

(1972, 32 pages, open) *North Texas State University Oral History Collection*

HELLER, JANE HARRIS
Smith alumna, class of 1953; Community service volunteer

(1973, 1 hour, 30 pages) *Smith College MA*

HELLER, JOHN RODERICK, JR. (1905–)
Health science collection (50 pages, permission required, also at *National Library of Medicine MD*) *Columbia University NY*

National Institutes of Health MD

HELLRIEGAL, META
South Dakota experience (1971), South Dakota Oral History Project *University of South Dakota*

HED, SHLOMO
WORLD WAR II: THE HOLOCAUST—RESISTANCE AND RESCUE: (5) Hiding children in Belgium (Hebrew, 37 pages, open) *Hebrew University, Israel*

HEDERMAN, ALBERT (1920–)
Assistant district attorney, Alameda County

(79 pages, open) *John F. Kennedy Library MA*

(36 pages, open) *John F. Kennedy Library MA*

HILTON, JOE, AND PAULINE PEARSON
South Dakota experience (1953), South Dakota Oral History Project *University of South Dakota*

HIMMELSBACH, CLIFTON
National Institutes of Health MD

HINDE, EDGAR G.
Independence postmaster; Friend of Truman
Harry S. Truman Library MO

HINDEMITH, PAUL (1895-1963)
German composer
Hindemith project *Yale University School of Music CT*
Discussed in *Yale University School of Music CT* Ellsworth Grumman interview (1972-1973, American music project)

HINDS, JULIAN
Water resources collection (open) *University of California, Los Angeles*

HINES, JOHN FRANCES
South Dakota experience (1970), South Dakota Oral History Project *University of South Dakota*

HINGLE, PAT (1924-)
Popular arts collection (74 pages, open) *Columbia University NY*

HINGSON, ROBERT ANDREW, M.D.
Anesthesiologist
Wood Library—Museum of Anesthesiology IL

HINSDALE, MILDRED
University of Michigan

HINSHAW, LILLIAS DULLES (MRS. ROBERT HINSHAW)
John Foster Dulles' daughter
Dulles oral history collection (1966, 70 pages, open) *Princeton University NJ*

HIPP, SHIFTY LOGAN
Edward Hull Crump and his regime *Memphis Public Library and Information Center TN*

HIPSKIND, MILDRED
Teacher
(1972) *Wabash Carnegie Public Library IN*

HIRSCH, ELIZABETH
Active member, O.S.E., during World War II: Director, Foyer Israelite de Neuilly (France)
WORLD WAR II: THE HOLOCAUST—RESISTANCE AND RESCUE: (2) Rescue of Jews via Spain and Portugal (French, 21 pages, open) *Hebrew University, Israel*

HIRSCH, MAYER
Rabbi

Discussed in Western Jewish History Center CA Mrs. Joseph Kay interview

HIRSCH, SAM
Discussed in Western Jewish History Center CA Mrs. Joseph Kay interview

HIRSCH FAMILY, SAN FRANCISCO
Discussed in Western Jewish History Center CA Mrs. Joseph Kay interview

HIRSCHBERG, NELL
Smith alumna, class of 1928; Biologist
(1973, 1 hour, 38 pages) *Smith College MA*

HIRSCHHORN, KURT
Mount Sinai Hospital Investitures (24 pages, permission required, also at *Mount Sinai Medical Center NY*) *Columbia University NY*

HIRSHFELD, BARBARA, AND F. DANA PAYNE
Challenges to governance by students project (1970, 59 pages, permission required to cite or quote) *Cornell University NY*

HISPANO—AMERICAN WAR, 1898 *see* U.S.—History—War of 1898

HISS, ALGER (1904-)
Lawyer
Carnegie Corporation collection (1968, 67 pages, permission required) *Columbia University NY*
Discussed in Columbia University interviews with Jerome New Frank; Gardner Jackson; Devereux Colt Josephs; Frederick Osborn; Henry Merritt Wriston

HISTORIANS, AMERICAN
American historians collection. Participants and pages: Bernard Bailyn, 83; Ray Allen Billington, 103; Stuart Bruchey, 92; Henry Steele Commager, 81; Robert D. Cross, 122; George Dangerfield, 82; Sigmund Diamond, 109; David Donald, 88; Clement Eaton, 89; Stanley Elkins, 87; Robert Ferrell, 111; Jack P. Greene, 161; Robert Heilbroner, 86; Richard Hofstadter, 58; Alfred Kazin, 82; Edward C. Kirkland, 67; Richard W. Leopold, 87; William E. Leuchtenburg, 99; Arthur S. Link, 96; Ernest R. May, 104; Richard B. Morris, 133; Robert K. Murray, 114; Roy F. Nichols, 81; Russell B. Nye, 101; David M. Potter, 82; Arthur M. Schlesinger, Jr., 73; T. Harry Williams, 103; C. Vann Woodward, 86 (1968, 2660 pages, permission required to cite or quote, interviews conducted and contributed by John A. Garraty) *Columbia University NY*

HISTORIC HOUSES
(1961, 100 hours, 2600 pages, permission required) *Charles B. Hosmer, Jr. Collection IL*

Colonial Williamsburg Foundation VA

Historic sites (Springfield, Illinois) (4 hours, 40 pages, open) *Sangamon State University IL*

HISTORY, ORAL *see* Oral History

HITCHINGS, RAYMOND (1892-)
(1965, 236 pages, permission required to cite or quote) *Cornell University NY*

HITLER, ADOLPH
German military opposition to Hitler *Harold C. Deutsch Collection DC*
Hungarian history *University of Southern California Library*
Discussed in Columbia University interviews with Lawrence Dennis; Luis F. Gay; Hans V. Kaltenborn

HO CHI MINH
Thomas A. Dooley collection *University of Missouri, St. Louis*

HO, FRANKLIN L.
Chinese oral history collection (450 pages, open, description of memoir available on request) *Columbia University NY*
Discussed by other participants in Columbia University Chinese oral history collection

HOBBS, NICHOLAS
Member, President's panel on mental retardation; Director of selection and research, Peace Corps
(32 pages, open) *John F. Kennedy Library MA*

HOBBY, OVETA CULP
Discussed in Columbia University interviews with Roswell Burchard Perkins; Leonard Andrew Scheele; Charles Irwin Schottland

HOBLER, ATHERTON
President, Benton and Bowles
(1968, 2 reels, 16 pages) *Broadcast Pioneers Library DC*

HOCHWALT, FREDERICK GEORGE (1909-1966)
Priest
(1962, 47 pages, open) *Columbia University NY*

HOCTOR, ALICE
Carnegie Corporation collection (48 pages, permission required) *Columbia University NY*

HODGE, FREDERICK WEBB (1864-1956)
Ethnologist
(1957, 264 pages) *University of California, Berkeley*

HODGE, WILLIAM
Discussed in Columbia University interview with Richard Gordon

HOLGATE, JEANNE
Hunt Institute for Botanical Documentation PA

HOLLAND, KENNETH (1907–)
Carnegie Corporation collection (35 pages, permission required) *Columbia University NY*

HOLLAND, LAWRENCE LaMOTTE (1895–)
Radio pioneers collection (25 pages, open) *Columbia University NY*

HOLLAND, MILDRED
Discussed in Columbia University interview with Richard Gordon

HOLLAND, VERNON
Professional football player
(1973) *Fisk University TN*

HOLLANDER, IRWIN (1927–)
Printer
(1970, 16 pages) *Archives of American Art—Smithsonian Institution NY*

HOLLANDER, JACOB
Discussed in Columbia University interview with Broadus Mitchell

HOLLANDER, LOUIS
Journalism lectures, Basic issues in the news: The labor movement (58 pages, permission required) *Columbia University NY*

HOLLANDER, SIDNEY
Shirley Camper Soman Collection NY

HOLLEMAN, CLARENCE H. (1890–)
China missionaries collection (95 pages, open, also at *Columbia University NY*) *Claremont Graduate School CA*

HOLLIS, MARK D. (1908–)
Health science collection (58 pages, permission required, also at *National Library of Medicine MD*) *Columbia University NY*

HOLLISTER, JOHN BAKER (1890–)
Executive director, Hoover Commission (1953); Director, International Cooperation Administration (1955–1957)
Eisenhower administration project (52 pages, open, also at *Dwight D. Eisenhower Library KS*) *Columbia University NY*
Robert A. Taft project (58 pages, permission required) *Columbia University NY*
Dulles oral history collection (1964, 71 pages, permission required to cite or quote) *Princeton University NJ*

HOLLISTER, SOLOMON C.
(91 pages) *Cornell University NY*

HOLLOWAY, JAMES LEMUEL, JR. (1898–)
U.S. naval officer

Naval history collection (1962, 187 pages, permission required, also at *Division of Naval History DC*) *Columbia University NY*

HOLLOWAY, MARTHA ALDRICH
Smith alumna, class of 1919; Community and college service volunteer
(1973, 2 hours, 39 pages) *Smith College MA*

HOLLYWOOD MOTION PICTURE AND TELEVISION MUSEUM
Edmund DePatie interview *University of California, Los Angeles*

HOLLYWOOD TEN
Samuel Guy Endore interview, Biographical collection *University of California, Los Angeles*
Robert Walker Kenny interview, Government and politics collection *University of California, Los Angeles*

HOLM, CELESTE (1919–)
Popular arts collection (96 pages, open) *Columbia University NY*

HOLMAN, CHARLES WILLIAM (1886–1971)
Agriculturist
(1953, 69 pages, also microfiche, permission required to cite or quote) *Columbia University NY*

HOLMAN, EZEKIEL L.
Ricks College ID

HOLMAN, STELLA MAY JACOBS
Ricks College ID

HOLMBERG, RUTH SULZBERGER
Smith alumna, class of 1943; Publisher, *Chattanooga Times*
(1973, 1 hour, 20 pages) *Smith College MA*

HOLMES, FRANK, III
U.S. Marine Corps Vietnam War veteran
(1972) *Fisk University TN*

HOLMES, JULIUS C. (1899–)
Diplomat
Dulles oral history collection (1965, 27 pages, open) *Princeton University NJ*

HOLMES, LULU
Dean of Women, Washington State University
Higher education for women in Japan (1946–1948) (1968, 54 pages, also at *Columbia University NY*) *University of California, Berkeley*

HOLMES, OLIVER W.
Discussed in Columbia University interviews with James McCauley Landis; John Lord O'Brian

HOLMES, ZEDEKIAH E.
Jazz musician
(1971) *Fisk University TN*

HOLSTROM, JOHN (1909–)
Berkeley police chief (1944–1960); Colleague of August Vollmer
(1972, 44 pages) *University of California, Berkeley*

HOLT, MABEL BROWN (MRS. MARMADUKE)
(1962) *State Historical Society of Colorado*

HOLTON, KARL (1897–)
Public administrator
(1972, 105 pages) *University of California, Berkeley*

HOLTTUM, RICHARD EPIC
Hunt Institute for Botanical Documentation PA

HOLTY, CARL (1900–1973)
Painter
(1964, 24 pages; 1964, 37 pages; 1965, 10 pages; 1968, 79 pages) *Archives of American Art—Smithsonian Institution NY*

HOLTZMAN, HARRY (1912–)
Painter
(1965, 24 pages) *Archives of American Art—Smithsonian Institution NY*

HOME ECONOMICS
New York State College of Human Ecology project *Cornell University NY*

HOMESTEAD GRAYS
Black St. Louis leaders collection *University of Missouri, St. Louis*

HONEY, JOHN C.
Carnegie Corporation collection (82 pages, permission required) *Columbia University NY*

HONEYWELL, EUGENIA (MRS. MARK C.)
(1973) *Wabash Carnegie Public Library IN*

HONEYWELL, MARK C.
Inventor; Founder, Honeywell, Inc.
Mark C. Honeywell collection (35 hours, permission required, also at *Columbia University NY*) *Wabash Carnegie Public Library IN*

HONEYWELL, INC.
Mark C. Honeywell collection (35 hours, permission required, also at *Columbia University NY*) *Wabash Carnegie Public Library IN*

HOOK, SIDNEY (1902–)
Philosophy professor, New York University
(1969, 77 pages, permission required) *Cornell University NY*

HOOKER, JOHN, SR.
Edward Hull Crump and his regime *Memphis Public Library and Information Center TN*

HOUSE, PATRICIA
Eisenhower administration project (46 pages, permission required to cite or quote, also at *Dwight D. Eisenhower Library KS*) *Columbia University NY*

HOUSEMAN, CLAIR *see John Badten*

HOUSTON, LYDA SUYDAM (1891–)
China missionaries collection (79 pages, open, also at *Columbia University NY*) *Claremont Graduate School CA*

HOUVOURAS, ANDREW
West Virginia political figure
(25 pages, open) *John F. Kennedy Library MA*

HOVING, WALTER
Discussed in Columbia University interview with William Lusk

HOWARD, ASBURY
United Steelworkers of America labor leader
(1968, 27 pages) *Pennsylvania State University*

HOWARD, BEN ODELL (1904–)
Aviation collection (67 pages, permission required to cite or quote, also at *United States Air Force Academy CO and University of the Air, Maxwell Air Force Base AL*) *Columbia University NY*

HOWARD, ERNEST (1910–)
American Medical Association official
(1967, 302 pages, permission required) *Columbia University NY*

HOWARD, KATHERINE GRAHAM (MRS. CHARLES P.) (1898–)
Eisenhower administration project
(1971, 600 pages, permission required, also at *Dwight D. Eisenhower Library KS*) *Columbia University NY*

HOWARD, ROBERT B.
Commissioner, Buffalo Fire Department
(1972) *Fisk University TN*

HOWE, HAROLD, II
Discussed in Columbia University interview with Benjamin W. Chidlaw

HOWE, JAMES E. (1907–), AND J. L. EVANS
United Transportation Union project (1971, 93 pages, permission required to cite or quote) *Cornell University NY*

HOWE, JAMES L.
Owner, WIRA (Fort Pierce FL)
(1965, 1 reel, 19 pages) *Broadcast Pioneers Library DC*

HOWE, JAMES WONG
Cinematographer
An oral history of the motion picture in America (open) *University of California, Los Angeles*

HOWE, LOUIS
James A. Farley collection *Scott E. Webber Collection NY*
Discussed in Columbia University interview with Marion Dickerman

HOWE, OSCAR
South Dakota experience (1954), South Dakota Oral History Project *University of South Dakota*

HOWE, QUINCY (1900–)
Journalist
(1962, 127 pages, also microfiche, permission required to cite or quote) *Columbia University NY*

HOWE, MRS. W. D.
(2 tapes, not transcribed, open) *University of Texas, El Paso*

HOWELL, REX
State Historical Society of Colorado

HOWELL, WARREN (1912–)
Bookman; Publisher
(1967, 73 pages) *University of California. Berkeley*

HOWELL, WILLIAM F.
World Bank (37 pages, open, also at *Brookings Institution DC*) *Columbia University NY*

HOWIE, JOHN
South Dakota experience (1971), South Dakota Oral History Project *University of South Dakota*

HOWSON, ALBERT SIDNEY (1881–1960)
Popular arts collection (42 pages, open) *Columbia University NY*

HOWZE, HAMILTON H.
U.S. Army general
United States Army Military Research Collection PA

HOY, ALVA
South Dakota experience (1971), South Dakota Oral History Project *University of South Dakota*

HOYNINGEN-HUENE, GEORGE
Biographical collection (open) *University of California, Los Angeles*

HOYTE, LESLIE
Musician; Steel drum maker
(1972) *Fisk University TN*

HU, C. T.
International negotiations project (18 pages, permission required) *Columbia University NY*

HU, SHIH
Chinese oral history collection (295 pages, open, description of memoir available on request) *Columbia University NY*

HUANG, FU
Chinese oral history collection (489 pages, open, description of memoir available on request) *Columbia University NY*

HUBBARD, NOAH
Northern Indiana Historical Society

HUBBARD, STANELY
Communications Workers of America collection *University of Iowa Libraries*

HUBBARD, THOMAS B.
South Dakota experience (1971), South Dakota Oral History Project *University of South Dakota*

HUBBELL TRADING POST
University of Utah

HUBELL, WILLIAM F.
University of Southern Mississippi

HUBER, REV. OSCAR
Priest (Dallas, TX)
(10 pages, open) *John F. Kennedy Library MA*

HUCKABY, ELIZABETH
Eisenhower administration project (62 pages, permission required to cite or quote, also at *Dwight D. Eisenhower Library KS*) *Columbia University NY*

HUCKER, GEORGE J. (1893–)
Bacteriologist
Food processing project (1964, 313 pages, open) *Cornell University NY*

HUDGENS, ROBERT WATTS (1896–)
U.S. government official
(1954, 290 pages, also microfiche, permission required to cite or quote) *Columbia University NY*

HUDSON, DONALD
Geographer
(1971, 10 minutes) *Plymouth State College NH*

HUEBSCH, BEN W. (1876–1964)
(1955, 492 pages, also microfiche, permission required to cite or quote) *Columbia University NY*

HUEMER, RICHARD
Animator; Director
An oral history of the motion picture in America (closed until May 7, 1976 or interviewee's death, whichever is earlier) *University of California, Los Angeles*

HUFF, EDGAR RICHARD (1919–)
Sergeant major, U.S. Marine Corps (service: 1942–1972)
(193 pages, permission required) *United States Marine Corps DC*

HUFF, HENRY P.
University of Washington Libraries WA

INGERSOLL, ROYAL E. (1883–)
U.S. naval officer
Naval history collection (1964, 126 pages, also microfiche, permission required to cite or quote, also at *Division of Naval History DC*) *Columbia University NY*

INGISON, KENNETH M.
Sales manager
(1964, 17 pages, permission required to cite or quote) *Cornell University NY*

INGRAHAM, MARY S.
Former member, New York City Board of Higher Education
Brooklyn College NY

INGRAM, CHARLES H. (1892–)
Weyerhaeuser Timber Company (12 pages, permission required) *Columbia University NY*

INSURANCE, SOCIAL
Social Security collection. Participants and pages: Arthur Altmeyer, 231 (*permission required to cite or quote*); Edward Annis, 84; Barbara Armstrong, 317 (*permission required*); Fred Arner, 47 (*closed during lifetime*); A. Henry Aronson, 173 (*closed during lifetime*); Robert M. Ball, 84 (*permission required*); Frank Bane, 121; Alexander Barkan, 10; Harry Becker, 40 (*closed during lifetime*); Bernice Bernstein, 125; Andrew Biemiller, 49 (*closed during lifetime*); Carter Bradley, 27; Howard Bray, 112 (*closed during lifetime*); James Brindle and Martin Cohen, 35; J. Douglas Brown, 105; Eveline M. Burns, 180; John Byrnes, 51; Winslow Carlton, 55; Blue Carstenson, 227; Ewan Clague, 152; Wilbur J. Cohen, 57; Nelson Cruikshank, 506; Charles U. Daly, 27; Alvin David, 27 (*closed during lifetime*); Michael M. Davis, 65; Richard Donahue, 74 (*closed during lifetime*); Loula F. Dunn, 73; John W. Edelman, 99; Martha Eliot, 115 (*closed during lifetime*); Thomas H. Eliot, 81; Katherine Ellickson, 285; Lavinia Engle, 184; Caldwell Esselstyn, 43; Oscar R. Ewing, 190; Clinton Fair, 75 (*closed during lifetime*); Isidore Falk, 289; Fedele Fauri, 59; Meyer Feldman, 29 (*closed during lifetime*); William K. Fitch, 100; Marion B. Folsom, 207 (*permission required to cite or quote*); Aime Forand, 77; Kathryn Goodwin, 80; Frank P. Graham, 24; William Haber, 78 (*closed during lifetime*); Alvin Hansen, 28; Joseph Harris, 44; Ray Henry, 135 (*closed during lifetime*); Arthur Hess, 102; Jane Hoey, 102 (*permission required to cite or quote*); Reinhard Hohaus, 141 (*closed during lifetime*); Marjorie Hunter, 26; William Hutton, 113; Leo Irwin, 76; Jacob Javits, 12; Jarold A. Kieffer, 21; Arlen Large, 66; Arthur Larson, 54; Murray Latimer, 50 (*closed during lifetime*); Katherine Lenroot, 173; Allen Lesser, 46; Leonard Lesser, 78; Manuel Levine, 34; Isador Lubin, 32; Dorothy McCamman, 79 (*permission required*); Walter J. McNerney, 34; Mike Manatos, 41 (*closed during lifetime*); Morton D. Miller, 61; William Mitchell, 140; Raymond Moley, 19; Maurine Mulliner, 303; Robert J. Myers, 94 (*permission required to cite or quote*); Robert R. Neal, 46; Ivan Nestingen, 109; Robert Novak, 46 (*closed during lifetime*); James C. O'Brien, 220; Charles Odell, 117; P. Kenneth O'Donnell, 40 (*permission required*); Michael O'Neill, 60 (*permission required to cite or quote*); Claude D. Pepper, 61; Roswell Perkins, 143; Robert Perrin, 48; Jerome Pollack, 47 (*closed during lifetime*); M. Allen Pond, 88; Jennings Randolph, 15; Paul and Elizabeth Raushenbush, 295 (*permission required to cite or quote*); William Reidy, 101; William A. Reynolds, 61; Elliot Richardson, 57 (*permission required to cite or quote*); Gerel Rubien, 41; Sidney Saperstein, 122 (*closed during lifetime*); Lisbeth B. Schorr, 105 (*permission required to cite or quote*); Charles Schottland, 167; Harold Sheppard, 104; Anton G. Singsen, 20; Herman M. Somers, 199 (*closed during lifetime*); Sidney Spector, 57; Joseph Stetler, 58; Jack B. Tate, 119; Russell Gordon Wagenet, 108; Elizabeth Wickenden, 211 (*permission required*); Alanson Willcox, 140 (*permission required to cite or quote*); Kenneth Williamson, 240; Edwin Winge, 48; Irwin Wolkstein, 255; Leonard Woodcock, 28 (1965–1968, 10,649 pages, open except as noted, also at *Social Security Administration MD*) *Columbia University NY*

INTELLECTUAL LIFE *see* Culture

INTELLIGENCE SERVICE *see* U.S. Intelligence Service

INTERNATIONAL ALLIANCE OF THEATRICAL STAGE EMPLOYEES AND MOVING PICTURE MACHINE OPERATORS OF THE UNITED STATES AND CANADA
Herbert Knott Sorrell interview, Motion picture and television collection (open) *University of California, Los Angeles*

INTERNATIONAL BROTHERHOOD OF TEAMSTERS, CHAUFFEURS, WAREHOUSEMEN, AND HELPERS OF AMERICA
University of California Institute of Industrial Relations

INTERNATIONAL BUSINESS MACHINES CORPORATION
International Business Machines Corporation NY

INTERNATIONAL FEDERATION OF WORKING WOMEN
Mary Anderson collection *Arthur and Elizabeth Schlesinger Library MA*

INTERNATIONAL LADIES GARMENT WORKERS UNION
Socialists of St. Louis and Missouri collection *University of Missouri, St. Louis*
University of California Institute of Industrial Relations

INTERNATIONAL RELATIONS
International negotiations project. Participants and pages: John M. Allison, 23; Davis Bobrow, 41; Emerson Chapin, 25; Theodore Chen, 26; Frank Tillman Durdin, 20; Robert S. Elegant, 33; John Fairbank, 25; C. T. Hu, 18; Harold Isaacs, 9; T. B. Koh, 28; Daniel Lerner, 15; John Lindbeck, 18; Sidney Liu, 28; Ithiel de Sola Pool, 20; Lucien Pye, 32; I. Milton Sacks, 26; Sol Sanders, 52; Ezra Vogel, 23 (1970, 462 pages, permission required) *Columbia University NY*

Manlio Brosio, 24; Arthur J. Goldberg, 51; W. Averell Harriman, 353; Sir Geoffrey Harrison, 34; Joseph E. Johnson, 66; Theodore H. Kheel, 43; John J. McCloy, 24; Llewellyn Thompson, 29; Vladimir Velebit, 80 (1970–1972, 704 pages, permission required) *Columbia University NY*

See also John Foster Dulles; David Nunnerly

INTERNATIONAL TYPOGRAPHIC UNION OF LOS ANGELES
University of California Institute of Industrial Relations

INTERNATIONAL UNION UNITED AUTOMOBILE, AIRCRAFT AND AGRICULTURAL IMPLEMENT WORKERS OF AMERICA
Wyndham Mortimer interview, Biographical collection *University of California, Los Angeles*

INWOOD, PAUL
Northern Indiana Historical Society

IOWA
Bettendorf Public Library IA
Dana College NE
Iowa State University of Science and Technology
Public Library of Des Moines IA
Progressive Party of 1948 (4 hours, 68 pages) *University of Iowa Libraries*

IOWA STATE UNIVERSITY
Iowa State University of Science and Technology

IRAZUSTA, JULIO
Argentina in the 1930s (Spanish, 51 pages, permission required to cite or quote) *Columbia University NY*

IRISH LITERATURE
Southern Illinois University

IRRIGATION *see* Water resources Development

IRVIN, LAWRENCE
Adlai E. Stevenson project (1969, 72 pages, permission required) *Columbia University NY*

IRVIN, LESLIE LeROY (1895–1966)
Aviation collection (37 pages, permission required to cite or quote, also at *United States Air Force Academy CO* and *University of the Air, Maxwell Air Force Base AL*) *Columbia University NY*

JENKINS, PAUL (1923–)
Painter
(1968, 50 pages) *Archives of American Art—Smithsonian Institution NY*

JENNEWEIN, FRED
South Dakota experience (1951), South Dakota Oral History Project *University of South Dakota*

JENNINGS, B. A. (1895-1964)
Agricultural engineer
Agricultural leaders project (1964, 23 pages, open) *Cornell University NY*

JENNINGS, HARRY E.
South Dakota experience (1970), South Dakota Oral History Project *University of South Dakota*

JENNINGS, MORLEY
Athletic boom in West Texas (open) *Texas Tech University*

JENNINGS, WILLIAM HAROLD
Water resources collection (open) *University of California, Los Angeles*

JENSEN, HANS
Ricks College ID

JENSEN, JENS
Designer, Lincoln Memorial Gardens
Lincoln Memorial Gardens collection (open) *Sangamon State University IL*

JENSEN, JOSEPH
Water resources collection (open) *University of California, Los Angeles*

JENSEN, LEONEL, AND HOWARD STRICKLIN
South Dakota experience (1969), South Dakota Oral History Project *University of South Dakota*

JENSEN, LOUIS J.
South Dakota experience (1968), South Dakota Oral History Project *University of South Dakota*

JENSEN, LOWELL
District attorney, Alameda County
Earl Warren oral history project (in process) *University of California, Berkeley*

JENSEN, OLIVER (1914–)
Editor: Writer
(1959, 29 pages, open) *Columbia University NY*

JEPSEN, DR. GLENN
with Ray Lemley
Geologist

South Dakota experience (1970), South Dakota Oral History Project *University of South Dakota*

JERGENSEN, ELI MORONI
Ricks College ID

JERGENSEN, MARY ALBERTA ORME
Ricks College ID

JERNEGAN, JOHN
U.S. ambassador to Iraq
(34 pages, permission of interviewee required) *John F. Kennedy Library MA*

JEROME, JOHN L.
Discussed in State Historical Society of Colorado James Grafton Rogers interview

JEROME, WILLIAM TRAVERS
Discussed in Columbia University interview with William Jay Schieffelin

JERSIG, HARRY
Lone Star Beer, Oral business history project *University of Texas, Austin*

JERSILD, ARTHUR T. (1902–)
Psychologist; Educator
(1967, 255 pages, also microfiche, permission required to cite or quote) *Columbia University NY*

JESFIELD, AUSTIN
South Dakota experience (1960), South Dakota Oral History Project *University of South Dakota*

JESSE, MR. AND MRS. RANDALL
Kansas City friends of Pres. Truman
Harry S. Truman Library MO

JESSEL, GEORGE
Discussed in Columbia University interview with Samson Raphaelson

JESSUP, FREDERICK P. (1920–)
U.S. government official
Eisenhower administration project (1972, 105 pages, permission required, also at *Dwight D. Eisenhower Library KS*) *Columbia University NY*

JESSUP, PHILIP CARYL (1897–)
Diplomat; Scholar
(1958, 388 pages, permission required) *Columbia University NY*
Journalism lectures, Basic issues in the news: The national state and the international community (85 pages, permission required) *Columbia University NY*
Discussed in Columbia University interview with James William Barco

JESSUP, WALTER A.
Discussed in Columbia University interviews with Morse Adams Cartwright; Robert MacDonald Lester; and in Carnegie Corporation collection

JESTER, LLOYD (1906–)
Inspector; Retired police chief
(1972, 74 pages) *University of California, Berkeley*

JESUITS
Georgetown University DC

JEWISH AGENCY
ANTECEDENTS TO THE STATE OF ISRAEL: (1) Jewish Agency executive in London (1938-1948), and other collections *Hebrew University, Israel*

JEWISH LABOR MOVEMENT
Yivo Institute for Jewish Research, Inc. NY

JEWISH LANGUAGE *see* Hebraica; Yiddish Language and Literature

JEWISH LITERATURE
Hebrew University, Israel

JEWISH MUSIC *see* Music, Jewish

JEWISH QUESTION *see* Zionism

JEWS
Hebrew University, Israel
Western Jewish History Center CA

JEWS IN AUSTRIA
WORLD WAR II: THE HOLOCAUST—RESISTANCE AND RESCUE: (6) Rescue of Jewish children *Hebrew University, Israel*

JEWS IN BELGIUM
WORLD WAR II: THE HOLOCAUST—RESISTANCE AND RESCUE: (4) Jews in the underground in Belgium *Hebrew University, Israel*
WORLD WAR II: THE HOLOCAUST—RESISTANCE AND RESCUE: (5) Hiding children in Belgium *Hebrew University, Israel*

JEWS IN BELORUSSIA
WORLD WAR II: THE HOLOCAUST—RESISTANCE AND RESCUE: (10) Belorussian Jewry *Hebrew University, Israel*

JEWS IN CENTRAL ASIA
JEWISH COMMUNITIES: (12) Jews of Bukhara (1900–1935) *Hebrew University, Israel*

JEWS IN CZECHOSLOVAKIA
WORLD WAR II: THE HOLOCAUST—RESISTANCE AND RESCUE: (6) Rescue of Jewish children *Hebrew University, Israel*
YOUTH MOVEMENTS: (1) Jewish youth movements in Czechoslovakia *Hebrew University, Israel*

JEWS IN EGYPT
JEWISH COMMUNITIES: (9) Jewish community in Egypt *Hebrew University, Israel*

JOHNSON, GILBERT HUBERT (1905-)
Sergeant major, U.S. Marine Corps (service: 1942-1956)
(108 pages, permission required) *United States Marine Corps DC*

JOHNSON, GLENN H., JR.
(1960) *State Historical Society of Colorado*

JOHNSON, GUION GRIFFIS (MRS. GUY B.)
Carnegie Corporation collection (67 pages, permission required) *Columbia University NY*

JOHNSON, GUY BENTON
Sociologist
Carnegie Corporation collection (64 pages, permission required) *Columbia University NY*

Southern intellectual leaders (1972, 171 pages, closed pending publication of a study) *Columbia University NY*

JOHNSON, HAROLD K.
U.S. Army general
United States Army Military Research Collection PA

JOHNSON, HIRAM
Discussed in Columbia University interview with Horace Marden Albright

JOHNSON, HOUSTON
Challenges to governance by students project (1969, 14 pages, permission required to cite or quote) *Cornell University NY*

JOHNSON, HUGH
Discussed in Columbia University interviews with Goldthwaite Higginson Dorr; Jerome New Frank; Henry Agard Wallace

JOHNSON, HURLEY
University of Southern Mississippi

JOHNSON, JAMES WELDON
Discussed in Columbia University interviews with George Samuel Schuyler; Carl Van Vechten

JOHNSON, JESSE CHARLES (1894-)
Adviser to U.S. delegation, International Conferences on Peaceful Uses of Atomic Energy (1955, 1958)
Eisenhower administration project (36 pages, permission required to cite or quote, also at *Dwight D. Eisenhower Library KS*) *Columbia University NY*

JOHNSON, JOHN B.
Discussed in Columbia University interview with William O'Dwyer

JOHNSON, JOHN C.
(1967) *State Historical Society of Colorado*

JOHNSON, JOHN J. (1915-)
United Transportation Union project (1970, 46 pages, transcript open, permission required to cite, quote, and reproduce tape) *Cornell University NY*

JOHNSON, JOSEPH ESREY (1906-)
Professor of history
(1951, 58 pages, closed during interviewee's lifetime) *Columbia University NY*
Carnegie Corporation collection (50 pages, permission required) *Columbia University NY*
International negotiations project (66 pages, permission required) *Columbia University NY*
United Nations Conference, San Francisco, 1945 (1951, 77 pages, open) *Columbia University NY*

JOHNSON, JOSIE R.
(1972) *Fisk University TN*

JOHNSON, LYDIA (1893-)
China missionaries collection (open, 38 pages, also at *Columbia University NY*) *Claremont Graduate School CA*

JOHNSON, LYNDON BAINES
U.S. President (1963-1968)
(1969, 1 reel) *Broadcast Pioneers Library DC*
John C. Stennis collection *Mississippi State University*
James A. Farley collection *Scott E. Webber Collection NY*
Lyndon B. Johnson project (1600 hours, 50,000 pages, varied restrictions, on-going) *University of Texas, Austin*
Discussed in Columbia University interviews with Edward Roland Annis; Milton Stover Eisenhower; Luther Harris Evans; Barry Morris Goldwater; D. B. Hardeman; Elizabeth Stevenson (Mrs. Ernest) Ives; Newton Norman Minow; John Sharon; Frank Stanton; Marietta (Mrs. Ronald) Tree; Elizabeth Wickenden

JOHNSON, MARY McCANN
Mining in Wood River *Idaho Bicentennial Commission*

JOHNSON, MAURICE E. (1909-)
Dairyman
(1965, 71 pages) *Cornell University NY*

JOHNSON, MIRIAM
Secretary of the King, Conner, Ramsay defense committee
Earl Warren oral history project (in process) *University of California, Berkeley*

JOHNSON, DR. MORDECAI
Educator
(1972) *Fisk University TN*

JOHNSON, NELSON TRUSLER (1887-1954)
Diplomat

(1954, 730 pages, also microfiche, permission required to cite or quote) *Columbia University NY*

JOHNSON, NUNNALLY
Screenwriter; Director
Popular arts collection (52 pages, open) *Columbia University NY*
An oral history of the motion picture in America (open) *University of California. Los Angeles*

JOHNSON, RAY (1927-)
Painter
(1968, 15 pages) *Archives of American Art—Smithsonian Institution NY*

JOHNSON, RICHARD
South Dakota experience (1971), South Dakota Oral History Project *University of South Dakota*

JOHNSON, ROBERT LIVINGSTON
Third president, Temple University
Temple University PA

JOHNSON, ROBERT S.
Aviation collection (35 pages, permission required to cite or quote, also at *United States Air Force Academy CO* and *University of the Air, Maxwell Air Force Base AL*) *Columbia University NY*

JOHNSON SPACE CENTER, HOUSTON
National Aeronautics and Space Administration DC

JOHNSON, U. ALEXIS (1908-)
Diplomat
(50 pages, portions closed, permission of interviewee required to cite, quote, or paraphrase) *John F. Kennedy Library MA*
Dulles oral history collection (1966, 42 pages, permission required to cite or quote) *Princeton University NJ*

JOHNSON, UNA
Curator
(1971) *Archives of American Art—Smithsonian Institution NY*

JOHNSON, WALTER, (1915-)
Adlai E. Stevenson project (37 pages, permission required) *Columbia University NY*

JOHNSTON, ELLEN SHOEMAKER (MRS. BARTLETT F.)
(1972, 2 hours), *Maryland Historical Society*

JOHNSTON, ERIC A. (1896-1963)
Popular arts collection (23 pages, open) *Columbia University NY*

JOHNSTON, MARGUERITE KULP
Social secretary to university president's wife; Former student leader
(1973, 52 pages) *University of California. Berkeley*

(1969, 16 pages, open) *University of Texas, El Paso*

JORDAHL, RUSSELL NELTON (1903–) Brigadier general, U.S. Marine Corps (service: 1926–1958)

(1970, 202 pages, open, also at *Columbia University NY* and *U.S. Naval Institute MD*) *United States Marine Corps DC*

JORDAN, BARBARA (1936–) Attorney; Member, Texas Senate (Houston)

(1972) *Fisk University TN*

Legislative project (1970, 63 pages, closed until her death) *North Texas State University Oral History Collection*

JORDAN, JOSEPH

Flying Tigers (38 pages, permission required to cite or quote) *Columbia University NY*

JORDAN, JULIE

Challenges to governance by students project (1969, tape, not transcribed, open) *Cornell University NY*

JORDON, VERNON J., JR.

(1972) *Fisk University TN*

JORGENSEN, ALBERT N.

University of Connecticut

JOSEPH, GLORIA

(1971, 69 pages, permission required to use, cite, or quote) *Cornell University NY*

Challenges to governance by students project (1969, permission required to use, cite, or quote) *Cornell University NY*

JOSEPHS, DEVEREUX COLT (1893–) Executive

Carnegie Corporation collection (1967, 150 pages, permission required) *Columbia University NY*

Discussed in Columbia University interviews with Morse Adams Cartwright; Charles Dollard; Caryl Parker Haskins; Edward Pendleton Herring; Robert MacDonald Lester

JOSEPHSON, MATTHEW (1899–)

La Follette Civil Liberties Committee interviews (75 pages, permission required to cite or quote) *Columbia University NY*

JOSEPHSON, WILLIAM

General counsel, Peace Corps

(69 pages, permission of interviewee required) *John F. Kennedy Library MA*

JOSLYN, MAYNARD

Wine (in process) *University of California, Berkeley*

JOURNALISM

Journalism lectures: Accounts of events. Participants and pages: Dean Acheson, 39; Justin Brooks Atkinson, 29; Hanson Baldwin,

17; Ross Barnett, 23; Watson Berry, 25; Herbert Block, 34; Robert Briscoe, 24; Ted Cott, 36; Norman Cousins, 26; E. Clifton Daniel, Jr. 76; Allen W. Dulles, 27; Benjamin Fine, 25; Max Freedman, 29; John V. Lindsay, 22; Walter Lippmann, 58; Samuel Lubell, 127; Malcolm X, 38; Lester Markel, 46; Herbert Mayes, 29; Sig Mickelson, 31; James B. Reston, 46; William A. Rusher, 66; Harrison E. Salisbury, 65; David Schoenbrun, 46; Harry S. Truman, 13; Tom Wicker, 40 (1037 pages, permission required to cite or quote) *Columbia University NY*

Journalism lectures: Basic issues in the news. Participants, topics, and pages: Adolf A. Berle on economics, 29; John Ray Dunning on nuclear energy, 104; Louis Hollander on the labor movement, 58; Philip Jessup on the national state and the international community, 85; Polykarp Kusch on physics, 17; Wallace S. Sayre on the problems of the city, 136. (1959–1963, 429 pages, permission required) *Columbia University NY*

Journalism lectures: Consumer reporting (1971–1972, 982 pages, permission required) *Columbia University NY*

Journalism lectures: Forum I: Grayson Kirk, moderator; Charles Frankel, Polykarp Kusch, Margaret Mead, Leo C. Rosten. Forum II: Edward W. Barrett, moderator; Hodding Carter, Max Lerner, Marya Mannes, Michael J. Ogden, Eric A. Sevareid. (1963, 105 pages, permission required to cite or quote) *Columbia University NY*

Field Enterprises IL

Henry James Forman interview, Biographical collection *University of California, Los Angeles*

See also Newspapers

JOY, JIMMY

Discussed in Texas Tech University "Big Band" era collection

JOYCE, GEORGE J.

New York political studies collection, Brooklyn politics (1930–1950) (45 pages, permission required) *Columbia University NY*

JOYCE, JAMES

Discussed in Columbia University interviews with Joseph Collins; Ben W. Huebsch

JUANENO INDIANS

Doris Duke American Indian Oral History Project *Arizona State Museum*

JUDD, DONALD (1928–) Sculptor

(1965, 11 pages; 1968, 77 pages) *Archives of American Art—Smithsonian Institution NY*

JUDD, DONALD AND FRANK STELLA

(1965, 21 pages) *Archives of American Art—Smithsonian Institution NY*

JUDD, WALTER H. (1898–) Physician; U.S. congressman

Eisenhower administration project (1970, 149 pages, permission required, also at *Dwight D. Eisenhower Library KS*) *Columbia University NY*

Dulles oral history collection (1965, 131 pages, access subject to special restriction) *Princeton University NJ*

JUDGES

Discussed in John Fujio Aiso interview *University of California, Los Angeles*

JUDSON, ARTHUR (1881–)

Radio pioneers collection (25 pages, open) *Columbia University NY*

Discussed in Columbia University interview with Howard Barlow

JUHAN, JO, AND GENEVIEVE FORDHAM JUHAN

(1964) *State Historical Society of Colorado*

JULIAN PETROLEUM COMPANY, LOS ANGELES

Robert Walker Kenny interview, Government and politics collection *University of California, Los Angeles*

JUNG, CARL

Discussed in Columbia University interview with Edward Glover

JUNKER, ERNEST

Manager, Scarab Club, Detroit

(1967, 21 pages) *Archives of American Art—Smithsonian Institution NY*

JURISCH, CLARENCE M.

South Dakota experience (1970), South Dakota Oral History Project *University of South Dakota*

JUSTICE, PHYLLIS (MRS. CLARENCE)

South Dakota experience (1971), South Dakota Oral History Project *University of South Dakota*

JUSTO, AGUSTIN P.

Discussed in Columbia University interviews with Jose Luis Pena; Dario Sarachaga

JUVENILE LITERATURE *see* Children's Literature

K

KOA RADIO, COLORADO

(1962) *State Historical Society of Colorado*

KADES, CHARLES LOUIS (1906–)

Occupation of Japan (78 pages, permission required to cite or quote) *Columbia University NY*

Discussed in Columbia University Occupation of Japan collection

KAPROW, ALLAN (1927–)
Painter

(1968, 35 pages) *Archives of American Art—Smithsonian Institution NY*

KARAM, JAMES

Eisenhower administration project (29 pages, closed during interviewee's lifetime, also at *Dwight D. Eisenhower Library KS*) *Columbia University NY*

KARAMANLIS, CONSTANTINOS
Prime minister of Greece

(4 pages, open) *John F. Kennedy Library MA*

KARCH, FREDERICK JOSEPH (1917–)
Brigadier general, U.S. Marine Corps (Service: 1940–1967)

(93 pages, restriction pending) *United States Marine Corps DC*

KARDINER, ABRAM (1891–)
Psychoanalyst

Psychoanalytic movement collection (1963, 127 pages, open except for specified pages) *Columbia University NY*

Hall–Brooke Hospital CT

KARITAS, JOSEPH
White House painter

(25 pages, open) *John F. Kennedy Library MA*

KARK, ALAN EUGENE (1921–)

Mount Sinai Hospital Investitures (14 pages, permission required, also at *Mount Sinai Medical Center NY*) *Columbia University NY*

KARKUKLI, EZRA
Ministry of Finance (Jerusalem)

JEWISH COMMUNITIES: (10) Jewish life in Iraq (Hebrew, 20 pages, open) *Hebrew University, Israel*

KARKUKLI, JOSEPH

JEWISH COMMUNITIES: (10) (Hebrew, translated from Arabic, 14 pages, open) *Hebrew University, Israel*

KARLA, CONSTANCE

Mill Valley Public Library CA

KARMI, ARIE

WORLD WAR II: THE HOLOCAUST—RESISTANCE AND RESCUE: (8) Theresienstadt ghetto (Hebrew, 96 pages, open) *Hebrew University, Israel*

KARON, DAVID
Member, Kibbutz Kfar-Menahem

JEWISH COMMUNITIES: (2) Jews in the Spanish Civil War (Hebrew, 41 pages, open) *Hebrew University, Israel*

KARP, IVAN (1926–)
Dealer

(1969, 62 pages) *Archives of American Art—Smithsonian Institution NY*

KARTVELI, ALEXANDER (1896–)

Aviation collection (43 pages, permission required to cite or quote, also at *United States Air Force Academy CO* and *University of the Air, Maxwell Air Force Base AL*) *Columbia University NY*

KASER, DAVID

Cornell University Libraries project (1972, 161 pages, open) *Cornell University NY*

KASPER, JOSEPH PHILIP (1897–)

Federated Department Stores project (45 pages, permission required) *Columbia University NY*

KASSLER, EDWIN S.

(1958) *State Historical Society of Colorado*

KASTENMEIER, ROBERT
U.S. representative (Wisconsin)

(18 pages, open) *John F. Kennedy Library MA*

KASTER, JAMES (1933–)

Travel agent; Pilot; Democratic member, Texas House of Representatives (El Paso)

Legislative project (1971, 57 pages, open) *North Texas State University Oral History Collection*

KATAN, DAISY
Ramat-Gan chemist

CULTURE AND EDUCATION: (2) Higher education among Iraqi Jews (Hebrew, 7 pages, open) *Hebrew University, Israel*

KATAN, KENNETH
Ramat-Gan radiologist

CULTURE AND EDUCATION: (2) Higher education among Iraqi Jews (Hebrew, 6 pages, open) *Hebrew University, Israel*

KATSCH, JESSE, AND VIDA FERN KENNEDY KATSCH

South Dakota experience (1971), South Dakota Oral History Project *University of South Dakota*

KATSMAN, LOUIS

University of Washington Libraries WA

KATZ, ALEX (1927–)
Painter

(1969, 34 pages) *Archives of American Art—Smithsonian Institution NY*

KATZ, MORDECHAI
Citrus Shipping Company employee (Tel-Aviv)

HISTORY OF THE YISHUV (PALESTINIAN JEWRY): (8) Revisionist "Ha 'apalah" (Hebrew, 10 pages, open) *Hebrew University, Israel*

KATZ, YITZHAK

YOUTH MOVEMENTS: (2) Netzach in Latvia (Hebrew, 31 pages, open) *Hebrew University, Israel*

KATZEN, LILA (1932–)
Sculptor

(1964, 8 pages) *Archives of American Art—Smithsonian Institution NY*

KATZEN, SALLY
Smith alumna, class of 1964; Lawyer

(1973, 2 hours, 35 pages) *Smith College MA*

KATZKI, HERBERT
Assistant executive vice-chairman, American Jewish Joint Distribution Committee

WORLD WAR II: THE HOLOCAUST—RESISTANCE AND RESCUE: (1) The Joint (American Jewish Joint Distribution Committee) (English, 28 pages, open Hebrew, based on English conversation, 4 pages, written interview) *Hebrew University Israel*

KATZNELBOIGEN, RAPHAEL
Jerusalem rabbi

HISTORY OF THE YISHUV (PALESTINIAN JEWRY): (4) Extreme Orthodox Jewry in Palestine (Hebrew, 94 pages, open) *Hebrew University, Israel*

KATZNELSON, GIDEON
Tel-Aviv literary critic

JEWISH COMMUNITIES: (2) Jews in the Spanish Civil War (Hebrew, 2 pages, open) *Hebrew University, Israel*

KAUFFMAN, CHARLES
Doctor; Neighbor of Charles Ives

Ives project (1969) *Yale University School of Music CT*

KAUFMAN, BORIS

Popular arts collection (33 pages, open) *Columbia University NY*

KAUFMAN, JACOB J. (1914–)
Professor of economics

United Transportation Union project (1970, 61 pages, permission required to cite or quote) *Cornell University NY*

KAUFMAN, RALPH

Mount Sinai Hospital Investitures (29 pages, permission required, also at *Mount Sinai Medical Center NY*) *Columbia University NY*

KAUFMAN, RUDOLPH, JR.

Ricks College ID

KAUFMANN, ARTHUR

Independence National Historical Park (21 pages, permission required) *Columbia University NY*

KAUL, BRIJ MOHAN (–1972)
Indian Army officer

(1964, 445 pages, permission required) *Columbia University NY*

KELLY, MARY
Oregon political figure

(27 pages, open) *John F. Kennedy Library MA*

KELLY, RICHMOND
United States Naval War College RI

KELLY, WILLIAM
Massachusetts political figure

(21 pages, open) *John F. Kennedy Library MA*

KELLY, MR. AND MRS. WILLIAM
State Historical Society of Colorado

KELSO, WINCHESTER (1895–   )
Benedum and the oil industry (13 pages, open) *Columbia University NY*

KELSON, JOHN
Journalist, *Boston Post*, Gannet papers

(44 pages, open) *John F. Kennedy Library MA*

KEMPER, JOHN MASON (1912–1971)
U.S. Army officer; Educator

(1963, 113 pages, permission required to cite or quote) *Columbia University NY*

KENAANI, ELIEZER
Director, Beit-Trumpeldor, Kibbutz Tel-Yosef

HISTORY OF THE YISHUV (PALESTINIAN JEWRY): (5) Gedud Ha-Avoda (Labor Brigade) (Hebrew, 18 pages, open) *Hebrew University, Israel*

KENDALL, DAVID WALBRIDGE (1903–   )
Assistant Secretary of the Treasury (1955–1957); Special counsel to the President (1958–1961)

Eisenhower administration project (85 pages, permission required, also at *Dwight D. Eisenhower Library KS) Columbia University NY*

KENDALL, EDWARD CALVIN (1886–1972)
Nobel Laureates collection (62 pages, permission required) *Columbia University NY*

KENDRICK, JOHN B.
Discussed in Columbia University interview with Joseph Christopher O'Mahoney

KENEN, PETER B. (1932–   )
Columbia crisis of 1968 (73 pages, permission required) *Columbia University NY*

KENISON, MR. AND MRS. REUBEN J.
South Dakota experience (1971), South Dakota Oral History Project *University of South Dakota*

KENNAN, GEORGE F. (1904–   )
Diplomat

(141 pages, portions closed) *John F. Kennedy Library MA*

Dulles oral history collection (1967, 52 pages, access subject to special restrictions) *Princeton University Library NJ*

Discussed in Columbia University interview with Frank W. Rounds, Jr.

KENNARD, MARIETTA CONWAY
Tacoma Public Library WA

KENNEDY, EINOR
Inventor

Idaho Bicentennial Commission

KENNEDY, ELSIE PARSONS (MRS. JOHN D.) (1903–1966)
with John D. Kennedy

(1962, 58 pages, permission required to cite or quote) *Columbia University NY*

KENNEDY, JACQUELINE
Discussed in Columbia University interview with Cass Canfield

KENNEDY, JOHN D.
Brief contribution to Columbia University interview with Elsie Parsons Kennedy

KENNEDY, JOHN FITZGERALD (1917–1963)
U.S. president

John F. Kennedy assassination (8 hours) *The Citadel Archives—Museum SC*

The Kennedy image in India *University of Bridgeport CT*

Radio interview with the author John F. Kennedy (1940) *Mayo Clinic Foundation MN*

Kennedy assassination reaction (4 hours, not transcribed) *Sangamon State University IL*

James A. Farley collection *Scott E. Webber Collection NY*

Presidential election of 1960 (400 pages, open) *University of Southern California Library*

Discussed in Columbia University interviews with Edward Roland Annis; Barry Bingham; Chester Bowles; Nelson Hale Cruikshank; Elizabeth Stevenson (Mrs. Ernest) Ives; Walter H. Judd; Carl McGowan; Almer Stillwell; Mike Monroney; Ivan Arnold Nestingen; Richard Elliott Neustadt; Charles Odell; John Sharon; Frank Thompson, Jr.; Marietta (Mrs. Ronald) Tree; Elizabeth Wickenden; Kenneth Williamson; Irwin Wolkstein; Wilson Watkins Wyatt; and in Journalism lectures collection

KENNEDY, JOSEPH P.
Discussed in Columbia University interviews with Eddie Dowling; Alan Goodrich Kirk; Emory Scott Land; James McCauley Landis

KENNEDY, ROSE FITZGERALD (MRS. JOSEPH P.) (1890–   )
Interview re Joseph P. Kennedy's associations with Herbert Hoover and Hoover Commission (no more than 2 pages may be copied,

also at *Herbert Hoover Oral History Program DC) John F. Kennedy Library MA*

KENNEDY, KEN
Program manager, WDAY (Fargo ND)

Radio pioneers collection (1963, 7 pages, also at *Broadcast Pioneers Library DC) Columbia University NY*

KENNEDY, LAWTON (1900–   )
Fine printer

(1967, 211 pages) *University of California, Berkeley*

KENNEDY, ROBERT F.
U.S. senator (New York)

Visit to Pine Ridge Indian Reservation (April 1968) *Chadron State College NE*

Special Robert F. Kennedy oral history program *John F. Kennedy Library MA*

James A. Farley collection *Scott E. Webber Collection NY*

Discussed in Columbia University interviews with Edward Costikyan; Elizabeth Stevenson (Mrs. Ernest) Ives

KENNEDY, W. KEITH
Black studies project (1971, 265 pages, permission required to cite or quote) *Cornell University NY*

Challenges to governance by students project (1969, permission required to cite or quote) *Cornell University NY*

Sugar beet industry in New York State (1968, permission required to cite or quote) *Cornell University NY*

KENNEDY FAMILY
Boston Public Library MA

KENNEDY SPACE CENTER, FLORIDA
National Aeronautics and Space Administration DC

KENNEL, DAVID, M.D.
St. Louis doctors for peace in Vietnam *Washington University School of Medicine MO*

KENNELL, WARREN (1898–   )
Engineer

Agricultural leaders project (1964, 82 pages, permission required to cite or quote) *Cornell University NY*

KENNERLEY, MITCHELL
Discussed in Columbia University interview with Alfred A. Knopf

KENNY, GEORGE C.
Discussed in Columbia University interview with Jarred V. Crabb

KENNY, ROBERT WALKER
Attorney general under Warren; Candidate for governor (1946)

Earl Warren oral history project (in process) *University of California, Berkeley*

KENNY, ROBERT WALKER (cont.)
Government and politics collection (open) *University of California, Los Angeles*

KENNY, WILLIAM F.
Discussed in Columbia University interview with Eddie Dowling

KENT, JAMES L. (1918–)
School custodian; U.S. Marine Corps veteran; Survivor of the siege of Corregidor
Prisoner-of-war project (1972, 77 pages, open) *North Texas State University Oral History Collection*

KENT, ROCKWELL (1882–1971)
Painter
(1969, 40 pages) *Archives of American Art—Smithsonian Institution NY*

Friends of the Columbia Libraries (20 pages, permission required to cite or quote) *Columbia University NY*

KENT, ROGER
California political figure
(57 pages, portion closed) *John F. Kennedy Library MA*

Earl Warren oral history project (in process) *University of California, Berkeley*

KENTUCKY
Alice Lloyd College KY
University of Louisville KY
Western Kentucky University

KENWORTHY, ELDON
Challenges to governance by students project (1969, 73 pages, permission required to cite or quote) *Cornell University NY*

KENYON, DOROTHY
Smith alumna, class of 1908; Lawyer; Municipal judge; Feminist; Civil rights activist
(1973, 2 hours, 39 pages) *Smith College MA*

KEOGH, EUGENE JAMES (1907–)
U.S. congressman
(1950, 82 pages, also microfiche, permission required to cite or quote) *Columbia University NY*
(21 pages, open) *John F. Kennedy Library MA*

KEPPEL, FRANCIS (1916–)
U.S. Commissioner of Education
Carnegie Corporation collection (61 pages, permission required) *Columbia University NY*
Discussed in Columbia University interview with Francis A. J. Ianni

KEPPEL, FREDERICK PAUL.
Discussed in Columbia University interviews with Florence Anderson; Roberta Capers; Morse Adams Cartwright; William Harold Cowley; Charles Dollard; and in Carnegie Corporation collection

KERBEL, JOE
Athletic boom in West Texas (open) *Texas Tech University*

KERES INDIANS
Doris Duke American Indian Oral History Project *Arizona State Museum*

KERR, AMELIA ANNA SCHMIDT (1914–)
Daughter of Baltimore seafood dealer
(1972, 6 pages, 30 minutes, open) *Maryland Historical Society*

KERR, BARBARA
Adlai E. Stevenson project (39 pages, permission required) *Columbia University NY*

KERR, CLARK
Head, University of California faculty committee during Warren's administration
Earl Warren oral history project (in process) *University of California, Berkeley*

KERR, ROBERT
Owner, WKER Radio
(1 reel) *Broadcast Pioneers Library DC*
Discussed in Columbia University interview with Herman Miles Somers

KERR, WALTER B. JR. (1911–)
Journalist
Dulles oral history collection (1964, 45 pages, open) *Princeton University NJ*

KERSTA, NORAN (NICK)
Pioneer NBC television executive
(1965, 1 reel, 44 pages) *Broadcast Pioneers Library DC*

KERBEL, JOE

KESHET (KESTENBAUM) AKIVA
Director, Religious Youth Section, Youth and He-Halutz Department, Jewish Agency (Jerusalem)
YOUTH MOVEMENTS: (1) Jewish youth movements in Czechoslovakia (Hebrew, 27 pages, open) *Hebrew University, Israel*

KESSLER, JOSEPH
Federal Communications Commission legal assistant to Commissioner Wadsworth
(1967, 1 reel) *Broadcast Pioneers Library DC*

KETLER, ERNESTINE
Suffragists (in process) *University of California, Berkeley*

KETTERING, CHARLES F. (1876–1958)
General Motors Corporation MI

KEYNES, JOHN MAYNARD
Discussed in Columbia University interview with Ansel Frank Luxford

KEYSERLING, LEON (1908–)
National Labor Relations Board (1969, 65 pages, open) *Cornell University NY*

KERN, JEROME
Discussed in Columbia University Popular arts collection
Discussed in Knox College IL Tribute to Otto Harbach

KERN COUNTY, CALIFORNIA
California State University, Bakersfield

KERNER, OTTO *see George W. Bunn*

KERNS, ETHEL
Richmond Public Library CA

KEROUAC, JACK
Author
Northport Public Library NY

KERR, ANNIE
Ricks College ID

KHOMAN, THANAT (1914–)
Minister of Foreign Affairs, Thailand
(8 pages, open) *John F. Kennedy Library MA*
Dulles oral history collection (1964, 18 pages, open) *Princeton University NJ*

KHRUSHCHEV, NIKITA
Chairman, Council of Ministers of the Soviet Union
(5 pages, open) *John F. Kennedy Library MA*
Discussed in Columbia University interviews with Evan Peter Aurand; James William Barco; Andrew Wellington Cordier, Ted Cott; Michel Gordey; James C. Hagerty; and in Journalism lectures collection

KIBBUTZ SYSTEM
Hebrew University, Israel

KIDD, CHARLES VINCENT (1914–)
Health science collection (59 pages, permission required, also at National Library of Medicine MD) *Columbia University NY*

KIDD, R. J.
Texas Interscholastic League, Oral business history project *University of Texas, Austin*

KIDRON, D.
WORLD WAR II: THE HOLOCAUST—RESISTANCE AND RESCUE: (15) Contacts between the Yishuv (Palestinian Jewry) and U.S.S.R. during W.W. II (Hebrew, 11 pages, open) *Hebrew University, Israel*

KGOSTSILE, WILLIE
with Aaron Douglas
(1971) *Fisk University TN*

KHAZUM, AVRAHAM ABOUDI (1914–)
JEWISH COMMUNITIES: (10) Jewish life in Iraq (Hebrew, translated from Arabic, 6 pages, open) *Hebrew University, Israel*

KHEEL, THEODORE WOODROW (1914–)
Lawyer; Mediator
International negotiations project (1969, 43 pages, permission required to cite or quote) *Columbia University NY*

KIDWELL, JEAN
Jackson Freedom Ride (closed during interviewee's lifetime), Biographical collection *University of California, Los Angeles*

KIEFFER, JAROLD ALAN (1923–   )
Social Security collection (21 pages, open, also at *Social Security Administration MD) Columbia University NY*

KIELY, JACK K.
Challenges to governance by students project (1969, 33 pages, permission required) *Cornell University NY*

KIENBUSCH, WILLIAM (1914–   )
Painter

(1968, 48 pages) *Archives of American Art—Smithsonian Institution NY*

KIERAN, JOHN
Discussed in Columbia University interview with Dan Golenpaul

KILCOYNE, FRANCIS P.
President emeritus, Brooklyn College

Brooklyn College NY

KILDAY, PAUL (1900–1968)
Attorney; Judge; U.S. congressman (San Antonio, 1939–1949)

Legislative project (1965, 97 pages, open) *North Texas State University Oral History Collection*

KILDEE, HERBERT
Iowa State *University of Science and Technology*

KILGORE, WILLIAM J.
Baylor project *Baylor University TX*

KILLENS, JOHN OLIVER
Author; Screenwriter; Playwright
(1972) *Fisk University TN*

KILLGO, CARLTON J. (1922–   )
U.S. Army Air Corps veteran

Prisoner-of-war project (1972, 115 pages, open) *North Texas State University Oral History Collection*

KILLIAN, GEORGE (1921–   )
U.S. Army veteran; Former member of the "Lost Battalion"

Prisoner-of-war project (1970, 110 pages, open) *North Texas State University Oral History Collection*

KILLIAN, JAMES R., JR. (1904–   )
Scientist

Eisenhower administration project (1970, 375 pages, closed until 1985, also at *Dwight D. Eisenhower Library KS) Columbia University NY*

KILLIAN, REV. WILLIAM A. (1930–   )
Roman Catholic priest involved in Rio Grande farm workers' movement (1966–1967)

(40 pages, open) *University of Texas, Arlington*

KILLION, GEORGE
Director, Department of Finance; National Democratic party treasurer

Earl Warren oral history project (in process) *University of California, Berkeley*

KILLPACK, MONT ROSE
Ricks College ID

KILPATRICK, CARROLL
Journalist, *Washington Post*

(19 pages, open) *John F. Kennedy Library MA*

KILPATRICK, JAMES J.
Cleveland State University Library OH

KILPATRICK, WILLIAM HEARD (1871–1965)
Educator

(1961, 212 pages, open) *Columbia University NY*

Discussed in Columbia University interviews with Harold Florian Clark; William Jansen; Arthur T. Jersild; Isaac Leon Kandel; John Kelley Norton; R. Bruce Raup; Goodwin Watson

KIMBALL, ARTHUR ALDEN (1908–   )
U.S. government official

Eisenhower administration project (1967, 104 pages, permission required to cite or quote, also at *Dwight D. Eisenhower Library KS) Columbia University NY*

KIMBALL, DAN
Discussed in Columbia University interview with William Morrow Fechteler

KIMBALL, DORIS FLEESON
Adlai E. Stevenson project (22 pages, permission required) *Columbia University NY*

KIMBALL, ELIZABETH McGREW
Smith alumna, class of 1901; Smith teacher

(1973, 2 hours, 36 pages) *Smith College MA*

KIMBRELL, MARVIN
James B. Duke project (24 pages, permission required, also at *Duke University NC) Columbia University NY*

KIMELMAN, HADASSA
HISTORY OF THE YISHUV (PALESTINIAN JEWRY): (1) Second Aliyah pioneers collection (Hebrew, 21 pages, open) *Hebrew University, Israel*

KIMMEL, HUSBAND
Discussed in Columbia University interviews with Ralph Chandler Parker; Omar Titus Pfeiffer; Harold C. Train

KIMMY, J. E.
Columbia television lectures (33 pages, open) *Columbia University NY*

KINANE, JOHN J. (1915–   )
(1965, 86 pages, permission required to cite or quote) *Cornell University NY*

KINCHER, MR. AND MRS. ARTHUR
(1960) *State Historical Society of Colorado*

KINDELBERGER, JAMES HOWARD (1895–1962)
Henry H. Arnold project (1960, 57 pages, permission required, also at *United States Air Force Academy CO) Columbia University NY*

KING, ASA (1877–1967) AND ANSON WRIGHT GIBSON (1892–   )
Educational administrators

Agricultural leaders project (1963, 16 pages, open) *Cornell University NY*

KING, EARL X.
Minister, Nashville

(1972) *Fisk University TN*

KING, ERNEST J.
Discussed in Columbia University interviews with Orvil A. Anderson; Walter Stratton Anderson; John Jennings Ballentine; Joseph James Clark; Donald Duncan; James Fife; John Lesslie Hall, Jr.; Thomas Charles Hart; Harry W. Hill; John Howard Hoover; Omar Titus Pfeiffer; William Augustus Read, Jr.; Merwin Hancock Silverthorn; William Sullivan; Eugene Edward Wilson

KING, HARRY T. (1894–   )
Chemist

(1964, 119 pages, permission required to cite or quote) *Cornell University NY*

KING, JIMMY, SR.
U.S. Marine Corps officer

(36 pages, permission required, also at *Columbia University NY and U.S. Naval Institute MD) United States Marine Corps DC*

KING, JOSEPH
Challenges to governance by students project (1969, 28 pages, permission required) *Cornell University NY*

KING, MARTIN LUTHER, JR.
Martin Luther King Library Documentation Project *GA*

Memphis events of 1968: Martin Luther King's assassination *Memphis State University TN*

Black St. Louis leaders collection *University of Missouri, St. Louis*

Discussed in Columbia University interviews with Lester B. Granger; John Lewis; Everett Frederic Morrow

KING, OTIS D.
(1961) *State Historical Society of Colorado*

KOCH, JOHN (1909–)
Painter
(1968, 64 pages) *Archives of American Art—Smithsonian Institution NY*

KOCH, LEA
WORLD WAR II: THE HOLOCAUST—RESISTANCE AND RESCUE: (5) Hiding children in Belgium. (French, 31 pages, open) *Hebrew University; Israel*

KOCH, RICHARD
Historic preservation *Charles B. Hosmer, Jr. Collection IL*

KOCHVA, ADINA
WORLD WAR II: THE HOLOCAUST—RESISTANCE AND RESCUE: (2) Rescue of Jews via Spain and Portugal (Hebrew, 7 pages, written interview, open) *Hebrew University; Israel*

KOCHVA, BARUCH
Deputy director, Tefahot Bank (Tel-Aviv)

KOEHLER, FRANK E.
Vice-president and manager, WDBJ (Roanoke VA)
(1964, 1 reel, 17 pages) *Broadcast Pioneers Library DC*

KOENIG, ROBERT P. (1904–)
Engineer; Geologist; Executive
(1964, 121 pages, closed during interviewee's lifetime) *Columbia University NY*
Mining engineers (26 pages, permission required to cite or quote) *Columbia University NY*

KOENIG, SAMUEL S. (1872–1955)
Lawyer; Politician
(1950, 53 pages, also microfiche, permission required to cite or quote) *Columbia University NY*

KOEPKE, ROY H. (1924–)
General chairman, UTU
United Transportation Union project (1970, 74 pages, open) *Cornell University NY*

KOFOED, LESLIE S. (1909–)
Trade association executive
(1971, 362 pages, open) *University of Nevada, Reno*

KOGER, HARRY (1893–), AND **GRACE KOGER**
Labor organizers
(61 pages, open) *University of Texas, Arlington*

KOH, T.B.
International negotiations project (28 pages, permission required) *Columbia University NY*

KOHLER, FOY D. (1908–)
Diplomat
Dulles oral history collection (1966, 1967, 36 pages, negotiations pending) *Princeton University NJ*

KOHLER, WALTER JODOK, JR. (1904–)
Wisconsin governor (1951–1956)
Eisenhower administration project (52 pages, permission required to cite or quote, also at *Dwight D. Eisenhower Library KS*) *Columbia University NY*

KOHLMAN, EDWINA
Book-of-the-Month-Club collection (18 pages, open) *Columbia University NY*

KOHLS, RICHARD L.
Purdue University School of Agriculture faculty member
(1970, 40 pages) *Purdue University Archives IN*

KOHN, CLYDE
Geographer
(1971, 10 minutes) *Plymouth State College NH*

KOHN, LOUIS A. (1907–)
Adlai E. Stevenson project (18 pages, permission required) *Columbia University NY*

KOHN, MAX
(1960) *State Historical Society of Colorado*

KOLB, LAWRENCE COLEMAN (1911–)
Health science collection (66 pages, permission required, also at *National Library of Medicine MD*) *Columbia University NY*

KOLBY, CLIFTON
Idaho Bicentennial Commission

KOLLMORGEN, WALTER
Geographer
(1970, 10 minutes) *Plymouth State College NH*

KONO, ICHIRO (1898–1966)
Secretary general, Japanese Liberal party
Dulles oral history collection (1964, Japanese and English, 26 pages, open) *Princeton University NJ*

KOO, VIKYUIN WELLINGTON (1888–)
Chinese oral history collection (in process) *Columbia University NY*

KOOK, HILLEL (BERGSON, PETER)
Investment company owner (Kfar-Shmaryahu)
HISTORY OF THE YISHUV (PALESTINIAN JEWRY): (7) Etzel and Lehi organizations (Hebrew, 111 pages, open) *Hebrew University; Israel*

KOONS, CHARLES V.
Communications Workers of America Collection *University of Iowa Libraries*

KOOPS, ROSE
Ricks College ID

KOOTZ, SAMUEL (1898–)
Art dealer
(1960, 8 pages; 1964, 10 pages) *Archives of American Art—Smithsonian Institution NY*

KOPPELBERG, PINCHAS
ANTECEDENTS TO THE STATE OF ISRAEL: (2) "Brichah" (organized escape) (Hebrew, 24 pages, open) *Hebrew University; Israel*

KORAK, STEVE
United Steelworkers of America labor leader
(1966, 16 pages) *Pennsylvania State University*

KORCZAK RUZKA
WORLD WAR II: THE HOLOCAUST—RESISTANCE AND RESCUE: (13) Underground activities of the Lithuanian Jews (Hebrew, 24 pages, open) *Hebrew University; Israel*

KORDT, ERICH
German military opposition to Hitler *Harold C. Deutsch Collection DC*

KOREN, FRIEDA
Former U.N.R.R.A. worker (Broumov); Histadrut employee (Tel-Aviv)
ANTECEDENTS TO THE STATE OF ISRAEL: (2) "Brichah" (organized escape) (Hebrew, 10 pages, open) *Hebrew University; Israel*

KORNBERG, ARTHUR (1918–)
Nobel Laureates collection (24 pages, permission required) *Columbia University NY*

KORNFELD, ERNEST
Pennsylvania State University

KORSON, GEORGE G.
King's College PA

KOSCIOLOWSKI, SOPHIE
Polish immigrant; Grievance committee member, United Packing House Workers of America
(1971, 1 hour, 39 pages) *Roosevelt University IL*

KOSHLAND, DANIEL E., SR. (1892–)
Businessman; Community leader; Philanthropist
(in process) Levi Strauss & Co. *University of California, Berkeley*
Philanthropy, Northern California Jewish Community series (1971, 325 pages, permission required, also at *University of California, Berkeley*) *Western Jewish History Center CA*

KOSHLAND, LUCILLE HEMING (1898–   )
Wife of community leader Daniel E. Koshland, Sr.; Participant in community affairs

Northern California Jewish Community series (1971, 79 pages, closed, also at *University of California, Berkeley*) *Western Jewish History Center CA*

KOTOK, E. I.
Forestry (in process) *University of California, Berkeley*

KOTT, JOSEPH
Chairman, Magen David Adom (Israel)

JEWISH COMMUNITIES: (4) Zionist movement in U.S.S.R. (1917–1935) (Hebrew, 24 pages, open) *Hebrew University, Israel*

KOURY, GEORGE (1922–   )
U.S. Marine Corps veteran; Bataan Death March survivor

Prisoner-of-war project (1972, 102 pages, open) *North Texas State University Oral History Collection*

KOVNER ABBA
Poet; Former leader, Ha-Shomer Ha-Tzair (Vilna ghetto)

ANTECEDENTS TO THE STATE OF ISRAEL: (2) "Brichah" collection (organized escape) (Hebrew, 67 pages, open) *Hebrew University, Israel*

WORLD WAR II: THE HOLOCAUST—RESISTANCE AND RESCUE: (13) Underground activities of the Lithuanian Jews (Hebrew, 56 pages, open) *Hebrew University, Israel*

KOZLOFF, MAX (1933–   )
Art critic

(1965, 8 pages) *Archives of American Art—Smithsonian Institution NY*

KRABINSKY, SHIMON

HISTORY OF THE YISHUV (PALESTINIAN JEWRY): (7) Etzel and Lehi organizations (Hebrew, 8 pages, open) *Hebrew University, Israel*

KRAFT, ALICE E.
McGraw-Hill, Inc. (45 pages, permission required) *Columbia University NY*

(31 pages, open) *John F. Kennedy Library MA*

KRAFT, JOSEPH
Columnist

KRAMER, DALE (–1966)

Farm Holiday Association (23 pages, open) *Columbia University NY*

KRAMER, ISAAC
Chicago rabbi

ANTECEDENTS TO THE STATE OF ISRAEL: (2) "Brichah" (organized escape) (Hebrew, 10 pages, open) *Hebrew University, Israel*

KRAMER, KENNETH (1904–   )
McGraw-Hill, Inc. (30 pages, permission required) *Columbia University NY*

KRANTZ, ARON

Aviation collection (60 pages, permission required to cite or quote, also at *United States Air Force Academy CO* and *University of the Air, Maxwell Air Force Base AL*) *Columbia University NY*

KRASNER, LEE
Painter

(1964, 28 pages; 1966, 21 pages; 1967, 1968, 22 pages) *Archives of American Art—Smithsonian Institution NY*

KRAUSE, AUREL
Hungarian history *University of Southern California Library*

KRAUSS, MOSHE
Former leader, He-Halu.tz and labor movement (Slovakia)

WORLD WAR II: THE HOLOCAUST—RESISTANCE AND RESCUE: (11) Jewish resistance in Slovakia (Hebrew, 29 pages, open) *Hebrew University, Israel*

KRAUSS, OTTO

WORLD WAR II: THE HOLOCAUST—RESISTANCE AND RESCUE: (8) Theresienstadt ghetto (Hebrew, 16 pages, open) *Hebrew University, Israel*

KRAVCHIK, MISHA
Zim employee (Haifa)

ANTECEDENTS TO THE STATE OF ISRAEL: (2) "Brichah" (organized escape) (Hebrew, 14 pages, open) *Hebrew University, Israel*

KREHBIEL, V. JOHN
Presidential election of 1960 *University of Southern California Library*

KREISER, RALPH (1908–   )
Newspaper reporter and editor; Bakersfield history hobbyist

(1971, 43 pages) *University of California, Berkeley*

KREMS, NATHAN
University of Washington Libraries WA

KRIS, ERNST
Discussed in Columbia University interviews with Heinz Hartmann; Rudolph Maurice Loewenstein

KRISTAL, AVRAHAM
Secretary, Manufacturers Association (Tel-Aviv)

HISTORY OF THE YISHUV (PALESTINIAN JEWRY): (2) Jewish private sector in Palestine (Hebrew, 10 pages, open) *Hebrew University, Israel*

KRISTENSEN, THORKIL
Minister of finance (1945–1947), Denmark

Harry S. Truman Library MO

KROCHMAL, MAX

ANTECEDENTS TO THE STATE OF ISRAEL: (2) "Brichah" (organized escape) (Hebrew, 29 pages, open) *Hebrew University, Israel*

KROCK, ARTHUR (1887–1974)
Newspaperman

(1950, 102 pages, also microfiche, permission required to cite or quote, also at *John F. Kennedy Library MA*) *Columbia University NY*

(27 pages, open) *John F. Kennedy Library MA*

Dulles oral history collection (1965, 40 pages, open) *Princeton University NJ*

KROENERT, LAWRENCE J. (1929–   )
Local chairman, UTU local 1299

United Transportation Union project (1970, 56 pages, permission required to cite or quote transcript and to use tape) *Cornell University NY*

KROLL, LEON (1884–   )
Artist

(1957, 259 pages, also microfiche, permission required to cite or quote) *Columbia University NY*

KRONHEIM, MILTON S., SR.
Friend of Truman; Washington DC businessman

Harry S. Truman Library MO

KRUEGER, MYRON E. (1890–   )
Professor of forestry

(1968, 27 pages) *University of California, Berkeley*

KRULAK, VICTOR HAROLD (1913–   )
Lieutenant general, U.S. Marine Corps (service: 1934–1968)

(1970, 269 pages, permission required, also at *Columbia University NY* and *U.S. Naval Institute MD*) *United States Marine Corps DC*

KRULEWITCH, MELVIN LEVIN (1895–   )
Major general, U.S. Marine Corps (service 1917–1956)

(125 pages, permission required, also at *Columbia University NY* and *U.S. Naval Institute MD*) *United States Marine Corps DC*

KRUSHENICK, NICOLAS (1929–   )
Painter

(1968, 52 pages) *Archives of American Art—Smithsonian Institution NY*

KRYSTALL, ERIC R.
Professor

Challenges to governance by students project (1969, 59 pages, open) *Cornell University NY*

LAUCK, CHESTER
(1969, 1 reel, 34 pages) Broadcast Pioneers Library DC

LAUDER, FRANK NEWTON
Ricks College ID

LAUGHLIN, JAMES WILLIAM (1876-)
Department store manager
(1955, 31 pages) University of California, Berkeley

LAUNDY, RODNEY
Vice-president, Miner Institute
(Open) Plattsburgh State University College NY

LAURENCE, WILLIAM LEONARD (1888-)
Science editor
(1954, 148 pages; 1964, 395 pages; also microfiche, permission required to cite or quote) Columbia University NY

LAURENS, JEAN
Discussed in Columbia University interview with Max Weber

LAURITZEN, J. DE LOS
Ricks College ID

LAVERY, EMMET GODFREY
Fine arts collection (open) University of California, Los Angeles

LAVI, JOSEPH
Solol Boneh Building Company chief engineer (Tel-Aviv)
ANTECEDENTS TO THE STATE OF ISRAEL: (2) "Brichah" (organized escape) (Hebrew, 4 pages, written interview, open) Hebrew University, Israel
WORLD WAR II: THE HOLOCAUST—RESISTANCE AND RESCUE: (13) Underground activities of the Lithuanian Jews (Hebrew, 29 pages, open) Hebrew University, Israel
WORLD WAR II: THE HOLOCAUST—RESISTANCE AND RESCUE: (13) Underground activities of the Lithuanian Jews (Hebrew, 47 pages, open) Hebrew University, Israel

LAW
Texas judicial systems project (7 hours, 242 pages) Baylor University TX
Legislative project (600 hours, 6000 pages) North Texas State University Oral History Collections
Social welfare history Shirley Camper Soman Collection NY
See also Judges

LAW ENFORCEMENT
South Dakota experience, South Dakota Oral History Project University of South Dakota IN

LAW ENFORCEMENT ASSISTANCE ADMINISTRATION
U.S. Department of Justice agency
(1971, 83 pages, 26 hours) Cornell University NY
Participants: Sanford Bates; James V. Bennett; R. L. Bradley; Lord Brockway (A. Fenner); Howard B. Gill; Hugh Klare; Peter B. Lejins; Austin H. MacCormick; Richard McGee; E. Preston Sharp; H. J. Taylor

LAWLER, OSCAR
Government and politics collection (open) University of California, Los Angeles

LAWLOR, GLENN JOSEPH (JAKE) (1907-)
Athletic coach; Teacher
(1971, 316 pages, open) University of Nevada, Reno

LAWRENCE, D. H.
Discussed in Columbia University interview with Ben W. Huebsch

LAWRENCE, DON
Weyerhaeuser Timber Company (66 pages, permission required) Columbia University NY

LAWRENCE, ERNEST
Discussed in Columbia University interview with Warren Weaver

LAWRENCE, GERTRUDE
Discussed in Columbia University interview with Richard Rodgers

LAWRENCE, JACOB (1917-)
Painter
(1968, 50 pages) Archives of American Art—Smithsonian Institution NY

LAWRENCE, T. E.
Discussed in Columbia University interview with James Freeman Curtis

LAWRENCE, W. C.
Jackson Hole Preserve (51 pages, permission required) Columbia University NY

LAWRENCE, WILLIAM HOWARD (1916-1972)
Journalist (New York Times, American Broadcasting Company)
Eisenhower administration project (1967, 37 pages, permission required to cite or quote, also at Dwight D. Eisenhower Library KS) Columbia University NY
(28 pages, open) John F. Kennedy Library MA

LAWSHE, CHARLES W.
University administrator, Purdue University Department of Psychology
(1970, 43 pages) Purdue University Archives IN

LAWSON, BELFORD
District of Columbia political figure; Civil rights advisor to Senator John Kennedy
(23 pages, open) John F. Kennedy Library MA

LAWSON, DOROTHY (1898-)
Educational administrator
(107 pages, in process) Cornell University NY

LAWSON, WILLIAM J. (ca. 1900-)
Former executive assistant to Governor W. Lee O'Daniel; former Texas secretary of state
Legislative project (1968, 55 pages, open) North Texas State University Oral History Collection

LAWTON, FREDERICK J.
Director, Bureau of the Budget (1950-1953)
Harry S. Truman Library MO

LAX, SALVADOR
CULTURE AND EDUCATION: (4) Jewish schools in Transylvania (Hebrew, translated from Hungarian, 15 pages, open) Hebrew University, Israel

LAY, BRIGID MAAS
Staff member, Voice of America
(1967, 1 reel, 12 pages) Broadcast Pioneers Library DC

LAZAR, HAIM
WORLD WAR II: THE HOLOCAUST—RESISTANCE AND RESCUE: (13) Underground activities of the Lithuanian Jews (Hebrew, 54 pages, open) Hebrew University, Israel

LAZARSFELD, PAUL FELIX (1901-)
Sociologist
(1962, 377 pages, closed during interviewee's lifetime) Columbia University NY

LAZARUS, CELIA ROSENTHAL (MRS. FRED, JR.)
Discussed in Columbia University interview with Frank Stanton

LAZARUS, CHARLES
Federated Department Stores project (99 pages, permission required) Columbia University NY

LAZARUS, ELEANOR AND MARGARET
Federated Department Stores project (21 pages, permission required) Columbia University NY

LAZARUS, FRED, JR. (1884-)
Merchandising executive
Federated Department Stores project (47 pages, permission required) Columbia University NY
Federated Department Stores project (1965, 1039 pages, permission required) Columbia University NY

Discussed in Columbia University Federated Department Stores project

LAZARUS, FRED, III (1912–)
Federated Department Stores project (42 pages, permission required) Columbia University NY

LAZARUS, IRMA MENDELSON (MRS. FRED, III)
Federated Department Stores project (40 pages, permission required) Columbia University NY

LAZARUS, JEFFREY L. (1894–)
Federated Department Stores project (32 pages, permission required) Columbia University NY

LAZARUS, MAURICE (1915–)
Federated Department Stores project (59 pages, permission required) Columbia University NY

LAZARUS, PAUL N., JR. (1913–)
Popular arts collection (41 pages, open) Columbia University NY

LAZARUS, RALPH (1914–)
Federated Department Stores project (54 pages, permission required) Columbia University NY

LAZARUS, MRS. RALPH
Federated Department Stores project (22 pages, permission required) Columbia University NY

LAZARUS, REUBEN AVIS (1895–1971)
Lawyer
(1951, 502 pages, permission required) Columbia University NY
New York political studies collection, New York election of 1949 (23 pages, permission required to cite or quote) Columbia University NY

LAZARUS, ROBERT (1890–1973)
Federated Department Stores project (32 pages permission required) Columbia University NY

LAZARUS, SIMON
Federated Department Stores project (44 pages, permission required) Columbia University NY

LAZY S RANCH
Ranching collection Texas Tech University

LEACH, ROBERT E.
Ohio judge
Life of Kingsley A. Taft Ohio Historical Society

LEAGUE OF NATIONS
Participants and pages: Thanassos Aghnides, 506; Pablo de Azcarate, 80; Pablo de Azcarate with Edouard de Haller and W. Van Asch Van Wijck, 156; Branko Lukac, 124

(1966–1969, French, individual restrictions apply, copies of memoirs also at Carnegie Endowment for International Peace NY and Geneva. Switzerland) Columbia University NY

LEAGUE OF WOMEN VOTERS
Ohio League of Women Voters Ohio Historical Society

LEAHY, WILLIAM
Discussed in Columbia University interviews with James Fife; Thomas Charles Hart

LEAR, WILLIAM POWELL (1902–)
Aviation collection (49 pages, permission required to cite or quote, also at United States Air Force Academy CO and University of the Air. Maxwell Air Force Base AL) Columbia University NY

LEAR SIEGLER, INC. see John Brooks, K. Robert Hahn, Robert W. Purcell, Phillip Smith

LEARNED, WILLIAM S.
Discussed in Columbia University Carnegie Corporation collection

LEARY, FAIRFAX
Discussed in Columbia University interview with James Fife

LEBOR, JOHN FRANCIS (1906–)
Federated Department Stores project (56 pages, permission required) Columbia University NY

LECKINGER, GERTRUDE
Secretary
(1964, 35 pages, permission required) Cornell University NY

LE CORBUSIER (CHARLES EDOUARD JEANNERET-GRIS)
Discussed in Columbia University interview with Robert Greenstein

LeCRON, JAMES D. (1885–1961)
U.S. Government official
(1953, 181 pages, open) Columbia University NY

LEDDY, DALE
M.L. Leddy & Sons, Oral business history project University of Texas, Austin

LEDDY, HOLLIS
M.L. Leddy & Sons, Oral business history project University of Texas, Austin

LEDDY, M. L., & SONS see Dale Leddy; Hollis Leddy

LEDERER, ARIE LEO
Official, Ata works

YOUTH MOVEMENTS: (1) Jewish youth movements in Czechoslovakia (German, 31 pages, open) Hebrew University, Israel

LEDUC, MONIQUE SCHMITZ
Daughter of R. Schmitz
Ives project (1971) Yale University School of Music CT

LEE, AMY FREEMAN
Biographical collection (open) Texas Tech University

LEE, C. C.
South Dakota experience (1970), South Dakota Oral History Project University of South Dakota

LEE, CARL
James B. Duke project (93 pages, permission required, also at Duke University NC) Columbia University NY

LEE, DON L.
Poet; Author
(1972) Fisk University TN
Discussed in Columbia University interview with William S. Paley

LEE, EDWARD
Former president, National Federation of Temple Brotherhoods; Lawyer
JEWISH COMMUNITIES: (5) Jewish nationalism and the reform movement in the United States (English, 21 pages, open) Hebrew University, Israel

LEE, GEORGE W.
Edward Hull Crump and his regime Memphis Public Library and Information Center TN

LEE, ISAAC HARVEY
Idaho Bicentennial Commission

LEE, JOSEPH BRACKEN (1899–)
Government official; Utah governor (1949–1957)
Eisenhower administration project (1967, 70 pages, permission required to cite or quote, also at Dwight D. Eisenhower Library KS) Columbia University NY

LEE, LILA
Popular arts collection (46 pages, open) Columbia University NY

LEE, ROBERT
Massachusetts political figure (16 pages, open) John F. Kennedy Library MA

LEE, RONALD F.
Historic preservation Charles B. Hosmer, Jr. Collection IL

LEE, RUSSEL VAN ARSDALE
Physician pioneering in prepaid group medicine
(1971, 84 pages) University of California. Berkeley

LEE, STELLA GARRETT
Smith alumna, class of 1918; Community service volunteer
(1973, 1 hour, 25 pages) *Smith College MA*

LEE, STEPHEN D.
Discussed in Columbia University interview with Cully Alton Cobb

LEE, TSUNG-DAO (1926–)
Nobel Laureates collection (23 pages, permission required) *Columbia University NY*

LEE, WARREN ISBELL (1874–1955)
U.S. congressman
(1950, 20 pages, open) *Columbia University NY*

LEE-SMITH, HUGHIE (1915–)
Painter
(1968, 34 pages) *Archives of American Art—Smithsonian Institution NY*

LEEDOM, SAMUEL R. (1896–1971)
Newspaperman; Water project administrator
(1967, 83 pages) *University of California, Berkeley*

LEEMAN, GEORGE with Pers Russell
South Dakota experience (1956), South Dakota Oral History Project *University of South Dakota*

LE FEVRE, ART
Communications Workers of America collection *University of Iowa Libraries*

LEFFINGWELL, ROBERT
Discussed in Columbia University interview with Alger Hiss

LEFFINGWELL, RUSSELL C.
Discussed in Columbia University interview with Frederick Osborn and in Carnegie Corporation collection

LE GATE, JAMES M.
General manager, WIOD (Miami FL)
(1965, 1 reel, 14 pages) *Broadcast Pioneers Library DC*

LEGROSS, R. E.
El Paso Fire Department (1968, 4 pages, open) *University of Texas, El Paso*

LE HAND, MARGUERITE
Discussed in Columbia University interview with Marion Dickerman

LEHI MOVEMENT
HISTORY OF THE YISHUV (PALESTINIAN JEWRY) (7) Etzel and Lehi organizations *Hebrew University, Israel*

LEHMAN, BENJAMIN H. (1889–)
Professor of English
(1969, 348 pages) *University of California, Berkley*

LEHMAN, HERBERT HENRY (1878–1963)
New York governor; U.S. senator
(1961, 785 pages, also microfiche, permission required to cite or quote, also at *John F. Kennedy Library MA*) *Columbia University NY*
Herbert H. Lehman project. Participants and pages: Helen Altschul, 13; Emanuel Celler, 3; Paul Douglas, 22; Julius Edelstein, 45; James A. Farley, 44; Carolin A. Flexner, 67; 12; Herbert H. Humphrey, 25; Estes Kefauver, 12; Herbert H. Lehman, 785; George Meany, 13; Henry Morgenthau, Jr., 8; Wayne Morse, 29; Charles Poletti, 32; Eleanor Roosevelt, 17; Anna M. Rosenberg, 14; Samuel I. Rosenman, 23; Marc Tanenbaum, 38; Roy Wilkins, 26 (1959, 1184 pages, permission required to cite or quote) *Columbia University NY*
New York political studies collection, New York election of 1949 (12 pages, permission required to cite or quote) *Columbia University NY*
Discussed in Columbia University interviews with Edward Costikyan; William Hammatt Davis; David Dressler; Justin N. Feldman; Jonah J. Goldstein; Philip Caryl Jessup

LEHMAN, MARTLEY
Discussed in Columbia University interview with Theresa Goell

LEHMAN, MAXWELL
New York political studies collection, Citizens Budget Commission (33 pages, permission required) *Columbia University NY*

LEHMANN-HAUPT, HELMUT
Friends of the Columbia Libraries (36 pages, permission required to cite or quote) *Columbia University NY*

LEIBOWITZ, ADOLF (–1969)
JEWISH COMMUNITIES: (7) Jewish life in Latin America (Spanish, 6 pages, open) *Hebrew University, Israel*

LEIBOWITZ, DAVID (–1969)
JEWISH COMMUNITIES: (4) Zionist movement in U.S.S.R. (1917–1935) (Hebrew, 24 pages, open) *Hebrew University, Israel*

LEIFER, ANN
American Federation of Teachers, Pittsburgh (1966, 16 pages) *Pennsylvania State University*

LEIGH, VERE C.
Member of Battery D, 129th Field Artillery, World War I
Harry S. Truman Library MO

LEIGHLEY, JOHN
Geographer
(1970, 10 minutes) *Plymouth State College NH*

LEIPER, HENRY SMITH (1891–)
Church official
Dulles oral history collection (1965, 46 pages, open) *Princeton University NJ*

LEITHEAD, BARRY T. (1907–)
Business executive
Eisenhower administration project (1968, 52 pages, permission required to cite or quote, also at *Dwight D. Eisenhower Library KS*) *Columbia University NY*

LEITZELL, CHARLES W.
Harwick College NY

LEJINS, PETER B.
Law Enforcement Assistance Administration project (1971, 1 hour 10 min) *Cornell University NY*

LEKACHMAN, ROBERT (1920–)
Danforth Foundation lectures (48 pages, permission required) *Columbia University NY*

LELAND, WALDO GIFFORD (1879–1966)
Historian
(1955, 63 pages, also microfiche, permission required to cite or quote) *Columbia University NY*

LEMAIRE, HENRY
Discussed in University of Nevada, Reno, René Watt Lemaire interview

LEMAIRE, RENE WATT (1903–)
Businessman; Politician
(1967, 29 pages, permission required to cite or quote) *University of Nevada, Reno*

LeMAISTRE, GEORGE
Civil rights in Alabama (1964, 31 pages, open) *Columbia University NY*

LEMASS, SEAN
Prime minister of Ireland
(23 pages, open) *John F. Kennedy Library MA*

LE MAY, CURTIS (1906–)
Former commander-in-chief, SAC
U.S. Air Force Academy project (107 pages, consult center for restriction, also at *United States Air Force Academy CO*) *Columbia University NY*
Dulles oral history collection (1966, 32 pages, permission required to cite or quote) *Princeton University NJ*

LEMLEY, PETE
South Dakota experience, South Dakota Oral History Project *University of South Dakota*

LEMLEY, DR. RAY
South Dakota experience (1970) South Dakota Oral History Project *University of South Dakota*

LEMLEY, DR. RAY, AND DR. GLENN JEPSEN
South Dakota experience (1970), South Dakota Oral History Project *University of South Dakota*

LEWIS, JOHN L.
Discussed in Columbia University interviews with John Brophy; William Hammatt Davis; Virginia Foster Durr; John Philip Frey; Albert John Hayes; Gardner Jackson; Edwin A. Lahey; James McCauley Landis; Lee Pressman; Boris Basil Shishkin; M. Hedley Stone

Discussed in Pennsylvania State University interview with David J. McDonald

Discussed in Sangamon State University IL Mining and John L. Lewis collection

LEWIS, KATHERINE HANDY
Popular arts collection (27 pages, open) *Columbia University NY*

LEWIS, KATHRYN (1911–)
Adlai E. Stevenson project (55 pages, permission required) *Columbia University NY*

LEWIS, L. A. "FAYETTE"
Anaheim Public Library CA

LEWIS, LEE ANDREW (1902–1972)
Labor organizer

(63 pages, open) *University of Texas, Arlington*

LEWIS, MORT
Author

Allan Nevins project (1970, 173 pages, closed until March 5, 1976) *Columbia University NY*

LEWIS, NORMAN (1909–)
Painter

(1968, 18 pages) *Archives of American Art—Smithsonian Institution NY*

LEWIS, OSCAR (1893–)
Author

(1965, 151 pages) *University of California. Berkeley*

LEWIS, RALPH
Historic preservation *Charles B. Hosmer, Jr. Collection IL*

LEWIS, ROBERT
Director, National headquarters, Farmers for Kennedy and Johnson; Deputy administrator, Commodity operations, Agricultural Stabilization and Conservation Service

(30 pages, open) *John F. Kennedy Library MA*

LEWIS, ROBERT (1909–)
Popular arts collection (61 pages, open) *Columbia University NY*

LEWIS, SAMUEL
Vice-president and general manager, Carlyle Hotel NY

(15 pages, open) *John F. Kennedy Library MA*

LEWIS, SINCLAIR
Discussed in Columbia University interview with Melville Henry Cane

Discussed in Sangamon State University IL George W. Bunn interview

LEWIS, SOLOMON
University of Southern Mississippi

LEWIS, W. W.
John Robert Gregg project (23 pages, permission required) *Columbia University NY*

LEWIS, WALTER "FURRY"
Memphis Public Library and Information Center TN

LEWKOWICZ, NASANEL AND DINA
Member, General Zionists, (Belgium)

WORLD WAR II: THE HOLOCAUST—RESISTANCE AND RESCUE: (4) Jews in underground in Belgium (French, 15 pages, open) *Hebrew University, Israel*

LI, HAN-HUN
Chinese oral history collection (239 pages, certain pages closed, description of memoir available on request) *Columbia University NY*

LI, HUANG (1895–)
Chinese oral history collection (1030 pages, closed) *Columbia University NY*

LI, SHU-HUA (1890–)
Chinese oral history collection (243 pages, certain pages closed, description of memoir available on request) *Columbia University NY*

LI, TSUNG-JEN (1890–)
Chinese oral history collection (4 vols., 54 chapters, permission required, description of memoir available on request) *Columbia University NY*

LIBBY, RUDOLF F.
Nobel Laureates collection (58 pages, permission required) *Columbia University NY*

LIBERTOVSKY, ISRAEL
ANTECEDENTS TO THE STATE OF ISRAEL: (3) "Ha 'apalah" (illegal immigration) (Hebrew, 42 pages, open; tape only, open) *Hebrew University, Israel*

LIBO, ALEXANDER
Physician; Chairman, Vilna Immigrants Association

JEWISH COMMUNITIES: (3) Lithuanian Jewry between the two world wars (Yiddish, 26 pages, open) *Hebrew University, Israel*

LIBOWSKY, HERMAN
New York City blackout project (14 pages) *Cornell University NY*

LIBRARIES *see* Cornell University; Friends of the Columbia Libraries

LICHTENFELD, LEON
Pioneer radio cellist

(1963, 22 pages, Radio pioneers collection also at *Broadcast Pioneers Library DC) Columbia University NY*

LICHTENSTEIN, HOWARD (1907–)
National Labor Relations Board (1969, 63 pages, open) *Cornell University NY*

LICHTENSTEIN, ROY (1923–)
Painter

(1963–1964, 166 pages; 1965, 16 pages) *Archives of American Art—Smithsonian Institution NY*

LICHTENSTEIN, ZALMAN J.
Discussed in Columbia University interviews with Ray Henry; Elizabeth Wickenden

LICHTER, FRANCES
Author

Montgomery County—Norristown Public Library PA

LICHTIG, ARIE
Jerusalem businessman

ANTECEDENTS TO THE STATE OF ISRAEL: (2) "Brichah" (organized escape) (Hebrew, 21 pages, open) *Hebrew University, Israel*

LICK OBSERVATORY
University of California, Santa Cruz

LIDOVSKY, ELIEZER
Israeli Labor Party

ANTECEDENTS TO THE STATE OF ISRAEL: (2) "Brichah" (organized escape) (Hebrew, 76 pages, open) *Hebrew University, Israel*

LIE, TRYGVE
Discussed in Columbia University interviews with Thanassos Aghnides; Andrew Wellington Cordier; Ernest A. Gross

LIEBEN, AVRAHAM
YOUTH MOVEMENTS: (1) Jewish youth movements in Czechoslovakia (Hebrew, 42 pages, open) *Hebrew University, Israel*

LIEBER, REV. ROBERT
German military opposition to Hitler *Harold C. Deutsch Collection DC*

LIEBERSON, GODDARD (1911–)
Composer; President, CBS Records

American cultural leaders collection (1966, 95 pages, closed pending publication of a study) *Columbia University NY*

Ives project (1969) *Yale University School of Music CT*

LIEBIG, CAROLINE
Discussed in Columbia University interview with Frank Stanton

LIEBIG, CAROLINE
Fine arts collection (open) *University of California, Los Angeles*

LISAGOR, PETER (1915–   )
Journalist

(85 pages, open) *John F. Kennedy Library MA*

Dulles oral history collection (1966, 49 pages, open) *Princeton University NJ*

LISKA, MRS. EMMA

(1966) *State Historical Society of Colorado*

LITERATURE
Claremont Graduate School CA

See also Black Literature; Children's Literature; Irish Literature; Journalism; Poetry

LITHUANIANS IN THE U.S.
Lithuanians in Luzerne County, Pennsylvania *King's College PA*

LITTAUER, KENNETH (–1968)

Aviation collection (30 pages, permission required to cite or quote, also at *United States Air Force Academy CO* and *University of the Air, Maxwell Air Force Base AL*) *Columbia University NY*

LITTLE, BERTRAM K.

Historic preservation *Charles B. Hosmer, Jr. Collection IL*

LITTLE, DONALD G. (1893–   )
Business executive

Radio pioneers collection (1951, 101 pages, open) *Columbia University NY*

LITTLE, LAWRENCE W. (1900–   )
Highway materials testing engineer

(1971) *University of Nevada, Reno*

LITVAK, MICHAEL ANATOLE (1902–   )

Popular arts collection (23 pages, open) *Columbia University NY*

LIU, J. HENG (1890–1961)

Chinese oral history collection (8 pages, closed) *Columbia University NY*

LIU, SIDNEY

International negotiations project (28 pages, permission required) *Columbia University NY*

LIUZZA, TED

Historic preservation *Charles B. Hosmer, Jr. Collection IL*

LIVNEH (LIVENSTEIN), ELIEZER
Jerusalem writer

JEWISH COMMUNITIES: (1) German Jewry (1933–35) (Hebrew, 13 pages, open) *Hebrew University, Israel*

LIVNEH, EPHRAIM

YOUTH MOVEMENTS: (2) Netzach in Latvia (Hebrew, 17 pages, open) *Hebrew University, Israel*

LLOYD, GLEN ALFRED (1895–   ) with Mrs. Lloyd

Adlai E. Stevenson project (30 pages, permission required) *Columbia University NY*

LLOYD, HAROLD CLAYTON (1893–1971)

Popular arts collection (76 pages, open) *Columbia University NY*

Discussed in Columbia University interview with Albert Edward Sutherland

LLOYD, R. McALLISTER

Carnegie Corporation collection (67 pages, permission required) *Columbia University NY*

LLOYD, TREVOR (1906–   )
Geographer

Carnegie Corporation collection (1968, 45 pages, permission required) *Columbia University NY*

LOBATO, EMILIO, SR.

(1962) *State Historical Society of Colorado*

LOBEL, OSWALD with Freida Lowy

YOUTH MOVEMENTS: (1) Jewish youth movements in Czechoslovakia (German, 45 pages, open) *Hebrew University, Israel*

LOBOS, ROBERTO

Argentina in the 1930s (Spanish, 55 pages, open) *Columbia University NY*

LOBSTER FISHERIES

Fishing and lobstering *University of Maine*

LOCHER, RALPH S.

Cleveland State University Library OH

LOCKE, EDWIN

Discussed in Columbia University interview with Joseph Charles Aub

LOCKE, EDWIN A., JR.
Special presidential assistant (1946)

Harry S. Truman Library MO

LOCKER, BERL
Former member, Jewish Agency executive (London)

ANTECEDENTS TO THE STATE OF ISRAEL: (1) Jewish Agency, (Hebrew, 127 pages, open) *Hebrew University, Israel*

LOCKWOOD, CHARLES A. (1890–1967)
U.S. naval officer

Naval history collection (1965, 720 pages, permission required to cite or quote, also at *Division of Naval History DC*) *Columbia University NY*

Discussed in Columbia University interview with James Fife

LODGE, HENRY CABOT (1902–   )
U.S. senator (Massachusetts); U.S. ambassador

(36 pages, portions closed) *John F. Kennedy Library MA*

Dulles oral history collection (1965, 44 pages, permission required to cite or quote) *Princeton University NJ*

Discussed in Columbia University interviews with Charles D. Cook; Luther Harris Evans; Claude Moore Fuess

LODGE, JOHN DAVIS (1903–   )
Government official; U.S. ambassador

Eisenhower administration project (1969, 195 pages, permission required to cite or quote, also at *Dwight D. Eisenhower Library KS*) *Columbia University NY*

LOEB, JAMES I. (1908–   )
Former U.S. ambassador to Peru; Guinea; Journalist

Harry S. Truman Library MO

(74 pages, permission of interviewee required) *John F. Kennedy Library MA*

LOEB, ROBERT

Discussed in Columbia University interviews with Dana Winslow Atchley; Jules Stahl

LOEMKER, DOROTHY ROWDEN

Carnegie Corporation collection (73 pages, permission required) *Columbia University NY*

LOENING, GROVER (1888–   )
Aircraft engineer

(1967, 43 pages, permission required to cite or quote) *Columbia University NY*

LOEVINGER, LEE
Assistant attorney general, Antitrust division, U.S. Department of Justice; Commissioner, Federal Communications Commission

(45 pages, open) *John F. Kennedy Library MA*

LOEW, MARCUS

Discussed in Columbia University interview with Eddie Dowling

LOEWENSTEIN, RUDOLPH MAURICE (1898–   )
Psychoanalyst

Psychoanalytic movement collection (1963, 149 pages, open except for specified pages, open protion also at *New York Psychoanalytic Institute*) *Columbia University NY*

Discussed in Columbia University interview with Heinz Hartmann

LOFTON, MARVIN F. (1908–   )
Chairman, UTU local 1732

United Transportation Union project (1971, 19 pages, open) *Cornell University NY*

LOGAN, DR. JIMMI
Opthalmologist

(1972) *Fisk University TN*

McCORD, JIM
Edward Hull Crump and his regime *Memphis Public Library and Information Center TN*

McCORD, ROBERT
American cultural leaders collection (50 pages, closed pending publication of a study) *Columbia University NY*

McCORMAC, KEITH
Leader, conservative, anti-Warren faction of Republican party; Organizer, 1952 delegation to Republican convention

Earl Warren oral history project (in process) *University of California, Berkeley*

McCORMACK, EDWARD
Massachusetts political figure

(38 pages, open) *John F. Kennedy Library MA*

McCORMACK, FRANCIS
Wisconsin political figure

(13 pages, open) *John F. Kennedy Library MA*

McCORMACK, HELEN
Historic preservation *Charles B. Hosmer, Jr. Collection IL*

McCORMACK, JOHN W. (1891–   )
U.S. congressman

Dulles oral history collection (1966, 28 pages, open) *Princeton University NJ*

MacCORMICK, AUSTIN H. (1893–   )
Law Enforcement Assistance Administration project (1971, 110 pages, 3 ½ hours) *Cornell University NY*

McCOSKER, M. JOSEPH
Independence National Historical Park (33 pages, permission required) *Columbia University NY*

McCOWEN, D. L.
Communications Workers of America collection *University of Iowa Libraries*

McCOY, ALVIN
Kansas political journalist *Kansas City Star*

(35 pages) *Dwight D. Eisenhower Library KS*

McCOY, JAMES
Staff representative, United Steelworkers of America

(1968, 20 pages) *Pennsylvania State University*

McCREA, JOEL (1905–   )
Popular arts collection (30 pages, open) *Columbia University NY*

McCRORY, CHARLES
Judge

Vigo County Public Library IN

McCRORY, JAMES
Eisenhower administration project (19 pages, closed during interviewee's lifetime, also at *Dwight D. Eisenhower Library KS*) *Columbia University NY*

McCUE, CONSTANCE
Carnegie Corporation collection (60 pages, permission required) *Columbia University NY*

McCULLERS, CARSON
Discussed in Columbia University interview with Dorothy Baker

McCULLOCH, FRANK
Chairman, National Labor Relations Board

(40 pages, open) *John F. Kennedy Library MA*

McCULLOCH, WALTER (1905–   )
Forestry school dean

(1968, 216 pages) *University of California, Berkeley*

McCULLOCH, WILLIAM H.
Cleveland State University Library OH

McCUNE, CAL
University of Washington Libraries WA

McCUNE, CAL
with Dave Royer and Bill Cunningham
University of Washington Libraries WA

McCUSKEY, CHARLES FLETCHER, M.D.
Anesthesiologist

Wood Library—Museum of Anesthesiology IL

McDANIEL, FRANCIS "FRANK"
South Dakota experience (1971), South Dakota Oral History Project *University of South Dakota*

McDANIEL, J. A.
Edward Hull Crump and his regime *Memphis Public Library and Information Center TN*

McDANIEL, ROLAND J., SR.
(1972) *Wabash Carnegie Public Library IN*

MacDANIELS, LAURENCE W. (1888–   )
(1967, 68 pages, open) *Cornell University NY*

McDERMOND, ALBERT J., AND NONA B. McDERMOND
South Dakota experience (1971), South Dakota Oral History Project *University of South Dakota*

McDERMOTT, EDWARD
Director, U.S. Office of Emergency Planning; Member, National Security Council

(67 pages, open) *John F. Kennedy Library MA*

McDERMOTT, EUGENE
Texas Instruments, Oral business history project *University of Texas, Austin*

McDERMOTT, ROBERT FRANCIS (1920–   )
U.S. Air Force officer

U.S. Air Force Academy project (1972, 207 pages, permission required, also at *United States Air Force Academy CO*) *Columbia University NY*

McDONALD, DAVID
President, United Steelworkers of America

(27 pages, open) *John F. Kennedy Library MA*

(1970, 56 pages) *Pennsylvania State University*

Discussed in Pennsylvania State University interviews with Mitchell F. Mazuca and Marvin Miller

MacDONALD, ELIZABETH, AND ISABELLE MacDONALD
(1967, 28 pages, most open) *Cornell University NY*

MacDONALD, GEORGE
Discussed in Columbia University interview with Hokan Bjornstrom Steffanson

MacDONALD, JEANETTE (1907–1965)
Popular arts collection (61 pages, open) *Columbia University NY*

McDONALD, JOSEPH F. (1891–1971)
Journalist

(1970, 227 pages, open) *University of Nevada, Reno*

McDONALD, JUNE
Communications Workers of America collection *University of Iowa Libraries*

McDONALD, MABEL RICE
(1967) *State Historical Society of Colorado*

MacDONALD, SIR THOMAS (1898–   )
Former New Zealand minister of external affairs

Dulles oral history collection (25 pages, permission required to cite or quote) *Princeton University NJ*

McDOUGAL, KATHERINE (MRS. EDWARD)
Adlai E. Stevenson project (42 pages, permission required) *Columbia University NY*

McDOWALL, RODDY (1928–   )
Popular arts collection (58 pages, open) *Columbia University NY*

McELROY, NEIL HOOSIER (1904–1972)
Business executive; Former U.S. Secretary of Defense

Eisenhower administration project (1967, 88 pages, permission required, also at *Dwight D. Eisenhower Library KS*) *Columbia University NY*

McGREGOR, MALCOLM (1892–   )
Attorney; Former state legislator (1954–1964)

Legislative project (1965, 115 pages, closed until notification by interviewee) *North Texas State University Oral History Collection*

McGREGOR, TRACY
Discussed in Columbia University interviews with James Murray McGregor; William John Norton

McGUIRE, EDWARD PERKINS (1904–   )
Eisenhower administration project (97 pages, permission required to cite or quote, also at *Dwight D. Eisenhower Library KS*) *Columbia University NY*

McGUIRE, MARIE
Commissioner, U.S. Public Housing Administration

(51 pages, open) *John F. Kennedy Library MA*

McGUIRE, TOM
with Reid Robinson and Chase Powers
Labor leaders

(1969, 132 pages) Mine, Mill and Smelter Workers Union *Pennsylvania State University*

MACHADO, LUIS (1899–   )
Diplomat

World Bank (1961, 35 pages, permission required to cite or quote, also at *Brookings Institution DC*) *Columbia University NY*

McHARG, ORMSBY (1871–   )
Lawyer; Politician

(1951, 126 pages, also microfiche, permission required to cite or quote) *Columbia University NY*

McHARGUE, ROBERT
Education collection (open) *University of California, Los Angeles*

MACHLIN, SHELDON (1918–   )
Sculptor

(1965, 10 pages) *Archives of American Art — Smithsonian Institution NY*

McHUGH, JAMES FRANCIS (1894–   )
Popular arts collection (82 pages, open) *Columbia University NY*

McHUGH, MATTHEW F.
Challenges to governance by students project (1969, 35 pages, permission required to cite or quote) *Cornell University NY*

McINTIRE, RAYMOND E.
Ricks College ID

McINTOSH, MILLICENT CAREY (1898–   )
Educator

(1966, 695 pages, permission required) *Columbia University NY*

MacINTOSH, SIR ROBERT
Men of anesthesia collection *Wood Library — Museum of Anesthesiology IL*

McIVER, PEARL
Nursing Archive *Boston University MA*

MacIVER, ROBERT MORRISON (1882–1970)
Sociologist

(1962, 99 pages, permission required) *Columbia University NY*

MACK, WALTER STAUNTON, JR. (1895–   )
Executive

(1950, 74 pages, also microfiche, permission required to cite or quote) *Columbia University NY*

McKAY, FRANK
University of Michigan

McKAY, HUGH C.
Ricks College ID

MACKAY, JOHN A. (1889–   )
Clergyman

Dulles oral history collection (1965, 50 pages, permission required to cite or quote) *Princeton University NJ*

McKEAN, JOSEPHINE
Occupation of Japan (79 pages, permission required to cite or quote) *Columbia University NY*

McKEEVER, MR. AND MRS. JOHN
Aberdeen American editor and publisher (1909–1929)

South Dakota experience (1970), South Dakota Oral History Project *University of South Dakota*

McKELDIN, THEODORE ROOSEVELT (1900–1974)
Maryland governor (1959–1950); Baltimore mayor (1943–1947, 1963–1967)

Discussed in Columbia University interview with Gordon R. Browning

MacKENNA, KENNETH (1899–   )
Popular arts collection (44 pages, open) *Columbia University NY*

MacKENZIE, DONALD

(17 pages, permission required to quote, also at *Columbia University NY*) *Forest History Society CA*

MacKENZIE, MR. AND MRS. FINDLAY
Friends of Ives

Ives project (1971) *Yale University School of Music CT*

McKENZIE, FRED F. (1900–   )
(1967, 68 pages, most open) Development of artificial insemination project *Cornell University NY*

MacKENZIE, JOHN, JR.
Ranching collection *Texas Tech University*

MacKENZIE, MURDO
Ranching collection *Texas Tech University*

MacKENZIE, VERNON
Chief, Division of Air Pollution, U.S. Public Health Service

(24 pages, open) *John F. Kennedy Library MA*

MACKESEY, THOMAS
(1969, 72 pages, open) *Cornell University NY*

MACKEY, GUY J.
Purdue University administrator

(1970, 25 pages) *Purdue University Archives IN*

McKIM, EDWARD D.
Chief administrative assistant to the President (1945)

Harry S. Truman Library MO

McKINLEY, WILLIAM
Discussed in Columbia University interview with Hobart Stanley Bird

McKINNEY, ERNEST RICE (1886–   )
Labor organizer

(1961, 116 pages, open) *Columbia University NY*

McKINNEY, REV. SAMULE
with Howard Droker and Alfred J. Westbex
University of Washington Libraries WA

McKINSTRY, ARTHUR F.
South Dakota experience (1970), South Dakota Oral History project *University of South Dakota*

McKISSACK, DEBERRY
Nashville architect

(1972) *Fisk University TN*

McKITTRICK, THOMAS HARRINGTON (1889–1970)
Banker

(1952, 43 pages, permission required to cite or quote) *Columbia University NY*

Dulles oral history collection (1964, 47 pages, permission required) *Princeton University NJ*

MACKLEM, STANLEY (1895–   )
Food processor

(1964, 132 pages, permission required to cite or quote) *Cornell University NY*

Dulles oral history collection (1966, 62 pages, permission required to cite or quote) *Princeton University NJ*

MACOMBER, WILLIAM BUTTS, JR. (1921–)
Assistant Secretary of State for congressional relations; U.S. ambassador to Jordan
(29 pages, permission of interviewee required to cite, quote, or paraphrase) *John F. Kennedy Library MA*

MACOUN, WILLIAM TERRIL
Hunt Institute for Botanical Documentation PA

McPEAK, WILLIAM
Discussed in Columbia University Association for the aid of Crippled Children collection

McPHEE, HENRY ROEMER, JR. (1925–)
U.S. government official (1954–1957)
Eisenhower administration project (58 pages, permission required to cite or quote, also at *Dwight D. Eisenhower Library KS*) *Columbia University NY*

McPHERSON, AIMEE SEMPLE
Discussed in Columbia University interview with Herbert Clark Hoover

McPHILLIPS, JAMES
United Steelworkers of America member
(1967, 34 pages) *Pennsylvania State University*

McQUAID, KAY
Adlai E. Stevenson project (6 pages, permission required) *Columbia University NY*

McQUAIN, MARY JANE BENN
(1968) *State Historical Society of Colorado*

McQUEEN, JOHN CRAWFORD (1899–)
Lieutenant general, U.S. Marine Corps (Service: 1921–1958)
(161 pages, open, also at *Columbia University NY* and *U.S. Naval Institute MD*) *United States Marine Corps DC*

McRAE, GORDON
Tribute to Otto Harbach *Knox College IL*

MACREADY, JOHN A.
Aviation collection (69 pages, permission required to cite or quote, also at *United States Air Force Academy CO* and *University of the Air, Maxwell Air Force Base AL*) Columbia University NY

McREYNOLDS, DAVID
Socialist movemen project (34 pages, permission required to cite or quote) *Columbia University NY*

McSHANE, JAMES
Head, Executive office for U.S. Marshals, U.S. Department of Justice
(34 pages, open) *John F. Kennedy Library MA*

MacVEAGH, FRANKLIN
Discussed in Columbia University interview with James Freeman Curtis

McWILLIAMS, CAREY (1905–)
Writer; California housing administrator
La Follette Civil Liberties Committee interviews (20 pages, permission required to cite or quote) *Columbia University NY*
Earl Warren oral history project (in process) *University of California, Berkeley*

MACY, GEORGE (1900–1956)
Founder of Limited Editions Club
Discussed in Columbia University Helen Macy interview

MACY, HELEN (MRS. GEORGE)
(In process) *Columbia University NY*

MACY, JOHN
Chairman, Civil Service Commission
(104 pages, open) *John F. Kennedy Library MA*

MADDEN, JOSEPH WARREN (1890–1972)
Judge
(1957, 170 pages, permission required) *Columbia University NY*
National Labor Relations Board (1968, 299 pages, written permission required) *Cornell University NY*

MADDOX, JACQUELINE SUE
Nashville news reporter
(1972) *Fisk University TN*

MADGETT, NAOMI LONG
Poet
(1972) *Fisk University TN*

MADIGAN, MICHAEL J. (1894–)
Robert P. Patterson project (47 pages, closed until January 1, 1980) *Columbia University NY*

MADISON, LEONA
(1962) *State Historical Society of Colorado*

MAFIA
Texas crime collection *Texas Tech University*

MAGEE, DAVID (1905–)
Publisher; Editor; Author; Bookman
(1969, 77 pages) *University of California, Berkeley*

MAGEE, RUBY
University of Southern Mississippi

MAGEN (LIFSHITZ), DOV
ANTECEDENTS TO THE STATE OF ISRAEL: (3) "Ha'apalah" (illegal immigration) (Tape only, open) *Hebrew University, Israel*

MAGGI, JUAN
Argentina in the 1930s (Spanish, 123 pages, open) *Columbia University NY*

MAGID, ELHANAN
Foreman, Netanya factory
WORLD WAR II: THE HOLOCAUST—RESISTANCE AND RESCUE: (13) Underground activities of the Lithuanian Jews (Hebrew, 30 pages; Hebrew, 45 pages; open) *Hebrew University, Israel*

MAGIDSON, JOSEPH
U.S. Army Medical Corps (World War I)
Washington University School of Medicine MO

MAGNIN, EDGAR F.
Rabbi
Northern California Jewish Community series (permission required to quote, also at *University of California, Berkeley*) *Western Jewish History Center CA*

MAGNUSON, PAUL BUDD (1884–1970) with Mrs. Magnuson
Adlai E. Stevenson project (32 pages, permission required) *Columbia University NY*

MAGRIEL, PAUL (1906–)
Collector; Author
(1970, 46 pages) *Archives of American Art—Smithsonian Institution NY*

MAGRUDER, CARTER B.
General, U.S. Army
United States Army Military History Research Collection PA

MAGUIRE, EDNA
Mill Valley Public Library CA

MAHADY, J. L.
Communications Workers of America collection *University of Iowa Libraries*

MAHARAL, AVRAHAM
YOUTH MOVEMENTS: (2) Netzach in Latvia (Hebrew, 29 pages, open) *Hebrew University, Israel*

MAHARAL, IDA
YOUTH MOVEMENTS: (2) Netzach in Latvia (Hebrew, 29 pages, open) *Hebrew University, Israel*

MAHARSHAK, PAULA
YOUTH MOVEMENTS: (2) Netzach in Latvia (Hebrew, 29 pages, open) *Hebrew University, Israel*

MAHLER, HERMAN
(1959) *State Historical Society of Colorado*

MANHART, ALBERT W.
(1968) *State Historical Society of Colorado*

MANHEIM, SYLVAN (1897–   )
Mount Sinai Hospital (50 pages, permission required; also at *Mount Sinai Medical Center NY*) *Columbia University NY*

MANKIEWICZ, JOSEPH LEO (1909–   )
Popular arts collection (47 pages, open) *Columbia University NY*

MANKOWSKI, JOHN
Staff representative, United Auto Workers
(In process) *Pennsylvania State University*

MANLEY, NORMAN
Premier of Jamaica; Leader of the opposition
(11 pages, open) *John F. Kennedy Library MA*

MANN, ABBY
Television screenwriter
An oral history of the motion picture in America (open) *University of California, Los Angeles*

MANN, DELBERT (1920–   )
Popular arts collection (61 pages, open) *Columbia University NY*

MANN, FRANK C., M.D.
Mayo Clinic Foundation MN

MANN, MAE
Communications Workers of America collection *University of Iowa Libraries*

MANN, SELUCHA
ANTECEDENTS FOR THE STATE OF ISRAEL: (2) "Brichah" (organized escape) (Hebrew, 43 pages, open) *Hebrew University, Israel*

MANN, SHLOMO
ANTECEDENTS TO THE STATE OF ISRAEL: (2) "Brichah" (organized escape) (Hebrew, 20 pages; Hebrew, 43 pages; open) *Hebrew University, Israel*

MANN, THOMAS CLIFTON (1912–   )
U.S. government official; Diplomat
Eisenhower administration project (1968, 60 pages, permission required; also at *Dwight D. Eisenhower Library KS*) *Columbia University NY*
(58 pages, permission of interviewee required) *John F. Kennedy Library MA*
Dulles oral history collection (1966, 19 pages, open) *Princeton University NJ*
Discussed in Columbia University interview with Alfred A. Knopf

MANN, WALTER (1889–   )
Photoengraver (1910–1969)
(1973, 94 pages) *University of California, Berkeley*

MANNES, MARYA (1904–   )
Journalism lectures, Forum II (permission required to cite or quote) *Columbia University NY*

MANNING, HELEN TAFT
Professor; Dean, Bryn Mawr *Bryn Mawr College Alumnae Association PA*
Robert A. Taft project (83 pages, permission required) *Columbia University NY*

MANNING, STANLEY RUTTER (1891–   )
Radio pioneers collection (16 pages, open) *Columbia University NY*

MANOR, GIDEON (MENDL, GEORG)
Ministry of Agriculture employee (Israel)
YOUTH MOVEMENTS: (1) Jewish Youth movements in Czechoslovakia (Hebrew, 34 pages, open) *Hebrew University, Israel*

MANSEAU, BENJAMIN
Discussed in Columbia University interview with William Sullivan

MANSFIELD, KATHERINE
Discussed in Columbia University interview with Alfred A. Knopf

MANSFIELD, MICHAEL J. (1903–   )
U.S. senator (Montana); Senate majority leader
(46 pages, open) *John F. Kennedy Library MA*
Dulles oral history collection (1966, 17 pages, open) *Princeton University NY*

MANSFIELD, PORTIA
Smith alumna, class of 1910; Dancer; Teacher
(1973, 2 hours, 37 pages) *Smith College MA*

MANSFIELD, RICHARD ROBINSON
South Dakota experience (1970), South Dakota Oral History Project *University of South Dakota*

MANSHIP, PAUL (1885–1966)
Sculptor
(1959, 33 pages) *Archives of American Art—Smithsonian Institution NY*
(1956, 71 pages, open) *Columbia University NY*

MANSO, LEO (1914–   )
Painter
(1965, 15 pages) *Archives of American Art—Smithsonian Institution NY*

MANTER, JERAULD
University of Connecticut

MANTL, THOMAS
WORLD WAR II: THE HOLOCAUST—RESISTANCE AND RESCUE: (8) Theresienstadt ghetto (German, 82 pages, open) *Hebrew University, Israel*

MANTON, IRENE
Hunt Institute for Botanical Documentation PA

MANUCY, ALBERT
Historic preservation *Charles B. Hosmer, Jr. Collection IL*

MAOR, YITZHAK
YOUTH MOVEMENTS: (2) Netzach in Latvia (Hebrew, 42 pages, open) *Hebrew University, Israel*

MAORI AGRICULTURAL COLLEGE, NEW ZEALAND
Interviews with men who attended the college between 1913 and 1931 *Church College of Hawaii*

MAPLES, CLEM
University of Southern Mississippi

MAPP, JAMES
President, Chattanooga NAACP
(1972) *Fisk University TN*

MAPP, LOIS
Artist
Montgomery County—Norristown Public Library PA

MARA, BILL
with John Sills and Michele Whitham
Perception of change in Ithaca school district project (1973, 3 hours) *Cornell University NY*

MARA, TIM
Discussed in Columbia University interview with Eddie Dowling

MARABLE, FATE
Jazzmen on the Mississippi *University of Missouri, St. Louis*

MARANTZ, PAUL
Challenges to governance by students project (1969, 62 pages, permission required to cite or quote) *Cornell University NY*

MARBURY, WILLIAM LUKE (1901–   )
Robert P. Patterson project (40 pages, closed until January 1, 1980) *Columbia University NY*

MARCA-RELLI, CONRAD (1913–   )
Painter
(1965, 29 pages) *Archives of American Art—Smithsonian Institution NY*

MARCANTONIO, VITO (1902–1954)
New York political studies collection. New York election of 1949 (7 pages, permission required to cite or quote) *Columbia University NY*
Discussed in Columbia University interviews with Virginia Foster Durr; Paul O'Dwyer

MAXWELL, WILLIAM L.
Auditor; Controller

Weyerhaeuser Timber Company (1956, 112 pages, permission required) *Columbia University NY*

MAY, ELIZABETH STOFFREGEN
Smith alumna, class of 1928; Dean and acting president, Wheaton College; Economist

(1973, 2 hours, 41 pages) *Smith College MA*

MAY, ERNEST RICHARD (1928–)

American historians collection (104 pages, permission required to cite or quote) *Columbia University NY*

MAY, EVERETTE
National Institutes of Health MD

MAY, HERBERT LOUIS (1877–1966)
Lawyer; Diplomat

(1951, 92 pages, also microfiche, permission required to cite or quote) *Columbia University NY*

MAY, MRS. MILLARD
William H. Miner philanthropic activities (10 minutes, open) *Plattsburgh State University College NY*

MAYER, ARTHUR LOEB (1886–)

Popular arts collection (43 pages, open) *Columbia University NY*

MAYER, GRACE
Curator

(1970, 59 pages) *Archives of American Art—Smithsonian Institution NY*

MAYER, HANS (–1968)

WORLD WAR II: THE HOLOCAUST—RESISTANCE AND RESCUE: (1) The Joint (American Jewish Joint Distribution Committee) (English, 3 pages, written interview) *Hebrew University, Israel*

MAYER, HAROLD M.
Geographer

(1972, 10 minutes) *Plymouth State College NH*

MAYER, LOUIS B.

Discussed in Columbia University interview with Eddie Dowling and in Popular arts collection

MAYER, MARIA GOEPPERT (1906–1972)

Nobel Laureates collection (51 pages, permission required) *Columbia University NY*

MAYER, RENE (1895–)
Former French prime minister

Dulles oral history collection (1964, French, 17 pages, closed until 10 years after interviewee's death) *Princeton University NY*

MAYER, ROBERT

James B. Duke project (69 pages, permission required, also at *Duke University NC*) *Columbia University NY*

MAYES, HERBERT RAYMOND (1900–)

Journalism lectures (29 pages, permission required to cite or quote) *Columbia University NY*

MAYHEW, HOUSTON
U.S. veteran of Vietnam War

(1972) *Fisk University TN*

MAYNARD, LEONARD A. (1887–)
Chemist

Agricultural leaders project (1964, 114 pages, permission required to cite or quote) *Cornell University NY*

MAYNOR, DOROTHY
Concert artist; Teacher

(1971) *Fisk University TN*

MAYO, LEONARD W. (1899–)

Chairman, President's panel on mental retardation; Executive director, Association for the Aid of Crippled Children

Association for the Aid of Crippled Children (71 pages, permission required) *Columbia University NY*

Health science collection (54 pages, permission required, also at *National Library of Medicine MD*) *Columbia University NY*

MAYO CLINIC
Mayo Clinic Foundation MN

MAYO INSTITUTIONS
Mayo Clinic Foundation MN

MAYOR, A. HYATT (1901–)
Curator; Author

(1969, 63 pages) *Archives of American Art—Smithsonian Institution NY*

MAYS, EUGENE

Communications Workers of America collection *University of Iowa Libraries*

MAZIA, FREDKA
Tel-Aviv teacher

ANTECEDENTS TO THE STATE OF ISRAEL: (2) "Brichah" (organized escape) (Hebrew, 37 pages, open) *Hebrew University, Israel*

MAZLUBATI, MOSHE
Tel-Aviv shopkeeper

HISTORY OF THE YISHUV (PALESTINIAN JEWRY): (6) Ha-Poel Ha-Mizrachi movement in Palestine (Hebrew, 50 pages with a deposition of 2 pages in writing attached, open) *Hebrew University, Israel*

MAZO, EARL (1919–)

Eisenhower administration project (52 pages, closed during interviewee's lifetime, also at *Dwight D. Eisenhower Library KS*) *Columbia University NY*

MAZUCA, MITCHELL F.
United Steelworkers of America member

(1967, 39 pages) *Pennsylvania State University*

MAZUR, PAUL MYER (1892–)

Federated Department Stores project (59 pages, permission required) *Columbia University NY*

MBOYA, THOMAS
Minister of Labor, Minister of Justice and Constitutional Affairs, Kenya

(8 pages, open) *John F. Kennedy Library MA*

MEAD, GENEVIEVE NICHOLS
Smith alumna, class of 1949; Community service volunteer

(1973, 2 hours, 27 pages) *Smith College MA*

MEAD, MARGARET (1901–)

Journalism lectures, Forum I (permission required to cite or quote) *Columbia University NY*

MEADE, EDWARD

Children's Television Workshop (14 pages, open) *Columbia University NY*

MEADER, GEORGE

Assistant counsel, Special U.S. Senate committee investigating the National Defense Program (1943–1945)

Harry S. Truman Library MO

MEADER, RALPH G.
National Institutes of Health MD

MEAKINS, MR. AND MRS. HARLEY

South Dakota experience (1971), South Dakota Oral History Project *University of South Dakota*

MEANY, GEORGE (1894–)
President, AFL-CIO

Herbert H. Lehman project (13 pages, permission required to cite or quote) *Columbia University NY*

(53 pages, open) *John F. Kennedy Library MA*

Discussed in Columbia University interviews with Nelson Hale Cruikshank; William Hammatt Davis

Discussed in Sangamon State University IL Mining and John L. Lewis collection

MEANS, HELEN HOTCHKIN
Smith alumna, class of 1919; President, Girl Scouts of America

(1973, 1 hour, 20 pages) *Smith College MA*

MEARA, FRANK S.

Discussed in Columbia University interview with Connie Myers Guion

MECHAM, J. LLOYD
Special projects *Baylor University TX*

MELTZER, NANCY (MRS. LEO) (1922–)

Perception of change in Ithaca school district project (1973, 26 pages, 35 minutes, permission required to cite or quote transcript or to use tape) *Cornell University NY*

MELVILLE, WARD

Historic preservation *Charles B. Hosmer, Jr. Collection IL*

MEMPHIS, TENNESSEE

Memphis Public Library and Information Center TN

Memphis State University TN

MENCKEN, AUGUST (1889–1967)

Engineer; Author

(1958, 150 pages, permission required) *Columbia University NY*

MENCKEN, H. L.

Discussed in Columbia University interviews with Mildred Gilman; Ben W. Huebsch; Alfred A. Knopf; Ellen Coyne (Mrs. Edgar Lee) Masters; August Mencken; J. Hamilton Owens; George Samuel Schuyler; and in Forest History Society collection

MENDEL, DAVID JACOB

South Dakota experience (1970), South Dakota Oral History Project *University of South Dakota*

MENDELS, MORTON M. (1908–)

Lawyer

World Bank (1961, 76 pages, permission required to cite or quote, also at *Brookings Institution DC*) *Columbia University NY*

MENDES FRANCE, PIERRE (1907–)

Former prime minister, France

Dulles oral history collection (1964, 46 pages, permission required to cite or quote; may not be copied in any form) *Princeton University NJ*

MENNONITES

Schowalter collection on conscientious objection during World War I (250 hours) *Bethel College KS*

MENON, KRISHNA

Discussed in Columbia University interviews with Roger Nash Baldwin; Charles D. Cook; Brij Mohan Kaul

MENSER, CLARENCE L.

Former NBC vice-president in charge of programming

(1965, 2 reels, 57 pages) *Broadcast Pioneers Library DC*

MENTAL HEALTH

Mental health care changes (9 hours, 224 pages, open) *Sangamon State University IL*

See also Psychology

MENZIES, COLIN, JR.

Mill Valley Public Library CA

MERCHANDISING *see* Retail Trade

MERCHANT, LIVINGSTON TALLMADGE (1903–)

U.S. government official; Diplomat

Eisenhower administration project (1967, 86 pages, permission required to cite or quote, also at *Dwight D. Eisenhower Library KS*) *Columbia University NY*

Marshall Plan (3 pages, permission required to cite or quote) *Columbia University NY*

(194 pages, portions closed) *John F. Kennedy Library MA*

Dulles oral history collection (1965, 107 pages, Section I, permission required to cite, quote, or copy in any form; Sections II–IV, permission required to read, cite, quote, or copy in any form) *Princeton University NJ*

MERIALDO, BERNARDO

Eureka County NV pioneer

Discussed in University of Nevada, Reno, Peter Merialdo interview

MERIALDO, PETER (1899–)

Insurance agent; Politician

(1967, 149 pages, permission required) *University of Nevada, Reno*

MERIDITH, JAMES

Missouri political figure

(14 pages, open) *John F. Kennedy Library MA*

University of Southern Mississippi

MERIDOR, YAAKOV

Owner, Tel-Aviv fruit transport company

HISTORY OF THE YISHUV (PALESTINIAN JEWRY): (7) Etzel and Lehi organizations (Hebrew, 333 pages, open) *Hebrew University, Israel*

MERKLE, EDWARD ARROL (1909–)

Financial executive

(1968, 106 pages, permission required) *Columbia University NY*

MEROM (MERIMOVITZ), YITZHAK

Histadrut official

WORLD WAR II: THE HOLOCAUST—RESISTANCE AND RESCUE: (15) Contacts between the Yishuv (Palestinian Jewry) and U.S.S.R. during W.W. II (Hebrew, 7 pages, open) *Hebrew University, Israel*

MERRIAM, ROBERT EDWARD (1918–)

Business executive

Eisenhower administration project (1969, 209 pages, permission required, also at *Dwight D. Eisenhower Library KS*) *Columbia University NY*

MERRICK, MR. AND MRS. E. R.

James B. Duke project (70 pages, permission required, also at *Duke University NC*) *Columbia University NY*

MERRICK, SAMUEL

Former special assistant, Office of Legislative Liaison, U.S. Department of Labor

(129 pages, permission of interviewee required) *John F. Kennedy Library MA*

MERRIL, MARCELLUS, AND GERALDINE MERRIL

(1971) *State Historical Society of Colorado*

MERRILL, ELMER DREW

Hunt Institute for Botanical Documentation PA

MERRILL, LARUUE HENDRICKS

Ricks College ID

MERRILL, MALCOLM H. (1903–)

Public health administrator; Bacteriologist

(1972, 153 pages) *University of California, Berkeley*

MERRITT, MRS. ORRIN

South Dakota experience (1970), South Dakota Oral History Project *University of South Dakota*

MERRITT, RALPH PALMER (1883–1963)

Comptroller and regent, University of California

(1962, 137 pages) *University of California, Berkeley*

University history collection (open), *University of California, Los Angeles*

MERSON, MARTIN (1906–)

Former consultant, IIA

Dulles oral history collection (1966, 59 pages, open, may not be copied in any form) *Princeton University NJ*

MERWIN, LORING CHASE (1906–1972)

Adlai E. Stevenson project (55 pages, permission required) *Columbia University NY*

MESERVE, FREDERICK HILL (1865–1962)

Lincoln collector

(1953, 96 pages, open) *Columbia University NY*

MESSER, THOMAS (1920–)

Museum director

(1970, 31 pages) *Archives of American Art—Smithsonian Institution NY*

MESSERSCHMITT, WILLY (1898–)

Aviation collection (14 pages, permission required to cite or quote, also at *United States Air Force Academy CO* and *University of the Air, Maxwell Air Force Base AL*) *Columbia University NY*

METADOR LAND & CATTLE COMPANY, LTD.

Ranching collection *Texas Tech University*

METAL WORKERS

Pennsylvania State University

Swedes in North America *Swedish Pioneer Historical Society IL*

South Dakota experience, South Dakota Oral History Project *University of South Dakota*

University of Texas, Arlington

Afro-American study; Japanese-American study; Jewish-American study *University of Washington Libraries WA*

Harbin Jews *Western Jewish History Center CA*

See also Discrimination; Segregation

MINOW, NEWTON NORMAN (1926-)
Lawyer; Federal Communications Commission chairman

Adlai E. Stevenson project (1969, 122 pages, permission required) *Columbia University NY*

MINOW, NEWTON NORMAN
with Regulatory Agencies Panel

(187 pages, portions closed) *John F. Kennedy Library MA*

MINSHALL, WILLIAM E.
Cleveland State University Library OH

MINSTER, LEONARD
Federated Department Stores project (26 pages, permission required) *Columbia University NY*

MINTENER, BENJAMIN D.
South Dakota experience (1970), South Dakota Oral History Project *University of South Dakota*

MINTENER, JAMES BRADSHAW (1902-)
Lawyer

Eisenhower administration project (1968, 65 pages, closed during interviewee's lifetime, also at *Dwight D. Eisenhower Library KS*) *Columbia University NY*

MISSIONS AND MISSIONARIES
China missionaries collection. Participants and pages: Netta Powell Allen, 83; James Chamberlain Baker, 26; Earl Cranston, 130; Rowland McLean Cross, 200 (*certain pages closed*); Helen Dizney, 23; Leslie and Mary Fairfield, 75; Edward Pearce Hayes, 23; Clarence H. Holleman, 95; Lyda Suydam Houston, 79; Lydia Johnson, 38; Francis Price Jones, 69; Lucile Williams Jones, 47; Alice Clara Reed, 122; Roderick Scott, 113; Marjorie Rankin Steurt, 33; George Thomas Tootell, 34; William Hill Topping, 25; Martha Wiley, 106; Pearl Fosnot Winans, 47 (1969-1971, 1368 pages, open, also at *Columbia University NY*) *Claremont Graduate School CA*

MISSISSIPPI
Mary Holmes College MS

Citizens Council *Millsaps College MS*

Elections of 1955, 1959, 1963 *Millsaps College MS*

Mississippi politics since 1930 *Millsaps College MS*

Ole Miss Crisis of 1962 *Millsaps College MS*

John C. Stennis collection *Mississippi State University*

University of Southern Mississippi

MISSISSIPPI CIVIL RIGHTS ADVISORY COUNCIL
Millsaps College MS

MISSOURI
Daviess County Library MO

University of Missouri, St. Louis

MITCHEL, JOHN PURROY
Discussed in Columbia University interviews with Frederic René Coudert; Bertram D. Cruger; Frances Perkins; Louis Heaton Pink; Morris Lincoln Strauss

MITCHELL, BROADUS (1892-)
Economic historian

Southern intellectual leaders (165 pages, closed pending publication of a study) *Columbia University NY*

MITCHELL, CLARENCE
Director, Washington bureau, NAACP

(48 pages, open) *John F. Kennedy Library MA*

MITCHELL, DR. EDWIN
Civil rights leader

(1972) *Fisk University TN*

Race Relations Information Center TN

MITCHELL, GEORGE S.
Discussed in Columbia University interview with Broadus Mitchell

MITCHELL, GEORGE WILDER (1904-)

Adlai E. Stevenson project (37 pages, permission required) *Columbia University NY*

MITCHELL, HARRY LELAND (1906-)
Union official

(1957, 191 pages, also microfiche, permission required to cite or quote) *Columbia University NY*

MITCHELL, HUGH B.
University of Washington Libraries WA

MITCHELL, JAMES P. (1900-1964)
Former U.S. Secretary of Labor

Dulles oral history collection (1964, 20 pages, open) *Princeton University NJ*

MITCHELL, JOSEPH (1875-)
Discussion of late 1800s and life as Adirondack guide (2-3 cassettes, open) *Plattsburgh State University College NY*

MITCHELL, LUCY SPRAGUE (1878-1967)
Educator

(1962, 174 pages, also at *Columbia University NY*) *University of California, Berkeley*

MITCHELL, MORRIS
Discussed in Columbia University interview with Broadus Mitchell

MITCHELL, RALPH JOHNSON (1891-1970)
Lieutenant general, U.S. Marine Corps (service: 1915-1948)

(29 pages, open, also at *Columbia University NY* and *U.S. Naval Institute MD*) *United States Marine Corps DC*

MITCHELL, SAMUEL CHILES
Discussed in Columbia University interview with Broadus Mitchell

MITCHELL, STEPHEN ARNOLD (1903-)
Lawyer

Adlai E. Stevenson project (1967, 173 pages, permission required) *Columbia University NY*

MITCHELL, WESLEY CLAIR
Discussed in University of California, Berkeley, interview with Lucy Sprague Mitchell

MITCHELL, WILLIAM
Discussed in Columbia University interviews with Joseph James Clark; Jerome Clarke Hunsaker; John Francis Victory; Eugene Edward Wilson; and in Aviation collection; Henry H. Arnold project

MITCHELL, WILLIAM A.
Harvard University Graduate School of Business MA

MITCHELL, WILLIAM L. (1900-)
Deputy commissioner (1946-1959) and commissioner (1959-1961), Social Security Administration

Eisenhower administration project (84 pages, open, also at *Dwight D. Eisenhower Library KS*) *Columbia University NY*

Social Security collection (140 pages, open, also at *Social Security Administration MD*) *Columbia University NY*

MITCHELL, WILLIAM W.
Discussed in Columbia University interview with Eleanor Arnold

MITELMAN, ELIAHU
WORLD WAR II: THE HOLOCAUST—RESISTANCE AND RESCUE: (3) Jewish underground movement in wartime France (Hebrew, 3 pages, open) *Hebrew University, Israel*

MITELMAN, ELIAHU
with Eytan Ginat
WORLD WAR II: THE HOLOCAUST—RESISTANCE AND RESCUE: (3) Jewish underground movement in wartime France (Hebrew, 49 pages, open) *Hebrew University, Israel*

20

MORTIMER, WYNDHAM

Biographical collection (open) *University of California, Los Angeles*

MORTON, ALFRED H.

Former NBC vice-president

(1965, 1 reel, 22 pages) *Broadcast Pioneers Library DC*

MORTON, THRUSTON (1907–)

U.S. senator (Kentucky); Chairman, Republican national committee

(25 pages, open) *John F. Kennedy Library MA*

Dulles oral history collection (1966, 46 pages, open) *Princeton University NJ*

University of Kentucky

MOSBY, ARTHUR J.

Broadcast pioneer since 1925

(1966, 1 reel, 22 pages) *Broadcast Pioneers Library DC*

MOSCOW, WARREN (1908–)

Journalist

(1953, 83 pages, also microfiche, permission required to cite or quote) *Columbia University NY*

MOSES, CORAL
with S. Spring and Della Moses

University of Washington Libraries WA

MOSES, DELLA
with S. Spring and Coral Moses

University of Washington Libraries WA

MOSES, GENERAL LLOYD

South Dakota experience (1971), South Dakota Oral History Project *University of South Dakota*

MOSES, ROBERT

Discussed in Columbia University interviews with Stanley Myer Isaacs; Abraham Kazan; Paul O'Dwyer; William O'Dwyer; Joseph M. Proskauer; Emily Smith (Mrs. John) Warner

MOSES, SIEGFRIED

Former Israeli state controller; President, Central European Immigration Association

BIOGRAPHICAL INTERVIEWS (German, in process) *Hebrew University, Israel*

JEWISH COMMUNITIES: (1) German Jewry (1933–1935) (German, 7 pages, closed) *Hebrew University, Israel*

MOSHEATEL, REBECCA (MORHAIME)

University of Washington Libraries WA

MOSHER, CHUCK

Athletic boom in West Texas (open) *Texas Tech University*

MOSHER, FREDERIC A.

Discussed in Columbia University Carnegie Corporation collection

MOSHOWITZ, YITZHAK

YOUTH MOVEMENTS: (3) He-Halutz movement (Hebrew, 3 pages, open) *Hebrew University, Israel*

MOSKOWITZ, BELLE

Discussed in Columbia University interview with Emily Smith (Mrs. John) Warner

MOSS, FRANKLIN

Challenges to governance by students project (1969, 70 pages, open, but no copy to federal, state, or local agents without written permission) *Cornell University NY*

MOSS, HYRUM THOMAS

Ricks College ID

MOSS, JACK (1924–)

Businessman; Army veteran; Former "Lost Battalion" member

Prisoner-of-war project (1970, 60 pages, open) *North Texas State University Oral History Collection*

MOSS, JANIE McKINLEY

Ricks College ID

MOSS, JOHN

U.S. representative (California)

(19 pages, open) *John F. Kennedy Library MA*

MOSS, MAXIMILIAN

Discussed in Columbia University interview with William O'Dwyer

MOSSADEGH, MOHAMMED

Discussed in Columbia University interview with Morris M. Marcus

MOSSAFER, DAVID

University of Washington Libraries WA

MOSSBAUER, RUDOLF LUDWIG (1929–)

Nobel Laureates collection (38 pages, permission required) *Columbia University NY*

MOSSERI, MAZAL MATHILDE

JEWISH COMMUNITIES: (9) Jewish community in Egypt (Hebrew, 24 pages, open) *Hebrew University, Israel*

MOTHERWELL, ROBERT (1915–)

Painter

(1965, 11 pages) *Archives of American Art—Smithsonian Institution NY*

MOTLEY, CONSTANCE BAKER

Peggy Lamson collection *Arthur and Elizabeth Schlesinger Library MA*

MOTT, LUCRETIA

Discussed in Columbia University interview with Anna Lord Strauss

MOTTLE, RONALD M.

Cleveland State University Library OH

MOUDY, MARTHA

Communications Workers of America collection *University of Iowa Libraries*

MOUNT SINAI MEDICAL CENTER

Mount Sinai Hospital. Participants and pages: George Baehr, 36; Bryan Brooke, 46; Ralph Colp, 22; B. B. Crohn, 11; John Gerster, 21; Leon Ginzberg, 31; Abraham Hyman, 33; George James, 37; Hillard Jason, 49; Samuel Klein, 44; Percy Klingenstein, 29; Sylvan Manheim, 50; Hans Popper, 34; Coleman Rabin, 20; Martin Steinberg, 80; Joseph Turner, 37; Peter Vogel, 17; Harry Wessler, 15; Ashe Winkelstein, 23. Faculty Meetings, 269; Investitures: Morris P. Bender, 24; Kurt Hirschhorn, 24; George James, 26; Alan Eugene Kark, 14; Ralph Kaufman, 29; Hans Popper, 28; Memorial Dr. Garlock 15; Seminars, 148 (1965–1969, 1212 pages, permission required, also at *Mount Sinai Medical Center NY*) *Columbia University NY*

MOUNTIN, JOSEPH

Discussed in Columbia University interview with John B. Grant

MOVING PICTURE INDUSTRY

American Film Institute CA

Hollywood Center for the Audio-Visual Arts CA

An oral history of the motion picture in America (87 hours, 2869 pages, open except for Richard Huemer interview) *University of California, Los Angeles*

MOVING PICTURES

Motion picture and television collection *University of California, Los Angeles*

Interviews with James Kirkwood, Morgan Farley, Robert Warwick, and Ernest Truex, plus 300 general discussion tapes (6 hours, 300 pages, open), Cinema collection *University of Southern California Library*

MOVSHOWITZ, HENIA

YOUTH MOVEMENTS: (3) He-Halutz movement (Hebrew, 3 pages, open) *Hebrew University, Israel*

MOY, SEONG (1921–)
Painter; Printmaker

(1971, 34 pages) *Archives of American Art—Smithsonian Institution NY*

MOYE, EARL

Communications Workers of America collection *University of Iowa Libraries*

MOYNE, LORD

Discussed in Columbia University interview with James McCauley Landis

MUALLEM, DAVID

Cantor; Member, Ramleh Religious Council

JEWISH COMMUNITIES: (10) Jewish life in Iraq (Hebrew, translated from Arabic, 50 pages, open) *Hebrew University, Israel*

MURO DE NADAL, FRANCISCO (1908–)
Businessman

Argentina in the 1930s (1971, Spanish, 59 pages, open) *Columbia University NY*

MURPHEY, BOB (1921–)
Attorney; Former sergeant-at-arms, Texas House of Representatives

(1969, 75 pages, open) *North Texas State University Oral History Collection*

MURPHY, CHARLES
Former Under-secretary of Agriculture

(31 pages, open) *John F. Kennedy Library MA*

MURPHY, CHARLES F.

Discussed in Columbia University interviews with Arthur Krock; Ferdinand Pecora; Herbert Claiborne Pell

MURPHY, CHARLES J. V. (1904–)
Editor; Writer

Dulles oral history collection (1966, 28 pages, closed until Dulles's official papers are open) *Princeton University NJ*

MURPHY, CHARLES SPRINGS (1909–)
Special presidential assistant (1947–1950); Special counsel to the President (1950–1953)

James Lawrence Fly project (13 pages, closed until January 1, 1982) *Columbia University NY*

Harry S. Truman Library MO

MURPHY, DONALD RIDGWAY (1895–)
Farm Holiday Association (32 pages, open) *Columbia University NY*

MURPHY, FRANK

Assian Sweet murder trial in Detroit *University of Michigan*

Discussed in Columbia University interview with Gordon Evans Dean

MURPHY, FRANKLIN MURPHY (1916–)

Discussed in University of California, Los Angeles, Andrew Jackson Hamilton interview (University history collection)

MURPHY, GEORGE
University of Michigan

MURPHY, JAMES
Massachusetts political figure

(23 pages, open) *John F. Kennedy Library MA*

MURPHY, JAY
Civil rights in Alabama (1964, 20 pages, open) *Columbia University NY*

MURPHY, KATHERINE PRENTIS (1882–1969)
Art collector

(1957, 50 pages, open) *Columbia University NY*

MURPHY, MATTHEW J. (1920–)
McGraw-Hill, Inc. (43 pages, permission required) *Columbia University NY*

MURPHY, RENA ELNIMA WHITMAN
South Dakota experience (1970), South Dakota Oral History Project *University of South Dakota*

MURPHY, ROBERT D. (1894–)
Former Under-secretary of State for political affairs

Eisenhower administration project (45 pages, permission required to cite or quote, also at *Dwight D. Eisenhower Library KS*) *Columbia University NY*

Dulles oral history collection (1965, 83 pages, open) *Princeton University NJ*

MURPHY, WILLIAM PARRY (1892–)
Nobel Laureates collection (37 pages, permission required) *Columbia University NY*

MURRAY, GEORGE WELWOOD

Discussed in Columbia University interview with Harrison Tweed

MURRAY, JAMES
U.S. senator

Discussed in Columbia University interview with William Reidy

MURRAY, JAMES P. (1892–)
Aviation collection (36 pages, permission of interviewee required to cite or quote, also at *United States Air Force Academy CO* and *University of the Air, Maxwell Air Force Base AL*) *Columbia University NY*

MURRAY, MAE (–1965)
Popular arts collection (28 pages, open) *Columbia University NY*

MURRAY, PHILIP

Discussed in Columbia University interviews with John Brophy; Edwin A. Lahey; Lee Pressman

Discussed in several Pennsylvania State University interviews, including those with Philip Curran and David J. McDonald

MURRAY, ROBERT K.

American historians collection (114 pages, permission required to cite or quote) *Columbia University NY*

MURRAY, TOM
United Steelworkers of America assistant to Walter Burke, Pittsburgh

(1967, 37 and 21 pages) *Pennsylvania State University*

MURROW, EDGAR R.

Discussed in Guilford College Library NC J. Edgar Murrow interview

MURROW, J. EDGAR
Uncle of Edgar R. Murrow

Guilford College Library NC

MURTAUGH, JOSEPH STUART (1912–)
Health science collection (44 pages, permission required, also at *National Library of Medicine MD*) *Columbia University NY*

MUSEUMS

Archives of American Art—Smithsonian Institution NY

Arts in Columbus (1960–1970) *Ohio Historical Society*

MUSHIER, CAROLE
Associate professor of physical education

Collective bargaining at SUNY project (1973, 43 minutes) *Cornell University NY*

MUSIC, AFRICAN
Fisk University TN

MUSIC, AMERICAN
Fisk University TN

Archives of traditional music *Indiana University*

Arts in Columbus (1960–1970) *Ohio Historical Society*

"Big Band" era *Texas Tech University*

Peter Yates interview, Fine arts collection *University of California, Los Angeles*

Yale University School of Music CT

MUSIC, BAROQUE

Alice Ehlers interview, Fine arts collection *University of California, Los Angeles*

MUSIC, BLACK *see* Black music

MUSIC, JEWISH

Rose Rinder interview, Northern California Jewish Community series (1971, 185 pages, permission required, also at *University of California, Berkeley*) *Western Jewish History Center CA*

MUSICIANS
University of Louisville KY

See also Pianists

MUSICA, PHILIP

Discussed in Columbia University interview with Edmund Delong

MUSKIE, EDMUND
U.S. senator (Maine)

(111 pages, permission of interviewee required) *John F. Kennedy Library MA*

MUSSER, CHARLES RIPLEY (1911–)
Weyerhaeuser Timber Company (27 pages, permission required) *Columbia University NY*

NOPPEN, LEONARD VAN
Discussed in Columbia University interview with Max Weber

NORBERG, DONALD
State chairman, Iowa Democratic party; Department of Agriculture official for congressional liaison

(27 pages, open) *John F. Kennedy Library MA*

NORDAHL, KONRAD
Chairman, Federation of Labor Unions (1939–), Norway

Harry S. Truman Library MO

NORMAN, ROBERT C.
Participant in battle of Wounded Knee

South Dakota experience (1963), South Dakota Oral History Project *University of South Dakota*

NORMAN, YITZHAK
JEWISH COMMUNITIES: (12) Jews of Bukhara (1900–1935) (Hebrew, 19 pages, open) *Hebrew University, Israel*

NORRIS, GEORGE
Discussed in Columbia University interview with Burton Kendall Wheeler

NORRIS, KATHLEEN (1880–1966)
Author

(1959, 264 pages) *University of California, Berkeley*

NORRIS, RALPH
Newspaper editor

Jennings County Public Library IN

NORRIS, STEWART (1912–)
Production executive, Stecher-Traung-Schmidt Corporation

(1969, 55 pages) *University of California, Berkeley*

NORSTAD, LAURIS (1907–)
Former Supreme Allied Commander in Europe, SHAPE

Dulles oral history collection (1967, 40 pages, open) *Princeton University NJ*

NORTH AMERICAN AVIATION, INC.
Wyndham Mortimer interview, Biographical collection *University of California, Los Angeles*

NORTH AMERICAN INDIANS *see Indians* of North America and Mexico

NORTH CAROLINA
Appalachian State University NC

Guilford College Library NC

University of North Carolina, Chapel Hill

University of North Carolina, Charlotte

NORTH CHURCH, BRIDGEWATER, SOUTH DAKOTA
75th Anniversary, South Dakota experience (1953), South Dakota Oral History Project *University of South Dakota*

NORTH COUNTRY REFERENCE AND RESEARCH RESOURCES COUNCIL
Indian affairs in northern New York (2 cassettes, open) *Plattsburgh State University College NY*

NORTH DAKOTA
Carnegie-Bookmobile ND

NORTHCLIFFE, LORD
Discussed in Columbia University interview with Sir Norman Angell

NORTHEASTERN STATE COLLEGE
Northeastern State College OK

NORTHROP, JOHN K.
Oral history project, National Air and Space Museum *Smithsonian Institution DC*

NORTHROP, JOHN T.
Aviation industry (Lockheed Bros.); Santa Barbara reminiscences *University of California, Santa Barbara*

NORTHWESTERN MUTUAL LIFE INSURANCE COMPANY
Marquette University Archives WI

NORTON, CLEMENT
Massachusetts political figure

Boston Public Library MA

(28 pages, open) *John F. Kennedy Library MA*

NORTON, HORTON (1883–)
(1964, 24 pages, open) *Cornell University NY*

NORTON, JOHN KEELEY (1893–)
Educator

(1963, 270 pages, permission required until March 1, 1975) *Columbia University NY*

NORTON, WILLIAM JOHN (1883–)
Social worker

(1954, 67 pages, open) *Columbia University NY*

NOSS, MR. AND MRS. LUTHER
Yale faculty colleagues and friends of Paul Hindemith (composer)

Hindemith project (1973) *Yale University School of Music CT*

NOTESTEIN, ADA COMSTOCK
Smith alumna, class of 1897; Educator; Administrator

(1973, 1 hour, 23 pages) *Smith College MA*

NOTTI, ROBERT
Democratic campaign (1960) organizer; Regional director of administration, Housing and Home Finance Agency (Chicago)

(33 pages, open) *John F. Kennedy Library MA*

NOURSE, DR. EDWIN G. (1883–)
Agricultural economist

(1968, 798 pages) *Cornell University NY*

NOVAK, ROBERT
Social Security collection (46 pages, closed during interviewee's lifetime, also at *Social Security Administration MD*) *Columbia University NY*

NOVINSKY, STANLEY M.
Wisconsin teacher

ANTECEDENTS TO THE STATE OF ISRAEL: (2) "Brichah" (organized escape) (English, 6 pages, open) *Hebrew University, Israel*

NOVOTNY, FRANK
Communications Workers of America collection *University of Iowa Libraries*

NOYES, BLANCHE
Aviation collection (68 pages, permission required to cite or quote; also at *United States Air Force Academy CO* and *University of the Air, Maxwell Air Force Base AL*) *Columbia University NY*

NTOYI, MARY
South African centenarian

(1972) *Fisk University TN*

NUCLEAR ENERGY *see* Atomic Energy

NUGENT, ELLIOTT (1900–)
Popular arts collection (85 pages, open) *Columbia University NY*

NUGENT, RICHARD
Discussed in Columbia University Occupation of Japan collection

NUNBERG, H.
Discussed in Columbia University interview with Willi Hoffer

NUNN, LINDSAY, AND GILMORE NUNN
Owners, WLEX (Lexington KY)

(1967, 2 reels) *Broadcast Pioneers Library DC*

NUNNERLY, DAVID
British-American relations during the 1960s (transcripts and notes of interviews with 64 British and American political and diplomatic leaders; permission of Dr. Nunnerly required) *John F. Kennedy Library MA*

NURICK, LESTER
World Bank (35 pages, closed during interviewee's lifetime, also at *Brookings Institution DC*) *Columbia University NY*

NURIEL, ASHER
JEWISH COMMUNITIES: (10) Jewish life in Iraq (Hebrew, 26 pages, open) *Hebrew University, Israel*

O'DONNELL, PHILLIP KENNETH
(1924–   )
Social Security collection (40 pages, permission required, also at *Social Security Administration MD) Columbia University NY*

O'DWYER, PAUL (1907–   )
Lawyer; Politician
New York political studies collection, Brooklyn politics (1930–1950) (1962, 245 pages, permission required) *Columbia University NY*

O'DWYER, WILLIAM (1890–1964)
Former New York mayor
New York political studies collection, Brooklyn politics (1930–1950) (1962, 1783 pages, permission required) *Columbia University NY*

Discussed in Columbia University interviews with Samuel J. Battle; Harry James Carman; Justin N. Feldman; Jonah J. Goldstein; Stanley Myer Isaacs; Solomon A. Klein; Reuben Avis Lazarus; Frederick Charles McLaughlin; Warren Moscow; Paul O'Dwyer; Laurence Arnold Tanzer

OFRI, AHRON
Israeli ambassador to Central African Republic
ANTECEDENTS TO THE STATE OF ISRAEL: (2) "Brichah" (organized escape) (Hebrew, 60 pages, open) *Hebrew University, Israel*

O'GARA, ROGER W.
National Institutes of Health MD

OGDEN, MICHAEL J. (1911–   )
Journalism lectures, Forum II (permission required to cite or quote) *Columbia University NY*

OGDEN, ROLLO
Discussed in Columbia University interview with Allan Nevins

OGG, OSCAR (1909–1971)
Book-of-the-Month Club collection (25 pages, open) *Columbia University NY*

OGLE, HAROLD H.
Weyerhaeuser Timber Company (47 pages, permission required) *Columbia University NY*

OGLE, MARBURY B., JR.
Dean, Purdue University School of Humanities, Social Science, and Education
(1970, in preparation) *Purdue University Archives IN*

O'HAIR, MADALYN M.
Religion and culture project *Baylor University TX*

O'HARE, JOHN (1881–   )
Labor unionist

(1957, 108 pages, also microfiche, permission required to cite or quote) *Columbia University NY*

OHIO
Ohio Historical Society

OHIO—POLITICS AND GOVERNMENT
City Club of Cleveland Debates *Cleveland State University Library OH*
The governor's office *Ohio Historical Society*
Ohio political parties since 1945 *Ohio Historical Society*
Life of Kingsley A. Taft *Ohio Historical Society*

OHIO STATE UNIVERSITY
The arts in Columbus, 1960–1970 *Ohio Historical Society*

OIEN, CARL
South Dakota experience (1970), South Dakota Oral History Project *University of South Dakota*

OKADA, KENZO (1902–   )
Painter
(1968, 22 pages) *Archives of American Art—Smithsonian Institution NY*

OKAZAKI, KATSUO (1897–1965)
Former Japanese foreign minister
Dulles oral history collection (1964, 31 pages, open) *Princeton University NJ*

O'KELLY, JAMES R. (JAKE)
Former master control engineer, NBC
(1965, 1 reel, 12 pages) *Broadcast Pioneers Library DC*

OKLAHOMA
Northeastern State College OK
Oklahoma Christian College
Tulsa County Historical Society OK
University of Oklahoma
University of Oklahoma Medical Center OK

OKLAHOMA CITY, OKLAHOMA
Oklahoma Christian College

OKTAVEK, RICHARD
Painter of "Baltimore screens"
(1972, in preparation) *Maryland Historical Society*

OLCOTT, DR. CHARLES T.
(1968, 32 pages) *Cornell University NY*

OLD STANLEY HISTORY SOCIETY
South Dakota experience (1966), South Dakota Oral History Project *University of South Dakota*

OLDENBURG, CLAES (1929–   )
Sculptor
(1965, 36 pages) *Archives of American Art—Smithsonian Institution NY*

OLDER, CHARLES
Flying Tigers (38 pages, permission required to cite or quote) *Columbia University NY*

OLIPHANT, HERMAN
Discussed in Columbia University interview with Edward Samuel Greenbaum

OLIPHANT, PAUL, AND F. C. SOWELL
Radio pioneers collection (32 pages, open) *Columbia University NY*

OLIVER, HARRY
Art director
An oral history of the motion picture in America (open) *University of California, Los Angeles*

OLIVER, "KING" JOE
Tulane University LA

OLIVER, MARIA ROSA (1904–   )
Author
Argentina in the 1930s (1971, Spanish, 57 pages, open) *Columbia University NY*

OLIVER, R. J.
Captain, U.S. Navy (Ret.); Flag lieutenant to Commander Cruiser Division 5 (1942)
(2 hours, 55 pages) *United States Naval War College RI*

OLIVER, RUTH LAW (1891–1970)
Aviation collection (33 pages, permission required to cite or quote, also at *United States Air Force Academy CO* and *University of the Air, Maxwell Air Force Base AL*) *Columbia University NY*

OLIVER, WILLIAM
Chief clerk for Warren
Earl Warren oral history project (in process) *University of California, Berkeley*

OLIVEY, ALEXANDER P. (1866–   )
Benedum and the oil industry (43 pages, open) *Columbia University NY*

OLMAN, ADOLPH
Popular arts collection (29 pages, open) *Columbia University NY*

OLMO, HAROLD P.
Wine (in process) *University of California. Berkeley*

OLMSTED, MILDRED SCOTT
Smith alumna, class of 1912; Women's suffragist; Recipient, SANE 1972 peace award
(1973, 2 hours, 51 pages) *Smith College MA*

OLNEY, GEORGE J. (1890–   )
Food processor; Machinery manufacturer
(1964, 69 pages, permission required to cite or quote) *Cornell University NY*

OLNEY, MARY McLEAN (1873–1965)
(1963, 169 pages) *University of California. Berkeley*

Eisenhower administration project (1967, 41 pages, permission required to cite or quote, also at *Dwight D. Eisenhower Library KS*) *Columbia University NY*

ORPIN, MR. AND MRS. EDGAR
Historic preservation in Nantucket (1969, 58 pages, most open) *Cornell University NY*

ORR, JAMES
Communications Workers of America collection *University of Iowa Libraries*

ORTMAN, GEORGE (1926–)
Painter
(1963, 143 pages) *Archives of American Art—Smithsonian Institution NY*

ORTNER, MOSHE
JEWISH COMMUNITIES: (1) German Jewry (1933–1935) (German, 57 pages, open) *Hebrew University, Israel*
(1950, 136 pages, also microfiche, permission required to cite or quote) *Columbia University NY*

OSBORN, FREDERICK (1889–)
Corporation executive; Public figure
Carnegie Corporation collection (1967, 140 pages, permission required) *Columbia University NY*
Dulles oral history collection (1966, 21 pages, open) *Princeton University NJ*

OSBORNE, LITHGOW (1892–)
Diplomat
(1953, 228 pages, also microfiche, permission required to cite or quote) *Columbia University NY*

OSBY, WILLIAM C., SR.
University of Michigan

OSBY, WILLIAM J.
Challenges to governance by students project (1970, 145 pages, permission required) *Cornell University NY*

OSLER, SIR WILLIAM
Discussed in Columbia University interview with Joseph Collins

OSSIA, SHMUEL
Engineer, Mekorot (Tel-Aviv)
ANTECEDENTS TO THE STATE OF ISRAEL: (3) "Ha'apalah" (illegal immigration) (Hebrew, 97 pages, open) *Hebrew University, Israel*

OSSORIO, ALFONSO (1916–)
Painter
(1968, 34 pages) *Archives of American Art—Smithsonian Institution NY*

OSTERBERG, ARNOLD E.
National Institutes of Health MD

OSTERHAUS, HUGO
Discussed in Columbia University interview with Walter Stratton Anderson

OSTHIMER, HARRY (–1972)
(1972) *Wabash Carnegie Public Library IN*

OSTROFF, ISIDOR
Independence National Historical Park (40 pages, permission required) *Columbia University NY*

OTENASEK, DR. MILDRED (1914–)
National Democratic committee member (1956–1973); President, United Democratic Women's Clubs of Maryland (1955–); Instructor
(1972, 38 pages, open) *Maryland Historical Society*

OTEY, EDITH
Widow of Flem B. Otey III, Nashville
(1973) *Fisk University TN*

OTEY, FLEM B., III
Nashville businessman
(1973) *Fisk University TN*

OTEY, INMAN
Nashville businessman
(1973) *Fisk University TN*

OUMANSKY, DAVID
WORLD WAR II: THE HOLOCAUST—RESISTANCE AND RESCUE: (6) Rescue of Jewish children (Hebrew, 58 pages, open) *Hebrew University, Israel*

OUNGRE, LOUIS (–1966)
JEWISH COMMUNITIES: (7) Jewish life in Latin America (French, 28 pages, open) *Hebrew University, Israel*

OURAY, CHIEF
University of Utah

OUTLAND, GEORGE
Democratic party leader, opposed Warren; U.S. congressman (Santa Barbara)
Earl Warren oral history project (in process) *University of California, Berkeley*

OVADIA, ALBERT
University of Washington Libraries WA

OVERTON, DOUGLAS
Occupation of Japan (51 pages, permission required to cite or quote) *Columbia University NY*

OWEN, CHANDLER
Discussed in Columbia University interviews with Asa Philip Randolph; George Samuel Schuyler

OWENS, DANIEL E.
Nashville broadcaster
(1972) *Fisk University TN*

OWENS, J. HAMILTON (1888-1967)
Editor
(1958, 70 pages, open) *Columbia University NY*

OWENS, J. STANLEY
University of Connecticut

OWENS, JESSE
Illinois State Historical Library

OWENS, WILLIAM A.
Folklorist; Historian; Author
Scott E. Webber Collection NY

OWINGS, DORSEY
Retired field representative, BMI
Radio pioneers collection (1963, 16 pages, also at *Broadcast Pioneers Library DC*) *Columbia University NY*

OYER, EDWIN B.
Challenges to governance by students project (1969, 70 pages, permission required to cite or quote) *Cornell University NY*

OZARK MOUNTAINS
Folk culture of the central Ozarks *Memphis State University TN*

P

P.A.
Jewish refugee (Spain); American Jewish Joint Distribution Committee member (Spain)
WORLD WAR II: THE HOLOCAUST—RESISTANCE AND RESCUE: (2) Rescue of Jews via Spain and Portugal (Hebrew, 4 pages, based on a Spanish conversation, open) *Hebrew University, Israel*

PAAMONI, JOSEPH (–1965)
HISTORY OF THE YISHUV (PALESTINIAN JEWRY): (7) Etzel and Lehi organizations (Hebrew, 50 pages, open) *Hebrew University, Israel*

PAARLBERG, DON (1911–)
Official, U.S. Department of Agriculture; Educator
Eisenhower administration project (1968, 164 pages, permission required, also at *Dwight D. Eisenhower Library KS*) *Columbia University NY*

PACE, GLENN W. (1920–)
U.S. Army veteran; "Lost Batallion" member
(1972, 28 pages, open) *North Texas State University Oral History Collection*

PACH, AVRAHAM
Former Dutch He-Halutz member
WORLD WAR II: THE HOLOCAUST—RESISTANCE AND RESCUE: (2) Rescue of Jews via Spain and Portugal (Hebrew, 20 pages, open) *Hebrew University, Israel*

PACIFIC ISLANDS *see* Islands of the Pacific

PARISIUS, HERBERT W. (1895–   )
U.S. government official

(1954, 226 pages plus papers, closed until 5 years after interviewee's death) *Columbia University NY*

Discussed in Columbia University interviews with Samuel B. Bledsoe; Gardner Jackson

PARK, HELEN VAN CLEAVE
Mill Valley Public Library CA

PARK, LUELLA WILDING
Ricks College ID

PARK, ROBERT E.
Discussed in Fisk University TN Margaret Park Redfield interview

PARK COLLEGE
Park College MO

PARKER, A. REEVE
Challenges to governance by students project (1969, 46 pages, permission required) *Cornell University NY*

PARKER, ALFRED
Former school teacher; Author; Vollmer's biographer

August Vollmer collection (1972, 10 pages) *University of California, Berkeley*

PARKER, DOROTHY ROTHSCHILD (1893–1967)

Popular arts collection (20 pages, open) *Columbia University NY*

Writers and authors collection *University of Southern California Library*

PARKER, HORATIO
Discussed in Columbia University interview with Roger Huntington Sessions

PARKER, JAMES
Associate professor of sociology and anthropology

Collective bargaining at SUNY project (1973, 19 minutes, 13 pages) *Cornell University NY*

PARKER, RACHEL NEELY
Smith alumna, class of 1930; Social worker

(1973, 2 hours, 42 pages) *Smith College MA*

PARKER, RALPH CHANDLER (1883–   )
U.S. naval officer

Naval history collection (1963, 146 pages, also at *Division of Naval History DC*) *Columbia University NY*

PARKER, WALT (1918–   )
Builder; Farmer-rancher; Democratic member, Texas House of Representatives (Denton)

Legislative project (1970, 31 pages; 1971, 53 pages; closed until 2 years after interviewee leaves political office) *North Texas State University Oral History Collection*

PARKHURST, NELSON M.
Administrator, Purdue University

(1970, in preparation) *Purdue University Archives IN*

PARKIN, GEORGE RALEIGH (1896–   )
Business executive

Carnegie Corporation collection (1968, 152 pages, permission required) *Columbia University NY*

PARKINSON, MRS. E. BLISS
Art collector

(1970, 48 pages) *Archives of American Art—Smithsonian Institution NY*

PARRAN, THOMAS (1896–1968)
Health science collection (133 pages, permission required, also at *National Library of Medicine MD*) *Columbia University NY*

PARRIOTT, FOSTER BROOKS (1878–1957)
Benedum and the oil industry (30 pages, open) *Columbia University NY*

PARSONS, BETTY (1900–   )
Art dealer; Collector; Artist

(1969, 35 pages) *Archives of American Art—Smithsonian Institution NY*

PARSONS, ELSIE CLEWS
Anthropologist
University of Utah

PARSONS, GEOFFREY (1879–1956)
Journalist; Lawyer

(1949, 26 pages, open) *Columbia University NY*

PARSONS, LOUELLA O. (1893–1972)
Popular arts collection (35 pages, open) *Columbia University NY*

PARSONS, M. R.
(1962) *State Historical Society of Colorado*

PARSONS, TALCOTT (1902–   )
Carnegie Corporation collection (41 pages, permission required) *Columbia University NY*

PARTON, JAMES (1912–   )
Publisher; Editor

(1959, 24 pages, open) *Columbia University NY*

Discussed in Columbia University interview with Oliver Jensen

PARTRIDGE, MRS. ALBERT
South Dakota experience (1971), South Dakota Oral History Project *University of South Dakota*

PASEUR, HERB
Caudill, Rowlett & Scott, Oral business history project *University of Texas, Austin*

PASSMAN, CHARLES
HISTORY OF THE YISHUV (PALESTINIAN JEWRY): (1) Jewish private sector in Palestine (Hebrew, 17 pages, open) *Hebrew University, Israel*

WORLD WAR II: THE HOLOCAUST—RESISTANCE AND RESCUE: (1) The Joint (American Jewish Joint Distribution Committee) (Hebrew, 17 pages, open) *Hebrew University, Israel*

PATT, JOHN FRANCIS (1905–1971)
(1 reel, 13 pages) *Broadcast Pioneers Library DC* Radio pioneers collection (73 pages, open, also at *Broadcast Pioneers Library DC*) *Columbia University NY*

PATTBERG, EMIL (1910–   )
with George Martin
World Bank (25 pages, open, also at *Brookings Institution*) *Columbia University NY*

PATTERSON, AUDREY
Communications Workers of America collection *University of Iowa Libraries*

PATTERSON, BRADLEY H., JR.
U.S. government official

Eisenhower administration project (65 pages, permission required to cite or quote, also at *Dwight D. Eisenhower Library KS*) *Columbia University NY*

(57 pages, open) *John F. Kennedy Library MA*

PATTERSON, EDGAR
Warren's chauffeur; Family aide

Earl Warren oral history project (in process) *University of California, Berkeley*

PATTERSON, ELLIS ELWOOD
Government and politics collection (Open) *University of California, Los Angeles*

PATTERSON, GEORGE
Staff representative, United Steelworkers of America, District 33 (Duluth MN)

(1967, 65 pages) *Pennsylvania State University*

PATTERSON, GEORGE, AND DOROTHY PATTERSON

(1967, 15 pages) *Pennsylvania State University*

PATTERSON, HUGH BASKIN, JR. (1915–   )

Eisenhower administration project (85 pages, closed during interviewee's lifetime, also at *Dwight D. Eisenhower Library KS*) *Columbia University NY*

PATTERSON, JOHN MALCOLM (1921–   )
Lawyer; Alabama governor

(46 pages, portions closed) *John F. Kennedy Library MA*

Independence National Historical Park (47 pages, permission required) *Columbia University NY*

PETERSON, CURT
Former employee, McCann Erickson

(1968, 1 reel, 21 pages) *Broadcast Pioneers Library DC*

PETERSON, ESTHER
Peggy Lamson collection *Arthur and Elizabeth Schlesinger Library MA*

PETERSON, HOUSTON (1897–)
Educator

(1967, 398 pages, permission required) *Columbia University NY*

PETRI, LOUIS A. (1912–)
Wine industry executive

(1971, 67 pages) *University of California, Berkeley*

PETRIE, DANIEL

Radio pioneers collection (48 pages, open) *Columbia University NY*

PETROLEUM INDUSTRY AND TRADE
Benedum and the oil industry. Participants and pages: John Charles Adams, 32; William W. Arnold, 15; Darwin Benedum, 6; James Claxton Benedum, 16; Michael Late Benedum, 144; Paul Benedum, 87; Sophie and Pearl Benedum, 30; Charles E. Beyer, 38; Al A. Buchanan, 14; Clem S. Clarke, 17; A. B. Dally, Jr., 36; Margaret E. Davis, 71; John W. Dieringer, 13; Bascom Giles, 18; William Morris Griffith, 22; Walter Simms Hallanan, 63; Houston Harte, 37; Harry B. Hickman, 26; David Dean Johnson, 42; Caswell S. Jones, Thomas J. Newlin and Alex U. McCandless, 18; William J. Jones, 22; Winchester Kelso, 13; W. B. Lane and Roy Gardner, 44; Charles A. McClintock, 11; Will E Odom, 16; Alexander P. Olivey, 43; Foster B. Parriott, 30; Andrew Donaldson Robb, 13; Ovid Daniel Robinson, 71; Frank B. Shepard, 17; Tom Slick, 38; Ernest A. Stiller, 14; Milton E. Witherspoon, 8 (1951, 1085 pages, open) *Columbia University NY*

Oklahoma Christian College

Oil industry collection (15 hours, 210 pages, open) *Texas Tech University*

Tulsa County Historical Society OK

University of Texas, Arlington

Oral history of the Texas oil industry, University of Texas Archives *University of Texas, Austin*

PETTUS, TERRY
University of Washington Libraries WA

PETUCHOWSKI, YAAKOV
Professor of Jewish studies, Hebrew Union College

JEWISH COMMUNITIES: (5) Jewish nationalism and the Reform movement in the United States (English, 22 pages, open) *Hebrew University, Israel*

PETWAY, CARLTON
Attorney; Councilman

(1973, in process) *Fisk University TN*

PEVZNER, AVIGDOR

JEWISH COMMUNITIES: (12) Jews of Bukhara (1900–1935) (Hebrew, 9 pages, open) *Hebrew University, Israel*

PEWETT, JAMES W.
Challenges to governance by students project (1969, 46 pages, permission required) *Cornell University NY*

PEYSER, JEFFERSON E.
Attorney

(1973, 70 pages) *University of California, Berkeley*

PEYTON, CORSE
Discussed in Columbia University interview with Richard Gordon

PFAEHLER, RICHARD
James B. Duke project (20 pages, permission required, also at *Duke University NC*) *Columbia University NY*

PFANN, GEORGE R.
Challenges to governance by students project (1969, 41 pages, open) *Cornell University NY*

PFEIFFER, LOUIS
John Robert Gregg project (17 pages, permission required) *Columbis University NY*

PFEIFFER, OMAR TITUS (1895–)
Major general. U.S. Marine Corps (service: 1917–1950)

(1968, 461 pages, open, also at *Columbia University NY* and *U.S. Naval Institute MD*) *United States Marine Corps DC*

PFEIFFER, TIMOTHY N. (1886–)
Classmate of John Foster Dulles

Dulles oral history collection (1965, 7 pages, permission required to cite or quote) *Princeton University NJ*

PFEIFFER, WILLIAM LOUIS (1907–)
New York political studies collection, New York election of 1949 (9 pages, permission required to cite or quote) *Columbia University NY*

PHELPS, RALPH A., JR.
Religion and culture project *Baylor University TX*

PHILANTHROPY *see* Charities

PHILBRICK, OTIS (1888–)
Painter; Printmaker

(1971, 14 pages) *Archives of American Art—Smithsonian Institution NY*

PHILIPPINE ISLANDS
William Jarvis Carr interview, Government and politics collection *University of California, Los Angeles*

Verne Dyson interview, Biographical collection *University of California, Los Angeles*

Frank Murphy oral history project *University of Michigan*

PHILLIPS, SAMUEL COCHRAN (1921–)
General, U.S. Air Force; Director, NASA Apollo program (1964–1969)

National Aeronautics and Space Administration DC

PHILLIPS, DR. ALICE
Careers of New England women in medicine *Arthur and Elizabeth Schlesinger Library MA*

PHILLIPS, BRAD
(1952, 1 reel) *Broadcast Pioneers Library DC*

PHILLIPS, HERBERT
Political editor, Sacramento *Bee*, during Warren's governorship

Earl Warren oral history project (in process) *University of California, Berkeley*

PHILLIPS, KATHRYN SISSON (1879–1968)
Educator

(1962, 98 pages, also microfiche, permission required to cite or quote) *Columbia University NY*

PHILLIPS, REUBEN
Conductor; Director

(1972) *Fisk University TN*

PHILLIPS, WILLIAM (1878–1968)
Diplomat

(1951, 165 pages, also microfiche, permission required to cite or quote) *Columbia University NY*

PHILLIPS, WILLIAM F.

South Dakota experience (1971, South Dakota Oral History Project *University of South Dakota*

PHILOSOPHY

Claremont Graduate School CA

Southern Illinois University

PHLEGER, HERMAN (1890–)
Former legal adviser, State Department

Dulles oral history collection (1964, 96 pages, permission required to cite or quote) *Princeton University NJ*

PHOTOGRAPHERS

Archives of American Art—Smithsonian Institution NY

George Hoyingen-Huene interview *University of California, Los Angeles*

PIUS XII, POPE
German military opposition to Hitler *Harold C. Deutsch Collection DC*

PLA, ALFREDO *see Jamie Bran*

PLANT, ELTON M. (1903–   )
Radio pioneers collection (45 pages, open) *Columbia University NY*

PLANT, THOMAS G. (1889–   )
American-Hawaiian steamship company (1956, 84 pages, closed during interviewee's lifetime also at *University of California Institute of Industrial Relations) University of California, Berkeley*

PLATE, CHARLES
Member, local 2599, Bethlehem Steel Corp.
(1968, 7 pages) *Pennsylvania State University*

PLATT, ALEXANDER B.
Columbia crisis of 1968 (41 pages, permission required) *Columbia University NY*

PLAYER, DR. WILLA
Educator
(1972) *Fisk University TN*

PLIMPTON, FRANCIS TAYLOR PEARSONS (1900–   )
Deputy U.S. representative to the United Nations
Adlai E. Stevenson project (74 pages, permission required) *Columbia University NY*
(73, pages, open) *John F. Kennedy Library MA*

PLOTKIN, HARRY
James Lawrence Fly project (36 pages, closed until January 1, 1982) *Columbia University NY*

PLOWDEN, EDWIN NOEL
Chairman, Economic Planning Board
(1947–1953), Great Britain *Harry S. Truman Library MO*

PLUMMER, MRS. HENRY S.
Mayo Clinic Foundation MN

PLYLER, JOHN LANEY (1894–   )
James B. Duke project (78 pages, permission required, also at *Duke University NC) Columbia University NY*

POAGE, W. R. (BOB)
Special projects *Baylor University TX*

POCOCK, MARY AGARD
Hunt Institute for Botanical Documentation PA

POETRY
Poets on their poetry collection. Participants and pages: Gregory N. Corso, 131; James Dickey, 42; James Wright, 29 (1972, 202 pages, permission required) *Columbia University NY*

Fisk University TN
Tacoma Public Library WA

POHORILES, HENRY
M.J.S. member and A.J. member (Nice)
WORLD WAR II: THE HOLOCAUST—RESISTANCE AND RESCUE: (3) Jewish underground movement in wartime France (French, 33 pages, open) *Hebrew University, Israel*

POINDEXTER, ELINOR
Art dealer; Collector
(1970, 15 pages) *Archives of American Art—Smithsonian Institution NY*

POLES IN THE U.S.
Alliance College PA

POLETTI, CHARLES (1903–   )
Herbert H. Lehman project (32 pages, permission required to cite or quote) *Columbia University NY*

POLICAR, HARRY
University of Washington Libraries WA

POLICE
Chicago Police Department *Chicago State College IL*
See also Crime and Criminals

POLITICAL ECONOMY *see* Economics

POLITICAL PARTIES
Democratic-Farmer-Labor party (in Minnesota) *Minnesota Historical Society*
Farmer-Labor party *Minnesota Historical Society*
Democratic party: Paul Ziffren interview, Government and politics collection *University of California, Los Angeles*
Progressive party: Several interviews, Government and politics collection *University of California, Los Angeles*
Fred W. Stover Progressive party of 1948 materials (4 hours, 68 pages) *University of Iowa Libraries*
Democratic party in Michigan *University of Michigan*
Peace and Freedom party in the election of 1968 *University of Michigan*

POLITICAL SCIENCE
Fisk University TN
Development of the new left *State Historical Society of Wisconsin*
Government and politics collection (197 hours, 5978 pages, open except for Paul Ziffren interview) *University of California, Los Angeles*
University of Delaware
See also Law; Political Parties; Socialism

POLK, ERNEST
(4 tapes, not transcribed, open) *University of Texas, El Paso*

POLK, JAMES H.
General, U.S. Army
United States Army Military Research Collection PA

POLLACK, JEROME
Social Security collection (47 pages, closed during interviewee's lifetime, also at *Social Security Administration MD) Columbia University NY*

POLLOCK, JACKSON (1912–1956)
Painter
(1954, 3 pages) *Archives of American Art—Smithsonian Institution NY*

POLLOCK, ROBERT
Communications Workers of America collection *University of Iowa Libraries*

POLLOCK, WILLIAM (1899–   )
Union official
(1957, 74 pages, also microfiche, permission required to cite or quote) *Columbia University NY*

POLUNIN, NICHOLAS
Hunt Institute for Botanical Documentation PA

POLUGSHKO, ELIEZER
Member, Kibbutz Yagur
JEWISH COMMUNITIES: (4) Zionist movement in U.S.S.R. (1917–1935) (Hebrew, 23 pages, open) *Hebrew University, Israel*

POLYNESIA *see* Islands of the Pacific

POMBRIO, RALPH
Anecdotes re William H. Miner (open) *Plattsburgh State University College NY*

POMERANITZ, HILDA
Right Poale Zion member; C.D.J. member; Lecturer, University of Beer-Sheva
WORLD WAR II: THE HOLOCAUST—RESISTANCE AND RESCUE: (4) Jews in the underground in Belgium (Hebrew, 17 pages, open) *Hebrew University, Israel*

POMERANZ, HANS
Director, Military History Library, Tel-Aviv University

JEWISH COMMUNITIES: (1) German Jewry (1933–1935) (German, 35 pages, open) *Hebrew University, Israel*

POMEROY, KENNETH B.
Chief forester, American Forestry Association
(1968, 21 pages) *University of California, Berkeley*

POMONA, CALIFORNIA
Pomona Public Library CA

PROHIBITION
Southwest Minnesota State College

PROSKAUER, JOSEPH M. (1877–1971)
Judge

(1961, 141 pages, permission required) *Columbia University NY*

Joseph M. Proskauer project. Participants and pages: Albert Fiorello, 20; Jacob Goldberg, 26; Kate Pantell, 32; Joseph M. Proskauer, 141; James N. Rosenberg, 32; Abram S. Sacher, 21; Ruth Proskauer Smith, 27 (1966, 299 pages, permission required) *Columbia University NY*

PROSTITUTION
Several interviews. South Dakota experience, South Dakota Oral History Project *University of South Dakota*

PROXMIRE, WILLIAM
U.S. senator (Wisconsin)

(17 pages, open) *John F. Kennedy Library MA*

PRUDEN, WESLEY

(1972) *Fisk University TN*

PRUITT, CHARLES
Tennessee legislator

PRUSS, MAX (–1960)

Aviation collection (20 pages, permission required to cite or quote, also at *United States Air Force Academy CO* and *University of the Air, Maxwell Air Force Base AL*) *Columbia University NY*

PRYOR, DAVID
Arkansas Constitutional Revision collection *State College of Arkansas*

PRYOR, HAROLD J. (1920–   )

United Transportation Union project (1972, 57 pages, permission required) *Cornell University NY*

PSYCHIATRY
American Psychiatric Association DC

Careers of New England women in medicine *Arthur and Elizabeth Schlesinger Library MA*

Washington School of Psychiatry DC

PSYCHOANALYSIS
Psychoanalytic movement. Participants and pages: Michael Balint, 78; Edward Glover, 108; Heinz Hartmann, 145; Willi Hoffer, 116; Abram Kardiner, 712; Rudolf Loewenstein, 149; Sandor Rado, 317; Raymond de Saussure, 73; René Spitz, 104; *in process:* Margaret Mahler. Joseph Sandler (1963–1966, 1802 pages, individual restrictions apply) *Columbia University NY*

Los Angeles Psychoanalytic Society CA

See also Psychology

PSYCHOLOGY
Archives of the History of American Psychology OH

See also Psychoanalysis

PUBLIC HEALTH
Health science collection. Participants and pages: Ernest Allen, 77; Carl Baker, 172; W. Ray Bryan, 82; Leroy Burney, 46; George Robert Coatney, 90; L. T. Coggeshall, 52; Martin Cummings, 28; Warren Palmer Dearing, 95; Warren Draper, 77; Rolla Dyer, 24; Kenneth M. Endicott, 45; I. S. Falk, 79; Robert Felix, 63; Arthur B. Flemming, 42; Marion B. Folsom, 101; Victor Haas, 137; John R. Heller, 50; Herman E. Hilleboe, 147; Vane Hoge, 33; Mark D. Hollis, 58; James M. Hundley, 62; Carlyle Jacobson, 59; Charles V. Kidd, 59; Lawrence C. Kolb, 66; Alexander Langmuir, 56; Esmond R. Long, 119; Jack Masur, 30; Leonard W. Mayo, 54; Joseph Murtaugh, 44; Thomas Parran, 133; John R. Paul, 34; George Perrott, 58; David E. Price, 41; Leonard A. Scheele, 57; William H. Sebrell, Jr., 72; W. P. Shephard, 40; Wilson G. Smillie, 50; Roscoe Spencer, 142; Harold J. Stewart, 63; Frederick L. Stone, 41; Norman H. Topping, 64; C. J. Van Slyke, 63 (1962–1967, 2905 pages, permission required, also at *National Library of Medicine MD*) *Columbia University NY*

National Library of Medicine MD

University of California, San Francisco

See also Medical care

PUBLIC SCHOOLS
University of Delaware

PUBLIC WELFARE
Fisk University TN

Ohio Historical Society

Shirley Camper Soman Collection NY

PUBLISHERS AND PUBLISHING *see* Book-of-the-Month Club; McGraw Hill, Inc.

PUEBLO INDIANS
Doris Duke American Indian Oral History Project *Arizona State Museum*

PULITZER, JOSEPH, JR. (1885–1955)
Editor

(1954, 193 pages, permission required) *Columbia University NY*

PULLEN, DON "Q"
Musician

(1972) *Fisk University TN*

PULLEN, DR. THOMAS GRANVILLE
Educator; Administrator; State superintendent in Maryland and Virginia public schools

(1971, 7 hours, 121 pages, open) *Maryland Historical Society*

PUPIN, MICHAEL
Discussed in Columbia University interview with William Fondiller

PUR, DAVID
WORLD WAR II: THE HOLOCAUST—RESISTANCE AND RESCUE: (13) Underground activities of the Lithuanian Jews (Hebrew, 24 pages, open) *Hebrew University, Israel*

PURCELL, E. M.
Educator, Purdue University

(1970, in preparation) *Purdue University Archives IN*

PURCELL, EDWARD MILLS (1912–   )
Nobel Laureates collection (35 pages, permission required) *Columbia University NY*

PURCELL, ROBERT
Lear Siegler, Inc., Oral business history project *University of Texas, Austin*

PURCELL, ROBERT W. (1911–   )
Lawyer

Dulles oral history collection (1965, 43 pages, open) *Princeton University NJ*

PURDUE UNIVERSITY
Purdue University Archives IN

PURDY, LA ROY
Communications Workers of America collection *University of Iowa Libraries*

PURDY, LAWSON (1863–1959)
Lawyer; Civic worker

(1948, 47 pages, open) *Columbia University NY*

PURNELL, THOMAS F. (1905–   )
Asst. State Legislative Director

United Transportation Union project (1970, 78 pages, permission required to cite, quote, or use) *Cornell University NY*

PUSEY, NATHAN
President, Harvard University

(36 pages, open) *John F. Kennedy Library MA*

PUTNAM, WALLACE

(1973, 28 pages, permission required to cite or quote until his article is published, then open) *Cornell University NY*

PYE, LUCIEN (1921–   )
International negotiations project (32 pages, permission required) *Columbia University NY*

PYE, W. S.
Discussed in Columbia University interview with Harold C. Train

PYLE, GLADYS
Politician

South Dakota experience (1971), South Dakota Oral History Project *University of South Dakota*

PYLE, HOWARD (1906-), AND CHARLES F. MASTERSON
Eisenhower administration project (134 pages, closed during interviewee's lifetime, also at *Dwight D. Eisenhower Library KS*) *Columbia University NY*

PYUN YUNG TAI (1892-)
Former prime minister of Korea
Dulles oral history collection (1964, 22 pages, open) *Princeton University NJ*

Q

QUAKERS *see* Friends, Society of

QUALEY, CARLTON CHESTER (1904-)
Historian; Educator
(1968, 9 pages, permission required) *Columbia University NY*

QUECHAN INDIANS
Doris Duke American Indian Oral History Project *Arizona State Museum*

QUESADA, ELWOOD RICHARD (1904-)
Aviation collection (76 pages, permission required to cite or quote, also at *United States Air Force Academy CO* and *University of the Air, Maxwell Air Force Base AL*) *Columbia University NY*
Eisenhower administration project (89 pages, permission required to cite or quote, also at *Dwight D. Eisenhower Library KS*) *Columbia University NY*
Henry H. Arnold project (18 pages, permission required, also at *United States Air Force Academy CO*) *Columbia University NY*

QUIGG, MURRAY T. (-1956)
Theodore Roosevelt Association (28 pages, permission required to cite or quote) *Columbia University NY*

QUIGLEY, MARTIN JOSEPH (1890-)
Popular arts collection (26 pages, open) *Columbia University NY*

QUIGLEY, THOMAS
Director, Outpatient Clinic, Veterans Administration, Boston
(7 pages, open) *John F. Kennedy Library MA*

QUILL, MICHAEL
Discussed in Columbia University interview with William O'Dwyer

QUIMBY, THOMAS
Michigan political figure; Peace Corps director of recruitment
(60 pages, open) *John F. Kennedy Library MA*

QUINE, RICHARD (1920-)
Popular arts collection (35 pages, open) *Columbia University NY*

QUINN, JOHN
Discussed in Columbia University interview with Ben B. W. Huebsch

QUINN, JOHN ROBERTSON
Government and politics collection (open) *University of California, Los Angeles*

QUINN, RALPH M. (MEL)
Voice of America staff member
(1963, 1 reel, 21 pages) *Broadcast Pioneers Library DC*

QUITZOW, CHARLES
Quitzow-Dance in Berkeley (in process) *University of California, Berkeley*

QUITZOW, SULGWYNN
Quitzow-Dance in Berkeley (in process) *University of California, Berkeley*

QUITZOW, VOL
Quitzow-Dance in Berkeley (in process) *University of California, Berkeley*

R

RABB, MAXWELL M. (1910-)
Former presidential assistant and Cabinet secretary
Eisenhower administration project (38 pages, permission required, also at *Dwight D. Eisenhower Library KS*) *Columbia University NY*
Dulles oral history collection (1965, 42 pages, in process) *Princeton University NJ*

RABBITT, JOHN L. (1919-)
Chairman, B & M, UTU local T-311
United Transportation Union project (1971, 37 pages, permission required) *Cornell University NY*

RABEN, SHERWOOD
Grievance committee, local 2610, Baltimore
(1969, 10 pages) *Pennsylvania State University*

RABETZ, LEVI
Yuval-Gad Construction Company engineer
YOUTH MOVEMENTS: (2) Netzach in Latvia (Hebrew, 7 pages, open) *Hebrew University, Israel*

RABI, ISIDOR ISAAC (1898-)
Physicist
(In process) *Columbia University NY*
Nobel Laureates collection (44 pages, permission required) *Columbia University NY*
Discussed in Columbia University interview with Norman Ramsey

RABIN, BEN-ZION
JEWISH COMMUNITIES: (12) Jews of Bukhara (1900-1935) (Hebrew, 21 pages, open) *Hebrew University, Israel*

RABIN, COLEMAN BERLEY (1900-)
Mount Sinai Hospital (20 pages, permission required, also at *Mount Sinai Medical Center NY*) *Columbia University NY*

RABINOFF, MAX (1878-1966)
Impresario
(1963, 48 pages, open) *Columbia University NY*

RABINOWITZ (NEE SOLTZ), HANA
Holon teacher
WORLD WAR II: THE HOLOCAUST—RESISTANCE AND RESCUE: (13) Underground activities of the Lithuanian Jews (Hebrew, 24 pages, open) *Hebrew University, Israel*

RABINOWITZ, LEIB
Survey Department director (Northern District of Israel)
JEWISH COMMUNITIES: (3) Lithuanian Jewry between the two world wars (Hebrew, 42 pages, open) *Hebrew University, Israel*

RABINOWITZ, LOUIS (1887-1957)
Manufacturer; Philanthropist
(1957, 42 pages, also microfiche, permission required to cite or quote) *Columbia University NY*

RABINOWITZ, OSCAR (-1969)
YOUTH MOVEMENTS: (1) Jewish youth movements in Czechoslovakia (German, 40 pages, open) *Hebrew University, Israel*

RABINOWITZ, YITZHAK (-1968)
JEWISH COMMUNITIES: (4) Zionist movement in U.S.S.R. (1917-1935) (Hebrew, 124 pages, open) *Hebrew University, Israel*
WORLD WAR II: THE HOLOCAUST—RESISTANCE AND RESCUE: (15) Contacts between the Yishuv (Palestinian Jewry) and the U.S.S.R. during W.W. II (Hebrew, 105 pages, open) *Hebrew University, Israel*

RACHMAN (REICHIK), YAAKOV
WORLD WAR II: THE HOLOCAUST—RESISTANCE AND RESCUE: (8) Theresienstadt ghetto (Hebrew, 29 pages, open) *Hebrew University, Israel*

RADFORD, ARTHUR W. (1896-)
Former chairman, Joint Chiefs of Staff
Dulles oral history collection (81 pages, written permission required to read) *Princeton University NJ*
Discussed in Columbia University interviews with Joseph James Clark; Felix Budwell Stump

RADIO
(1950- , 140 hours, partially transcribed, 3965 pages, partially edited, most tapes tempo-

rarily restricted, some transcripts restricted) *Broadcast Pioneers Library DC*

Radio pioneers collection. Participants and pages: Ernest Frederick Werner Alexanderson, 61; Ed Allen, 7; Frank Atkinson Arnold, 101; Walter Ransom Gail Baker, 20; Harry Ray Bannister, 62; Howard Barlow, 213; Patrick Henry Barnes, 35; Joseph M. Barnett, 30; Gustave A. Bosler, 21; Everett L. Bragdon, 20; Harry P. Breitenbach, 10; William Wilbur Brown, 28; Lyman Lloyd Bryson, 254; Orestes Hampton Caldwell, 28; Joseph D. Cappa, 22; Phillips Carlin, 27; Abram Chasins, 89; Thomas Edward Clark, 38; Norman Corwin, 100; Louis Cowan, 225 *(permission required to cite or quote)*; Thomas H. Cowan, 119; Roderick Cupp, 12; Lee DeForest, 9; Richard K. Doan, 26; Glen Dolberg, 8; Lloyd Espenschied, 48; Walter Chew Evans, 65; Edgar Felix, 55; John Earl Fetzer, 115; Fred Friendly, 50; Robert Fuller, 13; Wayland Fullington, 24; John Gambling, 39; George Gingell, 14; Harry Goodman, 8; Dorothy Gordon, 168; Ben Grauer, 65; Gordon Gray, 2; Gordon Greb, 29; Rosaline Greene, 42; Wilton Gunzendorfer, 10; Raymond Frederick Guy, 78; Joseph Anthony Haeffner, 30; Kolin Hager, 36; Richard F. Hanser, 32; William E. Harkness, 99; Herschell Hart, 21; Laurence Ashley Hawkins, 28; William Saxby Hedges, 123; John E. Hill, 8; Lawrence LaMotte Holland, 25; Herbert Clark Hoover, 21; Albert Wallace Hull, 31; E. P. H. James, 17; Eddie Janis, 25; Arthur Judson, 25; William J. Kaland, 7; H. V. Kaltenborn, 248; Ken Kennedy, 2; Alfred Henry Kirchhofer, 21; Kirk Knight, 34; Chester Henry Lang, 29; Leon Lichtenfeld, 22; Donald G. Little, 101; Edgar J. Love, 15; Ruth Lyons, 7; Stanley Rutter Manning, 16; Carlton E. Morse and Michael Rafeto, 18; Ray Newby, 38; Paul Oliphant and F. C. Sowell, 32; Dorsey Ownings, 16; John F. Patt, 73; Daniel Petrie, 48; James A. Pike, 18; Elton M. Plant, 45; Herbert Ponting, 10; Robert L. Pratt, 7; Harry Rasky, 42; Philip H. Reisman, 60 *(permission required to cite or quote)*; Lord John Reith, 25; Bruce Robertson, 15; Otis E. Robinson, 17; William N. Robson, 41; Manuel Rosenberg, 8; John Harold Ryan, 7; Abel Alan Schechter, 33; William Edmund Scripps, 33; Robert L. Shayon, 41; John L. Slaton, 7; Robert Smiley, 18; Ira D. Smith and Fred J. Hart, 82; Sigmund Spaeth, 121; Jeff Sparks, 60; Davidson Taylor, 82; Sybil True, 23; Edwin Lloyd Tyson, 32; Clyde D. Wagoner, 34; James Truman Ward, 10; Gene Waters, 8; Irving Reid Weir, 31; Grover A. Whalen, 27; Rex G. White, 19; William Cummings White, 20; Mark Woods, 120; William R. Yates, 50 (1950–   , 4789 pages, open except as noted) *Columbia University NY*

Mass Communications History Center *State Historical Society of Wisconsin*

See also James Lawrence Fly; Dan Golenpaul; Carl Haverlin; William Paley; Frank Stanton

RADO, SANDOR (1890–1972)
Psychoanalyst

Psychoanalytic movement (1965, 317 pages, permission required to cite or quote) *Columbia University NY*

RADRIZZI, MAURICE F.
State legislative board member

United Transportation Union project (1972, 100 pages, special permission required) *Cornell University NY*

RAFETTO, MICHAEL
with Carlton E. Morse

Radio pioneers collection (18 pages, open, also at Broadcast Pioneers Library DC) *Columbia University NY*

RAFT, GEORGE

Black St. Louis leaders collection *University of Missouri, St. Louis*

RAILROADS

History of the railroad in east Texas *East Texas State University*

Southern Utah State College Library

University of Wisconsin, River Falls

RAINEY, HOMER P. (1896–   )
Former president, University of Texas; Professor of higher education, University of Colorado

(1967, 205 pages, open) *North Texas State University Oral History Collection*

RAIRDON, HORACE

Communications Workers of America collection *University of Iowa Libraries*

RAISH, EDGAR (1887–   )

(1965, 119 pages, open) *Cornell University NY*

RALKOWSKI, HENRY
University of Washington Libraries WA

RAM, YITZHAK
Israeli police officer (Tel-Aviv)

ANTECEDENTS to the STATE of ISRAEL: (2) "Brichah" (organized escape) (Hebrew, 52 pages, open) *Hebrew University, Israel*

RAMICONE, LUIS (1901–   )
Union official

Argentina in the 1930s (1971, Spanish, 43 pages, open) *Columbia University NY*

RAMMELL, ARTHUR LEON
Ricks College ID

RAMMELL, PEARL DANIELS
Ricks College ID

RAMSAY, ERNEST G. (1909–   )
Marine Fireman's Union port agent

RAMSAY, MRS. JOHN B., JR. (1904–   )
President, Baltimore League of Women Voters (1947–1951)

(1971, 2 hours, open) *Maryland Historical Society*

RAMSAY, NORMAN (1915–   )
Physicist

(1960, 358 pages, permission required) *Columbia University NY*

RANCH LIFE

Rancho Laguna de los Palos Colorados *Moraga Historical Society Archives CA*

Ranching collection (160 hours, 2400 pages, open) *Texas Tech University*

South Dakota experience, South Dakota Oral History Project *University of South Dakota*

RANDALL, CLARENCE B. (1891–   )
Former special presidential assistant on foreign economic policy

Dulles oral history collection (1966, 37 pages, permission required to cite or quote) *Princeton University NJ*

RANDALL, DUDLEY
Publisher; Poet; Librarian

(1972) *Fisk University TN*

RANDALL, PAUL
Director, Temple University Theater (1930–1969) *Temple University PA*

RANDALL, TONY

Popular arts collection (63 pages, open) *Columbia University NY*

RANDOLPH, ASA PHILIP (1889–   )
Labor leader

(In process) *Columbia University NY*

Black St. Louis leaders collection *University of Missouri, St. Louis*

Discussed in Columbia University interviews with Benjamin McLaurin; George Samuel Schuyler

RANDOLPH, JENNINGS (1902–   )
U.S. senator (West Virginia)

Social Security collection (15 pages, open, also at Social Security Administration MD) *Columbia University NY*

(15 pages, open) *John F. Kennedy Library MA*

RANK, OTTO

Discussed in Columbia University interviews with Abram Kardiner; Theodor Reik

RANKIN, GRADY
with Norman A. Cocke

James B. Duke project (41 pages, permission required, also at Duke University NC) *Columbia University NY*

RANKIN, JEANNETTE

Suffragist (in process) *University of California, Berkeley*

(1973, 48 pages) *University of California, Berkeley*

REID, CLEMENT
Discussed in Columbia University Association for the Aid of Crippled Children collection

REID, DR. INEZ SMITH
Educator; Author
(1972) *Fisk University TN*

REID, OGDEN ROGERS (1925–)
Congressman; U.S. ambassador; Editor
Eisenhower administration project (1967, 22 pages, permission required to cite or quote, also at *Dwight D. Eisenhower Library KS*) *Columbia University NY*
Dulles oral history collection (1967, 21 pages, permission required to cite or quote) *Princeton University NJ*

REID, RALPH WALDO EMERSON (1915–)
Eisenhower administration project (51 pages, permission required to cite or quote, also at *Dwight D. Eisenhower Library KS*) *Columbia University NY*

REIDY, WILLIAM
Social security collection (1966, 101 pages, open, also at *Social Security Administration MD*) *Columbia University NY*
Discussed in Columbia University interview with Harold Sheppard

REIK, THEODOR (1888–1969)
Psychoanalyst
(1965, 99 pages, also microfiche, permission required to cite or quote) *Columbia University NY*

REIFEL, BEN
South Dakota experience (1957), South Dakota Oral History Project *University of South Dakota*

REILLY, GEORGE
Member, Board of Equalization (35 years)
Earl Warren oral history project (in process) *University of California, Berkeley*

REILLY, JAMES
District of Columbia political figure; Member, Post Office Advisory Board
(7 pages, open) *John F. Kennedy Library MA*

REILLY, JEAN BURT
Motion picture and television collection (open) *University of California, Los Angeles*

REILLY, WALLACE C. (1898–1972)
Owner-editor, *Dallas Craftsman;* Former officer, International Typographical Union (Dallas local) and Texas State Federation of Labor
(62 pages, open) *University of Texas, Arlington*

REINHARDT, AD (1913–1967)
Painter
(1964, 28 pages, open) *Archives of American Art—Smithsonian Institution NY*

REINHARDT, G. FREDERICK (1911–)
U.S. ambassador to Italy
Dulles oral history collection (1965, 41 pages, permission required to cite or quote) *Princeton University NJ*

REINHARDT, GOTTFRIED
Popular arts collection (39 pages, open) *Columbia University NY*

REINSCH, J. LEONARD
White House radio advisor (1945–1952); Executive director, Democratic national convention (1960, 1964)
(59 pages, open) *John F. Kennedy Library MA*
Harry S. Truman Library MO

REINSTEIN, JACQUES J. (1911–)
Foreign Service officer
Dulles oral history collection (1966, 1967, 51 pages, permission required to cite or quote) *Princeton University NJ*

REIS, CLAIRE
Director, League of Composers
American music project (1973) *Yale University School of Music CT*

REISMAN, PHILIP H.
Radio pioneers collection (1968, 60 pages, permission required to cite or quote) *Columbia University NY*

REISNER, JOHN (1888–)
(1964, 10 pages, open) *Cornell University NY*

REITER, BELA Z. (1890–1957)
McGraw-Hill, Inc. (46 pages, permission required) *Columbia University NY*

REITH, LORD JOHN (–1971)
Radio pioneers collection (25 pages, open) *Columbia University NY*

REITSCH, HANNA
Aviation collection (44 pages, interviewee required to cite or quote, permission of interviewee required, also at *United States Air Force Academy CO* and *University of the Air, Maxwell Air Force Base AL*) *Columbia University NY*

REIWAN, GEORGE
Holon tailor
JEWISH COMMUNITIES: (10) Jewish life in Iraq (Hebrew, translated from Arabic. 15 pages, open) *Hebrew University, Israel*

RELIGION
Religion and culture project *Baylor University TX*
American Indian research project *University of South Dakota*
South Dakota experience, South Dakota Oral History Project *University of South Dakota*

RELIGIOUS EDUCATION
Hebrew University Israel
University of Notre Dame IN

RENNAHAN, RAY
Cinematographer, *Duel in the Sun*
An oral history of the motion picture in America (open) *University of California, Los Angeles*

RENO, MILO
Discussed in Columbia University Farm Holiday Association collection

RENOIR, JEAN (1894–)
Popular arts collection (23 pages, open) *Columbia University NY*

RENTSCHLER, FREDERICK B.
Discussed in Columbia University interview with Eugene Edward Wilson

REPETTO, VICTOR
Wine (in process) *University of California, Berkeley*

RESEK, BELLA
Mill Valley Public Library CA

RESNER, HERBERT
King, Conner, Ramsay defense attorney
Earl Warren oral history project (in process) *University of California, Berkeley*

RESNIK, NISSAN
Ramat-Gan accountant
WORLD WAR II: THE HOLOCAUST—RESISTANCE AND RESCUE: (13) Underground activities of the Lithuanian Jews (Hebrew, 33 pages, open) *Hebrew University, Israel*

RESTON, JAMES B. (1909–)
Journalist
Journalism lectures (46 pages, permission required to cite or quote) *Columbia University NY*
Dulles oral history collection (1965, 34 pages, open) *Princeton University NJ*

RETAIL TRADE
Federated Department Stores project (1965, 2911 pages, permission required) *Columbia University NY*

RETTIG, FRANK A.
(1973) *Wabash Carnegie Public Library IN*

REUSS, HENRY
U.S. representative (Wisconsin)
(97 pages, open) *John F. Kennedy Library MA*

REUTER, RICHARD
Executive director, CARE, Inc.; Director, Food for Peace
(27 pages, open) *John F. Kennedy Library MA*

REUTHER, WALTER
Discussed in Columbia University interviews with Edward Roland Annis; John Brophy; Nelson Hale Cruikshank; Lee Pressman; M. Hedley Stone; Rolland Jay Thomas

REUVENI, YAAKOV AND LUBA
Tel-Aviv lawyer
WORLD WAR II: THE HOLOCAUST—RESISTANCE AND RESCUE: (13) Underground activities of the Lithuanian Jews (Hebrew, 44 pages, open) *Hebrew University, Israel*

REYBURN, BERTIE RUTH PERRY
Ricks College ID

REYBURN, WILLIAM BAILEY
Ricks College ID

REYHER, REBECCA HOURWICH
Suffragist (in process) *University of California, Berkeley*

REYNOLDS, BARBARA FISHER
Smith alumna, class of 1961; Community service worker
(1971, 3 hours, 91 pages) *Smith College MA*

REYNOLDS, HORACE C. (1897-1969)
Sugar beet industry in New York State (1967, 40 pages, open) *Cornell University NY*

REYNOLDS, JACKSON E. (1873-1958)
Lawyer; Banker
(1949, 179 pages, also microfiche, permission required to cite or quote) *Columbia University NY*

REYNOLDS, WILLIAM A.
Social Security collection (61 pages, open, also at *Social Security Administration MD*) *Columbia University NY*

REYNOLDS, WILLIAM A., AND MILDRED WALK REYNOLDS
State Historical Society of Colorado

RHEE, SYNGMAN
Discussed in Columbia University interview with Walter Spencer Robertson

RHIND, FLORA MACDONALD (1904-)
Foundation officer
(1969, 1520 pages, permission required) *Columbia University NY*

RHODE ISLAND
Women in Rhode Island collection (14 hours) *Arthur and Elizabeth Schlesinger Library MA*
Rhode Island Department of State Library Services
University of Rhode Island

RHODEN, JOHN (1918-)
Sculptor
(1968, 33 pages) *Archives of American Art—Smithsonian Institution NY*

RHODES, ALFRED H., AND LEE MARTIN
Challenges to governance by students project: Student activism—Jackson State College (1971, 25 minutes; 1972, 18 pages; permission required) *Cornell University NY*

RHODES, GEORGE
South Dakota experience (1967), South Dakota Oral History Project *University of South Dakota*

RHODES, JAMES A.
Cleveland State University Library OH

RHODES, JOHN J.
U. S. congressman
Carl Hayden project *Arizona State University*

RIBAKOFF-DAGIM, ARIE
JEWISH COMMUNITIES: (12) Jews of Bukhara (1900-1935) (Hebrew, 20 pages, open) *Hebrew University, Israel*

RIBICOFF, ABRAHAM
Discussed in Columbia University interviews with Blue Carstenson; Nelson Hale Cruikshank; Irwin Wolkstein
(1961, 290 pages, permission required) *Columbia University NY*

RICE, MONSIGNOR CHARLES OWEN
Labor priest, Pittsburgh
(1967, 31 pages; 1968, 25 pages) *Pennsylvania State University*

RICE, CYRUS
Journalist, *The Milwaukee Sentinel*
(17 pages, open) *John F. Kennedy Library MA*

RICE, HAROLD E.
(1963) *State Historical Society of Colorado*

RICE, MARTIN P.
Discussed in Columbia University interview with Chester Henry Lang

RICE UNIVERSITY
Rice University TX

RICH, CLIFFORD S. (1895 or 1896-1973)
(1972, 114 pages, open transcript, permission required to reproduce tape) *Cornell University NY*

RICH, DANIEL CATTON (1904-)
Museum director
(1970, 38 pages) *Archives of American Art—Smithsonian Institution NY*

RICH, FRANCES
Smith alumna, class of 1931; Sculptor; Smith College public relations director
(1973, 4 hours, 96 pages) *Smith College MA*

RICHARD, AUGUSTE (1890-)
Robert P. Patterson project (23 pages, closed until January 1, 1980) *Columbia University NY*

RICHARDS, BERNARD G. (1877-1971)
Jewish leader
(1960, 360 pages, also microfiche, permission required to cite or quote) *Columbia University NY*
JEWISH COMMUNITIES: (6) American Jewry (English, 36 pages, open) *Hebrew University, Israel*

RICHARDS, BESSIE LAUNDER (1885-1969)
Mining town memories—Colorado and Mexico (1967, 115 pages) *University of California, Berkeley*

RICHARDS, DICKINSON W. (1895-)
Nobel Laureates collection (20 pages, permission required) *Columbia University NY*

RICHARDS, HOMER C.
Jackson Hole Preserve (53 pages, permission required) *Columbia University NY*

RICHARDS, JAMES P. (1894-)
Former U.S. congressman
Dulles oral history collection (1965, 40 pages, open) *Princeton University NY*

RICHARDS, MARGARET (1900-)
McGraw-Hill, Inc. (32 pages, permission required) *Columbia University NY*

RICHARDS, RICHARD
Presidential election of 1960 *University of Southern California Library*

RICHARDSON, ALMON T.
Newspaper publisher
(1962, 41 pages) *Los Angeles County Public Library System CA*

RICHARDSON, BERT
South Dakota experience (1971), South Dakota Oral History Project *University of South Dakota*

RICHARDSON, DOC
with Bob Blyer
Flying Tigers (21 pages, permission required to cite or quote) *Columbia University NY*

RICHARDSON, ELLIOT LEE (1920-)
Social Security collection (57 pages, permission required to cite or quote, also at *Social Security Administration MD*) *Columbia University NY*

RICHARDSON, HOLDEN C. (-1960)
Aviation collection (29 pages, permission required to cite or quote, also at *United States Air Force Academy CO* and *University of the Air, Maxwell Air Force Base AL*) *Columbia University NY*

RICHARDSON, IRA
Adams State College president
(1958) *State Historical Society of Colorado*

RICHARDSON, LEON J. (1868-1965)
Professor; Director of university extension
(1962, 248 pages, open) *University of California, Berkeley*

RICHARDSON, STEPHEN A. *see* Herbert Birch

RICHARDSON, WILLIAM
West Virginia political figure
(43 pages, open) *John F. Kennedy Library MA*

RICHMOND, CALIFORNIA
Richmond Public Library CA

RICHMOND, VIRGINIA
Historic preservation *Charles B. Hosmer, Jr. Collection IL*

RICHMOND PUBLIC LIBRARY, CALIFORNIA
Richmond Public Library CA

RICHTMYER, F. K.
Discussed in Columbia University Association of Physics Teachers collection

RICHTMYER, NELSON K.
National Institutes of Health MD

RICKENBACKER, EDWARD VERNON (1890-1973)
Aviation collection (1961, 19 pages, permission required to cite or quote, also at *United States Air Force Academy CO* and *University of the Air, Maxwell Air Force Base AL*) *Columbia University NY*
U.S. Air Force Academy project (19 pages, consult center for restriction, also at *United States Air Force Academy CO*) *Columbia University NY*

RICKEY, GEORGE (1908-)
Sculptor
(1968, 53 pages) *Archives of American Art—Smithsonian Institution NY*

RICKLES, JULIUS
University of Washington Libraries WA

RICKOVER, HYMAN
Chief, Bureau for Nuclear Propulsion, Bureau of Ships; Chief, Naval Reactors Branch, Atomic Energy Commission
(12 pages, open) *John F. Kennedy Library MA*

RICKS, THOMAS E.
Ricks College ID

RIDDLEBERGER, JAMES W. (1904-)
Diplomat
Dulles oral history collection (1965, 40 pages, open) *Princeton University NJ*

RIDELNIK, ISRAEL
An-Oved Publishing Company employee (Haifa)
ANTECEDENTS TO THE STATE OF ISRAEL: (2) "Brichah" (organized escape) (Hebrew, 37 pages, open) *Hebrew University, Israel*

RIDGWAY, MATTHEW B. (1895-)
General, U.S. Army
Dulles oral history collection (1964, 36 pages, open) *Princeton University NJ*
United States Army Military Research Collection PA

RIEGELHUTH, KATHERINE M. (1876-1973)
Educator
(1966, 57 pages, open) *University of Nevada, Reno*

RIESMAN, DAVID (1909-)
Carnegie Corporation collection (84 pages, permission required) *Columbia University NY*

RIFKIND, SIMON with Mr. Eno
Judge; Adviser on Jewish affairs to American Military Command (Europe) (1945-1964)
(1973, 1 hour, 16 pages) *Smith College MA*

RIGBY, ELEANOR GRANT
Smith alumna, class of 1918; College administrator
(52 pages, open) *Smith College MA*

RIGGS, JOSEPH
Edward Hull Crump and his regime *Memphis Public Library and Information Center TN*

RILEY, ARCH
West Virginia legislator; Vice-chairman, Ohio County Democratic executive committee
(52 pages, open) *John F. Kennedy Library MA*

RILEY, EDWARD
Independence National Historical Park (40 pages, permission required) *Columbia University NY*

RILEY, HOWARD W. (1879-)
Agricultural engineer
(1964, 48 pages, open) *Cornell University NY*

RILEY, LEO M. (1908-)
United Transportation Union project (1971, 52 pages, open) *Cornell University NY*

RINDER, REUBEN R.
Cantor for life, Temple Emanu-El, San Francisco CA
Discussed in Western Jewish History Center CA interview with Rose Rinder

RINDER, ROSE (1894-)
Widow of Cantor Reuben R. Rinder; Jewish communal affairs worker
Northern California Jewish Community series (1971, 185 pages, also at *University of California, Berkeley*) *Western Jewish History Center CA*

RINES, JOE
Pioneer orchestra leader; Agency executive
(1966, 3 reels, 57 pages) *Broadcast Pioneers Library DC*

RING, BLANCHE (1872-1961)
Popular arts collection (18 pages, open) *Columbia University NY*

RING, FRANCES
Discussed in Columbia University interview with Richard Gordon

RING, ROBERT A. (1913-)
Cassino official
(1972) *University of Nevada, Reno*

RINGLAND, ARTHUR C. (1882-)
Conservationist
(1970, 538 pages) *University of California, Berkeley*

RIOS, THEODORE
Doris Duke American Indian Oral History project *Arizona State Museum*

RIPMAN, HUGH
World Bank (29 pages, permission of interviewee required to cite or quote, also at *Brookings Institution DC*) *Columbia University NY*

RISSER, JOHN
Communications Workers of America collection *University of Iowa Libraries*

RIST, LEONARD BERNSTEIN (1905-)
Banker; Economist
World Bank (1961, 62 pages, open, also at *Brookings Institution DC*) *Columbia University NY*

RITCHIE, A. F. MILLER
Harwick College NY

RITCHIE, WARD
Printing and book trade collection (open) *University of California, Los Angeles*

RITOV, ISRAEL
JEWISH COMMUNITIES: (4) Zionist movement in U.S.S.R. (1917-1935) (Hebrew, 24 pages, open) *Hebrew University, Israel*
ANTECEDENTS OF THE STATE OF ISRAEL: (2) "Brichah" (organized escape) (Hebrew, 25 pages, open) *Hebrew University, Israel*

RITTER, ZEEV
Ministry of Defense employee (Haifa)

WORLD WAR II: THE HOLOCAUST—RESIS-TANCE AND RESCUE: (6) Rescue of Jewish children (Hebrew, 18 pages, open) *Hebrew University, Israel*

RIVERA, DIEGO
Discussed in Columbia University interview with Ben Shahn

RIVERBOATS
Jazzmen on the Mississippi *University of Missouri, St. Louis*

RIVERS, LARRY (1923–)
Painter

(1960, 8 pages; 1968, 21 pages) *Archives of American Art—Smithsonian Institution NY*

RIVLIN, JOSEPH JOEL
Professor

HISTORY OF THE YISHUV (PALESTINIAN JEWRY): (8) Revisionist "Ha-apalah" (illegal immigration) (Hebrew, 14 pages, open) *Hebrew University, Israel*

ROACH, HAL
Memories of a film career (1965, 45 pages) *Los Angeles County Public Library System CA*

ROADS
National Park Service Archives WV

ROBB, AGNES
University history (in process) *University of California, Berkeley*

ROBB, ANDREW DONALDSON
Bendum and the oil industry (13 pages, open) *Columbia University NY*

ROBB, JAMES
Former president, District 30, United Steel workers of America, Indianapolis

(1968, 47 pages; 1969, 42 pages) *Pennsylvania State University*

ROBB, MARGARET
Professor of physical education

Collective bargaining at SUNY project (1973, 56 minutes, 25 pages) *Cornell University NY*

ROBB, ROGER

National Labor Relations Board (1970, 19 pages, open) *Cornell University NY*

ROBBINS, FREDERICK CHAPMAN (1916–)
Nobel Laureates collection (37 pages, permission required) *Columbia University NY*

ROBBINS, MORRIS
University of Washington Libraries WA

ROBBINS, THOMAS H., JR.
Rear admiral, U.S. Navy (Ret.); President, Naval War College (1953–1954)

(3 hours, 58 pages) *United States Naval War College RI*

ROBBINS, WILLIAM JACOB
Hunt Institute for Botanical Documentation PA

ROBERTS, ANNA
University of Southern Mississippi

ROBERTS, CARSON ABLE (1905–)
Lieutenant general, U.S. Marine Corps (service: 1929–1964)

(128 pages, open, also at Columbia University NY and *U.S. Naval Institute MD) United States Marine Corps DC*

ROBERTS, CHALMERS McGEAGH (1910–)
Journalist

Eisenhower administration project (1967, 36 pages, permission required to cite or quote, also at *Dwight D. Eisenhower Library KS) Columbia University NY*

Dulles oral history collection (1966, 39 pages, open) *Princeton University NJ*

ROBERTS, CHARLES (1916–)
Newsweek contributing editor

Eisenhower administration project (35 pages, closed during interviewee's lifetime, also at *Dwight D. Eisenhower Library KS) Columbia University NY*

(58 pages, portion closed) *John F. Kennedy Library MA*

ROBERTS, CLIFFORD (1904–)
Business executive

Eisenhower administration project (1972, 878 pages, closed until 20 years after interviewee's death, also at *Dwight D. Eisenhower Library KS) Columbia University NY*

ROBERTS, EDDIE
Tennessee agrarian

(1972) *Fisk University TN*

ROBERTS, GEORGE
Copyist

Ives project (1969) *Yale University School of Music CT*

ROBERTS, MRS. GEORGE

Ives project (1969) *Yale University School of Music CT*

ROBERTS, MARCUS D.
Educator; Director of Purdue University Office of Counseling Services

(1970, 37 pages) *Purdue University Archives IN*

ROBERTS, O. D.
Administrator, Purdue University

(1970, in preparation) *Purdue University Archives IN*

ROBERTS, PAUL H.
Forestry (in process) *University of California, Berkeley*

ROBERTS, PAULUS
(1967) *State Historical Society of Colorado*

ROBERTSON, BRUCE
Radio pioneers collection (15 pages, open) *Columbia University NY*

ROBERTSON, JAMES
University of Southern Mississippi

ROBERTSON, WALTER SPENCER (1893–1970)
Diplomat

Eisenhower administration project (1967, 194 pages, permission required, also at *Dwight D. Eisenhower Library KS) Columbia University NY*

Dulles oral history collection (1965, 112 pages, in process) *Princeton University NJ*

ROBESON, PAUL
Discussed in Columbia University interview with David A. Morse

ROBINSON, ARTHUR H.
Geographer

(1972, 10 minutes) *Plymouth State College NH*

ROBINSON, BENJAMIN LINCOLN
Hunt Institute for Botanical Documentation PA

ROBINSON, BEVERLY RANDOLPH (1876–1951)
Lawyer

(1949, 95 pages, permission required to cite or quote) *Columbia University NY*

ROBINSON, E. A.
Discussed in Columbia University interviews with William Stanley Beaumont Braithwaite; John Hall Wheelock

ROBINSON, DR. FLORENCE C.
Musician; Composer

(1971) *Fisk University TN*

ROBINSON, FREDERICK B.
Discussed in Columbia University interview with Charles Henry Tuttle

ROBINSON, HAROLD
(1958) *State Historical Society of Colorado*

ROBINSON, HAROLD G.
Chief investigator, special U.S. senate committee investigating the national defense program (1941–1945)

Harry S. Truman Library MO

ROBINSON, HELEN R. ROOSEVELT
Theodore Roosevelt Association (35 pages, permission required to cite or quote) *Columbia University NY*

RODEWALD, DON AND WILFRED SCHAPER
Flying Tigers (40 pages, permission required to cite or quote) Columbia University NY

RODGERS, CLEVELAND (1885–1956)
Editor

(1950, 288 pages plus papers, open) Columbia University NY

RODGERS, HENRY L.
Judge

University of Southern Mississippi

RODGERS, KATHRYN
Smith alumna, class of 1970; Lawyer

(1973, 2 hours, 62 pages) Smith College MA

RODGERS, RICHARD (1902–)
Composer

(1968, 392 pages, permission required to cite or quote, certain pages closed during interviewee's lifetime) Columbia University NY

Theatre on film and tape New York Public Library at Lincoln Center

RODRIGUEZ, JUAN (1903–)
Union and government official

Argentina in the 1930s (1971, Spanish, 70 pages, open) Columbia University NY

RODRIGUEZ, LUIS MARIA
Railroad union official

Argentina in the 1930s (1970, Spanish, 21 pages, open) Columbia University NY

RODRIGUEZ, PEDRO (1914–)
Smelter worker; Member, United Steelworkers of America, Laredo local

(43 pages, open) University of Texas, Arlington

RODRIGUEZ-CABALLERO, RAFAEL LUCAS
Hunt Institute for Botanical Documentation PA

ROGERS, FORD OVID (1894–1972)
Major general, U.S. Marine Corps (service: 1917–1946)

(108 pages, open except for specific pages, also at Columbia University NY and U.S. Naval Institute MD) United States Marine Corps DC

ROGERS, GERALD W. (1926–)
State legislative director, UTU

United Transportation Union project (1970, 68 pages, permission required to cite or quote) Cornell University NY

ROGERS, HAROLD
Author; Professor of history

(1973) Fisk University TN

ROGERS, HENERY
North County collection (open) Plattsburgh State University College NY

ROGERS, JAMES GRAFTON
State Historical Society of Colorado

ROGERS, LINDSAY (1891–1970)
Political scientist

(1958, 106 pages; 1965, 21 pages; open) Columbia University NY

ROGERS, NORMAN J. (1928–)
Chairman, UTU local C-155

United Transportation Union project (1970, 25 pages, permission required to cite, quote, or reproduce) Cornell University NY

ROGERS, PAUL
U.S. representative (Florida)

(14 pages, open) John F. Kennedy Library MA

ROGERS, T. Y.
Civil rights in Alabama (60 pages, open) Columbia University NY

ROGERS, WILLIAM
Associate professor of physics

Collective bargaining at SUNY project (1973, 1 hour) Cornell University NY

ROGERS, WILLIAM P. (1913–)
Government official

Eisenhower administration project (1968, 51 pages, closed until 1977, also at Dwight D. Eisenhower Library KS) Columbia University NY

Discussed in Columbia University interview with Arthur Joseph Goldberg

ROGERS, WILLIAM WALTER (1893–)
Major general, U.S. Marine Corps (service: 1917–1946)

(99 pages, open, also at Columbia University NY and U.S. Naval Institue MD) United States Marine Corps DC

ROGNESS, ANNA TROEN
South Dakota experience (1970), South Dakota Oral History Project University of South Dakota

ROITMAN, ARIE (LEO)
Tel-Aviv engineer

WORLD WAR II: THE HOLOCAUST—RESISTANCE AND RESCUE: (2) Rescue of Jews via Spain and Portugal (Hebrew, 7 pages, open) Hebrew University, Israel

ROITMAN, JACQUES
Paris physician

WORLD WAR II: THE HOLOCAUST—RESISTANCE AND RESCUE: (2) Rescue of Jews via Spain and Portugal (French, 37 pages, with a further 9-page deposition in French, open) Hebrew University, Israel

ROITMAN, PAUL
Central figure, A.J.: Rabbi; Jewish Agency (Paris)

WORLD WAR II: THE HOLOCAUST—RESISTANCE AND RESCUE: (3) Jewish underground movement in wartime France (Hebrew, 33 pages, open) Hebrew University, Israel

ROLL, GEORGE ARTHUR (1913–)
Brigadier general, U.S. Marine Corps (service: 1935–1959)

(1968, 196 pages, open, also at Columbia University NY and U.S. Naval Institute MD) United States Marine Corps DC

ROLLINS, CHARLEMAE
Children's librarian; Author

(1972) Fisk University TN

ROLLINS, MABEL (1909–)
Economist

(1964, 107 pages, permission required) Cornell University NY

ROMAN, GISELE
WORLD WAR II: THE HOLOCAUST—RESISTANCE AND RESCUE: (6) Rescue of Jewish children (French, 28 pages, open) Hebrew University, Israel

ROMAN CATHOLIC CHURCH see Catholic Church in the U.S.

ROMANS, VIVIAN B.
Challenges to governance by students project: Student activism—Jackson State College (1970, 52 minutes, 37 pages, permission required to use, cite, or quote) Cornell University NY

ROMNEY, VERNON (1896–)
Robert A. Taft project (43 pages, permission required) Columbia University NY

ROMULO, CARLOS P. (1901–)
Former Philippine Secretary of Foreign Affairs

Brandeis University MA

Dulles oral history collection (1964, 48 pages, permission required to cite or quote) Princeton University NJ

RONALD, WILLIAM (1926–)
Painter

(1963, 37 pages) Archives of American Art—Smithsonian Institution NY

RONCALIO, TENO
Wyoming political figure

(65 pages, open) John F. Kennedy Library MA

RONDEAU, NOAH JOHN
Adirondack hermit

Adolph Dittmar interview Plattsburgh State University College NY

RONEN (ROSENBERG), YAAKOV
Former leader, Ha-Shomer, Ha-Tzair, (Slovakia)

RONEN (ROSENBERG), YAAKOV (cont.)

WORLD WAR II: THE HOLOCAUST—RESISTANCE AND RESCUE: (11) Jewish resistance in Slovakia (Hebrew, 53 pages; Hebrew, 42 pages; German, 33 pages; open) *Hebrew University, Israel*

ROOSA, ROBERT VINCENT (1918–   )
Banker

Eisenhower administration project (98 pages, closed during interviewee's lifetime; also at *Dwight D. Eisenhower Library KS*) *Columbia University NY*

Discussed in Columbia University interview with Prescott Bush

ROOSEVELT, ELEANOR (MRS. FRANKLIN D.) (1884–1964)

Herbert H. Lehman project (17 pages, permission required to cite or quote) *Columbia University NY*

Scott E. Webber Collection NY

Discussed in Columbia University interviews with Roger Nash Baldwin; Samuel J. Battle; Chester Bowles; Cass Canfield; Edward Costikyan; Jonathan Worth Daniels; Marion Dickerman; Virginia Foster Durr; Justin N. Feldman; Katharine F. Lenroot; Harold C. Train; Marietta (Mrs. Ronald) Tree; Wilson Watkins Wyatt

ROOSEVELT, FRANKLIN D.
Scott E. Webber Collection NY

Black St. Louis leaders collection *University of Missouri, St. Louis*

Discussed in Columbia University interviews with Horace Marden Albright; Will Winton Alexander; Orvil A. Anderson; Charles Ascher; William Stiles Bennet; Adolf Augustus Berle; Edward L. Bernays; Chester Bowles; Henry Bruere; Cass Canfield; Ewan Clague; Lucius DuBignon Clay; Jonathan Worth Daniels; Goldthwaite Higginson Dorr; Virginia Foster Durr; Thomas Irwin Emerson; Isidore Sydney Falk; James Aloysius Farley; John Philip Frey; Thomas Charles Hart; Frederick W. Henshaw; H. Kent Hewitt; Marvin Jones; Emory Scott Land; James McCauley Landis; Herbert Lehman; Walter Lippmann; Lewis L. Lorwin; Langdon Parker Marvin; Eugene Meyer; Frances Perkins; Omar Titus Pfeiffer; Joseph M. Proskauer; Samuel Irving Rosenman; John Roy Steelman; Henry Lewis Stimson; Francis Russell Stoddard; Norman Mattoon Thomas; Emily Smith (Mrs. John) Warner; Burton Kendall Wheeler; James Thomas Williams, Jr.; Milburn Lincoln Wilson; and in Socialist movement collection

Discussed in Sangamon State University IL Mining and John L. Lewis collection

ROOSEVELT, FRANKLIN, JR.
Discussed in Columbia University interview with John L. Lewis collection

ROOSEVELT, FRANKLIN D.
Discussed in Columbia University interview with Justin N. Feldman

ROOSEVELT, JAMES
Discussed in Columbia University interview with Gerald Carthrae Thomas

ROOSEVELT, THEODORE (1858–1919)
U.S. President

Theodore Roosevelt Association. Participants and pages: Karl Howell Behr, 19; William Merriam Chadbourne, 34; William Sheffield Cowles, 118; F. Trubee Davison, 7; Barclay H. Farr, 33; Stanley Myer Isaacs, 28; Jesse Langdon, 67; Samuel McCune Lindsay, 49; Alice R. Longworth, 41; Ezra Parmalee Prentice, 5; Murray T. Quigg, 28; Helen R. Roosevelt Robinson, 35; William Savacool, 30; Henry R. Stern, 21 (515 pages, permission required to cite or quote) *Columbia University NY*

Discussed in Columbia University interviews with George William Alger; Frederic Morgan Davenport; Goldthwaite Higginson Dorr; John Philip Frey; Lloyd Carpenter Griscom; Thomas Charles Hart; John T. Hettrick; Stanley Myer Isaacs; Emory Scott Land; John Lord O'Brian; William Ambrose Prendergast; Beverly Randolph Robinson; Frederick Chauncey Tanner; Henry Williams; James Thomas Williams, Jr.

ROPES, DR. MARION
Careers of New England women in medicine *Arthur and Elizabeth Schlesinger Library MA*

ROSANDER, OSCAR
South Dakota experience (1971), South Dakota Oral History Project *University of South Dakota*

ROSATI, JAMES (1912–   )
Sculptor
(1968, 52 pages) *Archives of American Art—Smithsonian Institution NY*

ROOT, ELIHU (1845–1937)
Lawyer, Statesman
Discussed in Columbia University interviews with John Lord O'Brian; Stanley Washburn

ROOT, ELIHU, JR. (1881–1967)
Robert P. Patterson project (15 pages, closed until January 1, 1980) *Columbia University NY*

ROSE, ARNOLD
Discussed in Columbia University interview with Gunnar Karl Myrdal

ROSE, BILLY
Discussed in Columbia University interview with Richard Rodgers

ROSE, HAROLD M.
Geographer
(1972, 10 minutes) *Plymouth State College NH*

ROSE, WICKLIFFE
Discussed in Columbia University interview with John B. Grant

ROSE, WILLIAM C.
Organic chemist
University Archives *University of Illinois IL*

ROSENBERG, MANUEL
Publisher of *Markets of America*
Radio pioneers collection (1963, 8 pages, open; also at *Broadcast Pioneers Library DC*) *Columbia University NY*

ROSENBERG, MOSHE
Tel-Aviv businessman
HISTORY OF THE YISHUV (PALESTINIAN JEWRY): (7) Etzel and Lehi organizations (Hebrew, 41 pages, open) *Hebrew University, Israel*

ROSENBLATT, BERNARD (–1969)
Judge
JEWISH COMMUNITIES: (6) American Jewry (English, 156 pages, open) *Hebrew University, Israel*

ROSENBLATT, FRANK
Challenges to governance by students project (1969, 132 pages, open) *Cornell University NY*

ROSENBLUM, FRANK
Former secretary-treasurer, Amalgamated Clothing Workers' Union
(1970, 2 hours, 40 pages) *Roosevelt University IL*

ROSECRANS, WILLIAM STARKE, III
Recollections of life on the Rosecrans Ranch (1963, 65 pages) *Los Angeles County Public Library System CA*

ROSEN, PINCHAS
Former Israeli minister of justice; Independent Liberal Party president
BIOGRAPHICAL INTERVIEWS (Hebrew, in process) *Hebrew University, Israel*

ROSEN, A. J. (1909–   )
McGraw-Hill, Inc. (36 pages, permission required) *Columbia University NY*

ROSENBERG, ANNA M. (MRS. PAUL HOFFMAN) (1902–   )
Herbert H. Lehman project (14 pages, permission required to cite or quote) *Columbia University NY*

Discussed in Columbia University interviews with William Benton; Herbert Brownell; Lavinia Engle

ROSENBERG, JAMES N.
Central personality, American Jewish Joint Distribution Committee
Joseph M. Proskauer project (32 pages, permission required) *Columbia University NY*

WORLD WAR II: THE HOLOCAUST—RESISTANCE AND RESCUE: (1) The Joint (American Jewish Joint Distribution Committee) (English, 10 pages, written interview, correspondence appended) *Hebrew University, Israel*

ROSENBERG, JULIUS
Discussed in Columbia University interview with Herbert Brownell

ROSENFELD, LEO

WORLD WAR II: THE HOLOCAUST—RESISTANCE AND RESCUE: (11) Jewish resistance in Slovakia (Hebrew, 53 pages; German, 33 pages; open) *Hebrew University, Israel*

ROSENFELD, SHULAMIT

HISTORY OF THE YISHUV (PALESTINIAN JEWRY): (1) Second Aliyah pioneers (Hebrew, 18 pages, open) *Hebrew University, Israel*

ROSENFIELD, NANCY SCHULKIND

Smith alumna, class of 1964; Radiologist

(1973, 1 hour, 23 pages) *Smith College MA*

ROSENHEIM, KATE

WORLD WAR II: THE HOLOCAUST—RESISTANCE AND RESCUE: (6) Rescue of Jewish children (English, 7 pages, written interview, open) *Hebrew University, Israel*

ROSENMAN, SAMUEL IRVING (1896–)

Judge

(1959, 233 pages, closed until 5 years after interviewee's death) *Columbia University NY*

Herbert H. Lehman project (23 pages, permission required to cite or quote) *Columbia University NY*

Harry S. Truman Library MO

ROSENQUIST, JAMES (1933–)

Painter

(1965, 8 pages) *Archives of American Art—Smithsonian Institution NY*

ROSENSAFT, JOSEPH

Businessman; Head, Bergen-Belsen Survivors' Association

ANTECEDENTS TO THE STATE OF ISRAEL: (2) "Brichah" (organized escape) (Yiddish, 12 pages, open) *Hebrew University, Israel*

ROSENSTEIL, HANS

WORLD WAR II: THE HOLOCAUST—RESISTANCE AND RESCUE: (2) Rescue of Jews via Spain and Portugal (German, only on tape) *Hebrew University, Israel*

ROSENSTEIN-RODAN, PAUL

World Bank (51 pages, closed during interviewee's lifetime, also at *Brookings Institution DC*) *Columbia University NY*

ROSENSTOCK-HUESSY, EUGEN

Danforth Foundation lectures (87 pages, permission required) *Columbia University NY*

ROSENTEIL, LOUIS

Industrialist

Brandeis University MA

ROSENTHAL, BERNARD (1914–)

Sculptor

(1968, 33 pages) *Archives of American Art—Smithsonian Institution NY*

ROSENTHAL, JULIUS

Discussed in Columbia University interview with Joseph J. Klein

ROSENTHAL, MORRIS SIGMUND (1897–1958)

Foreign trade consultant

(1953, 484 pages, permission required to cite or quote) *Columbia University NY*

ROSENTHAL, SANFORD

National Institutes of Health MD

ROSENWALD, JULIUS

Discussed in Columbia University interviews with Will Winton Alexander, James Madison Barker

ROSETTE, MOSHE (MAURICE)

Former Jewish Agency official (London); Former Knesset clerk (Jerusalem)

ANTECEDENTS TO THE STATE OF ISRAEL: (1) Jewish Agency (English, 49 pages, open) *Hebrew University, Israel*

ROSIN, ARNOST

WORLD WAR II: THE HOLOCAUST—RESISTANCE AND RESCUE: (9) Resistance to the "final solution" in Auschwitz (Czech, 20 pages, closed) *Hebrew University, Israel*

ROSIN, AXEL G. (1907–)

Book-of-the-Month Club collection (45 pages, open) *Columbia University NY*

ROSMAN, MORDECHAI

ANTECEDENTS TO THE STATE OF ISRAEL: (2) "Brichah" (organized escape) (Hebrew, 58 pages, closed) *Hebrew University, Israel*

ROSNER, AVRAHAM

BIOGRAPHICAL INTERVIEWS (Hebrew, 18 pages, open) *Hebrew University, Israel*

ROSS, ALVIN (1920–)

Painter

(1964, 8 pages) *Archives of American Art—Smithsonian Institution NY*

ROSS, MRS. JESSE EVANS

Federated Department Stores project (34 pages, permission required) *Columbia University NY*

ROSS, ORRIN (1885–)

(1965, 61 pages, open) *Cornell University NY*

ROSS, PAUL L.

Lawyer

(1950, 135 pages, permission required to cite or quote) *Columbia University NY*

New York political studies collection, New York election of 1949 (35 pages, permission required to cite or quote) *Columbia University NY*

ROSS, SILAS E. (1887–)

Funeral director

(1969, 624 pages, open) *University of Nevada, Reno*

ROSS, VERN L.

South Dakota experience (1970), South Dakota Oral History Project *University of South Dakota*

ROSSI, EDMUND A. (1888–)

Winemaker

(1971, 103 pages) *University of California, Berkeley*

ROSSITER, CLINTON

Challenges to governance by students project (1969, 65 pages, permission required) *Cornell University NY*

ROSTEN, LEO CALVIN (1908–)

Journalism lectures, Forum I (permission required to cite or quote) *Columbia University NY*

Popular arts collection (116 pages, open) *Columbia University NY*

ROSTON, JAMES A., JR.

University of Washington Libraries WA

ROSTOW, WALT

Discussed in Columbia University interview with Frederick P. Jessup

ROSZAK, THEODORE (1907–)

Sculptor

(1963, 254 pages) *Archives of American Art—Smithsonian Institution NY*

ROTH, MANIA

YOUTH MOVEMENTS: (2) Netzach in Latvia (Hebrew, 46 pages, open) *Hebrew University, Israel*

ROTH, MIRIAM

Teacher, Oranim Seminary

YOUTH MOVEMENTS: (1) Jewish youth movements in Czechoslovakia (Hebrew, 24 pages, open) *Hebrew University, Israel*

ROTH, YEHUDA

YOUTH MOVEMENTS: (1) Jewish youth movements in Czechoslovakia (Hebrew, 27 pages, open) *Hebrew University, Israel*

ROTHENBERG, DR. AND MRS. J.

(41 pages) *Cornell University NY*

ROTHMAN, DAVID

Columbia crisis of 1968 (68 pages, permission required) *Columbia University NY*

ROTHSCHILD, ROSA

WORLD WAR II: THE HOLOCAUST—RESISTANCE AND RESCUE: (5) Hiding children in Belgium (German, 7 pages, open) *Hebrew University, Israel*

ROTHWELL, JAMES L. (1895–)

Accountant

(1964, 85 pages, permission required to cite or quote) *Cornell University NY*

RUBOTTOM, ROY RICHARD, JR. **(1912–   )**
Diplomat

Eisenhower administration project (1969, 95 pages, closed during interviewee's lifetime, also at *Dwight D. Eisenhower Library KS*) *Columbia University NY*

Dulles oral history collection (1966, 88 pages, permission required to cite or quote) *Princeton University NY*

RUBY, HARRY (1895–   )
Popular arts collection (39 pages, open) *Columbia University NY*

RUCKDASCHEL, ABE, RALPH ANDERSON, HERBERT HEGNA, AND JOE COOPER
South Dakota experience (1971), South Dakota Oral History Project *University of South Dakota*

RUDE, IKE
Ranching collection *Texas Tech University*

RUDHYAR, DANE
Composer; Philosopher

American music project (1970) *Yale University School of Music CT*

Ives project (1970) *Yale University School of Music CT*

RUDZINSKI, ALEKSANDER WITOLD
Diplomat

(221 pages, permission required) *Columbia University NY*

RUFFIN, JAMES E.
Special assistant to the U.S. attorney general (1935–1954)

Harry S. Truman Library MO

RUGG, HAROLD
Discussed in Columbia University interviews with William Heard Kilpatrick; R. Bruce Raup

RUGGLES, CARL
Composer

Ives project (1969) *Yale University School of Music CT*

RUGGLES, CHARLES (1892–1971)
Actor

Popular arts collection (1959, 42 pages, open) *Columbia University NY*

RUGGLES, MICAH
Ives project *Yale University School of Music CT*

RUHMANN, JAMES (ca. 1910–   )
Businessman

(1969, 10 pages, open) *North Texas State University Oral History Collection*

RUHOFF, RONALD F.
State Historical Society of Colorado

RULFO
Latin author

Discussed in University of Texas, El Paso, Chester Christian interview (one tape)

RUMBOUGH, STANLEY MADDOX, JR. **(1920–   )**
Industrialist

Eisenhower administration project (1967, 43 pages, open, also at *Dwight D. Eisenhower Library KS*) *Columbia University NY*

RUMFORD, WILLIAM BYRON **(1908–   )**
Assemblyman; Pharmacist; Legislator for fair employment, fair housing, and public health

(1973, 139 pages) *University of California. Berkeley*

RUML, BEARDSLEY
Discussed in Columbia University with Flora Macdonald Rhind; and in Carnegie Corporation collection

RUMPF, AUGUST J.
(1972) *Wabash Carnegie Public Library IN*

RUMSEY, FRED (1870–1967)
(1964, 46 pages, open) *Cornell University NY*

RUMSFELD, DONALD
Cost of Living Council DC

RUNDLE, GEORGIANA RICE (MRS. E. H.)
(1959) *State Historical Society of Colorado*

RURAL ELECTRIFICATION ASSOCIATION (REA)
Southwest Minnesota State College

RURAL LIFE *see* Country Life

RUSHER, JAMES SARGENT (1903–   )
Aviation collection (51 pages, permission of interviewee required to cite or quote, also at *United States Air Force Academy CO* and *University of the Air, Maxwell Air Force Base AL*) *Columbia University NY*

RUSHER, WILLIAM ALLEN (1923–   )
Journalism lectures (66 pages, permission required to cite or quote) *Columbia University NY*

RUSHMORE, DR. CHARLES
Alcohol abuse workshop *Vigo County Public Library IN*

RUSK, DEAN (1909–   )
Former Secretary of State

(401 pages, closed) *John F. Kennedy Library MA*

Dulles oral history collection (1965, 26 pages, written permission required to read) *Princeton University NJ*

RUSK, HOWARD
Discussed in Columbia University Association for the Aid of Crippled Children collection

RUSSELL, ALBERT LEE
National Institutes of Health MD

RUSSELL, ALLIE
University of Michigan

RUSSELL, BERTRAND
Discussed in Columbia University interview with Ordway Tead

RUSSELL, CHARLES
University of Washington Libraries WA

RUSSELL, CHARLES H. (1903–   )
Politician

(1966, 264 pages, permission required) *University of Nevada, Reno*

RUSSELL, CHARLES M.
Artist

Discussed in Columbia University interview with Edward S. Edwin

RUSSELL, FRANCIS H. (1904–   )
Diplomat

Dulles oral history collection (1966, 19 pages, permission required to cite or quote) *Princeton University NJ*

RUSSELL, GEORGE
Discussed in Columbia University interview with Milburn Lincoln Wilson

RUSSELL, HUBBARD S.
Cattle rancher

(1962, 28 pages) *Los Angeles County Public Library System CA*

RUSSELL, JACK P.
Cleveland State University Library OH

RUSSELL, JAMES E.
Discussed in Columbia University interviews with Charlotte Garrison; Arthur T. Jersild; William Heard Kilpatrick; Goodwin Watson; and in Carnegie Corporation collection

RUSSELL, JOHN McFARLANE **(1903–   )**
Foundation president

Carnegie Corporation collection (1967, 290 pages, permission required) *Columbia University NY*

Discussed in Columbia University interview with George Raleigh Parkin

RUSSELL, PERS, AND GEORGE LEEMAN
South Dakota experience (1956), South Dakota Oral History Project *University of South Dakota*

RUSSELL, RICHARD
John C. Stennis collection *Mississippi State University*

SAIGON

Thomas A. Dooley collection *University of Missouri, St. Louis*

SAILLE, LEWIS

Federated Department Stores project (28 pages, permission required) *Columbia University NY*

SAILORS, LOUISE (MRS. JAMES)

(1973) *Wabash Carnegie Public Library IN*

ST. AUGUSTINE, FLORIDA

Historic preservation *Charles B. Hosmer, Jr. Collection IL*

ST. CROIX RIVER, WISCONSIN

University of Wisconsin, River Falls

ST. DENIS, RUTH

Fine arts collection (open) *University of California, Los Angeles*

ST. LOUIS, LEONE MORGAN

(1971) *State Historical Society of Colorado*

ST. LOUIS, MISSOURI

Historic preservation *Charles B. Hosmer, Jr. Collection IL*

Washington University Library MO

ST. LOUIS SCHOOL BOARD

St. Louis Teachers' Strike collection *University of Missouri, St. Louis*

ST. LOUIS TEACHERS ASSOCIATION

St. Louis Teachers' Strike collection *University of Missouri, St. Louis*

ST. MARY'S HOSPITAL

Mayo Clinic Foundation MN

ST. SURE, JOSEPH PAUL

Labor relations counsel

(1957, 737 pages) *University of California Institute of Industrial Relations*

SAKOWITZ, BERNARD

Sakowitz Brothers, Oral business history project *University of Texas, Austin*

SAKOWITZ, ROBERT

Sakowitz Brothers, Oral business history project *University of Texas, Austin*

SAKOWITZ BROTHERS *see* Robert Sakowitz, Bernard Sakowitz

SAKOWSKI, CLIFF *see* Arthur Ashem

SALADIN, RAYMOND
with Leon Bathiat

Aviation collection (8 pages, permission required to cite or quote, also at *United States Air Force Academy CO* and *University of the Air, Maxwell Air Force Base AL*) *Columbia University NY*

SALANT, WALTER S.

Economist, Council of Economic Advisers (1946–1952)

Harry S. Truman Library MO

SALCHOW, HUGO K.

Member, Polar Bear expedition to Archangel during World War I

University of Michigan

SALE, ELIZABETH

Tacoma Public Library WA

SALES, RENO

Mining engineers (28 pages, permission required to cite or quote) *Columbia University NY*

SALISBURY, GLENN W. (1910–   )

Development of artificial insemination project (1967, 104 pages, most open) *Cornell University NY*

SALISBURY, HARRISON EVANS (1980–   )

Eisenhower administration project (23 pages, permission required to cite or quote, also at *Dwight D. Eisenhower Library KS*) *Columbia University NY*

Journalism lectures (65 pages, permission required to cite or quote) *Columbia University NY*

SALMON, RONALD D. (1909–   )

Brigadier general, U.S. Marine Corps (service: 1930–1960)

(1971, in process) *United States Marine Corps DC*

SALMON, W. W. (1909–   )

Banker

(1971, 30 pages, open) *North Texas State University Oral History Collection*

SALOMON, ANDRE

Member, O.S.E. (France)

WORLD WAR II: THE HOLOCAUST—RESISTANCE AND RESCUE: (3) Jewish underground movement in wartime France (French, 36 pages, open) *Hebrew University, Israel*

WORLD WAR II: THE HOLOCAUST—RESISTANCE AND RESCUE: (6) Rescue of Jewish children (German, 38 pages; French, 34 pages; open) *Hebrew University, Israel*

SALOMON, IRVING

Eisenhower administration project (39 pages, permission required to cite or quote, also at *Dwight D. Eisenhower Library KS*) *Columbia University NY*

SALOMON, ISRAEL

WORLD WAR II: THE HOLOCAUST—RESISTANCE AND RESCUE: (2) Rescue of Jews via Spain and Portugal (Hebrew, based on a German conversation, 5 pages, written interview, open) *Hebrew University, Israel*

SALSMAN, BYRL (1906–   )

Judge; State senator

(1971, 45 pages) *University of California, Berkeley*

SALTER, WILLIAM

Discussed in Columbia University interview with Joseph Charles Aub

SALTONSTALL, LEVERETT (1892–   )

U.S. senator (Massachusetts, 1944–1967)

Eisenhower administration project (1967, 151 pages, permission required to cite or quote, also at *Dwight D. Eisenhower Library KS*) *Columbia University NY*

(72 pages, open) *John F. Kennedy Library MA*

Dulles oral history collection (1966, 21 pages, open) *Princeton University NJ*

SALTZMAN, CHARLES E. (1903–   )

Former Under-secretary of State for administration

Dulles oral history collection (1967, 24 pages, open) *Princeton University NJ*

SALVERSON, MELVIN, AND RICHARD SALVERSON

South Dakota experience (1971), South Dakota Oral History Project *University of South Dakota*

SALZ, HELEN

Northern California Jewish Community series (permission required to quote, also at *University of California, Berkeley*) *Western Jewish History Center CA*

SAMARAS, LUCAS (1936–   )

Sculptor

(1968, 104 pages) *Archives of American Art—Smithsonian Institution NY*

SAMPSON, EDITH

Municipal judge; United Nations delegate

(1972) *Fisk University TN*

SAMPSON, GORDON A. (1898–   )

Business analyst

(1967, 531 pages, portion closed) *University of Nevada, Reno*

SAMPSON, MYRA

Smith alumna, class of 1909; Zoologist; Professor

(1973, 2 hours, 38 pages) *Smith College MA*

SAMS, L. L. & SONS

Texas economic history project *Baylor University TX*

SAMSON, SIR GEORGE (1883–1965)

Diplomat; Orientalist

(1957, 96 pages, open) *Columbia University NY*

SARGEANT, HOWLAND
Member, U.S. Joint Chiefs of Staff (1944–1946); President, 1951 UNESCO general conference

Eisenhower administration project (26 pages, permission required to cite or quote, also at *Dwight D. Eisenhower Library KS) Columbia University NY*

SARNOFF, DAVID (1891–1971)

Robert P. Patterson project (9 pages, closed until January 1, 1980) *Columbia University NY*

Discussed in Columbia University interview with Chester Henry Lang

SARON, GUSTAV
Secretary, South African Jewish Board of Deputies

JEWISH COMMUNITIES: (14) Individual interview (English, 91 pages, open) *Hebrew University, Israel*

SARTON, MAY

Discussed in Columbia University interview with Dorothy Baker

SASAKI, MIYOKO
Smith alumna, class of 1959; Teacher; Writer

(1973, 3 hours, 76 pages) *Smith College MA*

SASSON, BINYAMIN
with Yehoshua Battat

JEWISH COMMUNITIES: (10) Jewish life in Iraq (Hebrew, 31 pages, open) *Hebrew University, Israel*

SASSON, MEIR
Tel-Aviv urologist

SASSON, MOSHE

JEWISH COMMUNITIES: (13) Jews in the Far East (Hebrew, based on conversation in Arabic, 9 pages, open) *Hebrew University, Israel*

SASSON, SIMAN-TOV
Director, Burial Society of Kurdish community, (Jerusalem)

JEWISH COMMUNITIES: (10) Jewish life in Iraq (Hebrew, 23 pages, open) *Hebrew University, Israel*

SATTERTHWAITE, JOSEPH C.
(1900–   )
Diplomat

Dulles oral history collection (1966, 23 pages, open) *Princeton University NJ*

SATTLE, ALFRED *see* Arthur Ashem

SAUER, ALICE E. (1877–1972)
Teacher; Housewife

(1966, 50 pages, open) *University of Nevada. Reno*

SAUER, CARL
Geographer

(1970, 30 minutes) *Plymouth State College NH*

SAUER, MR. AND MRS. MARTIN

South Dakota experience (1971), South Dakota Oral History Project *University of South Dakota*

SAUER, WILLIAM F. (1878–1966)
Rancher

(1966, 51 pages, open) *University of Nevada. Reno*

SAUL, JOHN

South Dakota experience (1968), South Dakota Oral History Project *University of South Dakota*

SAULNIER, RAYMOND J. (1908–   )
Economist

Eisenhower administration project (1967, 71 pages, open, also at *Dwight D. Eisenhower Library KS) Columbia University NY*

Discussed in Columbia University interview with Neil H. Jacoby

SAUNDERS, ALFRED W.
Designing engineer, NBC

(1965, 1 reel, 19 pages) *Broadcast Pioneers Library DC*

SAUNDERS, CORNELIA
University of Washington Libraries WA

SAUNDERS, JAMES HENRY (1893–   )
Builder; Former Pullman porter

(33 pages, open) *University of Texas, Arlington*

SAUNDERS, ROBERT
University of Washington Libraries WA

SAUSSURE, RAYMOND DE (–1971)
Psychoanalyst

Psychoanalytic movement collection (1965, 73 pages, permission required) *Columbia University NY*

SAVACOOL, WILLIAM

Theodore Roosevelt Association (30 pages, permission required to cite or quote) *Columbia University NY*

SAVAGE, CHARLES J.

(1964) *State Historical Society of Colorado*

SAXBE, WILLIAM B.
Cleveland State University Library OH

SAXE, MARTIN (1874–1967)
Lawyer; Politician

(1949, 40 pages, also microfiche, permission required to cite or quote) *Columbia University NY*

SAYERS, FRANCES CLARK
Tacoma Public Library WA

SAYRE, CHARLES (1891–   )

(1964, 28 pages, permission required) *Cornell University NY*

SAYRE, E. BERTHOL

Columbiana (16 pages, open) *Columbia University NY*

SAYRE, REV. FRANCIS
Dean, Washington Cathedral; Chairman, U.S. Committee for Refugees

(17 pages, open) *John F. Kennedy Library MA*

SAYRE, FRANCIS BOWES (1885–1972)
Diplomat

(1952, 127 pages, permission required) *Columbia University NY*

SAYRE, WALLACE STANLEY (1905–1972)

Journalism lectures, Basic issues in the news: Problems of the city (136 pages, permission required) *Columbia University NY*

SAZ, ARTHUR K.
National Institutes of Health MD

SCALES, LAURA LORD
Smith alumna, class of 1901; Educator; Administrator; Smith warden (1922–1944)

(1973, 2 hours, 36 pages) *Smith College MA*

SCANDRETT, RICHARD B., JR. (–1969)
Lawyer; Republican party worker

(1967, 307 pages, permission required to cite or quote) *Cornell University NY*

SCANTLEBURY, RONALD E.
National Institutes of Health MD

SCARLETT, CHARLES E. (1908–   )
President, Steamship Trade Association (1951–1952) and National Association of Stevedores

(1971, 39 pages, 2 hours, open) *Maryland Historical Society*

SCHAAR, WALTER

Communications Workers of America collection *University of Iowa Libraries*

SCHACHT, HJALMAR
German military opposition to Hitler *Harold C. Deutsch Collection DC*

SCHACHT, JACOB J.

Communications Workers of America collection *University of Iowa Libraries*

SCHACHTMAN, MAX

Socialist movement project (76 pages, permission required to cite or quote) *Columbia University NY*

SCHAEFER, BERTHA
Art dealer; Interior designer

(1970, 47 pages) *Archives of American Art—Smithsonian Institution NY*

SCHAEFER, WALTER VINCENT (1904-)
Adlai E. Stevenson project (78 pages, permission required) *Columbia University NY*

SCHAFFER, LENA SCHADE
(1973) *Wabash Carnegie Public Library IN*

SCHAPER, WILFRED with Don Rodewald
Flying Tigers (40 pages, permission required to cite or quote) *Columbia University NY*

SCHAPER, WILFRED with Don Rodewald and Harvey Wirta
Flying Tigers (57 pages, permission required to cite or quote) *Columbia University NY*

SCHAPPES, MORRIS U. (1907-)
Member, Communist unit, New York City College, 1930s
(1968, 64 pages, mostly open) *Cornell University NY*

SCHARRENBERG, PAUL (1877-)
Labor leader, sailors' union; Editor, *Seaman's Journal*
(1954, 133 pages, also at *University of California Institute of Industrial Relations*) *University of California, Berkeley*

SCHARY, DORE (1905-)
Popular arts collection (87 pages, closed during interviewee's lifetime) *Columbia University NY*
Theatre on film and tape *New York Public Library at Lincoln Center*

SCHEAF, ORAL
Federated Department Stores project (40 pages, permission required) *Columbia University NY*

SCHECHTER, JOSEPH
ANTECEDENTS TO THE STATE OF ISRAEL: (2) "Brichah" (organized escape) (Hebrew, 37 pages, open) *Hebrew University, Israel*

SCHECTER, ABEL ALAN (1907-)
Radio pioneers collection (33 pages, open) *Columbia University NY*

SCHEELE, LEONARD ANDREW (1907-)
Surgeon general, U.S. Health Service (1948-1956)
Eisenhower administration project (1968, 44 pages, permission required to cite or quote, also at *Dwight D. Eisenhower Library KS*) *Columbia University NY*

SCHEFTEL, ARIE
Director, Brit Ivrit Olamit (Jerusalem)
WORLD WAR II: THE HOLOCAUST—RESISTANCE AND RESCUE: (13) Underground activities of the Lithuanian Jews (Hebrew, 16 pages, open) *Hebrew University; Israel*

SCHENCK, EDA
South Dakota experience (1971), South Dakota Oral History Project *University of South Dakota*

SCHENKEL, ARTHUR
(1972) *Wabash Carnegie Public Library IN*

SCHENKER, ANDRE
University of Connecticut

SCHERER, RAYMOND LEWIS (1919-)
Journalist
Eisenhower administration project (1968, 54 pages, open, also at *Dwight D. Eisenhower Library KS*) *Columbia University NY*
(62 pages, open) *John F. Kennedy Library MA*

SCHERMAN, HARRY (1887-1969)
Book club executive; Author
Book-of-the-Month Club collection (1955, 367 pages, also microfiche, permission required to cite or quote) *Columbia University NY*
Discussed in Columbia University Book-of-the-Month Club collection

SCHICK, VENA V. HICKS
South Dakota experience (1971), South Dakota Oral History Project *University of South Dakota*

SCHICKEL, NORBERT H., JR.
Ithaca Festival (Center for the Arts of Ithaca) project (1969, 210 pages, permission required to cite or quote transcript, permission required to use tape) *Cornell University NY*

SCHIEFFELIN, BAYARD (1903-)
Robert P. Patterson project (22 pages, closed until January 1, 1980) *Columbia University NY*

SCHIEFFELIN, WILLIAM JAY (1866-1955)
Businessman; Civic worker
(1949, 126 pages, also microfiche, permission required to cite or quote) *Columbia University NY*

SCHILANSKI, DOV
Tel-Aviv lawyer
WORLD WAR II: THE HOLOCAUST—RESISTANCE AND RESCUE: (13) Underground activities of the Lithuanian Jews (Hebrew, 65 pages, open) *Hebrew University; Israel*

SCHILLING, EDWARD LEWIS
National Institutes of Health MD

SCHILT, CHRISTIAN FRANKLIN (1895-)
General, U.S. Marine Corps (service: 1917-1957)
(1969, 136 pages, open, also at *Columbia University NY* and *U.S. Naval Institute MD*) *United States Marine Corps DC*

SCHINE, GERARD DAVID (1927-)
Eisenhower administration project (24 pages, permission required to cite or quote, also at *Dwight D. Eisenhower Library KS*) *Columbia University NY*
Aviation collection (23 pages, permission of interviewee required to cite or quote, also at *United States Air Force Academy CO* and *University of the Air, Maxwell Air Force Base AL*) *Columbia University NY*

SCHLEI, NORBERT
Assistant attorney general, Justice Department office of legal counsel
(62 pages, open) *John F. Kennedy Library MA*

SCHLEMAN, HELEN B.
Purdue University administrator
(1970, in preparation) *Purdue University Archives IN*

SCHLENCK, HUGO
Weyerhaeuser Timber Company (113 pages, permission required) *Columbia University NY*

SCHLESINGER, ARTHUR MEIER (1888-1965)
Historian
(1959, 1266 pages, permission required) *Columbia University NY*
Discussed in Columbia University interview with Gardner Jackson

SCHLESINGER, ARTHUR MEIER, JR. (1917-)
Adlai E. Stevenson project (43 pages, permission required to cite or quote) *Columbia University NY*
Richard Hofstadter project (14 pages, permission required to cite or quote) *Columbia University NY*
American historians collection (73 pages, permission required to cite or quote) *Columbia University NY*
Discussed in Columbia University interview with Newton Norman Minow

SCHLESINGER, DR. FALK (-1968)
HISTORY OF THE YISHUV (PALESTINIAN JEWRY): (4) Extreme Orthodox Jewry in Palestine (Hebrew, 51 pages, open) *Hebrew University; Israel*

SCHLESS, HOWARD
Columbia crisis of 1968 (10 pages, permission required) *Columbia University NY*

SCHLOSS, ANN LAZARUS
Federated Department Stores project (47 pages, permission required) *Columbia University NY*

SCHLOSSBERG, JOSEPH (1901-)
Socialist movement project (51 pages, permission required to cite or quote) *Columbia University NY*

SCHMETTERER, YAAKOV
ANTECEDENTS OF THE STATE OF ISRAEL: (2) "Brichah" (organized escape) (Hebrew, 108 pages, open) *Hebrew University, Israel*

SCHMIDT, BENNO
Member, Bedford-Stuyvesant Development and Services Corporation; Businessman
(67 pages, part of special Robert F. Kennedy oral history program, open) *John F. Kennedy Library MA*

SCHMIDT, BERNHARD (1884–   )
Factory superintendent, Schmidt Lithograph Company
(1968, 99 pages) *University of California, Berkeley*

SCHMIDT, KATHERINE (1898–   )
Painter
(1969, 55 pages) *Archives of American Art— Smithsonian Institution NY*

SCHMIDT, LORENZ (1913–   )
Past president, Schmidt Lithograph Company
(1969, 49 pages) *University of California, Berkeley*

SCHMIDT, MAX, JR. (1882–   )
Head of factory office, Schmidt Lithograph Company
(1968, 19 pages) *University of California, Berkeley*

SCHMIDT, ORVIS ADRIAN
World Bank (23 pages, permission of interviewee required to cite or quote, also at *Brookings Institution DC*) *Columbia University NY*

SCHMIDT, WILLIAM F.
Ithaca Festival (Center for the Arts at Ithaca) project (1966, 114 pages, open) *Cornell University NY*

SCHNEERSOHN, PINCHAS
HISTORY OF THE YISHUV (PALESTINIAN JEWRY): (5) Gedud Ha-Avoda (Labor Brigade) (Hebrew, 63 pages, open) *Hebrew University, Israel*

SCHNEIDER, ALAN
Ithaca Festival (Center for the Arts at Ithaca) project (1967, 229 pages, permission required to use for 20 years) *Cornell University NY*

Theatre on film and tape *New York Public Library at Lincoln Center*

SCHNEIDER ALAN
with Edward Albee
Popular arts collection (86 pages, permission required) *Columbia University NY*

SCHNEIDER, LOUIS J., JR.
Ohio judge
Life of Kingsley A. Taft *Ohio Historical Society*

SCHNEIDER, W. M.
Cedar Rapids and Iowa City Railway *University of Iowa Libraries*

SCHNEIDEREITH, WILLIAM, SR. (1886–   )
President, Schneidereith and Sons printing company
(1970, 45 pages, 3 hours, open) *Maryland Historical Society*

SCHOEN, ARNOLD F., JR.
Vice-president, WDBO-AM-FM-TV (Orlando)
(1965, 1 reel, 29 pages) *Broadcast Pioneers Library DC*

SCHOENBRUN, DAVID (1915–   )
News correspondent
Journalism lectures (46 pages, permission required to cite or quote) *Columbia University NY*

Cleveland State University Library OH

Dulles oral history collection (1964, 107 pages, open) *Princeton University NJ*

SCHOENWERK, OTTO C.
Weyerhaeuser Timber Company (40 pages, permission required) *Columbia University NY*

SCHOFIELD, JAMES R.
Baylor project *Baylor University TX*

SCHOFIELD, WILLIAM R. (1894–1973)
Lobbyist; Forester; Trade organization executive
(1968, 159 pages) *University of California, Berkeley*

SCHOLEM, GERSHOM
Hebrew University professor
YOUTH MOVEMENTS: (1) Jewish youth movements in Czechoslovakia (Hebrew, 30 pages, open) *Hebrew University, Israel*

SCHOMBURG, THOMAS A.
(1971) *State Historical Society of Colorado*

SCHOOL INTEGRATION see Segregation in Education

SCHOOL OF THE OZARKS
School of the Ozarks project *Cornell University NY*
Participants: M. Bailey; Linda Burk; M. Graham Clark; Sylvia Fletcher; Michael M. Foster; Robert M. Good; Everett Isaacs; Lola M. Jones; Mary Ann Seiler; Francis J. Wheeler; Gary L. Wortman

SCHOOL SUPERINTENDENTS COUNCIL
(1968, 92 pages) *Cornell University NY*

SCHOOLMAN, ABBA
JEWISH COMMUNITIES: (6) American Jewry (English, introduction and questions in Hebrew, 21 pages, open) *Hebrew University, Israel*

SCHOOLS
One room school collection (9 hours, 44 pages, open) *Sangamon State University IL*

University of Delaware
See also Education

SCHOONOVER, FRANK (1877–1972)
Illustrator
(1966, 11 pages) *Archives of American Art— Smithsonian Institution NY*

SCHORR, LISBETH BAMBERGER
Social Security collection (1967, 105 pages, permission required to cite or quote, also at *Social Security Administration MD*) *Columbia University NY*

SCHOTTLAND, CHARLES IRWIN (1906–   )
University dean; U.S. government official
Social Security collection (1965, 167 pages, open, also at *Social Security Administration MD*) *Columbia University NY*
(1973, 95 pages) *University of California, Berkeley*

SCHRAG, KARL (1912–   )
Painter
(1970, 34 pages) *Archives of American Art— Smithsonian Institution NY*

SCHREIBER, GEORGES (1904–   )
Illustrator
(1965, 8 pages) *Archives of American Art— Smithsonian Institution NY*

SCHREMP, PAUL
Director, United Steelworkers of America District 28 (Cleveland)
(1967, 19 pages) *Pennsylvania State University*

SCHROEDER, THEODORE
Discussed in Columbia University interview with Roger Nash Baldwin

SCHUB, BARUCH
Ramat-Gan engineer
WORLD WAR II: THE HOLOCAUST—RESISTANCE AND RESCUE: (13) Underground activities of the Lithuanian Jews (Hebrew, 60 pages, open) *Hebrew University, Israel*

SCHULMAN, JAY
Challenges to governance by students project: Pentagon march (1967) (1968, 160 pages, open) *Cornell University NY*

SCHULTZ, JAMES A. (1917–   )
Vice-president, Public Relations Association of American Railroads
United Transportation Union project (1970, 30 pages, open) *Cornell University NY*

SCHULTZE, ERICH
German military opposition to Hitler *Harold C. Deutsch Collection DC*

SCHULZ, ROBERT L. (1907–)
U.S. Army officer; Presidential aide
Eisenhower administration project (1968, 293 pages, closed until 1993, also at Dwight D. Eisenhower Library KS) *Columbia University NY*
Discussed in Columbia University interview with Edward Latimer Beach

SCHUSTER, MAX LINCOLN (1897–1970)
Editor; Publisher
(1964, 226 pages, permission required to cite or quote) *Columbia University NY*

SCHUTAN, MOSHE
WORLD WAR II: THE HOLOCAUST—RESISTANCE AND RESCUE: (13) Underground activities of the Lithuanian Jews (Yiddish, 45 pages, open) *Hebrew University, Israel*

SCHUTT, CALEB (1885–)
Food processor
(1964, 111 pages, open) *Cornell University NY*

SCHUYLER, GEORGE SAMUEL (1895–)
Author; Journalist
(1960, 723 pages, also microfiche, permission required to cite or quote) *Columbia University NY*

SCHWAB, CARL A. (–1973)
(1972) *Wabash Carnegie Public Library IN*

SCHWANDT, MRS. EMMA
South Dakota experience (1970), South Dakota Oral History Project *University of South Dakota*

SCHWARTZ, A. R. (1926–)
Attorney; Texas state senator (Galveston); Democrat
Legislative project (1970, 56 pages, pages 23, 25, 26, and 30 restricted until interviewee's political retirement) *North Texas State University Oral History Collection*

SCHWARTZ, ARTHUR (1900–)
Popular arts collection (20 pages, open) *Columbia University NY*

SCHWARTZ, BRYAN
(1968) *State Historical Society of Colorado*

SCHWARTZ, MR. AND MRS. BRYAN
(1968) *State Historical Society of Colorado*

SCHWARTZ, FELICE NIERENBERG
Smith alumna, class of 1946; Business executive
(1973, 2 hours, 51 pages) *Smith College MA*

SCHWARTZ, JOSEPH J.
Former director-general, American Jewish Joint Distribution Committee (Europe); Executive vice-president, Israel Bonds Organization (New York)
ANTECEDENTS TO THE STATE OF ISRAEL: (2) "Brichah" (organized escape) (English, 31 pages, open) *Hebrew University, Israel*
WORLD WAR II: THE HOLOCAUST—RESISTANCE AND RESCUE: (1) The Joint (American Jewish Joint Distribution Committee) (English, 51 pages, open) *Hebrew University, Israel*
WORLD WAR II: THE HOLOCAUST—RESISTANCE AND RESCUE: (2) Rescue of Jews via Spain and Portugal (English, 25 pages, open) *Hebrew University, Israel*

SCHWARTZ, LEO W. (–1968)
ANTECEDENTS TO THE STATE OF ISRAEL: (2) "Brichah" (organized escape) (English, 10 pages, open) *Hebrew University, Israel*

SCHWARTZ, WILLIAM S.
Illinois State Historical Library

SCHWARTZ, WALTER
ABC Radio, Oral business history project *University of Texas, Austin*

SCHWEITZER, URI
Director, Bank Ha-Poalim (Tel-Aviv)
ANTECEDENTS TO THE STATE OF ISRAEL: (2) "Brichah" (organized escape) (Hebrew, 62 pages, open) *Hebrew University, Israel*

SCHWENDIMAN, JOHN
Ricks College ID

SCHWIEGER, WILLIAM D. (1932–)
Chairman, UTU local 1895
United Transportation Union project (1972, 65 pages, special permission required) *Cornell University NY*

SCIENCE
National Institute of Health MD
University archives *University of Illinois*
See also Botany; Physics

SCIENTISTS
Nobel Laureates on scientific research. Participants and pages: Carl D. Anderson, 46; John Bardeen, 43; George Beadle, 46; Felix Bloch, 24; Walter H. Brattain, 54; Melvin Calvin, 12; Owen Chamberlain, 44; Carl Cori, 52; André Cournand, 54; E. A. Doisy, 30; Vincent du Vigneaud, 33; Joseph Erlanger, 30; Robert L. Hofstadter, 32; Edward C. Kendall, 62; Arthur Kornberg, 24; Polykarp Kusch, 49; T. D. Lee, 23; Rudolf F. Libby, 58; Fritz Lippmann, 41; Edwin M. McMillan, 49; Maria Goeppert Mayer, 51; Rudolf L. Mossbauer, 38; Hermann J. Muller, 57; William Parry Murphy, 37; Linus Pauling, 51; Edward Mills Purcell, 35; Isidor Isaac Rabi, 44; Dickinson W. Richards, 20; Frederick C. Robbins, 37; Glenn T. Seaborg, 20; Emilio Segrè, 50; William Shockley, 51; Wendell M. Stanley, 36; Albert Szent-Györgyi, 49; Edward Lawrie Tatum, 32; Max Theiler, 42; Harold C. Urey, 44; Eugene P. Wigner, 60; Chen Ning Yang, 67 (1964, 1525 pages, permission required) *Columbia University NY*
Scientist as citizen collection. Participants and pages: Kenneth T. Bainbridge, 150; Charles Du Bois Coryell, 441; Albert Crary, 87; Theodosius Dobzhansky, 637; Leslie Clarence Dunn, 1086; J. George Harrar (in process); Joseph Kaplan, 82; James R. Killian, Jr., 375; Polykarp Kusch, 212, 297; Isidor Isaac Rabi (in process); Norman Ramsey, Elvin C. Stakman, 1687; Sir Robert Watson-Watt, 568; Warren Weaver, 783 *Columbia University NY*

SCIUTTO, JOE
Dental history (in process) *University of California, Berkeley*

SCOFIELD, FRANK H.
Discussed in Columbia University interview with Harold C. Train

SCOGGINS, VERNE
Public relations consultant; Journalist; Governor Warren's press secretary
(1973, 94 pages) *University of California, Berkeley*

SCOROHOD, FREIDA
WORLD WAR II: THE HOLOCAUST—RESISTANCE AND RESCUE: (10) Belorussian Jewry (Hebrew, 57 pages, open) *Hebrew University, Israel*

SCOTT, AUSTIN WAKEMAN (1884–)
Robert P. Patterson project (3 pages, closed until January 1, 1980) *Columbia University NY*

SCOTT, EDDIE B. (1928–)
Civil rights leader
(1968) *University of Nevada, Reno*

SCOTT, ERNEST LYMAN (1878–1966)
Scientist
(1964, 11 pages plus papers, open) *Columbia University NY*

SCOTT, HARDY (1907–)
Independence National Historical Park (11 pages, permission required) *Columbia University NY*

SCOTT, JOE
Folk-poet
Folksongs and their makers *University of Maine*

SCOTT, MARY WINGFIELD
Historic preservation *Charles B. Hosmer, Jr. Collection IL*

SCOTT, REED
Biographical collection (open) *University of California, Los Angeles*

SCOTT, RODERICK (1885–)
China missionaries collection (113 pages, open, also at *Columbia University NY*) *Claremont Graduate School CA*

SCOTT, SHARON
Student
(1972) *Fisk University TN*

SCOTT, THOMAS W. (1929–)
Sugar beet industry in New York State (1966, 42 pages, permission required to cite or quote) *Cornell University NY*

SCOTT, WALLY
Caudill, Rowlett & Scott, Oral business history project *University of Texas, Austin*

SCOTT, ZACHARY (1914–1965)
Popular arts collection (39 pages, open) *Columbia University NY*

SCOVILLE, GAD PARKER (1885–)
(1964, 52 pages, permission required to cite or quote) *Cornell University NY*

SCRANTON, WILLIAM WARREN (1917–)
Former special assistant to the Secretary of State for public relations
Dulles oral history collection (1965, 22 pages, open) *Princeton University NJ*

SCRIBNER, CHARLES
Discussed in Columbia University interview with John Hall Wheelock

SCRIBNER, FRED C., JR. (1908–)
Lawyer
Eisenhower administration project (83 pages, permission required to cite or quote, also at *Dwight D. Eisenhower Library KS*) *Columbia University NY*

SCRIPPS, WILLIAM EDMUND (1882–1952)
Radio pioneers collection (33 pages, open) *Columbia University NY*

SCROGGS, JACK B. (1919–)
Professor
(1971, 83 pages, closed during C. C. Nolen's tenure as North Texas State University president and during tenure of university regents A. M. Willis, Dean Davis, David James Lawson, E. C. Pannell, and E. Bruce Street) *North Texas State University Oral History Collection*

SCUDDER, KENYON JUDSON
Sociologist
(1972, 46 pages; 421 pages) *University of California, Berkeley*
State and local history collection (open) *University of California, Los Angeles*

SCULPTORS
Archives of American Art—Smithsonian Institution NY

SEABORG, GLENN THEODORE (1912–)
Nobel Laureates collection (20 pages, permission required) *Columbia University NY*

SEABURY, SAMUEL
Discussed in Columbia University interviews with Thomas Edmund Dewey; Frances Perkins

SEAMAN, JONATHAN O. (1918–)
Lieutenant general, U.S. Army
United States Army Military Research Collection PA

SEAMANS, ROBERT CHANNING, JR. (1918–)
Associate administrator, NASA
(46 pages, closed to newspaper reporters and writers in current periodicals) *John F. Kennedy Library MA*
National Aeronautics and Space Administration DC

SEARS, GEORGE (1887–1960)
McGraw-Hill, Inc. (15 pages, permission required) *Columbia University NY*

SEATON, GEORGE (1911–)
Popular arts collection (46 pages, open) *Columbia University NY*

SEBALD, WILLIAM J. (1901–)
Diplomat
Dulles oral history collection (1965, 122 pages, permission required to cite or quote, may not be copied in any form) *Princeton University NJ*

SEBRELL, WILLIAM HENRY, JR. (1901–)
Public health officer
Health science collection (1962, 72 pages, permission required, also at *National Library of Medicine MD*) *Columbia University NY*

SECOR, GARY
(1963) *State Historical Society of Colorado*

SEDGWICK, ELLERY
Discussed in Columbia University interview with Quincy Howe

SEEDS, CORINNE ALDINE
University history collection (open) *University of California, Los Angeles*

SEEGER, CHARLES LOUIS
Musicologist; Composer
Fine arts collection (open) *University of California, Los Angeles*
American music project (1970) *Yale University School of Music CT*
Ives project (1970) *Yale University School of Music CT*

SEGAL, GEORGE (1924–)
Sculptor
(1965, 10 pages) *Archives of American Art—Smithsonian Institution NY*

SEGER, GERHART HENRY (1896–1967)
Editor; Author; Lecturer
(1950, 154 pages, also microfiche, permission required to cite or quote) *Columbia University NY*

SEGRE, EMILIO (1905–)
Nobel Laureates collection (50 pages, permission required) *Columbia University NY*

SEGREGATION IN EDUCATION
The model school controversy in Montgomery County, Maryland (30 hours, 460 pages, open) *George Washington University DC*
Millsaps College MS

SEH-LAVAN, JOSEPH
Tel-Aviv teacher
YOUTH MOVEMENTS: (2) Netzach in Latvia (Hebrew, tape only, open) *Hebrew University, Israel*

SEIDMAN, HAROLD D.
Bureau of the Budget, staff member and administrator (1943–1968)
Harry S. Truman Library MO

SEIDMAN, JOEL
Professor, University of Chicago School of Business
(1970, 1 hour, 30 pages) *Roosevelt University IL*

SEILER, MARY ANN
Challenges to governance by students project: School of the Ozarks (1969, 35 pages, most open) *Cornell University NY*

SEIM, BESSIE
South Dakota experience (1971), South Dakota Oral History Project *University of South Dakota*

SEITER, KARL W. (1893–)
Chemist
(1964, 59 pages, open) *Cornell University NY*

SELA (STEINER), YITZHAK
ANTECEDENTS TO THE STATE OF ISRAEL: (2) "Brichah" (organized escape) (Hebrew, 17 pages, open) *Hebrew University, Israel*

SELDEN, ARMISTEAD I., JR. (1921–)
U.S. congressman
Dulles oral history collection (1966, 9 pages, open) *Princeton University NJ*

SELF, SIR HENRY (1890–)
Henry H. Arnold project (56 pages, permission required, also at *United States Air Force Academy CO*) *Columbia University NY*

SHABBO, YAAKOV
Jerusalem civil servant
JEWISH COMMUNITIES: (10) Jewish life in Iraq (Hebrew, 47 pages, open) *Hebrew University, Israel*

SHACHAR (SCHWARTZ), MEIR
HISTORY OF THE YISHUV (PALESTINIAN JEWRY): (5) Gedud Ha-Avoda (Labor Brigade) (Hebrew, 8 pages, open) *Hebrew University, Israel*

SHACHEWITZ, MICHAEL (–1968)
JEWISH COMMUNITIES: (4) Zionist movement in U.S.S.R. (1917–1935) (Hebrew, 26 pages, open) *Hebrew University, Israel*

SHACHTMAN, MAX (1903–1972)
Trotskyite
(1963, 522 pages, also microfiche, permission required to cite or quote) *Columbia University NY*

SHADEGG, STEPHEN (1909–)
Author
Eisenhower administration project (1967, 30 pages, closed during interviewee's lifetime; also at *Dwight D. Eisenhower Library KS*) *Columbia University NY*

SHADMI (SCHONFELD), ELI
Secondary school teacher
YOUTH MOVEMENTS: (1) Jewish youth movements in Czechoslovakia (Hebrew, 24 pages, open) *Hebrew University, Israel*

SHADMI, HANAN
Teacher, Kibbutz Oranim Seminary
YOUTH MOVEMENTS: (2) Netzach in Latvia (Hebrew, 26 pages; Hebrew, 33 pages; Hebrew, 39 pages; open) *Hebrew University, Israel*

SHADMI, MENASHE
YOUTH MOVEMENTS: (2) Netzach in Latvia (Hebrew, 31 pages, open) *Hebrew University, Israel*

SHAFRIRI, JOSEPH
Member, Kvutzat Kinneret
HISTORY OF THE YISHUV (PALESTINIAN JEWRY): (8) Revisionist "Ha 'apalah" (illegal immigration) (Hebrew, 32 pages, open) *Hebrew University, Israel*

SHAHAM, MISHAEL
Colonel, Israeli army

SHAHN, BEN (1898–1968)
Painter
(1968, 36 pages) *Archives of American Art—Smithsonian Institution NY*
(1960, 136 pages, permission required to cite or quote) *Columbia University NY*

SHAHN, NAVA
Actress, Haifa Municipal Theater
WORLD WAR II: THE HOLOCAUST—RESISTANCE AND RESCUE: (8) Theresienstadt ghetto (German, 83 pages, open) *Hebrew University, Israel*

SHALLON, SELIM
JEWISH COMMUNITIES: (9) Jewish community in Egypt (French, 50 pages, open) *Hebrew University, Israel*

SHAMBERGER, HUGH A. (1900–)
Engineer
(1966, 221 pages, open) *University of Nevada, Reno*

SHAMDI, HANAN
YOUTH MOVEMENTS: (2) Netzach in Latvia (Hebrew, 31 pages, open) *Hebrew University, Israel*

SHAMGAR, SHLOMO
Former secretary, Portuguese Zionist Federation; Tel-Aviv journalist
WORLD WAR II: THE HOLOCAUST—RESISTANCE AND RESCUE: (2) Rescue of Jews via Spain and Portugal (Hebrew, 8 pages, open) *Hebrew University, Israel*

SHANE, MARY D.
(1972) *Fisk University TN*

SHANKS VILLAGE, NEW YORK
Scott E. Webber Collection NY

SHANLEY, BERNARD M. (1903–)
President Eisenhower's secretary
Dulles oral history collection (1966, 48 pages, permission required to cite or quote) *Princeton University NJ*

SHANNON, EDNA E. YOUNG
First black WAVE, U.S. Navy
(1973) *Fisk University TN*

SHANNON, SAMUEL H.
Fisk University TN

SHANNON, WILLIAM
U.S. Navy
(1973) *Fisk University TN*

SHAPIRA, BINYAMIN
HISTORY OF THE YISHUV (PALESTINIAN JEWRY): (8) Revisionist "Ha 'apalah" (illegal immigration) (Hebrew, 32 pages, open) *Hebrew University, Israel*

SHAPIRO, SHALOM
Manager, Otzar Ha-Hayal Bank (Haifa)
WORLD WAR II: THE HOLOCAUST—RESISTANCE AND RESCUE: (13) Underground activities of the Lithuanian Jews (Hebrew, 47 pages; Hebrew, 28 pages; open) *Hebrew University, Israel*

SHAPLEY, ALAN (1903–)
Lieutenant general, U.S. Marine Corps (service: 1927–1962)
(161 pages, permission required, also at *Columbia University NY* and *U.S. Naval Institute MD*) *United States Marine Corps DC*

SHAPLEY, S. REUBEN (1906–)
(1964, 34 pages, open) *Cornell University NY*

SHARECROPPING see Farm Tenancy

SHAREFKIN, MARK
Challenges to governance by students project (1969, 59 pages, open) *Cornell University NY*

SHARFMAN, PETER J.
Cornell professor
Challenges to governance by students project (1969, 106 pages, permission required to use while interviewee remains at Cornell, then open) *Cornell University NY*

SHARON, JOHN
Congressman Howell's legislative assistant; Democratic campaign (1960) organizer; Presidential adviser on foreign policy
(35 pages, permission of interviewee required) *John F. Kennedy Library MA*

SHARP, CATHERINE
Housewife
(1964, 26 pages, open) *Cornell University NY*

SHARP, DUDLEY CRAWFORD (1905–)
U.S. government official
Eisenhower administration project (1969, 67 pages, permission required to cite or quote, also at *Dwight D. Eisenhower Library KS*) *Columbia University NY*

SHARP, E. PRESTON (1904–)
Law Enforcement Assistance Administration project (56 pages) *Cornell University NY*

SHARP, GEORGE C. (1897–)
Partner, Sullivan & Cromwell
Dulles oral history collection (1964, 69 pages, permission required to cite or quote) *Princeton University NJ*

SHASHA, SHAUL S.
Jerusalem merchant
JEWISH COMMUNITIES: (10) Jewish life in Iraq (Hebrew, translated from Arabic, 14 pages, open) *Hebrew University, Israel*

SHATTNER, MORDECHAI (DECEASED)
WORLD WAR II: THE HOLOCAUST—RESISTANCE AND RESCUE: (6) Rescue of Jewish children (Hebrew, 58 pages, open) *Hebrew University, Israel*

SHATTUCK, EDWARD
Presidential election of 1960 *University of Southern California Library*

SHATTUCK, FRED
Discussed in Columbia University interview with Joseph Charles Aub

SHATTUCK, JESS L.
Vice-president, UTU
United Transportation Union project (1971, 91 pages, permission required) *Cornell University NY*

SHATTUCK, ROGER
with William Arrowsmith
American cultural leaders collection (16 pages, closed pending publication of a study) *Columbia University NY*

SHAUL, KENNETH A. (1887–1968)
Milk marketing in New York project (1968, 123 pages) *Cornell University NY*

SHAW, CHARLES (1912–)
Painter
(1968, 58 pages) *Archives of American Art—Smithsonian Institution NY*

SHAW, EDWIN H. JR.
South Dakota experience (1972), South Dakota Oral History Project *University of South Dakota*

SHAW, H.
Aviation collection (57 pages, permission required to cite or quote, also at *United States Air Force Academy CO* and *University of the Air, Maxwell Air Force Base AL*) *Columbia University NY*

SHAW, H. H. W. (1904–)
McGraw-Hill, Inc. (14 pages, permission required) *Columbia University NY*

SHAW, MARY
Journalist
(1971, 28 pages) *University of California, Berkeley*

SHAW, MARY THATCHER
Ricks College ID

SHAW, SAMUEL ROBERT (1911–)
Brigadier general, U.S. Marine Corps (service: 1928–1962)
(1970, 495 pages, permission required, also at *Columbia University NY* and *U.S. Naval Institute MD*) *United States Marine Corps DC*

SHAYON, ROBERT LEWIS (1912–)
Radio pioneers collection (41 pages, open) *Columbia University NY*

SHAZAR, RACHEL
Wife of President Shazar
HISTORY OF THE YISHUV (PALESTINIAN JEWRY): (8) Revisionist "Ha 'apalah" (illegal immigration) (Hebrew, 29 pages, open), *Hebrew University, Israel*

SHEA, ROBERT
with John Wilson
Vice-president, American National Red Cross; Cuban prisoner exchange participant (28 pages, open) *John F. Kennedy Library MA*

SHEA, WILLARD W. (1880–)
Public defender
(1971, 55 pages) *University of California, Berkeley*

SHEAR, MURRAY J.
Physician
National Institutes of Health MD

SHEARON, MARJORIE
Discussed in Columbia University interview with Elizabeth Wickenden

SHEATS, PAUL HENRY
University history collection (open) *University of California, Los Angeles*

SHEBEKO, BORIS (1900–)
Russian emigré
California-Russian emigré series (1961, 284 pages) *University of California, Berkeley*

SHEDD, EDWARD J.
Classmate of John Foster Dulles
Dulles oral history collection (1966, 30 pages, open) *Princeton University NJ*

SHEELER, CHARLES (1883–1965)
Painter
(1958, 59 pages; 1959, 60 pages) *Archives of American Art—Smithsonian Institution NY*

SHEELE
Health science collection (57 pages, permission required, also at *National Library of Medicine MD*) *Columbia University NY*

SHEEP
Brigham Young University UT

SHEFFER, EUGENE
Columbiana (55 pages, open) *Columbia University NY*

SHEFFIELD, FREDERICK (1902–)
Carnegie Corporation collection (61 pages, permission required) *Columbia University NY*

SHELDON, A. O.
Weyerhaeuser Timber Company (41 pages, permission required) *Columbia University NY*

SHELDON, BOBBY
Alaskan pioneers project (36 pages, open) *Columbia University NY*

SHELDON, EDWARD
Discussed in Columbia University interview with John Hall Wheelock

SHELDON, JOSEPH S.
Republican Party leader, Texas
Eisenhower administration project (1969, 28 pages, permission required to cite or quote, also at *Dwight D. Eisenhower Library KS*) *Columbia University NY*

SHELDON, PAUL
Physician
Dulles oral history collection (1966, 16 pages, open) *Princeton University NJ*

SHELFORD, VICTOR
Ecologist
University Archives *University of Illinois*

SHELL, JOSEPH
Conservative Republican: Leader of anti-Warren forces; Oil industry spokesman
Earl Warren oral history project (in process) *University of California, Berkeley*
Presidential election of 1960 *University of Southern California Library*

SHELLWORTH, H. C.
Weyerhaeuser Timber Company (77 pages, permission required) *Columbia University NY*

SHELTON, ROBERT
Civil rights in Alabama (59 pages, open) *Columbia University NY*

SHELTON, WILLIAM T.
City editor, *Arkansas Gazette*, during Little Rock school integration crisis
Eisenhower administration project (35 pages, permission required to cite or quote, also at *Dwight D. Eisenhower Library KS*) *Columbia University NY*

SHEMESH, YEHEZKIEL
Manager, Shemesh Restaurant (Jerusalem)
JEWISH COMMUNITIES: (10) Jewish life in Iraq (Hebrew, 23 pages, open) *Hebrew University, Israel*

SHEMESH, ZADOK
Director, Shekem (Tiberias)
JEWISH COMMUNITIES: (11) Jewish community of Iran (Hebrew, 56 pages, open) *Hebrew University, Israel*

SHENANDOAH VALLEY
Madison College VA

SHENKMAN, GRISHA
Director, Kfar-Giladi quarry
YOUTH MOVEMENTS: (2) Netzach in Latvia (Hebrew, 28 pages, open) *Hebrew University, Israel*

SHENTON, JAMES P.
Columbia crisis of 1968 (8 pages, permission required) *Columbia University NY*

SHEPARD, ALAN
Project Mercury astronaut

(21 pages, open) *John F. Kennedy Library MA*

SHEPARD, FRANK B. (1888–)
Benedum and the oil industry (17 pages, open) *Columbia University NY*

SHEPARD, HAROLD B.
Project leader, Forest Insurance Study
(1967, 6 pages) *University of California, Berkeley*

SHEPARDSON, WHITNEY H.
Discussed in Columbia University interviews with Cornelis Willem deKiewiet; Alger Hiss; Trevor Lloyd; George Raleigh Parkin; and in Carnegie Corporation collection

SHEPHARD, W. P.
Health science collection (40 pages, permission required, also at *National Library of Medicine MD*) *Columbia University NY*

SHEPHERD, LEMUEL CORNICK, JR. (1896–)
General, U.S. Marine Corps (service: 1917–1956)
(1967, 517 pages, open, also at *Columbia University NY* and *U.S. Naval Institute MD*) *United States Marine Corps DC*

SHEPHERD, VERN see Arthur Ashem

SHEPLEY, ETHAN A. H.
Former chancellor, Washington University MO
Washington University MO
The Washington University Medical School and Associated Hospitals, Inc. (WUM-SAH) *Washington University School of Medicine MO*

SHEPLEY, JAMES ROBINSON (1917–)
Journalist
Eisenhower administration project (1967, 39 pages, permission required to cite or quote, also at *Dwight D. Eisenhower Library KS*) *Columbia University NY*
Dulles oral history collection (1965, 39 pages, open) *Princeton University NJ*

SHEPPARD, HAROLD
Social Security collection (1967, 104 pages, permission required to cite or quote, also at *Social Security Administration MD*) *Columbia University NY*

SHER, DAVID (1908–)
New York political studies collection, New York election of 1949 (4 pages, permission required to cite or quote) *Columbia University NY*

SHERMAN, AREATHA CHENEY
Ricks College ID

SHERMAN, DAN
Hartwick College NY

SHERMAN, FORREST
Discussed in Columbia University interview with William Morrow Fechteler

SHERMAN, MABEL DE FORREST
Hartwick College NY

SHERMAN, STUART PRATT
Discussed in Columbia University interview with Allan Nevins

SHERMARKE, ABDIRASCID
Prime minister of Somalia
(21 pages, portions closed) *John F. Kennedy Library MA*

SHERROD, ROBERT LEE (1909–)
Eisenhower administration project (53 pages, permission required to cite or quote, also at *Dwight D. Eisenhower Library KS*) *Columbia University NY*

SHERRY, ARTHUR
Deputy district attorney under Warren; State Crime Study Commission member
Earl Warren oral history project (in process) *University of California, Berkeley*

SHERWIN, WILLIAM R.
Alaskan pioneers project (40 pages, open) *Columbia University NY*

SHEW, RANDALL E. (1929–)
Ithaca Festival (center for the Arts at Ithaca) project (1966, 36 pages, most open) *Cornell University NY*

SHIELDS, PETER J. (1862–)
Judge; Founder of Davis campus
(1954, 110 pages) *University of California, Berkeley*

SHIELDS, ROBERT HAZEN (1905–)
Agriculturist
(1954, 572 pages, closed during interviewee's lifetime) *Columbia University NY*

SHILLER, BERTHA
South Dakota experience (1970), South Dakota Oral History Project *University of South Dakota*

SHILOAH (LANGSAM), ZVI
Ministry of Labor employee (Tel-Aviv)
ANTECEDENTS TO THE STATE OF ISRAEL: (2) "Brichah" (organized escape) (Hebrew, 29 pages, open) *Hebrew University, Israel*

SHIMKIN, LEON (1907–)
with Freeman Lewis
(1955, 63 pages, also microfiche, permission required to cite or quote) *Columbia University NY*

SHIMKIN, MICHAEL B.
National Institutes of Health MD

SHIMKO, MARGARET RICHARDS
with Charles Lee Swem
John Robert Gregg project (82 pages, permission required) *Columbia University NY*

SHIMONOWITZ, RACHEL
WORLD WAR II: THE HOLOCAUST—RESISTANCE AND RESCUE: (10) Belorussian Jewry (Yiddish, 68 pages, open) *Hebrew University, Israel*

SHIMONOWITZ, YITZHAK
WORLD WAR II: THE HOLOCAUST—RESISTANCE AND RESCUE: (10) Belorussian Jewry (Yiddish, 54 pages, open) *Hebrew University, Israel*

SHINA, SALMAN
Tel-Aviv lawyer
JEWISH COMMUNITIES: (10) Jewish life in Iraq (Hebrew, 23 pages, open) *Hebrew University, Israel*

SHIN'AN, MARY
Tel-Aviv teacher
YOUTH MOVEMENTS: (2) Netzach in Latvia (Hebrew, 29 pages, open) *Hebrew University, Israel*

SHINAN, ZALMAN
Chief engineer, Yuval-Gad, Ashkelon
YOUTH MOVEMENTS: (2) Netzach in Latvia (Hebrew, 4 pages, open) *Hebrew University, Israel*

SHINER BREWERY see Cecile Spootzel

SHIPPING
University of California Institute of Industrial Relations

SHIRIN, YITZHAK
JEWISH COMMUNITIES: (10) Jewish life in Iraq (Hebrew, translated from Arabic, 5 pages, open) *Hebrew University, Israel*

SHIRLEY, DR. AARON
Challenges to governance by students project: Student activism—Jackson State College (1970, 29 pages, permission required) *Cornell University NY*

SHIRPSER, CLARA
Women in politics (in process) *University of California, Berkeley*

SHISHKIN, BORIS BASIL (1906–)
Economist
(1957, 872 pages, permission required) *Columbia University NY*

SHIVERS, ALLAN (1907–)
Texas governor
Eisenhower administration project (1969, 58 pages, permission required to cite or quote, also at *Dwight D. Eisenhower Library KS*) *Columbia University NY*

SMATHERS, GEORGE
U.S. senator (Florida)

(68 pages, portions closed) *John F. Kennedy Library MA*

Discussed in Columbia University interview with Edward Roland Annis

SMEBAKKEN, MR. AND MRS. GEORGE
South Dakota experience (1970), South Dakota Oral History Project *University of South Dakota*

SMEDLEY, CHESTER, AND CLYDE SMEDLEY
(1962) *State Historical Society of Colorado*

SMILEY, ALBERT K., JR., AND DANIEL SMILEY
(1968, 87 pages, permission required to cite or quote) *Cornell University NY*

SMILEY, JOSEPH R.
Former president, University of Texas, El Paso

(1970, 18 pages, open) *University of Texas, El Paso*

SMILEY, ROBERT
Program director, WGAR (Cleveland OH)

Radio pioneers collection (1963, 18 pages, also at *Broadcast Pioneers Library DC*) *Columbia University NY*

SMILLIE, WILSON GEORGE (1886–)
Health science collection (50 pages, permission required, also at *National Library of Medicine MD*) *Columbia University NY*

SMITH, ALFRED E.
Discussed in Columbia University interviews with Geroge Fletcher Chandler; Marion Dickerman; Eddie Dowling; Jonah J. Goldstein; Herbert Henry Lehman; John Lord O'Brian; Frances Perkins; Joseph M. Proskauer; William Jay Schieffelin; Francis Russell Stoddard; Emily Smith (Mrs. John) Warner

Discussed in Scott E. Webber Collection NY James A. Farley collection

SMITH, ALICE SCOFIELD
South Dakota experience (1971), South Dakota Oral History Project *University of South Dakota*

SMITH, ANTONIO MACEO
Federal housing official (Dallas)

(1972) *Fisk University TN*

SMITH, BLAKE
Religion and culture project *Baylor University TX*

SMITH, BROMLEY
Eisenhower administration project (36 pages, permission required to cite or quote, also at *Dwight D. Eisenhower Library KS*) *Columbia University NY*

SMITH, BRUCE
Columbia crisis of 1968 (74 pages, permission required) *Columbia University NY*

SMITH, CARLETON D.
Former NBC and RCA vice-president

(1967, 1 reel, 18 pages) *Broadcast Pioneers Library DC*

SMITH, CHARLES (1842–)
Black cowboy

(1963, 52 pages, open) *Columbia University NY*

SMITH, CHARLIE
Oldest man in United States (1972)

(1972) *Fisk University TN*

SMITH, CHESTER
Charlie Smith's son

(1972) *Fisk University TN*

SMITH, CLARENCE W. (1905–)
Agricultural businessman

(1965, 68 pages, open) *Cornell University NY*

SMITH, CYRUS ROWLETT (1899–)
Aviation collection (48 pages, permission required to cite or quote, also at *United States Air Force Academy CO* and *University of the Air, Maxwell Air Force Base AL*) *Columbia University NY*

SMITH, DAVID
Ithaca Festival (Center for the Arts at Ithaca) project (98 pages, open) *Cornell University NY*

SMITH, DAVID (1906–1965)
Sculptor

(1961, 10 pages; 1964, 7 pages) *Archives of American Art—Smithsonian Institution NY*

SMITH, DEAN
Aviation collection (77 pages, permission required to cite or quote, also at *United States Air Force Academy CO* and *University of the Air, Maxwell Air Force Base AL*) *Columbia University NY*

SMITH, DR. *see* Victor Rubert

SMITH, DUANE A.
(1968) *State Historical Society of Colorado*

SMITH, EDWARD
University of Washington Libraries WA

SMITH, EDWIN S. (1891–)
National Labor Relations Board (1968, 103 pages, permission required to cite or quote) *Cornell University NY*

SMITH, FREDDIE
U.S. Marine Corps Vietnam War veteran

(1972) *Fisk University TN*

SMITH (GARRETT) FAMILY
One of first black families in South Bend

Discussed in Northern Indiana Historical Society Noah Hubbard interview

SMITH, GERARD C. (1914–)
Assistant Secretary of State for policy planning

Dulles oral history collection (1965, 52 pages, permission required to cite or quote) *Princeton University NJ*

SMITH, GIRARD E.
Mill Valley Public Library CA

SMITH, H. ALEXANDER (1880–1966)
U.S. senator

(1963, 595 pages, also microfiche, permission required to cite or quote) *Columbia University NY*

SMITH, HARVEY
Sugar beet industry in New York State (1968, 28 pages, permission required to cite or quote) *Cornell University NY*

SMITH, HENRY DEWITT
Mining engineers (22 pages, permission required to cite or quote) *Columbia University NY*

SMITH, HERMON DUNLAP (1900–), AND MRS. SMITH
Adlai E. Stevenson project (58 pages, permission required) *Columbia University NY*

SMITH, HILDA JANE
History of workers education project (in process) *Pennsylvania State University*

SMITH, HILDA W.
Bryn Mawr Summer School for Women Workers *Bryn Mawr College Alumnae Association PA*

SMITH, HOLLAND M.
United States Naval War College RI

Discussed in Columbia University interviews with Graves Blanchard Erskine; Harry W. Hill; Robert Edward Hogaboom; Victor Harold Krulak

SMITH, HOWARD
(1972) *Wabash Carnegie Public Library IN*

SMITH, HOWARD W. (1883–)
Judge

National Labor Relations Board (1969, 68 pages, open) *Cornell University NY*

SMITH, HOWARD KINGSBURY (1914–)
Journalist

Eisenhower administration project (1968, 44 pages, permission required to cite or quote, also at *Dwight D. Eisenhower Library KS*) *Columbia University NY*

SNIPES, KENNETH
Executive director, Karamu House (Cleveland OH)

(1972) *Fisk University TN*

SNITOW, ALAN M.
Challenges to governance by students project: Pentagon March (1967) (1968, 33 pages, open) *Cornell University NY*

SNOW, FLORENCE
Smith alumna, class of 1904: Founder, Smith Alumnae Association

(1973, 1 hour, 30 pages) *Smith College MA*

SNOW, WILBERT
University of Connecticut

SNOY, JEAN CHARLES
Chairman, Organization of European Economic Cooperation (1948–1950), Belgium

Harry S. Truman Library MO

SNYDER, ANITA
University of Washington Libraries WA

SNYDER, BILL, TRIO *see* Bill Snyder Trio

SNYDER, HOWARD
Discussed in Columbia University interview with Edward Delos Churchill

SNYDER, MURRAY (1911–   )
Public relations executive
Eisenhower administration project (1967, 67 pages, permission required to cite or quote, also available at *Dwight D. Eisenhower Library KS*) *Columbia University NY*

SNYDER, TEXAS
Oil industry collection *Texas Tech University*

SOBELOFF, HON. SIMON (1894–1973)
Chief judge, Maryland court of appeals; U.S. solicitor general; Chief judge, U.S. court of appeals (1956–1964)

(1971, 30 pages, 2 hours) *Maryland Historical Society*

SOCIAL PROBLEMS
Shirley Camper Soman Collection NY
See also Crime and criminals; Immigration and Emigration; Public health; Woman—Employment

SOCIAL SECURITY *see* Insurance, Social; Public Welfare

SOCIAL WELFARE *see* Public Welfare; Social work

SOCIAL WORK
Field Enterprises IL

Shirley Camper Soman Collection NY
See also Public Welfare

SOCIALISM
Socialist movement project Participants and pages: Irving Barshop, 27; Daniel Bell, 49; John Bennett, 30; Thomas Clement, 39; Morris L. Ernst, 33; Paul Feldman, 23; Harry Fleischman, 38; Samuel Friedman, 54; Gerry Gelles, 50; Maurice Goldbloom, 37; Eric Hass, 33; Adolph Held, 28; Harry W. Laidler, 50; Aaron J. Levenstein, 43; David McReynolds, 34; Nathaniel Minkoff, 28; A. J. Muste, 26; Robin Myers, 53; Pauline Newman, 33; D. Ernst Papanek, 62; Joseph Schlossberg, 51; Max Shachtman, 76; Herman Singer, 23; Mark Starr, 42; Seymour Steinsapir, 24; Irwin Suall, 43; Paul Sweezy, 14; Norman M. Thomas, 25; Gus Tyler, 28; James Weinstein, 45 (1965, 1141 pages, permission required to cite or quote) *Columbia University NY*

Early socialists in California *Immaculate Heart College CA*

Bridgeport Socialist Party *University of Bridgeport CT*

Government and politics collection *University of California, Los Angeles*

Socialists of St. Louis and Missouri collection (5 hours, on-going) *University of Missouri, St. Louis*

SOCIETY ISLANDS
The Genealogical Society of the Church of Jesus Christ of Latter-Day Saints UT

SOCIETY OF FRIENDS *see* Friends, Society of

SOCIETY OF THE HOLY CHILD JESUS (SHCJ)
Society of the Holy Child Jesus PA

SOCIETY OF JESUS *see* Jesuits

SODOMA, JOHN
Sugar beet industry in New York State (1966–1968, 65 pages, open) *Cornell University NY*

SOFER, MOSHE
JEWISH COMMUNITIES (10) Jewish life in Iraq (Hebrew, 21 pages, open) *Hebrew University, Israel*

SOHN WON YIL
Former Korean minister of defense
Dulles oral history collection (1964, 17 pages, open) *Princeton University, NJ*

SOKOLSKY, GEORGE EPHRAIM (1893–1962)
Columnist; Author

(1962, 126 pages, also microfiche, permission required to cite or quote) *Columbia University, NY*

SOLA, FERNANDO (1906–   )
Lawyer

Argentina in the 1930s (1971, Spanish, 50 pages, open) *Columbia University, NY*

SOLBERG, HARRY L.
Educator, Purdue Research Foundation

(1970, 55 pages) *Purdue University Archives IN*

SOLINS, SAMUEL
West Virginia political figure

(22 pages, open) *John F. Kennedy Library MA*

SOLOMON, AVRI
Wartime leader, Slovakian Betar movement; Israel Electric Company official (Haifa)

WORLD WAR II—THE HOLOCAUST—RESISTANCE AND RESCUE. (11) Jewish resistance in Slovakia (Hebrew, 53 pages; Hebrew, 18 pages; German, 33 pages; open) *Hebrew University, Israel*

SOLOMON, SIDNEY L. (1902–   )
Federated Department Stores Project (42 pages, permission required) *Columbia University NY*

SOLTZ, MISHA
WORLD WAR II: THE HOLOCAUST—RESISTANCE AND RESCUE: (13) Underground activities of the Lithuanian Jews (Hebrew, 39 pages, open) *Hebrew University, Israel*

SOMERS, A. NORMAN
National Labor Relations Board (1969, 34 pages, permission required to cite or quote) *Cornell University NY*

SOMERS, HERMAN MILES (1911–   )
Economist
Social Security collection (1968, 199 pages, closed during interviewee's lifetime, also at *Social Security Administration MD) Columbia University NY*

SOMMERS, DAVIDSON
World Bank (74 pages, permission required to cite or quote, also at *Brookings Institution DC) Columbia University NY*

SOMMERS, EARL, AND ERNEST D. SOMMERS

(1962) *State Historical Society of Colorado*

SOMMERVILLE, JOHN
Early black dentist in Los Angeles
Miscellaneous collection *University of Southern California Library*

SONDHEIM, WALTER (1908–   )
Vice-chairman, Charles Center-Inner Harbor Management, Inc.

(1971, 31 pages, 1 hour) *Maryland Historical Society*

SONNENHOL, GUSTAV A.
Information officer, Marshall Plan ministry (1949–1954, Germany)

Harry S. Truman Library MO

SPARKS, MRS. WALTER (1905–   )

(1969, 19 pages, open) *North Texas State University Oral History Collection*

SPARKS, WILBUR D.
Truman Committee staff investigator (1941–1946)

Harry S. Truman Library MO

SPATHELF, VICTOR F.
President emeritus, Ferris State College

Ferris State College MI

SPAULDING, CHARLES
Kennedy friend and campaign aide

(110 pages, portion closed) *John F. Kennedy Library MA*

(88 pages, part of special Robert F. Kennedy oral history program, portions closed) *John F. Kennedy Library MA*

SPAULDING, SARAH G.

(1959) *State Historical Society of Colorado*

SPAULDING, VIRGINIA STOLTE
Mill Valley Public Library CA

SPEARMAN, ELIHU
University of Washington Libraries WA

SPEARMAN, VIVIAN
University of Washington Libraries WA

SPECTOR, SIDNEY
Social Security collection (57 pages, open, also at *Social Security Administration MD*) *Columbia University NY*

Discussed in Columbia University interview with Harold Sheppard

SPEDDING, FRANK H.
Iowa State University Libraries

SPEED, KEATS (1879–1952)
Newspaperman

(1950, 64 pages, open) *Columbia University NY*

SPEIRS, NEIL P. (1912–   )
Labor member, Railroad Retirement Board

United Transportation Union project (1971, 142 pages, open, permission required to reproduce tape) *Cornell University NY*

SPELLMAN, A. B.

(1972) *Fisk University TN*

SPENCE, HERSEY EVERETT (1882–   )

James B. Duke project (78 pages, permission required, also at *Duke University NC*) *Columbia University NY*

SPENCE, HOMER R. (1891–1973)
California Supreme Court justice, retired; Attorney; Legislator

(1972, 78 pages) *University of California. Berkeley*

SPENCE, RALPH
Discussed in Columbia University interview with Albert Edward Sutherland

SPENCER, EMORY M. (1905–   )
Attorney

(1971, 64 pages, open) *North Texas State University Oral History Collection*

SPENCER, J. E.
Geographer

(1970, 20 minutes) *Plymouth State College NH*

SPENCER, LELAND (1895–   )

Milk marketing in New York project (1967, 202 pages, permission required to cite or quote, tape open) *Cornell University NY*

SPENCER, LEN
Chief engineer, CKAC (Montreal, Canada)

(1966, 1 reel) *Broadcast Pioneers Library DC*

SPENCER, ROSCOE
Health science collection (142 pages, permission required, also at *National Library of Medicine MD*) *Columbia University NY*

SPENDER, SIR PERCY (1897–   )
Former Australian ambassador to the United States

Dulles oral history collection (1964, 27 pages, permission required to cite or quote) *Princeton University NJ*

SPENGLER, EDWIN
Dean emeritus, Brooklyn College

Brooklyn College NY

SPERISEN, ALBERT (1908–   )
Fine printer; Advertising art director

(1966, 91 pages) *University of California. Berkeley*

SPERRY, JESSIE (1888–   )

(1963, 62 pages, permission required to use) *Cornell University NY*

SPEWACK, BELLA LOEBEL (1899–   )
with Samuel Spewack

Popular arts collection (49 pages, open) *Columbia University NY*

SPEWACK, SAMUEL (1899–   ), AND BELLA LOEBEL SPEWACK

Popular arts collection (49 pages, open) *Columbia University NY*

SPIEGEL, MATHIAS L.
New York political studies, Citizens Budget Commission (67 pages, closed until January 1, 1975) *Columbia University NY*

SPIEGELBERG, GEORGE ALFRED (1897–   )
Lawyer

Robert P. Patterson project (20 pages, closed until January 1, 1980) *Columbia University NY*

SPINAR, LEO
SDSU engineering controversy (1969–1971). South Dakota experience, South Dakota Oral History Project (1971, restricted until 1981 or permission from interviewee) *University of South Dakota*

SPINGARN, ARTHUR B. (1878–1971)
Lawyer

(1966, 101 pages, closed until December 2, 1976) *Columbia University NY*

SPITALNY, H. LEOPOLD
Conductor and former contractor for NBC musicians

(1965, 1 reel, 31 pages) *Broadcast Pioneers Library DC*

SPITZ, RENE
Psychoanalyst

Psychoanalytic movement collection (1965, 104 pages, permission required) *Columbia University NY*

SPITZER, ARTHUR
Challenges to governance by students project (1969, 161 pages, open) *Cornell University NY*

SPITZER, MOSHE
Owner, Tarshish Books Publishing House, (Jerusalem)

JEWISH COMMUNITIES: (1) German Jewry (1933–1935) (Hebrew, 32 pages, open) *Hebrew University, Israel*

YOUTH MOVEMENTS: (1) Jewish youth movements in Czechoslovakia (Hebrew, 24 pages, open) *Hebrew University, Israel*

SPIVACKE, HAROLD (1904–   )
Musicologist

Carnegie Corporation collection (1968, 76 pages, permission required) *Columbia University NY*

SPOCK, BENJAMIN
Cleveland State University Library OH

SPOETZEL, CECILE
Shiner Brewery, Oral business history project *University of Texas, Austin*

SPOKANE PUBLIC LIBRARY
Spokane Public Library WA

SPORTS
Athletic boom in West Texas (open) *Texas Tech University*

See also Olympic Games; Rodeos

SPRAGUE, MANSFIELD DANIEL (1910–   )
Lawyer

Eisenhower administration project (1968, 57 pages, permission required to cite or quote, also at *Dwight D. Eisenhower Library KS*) *Columbia University NY*

STANLEY, HAROLD R.
National Institutes of Health MD

STANLEY, KIM (MRS. ALFRED RYDER) (1925–)
Popular arts collection (41 pages, open) *Columbia University NY*

STANLEY, MILES
President, West Virginia Labor Federation (AFL-CIO)

(24 pages, open) *John F. Kennedy Library MA*

STANLEY, ROBERT M.
(1968) *State Historical Society of Colorado*

STANLEY, WENDELL MEREDITH (1904–)
Nobel Laureates collection (36 pages, permission required) *Columbia University NY*

STANS, MAURICE HUBERT (1908–)
Investment banker; Government official

Eisenhower administration project (1968, 83 pages, closed during interviewee's lifetime, also at *Dwight D. Eisenhower Library KS*) *Columbia University NY*

STANTON, FRANK (1908–)
Broadcasting executive

American cultural leaders collection (1968, 330 pages, closed pending publication of a study) *Columbia University NY*

Discussed in Columbia University interview with Paul Felix Lazarsfeld

STANTON, JAMES V.
Cleveland State University Library OH

STANTON, DR. PHOEBE
Professor of art, Johns Hopkins University

(1971, 31 pages, 1 1/2 hours, open) *Maryland Historical Society*

STANTON, R. MILLER (1900–)
(1965, 83 pages, permission required to cite or quote) *Cornell University NY*

STANTON, RUTH C. *see* Sam Young

STANTON, TOM
SDSU engineering controversy (1970–1971). South Dakota experience, South Dakota Oral History Project (1971, restricted, permission of interviewee required) *University of South Dakota*

STAPLETON, BENJAMIN FRANKLIN
State Historical Society of Colorado

STAPLETON, MAUREEN (1925–)
Popular arts collection (79 pages, permission required) *Columbia University NY*

STAPP, JOHN PAUL (1910–)
Aviation collection (28 pages, permission required to cite or quote, also at *United States Air Force Academy CO* and *University of*

the Air, Maxwell Air Force Base AL) *Columbia University NY*

STARK, HAROLD
Discussed in Columbia University interview with Thomas Charles Hart

STARK, HEMAN G.
Public administrator

(1972, 60 pages) *University of California, Berkeley*

STARKMAN (NEE VERLINSKI), MIRIAM
Chief magistrate (Haifa)

JEWISH COMMUNITIES: (4) Zionist movement in U.S.S.R. (1917–1935)(Hebrew, 12 pages, open) *Hebrew University, Israel*

STARKWEATHER, WILLIAM E. B.
William E. B. Starkweather on Sorolla *Hispanic Society of America NY*

STARR, MARK (1894–)
Socialist movement project (42 pages, permission required to cite or quote) *Columbia University NY*

STARR, RAYMOND W.
Federal judge

Ferris State College MI

STASON, E. BLYTHE
University of Michigan

STASSEN, HAROLD EDWARD (1907–)
Lawyer

Eisenhower administration project (1967, 68 pages, closed until 1985, also at *Dwight D. Eisenhower Library KS*) *Columbia University NY*

Dulles oral history collection (1965, 59 pages, open) *Princeton University NJ*

Discussed in Columbia University interviews with Hugh Meade Alcorn, Jr.; Richard Mervin Bissell, Jr.

STATE COLLEGE OF ARKANSAS
History of the State College of Arkansas collection (open, must be used in library or office) *State College of Arkansas*

STATE UNIVERSITY OF NEW YORK (SUNY), CORTLAND
Collective bargaining at SUNY project *Cornell University NY*
Participants: Manry Beilby; Hiram Bleeker; Daniel Brennan; Rozanne Brooks; William T. Corey; Richard Correnti; Nicholas Esposito; Dottie Gutenkauf; Fred Hanga, Richard C. Jones; Donald Leon; Joseph Ludewig; Richard L. Margison; Delmar Palm; Anthony Papalia; James Parker; Charles Poskanzerin; G. Frank Ray; William Rogers; Margaret Robb; Louis Rzepka; Donald H. Stewart; Phil Swarr, William W. Taylor; Kenneth Wickman; Alan Willsey

STATES, M. N.
American Association of Physics Teachers (31 pages, permission required to cite or quote, also at *American Institute of Physics NY*) *Columbia University NY*

STAUFFACHER, JACK W. (1920–)
Printer

(1969, 104 pages) *University of California, Berkeley*

STEAD, FRANK M. (1906–)
Public health administrator; Environmental engineer

(1972, 78 pages) *University of California, Berkeley*

STEAMBOATS
University of Wisconsin, River Falls

STEARN, WILLIAM THOMAS
Hunt Institute for Botanical Documentation PA

STEARNS, ALFRED
Discussed in Columbia University interview with Claude Moore Fuess

STEBBINS, GEORGE LEDYARD
Hunt Institute for Botanical Documentation PA

STECK-VAUGHN *see* E. H. Porter

STECK-WARLICK *see* E. B. Moody; William Hart

STEDMAN, ALFRED
Discussed in Columbia University interview with Frederick W. Henshaw

STEEL, FREEMAN, SR.
with George Beesman et al.
South Dakota experience (1952), South Dakota Oral History Project *University of South Dakota*

STEELE, CLINTON
(1962) *State Historical Society of Colorado*

STEELE, EDWARD C. (1922–)
Food processor

(1964, 75 pages, permission required to cite or quote) *Cornell University NY*

STEELMAN, JOHN ROY (1900–)
Labor administrator; Presidential adviser (1946–1953)

(1957, 378 pages, closed until 1985) *Columbia University NY*

Eisenhower administration project (1968, 89 pages, closed until 1990, also at *Dwight D. Eisenhower Library KS*) *Columbia University NY*

Harry S. Truman Library MO

Discussed in Columbia University interview with Ewan Clague

STETTINIUS, EDWARD (1900–1949)
Financier; Statesman

Discussed in Columbia University interview with William Lockhart Clayton

STETTINIUS, EDWARD, SR.

Discussed in Columbia University interview with Boris Alexander Bakhmeteff

STEURT, MARJORIE RANKIN (1888–   )

China missionaries collection (33 pages, open, also at *Columbia University NY) Claremont Graduate School CA*

STEVENS, ARTHUR GRANT (1912–   )

Marshall Plan (4 pages, permission required to cite or quote) *Columbia University NY*

STEVENS, BOSWELL
University of Southern Mississippi

STEVENS, FRANK C. (1885–1965)
Executive secretary to University of California presidents (1905–1945)

(1959, 189 pages) *University of California. Berkeley*

STEVENS, JAMES FLOYD (1892–   )

Forest History Society (33 pages, permission required to quote, also at *Columbia University NY) Forest History Society CA*

STEVENS, JAMES FLOYD (1892–   ) with Arthur Priaulx

Weyerhaeuser Timber Company (75 pages, permission required) *Columbia University NY*

STEVENS, M. JAMES
University of Southern Mississippi

STEVENS, MONTAGUE

Ranching in New Mexico, Pioneers Foundation (also at *University of Arizona) University of New Mexico*

STEVENS, ROGER

Special presidential assistant on the arts; Chairman, National Council on the Arts

(28 pages, open) *John F. Kennedy Library MA*

STEVENSON, ADLAI E. (1900–1965)
Lawyer; Diplomat; Illinois governor

Adlai E. Stevenson project. Participants and pages: Mr. and Mrs. Warwick Anderson, 35; Jacob M. Arvey, 59; William Attwood, 33; Lauren Bacall, 76; George W. Ball, 29; Elizabeth Beale, 36; Robert S. Benjamin, 39; Richard Bentley, 35; William Benton, 40; Barry Bingham, 117; William McCormick Blair, Jr., 94; Joseph E. Bohrer, 46; John Brademas, 23; John Paulding Brown, 24; Mrs. John Carpenter, 14; Marquis W. Childs, 35; Jonathan W. Daniels, 19; Kenneth S. Davis, 91; James Edward Day, 40; Jane Dick, 102; Sherwood Dixon, 87; Carol Evans, 74; Margaret M. Farwell, 31; Ruth Field, 26; Thomas K. Finletter, 62; Thomas Finney, 33; Walter T. Fisher, 27;

Clayton Fritchey, 27; Katherine Clark Gibbons, 73; Richard Graebel, 39; Phyllis Gustafson, 44; John Marshall Harlan, 23; Marian Heiskell, 27; Juanda Higgins, 41; Alicia Hoge, 51; Stephen Y. Hord, 41; Edd Hyde, 24; Lawrence Irvin, 72; Elizabeth Stevenson Ives, 309; Ernest Ives, 36; Walter Johnson, 37; Barbara Kerr, 39; Doris Fleeson Kimball, 22; Louis A. Kohn, 18; Kathryn Lewis, 55; Glen A. Lloyd and Mrs. Lloyd, 30; Edward Bohrer McDougal, 67; Katherine McDougal, 42; Nan McEvoy, 42; Carl McGowan, 252; Thomas S. Matthews, 39; Maury Maverick, Jr., 24; Loring C. Merwin, 55; Newton Minow, 122; George W. Mitchell, 37; Stephen A. Mitchell, 173; A. S. Mike Monroney, 128; Michael Monroney, 50; Arthur Moore, 13; Theodore Myers, 50; John U. Nef, 20; Richard Nelson, 79; James F. Oates, 20; Elizabeth Paepcke, 46; Howard C. Petersen, 69; Francis T. P. Plimpton, 74; Viola Reardy, 99; Richard Reed, 22; Mr. and Mrs. Lawrence Rust, 36; Walter V. Schaefer, 78; Arthur M. Schlesinger, Jr., 43; Eric A. Sevareid, 47; John Sharon, 148; Mr. and Mrs. Hermon Dunlap Smith, 58; John Sparkman, 43; Adlai E. Stevenson III, 75; Ed M. Stevenson, 60; John Fell Stevenson, 28; Nancy Anderson Stevenson, 47; Carroll Sudler, 35; Joseph Tally, 13; Chalmer C. Taylor (with Mrs. Taylor), 41; Marietta Tree, 161; Mr. and Mrs. Clifton Utley, 55; Mrs. A. L. Voigt, 70; Kenneth Walker, 35; James A. Wechsler, 21; Harriet Welling, 26; Franklin Hall Williams, 13; William Willard Wirtz, 87; Samuel W. Witwer, 49; Wilson W. Wyatt, 161 (1966–1970, 5326 pages, permission required) *Columbia University NY*

Discussed in Columbia University interviews with Chester Bowles; Cass Canfield; Charles D. Cook; Edward Costikyan; Louis G. Cowan; Luther Hartwell Hodges; Eric Hodgins; Robert Edward Merriam; Alan Shivers; Elizabeth Wickenden

STEVENSON, ADLAI E., III (1930–   )

Adlai E. Stevenson project (75 pages, permission required) *Columbia University NY*

STEVENSON, ALEXANDER

World Bank (28 pages, permission required to cite or quote, also at *Brookings Institution DC) Columbia University NY*

STEVENSON, COKE R. (1888–   )
Former member, Texas House of Representatives; Speaker of the House, Lieutenant governor, Governor (Texas, 1941–1946)

(1967, 1969, 138 pages, in process) *North Texas State University Oral History collection*

STEVENSON, ED M.

Adlai E. Stevenson project (60 pages, permission required) *Columbia University NY*

STEVENSON, ELEANOR BUMSTEAD
World War II Red Cross worker; Oberlin College president's wife (1946–1960)

(1973, 2 hours, 50 pages) *Smith College MA*

STEVENSON, JOHN FELL (1936–   )
Adlai E. Stevenson project (28 pages, permission required) *Columbia University NY*

STEVENSON, NANCY ANDERSON (MRS. ADLAI E., III)
Smith alumna, class of 1955; Illinois senator's wife

Adlai E. Stevenson project (47 pages, permission required) *Columbia University NY*

STEVENSON, RAY
Member, United Steelworkers of America education department, Toronto

(1968, 58 pages) *Pennsylvania State University*

STEVENSON, WILLIAM
U.S. ambassador to the Philippines

(136 pages, portions closed) *John F. Kennedy Library MA*

STEWART, BELLE, AND QUEENA JEAN
South Dakota experience (1971), South Dakota Oral History Project *University of South Dakota*

STEWART, BUELL H.
Mexican American project *Baylor University TX*

STEWART, DR. DEWEY
Sugar beet industry in New York State (1969, 31 pages, open) *Cornell University NY*

STEWART, DONALD H.
Professor of History

Collective bargaining at SUNY project (1973, 33 minutes) *Cornell University NY*

STEWART, GEORGE R.
Emeritus professor of English

(1972, 319 pages) *University of California. Berkeley*

STEWART, HAROLD JULIAN (1896–   )

Health science collection (63 pages, permission required, also at *National Library of Medicine MD) Columbia University NY*

STEWART, IRVIN

Discussed in Columbia University Carnegie Corporation collection

STEWART, ISABEL MAITLAND (1878–1963)
Professor of nursing

(1960, 459 pages, also microfiche, permission required to cite or quote) *Columbia University NY*

STEWART, JOHN POGUE
Hunt Institute for Botanical Documentation PA

STEWART, JOSEPH LESTER (1915–   )
Brigadier general, U.S. Marine Corps (service: 1937–1965)

STOREY, ROBERT GERALD (1893–)
Eisenhower administration project (63 pages, permission required to cite or quote, also at *Dwight D. Eisenhower Library KS) Columbia University NY*

STORIE, WILLIAM G.
President, San Francisco employers' council

(1958, 1959, 378 pages) *University of California Institute of Industrial Relations*

STORY, HAROLD HADLEY
Government and politics collection (open) *University of California, Los Angeles*

STOUFFER, SAMUEL A.
Discussed in Columbia University interview with Paul Felix Lazarsfeld and in Carnegie Corporation collection

STOUT, MYRON (1908–)
Painter

(1965, 12 pages) *Archives of American Art—Smithsonian Institution NY*

STOWE, MICHAEL
Tacoma Public Library WA

STOWELL, ADA HELQUIST
Ricks College ID

STOWELL, ELIZABETH
Ricks College ID

STOWELL, EUGENE
Ricks College ID

STRADER, JESSE *see* John Badten

STRANGMAN, HENRY WYMAN
Henry H. Arnold project (38 pages, permission required, also at *United States Air Force Academy CO) Columbia University NY*

STRATEGIC AIR COMMAND
(125 hours, 1800 pages, partially restricted, partially undetermined) *Strategic Air Command NE*

STRAUS, ELLEN SULZBERGER
Smith alumna, class of 1946; Originator and director of "Call for Action"; Writer

(1973, 1 hour, 27 pages) *Smith College MA*

STRAUS, NATHAN (1889–1961)
Businessman; Publisher

(1950, 139 pages, open) *Columbia University NY*

STRAUSS, ANNA LORD (1899–)
Civic leader

(1972, 571 pages, open) *Columbia University NY*

STRAUSS, LEWIS LICHTENSTEIN (1896–)
U.S. government official; Financier

Eisenhower administration project (177 pages, closed until 1985, also at *Dwight D. Eisenhower Library KS) Columbia University NY*

Harry S. Truman Library MO

Discussed in Columbia University interviews with Edward Latimer Beach; Paul F. Foster; Norman Ramsey

STRAUSS, MORRIS LINCOLN (1877–1953)
Lawyer

(1952, 436 pages, permission required to cite or quote) *Columbia University NY*

STRAVINSKY, IGOR
Discussed in Columbia University interview with Roger Huntington Sessions

STRAYER, GEORGE
Discussed in Columbia University interviews with Hollis Caswell; William Jansen; John Kelley Norton; Goodwin Watson

STREIBERT, THEODORE C. (1899–)
Director, U.S. Information Agency (1953–1956); Member, Nelson and Laurance Rockefeller's business staff (1957–1960)

(36 pages) *Dwight D. Eisenhower Library KS*

Dulles oral history collection (1964, 48 pages, open) *Princeton University NJ*

STRICK, GEORGE
Communication's Workers of America collection *University of Iowa Libraries*

STRICKLER, DAVID P. (–1962)
State Historical Society of Colorado

STRICKLIN, HOWARD *see* Leonel Jensen

STRIEGLER, KATHLEEN ROBERTS
University of Southern Mississippi

STRIKES AND LOCKOUTS
Flint (1937) *University of Michigan*

Michigan copper strike (1913), O'Brien interview *University of Michigan*

St. Louis Teachers' Strike collection *University of Missouri, St. Louis*

Gas house workers' strike of 1934, Socialists of St. Louis and Missouri collection *University of Missouri, St. Louis*

See also Labor Unions

STRINGHAM, DAVID V.W. (1948–)
Challenges to governance by students project: Open House Ithaca (1971, 189 pages, permission required) *Cornell University NY*

STRINGHAM, LUTHER
Program analysis officer, HEW; Consultant on mental retardation; Member, President's committee on employement of the handicapped

(28 pages, open) *John F. Kennedy Library MA*

STRONG, EVA
University of Washington Libraries WA

STRONG, VERNON L.
Ricks College ID

STRONG, WILLIAM
Discussed in Columbia University interview with William Jay Schieffelin

STROTHER, DEAN C.
U.S. Air Force Academy project (76 pages, consult center for restriction, also at *United States Air Force Academy CO) Columbia University NY*

STROTHER, MRS.
Explaining weaving *Appalachian State University NC*

STROUD, JAMES (1914–)
Retired civil service administrator; Democratic member, Texas House of Representatives (Dallas)

Legislative project (1971, 73 pages, closed until interviewee's death) *North Texas State University Oral History Collection*

STROUP, JOHN M. (1891–)
Food processor

(1964, 20 pages, permission required to cite or quote) *Cornell University NY*

STROUT, S. CUSHING, JR.
Challenges to governance by students project (1969, 59 pages, permission required to cite or quote) *Cornell University NY*

STRUNK, OLIVER
Musicologist

American music project (1973) *Yale University School of Music CT*

STRUNSKY, MORRIS
Discussed in Columbia University interview with Charles Abrams

STRUNSKY, SIMEON
Discussed in Columbia University interview with Allan Nevins

STRUSS, KARL
Cinematographer

An oral history of the motion picture in America (open) *University of California, Los Angeles*

STUART, REGINALD
TV journalist

(1972) *Fisk University TN*

STUCKEY, M. S. (1919–)
United Transportation Union project (1972, 43 pages, permission required) *Cornell University NY*

STUDENT MOVEMENT *see* Youth Movement

SWAIN, GEORGE F.
Discussed in Columbia University interview with James Madison Barker

SWAINBANK, LOUISE ROBINSON
Smith alumna, class of 1939; Teacher; Member, Vermont state legislature

(1973, 2 hours, 54 pages) *Smith College MA*

SWAINE, PHILIP WILLIAM (1889–1958)
McGraw-Hill, Inc. (32 pages, permission required) *Columbia University NY*

SWAN, W. GORDON
Pioneer program manager, WBZ (Boston)

(1965, 1 reel, 41 pages) *Broadcast Pioneers Library DC*

SWANSON, CARL O.
South Dakota experience (1970), South Dakota Oral History Project *University of South Dakota*

SWANSON, GLORIA (1889–   )
Popular arts collection (50 pages, open) *Columbia University NY*

SWANSON, LESTER
South Dakota experience (1969), South Dakota Oral History Project *University of South Dakota*

SWANSON, SAM
Retired staff representative, Steel Workers Organizing Committee (Deluth)

(1967, 65 pages) *Pennsylvania State University*

SWANTICK, ROBERT
Peace Corps project (1970, 54 pages, open) *Cornell University NY*

SWARR, PHIL
Associate director, Institutional Planning

Collective bargaining at SUNY project (1973, 80 minutes) *Cornell University NY*

SWARTLEY, WILLIAM C.
Vice-president, Westinghouse, WBZ (Boston)

(1965, 1 reel, 24 pages) *Broadcast Pioneers Library DC*

SWARTZ, DORIS DOYLE (MRS. EMERSON A.)
John Foster Dulles's secretary

Dulles oral history collection (1965, 53 pages, open) *Princeton University NJ*

SWAYZE, BENJAMIN (1909–   )
Sugar beet industry in New York State (1966–1968 53 pages, open) *Cornell University NY*

SWEENEY, JAMES
South Dakota experience (1971), South Dakota Oral History Project *University of South Dakota*

SWEENEY, JAMES JOHNSON (1900–   )
Museum director

(1962, 6 pages) *Archives of American Art—Smithsonian Institution NY*

SWEET, OSSIAN
Ossian Sweet murder trial in Detroit *University of Michigan*

SWEET, OTIS
Ossian Sweet murder trial in Detroit *University of Michigan*

SWEETS, WILLIAM N.
Pioneer writer; Producer; Director

(1965, 1 reel, 35 pages) *Broadcast Pioneers Library DC*

SWEEZY, PAUL
Socialist movement project (14 pages, permission required to cite or quote) *Columbia University NY*

SWEIGERT, WILLIAM T.
Governor Warren's secretary; Judge

Earl Warren oral history project (in process) *University of California, Berkeley*

SWEM, CHARLES L. (–1956) with Margaret Richards Shimko
John Robert Gregg project (82 pages, permission required) *Columbia University NY*

SWERI, MENACHEM
Jerusalem lawyer

JEWISH COMMUNITIES: (10) Jewish life in Iraq (Hebrew, 27 pages, open) *Hebrew University, Israel*

SWETT, FRANK T. (1869–1969)
Farmer

(1968, 125 pages) *University of California, Berkeley*

SWIDLER, JOSEPH with Regulatory Agencies Panel
Federal Power Commission chairman

(187 pages, portions closed) *John F. Kennedy Library MA*

SWIFT, LLOYD
Chief, U.S. Forest Service, division of wildlife management

(1968, 29 pages) *University of California, Berkeley*

SWIG, BEN
Close friend of Earl Warren

Earl Warren oral history project (in process) *University of California, Berkeley*

SWING, JOSEPH (1894–   )
U.S. Army officer

Eisenhower administration project (1967, 76 pages, closed during interviewee's lifetime, also at *Dwight D. Eisenhower Library KS*) *Columbia University NY*

SWINYARD, CHESTER A.
Association for the Aid of Crippled Children (52 pages, permission required) *Columbia University NY*

SWIRSKI, AVRAHAM (LOVA)
Ramat-Gan contractor

WORLD WAR II: THE HOLOCAUST—RESISTANCE AND RESCUE: (13) Underground activities of the Lithuanian Jews (Hebrew, 28 pages, open) *Hebrew University, Israel*

SWIRSKY, DAVID AND BLUMA
Tel-Aviv accountant

WORLD WAR II: THE HOLOCAUST—RESISTANCE AND RESCUE: (13) Underground activities of the Lithuanian Jews (Hebrew, 45 pages, open) *Hebrew University, Israel*

SWITKAY, MARY ECKMAN
Smith alumna, class of 1949; Community service volunteer

(1973, 1 hour, 17 pages) *Smith College MA*

SWOPE, GERARD (1872–1957)
Electrical engineer

(1955, 116 pages, also microfiche, permission required to cite or quote) *Columbia University NY*

SWOPE, HERBERT B.
Discussed in Columbia University interview with Allan Nevins

SYDENSTICKER, EDGAR
Discussed in Columbia University interview with Isidore Sydney Falk

SYKES, C. S. (1913–   ), AND RUTH SYKES (1915–   )
The Japanese attack on Pearl Harbor (1971, 75 pages, open) *North Texas State University Oral History Collection*

SYMINGTON, JAMES
Missouri political figure; Deputy director, Food for Peace

(31 pages, open) *John F. Kennedy Library MA*

SYMINGTON, STUART
Discussed in Columbia University interview with Kenneth Claiborne Royall

SYNANON FOUNDATION
State and local history collection (open) *University of California, Los Angeles*

SYNANON, SANTA MONICA, CALIFORNIA
Samuel Guy Endore interview, Biographical collection *University of California, Los Angeles*

SZEMAK, DR. JENO
Hungarian history *University of Southern California Library*

TANNER, GEORGE S.
Ricks College ID

TANNER, MILDRED LOUISE HOGUE
Ricks College ID

TANSLEY, ARTHUR GEORGE
Hunt Institute for Botanical Documentation PA

TANZER, LAURENCE ARNOLD (1874–1963)
Lawyer
(1949, 73 pages, also microfiche, permission required to cite or quote) *Columbia University NY*

TAPP, JESSE WASHINGTON (1900–1967)
Agricultural economist
(1953, 225 pages, open) *Columbia University NY*

TARBELL, IDA
Discussed in Columbia University interview with Burton Jesse Hendrick

TARNOPOLER, LEIBISH
Al Ha-Mishmar newspaper employee

WORLD WAR II: THE HOLOCAUST—RESISTANCE AND RESCUE: (16) Contacts between the Yishuv (Palestinian Jewry) and the U.S.S.R. after W.W. II (Hebrew, 32 pages, open) *Hebrew University. Israel*

TARR, FRANK
Weyerhaeuser Timber Company (17 pages, permission required) *Columbia University NY*

TARRANT, WILLIAM THEODORE (1878–)
U.S. naval officer
Naval history collection (1963, 53 pages, open, also at *Division of Naval History DC*) *Columbia University NY*

TARSHISH, YEHUDA
Tel-Aviv contractor

WORLD WAR II: THE HOLOCAUST—RESISTANCE AND RESCUE: (13) Underground activities of the Lithuanian Jews (Hebrew, 52 pages, closed) *Hebrew University, Israel*

TARTAKOWER, ARIE
Professor; Head, Israeli executive, World Jewish Congress

WORLD WAR II: THE HOLOCAUST—RESISTANCE AND RESCUE: (16) Contacts between the Yishuv (Palestinian Jewry) and the U.S.S.R. after W.W. II (Hebrew, 2 pages, written interview, open) *Hebrew University. Israel*

TASSMAN, HINDA

WORLD WAR II: THE HOLOCAUST—RESISTANCE AND RESCUE: (10) Belorussian Jewry (Yiddish, 87 pages, open) *Hebrew University, Israel*

TATE, ALLEN (1899–)
Hart Crane project (35 pages, closed during interviewee's lifetime) *Columbia University NY*

TATE, JACK BERNARD (1902–1968)
Lawyer
Social Security collection (1965, 119 pages, also at *Social Security Administration MD*) *Columbia University NY*

Discussed in Columbia University interviews with Adolf Augustus Berle; Bernice Bernstein; Alanson Work Willcox

TATE, ROBERT
Mexican American Project *Baylor University TX*

TATUM, EDWARD LARWIE (1909–)
Nobel Laureates collection (32 pages, permission required) *Columbia University NY*

TAYLOR, AUGUSTA HAMPTON
University of Southern Mississippi

TAYLOR, CARL C. (1884–)
(1970, 80 pages) *Cornell University NY*

TAYLOR, CHALMER C. with Mrs. Taylor
Adlai E. Stevenson project (41 pages, permission required) *Columbia University NY*

TAYLOR, CHARLES E. (1883–1967)
Farm leader
(1967, 248 pages, closed until July 4, 1976) *Columbia University NY*

TAYLOR, CHARLES W.
University of Washington Libraries WA

TAYLOR, CLAYTON
Farmer
(1964, 73 pages, open) *Cornell University NY*

TAYLOR, DOC
Alice Lloyd College KY

TAYLOR, EDWARD DE WITT (1871–)
Printer
(1958, 45 pages) *University of California. Berkeley*

TAYLOR, EFFIE
Nursing Archive *Boston University MA*

TAYLOR, GEROGE
Kennedy Boston associate
(21 pages, open) *John F. Kennedy Library MA*

TAYLOR, GORDON BRINTON
Ricks College ID

TAYLOR, H. J. (1898–)
Law Enforcement Assistance Administration project (1971, 83 pages, 1 ½ hours) *Cornell University NY*

TAYLOR, HARDEN F. (1890–1966)
(1966, 101 pages, open) *Cornell University NY*

TAYLOR, HENRY
Discussed in Columbia University interview with Henry Williams

TAYLOR, HENRY CHARLES (1873–1969)
Agricultural economist
(1952, 170 pages, plus papers, open) *Columbia University NY*
Iowa State University of Science and Technology
Discussed in Columbia University interview with Oscar Clemen Stine

TAYLOR, HOBART
Executive vice-chairman, President's committee on Equal Employment Opportunity; Special assistant to the vice-president
(35 pages, open) *John F. Kennedy Library MA*

TAYLOR, JAMES DAVIDSON (1907–)
Radio pioneers collection (82 pages, open) *Columbia University NY*

TAYLOR, JOHN WHITFIELD (1914–)
McGraw-Hill, Inc. (27 pages, permission required) *Columbia University NY*

TAYLOR, DR. JULIUS H.
Physicist
(1973) *Fisk University TN*

TAYLOR, KATHARINE (1888–)
Educator, Francis W. Parker School, Chicago and Shady Hill, Boston
(1966, 570 pages, permission required to cite or quote) *Cornell University NY*

TAYLOR, LILY ROSS
Professor emeritus of Latin; Dean, Bryn Mawr Graduate School
Bryn Mawr College Alumnae Association PA

TAYLOR, MATTHEW
Dallas Indian urbanization project *Baylor University TX*

TAYLOR, MAXWELL D. (1901–)
General, U.S. Army; Government official
Dulles oral history collection (1966, 31 pages, permission required to cite or quote) *Princeton University NJ*
United States Army Military Research Collection PA

TAYLOR, PAUL SCHUSTER (1895–)
Emeritus professor of economics; California social scientist
(1973, 342 pages) *University of California. Berkeley*

Life experiences of persons who came to Texas as refugees from the Mexican Revolution (1910–1920) *Texas A & M University*

Cattle shoot of 1934–1935 (27 hours, 810 pages, open) *Texas Tech University*

Lubbock, Texas: tornado, May 11, 1970 (60 hours, 1800 pages, open) *Texas Tech University*

Oil industry collection (15 hours, 210 pages, open) *Texas Tech University*

Ranching collection *Texas Tech University*

Texas crime collection (26 hours, 26 pages, open) *Texas Tech University*

University of Texas, Arlington

History of the Texas oil industry, University of Texas Archives *University of Texas, Austin*

Oral business history project (on-going, 170 hours, 3000 pages) *University of Texas, Austin*

University of Texas, El Paso

TEXAS—POLITICS AND GOVERNMENT

Legislative project (600 hours, 6000 pages) *North Texas State University Oral History Collection*

Ex-governor's project (interviews with Allan Shivers, Price Daniel, Coke Stevenson) (200 hours, 2000 pages) *North Texas State University Oral History Collection*

TEXAS COFFIN COMPANY

Texas economic history project *Baylor University TX*

TEXAS COMMERCE BANK *see* Ben Love

TEXAS INSTRUMENTS *see* Cecil Green; Eugene McDermott; C. J. Thomsen

TEXAS INTERSCHOLASTIC LEAGUE *see* R. J. Kidd

TEXAS RANGERS

Oil industry collection *Texas Tech University*

TEXAS SHEEP & GOAT RANCHERS ASSOCIATION *see* Bill Sims

TEXAS TECH UNIVERSITY

Texas Tech University (40 hours, 850 pages, open) *Texas Tech University*

TEXAS WESTERN PRESS

Texas economic history project *Baylor University TX*

TEX-TAN *see* C. C. Welhausen

TEXTILE INDUSTRY AND FABRICS

Rhode Island Department of State Library Services

University of Rhode Island

See also Cotton Manufacture and Trade

THALBERG, IRVING

Discussed in Columbia University Popular arts collection

THALER, R. W. (GUM SHOE KID)

(1958) *State Historical Society of Colorado*

THATCHER, HERBERT B.

U.S. Air Force Academy project (122 pages, consult center for restriction, also at *United States Air Force Academy CO*) *Columbia University NY*

THATCHER, HOWARD R. (1879–1973)
Professor, Peabody Institute of Music; Organist; Composer

(1971, 1 hour, 25 pages, open) *Maryland Historical Society*

THATCHER, THOMAS DAY (1881–1950)
Judge

(1949, 108 pages, permission required to cite or quote) *Columbia University NY*

THAYER, ROBERT HELYER (1901–   )
Diplomat

Eisenhower administration project (44 pages, permission required to cite or quote, also at *Dwight D. Eisenhower Library KS*) *Columbia University NY*

Dulles oral history collection (1965, 37 pages, permission required to cite or quote) *Princeton University NJ*

THAYER, WALTER NELSON (1910–   )
Lawyer; Banker

Eisenhower administration project (1967, 52 pages, permission required to cite or quote, also at *Dwight D. Eisenhower Library KS*) *Columbia University NY*

THEATER

Theater on film and tape *New York Public Library; Lincoln Center*

Southern Illinois University

Emmet Godfrey Lavery interview. Fine arts collection *University of California, Los Angeles*

See also Acting; Actors and Actresses; Moving Pictures

THEILER, MAX (1899–1972)

Nobel Laureates collection (42 pages, permission required) *Columbia University NY*

THEIME, DR. DARIUS

Fisk University TN

THEIS, WILLIAM
Steel union leader

(1969, 72 pages) *Pennsylvania State University*

THELEN, EDWARD F.

Associate of Truman in Reserve Officers Training Corps (1930–1940)

Harry S. Truman Library MO

THELEN, MAX (1880–1972)
California progressive; Railroad commissioner; Attorney

(1962, 100 pages) *University of California, Berkeley*

THEOBOLD, JOHN J. (1904–   )
Educator

(1966, 229 pages, plus papers, permission required) *Columbia University NY*

Discussed in Columbia University interview with Frederick Charles McLaughlin

THERESIENSTADT GHETTO

WORLD WAR II: THE HOLOCAUST—RESISTANCE AND RESCUE: (8) Theresienstadt ghetto *Hebrew University, Israel*

THERNES, FRANK

Communications Workers of America collection *University of Iowa Libraries*

THOM, ALTIA M.

South Dakota experience (1970), South Dakota Oral History Project *University of South Dakota*

THOMAS, CAROLINE BEDELL, M.D.
Smith alumna, class of 1925: Cardiac researcher

(1973, 2 hours, 51 pages) *Smith College MA*

THOMAS, CHET
General manager, KXOK (St. Louis)

(1964, 1 reel, 9 pages) *Broadcast Pioneers Library DC*

THOMAS, CONSTANCE A. PITTER

University of Washington Libraries WA

THOMAS, CONSTANCE A. PITTER, AND EDWARD ALEXANDER PITTER

University of Washington Libraries WA

THOMAS, DOROTHY QUINSY HANCOCK (MRS. JAMES A. THOMAS)
Personal friend and distant relative of the Dulles family

Dulles oral history collection (1964, 55 pages, open) *Princeton University NJ*

THOMAS, EUGENE M.

(1970, 9 pages, open) *University of Texas, El Paso*

THOMAS, EUGENE S.
Executive vice-president, KETV-TV (Omaha)

(1 reel) *Broadcast Pioneers Library DC*

THOMAS, G. HARRIS

Weyerhaeuser Timber Company (63 pages, permission required) *Columbia University NY*

THOMAS, GERALD CARTHRAE (1894–   )
General, U.S. Marine Corps (service: 1917–1956)

THOMAS, GERALD CARTHRAE (cont.)
(1966, 831 pages, permission required to cite or quote, also at Columbia University NY and U.S. Naval Institute MD) United States Marine Corps DC

THOMAS, J. PARNELL
Discussed in Columbia University interview with Robert Baumle Meyner

THOMAS, LOWELL.
(1968, 2 reels) Broadcast Pioneers Library DC

THOMAS, MINOR W.
Historic preservation Charles B. Hosmer, Jr. Collection IL

THOMAS, NORMAN MATTOON (1884-1968)
Clergyman; Politician
(1950, 217 pages, also microfiche; 1965, 152 pages, also microfiche; permission required to cite or quote) Columbia University NY
Discussed in Columbia University interview with Max Schachtman and in Socialist movement collection
Socialist movement project (25 pages, permission required to cite or quote) Columbia University NY
Socialists of St. Louis and Missouri collection University of Missouri, St. Louis
(1956, 270 pages, open) Columbia University NY

THOMAS, ROLLAND JAY (1900-1967)
Union official

THOMAS, WILLIAM L., JR.
Geographer
(1972, 10 minutes) Plymouth State College NH

THOMPSON, AILEEN (O'CONNOR)
Joseph McCarthy project (1967, 46 pages, most open) Cornell University NY

THOMPSON, ARTHUR
Administrative assistant to Iowa Governor Loveless; Director, Grain policy staff, Agricultural Stabilization and Conservation Service
(28 pages, open) John F. Kennedy Library MA

THOMPSON, DALE
Sugar beet industry in New York State (1968, 146 pages, open) Cornell University NY

THOMPSON, ERA BELL
Author, Editor
(1972) Fisk University TN

THOMPSON, EUGENE
Educator, Businessman
(1973) Fisk University TN

THOMPSON, FRANK, JR. (1918-)
U.S. congressman (New Jersey)
American cultural leaders collection (1967, 138 pages, closed pending publication of a study) Columbia University NY
(22 pages, open) John F. Kennedy Library MA

THOMPSON, FRED
Industrial Workers of the World organizer
(1970, 10 hours, 293 pages) Roosevelt University IL

THOMPSON, GORDON
New York City blackout (1965) (68 pages)

THOMPSON, HOMER C. (1885-)
Horticulturist
(1964, 125 pages, open) Cornell University NY

THOMPSON, JAMES STACY (1887-)
McGraw-Hill, Inc. (80 pages, permission required to cite or quote) Columbia University NY

THOMPSON, JOHN FAIRFIELD (1881-)
Industrialist
Dulles oral history collection (1964, 43 pages, permission required to cite or quote) Princeton University NJ

THOMPSON, JOHN S.
Insurance salesman
Ives project (1969) Yale University School of Music CT

THOMPSON, JOSEPH S.
Mill Valley Public Library CA

THOMPSON, LLEWELLYN E. (1904-1972)
Diplomat
International negotiations project (29 pages, permission required) Columbia University NY
Dulles oral history collection (1966, 27 pages, open) Princeton University NJ
(62 pages, permission of interviewee required) John F. Kennedy Library MA
(23 pages, portion closed) John F. Kennedy Library MA

THOMPSON, MRS. MARSHALL
American cultural leaders collection (37 pages, closed pending publication of a study) Columbia University NY

THOMPSON, PETER ARLANDO
Ricks College ID

THOMPSON, PHILLIP
Sheep rancher
Oral business history project University of Texas, Austin

THOMPSON, RALPH (1904-)
Book-of-the-Month Club collection (28 pages, open) Columbia University NY

THOMPSON, RALPH MARION
Ricks College ID

THOMPSON, ROY B.
Trucking industry (1958, 547 pages) University of California Institute of Industrial Relations

THOMSEN, C. J.
Texas Instruments, Oral business history project University of Texas, Austin

THOMSON, EDWARD H.
Agricultural businessman
(1964, 54 pages, open) Cornell University NY

THOMSON, MARGARET
Smith alumna, class of 1911; Missionary in China, Japan, Iran, Pakistan, Turkey, and Korea
(1973, 1 hour, 23 pages) Smith College MA

THONEY, CLINTON
Mill Valley Public Library CA

THORESEN, THOR
South Dakota experience (1971), South Dakota Oral History Project University of South Dakota

THORNDIKE, EDWARD LEE
Discussed in Columbia University interviews with Arthur T. Jersild; William Heard Kilpatrick, R. Bruce Raup; Goodwin Watson

THORNDIKE, JOSEPH J.
Discussed in Columbia University interview with Oliver Jensen

THORNE, FLORENCE CALVERT (1878-)
Aide to Samuel Gompers
(1957, 170 pages, closed during interviewee's lifetime) Columbia University NY

THORNEYCROFT, PETER
British minister of aviation; Minister of defense

THORNTON, DAN
(1952) State Historical Society of Colorado

THORNTON, DANIEL I. J.
Biographical collection (open) Texas University

THORNTON, JESSIE WILLOCK (MRS. DAN) (1912-)
Eisenhower administration project (41 pages, closed during interviewee's lifetime, also at Dwight D. Eisenhower Library KS) Columbia University NY

THORNTON, LES
Acting director, District 38, United Steelworkers of America
(in process) Pennsylvania State University

THORNTON, RAYMOND HOYT, JR.

Arkansas Constitutional Revision collection *State College of Arkansas*

THORPE, CLEATA

South Dakota experience (1971), South Dakota Oral History Project *University of South Dakota*

THORPE, JAMES

Allan Nevins project (3 pages, closed until March 5, 1976) *Columbia University NY*

THORPE, RAYMOND G.

Challenges to governance by students project (1969, 37 pages, permission required) *Cornell University NY*

THORSON, SELMER, AND BILLY SHOUN

South Dakota experience (1960), South Dakota Oral History Project *University of South Dakota*

THORSTENSON, MR. AND MRS. AUGUST

South Dakota experience (1971), South Dakota Oral History Project *University of South Dakota*

THULE, GREENLAND

Nuclear accident *Strategic Air Command NE*

THURMOND, STROM

Cleveland State University Library OH

THURSTON, FLORA R. (1890–)

(1965, 217 pages, permission required to cite or quote) *Cornell University NY*

THYE, EDWARD J. (1896–1969)

U.S. senator (Minnesota, 1946–1959)

Eisenhower administration project (1967, 76 pages, permission required to cite or quote, also at *Dwight D. Eisenhower Library KS*) *Columbia University NY*

THYGESON, SYLVIE G.

Suffragists (in process) *University of California, Berkeley*

TIBBETS, PAUL, JR.

Aviation collection (38 pages, permission required to cite or quote, also at *United States Air Force Academy CO* and *University of the Air, Maxwell Air Force Base AL*) *Columbia University NY*

TIESZEN, ABRAHAM V.

South Dakota experience (1970), South Dakota Oral History Project *University of South Dakota*

TIFFIN, JOSEPH H.

Educator, Purdue University

(1970, in preparation) *Purdue University Archives IN*

TIGUA INDIANS *see* Tiwa Indians

TILAYOFF, SHULAMIT

JEWISH COMMUNITIES: (12) Jews of Bukhara (1900–1935) (Hebrew, 27 pages, open) *Hebrew University, Israel*

TILDEN, FREEMAN

National Park Service Archives WV

TILL, EMMETT

Discussed in Columbia University interview with Herbert Brownell

TILLMAN, ROBERT

Edward Hull Crump and his regime *Memphis Public Library and Information Center TN*

TIMMONS, GERALD

Dean, Temple University School of Dentistry *Temple University PA*

TIMOTHY, BROTHER STEPHEN

Wine (in process) *University of California, Berkeley*

TINKER, EDWARD LAROQUE (1881–1968)

Author

(1964, 41 pages, permission required to cite or quote) *Columbia University NY*

TIOMKIN, DMITRI

Discussed in Columbia University interview with Henry Myers

TIPTON, ELDEN

State legislator

Vigo County Public Library IN

TIREY, RALPH NOBLE

President, Indiana State University

Vigo County Public Library IN

TIREY, MRS. RALPH NOBLE

Vigo County Public Library IN

TIROSH, DEVORAH

YOUTH MOVEMENTS: (2) Netzach in Latvia (Hebrew, 28 pages, open) *Hebrew University, Israel*

TISDALE, JAMES *see* Edward A. Davies

TIWA INDIANS

Doris Duke American Indian Oral History Project *Arizona State Museum*

TIZARD, HENRY

Discussed in Columbia University interviews with Sir Robert Alexander Watson-Watt; Warren Weaver

TLILL, AHMED

(1967, 65 pages, permission required to cite or quote) *Cornell University NY*

TOBIA, VINCENT A.

Chairman, UTU local 1309

United Transportation Union project (1971, 76 pages, special permission required) *Cornell University NY*

TOBIAS, SHEILA

Challenges to governance by students project (1969, 84 pages, permission required to cite or quote) *Cornell University NY*

TOBIN, MAURICE

Discussed in Columbia University interviews with John Brophy; Boris Basil Shishkin

TOBIN, THOMAS

Challenges to governance by students project (1969, 132 pages, permission required to cite, quote or use tape) *Cornell University NY*

TOBRINER, MATHEW O.

Lawyer for quasi-public associations

(1958–1959, 342 pages) *University of California Institute of Industrial Relations*

TOBRINER, WALTER

Commissioner of the District of Columbia

(6 pages, open) *John F. Kennedy Library MA*

TODD, H. P.

University of Southern Mississippi

TODD, JANE H. (–1966)

New York election of 1949 (23 pages, permission required to cite or quote) *Columbia University NY*

TODD, WEBSTER BRAY (1899–)

Eisenhower administration project (88 pages, permission required to cite or quote, also at *Dwight D. Eisenhower Library KS*) *Columbia University NY*

TOEPFER, LOUIS A.

Cleveland State University Library OH

TOIGO, AVINERE

Associate of Illinois Governor Horner

(6 hours, 125 pages, open) *Sangamon State University IL*

TOKARSKI, MIRIAM

WORLD WAR II: THE HOLOCAUST—RESISTANCE AND RESCUE: (10) Belorussian Jewry (Yiddish, 45 pages, open) *Hebrew University, Israel*

TOKARSKI, ZILIA

WORLD WAR II: THE HOLOCAUST—RESISTANCE AND RESCUE: (10) Belorussian Jewry (Yiddish, 7 pages, open) *Hebrew University, Israel*

TOLLEY, HOWARD ROSS (1889–1958)

Agricultural economist

(1954, 703 pages, open) *Columbia University NY*

Discussed in Columbia University interview with Frederick W. Henshaw

TOMLINSON, WILLIAM G.

Challenges to governance by students project (1969, 26 pages, open) *Cornell University NY*

TRESSLER, DONALD (1894–   )
Chemist

(1964, 80 pages, permission required to cite or quote) *Cornell University NY*

TRETICK, STANLEY
Photographer, *Look*, UPI

(50 pages, open) *John F. Kennedy Library MA*

TRILLING, LIONEL (1905–   )
Columbia crisis of 1968 (78 pages, permission required) *Columbia University NY*

TRIPPET, OSCAR
Presidential election of 1960 *University of Southern California*

TROBE, JACOB
Former American Jewish Joint Distribution Committee representative, (Germany)

ANTECEDENTS TO THE STATE OF ISRAEL: (2) "Brichah" (organized escape) (English, 9 pages, open) *Hebrew University, Israel*

TROHAN, WALTER (1903–   )
Robert A. Taft project (26 pages, permission required) *Columbia University NY*

TROOB, LESTER (1912–   )
Book-of-the-Month Club collection (26 pages, open) *Columbia University NY*

TROPLE, JACK, AND CORINA AND EMIL CARSTENSEN
South Dakota experience (1969), South Dakota Oral History Project *University of South Dakota*

TROTSKY, LEON
Discussed in Columbia University interviews with Cass Canfield; J. B. S. Hardman; Max Shachtman

TROTSKY, PAULINA
Givatayim dentist

WORLD WAR II: THE HOLOCAUST—RESISTANCE AND RESCUE: (4) Jews in the underground in Belgium (French, 52 pages, open) *Hebrew University, Israel*

TROTT, MRS. A. B.

(1963) *State Historical Society of Colorado*

TROTTER, MILDRED, M.D.
Anatomy *Washington University School of Medicine MO*

TROY, DAVID S.

Weyerhaeuser Timber Company (36 pages, permission required) *Columbia University NY*

TRUCKING INDUSTRY *see* Freight and Freightage

TRUDEAU, ARTHUR G.
Lieutenant general, U.S. Army

United States Army Military Research Collection PA

TRUDELL, CLYDE
Historic preservation *Charles B. Hosmer, Jr. Collection IL*

TRUE, SYBIL
Radio pioneers collection (23 pages, open) *Columbia University NY*

TRUE, VIRGINIA (1900–   )
Educator

(1964, 111 pages, permission required) *Cornell University NY*

TRUEX, ERNEST
Cinema collection *University of Southern California Library*

TRUITT, DR. REGINALD V.
Professor of zoology and agriculture, University of Maryland

(1971, 1 hour, 16 pages, open) *Maryland Historical Society*

TRUMAN, DAVID BICKNELL (1913–   )
Columbia crisis of 1968 (83 pages, permission required) *Columbia University NY*

TRUMAN, HARRY S. (1884–1972)
U.S. President

Journalism lectures (13 pages, permission required to cite or quote) *Columbia University NY*

Harry S. Truman Library MO

John C. Stennis collection *Mississippi State University*

James A. Farley collection *Scott E. Webber Collection NY*

Discussed in Columbia University interviews with Chester Bowles; Ewan Clague; Jonathan Worth Daniels; Goldthwaite Higginson Dorr; Dwight David Eisenhower; Milton Stover Eisenhower; Edward Lee Roy Elson; Edward Thomas Folliard; Gordon Gray; James Lemuel Holloway, Jr.; Chester Henry Lang; Stephen Arnold Mitchell; Edwin Wendell Pauley; Frances Perkins; Omar Titus Pfeiffer; Kenneth Claiborne Royall; John Sharon; John Roy Steelman; Anna Lord Strauss; Marietta (Mrs. Ronald) Tree; Burton Kendall Wheeler; James Thomas Williams, Jr.; Wilson Watkins Wyatt

Discussed in Sangamon State University IL Mining and John L. Lewis collection

TRUMBLE, THOMAS

Flying Tigers (78 pages, permission required to cite or quote) *Columbia University NY*

TRUSCOTT, LUCIAN
Discussed in Columbia University interview with Frederick P. Jessup

TRUSSELL, RAY ELBERT (1914–   )
Physician

(1966, 320 pages, permission required) *Columbia University NY*

TSALDARIS, CONSTANTINE
Prime minister of Greece (1946–47)

Harry S. Truman Library MO

TSCHETTER, DR. JOHN
South Dakota experience (1971), South Dakota Oral History Project *University of South Dakota*

TSIANG, TINGFU F.
Chinese oral history collection (250 pages, closed) *Columbia University NY*

TSO, SHUN-SHENG
Chinese oral history collection (489 pages, open, description of memoir available on request) *Columbia University NY*

TUAN, YI-FU
Geographer

(1972, 10 minutes) *Plymouth State College NH*

TUBBY, ROGER
Assistant Secretary of State for public affairs; Ambassador to United Nations, European office, Geneva, Switzerland

Harry S. Truman Library MO

(73 pages, permission of interviewee required) *John F. Kennedy Library MA*

TUBRIDY, DOROTHY
Kennedy family friend, Ireland

(38 pages, open) *John F. Kennedy Library MA*

TUCKER, BENJAMIN
Musician

(1972) *Fisk University TN*

TUCKER, EVERETT, JR.
Eisenhower administration project (62 pages, permission required, also at *Dwight D. Eisenhower Library KS*) *Columbia University NY*

TUCKER, JOSLYN
Newscaster; TV reporter

(1972) *Fisk University TN*

TUCKER, MADGE (MRS. WILLIAM BURKE MILLER)
Early producer of children's programs

(1965, 1 reel, 34 pages) *Broadcast Pioneers Library DC*

TUCKER, RALPH
Vigo County Public Library IN

TUCKER, RAYMOND J.
Black St. Louis leaders collection *University of Missouri, St. Louis*

TUCKER, WILLIAM
Massachusetts political figure; Commissioner, Interstate Commerce Commission

(25 pages, open) *John F. Kennedy Library MA*

(40 pages, open) *John F. Kennedy Library MA*

Dulles oral history collection (1965, 32 pages, open) *Princeton University NJ*

TYLER, WINFIELD D. (1913–)
Agricultural businessman

(1964, 145 pages, permission required to cite or quote) *Cornell University NY*

TYNES, EMILY WILSON
Smith alumna, class of 1961; Family and community service volunteer

(1973, 2 hours, 38 pages) *Smith College MA*

TYPOGRAPHY *see* Printing

TYREE, VIRGIL, AND VANISHING TRAILS EXPEDITION (1969)
South Dakota experience (1968), South Dakota Oral History Project *University of South Dakota*

TYSON, EDWIN LLOYD
Radio pioneers collection (32 pages, open) *Columbia University NY*

TYSON, J. D. (1903–)
Former representative, Singer Sewing Machine Co. (Baguio, Luzon, Philippine Islands)

(Prisoner-of-war project (1970, 1971, 178 pages, open) *North Texas State University Oral History Collection*

TZIPPOR, MOSHE (VOGEL, ERVIN)
Editorial staff member, Al Ha-Mishmar

YOUTH MOVEMENTS: (1) Jewish youth movements in Czechoslovakia (Hebrew, 29 pages, open) *Hebrew University, Israel*

U

UAW *see* United Automobile Workers of America

USSR *see* Russia

USWA *see* United Steelworkers of America

U THANT
Secretary general of the United Nations

(19 pages, open) *John F. Kennedy Library MA*

Discussed in Columbia University interviews with Thanassos Aghnides; Andrew Wellington Cordier

UCELLO, ANN

UCLA DAILY BRUIN
Peggy Lamson collection *Arthur and Elizabeth Schlesinger Library MA*

Andrew Jackson Hamilton interview, University history collection *University of California, Los Angeles*

UDALL, MORRIS K.
Congressman

Carl Hayden project *Arizona State University*

ULEN, HAROLD
Harvard swimming coach

(7 pages, open) *John F. Kennedy Library MA*

ULLMAN, EDWARD
Geographer

(1972, 18 minutes) *Plymouth State College NH*

ULLMAN, SOLOMON (–1965)
Rabbi; Acting Chief Rabbi during Nazi occupation of Belgium; chairman of A.J.B.

WORLD WAR II: THE HOLOCAUST—RESISTANCE AND RESCUE: (4) Jews in the underground in Belgium (German and French, 24 pages, with a further deposition of 2 pages, open) *Hebrew University, Israel*

ULMER, JACOB M.
National Institutes of Health MD

ULRICHS, HERMANN F.
University of Washington Libraries WA

UNDERHILL, JAMES LATHAM (1891–)
Lieutenant general, U.S. Marine Corps (service: 1913–1946)

(1968, 204 pages, open, also at Columbia University NY and U.S. Naval Institute MD) *United States Marine Corps DC*

UNDERHILL, ROBERT M. (1893–)
University of California financial officer

(1967, 421 pages) *University of California, Berkeley*

UNDERWOOD, VICTOR (1889–)
(1963, 65 pages, open) *Cornell University NY*

UNGERS, O. M.
Challenges to governance by students project (1969, 30 pages, open) *Cornell University NY*

UNION OIL COMPANY OF CALIFORNIA
William Jarvis Carr interview, Government and politics collection *University of California, Los Angeles*

Robert Field interview, Fine arts collection *University of California, Los Angeles*

UNIONS, LABOR *see* Labor Unions

UNITED AUTOMOBILE WORKERS OF AMERICA (UAW)
Wyndham Mortimer interview, Biographical collection *University of California, Los Angeles*

UNITED FARM WORKERS OF THE WORLD

UNITED METHODIST CHURCH
United Methodist Church collection *Emory and Henry College VA*

UNITED MINE WORKERS
Alice Lloyd College KY

UNITED NATIONS
United Nations Conference, San Francisco, 1945. Group discussion among Malcolm W. Davis, William T. R. Fox, Leland Goodrich, Joseph E. Johnson, and Grayson Kirk (1951, 77 pages, open) *Columbia University NY*

UNITED PUBLIC WORKERS UNION
University of Hawaii

U.S.—HISTORY
Alice Lloyd College KY

Columbia University NY

The Great Depression in east Texas *East Texas State University*

Depression in Western Kansas *Fort Hays Kansas State College*

Harry S. Truman Library MO

John F. Kennedy Library MA

Anniversaries of Lincoln-Douglas debate *Knox College IL*

George Grider *War Fish* memoir *Memphis Public Library and Information Center TN*

Memphis events of 1968 *Memphis State University TN*

Moorhead State College MN

Dulles oral history collection (279 interviews, 12,000 pages) *Princeton University NJ*

Southwest Minnesota State College

Man-land confrontation in the southwest (110 hours, 2000 pages, open) *Texas Tech University*

University of Delaware

University of Michigan

Black St. Louis leaders collection *University of Missouri, St. Louis*

South Dakota experience, South Dakota Oral History Project *University of South Dakota*

University of Texas, Arlington

Lyndon B. Johnson project *University of Texas, Austin*

University of Wisconsin, La Crosse

Effects of Great Depression on agriculture *Walla Walla College WA*

U.S.—HISTORY—CIVIL WAR
Civil War Centennial Participants and pages: Harold M. Hyman, 15; E. B. Long, 53; Bell I. Wiley, 44; T. Harry Williams, 31 (1965, 143 pages, permission required to cite or quote) *Columbia University NY*

See also Slavery in the U.S.

U.S. NAVY

Columbia University NY

Admiral Harold M. Martin *Memphis Public Library and Information Center TN*

U.S. Naval Institute MD

United States Naval War College RI

U.S. SENATE

John C. Stennis collection *Mississippi State University*

U.S. SUPREME COURT

Frank Murphy oral history project *University of Michigan*

U.S. WOMEN'S BUREAU

Mary Anderson collection *Arthur and Elizabeth Schlesinger Library MA*

U.S. WORKS PROJECTS ADMINISTRATION

John Anson Ford interview *University of California, Los Angeles*

UNITED STEELWORKERS OF AMERICA

Pennsylvania State University

UNITED TRANSPORTATION UNION

United Transportation Union project *Cornell University NY*

Participants: Michael R. Alamprese; Parnell M. Aimone; Donald S. Beattie; Charles N. Benner; Paul R. Bennett; George P. Blazin; Charles R. Bethge; John H. Blount; Francis B. Boardman; Louis J. Broten; John R. Burge; Beatrice M. Burgoon; Walter H. Callies; James T. Camp; Walter H. Canty; Willard W. Carson; Charles J. Chamberlain; Al H. Chesser; Louis E. Chester; Louis C. Chisholm; John F. Collins; Joseph R. Coyne; Donald J. Crabtree; Norman R. Dommermuth; William R. Donovan; Thomas J. Duggan; Merrill E. Eastman, Jr.; J. L. Evans and James E. Howe; Gale R. Field; Howard D. Fleenor; Quinton C. Gabriel; Henry E. Gilbert; Robert Godwin; Luis Gonzalez; Christopher V. Grady; Robert W. Groah; Maurice F. Radrizzi; Leo M. Riley; Gerald W. Rogers; Norman J. Rogers; James A. Schultz; William D. Schwieger; Jess L. Shattuck; Charles J. Sludden; John F. Spanfelner; Neil P. Speirs; M. S. Stuckey; George A. Stuebner; Jesse L. Summers, Jr.; Donald J. Swain; Vincent A. Tobia; Thomas A. Tracy; James B. Vanders; Calvin F. Watson; Ben L. Wedding; Pual C. Weixlmann; William R. Welch; Cue O. White; David J. Wykle; J. Frank Young; Charles W. Zies

UNIVERSAL PICTURES COMPANY

Black studies collection *University of California, Los Angeles*

Motion picture and television collection *University of California, Los Angeles*

UNIVERSITY OF BALTIMORE

University of Baltimore MD

UNIVERSITY OF CALIFORNIA

Milton Badt interview *University of Nevada, Reno*

UNIVERSITY OF CALIFORNIA, LOS ANGELES

University history collection (103 hours, 3062 pages, open except for Hansena Frederickson interview and portions of Rosalind Cassidy interview) *University of California, Los Angeles*

UNIVERSITY OF CALIFORNIA, SAN FRANCISCO

University of California, San Francisco

UNIVERSITY OF CALIFORNIA, SANTA BARBARA

University of California, Santa Barbara

UNIVERSITY OF CALIFORNIA, SANTA CRUZ

University of California, Santa Cruz

UNIVERSITY OF DELAWARE

University of Delaware

UNIVERSITY OF FLORIDA

University of Florida

UNIVERSITY OF ILLINOIS

University Archives *University of Illinois*

UNIVERSITY OF LOUISVILLE

University of Louisville KY

UNIVERSITY OF MICHIGAN

Administration of Alexander G. Ruthven (128 pages, open) *University of Michigan*

UNIVERSITY OF MISSISSIPPI

Ole Miss Crisis of 1962 *Millsaps College MS*

UNIVERSITY OF NEVADA, RENO

Interviews with students and faculty (1970) *University of Nevada, Reno*

UNIVERSITY OF NORTH CAROLINA AT CHARLOTTE

University of North Carolina, Charlotte

UNIVERSITY OF NOTRE DAME

University of Notre Dame IN

UNIVERSITY OF SOUTHERN CALIFORNIA, LOS ANGELES

Alice Ehlers interview (School of Music) Fine arts collection *University of California, Los Angeles*

UNIVERSITY OF SOUTH DAKOTA

University of South Dakota

UNIVERSITY OF TEXAS

North Texas State University Oral History Collection

UNIVERSITY OF WISCONSIN, LA CROSSE

University of Wisconsin, La Crosse

UNTERMEYER, LOUIS

Poet

Ives project (1971), *Yale University School of Music CT*

UPINGTON, GAYLORD M., AND LAFAYETTE STEPHENS

Weyerhaeuser Timber Company (75 pages, permission required) *Columbia University NY*

UPPER SNAKE RIVER VALLEY HISTORICAL SOCIETY

Ricks College ID

UPTON, MR. AND MRS. ERNEST

(1964) *State Historical Society of Colorado*

UPTON, WAYNE

Eisenhower administration project (64 pages, permission required to cite or quote, also at *Dwight D. Eisenhower Library KS*) *Columbia University NY*

URANIUM

Brigham Young University UT

(600 hours) *California State University, Fullerton*

URBACH, ARIE

Israeli police, Tel-Aviv

WORLD WAR II: THE HOLOCAUST—RESISTANCE AND RESCUE: (13) Underground activities of the Lithuanian Jews (Yiddish, 36 pages, open) *Hebrew University, Israel*

URBAN DEVELOPMENT *see City Planning*

URBAN LEAGUE (COLUMBUS)

Black history in Columbus (60 hours, 550 pages, mostly open) *Ohio Historical Society*

UREY, HAROLD

Discussed in Columbia University interview with Warren Weaver

UREY, HAROLD CLAYTON (1893-   )

Nobel Laureates collection (44 pages, permission required) *Columbia University NY*

UTAH

Settlement of Bluff, Blanding, and Monticello *Brigham Young University UT*

Southern Utah State College Library

Utah State Historical Society

UTESCH, MRS. ART, AND MRS. HENRY LORSHBAUGH

South Dakota experience, South Dakota Oral History Project *University of South Dakota*

UTLEY, CLIFTON MAXWELL (1904-   ), AND MRS. UTLEY

Adlai E. Stevenson project (55 pages, permission required) *Columbia University NY*

VON KLEMPERER, ELIZABETH GALLAHER
Smith alumna, class of 1944; Professor of English

(1973, 2 hours, 47 pages) *Smith College MA*

VON MERTENS, PETER
Peace Corps project (1969, 55 pages, open) *Cornell University NY*

VON SCHLABRENDORFF, FABIAN
German military opposition to Hitler *Harold C. Deutsch Collection DC*

VON SCHMIDT, HAROLD (1893–)
Illustrator

(1965, 48 pages) *Archives of American Art—Smithsonian Institution NY*

VON SUSSKIND, ALEXANDER
Deputy chief, Mission to the Organization of European Economic Cooperation (1949–1952), Germany

Harry S. Truman Library MO

VON WIEGAND, CHARMION (1899–)
Painter

(1968, 53 pages) *Archives of American Art—Smithsonian Institution NY*

VOORHEES, LILLIAN WELCH
(1973) *Fisk University Library TN*

VOORSANGER FAMILY, NORTHERN CALIFORNIA see Isabel Wiel

VOSE, OWSLEY (1908–)
National Labor Relations Board (1969, 55 pages, open) *Cornell University NY*

VOSHMIK, ROY
Weyerhaeuser Timber Company (16 pages, permission required) *Columbia University NY*

VOSKOVEC, GEORGE
Theatre on film and tape *New York Public Library at Lincoln Center*

VOSS, DR. CARL HERMAN
American Christian Palestine Committee head (U.S.)

JEWISH COMMUNITIES: (6) American Jewry (English, 48 pages, open) *Hebrew University, Israel*

VOUGHT, CHANCE M.
Discussed in Columbia University interview with Eugene Edward Wilson

VYTLACIL, VACLAV (1893–)
Painter

(1966, 11 pages) *Archives of American Art—Smithsonian Institution NY*

W

WABASH, INDIANA
Wabash Carnegie Public Library IN

WACHTEL, HYMAN
WORLD WAR II: THE HOLOCAUST—RESISTANCE AND RESCUE: (1) The Joint (American Jewish Joint Distribution Committee) (English, 2 pages, written interview, closed) *Hebrew University, Israel*

WADDELL, HARRY W. (1911–)
McGraw-Hill, Inc. (30 pages, permission required) *Columbia University NY*

WADHAMS, WILLIAM HENDERSON (1873–1952)
Lawyer

(1950, 118 pages, also microfiche, permission required to cite or quote) *Columbia University NY*

WADSWORTH, JAMES J. (1905–)
U.S. government official

Eisenhower administration project (1967, 248 pages, permission required to cite or quote, also at *Dwight D. Eisenhower Library KS*) *Columbia University NY*

Dulles oral history collection (1965, 41 pages, open) *Princeton University NJ*

WADSWORTH, JAMES WOLCOTT (1877–1953)
U.S. congressman

(1952, 458 pages, also microfiche, permission required to cite or quote) *Columbia University NY*

WADSWORTH, REVERDY (1914–)
Farmer

(1964, 50 pages, permission required to cite or quote) *Cornell University NY*

WADSWORTH, WILLIAM (1906–)
Farmer

(1964, 74 pages, permission required to cite or quote) *Cornell University NY*

WAGENET, RUSSELL GORDON (1890–)
U.S. government official

Social Security collection (1965, 108 pages, open, also at *Social Security Administration MD*) *Columbia University NY*

WAGNER, FRED
Central California coast collection (1966, 384 pages) *University of California, Santa Cruz*

WAGNER, HAYDEN
Henry H. Arnold project (35 pages, permission required, also at *United States Air Force Academy CO*) *Columbia University NY*

WAGNER, JACQUELYN
Smith alumna, class of 1957; Teacher; Political activist

(1973, 2 hours, 49 pages) *Smith College MA*

WAGNER, ROBERT F. (1910–)
New York political studies collection, Citizens Budget Commission (29 pages, permission required) *Columbia University NY*

Discussed in Columbia University interview with William H. Davis; Jonah J. Goldstein; Maurine Mulliner

WAGNER, ROBERT F. JR.
Discussed in Columbia University interviews with Harry Carman; Edward Costikyan; Justin Feldman; Frederick Charles McLaughlin; Pearl (Mrs. Louis W.) Max

WAGONER, CLYDE D. (–1963)
Radio pioneers collection (34 pages, open) *Columbia University NY*

WAHL, JOHN A.
Weyerhaeuser Timber Company (18 pages, permission required) *Columbia University NY*

WAHL, M. MARTIN (1899–)
Food processor

(1964, 47 pages, permission required to cite or quote) *Cornell University NY*

WAILES, LEE B.
(1965, 1 reel, 14 pages) *Broadcast Pioneers Library DC*

WAINHOUSE, DAVID W. (1900–)
Former director, UN office of political affairs

Eisenhower administration project (33 pages, permission required to cite or quote, also at *Dwight D. Eisenhower Library KS*) *Columbia University NY*

Dulles oral history collection (1965, 43 pages, closed during interviewee's lifetime) *Princeton University NJ*

WAJSBLUM, DAVID
Official, Ramat-Gan municipality

WORLD WAR II: THE HOLOCAUST—RESISTANCE AND RESCUE: (4) Jews in the underground in Belgium (Hebrew, 10 pages, open) *Hebrew University, Israel*

WAJSBLUM, GIZA
WORLD WAR II: THE HOLOCAUST—RESISTANCE AND RESCUE: (4) Jews in the underground in Belgium (Hebrew, 22 pages, open) *Hebrew University, Israel*

WAKE FOREST UNIVERSITY
Wake Forest University NC

WAKELY, PHILIP (1902–)
Forester

(1965, 131 pages, mostly open) *Cornell University NY*

WALRADTH, RACHEL LUNG

South Dakota experience (1970), South Dakota Oral History Project *University of South Dakota*

WALSER, DUKE

Tenneco, Oral business history project *University of Texas, Austin*

WALSH, DANIEL CLIFFORD

South Dakota experience (1971), South Dakota Oral History Project *University of South Dakota*

WALSH, JOE

Former editor, Pennsylvania AFL-CIO *News*

(1968, 32 pages) *Pennsylvania State University*

WALSH, PHYLLIS (1897–   )

Civic leader

(1973, open) *University of Nevada, Reno*

WALSH, THOMAS

Discussed in Columbia University interview with Burton Kendall Wheeler

WALSH, WILLIAM

Communications Workers of America collection *University of Iowa Libraries*

WALT, LEWIS

Cleveland State University Library OH

WALTER, ERICH

University of Michigan

WALTER, ISAAC I.

South Dakota experience (1970), South Dakota Oral History Project *University of South Dakota*

WALTER, PAUL

Robert A. Taft project (131 pages, permission required) *Columbia University NY*

WALTERS, JOSEPH

Long-time associate of Shepard in Providence and Boston (1928–1935)

(1967, 1 reel, 18 pages) *Broadcast Pioneers Library DC*

WALTNER, MRS. JOHN L.

South Dakota experience (1971), South Dakota Oral History Project *University of South Dakota*

WAN WAITHAYAKON, PRINCE KROMMUN NARADHIP BONGSPRABANDH (1891–   )

Former Thai minister of foreign affairs

Dulles oral history collection (1964, 19 pages, open) *Princeton University NJ*

WANZER, C. T.

James B. Duke project (54 pages, permission required) *Columbia University NY*

WARBURG, EDWARD M. M.

Son of Felix Warburg, founder of American Jewish Joint Distribution Committee; Art Collector

WORLD WAR II: THE HOLOCAUST—RESISTANCE AND RESCUE: (1) The Joint (American Jewish Joint Distribution Committee) (English, 33 pages, open) *Hebrew University, Israel*

(1971, 18 pages) *Archives of American Art—Smithsonian Institution NY*

WARBURG (UNGER), EVA

WORLD WAR II: THE HOLOCAUST—RESISTANCE AND RESCUE: (6) Rescue of Jewish children (Hebrew, 17 pages, open) *Hebrew University, Israel*

WARBURG, FELIX

Founder, American Jewish Joint Distribution Committee

WORLD WAR II: THE HOLOCAUST—RESISTANCE AND RESCUE: (1) The Joint (American Jewish Joint Distribution Committee) *Hebrew University, Israel*

Discussed in Columbia University interviews with Jonah J. Goldstein; Joseph J. Klein

WARBURG, JAMES PAUL (1896–1969)

Banker; Author

(1952, 1873 pages, permission required to cite or quote) *Columbia University NY*

WARD, A. W.

Dental history (in process) *University of California, Berkeley*

WARD, JAMES TRUMAN (1898–   )

Radio pioneers collection (10 pages, open) *Columbia University NY*

WARD, MARSHALL

Appalachian State University NC

WARD, ROBERT E.

Carnegie Corporation collection (81 pages, permission required) *Columbia University NY*

WARD, ROBERTSON DWIGHT (1905–   )

Carnegie Corporation collection (49 pages, permission required) *Columbia University NY*

WARDLAW, WALT

Sheep rancher

Oral business history project *University of Texas, Austin*

WARDWELL, ALLEN (1873–1953)

Lawyer

(1952, 124 pages, also microfiche, permission required to cite or quote) *Columbia University NY*

WARE, FLO

University of Washington Libraries WA

WARHAFTIG, ZERAH

Israeli minister for religious affairs

JEWISH COMMUNITIES: (3) Lithuanian Jewry between the two world wars (Hebrew, 90 pages, open) *Hebrew University, Israel*

WARING, ETHEL (1887–   )

Psychologist

(1965, 297 pages, open) *Cornell University NY*

WARING, FRED

Discussed in Texas Tech University "Big Band" era collection

WARING, HENRY C.

Business manager, University extension

(1960, 130 pages) *University of California, Berkeley*

WARING, JULIUS WATIES (1880–1968)

Judge

(1957, 449 pages plus papers, also microfiche, permission required to cite or quote) *Columbia University NY*

WARNER, EMILY SMITH (MRS. JOHN)

(1967, 118 pages, permission required to cite or quote) *Columbia University NY*

WARNSHUIS, ABBE LIVINGSTON (1877–1958)

Missionary secretary

(1952, 160 pages, also microfiche, permission required to cite or quote) *Columbia University NY*

WARREN, CARL L.

(1963, 70 pages, open) *Cornell University NY*

WARREN, CHARLES (1868–1954)

Lawyer

(67 pages, written interview, open) *Columbia University NY*

WARREN, EARL

Chief justice, U.S. Supreme Court

Earl Warren oral history project (in process) *University of California, Berkeley*

Discussed in Columbia University interviews with Sherman Adams; Earl C. Behrens; Goodwin Knight

WARREN, EARL, JR. (1930–   )

Judge; Son of Earl Warren

(1973, 63 pages) *University of California, Berkeley*

WARREN, ERNEST

Journalist, Associated Press

(25 pages, open) *John F. Kennedy Library MA*

WARREN, FLETCHER

Former U.S. ambassador

Autobiography of Fletcher Warren *East Texas State University*

WORLD WAR II: THE HOLOCAUST—RESISTANCE AND RESCUE: (10) Belorussian Jewry collection (Hebrew, 22 pages, open) *Hebrew University Israel*

WESSELS, GLENN (1895–)
Emeritus professor of art

(1967, 326 pages) *University of California. Berkeley*

WESSLER, HARRY

Mount Sinai Hospital (15 pages, permission required, also at *Mount Sinai Medical Center NY*) *Columbia University NY*

WEST, ANDREW

Mutual Broadcasting System reporter

(1968, 1 reel) *Broadcast Pioneers Library DC*

WEST, BINYAMIN

Writer; Chairman, "Magen" Association

JEWISH COMMUNITIES: (4) Zionist movement in U.S.S.R. (1917–1935) (Hebrew, 12 pages, open) *Hebrew University, Israel*

WORLD WAR II: THE HOLOCAUST—RESISTANCE AND RESCUE: (15) Contacts between the Yishuv (Palestinian Jewry) and the U.S.S.R. during W.W. II (Hebrew, 9 pages, open) *Hebrew University, Israel*

WEST, MARSHALL

Co-chairman, Hubert Humphrey's West Virginia campaign

(14 pages, open) *John F. Kennedy Library MA*

THE WEST
University of Wyoming

WEST VIRGINIA
Kanawha County Public Library WV

West Virginia University

WESTBEX, ALFRED J. with Howard Droker and Rev. Samule McKinney
University of Washington Libraries WA

WESTBROOK, JOHN
Baylor project *Baylor University TX*

WESTERGAARD, WALDEMAR CHRISTIAN

University history collection (open) *University of California, Los Angeles*

WESTERN MICHIGAN UNIVERSITY
Western Michigan University

WESTERN SAMOA
The Genealogical Society of the Church of Jesus Christ of Latter-day Saints UT

WESTFELL, BENTON B.
National Institutes of Health MD

WESTON, FRANK
Advertising executive

(1965, 1 reel, 45 pages) *Broadcast Pioneers Library DC*

WESTOVER, WENDELL

Discussed in Columbia University interview with Eleanor Arnold

WESTPHALL, POVL
Journalist, Denmark

Harry S. Truman Library MO

WESTWOOD, JEAN
Utah State Historical Society

WETHERILL, MARIETTA

Ranching in New Mexico, Pioneers Foundation (tapes also at *University of Arizona) University of New Mexico*

WETTSTEIN, FRED, AND STEPHEN GILLIGAN

Milk Wagon Drivers' Union local 226 (1958, 205 pages) *University of California Institute of Industrial Relations*

WETZLER, AVRAHAM AND SHIMSHON
Partners, Tel-Aviv cooperative

YOUTH MOVEMENTS: (1) Jewish youth movements in Czechoslovakia (German, 42 pages, open) *Hebrew University, Israel*

WEYAND, RUTH

National Labor Relations Board (1970, 89 pages, special, permission required) *Cornell University NY*

WEYERHAEUSER, C. D. with C. S. Martin

Weyerhaeuser Timber Company (98 pages, permission required) *Columbia University NY*

WEYERHAEUSER, CHARLES A.

Discussed in Columbia University interview with William L. Maxwell

WEYERHAEUSER, FREDERICK KING (1895–)
Industrialist

Weyerhaeuser Timber Company (1956, 167 pages, permission required) *Columbia University NY*

WEYERHAEUSER, JOHN PHILIP, JR. (1899–1956)

Weyerhaeuser Timber Company (41 pages, permission required) *Columbia University NY*

Discussed in Columbia University interview with Albert B. Curtis

WEYERHAEUSER TIMBER COMPANY

Participants and pages: Volume I: A. E. Aitchison, 85; John Aram, 98; David H. Bartlett, 59; Jack Bishop, 32; Ralph Boyd, 26; Hugh B. Campbell, 32; Norton Clapp, 32; R. V. Clute, 65; T. S. Durment, 45; O. D. Fisher, 73; A. N. Frederickson, 71; John H. Hauberg, 126; E. F. Heacox, C. S. Martin and C. D. Weyerhaeuser, 98; F. W. Hewitt, 66; Robert W. Hunt, 85; C. H. Ingram, 12; R. E. Irwin, 40; S. P. Johns, Jr., 46; Don Lawrence, 66; George S. Long, Jr., 46; R. R. Macartney, 44; Charles J. McGough, 66; William L. Maxwell, 112; Howard Morgan, 54; C. R. Musser, 27; Leonard H. Nygaard, 49; Harold H. Ogle, 47; Arthur Priaulx and James F. Stevens, 75; Al Raught, 54; Otto C. Schoenwerk, 40; A. O. Sheldon, 41; H. C. Shellworth, 77; Frank Tarr, 17; G. Harris Thomas, 63; David S. Troy, 36; Roy Voshmik, 16; John A. Wahl, 18; Frederick K. Weyerhaeuser, 167; J. Philip Weyerhaeuser, 41; Maxwell W. Williamson, 38. Volume II: Earl R. Bullock, 32; Albert B. Curtis, 103; Wells Gilbert, 26; Roy Huffman, 68; W. K. McNair, 33; Leslie Mallory, 13; S. G. and C. D. Moon, 32; Jack Morgan, 43; J. J. O'Connell, 77; R. E. Saberson, 81; Hugo Schlenck, 113; Gaylord M. Upington and Lafayette Stephens, 75 (1956, 2981 pages, permission required) *Columbia University NY*

WEYLAND, OTTO P. (1902–)

Aviation collection (71 pages, permission required to cite or quote, also at *United States Air Force Academy CO* and *Maxwell Air Force Base AL) Columbia University NY*

WHALEN, GROVER A. (1886–1962)

Radio pioneers collection (27 pages, open) *Columbia University NY*

WHALEN, JESSE LEO

South Dakota experience (1970), South Dakota Oral History Project *University of South Dakota*

WHARTON, ARTHUR

Discussed in Columbia University interview with Albert John Hayes

WHARTON, EDITH

Discussed in Columbia University interviews with Cass Canfield; Caroline King Duer

WHEAT, LEAN

South Dakota experience (1971), South Dakota Oral History Project *University of South Dakota*

WHEATON, ANNE W.

Director of women's publicity, Republican national committee (1939–1957); Associate White House press secretary (1957–1961)

Eisenhower administration project (1968, 178 pages, permission required to cite or quote, also at *Dwight D. Eisenhower Library KS) Columbia University NY*

WHEELER, BENJAMIN IDE (1854–1927)

Discussed in Columbia University interview with Newton Bishop Drury

Discussed in University of California, Los Angeles, Ralph Palmer Merritt interview (University history collection, open)

WILHELM, JOHN REMSON (1916–)
Diplomat
Dulles oral history collection (1965, 44 pages, closed until Dulles's official papers are open) *Princeton University NJ*

WILKINS, FRASER (1908–)
McGraw-Hill, Inc. (89 pages, permission required) *Columbia University NY*

WILKINS, JOHN W.
Challenges to governance by students project (1969, 48 pages, permission required) *Cornell University NY*

WILKINS, LAURA (MRS. EARL)
State Historical Society of Colorado

WILKINS, RAYMOND SANGER (1891–1971)

WILKINS, ROY (1901–)
Executive director, NAACP
(1960, 130 pages, permission required to cite or quote, also at *John F. Kennedy Library MA*) *Columbia University NY*

Herbert H. Lehman project (26 pages, permission required to cite or quote) *Columbia University NY*

Black St. Louis leaders collection *University of Missouri, St. Louis*

Discussed in Columbia University interviews with George Samuel Schuyler; Arthur B. Spingarn

WILKINSON, EDWARD G., AND FRANK M. READ
South Dakota experience (1970), South Dakota Oral History Project *University of South Dakota*

WILLARD, MARIAN (1904–)
Art dealer, Collector
(1969, 33 pages) *Archives of American Art—Smithsonian Institution NY*

WILKS, ULYSSES
U.S. Navy veteran
(1973) *Fisk University TN*

WILLCOX, ALANSON WORK (1901–)
Lawyer
Social Security collection (1966, 140 pages, open except for specified pages, also at *Social Security Administration MD*) *Columbia University NY*

Discussed in Columbia University interview with Kenneth Williamson

WILLETS, GILSON VANDER VEER
(1 reel, 51 pages)
Broadcast Pioneers Library DC

WILLIAMS, ALEX, SR.
U.S. Marine Corps officer
(21 pages, permission required, also at *Columbia University NY* and *U.S. Naval Institute MD*) *United States Marine Corps DC*

WILLIAMS, AVON, JR.
Black leader, Tennessee
Race Relations Information Center Library TN

WILLIAMS, B. M. G.
Rector emeritus, Church of St. Clemens, El Paso
(1968, 6 pages, open) *University of Texas, El Paso*

WILLIAMS, CLARENCE
(1972, 20 pages, permission required) *Cornell University NY*

WILLIAMS, DONALD
Administrator, Soil Conservation Service
(23 pages, open) *John F. Kennedy Library MA*

WILLIAMS, REV. COUNTEE ROBERT
Baptist
(1972) *Fisk University TN*

WILLIAMS, E. GRAINGER
President, Little Rock AR Chamber of Commerce during school integration crisis (1957–1959)
Eisenhower administration project (65 pages, permission required to cite or quote, also at *Dwight D. Eisenhower Library KS*) *Columbia University NY*

WILLIAMS, EDWARD EUGENE (1892–)
James B. Duke project (42 pages, permission required, also at *Duke University NC*) *Columbia University NY*

WILLIAMS, FRANK H.
Former NBC engineer
(1 reel, 43 pages) *Broadcast Pioneers Library DC*

WILLIAMS, FRANKLIN HALL (1917–)
Adlai E. Stevenson project (13 pages, permission required) *Columbia University NY*

WILLIAMS, G. MENNEN
University of Michigan

WILLIAMS, HENRY (1877–)
U.S. naval officer
Naval history collection (1963, 251 pages, also microfiche, permission required to cite or quote, also at *Division of Naval History DC*) *Columbia University NY*

WILLIAMS, IRVIN
White House gardener
(23 pages, open) *John F. Kennedy Library MA*

WILLIAMS, JAMES THOMS, JR. (1881–1969)
Editor
(1953, 966 pages, permission required to cite or quote) *Columbia University NY*

WILLIAMS, JOHN BELL
Former governor
University of Southern Mississippi

WILLIAMS, MRS. JOHN
James B. Duke project (64 pages, permission required, also at *Duke University NC*) *Columbia University NY*

WILLIAMS, OSCAR
Discussed in Columbia University interview with John Hall Wheelock

WILLIAMS, ROBIN H.
Challenges to governance by students project (1969, 44 pages, permission required) *Cornell University NY*

WILLIAMS, T. HARRY (1909–)
American historians collection (103 pages, permission required to cite or quote) *Columbia University NY*

Civil War Centennial (31 pages, permission required to cite or quote) *Columbia University NY*

WILLIAMS, TATE (1893–)
Businessman
(1966, 61 pages, open) *University of Nevada, Reno*

WILLIAMS, TENNESSEE
Discussed in Columbia University interview with Eddie Dowling

WILLIAMS, W. WALTER (1894–)
Banker
Eisenhower administration project (1967, 103 pages, closed during interviewee's lifetime, also at *Dwight D. Eisenhower Library KS*) *Columbia University NY*

WILLIAMS, WALTER
Artist
(1972) *Fisk University TN*

WILLIAMS, WALTER
Associate director, Manned Spacecraft Center, NASA
(25 pages, open) *John F. Kennedy Library MA*

WILLIAMSBURG, VIRGINIA
Charles B. Hosmer, Jr. Collection IL

WILLIAMSON, MRS. ADIE
South Dakota experience (ca. 1970), South Dakota Oral History Project *University of South Dakota*

WILLIAMSON, KENNETH
Social Security collection (1967, 240 pages, open, also at *Social Security Administration MD*) *Columbia University NY*

(1966, 53 pages, also microfiche, permission required to cite or quote) *Columbia University NY*

WITT, NATHAN (1903–)
Member, United Steel Workers of America legal staff

National Labor Relations Board (1969, 201 pages, most open) *Cornell University NY*

WITHERSPOON, MILTON E.
Benedum and the oil industry (8 pages, open) *Columbia University NY*

WITKOP, CARL, JR.
National Institutes of Health MD

WITMARK, JULIUS
Popular arts collection (23 pages, open) *Columbia University NY*

WITTE, EDWIN
Discussed in Columbia University interviews with Arthur Joseph Altmeyer; Barbara Armstrong; James Douglas Brown; Eveline Mabel Burns; Katherine Fredrica Lenroot; Herman Miles Somers

WITTER, JEAN CARTER (1892–)
Investment banker

(1968, 95 pages) *University of California, Berkeley*

WITTER, REV. RAY I.
Relative of Dwight D. Eisenhower

(41 pages) *Dwight D. Eisenhower Library KS*

WITWER, SAMUEL WEILER (1908–)
Lawyer

Adlai E. Stevenson project (49 pages, permission required) *Columbia University NY*

WOFFORT, LIOLA, AND BEULA HART
University of Washington Libraries WA

WOHL, YAAKOV
Government official (Tel-Aviv)

YOUTH MOVEMENTS: (1) Jewish youth movements in Czechoslovakia (Hebrew, 19 pages, open) *Hebrew University, Israel*

WOHLFORTH, ROBERT, AND MATTHEW JOSEPHSON
La Follette Civil Liberties Committee interviews (75 pages, permission required to cite or quote) *Columbia University NY*

WOLF, BENEDICT (1904–)
National Labor Relations Board (105 pages, permission required to reproduce pages 1–

62; open, pages 63–105) *Cornell University NY*

WOLFBEIN, SEYMOUR
Deputy manpower administrator for planning, research and evaluation, U.S. Department of Labor

(34 pages, open) *John F. Kennedy Library MA*

WOLFE, KENNETH B. (1896–1971)
Henry H. Arnold project (49 pages, permission required, also at *United States Air Force Academy CO*) *Columbia University NY*

WOLFE, MRS. LENA
South Dakota experience (1971), South Dakota Oral History Project *University of South Dakota*

WOLFE, THOMAS
Discussed in Columbia University interviews with Melville Henry Cane; Jonathan Worth Daniels; Carl Van Vechten; John Hall Wheelock

WOLFORD, FRANK
Hartwick College NY

WOLFS, MARIE
Smith alumna, class of 1908: Original member, Smith College Relief Unit which served in France in World War I; Pioneer in civilian rehabilitation

(1973, 45 minutes, 21 pages) *Smith College MA*

WOLKSTEIN, IRWIN
Social Security collection (1968, 255 pages, open, also at *Social Security Administration MD*) *Columbia University NY*

WOLL, MATTHEW
Discussed in Columbia University interview with Sydney Saperstein

WOLLENBERG, ALBERT C.
Assembly supporter of governor's legislation

Earl Warren oral history project (in process) *University of California, Berkeley*

WOLMAN, LEO (1890–1961)
Economist

(1960, 316 pages plus papers, open) *Columbia University NY*

WOLPE, STEFAN
Composer

American music project (1971) *Yale University School of Music CT*

WOMAN
Business and Professional Women's Foundation DC

Fisk University TN
Smith College MA

WOMAN—CIVIL RIGHTS
Mary Anderson collection *Arthur and Elizabeth Schlesinger Library MA*

WOMAN—EMPLOYMENT
Mary Anderson collection *Arthur and Elizabeth Schlesinger Library MA*

Working women in southern California (130 tapes) *Immaculae Heart College CA*

WOMAN—SUFFRAGE
Ohio League of Women Voters *Ohio Historical Society*

Grace McClure interview *University of Michigan*

WOMBLE, BUNYAN SNIPES (1882–)
James B. Duke project (81 pages, permission required, also at *Duke University NC*) *Columbia University NY*

WOMEN, BLACK
Fisk University TN

WOMEN IN MEDICINE
Careers of New England women in medicine *Arthur and Elizabeth Schlesinger Library MA*

WOMEN IN POLITICS
(30 hours, open) *Immaculate Heart College CA*

WOMEN IN SPORTS
Rodeos and rodeo performers *Texas Tech University*

Oral History Research Laboratory *University of Illinois*

WOMEN'S LIBERATION MOVEMENT
Women's Liberation movement collection (on-going, 10 hours, 11 pages, one tape, written permission required) *University of Missouri, St. Louis*

WOOD, BENJAMIN DE KALBE (1894–)
Professor; Author

Carnegie Corporation collection (1967, 123 pages plus papers, permission required) *Columbia University NY*

WOOD, GEORGE A.
Builder of Cedar City's Rock Church, El Escalante Hotel, and other buildings

Southern Utah State College Library

WOOD, GORDON
Athletic boom in West Texas (open) *Texas Tech University*

WOOD, GRANT
Discussed in Iowa State University of Science and Technology History of University collection

WOOD, IDA
Discussed in Columbia University interview with Joseph Aloysius Cox

and Emil Pattberg, 25 (open); Morton Mendels, 76; Lester Nurick, 35 (closed during lifetime); Hoyt Peck, 35; Hugh Ripman, 29; Leonard B. Rist, 62 (open); Paul Rosenstein-Rodan, 51 (closed during lifetime); Orvis A. Schmidt, 23; Davidson Sommers, 74; Alexander Stevenson, 28; Raymond A. Wheeler, 27 (open) (1961, 1392 pages, permission of individual contributor required to cite or quote, except as noted, also at Brookings Instuition DC) Columbia University NY

WORLD WAR, 1914-1918 see European War, 1914-1918

WORLD WAR, 1939-1945
Mormon chaplains of World War II Brigham Young University UT

Dwight D. Eisenhower Library KS

Hebrew University, Israel

Brigadier General Everett R. Cook memoir Memphis Public Library and Information Center TN

George Grider Warfish memoir Memphis Public Library and Information Center TN

Admiral Harold M. Martin (27 hours, 165 pages, open) Memphis Public Library and Information Center TN

Texas Tech University

United States Marine Corps DC

United States Military Academy NY

United States Naval War College RI

WORLD WAR, 1939-1945—CAMPAIGNS AND BATTLES
Sidney Forrester Mashbir interview University of California, Los Angeles

Philippine Campaign World Tapes for Education VA

WORNHAM, THOMAS ANDREWS (1903-)
Lieutenant general, U.S. Marine Corps (service: 1926-1961)

(1968, 127 pages, open, also at Columbia University NY and U.S. Naval Institute MD) United States Marine Corps DC

WORTHAM, GUS
American General Insurance, Oral business history project University of Texas, Austin

WORTHEN, E. L. (1882-1965)
(1964, 32 pages, open) Cornell University NY

WORTMAN, GARY
Challenges to governance by students project: School of the Ozarks (1969, 22 pages, most open) Cornell University NY

WORTON, WILLIAM ARTHUR (1897-)
Major general, U.S. Marine Corps (service: 1917-1949)

(1967, 328 pages, permission required, also at Columbia University NY and U.S. Naval Institute MD) United States Marine Corps DC

WRATHER, WILLIAM EMBRY (1883-1963)
Mining engineers (42 pages, permission required to cite or quote) Columbia University NY

WRAY, LAWRENCE (1899-)
McGraw-Hill, Inc. (40 pages, permission required) Columbia University NY

WRIGGINS, WILLIAM
(1972) Fisk University TN

WRIGHT, ALBERT (1879-)
(1963, 92 pages, permission required to cite or quote) Cornell University NY

WRIGHT, DR. DORIS J.
Pediatrician; Hematologist
(1972) Fisk University TN

WRIGHT, E. A.
(1968, 2 tapes, open) University of Texas, El Paso

WRIGHT, FRANK LLOYD (1869-1959)
Architect
(1957, 45 pages, open) Columbia University NY

WRIGHT, GEORGE A.
University of Washington Libraries WA

WRIGHT, HENRY L.
Discussed in Columbia University interview with Charles Ascher

WRIGHT, JAMES
Poets on their poetry collection (29 pages, permission required) Columbia University NY

WRIGHT, JOHN
Alice Lloyd College KY

WRIGHT, KATHRYN STUBBS
Smith alumna, class of 1935; Volunteer, especially in mental health
(1973, 1 hours, 26 pages) Smith College MA

WRIGHT, LEWIS H. WRIGHT, M.D.
Anesthesiologist
Wood Library—Museum of Anesthesiology IL

WRIGHT, MICHAEL J.
Challenges to governance by students project (1970, 64 pages, open) Cornell University NY

WRIGHT, ORVILLE
Discussed in Columbia University Henry H. Arnold project

WRIGHT, TERESA (1918-)
Popular arts collection (47 pages, open) Columbia University NY

WRIGHT, WILBUR
Discussed in Columbia University interviews with Ross Browne; Grover Loening

WRIGHT, WILLARD H.
National Institutes of Health MD

WRISTON, HENRY MERRITT (1889-)
Brown University president (1937-1955); U.S. government official

Carnegie Corporation collection (1967, 219 pages, permission required) Columbia University NY

Eisenhower administration project (1968, 51 pages, permission required to cite or quote, also at Dwight D. Eisenhower Library KS) Columbia University NY

Dulles oral history collection (1964, 42 pages, permission required to cite or quote) Princeton University NJ

WRITERS see Authors

WU, K. C.
Chinese oral history collection (391 pages, open, description of memoir available on request) Columbia University NY

WUNDERMAN, JAN (1922-)
Painter
(1965, 8 pages) Archives of American Art—Smithsonian Institution NY

WURSTER, C. V.
University of Michigan

WURSTER, WILLIAM WILSON (1895-)
Architect
(1964, 325 pages) University of California, Berkeley

WUTHMAN, ERNEST F. (1918-)
Sales executive, Stecher-Traung-Schmidt Corporation
(1969, 52 pages) University of California, Berkeley

WYATT, WILSON WATKINS (1905-)
Lawyer
(1964, 1 hours, 9 pages) Broadcast Pioneers Library DC

WYCOFF, OLIVER A.
(1968, 1 reel, 9 pages) Broadcast Pioneers Library DC

WYKLE, DAVID J. (1916-)
Assistant general chairman, Penn Central East (T-C)
United Transportation Union project (1970, 42 pages, open) Cornell University NY

WYLER, KARL
Owner and president, KTSM (El Paso TX)
(1964, 1 reel, 15 pages) Broadcast Pioneers Library DC

ZIPKIN, ISADORE
National Institutes of Health MD

ZIRLIN, AHARON

JEWISH COMMUNITIES: (4) Zionist movement in U.S.S.R. (1917–1935) (Hebrew, 24 pages, open) *Hebrew University, Israel*

ZMIRI, SHIMON

YOUTH MOVEMENTS: (2) Netzach in Latvia (Hebrew, 21 pages, open) *Hebrew University, Israel*

ZOGBAUM, WILFRED (1915–1965)
Sculptor

(1964, 8 pages) *Archives of American Art—Smithsonian Institution NY*

ZOHAR, ZEEV
Tel-Aviv diamond merchant

HISTORY OF THE YISHUV (PALESTINIAN JEWRY): (4) Extreme Orthodox Jewry in Palestine (Hebrew, 27 pages, open) *Hebrew University, Israel*

ZOLLINGER, CHARLES
Ricks College ID

ZONARICH, NICHOLAS
Director, AFL–CIO, department of industrial relations, Washington, DC

(37 pages; 45 pages) *Pennsylvania State University*

ZORACH, WILLIAM (1887–1966)
Sculptor

(1959, 25 pages) *Archives of American Art—Smithsonian Institution NY*

(1957, 348 pages, closed until 1977) *Columbia University NY*

ZQUOR (WEISS), DOV

WORLD WAR II: THE HOLOCAUST—RESISTANCE AND RESCUE: (11) Jewish resistance in Slovakia (Hebrew, 53 pages; German, 33 pages; open) *Hebrew University, Israel*

ZUCKERMAN, BARUCH

JEWISH COMMUNITIES: (6) American Jewry (Yiddish, 147 pages, and 116 pages, open) *Hebrew University, Israel*

ZUCROW, MAURICE J.
Professor emeritus of mechanical engineering, Purdue University

(1970, 37 pages) *Purdue University Archives IN*

ZUKERMAN, YITZHAK (ANTEK)

ANTECEDENTS TO THE STATE OF ISRAEL: (2) "Brichah" (organized escape) (Hebrew, 86 pages, open) *Hebrew University, Israel*

ZUKOR, ADOLPH (1873–   )
Popular arts collection (37 pages, open) *Columbia University NY*

Discussed in Columbia University interview with William S. Paley

ZVIGEL, JOSEPH
Director, Greenberg Institute (Jerusalem)

CULTURE AND EDUCATION: (3) Greenberg Seminary for Teachers of the Diaspora collection (Hebrew, 20 pages, open) *Hebrew University, Israel*

ZWEIG, STEFAN

Discussed in Columbia University interview with Ben W. Huebsch

ZWERMAN, PAUL J. (1911–   )

(1966, 40 pages, open) *Cornell University NY*

ZWINGLE, JAMES L.

Challenges to governance by students project (1969, 131 pages, permission required) *Cornell University NY*

U.S. Oral History Centers

ALABAMA

AUBURN UNIVERSITY
Department of Archives
Auburn, Alabama 36830
(205) 826-4000
Allen W. Jones, Director, Oral History Program

General information: 1966, on-going. Tapes: 560 interviews, 750 hours, partially transcribed, fully preserved. Transcriptions: 25 interviews, 400 pages, edited.

Accessibility: Catalog. Indexed. Available to scholars, with some restrictions placed by some interviewees.

Purpose of the program: To collect material about Auburn University and its history; to supplement manuscript collection on deposit in the Archives.

MARSHALL SPACE FLIGHT CENTER
Huntsville, Alabama
(205) 453-2121

Purpose of the program: To collect oral interviews that document the United States' efforts in space, especially those connected with the Marshall Space Flight Center.

ALASKA

ALASKA HISTORICAL LIBRARY
Alaska State Library
Pouch G
Juneau, Alaska 99801
(907) 465-2910

General information: 1970, on-going. Budget: government funding. Tapes: 15 hours, preserved.

Accessibility: Available to scholars applying in person and agreeing to the regulations established by the institution.

Purpose of the program: To document Alaskan history. Memoirs deserving special mention include pioneer memoirs, interviews with politicians and native folktales.

TANANA-YUKON HISTORICAL SOCIETY
Post Office Box 1794
Fairbanks, Alaska 99701
Alma H. Matlock

General information: Tapes: 100 recorded talks and memoirs, not transcribed.

Major collections: Alaskan pioneers during gold strike days.

TONGASS HISTORICAL SOCIETY
Post Office Box 674
Ketchikan, Alaska 99901
Virginia McGillvray, Museum Director

General information: 1960s. Tapes: 8 interviews, 5 hours, preserved.

Accessibility: Not indexed. Available to scholars applying in person and agreeing to the regulations established by the institution.

Purpose of the program: To record material on local and southeastern Alaska history.

ARIZONA

ARIZONA STATE MUSEUM
Doris Duke American Indian Oral History Project
University of Arizona
Tucson, Arizona 85721
(602) 884-2132

General information: 1966. Budget: $50,000. Tapes: many hours, most transcribed and preserved. Transcriptions: edited.

Accessibility: Catalog. Indexed. Interlibrary loan. Few restrictions.

Purpose of the program: To collect and preserve Indian history.

Note: Other institutions cooperating in the Doris Duke Indian Oral History Project are the Universities of Florida, Illinois, New Mexico, Oklahoma, South Dakota and Utah.

ARIZONA STATE UNIVERSITY
Tempe, Arizona 85272
(602) 965-3219; 965-6551
Ross R. Rice, Curator, Carl Hayden Project

General information: 1972. Budget: Not established as an oral history program per se; the taped interviews will be used to supplement the correspondence, books and materials that Hayden presented to the Arizona State University Library. Tapes: 7 hours, on-going, not transcribed.

Accessibility: Not indexed. Available to scholars applying in person and agreeing to the regulations established by the institution.

Purpose of the program: To investigate Senator Carl Hayden, the man and his times, with special emphasis on his early years in Arizona (formative and educational), early Arizona politics and his unrivaled experience in national politics. Areas will include water, land, immigration policies, appropriations, Senate

ARIZONA STATE UNIVERSITY (cont.)
rules and administration, the seniority principle, congressional committee structure and operation, Arizona and other western states.

UNIVERSITY OF ARIZONA
See Arizona State Museum

ARKANSAS

STATE COLLEGE OF ARKANSAS
Box 933
Conway, Arkansas 72032
(501) 329-2931, ext. 223
Waddy, William Moore, Director, Oral History Office

General information: 1967. Budget: $1,820 (not including salary of the director, who teaches a full load in addition to the oral history program). Tapes: 260 hours, transcribed, preserved. Transcriptions: 1600 pages, edited.

Accessibility: Catalog. Each transcript is indexed. No interlibrary loan. All material must be used in the college library or the office of the program with the exception of the Nurses project, in which case copies are deposited with the State Nurses Association for use.

Purpose of the program: To collect source materials on Arkansas history through the oral history memoirs.

Major collections:
1. Arkansas Constitutional Revision (200 hours, 780 pages, one typescript partially closed).
2. History of the State College of Arkansas (46 hours, 500 pages).
3. Health care. A joint venture with the Arkansas State Nurses Association, covering the past half century. Both institutions have copies of the tapes and transcripts (19 hours, 287 pages).

CALIFORNIA

AMERICAN AVIATION HISTORICAL SOCIETY
Post Office Box 99
Redondo Beach, California 90277
William W. Clarke, Coordinator, Oral History Library

General information: 1950 informally; 1969, formally. Tapes: 50 interviews, 120 hours, partially transcribed, fully preserved. Transcriptions: 10 interviews, 300 pages.

Accessibility: No catalog, a list of interviews available. Not indexed. Available to scholars applying in person and agreeing to the regulations established by the society.

Purpose of the program: To record the personal experiences of participants in the history of aviation and specific accounts of events, causes and effects of occurrences and decisions.

THE AMERICAN FILM INSTITUTE—CENTER FOR ADVANCED FILM STUDIES
501 Dohney Road
Beverly Hills, California 90210
(213) 278-8777
James Powers, Administrator, Film History Program

General information: 1969, on-going. Budget: $50,000. Tapes: 175 hours, transcribed, preserved. Transcriptions: 7000 pages, edited.

Accessibility: No catalog. Indexed. No interlibrary loan. Bonafide scholars, researchers and film historians may read the transcripts in the library. Permission to photocopy, quote or otherwise reproduce must be obtained from the oral history administrator. Tapes are not available to the public.

Purpose of the program: To preserve the history of the moving-picture industry.

Publications based on collection research:
Bogdanovich, Peter. *Allan Dwan.* New York: Praeger, 1971.
Labmert, Gavin. *On Cukor.* New York: Putnam, 1972.
Bronlow, Kevin. *The Parade's Gone By.* New York: Alfred Knopf, 1968.

ANAHEIM PUBLIC LIBRARY
500 West Broadway
Anaheim, California 92805
(714) 533-5254
Mary Elizabeth Wilkins, Curator, Mother Colony History Room

General information: 1969. Budget: Funding as needed provided by Friends of the Anaheim Public Library. Tapes: Not transcribed.

Accessibility: No catalog. Not indexed. No interlibrary loan. Must be used in Mother Colony History Room at the Anaheim Public Library.

Purpose of the program: To preserve historical data pertaining to Anaheim, California.

CALIFORNIA STATE COLLEGE, BAKERSFIELD
Bakersfield, California 93301
(805) 833-2011
or
Orville Armstrong
1655 Elm Street
Bakersfield, California 93301

General information: Tapes: 25 interviews made by the Kern County Oral History Conference.

CALIFORNIA STATE UNIVERSITY, FULLERTON
Fullerton, California 92631
(714) 870-2011
Gary L. Shumway

General information: 1966. Tapes: 800 interviews, 1200 hours, partially transcribed, fully preserved. Transcriptions: 300 interviews, 9000 pages, edited.

Accessibility: Not indexed. Available to scholars applying in person and agreeing to the regulations established by the college.

Purpose of the program: To obtain information through the oral history process that may be useful to scholars.

Major collections:
1. The Richard Nixon project. Interviews with persons who knew Nixon during the first 33 years of his life in the communities surrounding Fullerton (175 hours).
2. Uranium industry project. Sponsored jointly with the University of Utah; copies of tapes and transcriptions available at both institutions (600 hours).
3. Indian urbanization project. Sponsored jointly with the University of Utah; copies of tapes and transcriptions available at both institutions (75 hours).
4. Community history project. Interviews with persons significant in twentieth century southern California history (350 hours).

CALIFORNIA STATE COLLEGE, STANISLAUS
800 Monte Vista Avenue
Turlock, California 95380
(209) 634-9101
J. Carlyle Parker, Head of Public Services and Assistant Director

General information: 1964, on-going. Tapes: 12 hours, transcribed, preserved. Transcriptions: 500 pages, edited.

Accessibility: No catalog. Not indexed. Interlibrary loan. No restrictions.

Purpose of the program: Local history.

CHINESE CULTURE FOUNDATION OF SAN FRANCISCO
Folklore Workshop Project
Kearney at Washington Street
San Francisco, California 94108
(415) 986-1822
William D. Y. Wu

General information: 1970. Tapes: 30 interviews in Cantonese, usually Sze-Yap dialect, 40 hours, partially transcribed, fully preserved. Transcriptions: In process; some tapes have been transcribed in Chinese and English, many only in Chinese.

Accessibility: Collection is available to scholars applying in person and agreeing to the regulations established by the institution.

Purpose of the program: To collect oral history from the older generation of Chinese in the United States and to entertain the older generation as well as to learn about the history of the Chinese in America.

CLAREMONT GRADUATE SCHOOL
Oral History Program
Harper Hall 155
Claremont, California 91711
Enid H. Douglass, Director

General information: 1962. Tapes: 130 interviews, 270 hours, partially transcribed, fully preserved. Transcriptions: 5000 pages, edited.

Accessibility: Partially indexed. Available to scholars applying at the Honnold Library, which serves Claremont Colleges.

Major collections:
1. China missionaries (deposited in nine major universities and available at each).
2. Aviation.
3. California—state and local history.
4. Citrus industry.
5. Claremont Colleges and development of the Group Plan.
6. Paris expatriates.
7. Philosophy, psychology, education and literature.
8. Bolsa Chica Gun Club.

FOREST HISTORY SOCIETY
733 River Street
Post Office Box 1581
Santa Cruz, California 95060
(408) 426-3770
Elwood R. Maunder, Executive Director

General information: 1952. Budget: $40,000 in 1972. Tapes: 60 hours, transcribed and preserved. Transcriptions: 1200 pages, edited.

Accessibility: No catalog. Indexed. No interlibrary loan. No restrictions.

The purpose of the program: To record oral memoirs of active leaders in forestry and the forest industries, as one important aspect of an overall program of writing and researching North American forest history; an acquisition program aimed at preserving important papers of individuals, agencies, associations and companies involved with North American forests.

Publications based on collection research: Several volumes published by the Forest History Society.

FRESNO COUNTY FREE LIBRARY
2420 Mariposa Street
Fresno, California 93721
(209) 488-3208

General information: 1968. Tapes: Transcribed, not preserved. Transcriptions: 319 pages.

Accessibility: Catalog. Indexed. No interlibrary loan. The transcripts are limited to use in the building. Patrons are referred to them who clearly are attempting to pursue research in depth and of a serious nature—as opposed to students seeking sources of information for term papers or course work.

Purpose of the program: To obtain and make available for use local historical data otherwise unavailable and most likely permanently lost.

HOLLYWOOD CENTER FOR THE AUDIO-VISUAL ARTS
412 South Parkview
Los Angeles, California 90057
Clarence Inman

General information: 1962 (originally recorded by Hollywood Museum Associates; in 1968 the program transferred to Los Angeles City Recreation and Parks Department). Tapes: 400 interviews, preserved, not transcribed.

Accessibility: Restricted.

Purpose of the program: To supplement the collection of films, artifacts and memorabilia.

HOOVER INSTITUTION
Stanford University, Stanford, California
See Herbert Hoover Oral History Project Program, Washington, D.C.

IMMACULATE HEART COLLEGE
2021 North Western
Los Angeles, California 90027
(213) 462-1301
Knox Mellon, Director, Oral History Research Office

General information: 1966, on-going. Budget: $1500. Tapes: 30 hours plus 130 tapes, partially transcribed, fully preserved. Transcriptions: edited.

Accessibility: No catalog: Not indexed. Interlibrary loan. No restrictions.

Purpose of the program: To gather material to be used by interested researchers and to serve as a learning experience for students in the training and techniques of oral history. Areas of special emphasis include the working women in southern California, women in California politics, land development in Southern California, and early socialists in California.

Major collections:
1. Women in politics, an oral history of California women currently serving in elective political office (30 hours, on-going).
2. Working women in southern California (130 tapes, 35 transcribed).

JUDAH L. MAGNES MEMORIAL MUSEUM
See Western Jewish History Center

KERN COUNTY ORAL HISTORY CONFERENCE
See California State College, Bakersfield

KZSU (STANFORD STUDENT RADIO STATION)
Library of Recorded Sound
Stanford University
Stanford, California 94305
(415) 328-2000

General information: Program lasted ten weeks during summer, 1965. Tapes: 200 hours, mostly transcribed, fully preserved. Transcriptions: 2500 pages.

Accessibility: Available to scholars agreeing to the regulations established by the institution.

Purpose of the program: To record information on the civil rights movement interviewers visited over 50 civil rights projects in six states. Interviews were made with white civil rights workers, local blacks, "action tapes" of civil rights workers canvassing voters, conducting freedom schools or participating in demonstrations.

Accessibility: Available to scholars agreeing to the regulations established by the institution. Transcriptions: 450 pages, edited.

LONG BEACH PUBLIC LIBRARY
Long Beach, California 90802
(213) 597-3341
Roberta Nichols, Curator

General Information: 1963, on-going. Budget: $150 for tapes (co-sponsored by Friends of the Long Beach Public Library). Tapes: 111 interviews, running from 15 minutes to 3 hours each, 37 interviews are transcribed, all tapes preserved. Transcriptions: edited.

Accessibility: No catalog. Not indexed. No interlibrary loan. For research purposes only, permission is required to quote.

Purpose of the program: To explore Long Beach history from its beginnings as a part of the 27,000 acre Rancho Los Cerritos. Within this framework, the library has interviewed descendants of the owners of the Rancho, Mexican and Indian workers, and has collected folklore and superstitions. The collection covers land development and early government, the 1933 Long Beach earthquake, early days of aviation, and the harbor.

LOS ANGELES CITY RECREATION AND PARKS DEPARTMENT
See Hollywood Center for the Audio-Visual Arts

LOS ANGELES COUNTY PUBLIC LIBRARY SYSTEM
320 West Temple Street
Los Angeles, California 90012
(213) 974-6564
Palmer G. Brown, Oral History Librarian

General information: 1968–1969. Budget: $3,000–$5,000. Tapes: Transcribed, partially preserved. Transcriptions: 1,200 pages, edited.

Accessibility: No catalog. Indexed. No interlibrary loan. Transcripts may be read in the library; they may not be reproduced in any way. Some tapes have individual use restrictions.

Purpose of the program: Los Angeles County Public Library System cooperates with the oral history program of Claremont Colleges, Claremont, California (Enid H. Douglass, director) in the policy, planning, interviewing and funding of oral history projects on the San Gabriel Valley and the Greater Los Angeles area.

LOS ANGELES PSYCHOANALYTIC SOCIETY
9735 Wilshire Boulevard
Beverly Hills, California 90212
(213) 271-1368
Albert Kandelin, M.D.

General information: 1965. Tapes: 12 interviews, 30 hours, partially transcribed, fully preserved. Transcriptions: 450 pages, edited.

Accessibility: Available to scholars applying in person and agreeing to the regulations established by the institution.

Purpose of the program: The preservation and study of the history and development of psychoanalytic practice in California.

MILL VALLEY PUBLIC LIBRARY
375 Throckmorton Avenue
Mill Valley, California 94941
(415) 388-4245
Ruth W. Lescohier, Chairman, Oral History Committee

General information: 1968. Budget: Interviewers are volunteers, using their own equipment. Necessary expenditures are met by the Mill Valley Library Association (Friends of the Library). Tapes: approx. 35 hours, transcribed, preserved. Transcriptions: 500 pages, lightly edited.

Accessibility: No catalog. Indexed. Interlibrary loan: Copies of typed manuscripts furnished upon payment of cost for photocopying. Manuscripts are open for research purposes. All literary rights, including the right to publish, are reserved by the Mill Valley Public Library. No part of the manuscript may be quoted for publication without written permission of the librarian. Requests should include identification of specific passages to be quoted, anticipated use of passages and identification of the user.

Purpose of the program: To record the reminiscences of those who have interesting things to say about Mill Valley, past and present.

MORAGA HISTORICAL SOCIETY ARCHIVES
St. Mary's College
Moraga, California 94575
(415) 376-4411
Brother L. Dennis, FSC

General information: 1965, on-going. Budget: indefinite. Tapes: 60 hours, not transcribed.

Accessibility: No catalog. Indexed. Interlibrary loan. No restrictions.

Purpose of the program: Documentary history for the area of Rancho Laguna de los Palos Colorados from 1885 to 1940 is practically nonexistent. During that period close to 13,000 acres (including the area of a greater part of three towns and their suburbs) held residents who were tenant farmers for whom the county kept no records. This is the gap this oral history can fill.

ORANGE PUBLIC LIBRARY
101 North Center Street
Orange, California 92600
(714) 532-0391
Milan Pavlovich

General information: Tapes: 20 interviews, 30 hours, preserved.

Accessibility: Available to scholars applying in person and agreeing to the regulations established by the institution. Copies of tapes are on deposit both at the Orange Public Library and the California State University, Fullerton Library.

Purpose of the program: The social, economic and political history of the city of Orange (1895–1930).

POMONA PUBLIC LIBRARY
625 South Garey Avenue
Pomona, California 91766
(714) 620-2026

General information: 1963. Tapes: 29 hours, not transcribed, summarized only.

Accessibility: No catalog. Indexed. No interlibrary loan. For use in the library only.

Purpose of the program: A representative picture of the growth and changes in the Pomona Valley during the period between 1840 and 1920 is presented through interviews with 122 residents.

RICHMOND PUBLIC LIBRARY
Civic Center Plaza
Richmond, California 94804
(415) 234-6632
Theodora Johnson, City Librarian

General information: 1973. Tapes: 11 hours, not transcribed.

Accessibility: No catalog. Not indexed. No interlibrary loan. No restrictions.

Purpose of the program: To document local history, including the history of the city of Richmond, the history of the Richmond Public Library and biographical material on local residents.

SAN DIEGO HISTORICAL SOCIETY—SERRA MUSEUM AND LIBRARY
Post Office Box 81825
San Diego, California 92138
(714) 297-3258
Sylvia Arden, Research Librarian

General information: 1958, on-going. Budget: volunteer program. Tapes: Over 400 interviews, transcribed, preserved. Transcriptions: edited.

Accessibility: No catalog. Indexed on subject cards in library. No interlibrary loan. Nothing leaves the library and nothing can be entirely copied or published without the permission of the person interviewed.

Purpose of the program: History of San Diego County.

SAN FRANCISCO MARITIME MUSEUM
Foot of Polk
San Francisco, California 94109
(415) PR 6-1175
Karl Kortum, Museum Director

General information: 1957.

Accessibility: Catalog. Not indexed. No interlibrary loan. Use by special permission only.

Purpose of the program: West Coast maritime history, primarily San Francisco (Crowley Tugs, etc.).

STANFORD UNIVERSITY
See KZSU (Stanford Student Radio Station), Stanford, California; Herbert Hoover Oral History Program, Washington, D.C.

UNIVERSITY OF CALIFORNIA, BERKELEY
Regional Oral History Office
Bancroft Library
Berkeley, California 94720
(415) 642-7395
Willa K. Baum, Department Head

General information: 1954. Budget: Primarily by grants, gifts, and contracts. Tapes: several hundred interviews, transcribed, large portions preserved. Transcriptions: edited.

Accessibility: Out-of-date catalog, supplemented by lists of interviews by subject with content descriptions. Indexed. Interlibrary loan. Copies of transcripts may be obtained for deposit by manuscript repositories at cost of reproduction. Most interviews are open. All interviews require the written permission of the director of the Bancroft Library to quote for publication.

Purpose of the program: To record the memoirs of persons who have contributed significantly to the development of the West and the nation.

Publications based on collection research:
Teiser, Ruth and Harroun, Catherine. *Printing as a Performing Art.* San Francisco: Book Club of California, 1970.

Major collections:

1. Interviews on agriculture, water resources, and land use.
2. Agriculture interviews (3300 pages, interviews still in process).
3. Interviews on art, photography and architecture in the San Francisco Bay area (16 interviews).
4. Books and printing in the San Francisco Bay area (25 interviews, some interviews still in process, 2800 pages).
5. California-Russian emigré series (11 interviews, 2000 pages).
6. California wine industry interviews. Interviews with more than twenty wine men, including industry members and university research men, some of whose recollections go back to the first decade of the twentieth century. Their recollections are of particular value because the Prohibition period saw the disruption not only of grape growing and wine making, but also the orderly maintenance and preservation of records. There is a real paucity of information on the Prohibition years (1920–1933), although some wine making did continue under the supervision of the Prohibition Department (20 interviews, 1000 pages, some interviews still in process).
7. Forestry interviews. Conservation: State and National Parks (2650 pages).
8. Forestry interviews sponsored by the Forest History Society (16 interviews, 1000 pages, many interviews still in process).
9. Memoir of Harry L. Kingman.
10. Interviews on law, politics and public administration (24 interviews, 5000 pages).
11. Benjamin Lehman interview.
12. Interviews on literature, art and photography in the San Francisco Bay area (18 interviews).
13. Dillon Seymour Myer memoir (442 pages).
14. Arthur C. Ringland memoir (538 pages).
15. San Francisco Bay maritime history series (4 interviews).
16. Science interviews (6 interviews, 1200 pages, interviews still in process).
17. Interviews on the social history of northern California (19 interviews).
18. August Vollmer collection on police history (12 interviews, project still in process).
19. Earl Warren oral history project. Includes interviews on the subjects of labor, law enforcement, Earl Warren's Bakersfield, health insurance, Earl Warren and the Youth Au-

UNIVERSITY OF CALIFORNIA, BERKELEY (cont.)

thority, perspectives on the Alameda County district attorney's office, Earl Warren and the State Department of Mental Hygiene, the State Department of Public Health, the public, the press and the legislature as well as individual memoirs by other persons close to Earl Warren (59 interviews, 4800 pages, another 69 interviews still in process).

20. Interviews with outstanding women of northern California (21 interviews, 4300 pages).
21. Dental history (in process).
22. Quizow-Dance in Berkeley (in process).
23. Suffragists (in process).
24. Cutter Laboratories.
25. Jewish history.
26. Levi-Strauss & Company.
27. Sanitary engineering.
28. University history.
29. Women in politics.
30. Sierra Club.
31. Miscellaneous interviews.

UNIVERSITY OF CALIFORNIA, DAVIS

The Library
Davis, California 95616
(916) 752-4441
A.I. Dickman, Director

General information: 1971. Budget: included in university library. Tapes: 160 hours, tapes preserved. Transcriptions: 2000 pages.

Accessibility: No catalog. Indexed. Interlibrary loan. Manuscripts are available for research purposes. All literary rights, including the right to publish or to quote from, are reserved to the university library.

Purpose of the program: Biographical oral history; key figures in campus history who are also of special significance to the history of California agriculture; also, folk and institutional oral history.

UNIVERSITY OF CALIFORNIA, LOS ANGELES

Oral History Program
136 Powell Library
405 Hilgard Avenue
Los Angeles, California 90024
(213) 825-4932
Bernard Galm, Director

General information: 1959. Budget: $40,658. Tapes: transcribed, partially preserved. Transcriptions: edited.

Accessibility: Catalog. Subject entries appear in catalog. Department of Special Collections. Interlibrary loan only to UC campuses. The oral history manuscripts are made available for research purposes only. All literary rights, including the right to publication, are reserved to the University Library of the University of California, Los Angeles. No part of the manuscript may be quoted for publication without the written permission of the university librarian.

Purpose of the program: To supplement the research resources of the university library.

Publications based on collection research: "Early San Fernando: Memoirs of Catherine Hubbard Dace." Edited with an introduction by Elizabeth I. Dixon. *Southern California Quarterly*, vol. 44, no. 3, September 1962.

Major collections:
1. Biographical (157 hours, 6005 pages, on-going).
2. Black studies (12 hours, 335 pages, on-going).
3. Education (99 hours, 2526 pages, on-going).
4. Fine arts (124 hours, 3647 pages, on-going).
5. Government and politics (197 hours, 5978 pages, on-going).
6. Motion picture and television (65 hours, 1685 pages, on-going).
7. Printing and book trade (32 hours, 696 pages, on-going).
8. State and local history (92 hours, 2646 pages, on-going).
9. University history (102 hours, 3062 pages, on-going).
10. Water resources (65 hours, 1748 pages, on-going).
11. An oral history of the motion picture in America (87 hours, 2869 pages, completed).

UNIVERSITY OF CALIFORNIA, SAN FRANCISCO

History Collection, Library
San Francisco, California 94122
(415) 666-9000
Nancy W. Zinn

General information: 1964. Tapes: 45 interviews, 75 hours, preserved.

Accessibility: Available to scholars applying in person and agreeing to the regulations established by the institution.

Purpose of the program: To record information about the development of the various disciplines on the campus over the years. There are biographical memoirs of faculty members and information on the health sciences.

UNIVERSITY OF CALIFORNIA, SANTA BARBARA

Library
Santa Barbara, California 93106
(805) 961-3062
Christian Brun, Head, Department of Special Collections

General information: 1969. Budget: out of existing library budget. Tapes: 30 hours, transcribed and preserved. Transcriptions: 580 pages, edited.

Accessibility: Catalog. Not indexed. Interlibrary loan with permission of interviewee. Generally the typescripts will be made available to any interested reader for use in the department only. If the interviewee should desire to be notified if someone wishes to use the material, the library will do this.

Purpose of the program: Oral history interviews are conducted in three general areas: campus and alumni; local history of the Santa Barbara area; nationally and internationally known figures who live in the Santa Barbara area. Interviews are made of visiting writers, printers, etc. in relation to work being done relating to various collections in the Department of Special Collections.

Publications based on collection research: Several interviews have been published in the library's periodical *Soundings*; others have been used for reference.

UNIVERSITY OF CALIFORNIA, SANTA CRUZ

Regional History Project
University Library
Santa Cruz, California 95060
(415) 429-0111
Elizabeth Spedding Calciano

General information: 1963. Tapes: 41 interviews, 140 hours, transcribed and preserved. Transcriptions: 6500 pages, edited.

Accessibility: Annotated bibliography available. Indexed. Interlibrary loan: Copies of the manuscripts will be made on request for educational or research institutions for the cost of reproduction. Tapes are not generally open to the public. No part of any manuscript may be quoted for publication without the written permission of the university librarian. Some sections have been sealed by the interviewees until specified dates. With these provisions, the material is available.

Purpose of the program: To help preserve the history of the central California coast area and to record the growth and development of a new university campus.

Major collections:
1. Central California coast collection (88 hours, 3000 pages).
2. University history collection (including Lick Observatory) (56 hours, 3000 pages, 1400 pages of which are sealed).

UNIVERSITY OF CALIFORNIA INSTITUTE OF INDUSTRIAL RELATIONS
2521 Channing Way
Berkeley, California 94720
(415) 642-4441

General information: 1956, program now terminated due to lack of funds. Budget: none. Tapes: 25 individuals interviewed, tapes not preserved. Transcriptions: 25 volumes, edited.

Accessibility: Catalog. Indexed in regular library card catalog. No interlibrary loan. Transcripts may be used by qualified scholars and researchers in the library. Permission is required to quote or to photocopy. Certain interviews are restricted for a period of time.

Purpose of the program: To record reminiscences and experiences of leaders and other important persons involved in labor-management relations in California. Both labor and management representatives are included. The interviews cover topics other than labor and industrial relations if the interviewee was active in other fields.

UNIVERSITY OF SOUTHERN CALIFORNIA LIBRARY
University Park
Los Angeles, California 90007
(213) 746-6058
Robert Knutson, Head, Department of Special Collections

General information: 1960. Budget: None at present. Tapes: 60 hours, partially transcribed, partially preserved. Transcriptions: 1400 pages, edited.

Accessibility: Catalog. Partially indexed. No interlibrary loan. Collection available to scholars applying in person and agreeing to the regulations established by the institution.

Purpose of the program: Emphasis is on Hungarian history, California political campaigns, cinema, literary figures and aviation history.

Major collections:
1. Presidential election of 1960 (400 pages, open).
2. Writers and authors (20 hours, 75 pages, open).
3. Aeronautical history. Early aviation activities primarily in southern California (20 hours, open).
4. Hungarian history (6 interviews, 400 pages, open).
5. Cinema (6 hours, 300 pages, open).
6. Miscellaneous, primarily local history (6 hours, 140 pages, open).

VICTOR VALLEY COLLEGE
Bear Valley Road
Victorville, California 92392
(714) 245-4271
Paul Smith, Instructor

General information: 1971. Budget: Salary for instructor. Tapes: 25 hours, not transcribed.

Accessibility: No catalog. Not indexed. No interlibrary loan.

Purpose of the program: To deal with the last of the frontier people who settled the desert area of southern California.

WESTERN JEWISH HISTORY CENTER
Judah L. Magnes Memorial Museum
2111 Russell Street
Berkeley, California 94705
(415) 849-2710
Moses Rischin, Director; Ruth Rafael, Archivist

General information: 1968. Budget: $10,000 for all oral history projects. This is not an annual sum.

Accessibility: No catalog. Not indexed. For restrictions see individual collections below.

Purpose of the program: In addition to the Northern California Jewish Community Series, the archives cover immigrants to the United States, Jewish pioneers and leaders.

Major collections:
1. The Northern California Jewish Community Series represents five areas of inquiry: pioneer Jewish families, community leaders, religious and institutional leaders, Jews prominent in the development of California and representatives of early rural communities. This collection is carried on in conjunction with the Regional Oral History Office, Bancroft Library, University of California, Berkeley. All literary rights in the manuscript, including the right to publish, are reserved to the Bancroft Library, the trustees of the Judah L. Magnes Memorial Museum and the interviewee. No part of the manuscript may be quoted for publication without the written permission of the director of the Bancroft Library and the interviewee. Tapes are kept at the Regional Oral History Office and transcriptions are available at both the Regional Oral History Office and the Western Jewish History Center.

2. The Harbin Jews collection. Concerns a group of aging Russian Jews, many of whom spent their formative years and adulthood in Harbin, Manchuria-China where a flourishing Jewish community existed. Interviews will be with the Harbin Jews in America, particularly those belonging to a social and cultural club called The Far East Society. One of the topics explored will be how Jews retain their unique Jewish identity in circumstances where they are a minority group. Their practices and the inferences of these for Jewish continuity in America at the present time will also be explored. On-going collection, restrictions to be set when project is completed.

3. Western Jewish History Center on-site interviews. On-going, tapes transcribed and preserved, transcriptions edited, indexed by name; copies may be obtained through interlibrary loan with permission of person taped (approx. 3 hours, 32 pages to date).

4. Interviews by Dr. Robert Levinson. These tapes are copies of originals at the Bancroft Library, University of California, Berkeley.

WHITTIER COLLEGE
Nixon Oral History Project
Whittier, California 90600
(213) 693-0771

General information: 1970.

Purpose of the program: To examine the life of Richard M. Nixon up to the time he became Vice President.

COLORADO

DENVER PUBLIC LIBRARY
1357 Broadway
Denver, Colorado 80203
(303) 573-5152

DENVER PUBLIC LIBRARY (cont.)

General information: 1972, on-going but not ready for use yet.

Purpose of the program: To record an urban history of the city of Denver from the 1920s. The program is not active at present. There are 150 tapes, partially transcribed but not prepared for use. Major topics include Ku Klux Klan and city government.

DENVER PUBLIC LIBRARY—CONSERVATION LIBRARY
1357 Broadway
Denver, Colorado 80203
(303) 573-5152, ext. 254
Kay Collins, Conservation Specialist

General information: 1965. Tapes: 217 hours, not transcribed.

Accessibility: Card catalog. Partially indexed. Some tapes are sealed until specific dates. No original tape is loaned. Unless restricted, copies will be made at the expense of user.

Purpose of the program: To cover Forest Service history, Park Service history and some selected programs in the Colorado area. Topics included are land management, timber, grazing, wildlife, forestry, Forest Service.

Publications based on collection research:

Baldwin, D. N. The Quiet Revolution. Boulder, Colorado: Pruett Publishing Co., 1973.

METROPOLITAN STATE COLLEGE
Center for Urban History
250 West Fourteenth Avenue
Denver, Colorado 80204
(303) 292-5190
Stephen J. Leonard, Director

General information: 1968. Tapes: 25 interviews, 10 hours, partially transcribed, partially preserved. Transcriptions: 50 pages.

Accessibility: Interlibrary loan.

Purpose of the program: To collect information pertaining to the growth and development of Denver, including ethnic, Hispanic, Black and Chicano history.

PIKES PEAK REGIONAL LIBRARY DISTRICT
20 North Cascade Avenue
Post Office Box 1579
Colorado Springs, Colorado 80901
(303) 636-3948
Brenda G. Hawley, Librarian, Western History Department

General information: 1971. Budget: Not budgeted separately. Tapes: 15 hours, partially transcribed, fully preserved. Transcriptions: 50 pages.

Accessibility: No catalog. Not indexed. No interlibrary loan. Limited to adults interested in serious research.

Purpose of the program: To preserve the recollections of persons who have a first-hand knowledge of and insight into historical happenings in Colorado Springs and the immediate vicinity.

STATE HISTORICAL SOCIETY OF COLORADO
200 Fourteenth Avenue
Denver, Colorado 80203
(303) 892-2305
Maxine Benson, Curator of Documentary Resources

General information: Budget: principally volunteer personnel. Tapes: 205 interviews.

Purpose of the program: To collect material relating to the history of Colorado and the American West. Within this framework the program seeks to reflect all areas of historical, geographical and topical interest.

UNITED STATES AIR FORCE ACADEMY
Department of History
USAF Academy, Colorado 80840
(303) 472-1818
Lt. Col. Robert M. Burch, Director

General information: 1968. Tapes: 21 interviews, 50 hours, preserved and transcribed. Transcriptions: edited.

Accessibility: Interlibrary loan. Research and reproduction services available to those unable to come to the institution. Copies are on deposit at Columbia University, New York. Some transcripts are restricted.

Purpose of the program: To generate audiovisual material for military history courses, to collect previously unrecorded military aviation data and to provide oral memoirs by persons who made and shaped Air Force history.

CONNECTICUT

HALL-BROOKE HOSPITAL
A Division of Hall-Brooke Foundation, Inc.
47 Long Lots Road
Westport, Connecticut 06880
(203) 227-1251
Leo H. Berman, Director, Professional Services

General information: 1960, on-going. Budget: undesignated. Tapes: 60 hours, not transcribed.

Accessibility: No catalog. Indexed. Interlibrary loan. No restrictions.

Purpose of the program: To record the memoirs of those involved in the development of psychiatry and psychoanalysis, particularly those who have played prominent parts in the development of these specialties in Connecticut.

UNIVERSITY OF BRIDGEPORT
Oral History Research Project
10 Stamford Hall
Bridgeport, Connecticut 06602
(203) 384-0711

General information: 1968. Tapes: 45 interviews, 50 hours, partially transcribed, fully preserved. Transcriptions: 15 interviews, 300 pages, edited.

Accessibility: Available to scholars applying in person and agreeing to the regulations established by the institution.

Purpose of the program: To collect source materials for primary research on Jasper McLevy and the Bridgeport Socialist party, the Kennedy image in India. Interviews with Norman Thomas and the Bridgeport Socialists. A study of the Bridgeport black community is planned.

UNIVERSITY OF CONNECTICUT
Connecticut Oral History Project
Post Office Box U-106
Storrs, Connecticut 06268
(203) 486-4519
Morton J. Tenzer, Director

General information: 1968. Budget: $15,000. Tapes: preserved. Transcriptions: edited.

Accessibility: No catalog. Not indexed. No interlibrary loan. Subject to limitations stipulated by individual subjects; access to the collection is restricted to researchers approved by the director of the Oral History Project and the director of Special Collections, Wilbur Cross Library.

Purpose of the program: The Connecticut Oral History Project attempts to capture the recent political, social, and educational history of the state through interviews with prominent participants. Concentration is on former governors of the state, labor leaders, businessmen, and educators.

Publications based on collection research:

Johnson, Curtiss. *Raymond E. Baldwin Connecticut Statesman.* Sally Devaney, ed. Chester, Connecticut: Pequot Press, 1972.

YALE UNIVERSITY SCHOOL OF MUSIC

96 Wall Street
New Haven, Connecticut 06520
(203) 436-8740
Vivian Perlis, Director, Oral History Research, American Music

General information: 1971, on-going. Budget: Varies. Supported by outside funding, presently from the Rockefeller Foundation. Tapes: 50+ hours, transcribed and preserved. Transcriptions: Editing in process.

Accessibility: No catalog. Not indexed. No interlibrary loan. Permission of interviewee is usually required.

Purpose of the program: To collect source material relating to twentieth century American music by means of tape recorded interviews with composers and others important in musical activities. This program is an outgrowth of the Charles Ives project, a documentary oral history on this important American composer. The Ives project was sponsored by the Yale Music Library. The present program is affiliated with the School of Music.

Major collections:
1. American music (on-going).
2. Charles Ives oral history (completed 1971, 50 hours, 58 interviews).
3. Hindemith project (9 interviews, 1972, 1973, on-going).

DELAWARE

THE HAGLEY MUSEUM

Eleutherian Mills—Hagley Foundation, Inc.
Greenville, Delaware 19807
(302) 658-2401
Norman B. Wilkinson, Director, Hagley Museum Oral History Program

General information: 1955. Tapes: 90 interviews, 400 hours, partially transcribed, fully preserved. Transcriptions: 88 interviews, 3400 pages, edited.

Accessibility: No catalog. Not indexed. Available to scholars applying in person and agreeing to the regulations governing their use as established by the Foundation.

Purpose of the program: To supplement manuscript and published materials with the first-hand recollections of persons who worked and lived in the lower Brandywine Valley—Wilmington region.

UNIVERSITY OF DELAWARE

Newark, Delaware
(302) 738-2000
John A. Munroe, H. Rodney Sharp Professor of History

General information: 1966, on-going. Budget: $1,000. Tapes: 180 hours, partially transcribed, preserved. Transcriptions: not edited.

Accessibility: No catalog. Not indexed. No interlibrary loan. Use is restricted to serious students.

Purpose of the program: The aim is to collect material concerning Delaware and Delawareans that would not otherwise be recorded for posterity. Topics emphasized so far have been immigration, the public school, the university, the Depression and politics.

DISTRICT OF COLUMBIA

AMERICAN PSYCHIATRIC ASSOCIATION

1700 Eighteenth Street, N. W.
Washington, D. C. 20009
(202) 232-7878
Jean C. Jones, Librarian

General information: 1965. Tapes: 24 interviews, partially transcribed, fully preserved. Transcriptions: 15 interviews.

Accessibility: Available to scholars applying in person and agreeing to the regulations established by the institution.

Purpose of the program: To preserve the voice and personality of leaders in the psychiatric field, as well as to collect information about the history of psychiatry as they have experienced it.

BROADCAST PIONEERS LIBRARY

1771 N Street, N. W.
Washington, D. C. 20036
(202) 223-0088
Catherine Heinz, Director

General information: 1950 (library opened in 1971). Tapes: 140 hours, partially transcribed, fully preserved. Transcriptions: 3965 pages, partially edited.

Accessibility: Catalog in preparation. Index in preparation. Interlibrary loan. Because of their age, most tapes cannot be used until they have been transferred to 1 1/2 mil Mylar. A few of the transcripts have restrictions for use.

Purpose of the program: History of broadcasting (radio and television).

BUSINESS AND PROFESSIONAL WOMEN'S FOUNDATION

2012 Massachusetts Avenue, N. W.
Washington, D. C. 20036
(202) 293-1100
Jeanne Spiegel, Director

General information: 1966. Tapes: 38 interviews, partially transcribed.

Accessibility: Catalog. Indexed. Available to scholars applying in person and agreeing to the regulations established by the institution.

Purpose of the program: To present a picture of the status of women and the history of the National Federation of Business and Professional Women's Clubs, Inc.

THE CIVIL RIGHTS DOCUMENTATION PROJECT

1527 New Hampshire Avenue, N. W.
Washington, D. C. 20036
Vincent J. Browne, Director

THE CIVIL RIGHTS DOCUMENTATION PROJECT (cont.)

General information: 1966. Tapes: 650 interviews, 1500 hours, partially transcribed, fully preserved. Transcriptions: 370 interviews, 17,500 pages, edited.

Accessibility: Not indexed. Entire collection will be available, according to the terms specified by each interviewee, at an institution yet to be determined.

Purpose of the program: To tape record and transcribe interviews with persons significantly involved in civil rights activities and to collect unpublished written materials.

COST OF LIVING COUNCIL
History and Archives Division
Room 2006
2000 M Street, N.W.
Washington, D.C. 20508
(202) 254-3211
Harry P. Jeffrey, Director

General Information: 1973. Tapes: 135 hours, preserved. Transcriptions: Interviews are transcribed and edited.

Accessibility: Not indexed. Collection is closed; ultimately will be open to studies of wage and price controls.

Purpose of the program: Oral history of President Nixon's economic stabilization program (1971).

Major collection:

1. Economic stabilization program oral history project.

DEUTSCH, HAROLD C., COLLECTION
See Harold C. Deutsch Collection

GEORGE WASHINGTON UNIVERSITY
Continuing Education for Women
2130 H Street, N.W.
Washington, D.C. 20006
(202) 676-7036
Ruth Osborn, Director, Continuing Education for Women; Mary Jo Deering, Oral History Project Director

General information: 1971. Tapes: 45 hours, partially transcribed, partially time-indexed, fully preserved. Transcriptions: 500 pages, edited.

Accessibility: No catalog. Not indexed. No interlibrary loan. No restrictions.

Purpose of the program: The oral history projects have been conducted in conjunction with a survey course in oral history which has been offered for four years.

Major collections:

1. The development of the Continuing Education for Women program. An on-going project concerning the organization and development of the Continuing Education for Women program, its philosophy and rationale; includes case histories of graduates (15 hours, 40 pages, open).

2. The model school controversy in Montgomery County, Maryland. This one-year project, now completed, documented a school controversy in Montgomery County, Maryland, involving such issues as educational innovation, de facto segregation and busing, community control of schools, school system decision-making (30 hours, 460 pages, open).

GEORGETOWN UNIVERSITY
37th & O Streets, N.W.
Washington, D.C. 20007
(202) 625-4567; 625-4160
George M. Barringer, Special Collections Librarian; John K. Reynolds, Archivist/Manuscripts Librarian

General information: 1968. Budget: No designated amount. Tapes: 900 hours, transcribed, partially preserved. Transcriptions: Partially edited, at interviewees' discretion and by interviewee only.

Accessibility: No catalog. Not indexed. No interlibrary loan. With the exceptions of some interviews, which are restricted at the discretion of interviewees, all are open to qualified researchers. All will be open eventually.

Purpose of the program: To complete the work of the McCarthy historical project, whose collections were transferred to Georgetown in 1971; interest in the McCarthy 1968 campaign exclusively. To accumulate potentially valuable reminiscences of men, particularly Jesuits, who have served long tenures at Georgetown University or who have exercised powerful roles in her educational development; a program of the University Archives.

HAROLD C. DEUTSCH COLLECTION
National War College
Washington, D.C. 20319
(202) 693-8234
Harold C. Deutsch, Collector

General information: 1957. Budget: none. Tapes: 100 hours, mostly transcribed, fully preserved. Transcriptions: 400 hours, edited.

Accessibility: No catalog. Not indexed. No interlibrary loan. No specific restrictions. Each case would be considered by itself.

Purpose of the program: To provide source material for studies on the history of the German military opposition to Hitler. Major topics are the Blomberg and Fritsch affairs of 1938 as a background to the growth of military opposition, the plot against Hitler of September 1938, opposition efforts to develop a working relationship with the British and French governments, the role of the military conspiracy during the first months of the war, and that of Pope Pius XII in striving to mediate between the conspirators and the government.

Publications based on collected works:

The Conspiracy against Hitler in the Twilight War. Minneapolis: University of Minnesota Press, 1938 (German edition, Beck Verlag, Munich).

Hitler and the Generals. The Blomberg and Fritsch Affairs and the Wehrmacht Crisis of 1938. Minneapolis: University of Minnesota Press, 1973 (German language edition, Diana Verlag, Zurich).

HERBERT HOOVER ORAL HISTORY PROGRAM
1500 Massachusetts Avenue, N.W.
Suite 840
Washington, D.C. 20005
Raymond Henle, Director

General information: 1966. Tapes: 358 interviews, 400 hours. Transcriptions: will be edited, indexed.

Accessibility: No catalog. Not indexed. Restrictions pending on disposition of the tapes. The material is copyrighted; will be freely available for study, except for small restricted portions.

Purpose of the program: To fortify and add to the collection of Hoover materials in the presidential library, West Branch, Iowa, and Hoover Institution, Stanford University, California.

HOWARD UNIVERSITY
Department of History
Washington, D.C. 20001
(202) 636-6100
Elsie M. Lewis

General information: 1968.

Purpose of the program: To build a collection on black African tribal customs, including marriage customs, ceremonies upon death, birth of sons.

MARINE CORPS
See United States Marine Corps

NATIONAL AERONAUTICS AND SPACE ADMINISTRATION
Fourth & Maryland Avenue, S. W.
Washington, D. C. 20546
(202) 755-3612
Eugene M. Emme, NASA Historian

General information: 1959. Budget: Not separately budgeted. Tapes: 800 hours, partially (35 percent) transcribed, fully preserved. Transcriptions: 300 pages, partially (35 percent) edited.

Accessibility: No catalog. Indexed. No interlibrary loan. Tapes may not be used without permission of interviewee.

Purpose of the program: Oral history interviews are conducted by historians engaged on major projects concerning NASA history (1958–) and predecessor institutions (NACA, IGY, etc.). Tapes of major individuals are transcribed. Interviewees include top federal as well as industrial and other participants.

Publications based on collection research:

Green, Constance M. and Lomask, Milton. *Vanguard: A History.* Washington, D. C.: Smithsonian, 1971.

Major collections:

1. Oral history is employed in conjunction with project histories, and exit interviews of key officials or persons associated with NACA/NASA. Their purpose is to supplement historical research on matters not documentable. Related interviews were conducted for the John F. Kennedy Library, Waltham, Massachusetts, which controls access. All interviewees retain access clearance and some have or will be placing their transcripts in other collections (such as presidential libraries). Companion collections are maintained at the three manned flight centers (Johnson Spacecraft Center, Houston; Marshall Space Flight Center, Huntsville, Alabama; and Kennedy Space Center, Florida). By far the largest collection is maintained by the historical office at the Johnson Spacecraft Center.
2. Taped interviews with leading participants of NASA programs (Mercury, Gemini, Apollo, etc.).

NATIONAL WAR COLLEGE
See Harold C. Deutsch Collection

SMITHSONIAN INSTITUTION
Oral History Project
National Air and Space Museum
Washington, D. C. 20560
(202) 628-4422
E. W. Robischon, Director

General information: 1968. Tapes: 10 interviews, 20 hours, partially transcribed, fully preserved.

Accessibility: A few individuals have placed restrictions on interviews pending publication of histories or biographies.

Purpose of the program: To record the voices and memories of persons who participated in the development of air and space industry and technology.

See also Archives of American Art, Smithsonian Institution, New York

UNITED STATES MARINE CORPS
Historical Division
Headquarters, Commandant of the Marine Corps (Code HD)
U.S. Marine Corps
Washington, D. C. 20380
(202) OX 4-2460; OX 4-2846
Benis M. Frank, Head, Oral History Unit

General information: 1966. Budget: The budget is an integral part of the Historical division's overall budget; approximately $35,000 per year. Tapes: 900+ hours, transcribed and preserved. Transcriptions: 17,000+ pages, edited. *Note:* These statistics for interviews with retired distinguished Marines only. There are over 5000 individual, Vietnam-related interviews, classified from Top Secret to Unclassified, which have not been transcribed, and there is no way to determine what these interviews represent in total hours.

Accessibility: Catalog. Indexes to individual transcripts; also an index to overall collection of classified and unclassified Vietnam-related tapes. No interlibrary loan. At present, the Vietnam-related interviews have classifications imposed by their originators and range from Top Secret down to Official Use Only and Unclassified. Only researchers with an established "need to know" and a security clearance may use these interviews, which are not transcribed. Another collection of interviews of distinguished retired Marines is listed in this book by name with their individual restrictions.

Purpose of the program: The objectives of this program are to obtain personal narratives concerning noteworthy professional experiences and observations from active duty, reserve, and retired Marines through oral history interviews conducted at the scene of Fleet Marine Force operations and deployments, major exercises and manoeuvers, and with distinguished retired Marines. Interviews with retired Marines cover the pre-World War I period to the present, while operational-type interviews and the like are primarily concerned with operations in Vietnam.

Publications based on collection research: Vietnam-related interviews are currently being used by writers in the Historical division working on sequential monographs concerned with Marine Corps operations in Vietnam. Interviews with retired distinguished Marines have been used in the preparation of *Victory and Occupation—History of the U. S. Marine Corps Operations in World War II* by Benis M. Frank and Henry I. Shaw, Jr. and in "Living History," by Benis M. Frank, which appeared in *Marine Corps Gazette*, November 1970. Because the accessioned interviews with retired distinguished Marines have just recently been made available for research, there is no indication at present of how much in demand by researchers the transcripts and interviews will be.

Major Collections:

1. Interviews conducted by major Marine Corps interview centers.
2. Interviews conducted by major Fleet Marine Force commands at the scenes of crisis actions.
   Note: The above two collections are primarily concerned with Vietnam and comprise over 5000 interviews, covering the entire spectrum of the Marine Corps effort in support of U. S. policy.
3. Interviews with individual distinguished Marines. Copies of these transcripts of interviews with retired distinguished Marine Corps officers are on deposit also at Columbia University, New York, and at the U. S. Naval Institute, Maryland. A list of participants appears under the entry for the U. S. Marine Corps (900+ hours, 17,000+ pages).

WASHINGTON HOSPITAL CENTER
Medical Library
Room 2A-21
110 Irving Street, N. W.
Washington, D. C. 20010
(202) 541-0500
Jane M. Fulcher, Director

General information: 1963. Tapes: 8 interviews, 10 hours, partially transcribed, fully preserved. Transcriptions: 8 interviews, 137 pages, not edited.

Accessibility: No catalog. Not indexed. Available to scholars applying in person and agreeing to regulations established by the institution.

Purpose of the program: To collect information and anecdotes which could be used for writing the history of the center.

WASHINGTON SCHOOL OF PSYCHIATRY
1610 New Hampshire Avenue, N. W.
Washington, D. C.
(202) 667-3008
Robert N. Butler

General information: 1962. Tapes: 30 interviews, 100 hours, preserved.

Accessibility: Although the collection is restricted, it is available to scholars applying in person and agreeing to the regulations established by the institution.

Purpose of the program: To study creativity and the history of genomology.

FLORIDA

DERMATOLOGY FOUNDATION OF MIAMI
480 Casuarina Concourse
Coral Gables, Florida 33143
(305) 667-3224
Victor H. Witten, Director

General information: 1959. Tapes: 100+ hours, transcribed and preserved. Transcriptions: 680+ pages, not edited.

Accessibility: No catalog. Indexed. No interlibrary loan. At the present time the material collected is available for use only by special arrangement.

Purpose of the program: To interview famous dermatologists throughout the world in order to learn something about their personality, characteristics, hobbies, reasons for going into the field of dermatology, other dermatologists, and opinions on the subject of the many facets of dermatology today as compared with years ago.

FLORIDA STATE UNIVERSITY
Program in Oral History
425 Bellamy Building
Tallahassee, Florida 32306
(904) 599-3317
Edward F. Keuchel, Director

General information: 1970. Tapes: 15 interviews, 20 hours, partially transcribed, fully preserved. Transcriptions: edited.

Accessibility: Available to scholars applying in person and agreeing to the regulations established by the institution.

Purpose of the program: To study the development of north Florida and Tallahassee.

JOHN F. KENNEDY SPACE CENTER
Kennedy Space Center, Florida 32899

General information: Tapes: 60 interviews, 200 hours, transcribed, preserved. Transcriptions: 2400 pages, partially edited.

Accessibility: Available to scholars applying in person and agreeing to the regulations established by the institution.

Purpose of the program: To make material available for research.

UNIVERSITY OF FLORIDA
Oral History Program
Library West, 4th Floor
Gainesville, Florida 32601
(904) 392-3261
Samuel Procter, Director

Major collections:

1. Florida Indians (Seminole Project). Part of the Doris Duke Indian Oral History program. Other institutions cooperating in this program are the Arizona State Museum, and the Universities of Illinois, New Mexico, Oklahoma, South Dakota and Utah.
2. Florida political history.
3. University of Florida.

Purpose of the program: To make material available for research.

UNIVERSITY OF WEST FLORIDA
Library
Pensacola, Florida 32504
(904) 476-9500
James A. Servies, Director of Libraries

General information: 1970, on-going. Budget: None.

Accessibility: No catalog. Indexed within manuscript collection. Available to serious researchers.

Purpose of the program: Interviews with Pensacola old-timers. There is no actual oral history program as such, merely a few tapes, but these are of value for names and other information. This activity will be expanded in the future.

GEORGIA

EMORY UNIVERSITY
Atlanta, Georgia 30322
(404) 377-2411
James Harvey Young, Director

General information: 1967. Budget: Funded by the National Library of Medicine. Tapes: 10 interviews, 50 hours, partially transcribed, fully preserved. Transcriptions: 150 pages.

Accessibility: No catalog. Not indexed. A few interviews restricted by interviewee; the rest are available in accordance with regulations established by the institution. A copy of each transcript is also available at the National Library of Medicine, Bethesda, Maryland.

Purpose of the program: To acquire information from those associated with food and drug regulation in the United States.

MARTIN LUTHER KING LIBRARY DOCUMENTATION PROJECT
671 Beckwith Street, S. W.
Atlanta, Georgia 30314
(404) 524-1956
W. L. Harriford, Jr., Director

General information: 1970. Tapes: 30 interviews, 60 hours, preserved.

Accessibility: Restricted use at present.

Purpose of the program: To collect recollections of Dr. King and the civil rights movement. Interviews have been held with members of the family, the church, SCLC, school and college classmates and faculty and civil rights leaders.

SOUTHERN HIGHLANDS LITERARY FUND, INC.

Foxfire Magazine
Raban Gap, Georgia 30568
(404) 746-2561
B. Eliot Wigginton, President

General information: 1966. Budget: Funded by foundation grants, government grants, private donation and subscriptions. Tapes: 400 + interviews, over 500 hours, transcribed, preserved. Transcriptions: Edited if printed in *Foxfire* Magazine.

Accessibility: Brochure. Not indexed. No interlibrary loan. Available to scholars applying in person and agreeing to the rules established by the institution. Most interviews are printed in *Foxfire* Magazine.

Purpose of the program: To bridge the gaps and understand certain cultures, and to give high school students an opportunity to achieve rapport with their own roots, traditions, and environment.

HAWAII

CHURCH COLLEGE OF HAWAII

55-020 Kulanui Street
Laie, Hawaii 96762
(808) 293-9211
Kenneth W. Baldridge, Director

General information: 1972. Budget: None. Tapes: 17 hours, transcribed, preserved. Transcriptions: not edited.

Accessibility: No catalog. Not indexed. Interlibrary loan. No restrictions.

Purpose of the program: The program primarily deals with the early history of the Latter-Day Saints Church, especially in New Zealand and Hawaii, with hopes of expanding to include other areas of the Pacific.

UNIVERSITY OF HAWAII

Pacific Regional Oral History Program
Department of History
2550 Campus Road
Honolulu, Hawaii 96822
(808) 948-8486
Edward Beechert, Coordinator

General information: 1969. Budget: $1,200 and declining. Tapes: 100 hours, transcribed, preserved. Transcriptions: 500 + pages, not edited.

Accessibility: No catalog. Index in process. Interlibrary loan: possible. Generally restricted to scholarly activities. Most interviews are open by application to the program and referral of the application to the union involved.

Purpose of the program: The program focuses on Hawaiian labor primarily, with increasing attention being paid to ethnic groups. For the past year or more, the program has been assisting community groups in oral history programs, such as the Hawaii Chinese Historical Society. An oral history of a Filipino plantation worker is almost completed. A series on the formation of the United Public Workers Union in Hawaii (25 interviews) is available. Eight interviews covering Hawaiian

politics from 1938 to 1970, Senator William Hill, and supporting interviews from others are available. A series on longshore experiences is under way.

IDAHO

CASSIA COUNTY HISTORICAL SOCIETY AND MUSEUM

Main and Hiland
Post Office Box 331
Burley, Idaho 83318
(208) 678-7172
Lillian Dawson, Cataloger

General information: 1972. Budget: No specified budget. Tapes: 13 hours, not transcribed.

Accessibility: No catalog. Indexed. No interlibrary loan. At present the tapes in the collection have not been transcribed and it would be necessary to use the facilities of the Museum to listen to them. Approximately 8 hours of these tapes are at the Idaho Bicentennial Commission, 210 Main Street, Boise, Idaho 83702. Contact Diane Alters, Coordinator Oral History Project.

Purpose of the program: A. W. Dawson began taping area pioneers in 1968 in connection with his column, "Western Saga." When the Museum was opened in 1972, the program was expanded with the help of the Idaho Bicentennial Commission and the Cassia County Historical Society. The purpose is to tell the story of Cassia County.

Publications based on collection research:
Alson W. Dawson's column, "Western Saga."

COLLEGE OF IDAHO

See Snake River Regional Studies Center

IDAHO BICENTENNIAL COMMISSION

210 Main Street
Boise, Idaho 83702
(208) 384-3890
Diane Alters, Historian

General information: 1972. Budget: $10,000. Tapes: 30 hours, partially transcribed, fully preserved. Transcriptions: not edited.

Accessibility: No catalog. Indexed by name only. No interlibrary loan. Restrictions vary with individual interviews.

Purpose of the program: The Bicentennial Commission has acted as a coordinating center for other projects in Idaho by supplying material about method, encouraging communication between projects, transcribing tapes for other Idaho projects, and by serving as a central tape library for copies of oral history tape interviews conducted in the state. It has also started interviewing on the three topics listed below.

Major collections:
1. Land management and reclamation from the early 1900s.
2. Newspaper history in Idaho.
3. Mining history.

IDAHO FALLS PUBLIC LIBRARY

Idaho Falls, Idaho 83401
(208) 522-5498
Ruth James, Regional Assistant, Eastern Idaho Library Region

General information: This program is one of a number of oral history projects being initiated at the time of publication of this volume. It will concentrate on local history.

IDAHO HISTORICAL AUXILIARY
610 North Julia Davis Drive
Boise, Idaho 83706
(208) 384-2120
Mardi Keen, Chairman

General Information: 1967. Tapes: 120 hours. Transcriptions: 650 pages.

Accessibility: Catalog. Indexed.

IDAHO STATE HISTORICAL SOCIETY
Idaho Historical Auxiliary Oral History Program
610 North Julia Davis Drive
Boise, Idaho 83706
(208) 384-3356
Mrs. Robert Alexander

General information: 1968.

Purpose of the program: To study an interesting aspect of contemporary culture through an investigation of entertaining stories related by old-timers.

Accessibility: No catalog. Not indexed.

Purpose of the program: Taped interviews with pioneers of Latah County.

LATAH COUNTY PIONEER HISTORICAL MUSEUM ASSOCIATION
110 South Adams Street
Moscow, Idaho 83843
(208) 882-1004
Larry French, Museum Director

General information: 1972, on-going. Budget: $3,500 plus donations. Tapes: Program just beginning, tapes will be transcribed.

Accessibility: No catalog. Not indexed.

LEWIS-CLARK STATE COLLEGE
Lewiston, Idaho 83501
(208) 746-2341
Larry P. Quinn, Director, Oral History Project

General information: 1972, on-going. Budget: None. Tapes: 10 hours, not transcribed.

Accessibility: No catalog. Not indexed. No restrictions.

Purpose of the program: This is a random collection of social and economic history of Lewiston, Idaho and environs.

MINIDOKA COUNTY HISTORICAL SOCIETY
1941 Burton Avenue
Burley, Idaho 83318
Mr. and Mrs. Alvin Holmes

General information: This program is one of a number of Idaho oral history projects being initiated at the time of publication of this volume.

NORTH IDAHO COLLEGE
Coeur d'Alene, Idaho 83814
(208) 667-7422
James Crowe, Chairman

General information: This program is one of a number of Idaho oral history projects being initiated at the time of publication of this volume.

RICKS COLLEGE
Rexburg, Idaho 83440
(208) 356-2351
Jerry L. Glenn, Director, Oral History

General information: 1968. Budget: $100. Tapes: 200 hours, not transcribed.

Accessibility: No catalog. Indexed. No interlibrary loan. No restrictions.

Purpose of the program: To collect the history of the Upper Snake River Valley of Idaho.

THE SNAKE RIVER REGIONAL STUDIES CENTER
College of Idaho
Caldwell, Idaho 83605
(208) 459-5011
Pam Haddock, Research Coordinator

General information: This program is one of a number of Idaho oral history projects being initiated at the time of publication of this volume.

TWIN FALLS PUBLIC LIBRARY
434 Second Street East
Twin Falls, Idaho 83301
(208) 733-2964
Marilyn Jardine, Region IV Assistant

General information: This program is one of a number of Idaho oral history projects being initiated at the time of publication of this volume.

UNIVERSITY OF IDAHO LIBRARY
Moscow, Idaho 83843
(208) 885-6111
Charles Webber, Special Collections Librarian

General information: 1960, completed. Tapes: 15 interviews, 30 hours, partially transcribed, fully preserved.

Purpose of the program: Personal reminiscences of old times in the area, from politics to stage coach driving.

UPPER SNAKE RIVER VALLEY HISTORICAL SOCIETY
Post Office Box 244
Rexburg, Idaho 83440
Harold S. Forbush

General information: This program is one of a number of Idaho oral history projects being initiated at the time of publication of this volume.

ILLINOIS

AMERICAN MEDICAL ASSOCIATION
Archive Library
535 North Dearborn Street
Chicago, Illinois 60610
(312) 751-6000
Warren Albert, Associate Director

General information: 1966, on-going. Tapes: 15 hours, not transcribed (30 interviews) plus material described under Major collections.

Accessibility: Restricted.

Purpose of the program: To augment the written record of the association; to preserve for future internal and external use primary documentation of the association's views on issues of concern to organized medicine.

Major collections:
1. 30 interviews, 15 hours of tape, not transcribed.

2. 400 hours of tape recorded interviews with a variety of persons. Some are copies of disc recordings released for radio use in the late 1940s and early 1950s. These have not been transcribed, nor is the full import of these conversations known at present.

CHARLES B. HOSMER, JR. COLLECTION
Principia College
Post Office Box 155
Elsah, Illinois 62028
(618) 466-2608
Charles B. Hosmer, Professor of History, Private collector of oral history materials

General information: 1961. Budget: varies. Tapes: 100 hours, transcribed, preserved. Transcriptions: 2530 pages, edited.

Accessibility: No catalog. Index in process. Interlibrary loan. Permission of interviewee required.

Purpose of the program: The collection has been made with the idea of using the material for a proposed book on the history of historic preservation in the United States (1926–1949). Mr. Hosmer expects to add a few more interviews, bringing the total to about 80.

CHICAGO STATE COLLEGE
Oral History Research Office
6800 South Stewart
Chicago, Illinois 60621
(312) 995-2000
Thomas A. DePasquale, Director

General information: 1966. Tapes: 70 interviews, 225 hours, partially transcribed, fully preserved. Transcriptions: 55 interviews, 6000 pages, edited.

Accessibility: No catalog. Indexed. Available to scholars applying in person and agreeing to the regulations established by the institution.

Purpose of the program: To collect memoirs about Chicago State College and the city of Chicago. Memoirs deserving special mention include those with key members of the Chicago Police Department and people living in black ghettos.

ELMHURST HISTORICAL COMMISSION
107 Fellows Court
Wilder Park
Elmhurst, Illinois 60126
(312) 833-1457
Ruth Strand, Director

General information: 1971. Tapes: transcribed. Transcriptions: edited.

Accessibility: Indexed. Interlibrary loan: Research and reproduction services can be arranged for persons unable to come to the institution.

Purpose of the program: To preserve local history.

FIELD ENTERPRISES, INC.
Chicago Sun-Times
401 North Wabash Avenue
Chicago, Illinois 60611
(312) 321-2600
Herman Kogan

communications, journalism, social service, philanthropy, etc. Interviews have been made with past and present executives and employees of Field Enterprises, especially in the newspaper division.

HOSMER, CHARLES B., JR., COLLECTION
See Charles B. Hosmer, Jr. Collection

ILLINOIS STATE HISTORICAL LIBRARY
Old State Capitol
Springfield, Illinois 62706
(217) 525-4836

General information: 1961. Budget: None. Tapes: 60 hours, partially transcribed, fully preserved. Transcriptions: 800 pages, edited.

Accessibility: No catalog. Not indexed. No interlibrary loan. Not available for research at this time.

Purpose of the program: Illinois history.

KNOX COLLEGE
Galesburg, Illinois 61401
(309) 343-0112, ext. 207
Mrs. Philip Haring, Curator of Special Collections

General information: Tapes: Not transcribed.

Accessibility: No catalog. Indexed. No interlibrary loan. Restrictions vary with individual interviews.

Purpose of the program: The archives keeps materials pertaining to the college or city history.

PRINCIPIA COLLEGE
See Charles B. Hosmer, Jr. Collection

ROOSEVELT UNIVERSITY
430 South Michigan
Chicago, Illinois 60605
(312) 431-3763
Elizabeth Balanoff, Director, Oral History Project in Labor History

General information: 1970. Budget: Depends on grants; NEH funded it $14,000 for one year and $5,000 for another, averages $8,000. Tapes: 163 hours, on-going, transcribed, preserved. Transcriptions: 1447 pages, edited.

Accessibility: No catalog, complete list of transcripts. Not indexed. No interlibrary loan. Some completed transcripts are withheld from the public for a specified number of years. These are not listed in this volume. Permission of interviewee to cite is required during lifetime.

Purpose of the program: Roosevelt's major interest is in the labor history of Chicago and the surrounding area through the recollections of people who have participated in the labor movement at various levels, from top leaders to rank and file. The program is secondarily interested in recording immigrant history as reflected through the labor movement.

RUSH MEDICAL COLLEGE LIBRARY
1758 West Harrison
Chicago, Illinois 60612
(312) 942-5950
William Kona, Director

General information: 1970, on-going.

Accessibility: No catalog. Not indexed. No interlibrary loan. For internal use only.

Purpose of the program: To record and conserve the history and tradition of all our institutions.

SANGAMON STATE UNIVERSITY

Shepherd Road
Springfield, Illinois 62708
(217) 786-6656
Cullom Davis, Director; Mrs. Lewis Herndon, Coordinator

General information: 1971. Budget: $5,700. Tapes: 120 hours, partially transcribed, fully preserved. Transcriptions: 1700 pages, edited.

Accessibility: No catalog. Not indexed. Interlibrary loan. Some collections are subject to interlibrary regulations; some tapes carry restrictions.

Purpose of the program: The collection's emphasis is on subjects of local and regional nature: coal mining and unions in central and southern Illinois, ethnic populations in Springfield, local history, farming practices and politics in central Illinois, local businesses and other institutions. The collection consists of tape recorded interviews with several hundred persons. The basic unit of the collection is the personal memoir. Ultimately all of the memoirs will be available in finished transcript form as well as sound tape; at the present some are completed, some are in process and some are in tape form only.

Major collections:
1. Mining and John L. Lewis. Interviews with 21 coal miners on the mine war, John L. Lewis, F. D. Roosevelt, George Meany, Harry Truman, Arnold Miller, Governor Emmerson, Governor Horner (35 hours, on-going, 848 pages, some tapes restricted).
2. German Americans. Reactions of the German community to World War II (3 hours, open).
3. One room schools. Interviews with teachers, principals and students of one room schools (9 hours, 44 pages, open).
4. Historic sites. Discussion of the construction and reconstruction of the capitol, the old state capitol and the governor's mansion (4 hours, on-going, 40 pages, open).
5. Lincoln Scholars. Interviews with T. Harry Williams, George Cashman, R. Gerald McMurty about the myth of Lincoln (3 hours, open).
6. Kennedy assassination reaction (4 hours, not transcribed).
7. Grey Herndon memoirs: farming (12 hours, 237 pages, open).
8. Italian Americans. Ethnic experience of assimilation into American life, including prohibition, mining, education, World War I and the effects of the Depression and the church (7 hours, 155 pages, some tapes restricted).
9. Lincoln Memorial Gardens (3 hours, open).
10. Poston Brick Company (7 hours, open).
11. George W. Bunn memoir (3 hours, 67 pages, open).
12. Charles Shuman memoir (5 hours, 114 pages, open).
13. Robinson memoir: Life in Springfield (6 hours, open).
14. Mental health care changes. Interviews with a wide spectrum of people connected with the state mental hospital (9 hours, 224 pages, open).
15. Springfield during World War II. The effects of wartime on a central Illinois community (6 hours, 26 pages, open).
16. Avinere Toigo memoir (6 hours, 125 pages, open).
17. Nauvoo. Interviews with men instrumental in reconstructing the Mormon city of Nauvoo, Illinois (6 hours, open).
18. Willard Conlon memoirs (2 hours, 20 pages, open).

SOUTHERN ILLINOIS UNIVERSITY

Morris Library
Carbondale, Illinois 62901
(618) 549-3296; 549-2516
Kenneth W. Duckett, Curator of Special Collections

General information: 1966. Budget: Included in Special Collections budget. Tapes: 150 hours, some transcribed, fully preserved. Transcriptions: 700 pages, edited.

Accessibility: No catalog. Indexed: Cataloged by author; a few subjects in the main card index of Special Collections. Interlibrary loan. Restrictions vary with each interview.

Major collections:
1. John Dewey (19 hours, 423 pages, one tape closed, completed).
2. SIU activities (28 hours, on-going).
3. SIU faculty (35 hours, 142 pages, on-going, most tapes are restricted until after interviewee's death).
4. Southern Illinois regional history (17 hours, 60 pages, on-going).
5. General, to support collection in theatre, Irish literature, philosophy, expatriate writers (44 hours, 114 pages, on-going).

SWEDISH PIONEER HISTORICAL SOCIETY

5125 North Spaulding Avenue
Chicago, Illinois 60625
(312) 583-5722
P. Raymond Nelson

General information: 1972, on-going. Budget: not specific. Tapes: transcribed, preserved. Transcriptions: not edited.

Accessibility: No catalog. Not indexed. No interlibrary loan.

Purpose of the program: To preserve the dialects of immigrants from Sweden.

UNIVERSITY OF ILLINOIS

Doris Duke Indian Oral History Project
109 Davenport Hall
Urbana, Illinois 61801
(217) 333-1000
Edward Bruner, Department of Anthropology

Note: Other institutions cooperating in the Doris Duke Indian Oral History Project are the Arizona State Museum, and the Universities of Florida, New Mexico, Oklahoma, South Dakota and Utah.

UNIVERSITY OF ILLINOIS

Oral History Research Laboratory
155 Freer Gymnasium
Goodwin and Gregory
Urbana, Illinois 61801
(217) 333-3765
Marianna Trekell, Oral History Research Office Director

General information: 1965. Budget: Depends upon requests and need. Tapes: 35 hours, transcribed, preserved. Transcriptions: 700 pages, partially edited.

Accessibility: Catalog: in process. Indexed. No interlibrary loan. Open for scholarly and research work; material must be used on site.

Purpose of the program: To obtain source material and raw historical data, through tape-recorded interviews with persons who have made and are making important contributions to physical education and sports. Efforts are made to acquire information which can be used as primary sources in investigating persistent historical problems in physical education and sports and to obtain a biographical account of the person being interviewed.

UNIVERSITY OF ILLINOIS

University Archives
Room 19, The Library
Urbana, Illinois 61801
(217) 333-1000
Maynard Brichford, University Archivist

General information: 1964. Tapes: 22 interviews, 22 hours, partially transcribed, fully preserved. Transcriptions: Partial.

Accessibility: Indexed. Interlibrary loan: Research and reproduction services can be arranged for persons unable to come to the library. Available to scholars applying in person and agreeing to the regulations established by the institution. Restrictions vary; usually permission of archivist or interviewee is required.

Purpose of the program: To supplement existing documentation in the university archives and manuscript collections. Major topics include university history, history and science, and technology.

WOOD LIBRARY—MUSEUM OF ANESTHESIOLOGY
515 Busse Highway
Park Ridge, Illinois 60068
(312) 825-5586
John J. Leahy, M.D., Director of Oral History Project, American Society of Anesthesiologists

General information: 1965. Tapes: not transcribed (about 50 interviews).

Accessibility: Catalog. Not indexed.

Purpose of program: To build a heritage of the persons and events that have been involved in the development of the specialty of anesthesia. The program is conducted by the Wood Library—Museum of Anesthesiology under the sponsorship of the American Society of Anesthesiologists.

INDIANA

AMERICAN SOCIETY FOR MICROBIOLOGY
Indiana University
438 Jordan Hall
Bloomington, Indiana 47401
(812) 332-0211
L.S. McClung

General information: 1964. Tapes: 20 interviews, preserved.

Accessibility: Indexed. Available to scholars applying in person, with archivist's approval.

Purpose of the program: To preserve the history of American microbiology. Major topics include interviews with current presidents, former presidents and other officers of ASM, history symposia at national meetings, council meetings, and presidential addresses.

FRANKLIN COUNTY CENTENNIAL COMMITTEE
Post Office Box 201
Brookville, Indiana 47012
John J. Newman, Director

General information: 1970.

Purpose of the program: To use oral history interviews to update the history of Franklin County, Indiana, in time to celebrate the bicentennial of the founding of the United States. Teachers, businessmen, country leaders, and representatives of ethnic groups in and out of the country are being interviewed.

HAMMOND HISTORICAL SOCIETY
564 State Street
Hammond, Indiana 46320
(219) 931-5100
Florence Cleveland, Librarian

General information: 1967. Tapes: 80 hours, not transcribed.

Accessibility: No catalog. Indexed. No interlibrary loan. Reference use only.

Purpose of the program: Interviews with local citizens and tapes of speakers at Hammond Historical Society meetings.

INDIANA STATE LIBRARY
140 North Senate Avenue
Indianapolis, Indiana 46204
(317) 633-5440
Randall Jehs

General information: 1967. Tapes: 25 interviews, 49 hours, partially transcribed, fully preserved. Transcriptions: 7 interviews, 222 pages.

Accessibility: No catalog. Indexed. Available to scholars applying in person and agreeing to the regulations established by the institution.

Purpose of the program: To supplement present collection and to collect memoirs of prominent persons. Major topics include twentieth century Indiana politics and Indiana veterans of the Spanish-American War.

INDIANA UNIVERSITY
Archives of Traditional Music
Bloomington, Indiana 47401
Frank J. Gillis, Associate Director

General information: Extensive holdings of oral data on the subject of music. The archives is hoping to obtain funds to publish a catalog and to index its holdings.

INDIANA UNIVERSITY
Indiana University Sesquicentennial Project
706 Ballantine Hall
Bloomington, Indiana 47401

General information: 1967, on-going. Tapes: 45 interviews, 75 hours, transcribed, fully preserved. Transcriptions: 490 interviews, 1600 pages, edited.

Accessibility: Restrictions: policy not determined.

Purpose of the program: To augment materials needed to write sesquicentennial history of Indiana University and to augment holdings on Indiana history.

JENNINGS COUNTY PUBLIC LIBRARY
143 East Walnut
North Vernon, Indiana 47265
(812) 346-2091
Frances Fawcett, Librarian

General information: 1972. Budget: No special amount. Tapes: 3 hours, not transcribed.

Accessibility: No catalog. Indexed. No interlibrary loan. Tapes must be used in the library.

Purpose of the program: To tape personal accounts relating to local history.

NEW CASTLE—HENRY COUNTY PUBLIC LIBRARY
296 South Fifteenth Street
New Castle, Indiana 47362
(317) 529-0362
Marjorie J. Johnson, Director

General information: 1972, on-going. Tapes: transcribed, preserved. Transcriptions: not edited.

Accessibility: Catalog in process. Not indexed. No interlibrary loan. No restrictions.

Purpose of the program: To preserve local history of Henry County, Indiana.

NORTHERN INDIANA HISTORICAL SOCIETY
112 South Lafayette Boulevard
South Bend, Indiana 46601
(219) 284-9664
Jean Robertson, Curator of the Museum

General information: 1969. Budget: $35,000. Tapes: some transcribed. Transcriptions: some edited.

Accessibility: Catalog. Not indexed. No interlibrary loan. Must be used in the museum.

Purpose of the program: To make a record of local history from the older residents of the area who have personal knowledge of the past.

NOTRE DAME
See University of Notre Dame

PURDUE UNIVERSITY ARCHIVES
Purdue University Libraries
West Lafayette, Indiana 47907
(317) 749-2577

General information: 1970, on-going. Budget: not stated, released time for staff. Tapes: 50 hours, mostly transcribed, fully preserved. Transcriptions: 2000 pages, edited.

Accessibility: No catalog. Indexed by name only. Interlibrary loan. Transcripts are restricted for library use only; must be used at borrowing institution when out on interlibrary loan.

Purpose of the collection: To document the history and development of Purdue University by obtaining first hand experiences and observations from individuals who participated in the decisions influencing Purdue's development. Additionally, significant biographical material was collected from faculty members, administrative officers and alumni who were interviewed.

UNIVERSITY OF NOTRE DAME
Notre Dame, Indiana 46556
(219) 283-6447
Rev. Thomas E. Blantz, University Archivist

General information: 1970. Budget: Included in budget of University Archives.

Accessibility: No catalog. Not indexed. Most projects are still in process and restrictions and terms of use have not been determined.

Purpose of the program: Areas of special interest are the history of the University of Notre Dame, the history of Catholic education in the United States and recent changes in the American Catholic Church.

VIGO COUNTY PUBLIC LIBRARY
222 North Seventh Street
Terre Haute, Indiana 47801
(812) 232-5041
Frances Boyd, Head, Public Services; Alice L. Wert, Art and Music Specialist

General information: 1970. Budget: Adjusted to fit needs. Tapes: 21 hours, partially transcribed, fully preserved. Transcriptions: not edited.

Accessibility: No catalog. Indexed. Interlibrary loan. Permission to quote or publish any of the material must be obtained from the Vigo County Public Library.

Purpose of the program: Members of the library staff interview persons who can "tell it like it was" about life in the area with emphasis on local people of prominence in literary, political, educational or social fields vital to the community. The library also tapes some current local events that will have historical significance in the future.

WABASH CARNEGIE PUBLIC LIBRARY
188 West Hill Street
Wabash, Indiana 46992
(219) 563-2972
Linda Robertson, Library Director

General information: 1970, on-going. Budget: $150. Tapes: 55 hours, in process of transcription. Transcriptions: 300 + pages, not edited.

Accessibility: No catalog. Not indexed. Interlibrary loan: with permission. The oral histories will not circulated from the library; they may be used by students, historians and genealogists; permission for use must be obtained from the Wabash Carnegie Public Library and the Indiana State Library.

Publications based on collected works:
Indian Magazine of History, December 1972.

Major collections:
1. Mark C. Honeywell collection (35 hours, on-going, owned jointly by the library and Honeywell, Inc. Recently accepted by Columbia University, N.Y.).
2. Local history collection (25 hours, on-going).

IOWA

BETTENDORF PUBLIC LIBRARY
2211 Grant Street
Bettendorf, Iowa 57222
(319) 355-1551
Rosalind Meyer

General information: 1965, on-going. Budget: none. Tapes: 6 hours, transcribed, preserved. Transcriptions: edited.

Accessibility: No catalog. Not indexed. No interlibrary loan. Tapes must be used in the library.

Purpose of the program: To collect information on the local area and people.

DES MOINES PUBLIC LIBRARY
See Public Library of Des Moines

HERBERT HOOVER PRESIDENTIAL LIBRARY
West Branch, Iowa
See Herbert Hoover Oral History Program, Washington, D.C.

IOWA STATE UNIVERSITY OF SCIENCE AND TECHNOLOGY
Ames, Iowa 50010
(515) 294-6672
Stanley Yates, Head, Department of Special Collections

General information: 1958, on-going. Budget: none. Tapes: transcribed, partially preserved. Transcriptions: 1600 pages, edited.

Accessibility: No catalog. Not indexed. Interlibrary loan. No general restrictions, but individual interviews may have restrictions.

Purpose of the program: Used for interviewing faculty, staff, students and alumni for history of the university. Also has scattered tapes of persons outside the university in connection with the manuscript collection.

Major collections:
1. History of University
2. Joe C. Reasoner tapes (16 separate tapes dealing with life on an Iowa farm in the early 20th century).

PUBLIC LIBRARY OF DES MOINES
100 Locust
Des Moines, Iowa 50309
(515) 283-4152
Elaine G. Estes, Head, West Side Branch Library

General information: 1972. Budget: $800. Tapes: 1400 hours, partially transcribed, fully preserved. Transcriptions: 91 pages, edited.

Accessibility: Catalog. Indexed. Interlibrary loan. Circulate for one week.

Purpose of the program: The local history tapes are to gather and preserve by recording the voices and reminiscences of persons who have special knowledge or association with the area, primarily Des Moines. The Iowa history tapes were purchased to provide additional resource material.

Major collections:
1. Local history (on-going, 660 hours, 91 pages, tapes transcribed and preserved, transcriptions edited and indexed).
2. Iowa history (Ashmore Audio Production Company) (700 hours, indexed).

UNIVERSITY OF IOWA LIBRARIES
Iowa City, Iowa 52240
(319) 353-2121
Robert A. McCown, Manuscripts Librarian

Accessibility: No catalog. Indexed. No interlibrary loan. Restrictions vary.

Major collections:
1. Communications Workers of America (220 hours, 2400 pages, available to scholars agreeing to regulations set by the CWA and interviewee).
2. Progressive Party of 1948 (4 hours, 68 pages).
3. Cedar Rapids and Iowa City Railway collection (59 pages).

KANSAS

BETHEL COLLEGE
North Newton, Kansas 67117
(316) 283-2500
Keith L. Sprunger, Professor of History

General information: 1968, on-going. Budget: $1,000. Tapes: 250 hours, partially transcribed, fully preserved. Transcriptions: not edited.

Accessibility: Catalog. Indexed. No interlibrary loan. Restrictions: Materials must be used in the library. Some interviews are restricted.

Purpose of the program: To collect information on conscientious objection during World War I (primarily Mennonite).

Publications based on collection research:
"World War I and the Mennonite Migration to Canada to Avoid the Draft," Mennonite Quarterly Review, July 1971.

DWIGHT D. EISENHOWER LIBRARY
Eisenhower Oral History Project
Abilene, Kansas 67410
(913) 263-4751
Maclyn P. Burg, Historian

General information: 1964. Budget: Not carried as a separate item in the library's budget. Tapes: approx. 1000 hours, transcribed, preserved. Transcriptions: 29,486 pages (as of June, 1973), edited.

Accessibility: Catalog. Not indexed. No interlibrary loan. Materials are available on an equal basis to all researchers. Some parts of oral history interviews are closed in accordance with the wish of the donors. Restrictions on materials have not been indicated in the subject index because restricted or closed material is continually being reviewed and opened for research.

Purpose of the program: The Eisenhower Oral History Project is centered upon the life and career of President Dwight D. Eisenhower. Its purpose is to collect the reminiscences of those who were associated with the President at some time during his military and public service. In the course of this work interviews have been secured with a broad spectrum of donors representing such fields as: politics, government, the military services, the news media, science, business, the arts, and many of the professions. Naturally, the collection is particularly rich in terms of the Eisenhower administration years, but it also contains material which illuminates the President's service as a military officer, as president of Columbia University and his activities and services during the post-Presidential years, 1961 to 1968.

FORT HAYS KANSAS STATE COLLEGE
Western Kansas Regional Oral History Project
Department of History
Hays, Kansas 67601
(913) 628-5691
James L. Forsythe, Director

General information: 1971. Budget: No budget, but the approx. costs from various areas is $3,500. Tapes: 350 hours, transcribed, preserved. Transcriptions: 5000 pages, edited.

Accessibility: No catalog. Not indexed. Interlibrary loan. Permission must be obtained from the director either to use the collection or to have the material reproduced.

Purpose of the program: To collect an oral history of western Kansas. The concentration is on former faculty and students of Fort Hays Kansas State College; settlement; economic development; depression; retired professionals such as teachers, merchants, and bankers; county and regional history; and ethnic groups. There are interviews with World War I and World War II veterans as well as a few prisoners of war. The ultimate goal is to have a full oral history collection of interviews of the history of the college and of western Kansas.

KANSAS STATE UNIVERSITY LIBRARY
Manhattan, Kansas 66506
(913) 532-6516
Evan W. Williams, Special Collections Librarian

General information: 1971. Budget: none. Tapes: 14 hours, transcribed, preserved. Transcriptions: 225 pages, edited.

Accessibility: No catalog. Not indexed. Interlibrary loan. Some tapes and transcripts are to be available only after the death of the interviewee, or after termination of his employment with the university. Most are open to public use.

Purpose of the program: To collect the oral history of the university, especially since 1940, when the last history of the institution was published. Major topics are the personalities of KSU presidents, and recollections of student days by the interviewees.

KENTUCKY

ALICE LLOYD COLLEGE

Appalachian Oral History Project: A four-school consortium
Pippa Passes, Kentucky 41844
(606) 368-2101
William Weinberg, Project Director
Campus Directors: George Stevenson, Emory and Henry College, Emory, Virginia 24327; Mike Mullins, Alice Lloyd College, Pippa Passes, Kentucky 41844; Sari Tudiver, Lees Junior College, Jackson, Kentucky 41339; Joy Lamm, Appalachian State University, Boone, North Carolina 28607

General information: 1970. Budget: $69,923 for FY 1973–1974. Tapes: 600 hours, preserved, partially transcribed. Transcriptions: 10,500 pages, not edited.

Accessibility: Catalog. Indexed. Interlibrary loan: sometimes. Researchers should ordinarily plan to use materials at the college, although limited loans are possible in special situations.

Purpose of the program: To collect and preserve the history of Central Appalachia through taped interviews with the last generation of Appalachian residents to reach maturity before the advent of radio and television—thus the last generation to maintain an oral tradition. It is not only a research program but an educational one too. Since students are doing the interviewing, they are put in the position of both researcher and learner. They are developing research skills, learning history, and most importantly, gaining a better understanding of their own cultural heritage and therefore of themselves.

Publications based on collection research works:
Articles in *Appalachian Heritage and Mountain Life and Work.*

UNIVERSITY OF KENTUCKY

Archives and Special Collections, King Library
Lexington, Kentucky 40506
(606) 258-8661
Charles L. Atcher, Archivist

General information: 1972. Budget: $20,000. Tapes: 7 hours, preserved. Transcriptions: 350 pages, indexed and edited.

Accessibility: No catalog. Indexed. Interlibrary loan. No restrictions.

Purpose of the program: To strengthen the collections of Senator Thurston B. Morton and Chief Justice Fred M. Vinson.

Major collections:
1. Senator Thurston B. Morton.
2. Chief Justice Fred M. Vinson.

UNIVERSITY OF LOUISVILLE

Department of History
Belknap Campus
Louisville, Kentucky
(502) 636-4892
Charles R. Berry, Oral History Center

General information: 1968.

Purpose of the program: To preserve the history of the Louisville Orchestra and the University of Louisville, to collect memoirs of prominent Kentuckians, and to collect information on the early training of American concert musicians.

WESTERN KENTUCKY UNIVERSITY

Bowling Green, Kentucky 42101
(502) 745-0111
Robert S. Phillips

General information: 1965. Budget: $800. Tapes: 800 hours, partially transcribed, wholly preserved. Transcriptions: 4000 pages, not edited.

Accessibility: No catalog. Indexed. Interlibrary loan by permission. There is to be no duplication or publication without the permission of the director.

Purpose of the program: The program supports the masters degree program in folklore and provides researchers with information about Kentucky culture and history.

Publications based on collection research:
Montell, William L. *Saga of Coe Ridge.* Knoxville: University of Tennessee Press, 1970.

LOUISIANA

ALLEN PARISH LIBRARY

Box 400
Oberlin, Louisiana 70655
(318) 639-4338
Bess Johnson, Oakdale Branch Assistant

General information: 1968, on-going. Budget: none. Tapes: 3 hours, transcribed, preserved. Transcriptions: 18 pages, not edited.

Accessibility: Catalog. Not indexed. No interlibrary loan. Tapes can be copied but do not circulate to general public.

Purpose of the program: Local citizens tell local history.

TULANE UNIVERSITY

Howard Tilton Library
New Orleans, Louisiana 70118
(504) 865-6634
Richard B. Allen, Curator of the Archive of New Orleans Jazz

General information: 1958. Budget: $17,500. Tapes: 1500 hours, preserved, some (11 percent) transcribed, some (75 percent) tapes are in digest form and others (14 percent) have rough notes. Transcriptions: 22,000 pages, edited.

Accessibility: No catalog. Index incomplete. Interlibrary loan: No, but photocopies can be obtained rather than a recorded tape. The tapes themselves are not copied, but copies of transcriptions may be obtained at cost. Some interviews are restricted either by the interviewee or by Tulane.

Purpose of the program: Documentation of origin and development of New Orleans jazz. Interviews include biographical details as well as description and demonstration of the music and the way it functions in society. There are interviews with musicians and non-musicians.

Publications based on collected works:
Balliett, Whitney. *Such Sweet Thunder.* Indianapolis: Bobbs-Merrill Co., 1966.
Bellocq, E.J. *Storyville Portraits.* New York: Museum of Modern Art, 1970.
Dodds, Warren. *The Baby Dodds Story: Los Angeles: Contemporary Press, 1959.
Lawrence, Vera Brodsky. *The Collected Works of Scott Joplin.* New York: Belwin Mills Publishing, 1973.
Oster, Harry. *Living Country Blues.* Detroit: Folklore Association, 1969.
Schafer, William J. and Riedel, Johannes. *The Art of Ragtime.* Baton Rouge: Louisiana State University Press, 1973.
Williams, Martin T. *Jazz Masters of New Orleans.* New York: Macmillan Co., 1967.

MAINE

CARY LIBRARY
Houlton, Maine 04730
(207) 532-3967
Helen K. Atchison, Project Director; Charlotte L. Melvin, History Consultant

General information: 1971. Budget: The program was funded originally by LSCA funds, under Title I. These funds ($15,000) have been used and libraries are buying cassettes as they need them with no real budget. Tapes: 116 hours, not transcribed.

Accessibility: No catalog. Indexed. Interlibrary loan. Out-of-State borrowers should borrow the three sets held by the Maine State Library or use the two sets at the Library of Congress. No restrictions.

Purpose of the program: To preserve the flavor of by-gone days in the county, to reach senior citizens and draw them into the library as important contributing patrons, and to locate bits and pieces of forgotten history. Since the French and Swedes are important minorities in the area, their contributions were sought with the hope that they might be assured of their cultural influence in the county and would consider the many services available at the libraries in the county as one of their rights. Subjects include early farming, sports, railroading, folksongs, education, politics, church affairs, fires and floods, newspapers, Indian affairs, lumbering, customs in French and Swedish settlements, war memoirs, social organizations, socials, cemetaries, inns and hotels, early travel, libraries, peddlers, banks and banking, mining, local vocabulary, etc.

UNIVERSITY OF MAINE
Northeast Archives of Folklore and Oral History
Department of Anthropology
South Stevens Hall
Orono, Maine 04473
(207) 581-7466
Edward D. Ives, Director

General information: 1971. Budget: Department budget of $850 with work-study and other salary assistance additions. Tapes: 136 hours, transcribed, preserved. Transcriptions: 5875 pages, not edited.

Accessibility: Catalog. No index, Place-name, personal-name, special subject index in process. Interlibrary loan: Possibly, upon direct application to director only. Written permission of director required for any and all uses.

Purposes of the collection: Approx. 800 separate collections, many of which are miscellaneous collections of folklore materials. Special emphasis: the lumberman's life, lobstering and fishing, labor history, folksongs and their makers.

Publications based on collection research:
Larry Gorman: The Man Who Made the Songs and *Lawrence Doyle: Poet of Prince Edward Island* (both by Edward Ives). *Northeast Folklore*, Volumes IV–XIII. Several dissertations in process.

Major collections:
1. Fishing and lobstering. Interviews with lobstermen and men who have spent their lives as fishermen; descriptions of techniques, daily life, etc. (20 hours, 500+ pages, on-going).
2. Organized labor in Maine. Interviews with men who have played a significant part in the union movement in Maine (35 hours, 900+ pages, on-going).
3. Folksongs and their makers. Materials documenting the lives and songs of such folk-poets as Larry Gorman, Lawrence Doyle and Joe Scott (130 hours, 3,200+ pages, on-going).
4. The lumberman's life. Interviews with woodsmen and river-drivers about what life was like, including descriptions of camp and drive, logging operations, techniques, etc. (57 hours, 1,275 pages, on-going).

MARYLAND

MARYLAND HISTORICAL SOCIETY
201 West Monument Street
Baltimore, Maryland 21201
(301) 685-3750
Francis S. Key, Director, Oral History Office

General information: 1971. Budget: $5,000. Tapes: 63 hours, transcribed, preserved. Transcriptions: 680 pages, edited.

Accessibility: No catalog. Indexed. No interlibrary loan. Must be used at Historical Society Library. A few interviews have closed sections.

Purpose of the program: To collect interviews with Marylanders of note or more obscure people who can speak of something uniquely Maryland. Emphasis is necessarily on Baltimore. The program includes the development of oral history programs throughout the state and the assembly in a catalog of other Maryland oral history material.

NATIONAL INSTITUTES OF HEALTH
9000 Rockville Pike
Bethesda, Maryland 20014
(301) 496-3006
Wyndham D. Miles, Historian

General information: 1962. Budget: No separate budget. Tapes: 300 hours, not transcribed (a long abstract of each is made).

Accessibility: No catalog. Not indexed. Interlibrary loan: Copies of tapes will be loaned. No restrictions.

Purpose of the program: To provide historical and biographical information for persons interested in development of National Institutes of Health and Public Health Service or the history of medicine.

NATIONAL LIBRARY OF MEDICINE
8600 Rockville Pike
Bethesda, Maryland 20014
(301) 656-4000
Peter D. Olch, M.D., History of Medicine Division

General information: 1966. Tapes: 55 interviews, 290 hours, transcribed, preserved. Transcriptions: edited.

Accessibility: Indexed. Interlibrary loan: Extracts and copies of transcripts can be made within the restrictions set by the interviewee. Restrictions: Vary as set by interviewees. Limited reference service related to content of the collection can be provided by the library.

SOCIAL SECURITY ADMINISTRATION
Department of Health, Education and Welfare
832 Administration Building
Baltimore, Maryland 21235
(301) 594-1234
Abe Bortz, Historian

General information: 1964. Tapes: 112 interviews, 370 hours, transcribed, preserved. Transcriptions: 11,398 pages, edited.

SOCIAL SECURITY ADMINISTRATION (cont.)

This project was carried out by Columbia University's Oral History Office. All tapes and transcripts are deposited with that office.

Accessibility: Restrictions: Vary with wishes of interviewee.

Purpose of the program: To secure the personal memoirs of people involved in various aspects of the social security movement in the United States. Major emphasis is placed on experiences of the pioneers in the movement and those involved in Medicare. A detailed description of the collection appears under the entry for Columbia University and a list of participants, pages and restrictions appear under "Social Security" in the subject and name index.

U.S. NAVAL INSTITUTE

Annapolis, Maryland 21402
(301) 268-6110
John T. Mason, Director

General information: March 1969. Tapes 150 interviews, 1300 hours, transcribed, preserved. Transcriptions: 20,000 pages, edited; 12,500 pages not transcribed: 43 bound volumes; 45 volumes in process.

Accessibility: Indexed. Collection is open except for material that is closed until a specified date.

Purpose of the program: To collect materials of interest and value to naval historians and biographers. Major topics include naval aviation, the Coast Guard, oceanography, the Waves, Fleet Admiral Chester W. Nimitz, and other biographies.

Major collections:

In addition to the program described above, a copy of transcripts from the United States Marine Corps collection on retired Marine Corps officers is on deposit here. A full description of the collection is found under the entry for Columbia University, New York and a list of participants and pages can be found under the entry for "Marine Corps" in the name and subject index.

UNIVERSITY OF BALTIMORE

Langsdale Library
1420 Maryland Avenue
Baltimore, Maryland 21201
(301) 727-6350, ext. 285
Adele Newburger, Curator for Oral History Programs

Purpose of the program: To prepare a history of the university and to develop taped interviews supplementing urban archival collections held by the university's Baltimore Region Institutional Studies Center.

Accessibility: No catalog. Index in process. Interlibrary loan. No restrictions.

General information: 1972. Budget: $150. Tapes: partially transcribed, preserved. Transcriptions: 24 pages, edited.

MASSACHUSETTS

THE ARTHUR AND ELIZABETH SCHLESINGER LIBRARY ON THE HISTORY OF WOMEN IN AMERICA

Radcliffe College
3 James Street
Cambridge, Massachusetts 02138
(617) 495-8647
Jeannette Bailey Cheek, Director

General information: No formal program—just "pieces" of oral history. Budget: $2,000 gift to start program, other funds being sought. Tapes: 35 hours, mostly transcribed and wholly preserved. Transcriptions: edited.

Accessibility: Catalog. Not indexed. No interlibrary loan. To be used in the library. Permission to use two tapes must be obtained from the author.

Purpose of the program: Interviews thus far have tended to relate to major collections of papers in the library. Sometimes this has meant interviews with individual women who have made a distinguished contribution to American history in a given field. Sometimes it has been a matter of social history in general.

Publication based on collection research:

Lamson, Peggy. *Few Are Chosen: American Women in Political Life Today.* Boston: Houghton-Mifflin Co., 1968.

Major collections:

1. The careers of New England women in medicine (10 hours).
2. Mary Anderson (first director of the Women's Bureau) interviewed by Esther Peterson (2 hours).
3. Claudia White Harreld: Memoirs. Recollections of her mother, a former slave (2 hours).
4. Interviews with older women, many of them first generation immigrants to Rhode Island.
5. The career of Harriet Pilpel and the legal fight for liberalized abortion laws.
6. Peggy Lamson collection.

BOSTON PUBLIC LIBRARY

Copley Square
Boston, Massachusetts 02117
(617) 536-5400
Francis Moloney, Assistant Director; Mrs. H. B. Shepherd, Librarian; Philip J. McNiff, Oral History Program

General information: 1970. Tapes: 11 interviews, 33 hours, partially transcribed, fully preserved. Transcriptions: 24 pages.

Accessibility: Available to scholars applying in person and agreeing to the regulations established by the institution.

Purpose of the program: To record the observations and reminiscences of men and women who have been prominent in the public life of Boston or of Massachusetts during the present century. Major topics include political and governmental history of the city and state and the Sacco-Vanzetti Case.

BOSTON UNIVERSITY

771 Commonwealth Avenue
Boston, Massachusetts 02215
(617) 353-3696
M. A. Garrigan, Professor of Nursing, Nursing Archive Curator

General information: 1966, on-going. Budget: None; some support from Nursing Archive Fund. Tapes: 85 hours, partially transcribed, wholly preserved. Transcriptions: partially edited.

Accessibility: No catalog. Not indexed. No interlibrary loan. Material not available yet.

Purpose of the program: In 1965, the Nursing Archive was an outgrowth of a "centralization of libraries" project at Boston University. In every possible instance clients for whom a personal or institutional manuscript collection was established were interviewed.

BRANDEIS UNIVERSITY

Waltham, Massachusetts 02154
(617) 647-2000
David Westphal, Director, Dretzin Living Biographies Program

General information: 1967. Tapes: 6 interviews, 7 hours, wholly preserved, partially transcribed.

Accessibility: Collection is available to scholars applying in person and agreeing to the regulations established by the institution.

Purpose of the program: Memoirs of individuals such as David Ben Gurion, Carlos Romulo, Louis Rosentiel, and Dr. Grete Bebring.

HARVARD UNIVERSITY
Christian A. Herter Oral History Project
Charles Warren Center
Cambridge, Massachusetts 02138
(617) 495-1000
Charles T. Morrissey, Director

Purpose of the program: To preserve oral history about Christian A. Herter.

HARVARD UNIVERSITY GRADUATE SCHOOL OF BUSINESS
Baker Library
Boston, Massachusetts
(617) 495-6000
Robert W. Lovett, Curator of Manuscripts and Archives

General information: 1970. Tapes: 3 interviews, 4 hours, partially preserved, wholly transcribed. Transcriptions: 425 pages.

Accessibility: Not indexed. Available to scholars applying in person and agreeing to the regulations established by the institution. Some interviews restricted.

Purpose of the program: To record business history and the history of the business school.

IPSWICH PUBLIC LIBRARY
25 North Main
Ipswich, Massachusetts 01938
(617) 356-4646
Elizabeth Stanton

General information: 1971. Budget: $500. Tapes: 40 hours, not transcribed at present time.

Accessibility: No catalog. Not indexed. No interlibrary loan. Tapes must be used in the library.

Purpose of the program: To record in spoken and narrative form accounts, descriptions, and reminiscences relating to the town's history. Program fulfills two objectives: to bring local histories up to date and to supplement written records. A community-wide effort uniting schools, libraries, and historical groups, the project hopes to achieve the unification of fragmented random collections of oral history. Local industry and transportation are represented in this collection.

JOHN F. KENNEDY LIBRARY
380 Trapelo Road
Waltham, Massachusetts 02154
(617) 223-7250
Dan H. Fenn, Jr., Director; John F. Stewart, Assistant Director for Archives

General information: 1964. Budget: approx. $75,000. Tapes: 530 hours, transcribed, preserved. Transcriptions: 17,200 pages, edited according to wishes of donor.

Accessibility: No catalog. Interviews are name and subject indexed but index is not published. Interlibrary loan, except when restricted by donor. Restrictions vary by interview.

Purpose of the program: The oral history program records and preserves interviews with persons who have valuable recollections of events and personalities of interest to researchers who will use the Kennedy Library. The interviews are not conducted for publication or as memorials to President Kennedy, but to contribute to a more complete understanding of his career and administration and of major public events of his time. Persons interviewed include prominent public figures as well as less prominent people who helped develop and carry out the programs of the Kennedy administration. People who opposed Kennedy's policies as well as those who supported them are interviewed. Over 1000 persons have been interviewed.

Publications based on collection research:
Fitzsimons, Louise. *The Kennedy Doctrine.* New York: Random House, Inc., 1972.
Halberstam, David. *The Best and the Brightest.* New York: Random House, Inc., 1972
Navasky, Victor. *Kennedy Justice.* New York: Atheneum Publishers, 1971.

LAUREL HILL ASSOCIATION
Austen Riggs Center
Stockbridge, Massachusetts 01262
(413) 298-5511
Eugene Talbot, President

General information: Tapes: 20 interviews.

Accessibility: Not indexed. Research and reproduction permitted.

Purpose of the program: To record personal recollections of Stockbridge and other aspects of local history.

MASSACHUSETTS INSTITUTE OF TECHNOLOGY
See Neurosciences Research Program

NEUROSCIENCES RESEARCH PROGRAM
Massachusetts Institute of Technology
280 Newton Street
Brookline, Massachusetts 02146
(617) 253-1000
Theodore Melnechuk

General information: 1963. Tapes: 1000 hours, preserved.

Accessibility: Restrictions to be decided on an individual basis.

Purpose of the program: Tape recordings of NRP meetings. To permit eventual scholarly study of the history of science in brain research. Tapes are of invited groups of experts on a topic and not of individual interviews.

RADCLIFFE COLLEGE
See Arthur and Elizabeth Schlesinger Library on the History of Women in America

SMITH COLLEGE
Northampton, Massachusetts 01060
(413) 584-2700, ext. 502
Jacqueline Van Voris, Director, Smith Centennial Study

General information: 1971. Tapes: 260 hours, transcribed, preserved. Transcriptions: 5000 pages, edited.

Accessibility: No catalog. Indexed by name only. No interlibrary loan. Restricted to Smith College use until June 1, 1975. Permission of interviewees required to quote.

SMITH COLLEGE (cont.)

Purpose of the program: To provide a source of information about the importance of education in women's lives. The immediate goal is a publication commemorating the one hundredth anniversary of the opening of the college in 1875. This will not be a history of Smith College per se, but an assessment of its role in the contributions women's colleges have made to higher education in the United States. The emphasis is on the college, what the alumnae remember about it, their views on higher education, coeducation, feminist movements, community service, professions, what effect their Smith education had on their lives. In short: how does an educated woman look at her education? The respondents include some women with professional careers, some who represent those whose lives have been devoted to home, family, and community service (although this does not imply that those with paid jobs have not had families and given volunteer service as well).

UNIVERSITY OF MASSACHUSETTS

Labor Relations Oral History Project
Draper Hall
Amherst, Massachusetts 01002
(413) 545-0111

General information: 1967–1970, completed.

Purpose of the program: Labor history in Massachusetts during World War I.

WELLESLEY COLLEGE

Wellesley, Massachusetts 02181
(617) 235-0320
Jean Glasscock, Centennial Historian

General information: 1970–1971. Tapes: 100 hours and growing, transcribed, preserved. Transcriptions: Very slightly edited or not at all.

Accessibility: No catalog. Not indexed. Interlibrary loan. No restrictions except a genuine scholarly interest in the material and the intention to use it with integrity for an appropriate purpose.

Purpose of the program: The immediate purpose of the program is to provide fresh, authoritative data for use in connection with the history of the college which will be published as part of Wellesley's centennial in 1975. After that time, the project will be continued, focusing on various aspects of liberal arts education for women, in general, and on Wellesley in particular.

WORCESTER HISTORICAL SOCIETY

39 Salisbury Street
Worcester, Massachusetts 01608
(617) 753-8278
John Herron, Director, Worcester Historical Society; Daniel E. Dick, Curator, Oral History Program

General information: 1970. Budget: limited. Tapes: 20 hours, not transcribed.

Purpose of the program: A thorough and continuous oral history of the city, to fit into the larger history of Worcester project, whose purpose is to identify the nature, location and to acquire eventually all significant materials beginning with 1830. The major emphasis of the oral history aspects are: to reach as far into the past as memories will allow and to obtain historical testimony to the present where little other material exists, as in the case of the Spanish-speaking community.

Accessibility: No catalog. Indexed. Interlibrary loan. Restrictions as agreed upon with individual interviewees.

MICHIGAN

ALBION COLLEGE LIBRARY

Albion, Michigan 49224
(313) 629-5511
Charles Held, Librarian

General information: 1973.

Purpose of the program: This program has been initiated with funds secured from a Kellogg Foundation grant (Experiments in Relevance program). It will rely heavily on community participation to develop the project. Taped interviews will be used to trace the history of the city of Albion and the environs.

CENTRAL MICHIGAN UNIVERSITY

Clarke Historical Library
Mount Pleasant, Michigan 48858
(517) 774-3151
John Cumming

General information: 1964. Tapes: 23 interviews.

Purpose of the program: To record local history.

FERRIS STATE COLLEGE

901 South State Street
Big Rapids, Michigan 49307
(616) 796-9971
Goldie T. Nott, Director

General information: 1968. Budget: none. Tapes: 7 hours, not transcribed.

Accessibility: No catalog. Listed in card catalog. No interlibrary loan. To be used in the library.

Purpose of the program: An attempt is being made to interview alumni and former faculty members about their memories of Ferris State College. Tapes are made by the College Relations Department of significant programs and speeches.

FLINT PUBLIC LIBRARY

1026 East Kearsley Street
Flint, Michigan 48502
(313) 232-7111
Ransom L. Richardson, Oral History Program

General information: 1964. Tapes: 27 interviews, 37 hours, partially transcribed, fully preserved. Transcriptions: 205 pages.

Accessibility: Interlibrary loan of transcripts.

Purpose of the program: To strengthen the local history collection by adding personal reminiscences of longtime residents. Major topics include local history and recollections of the automotive industry.

FORD ARCHIVES

Henry Ford Museum and Greenfield Village
Dearborn, Michigan 48100
(313) 271-1620
Henry E. Edmunds, Oral History Section

General information: 1950. Tapes: 434 interviews, transcribed. Transcriptions: 26,000+ pages, edited.

Accessibility: Available to qualified scholars applying in person and agreeing to the regulations established by the institution.

Purpose of the program: To supplement and interpret Ford documentation. Major topics include Henry Ford, the Ford Motor Company, and related activities.

GENERAL MOTORS CORPORATION
Research Laboratories
General Motors Technical Center
Warren, Michigan 48090
(313) 575-2731
Robert W. Gibson, Jr., Head, Library Department

General information: 1960, on-going. Tapes: transcribed, preserved. Transcriptions: 1000 pages, edited.

Accessibility: Catalog. Indexed. No interlibrary loan. Available to serious students of the history of science and technology.

Purpose of the program: The oral history project, begun in 1960 under the direction of T. A. Boyd, Charles F. Kettering's biographer and scientific associate since 1918, led to interviews with those people associated with Kettering in engineering, scientific, medical, and other endeavors, as well as many of his personal friends.

MONROE COUNTY LIBRARY SYSTEM
3700 South Custer Road
Monroe, Michigan 48161
(313) 241-5277
Mary Daume, Director

General information: 1956. Budget: included in budget of reference department. Tapes: 4 hours, transcribed, preserved. Transcriptions: 700 pages, edited.

Accessibility: No catalog. Indexed. No interlibrary loan. Must be used in the library as there is only one copy, but pages may be photocopied.

Purpose of the program: To record the biographies of prominent men and women, as well as the history of Monroe County.

UNIVERSITY OF MICHIGAN
Michigan Historical Collections
160 Rackham
Ann Arbor, Michigan 48104
(313) 764-3482
Robert M. Warner

General information: 1960. Budget: no formal budget. Tapes: 550+ hours, some collections transcribed and preserved. Transcriptions: 7300 pages, some edited.

Accessibility: Card catalog. No interlibrary loan. No general restrictions; see specific collections below.

Purpose of the program: This oral history program is intended to complement the manuscript holdings. In many cases the program will cooperate with doctoral students who want to interview people of importance to the history of Michigan and the development of the University of Michigan. In the past, Michigan Historical Collections has supplied equipment to such persons and made transcriptions of their interviews available. Its major emphasis is Michigan politics and society and the history of the University of Michigan.

Publications based on collection research:
Fine, Sidney. *Automobile under the Blue Eagle: Labor, Management, and the Auto Manufacturing Code.* Ann Arbor: University of Michigan Press, 1963.

Major collections:
1. Institute of Labor and Industrial Relations (University of Michigan-Wayne State University) collection. This collection covers labor in the United States, a history of the United Auto Workers, particularly during the Depression, and Michigan and national politics (500 hours, approx. 5000 pages, transcribed and indexed. One must sign an agreement of use).
2. The relationship between the Board of Regents of the University of Michigan and the Michigan State legislature (4 hours, 46 pages, transcribed and indexed, open).
3. The administration of Alexander G. Ruthven, president of the University of Michigan (128 pages, transcribed, indexed, open).
4. The Ossian Sweet murder trial in Detroit, Michigan (1925) (119 pages, open).
5. Methadone treatment of drug rehabilitation (235 pages, permission required to publish).
6. Local history in Michigan (100 pages, open).
7. Michigan politics (200 pages, open).
8. Activities of the Peace and Freedom Party in the election of 1968 (4 hours, 60 pages, permission of donor required).
9. Frank Murphy oral history project covering national politics, the Philippine Islands, the U.S. Supreme Court, the Flint sit-down strike, and Michigan Democratic politics (1200 pages, transcribed, closed).
10. Gerald L. K. Smith oral history project covering the New Deal and national politics, 1930–present (100 pages, transcribed, preserved, closed).
11. Miscellaneous biographical and topical interviews.

WAYNE STATE UNIVERSITY
Archives of Labor History and Urban Affairs
Detroit, Michigan 48202
(313) 577-4024
Philip P. Mason, Director

General information: 1961. Budget: no separate budget at this time. Tapes: 600 hours, transcribed, preserved. Transcriptions: 22,000 pages, edited.

Accessibility: No catalog. Indexed. No interlibrary loan. Available to faculty members and graduate students doing directed research. All others must secure special permission.

Purpose of the program: To supplement and interpret the archival collection and provide historical information not available in written materials.

Publications based on collection research:
Fine, Sidney. *Automobile Under the Blue Eagle: Labor, Management, and the Auto Manufacturing Code.* Ann Arbor: University of Michigan Press, 1963.
Fine, Sidney. *Sit-Down: The General Motors Strike of 1936–1937.* Ann Arbor: University of Michigan Press, 1969.

Major collections:
1. Labor and the black worker (97 hours, 1160 pages).
2. Unionization of the auto industry: Development of UAW (500 hours, 20,000 pages).

WESTERN MICHIGAN UNIVERSITY
Kalamazoo, Michigan 49001
(616) 383-4917; 383-1826
Peter J. Schmitt, Director, INSIGHTS: The Data Bank for Living History

General information: 1973. Budget: grant support.

Accessibility: No catalog. Not indexed. For scholarly use; some materials have specific restrictions or are closed.

Purpose of the program: Insights is concerned with regional history materials in southwestern Michigan (a twelve county area). At present major topics include business history in Kalamazoo, agricultural transition in the twentieth century, growth of a regional university, special education experiences, and community political life.

MINNESOTA

MAYO CLINIC FOUNDATION
200 First Street, S.W.
Rochester, Minnesota 55901
(507) 282-2511
Clark W. Nelson, Director

General information: 1963. Tapes: 46 interviews, 60 hours, wholly preserved, partially transcribed. Transcriptions: edited.

Accessibility: Availability dependent upon prior application and research needs of scholar.

Purpose of the program: To document Mayo Institutions history using oral as well as visual and written means. The history of Mayo Institutions, staff and their relationship to American medicine, St. Mary's Hospital and Methodist Hospital are among the major topics.

MINNESOTA HISTORICAL SOCIETY
690 Cedar Street
St. Paul, Minnesota 55101
(612) 296-2489
Lila M. Johnson, Head, Audiovisual Library

General information: 1967. Budget: $12,000. Tapes: 400 hours, preserved, partially transcribed. Transcriptions: 5000 pages, edited.

Accessibility: Card catalog only. Indexed. No interlibrary loan. Restrictions vary with each interview; most are not restricted.

Purpose of the program: To collect information on the history of Minnesota, with emphasis on Minnesotans and Minnesota history. Major topics: public affairs, including state government, labor history, urban history.

MOORHEAD STATE COLLEGE
Northwest Minnesota Historical Center
Moorhead, Minnesota 56560
(218) 236-2812
Kenneth Smemo, Director

General information: 1973. Budget: $10,000. Tapes: program just started.

Accessibility: No catalog. Not indexed. Unless a donor places specific restrictions, materials will be open for scholarly use by anyone.

Purpose of the program: The oral history project portion of the center's activities is concerned primarily with collecting interviews from area residents regarding their memories and involvement in various movements and events germane to the Red River Valley past. The first thematic collecting is centering on the Red River Valley in the 1930s.

SOUTHWEST MINNESOTA STATE COLLEGE
Marshall, Minnesota 56258
(507) 537-6172
Warren Gardner and David Nass, Co-Directors

General information: 1972. Tapes: 35 taped interviews, transcribed, preserved. Transcriptions: edited.

Accessibility: No catalog. Index in process. Interlibrary loan: not decided yet. No restrictions.

Purpose of the program: To obtain taped interviews dealing with the Farm Holiday Association, Depression in the 1930s, early nationality settlements, prohibition, Non-Partisan League, the Rural Electrification Association, and Southwest Minnesota State College.

MISSISSIPPI

MARY HOLMES COLLEGE
West Point, Mississippi 39773
(601) 494-6820
Clarence M. Simmons, Director

General information: Tapes: 300 interviews, partially transcribed. Transcriptions: edited.

Purpose of the program: To engage students and faculty in joint research on rural Mississippi, especially sharecropping.

MILLSAPS COLLEGE
Jackson, Mississippi 39200
(601) 354-5201
Gordon Henderson, Department of Political Science

General information: 1965. Tapes: 50 interviews.

Accessibility: Some memoirs are restricted, but others are available for research and reproduction.

Purpose of the program: To document the civil rights movement, including school desegregation and voter registration, Theodore Bilbo, Mississippi politics since 1930, the cotton industry, elections, and the Citizens Council.

MISSISSIPPI STATE UNIVERSITY
Box 5408
Mississippi State, Mississippi 39762
(601) 325-4225
J. G. Shoalmire, Curator, John C. Stennis Collection

General information: 1972. Budget: varied. Tapes: 15 hours, transcribed and preserved (partial in cases of unusual editing). Transcriptions: 150 pages, edited.

Accessibility: No catalog. Index in process. Interlibrary loan for unrestricted material only. Restrictions vary with interviewee's wishes; some are very severe, others are open immediately after transcription. Many are closed subject to approval of researcher by the interviewee. Most under time seal follow Senator Stennis's requirement of 25 years from interview.

Purpose of the program: The program was initiated to utilize oral history in compiling information on Senator Stennis. The equipment acquired for that purpose is now beginning to be utilized by other interviewers on other topics. Primary emphasis at present, however, is Mississippi politics (1930–1950), Senator Stennis's 1947 campaign for the U.S. Senate and Senator Stennis's recollections of his career in the Senate and his colleagues there.

UNIVERSITY OF SOUTHERN MISSISSIPPI
Box 2175
Southern Station
Hattiesburg, Mississippi 39401
(601) 266-7245
Orley B. Caudill, Director, Mississippi Oral History Program

General information: 1971, on-going. Budget: $15,000. Tapes: 250 hours, transcribed, preserved. Transcriptions: 2750 pages, edited (in a limited manner, to eliminate false starts, etc.).

Accessibility: No catalog. Not indexed. No interlibrary loan. There are restrictions established by interviewees. Some are restricted in part for a period of years, one entire interview is restricted for five years.

Purpose of the program: The emphasis of the program is to document the rapid transition of the biracial, formerly segregated, primarily agrarian society of Mississippi into a more homogeneous, racially integrated and industrial-agricultural-service society and the effects of these changes upon both races. It also emphasizes the preservation of the unique aspects of minority group history including Blacks, Chinese, Indians and other ethnic groups. Included in this is the preservation of rapidly disappearing dialects of the various groups, especially the blacks.

MISSOURI

CONCORDIA HISTORICAL INSTITUTE
801 DeMun Avenue
St. Louis, Missouri 63105
(314) 721-5934; ext. 297, 351
August R. Suelflow, Director

General information: 1951. Budget: $200. Tapes: 100,000 hours, not transcribed.

Accessibility: No catalog. Partially indexed. No interlibrary loan. The material in the collection is not considered open for 25 years. Under ordinary circumstances the actual tapes are not used unless absolutely necessary. Access to Missouri Synod convention tapes requires permission of the synodical president.

Purpose of the program: The program is designed to gather information in oral form on the history of Lutheranism in America. One phase of the program has the goal of obtaining interviews with significant individuals at transition stages of their careers or at retirement. Another seeks to record worship services and work in foreign languages at various times and places, in mission fields, and by ethnic groups in their native languages. Another segment consists of recordings of the complete proceedings of the general conventions of the Lutheran Church-Missouri Synod.

DAVIESS COUNTY LIBRARY
Gallatin, Missouri 64640
(816) 663-3222
Ina Naylor, Administrative Librarian

General information: 1973, on-going. Budget: not yet.

Purpose of the program: The program will concentrate on county history as remembered by senior citizens.

HARRY S. TRUMAN LIBRARY
Independence, Missouri 64056
(816) 252-1141
James R. Fuchs, Chief, Oral History Project

General information: 1961. Tapes: 400 accessioned, 395 not yet accessioned, partially transcribed, a small segment of each is preserved. Transcriptions: 9612 pages (accessioned), edited.

Accessibility: Catalog. Interlibrary loan. Restrictions vary from transcript to transcript. Copies are not made to be placed in other collections. Publication in full is reserved for the Truman Library.

Purpose of the program: To document the career and administration of Harry S. Truman.

Publications based on collection research:
Cochran, Bert. *Harry Truman and the Crisis Presidency.* New York: Holt, Rinehart & Winston, 1973.
Truman, Margaret. *Harry S. Truman.* New York: William Morrow & Company, 1973.
Kish, Major Francis B. "Citizen-Soldier: Harry S. Truman, 1884-1972." *Military Review* 53 (February 1973): 30-44.

PARK COLLEGE
Parkville, Missouri 64152
(816) 741-2000
Frances Fishburn, College Historian

General information: 1966. Budget: None—supported by Alumni Association. Tapes: 15 hours, transcribed. Transcriptions: edited.

Accessibility: No catalog. Not indexed. No interlibrary loan. No restrictions.

Purpose of the program: To preserve the early history of the college through interviews with alumni.

UNIVERSITY OF MISSOURI
Western Historical Manuscript Collections
University of Missouri Library
Columbia, Missouri 65202
(314) 882-2121
Nancy C. Prewitt

General information: 1965-1970, completed. Tapes: 4 interviews, 8 hours, transcribed, not preserved. Transcriptions: 162 pages, edited.

Accessibility: Interlibrary loan. Research and reproduction services can be arranged for persons unable to come to the institution. Permission of interviewee required.

Purpose of the program: This was a pilot program on newspaper editors.

UNIVERSITY OF MISSOURI—ST. LOUIS
8001 Natural Bridge Road
St. Louis, Missouri 63121
(314) 453-5143
Irene E. Cortinovis, Director, Oral History Program

General information: 1970. Budget: $20,000. Tapes: 150 hours, some transcribed, preserved. Transcriptions: 2500 pages, not edited.

Accessibility: Catalog. Indexed. Interlibrary loan. No special restrictions. All tapes and transcriptions must be credited whenever used.

Purpose of the program: To record and preserve the personal recollections of individuals in the metropolitan St. Louis area. The aims are two-fold: to add to the picture of the cultural, social, political, and economic life of St. Louis which is presented to researchers of the future, and to provide immediate source material for student use.

Major collections:
1. Socialists of St. Louis and Missouri (5 hours, on-going).
2. Black St. Louis leaders (22 hours, 700 pages, on-going).
3. Jazzmen on the Mississippi (18 hours, 16 pages, on-going).
4. Women's liberation movement (10 hours, 11 pages, one tape required written permission, on-going).
5. Immigrants to St. Louis (30 hours, 300 pages, on-going).
6. Dr. Thomas A. Dooley, St. Louis doctor in Indo-China (58 hours, 1250 pages, completed).
7. St. Louis Teachers' Strike (15 hours, 213 pages, on-going).

WASHINGTON UNIVERSITY
Box 1061
Washington University Library
St. Louis, Missouri 63130
(314) 863-0100
William A. Deiss, University Archivist, University Archives and Research Collection

WASHINGTON UNIVERSITY (cont.)

General information: 1968. Tapes: 3 interviews, 35 hours, wholly preserved, partially transcribed. Transcriptions: 2 interviews, 400 pages, edited.

Accessibility: None of the material is open yet.

Purpose of the program: History of Washington University and of the St. Louis metropolitan area in the twentieth century.

WASHINGTON UNIVERSITY SCHOOL OF MEDICINE LIBRARY

4580 Scott Avenue
St. Louis, Missouri 63110
(314) 367-6400, ext. 3711
Darryl B. Podoll, Archivist

General information: 1969, on-going. Budget: none. Tapes: 9 hours, not transcribed.

Accessibility: No catalog. Indexed. No portion of the oral history tapes may be published without the express written permission of the librarian, Washington University School of Medicine.

Purpose of the program: The medicine oral history program has three objectives: to document the history of the Washington University School of Medicine; to document outstanding scientific achievements by faculty members in their particular medical specialities; and to publish selected portions of these interviews as a scholarly contribution to the study of medical history.

MONTANA

MONTANA STATE UNIVERSITY

Library Special Collections
Bozeman, Montana 59715
(406) 994-2841
Minnie Paugh, Special Collections Librarian

General information: The program started with a community history group and a Montana history class which permitted advanced students to substitute a taped interview for a research paper. Both the local history group and the students concentrated their efforts on the community history of Bozeman and Gallatin County. Neither the technical equipment or the budget is available to make transcriptions. If editing were done, it would be of the nature of notes to explain items included in the interview and to explain why the oldtimer merited the interview. Some tapes have linguistic value.

Accessibility: Materials must be used in the library unless the patron has the library copy the tape. All tapes are subject to restrictions placed on the material by the donor. No tape may be used for publication without the permission of the speaker or his heirs unless the library has a written release.

UNIVERSITY OF MONTANA

Missoula, Montana 59801
(406) 243-2053
Dale L. Johnson, Archivist

General information: 1967. Budget: none. Tapes: 5 interviews, 7 hours, preserved.

Accessibility: No catalog. Not indexed. Available to scholars applying in person and agreeing to the regulations established by the institution.

Purpose of the program: To supplement the historical manuscripts collection. Major topics include Montana and Northwest history, politics, business, and industry.

NEBRASKA

CHADRON STATE COLLEGE

Tenth & Main Street
Chadron, Nebraska 69337
(308) 432-5571
William Hueser, Media Specialist

General information: 1967. Tapes: transcribed, preserved. Transcriptions: edited.

Accessibility: No catalog. Indexed. Interlibrary loan: possibly. No restrictions.

Purpose of the program: To gather historical data and provide enriched instruction. There is an emphasis on local history and Indian and agricultural problems.

DANA COLLEGE

Blair, Nebraska 68008
(402) 426-4101, ext. 119
Ronald D. Johnson, Head Librarian

General information: 1973. Budget: none (special grant money at this time). Tapes: 15 hours, will be transcribed and preserved.

Accessibility: No catalog. Not indexed. No interlibrary loan.

Purpose of the program: To focus on local Danish-American history in eastern Nebraska and western Iowa, especially in Washington County, Nebraska.

NEBRASKA STATE HISTORICAL SOCIETY

1500 R Street
Lincoln, Nebraska 68502
(402) 432-2793
Donald D. Snoddy, Manuscript Curator

General information: 1954, on-going. Budget: none. Tapes: 60 hours, some transcribed, preserved. Transcriptions: 500 pages, edited.

Accessibility: No catalog. Interlibrary loan. No restrictions.

Purpose of the program: To collect materials relating to the history of Nebraska.

STRATEGIC AIR COMMAND

Office of the Historian
Offutt Air Force Base
Omaha, Nebraska 68113
(402) 294-2245
John T. Bohn, Command Historian

General information: 1962. Budget: Included in overall history program budget. Tapes: 125 hours, partially transcribed, partially preserved. Transcriptions: 1800 pages, edited.

Accessibility: No catalog. Indexed by name. No interlibrary loan. Some of the collection is classified and other parts are as yet undetermined.

Purpose of the program: Mostly interviews for historical documentation and for use in several books. The majority of the interviews are on Southeast Asia; many by non-SAC personnel. Some are part of the Air Force Corona Harvest Project. Other subjects covered are the Cuban Crisis, reconnaissance operations, and the nuclear accidents at Palomares, Spain, and Thule, Greenland.

Publications based on collection research: Classified Air Force histories and monographs.

NEVADA

UNIVERSITY OF NEVADA, RENO
33 Getchell Library
Reno, Nevada 89507
(702) 784-6932
Mary Ellen Glass, Head, Oral History Project

General information: 1965, on-going. Budget: $26,400. Tapes: transcribed, partially preserved. Transcriptions: 13,000 pages, edited.

Accessibility: Catalog. Indexed. Interlibrary loan. Optional restriction offered chroniclers.

Purpose of the program: History of the state of Nevada and western America, with special emphasis on interests in political science, anthropology, sociology, and education.

NEW HAMPSHIRE

PLYMOUTH STATE COLLEGE OF THE UNIVERSITY OF NEW HAMPSHIRE
Plymouth, New Hampshire 03264
(603) 536-1550
Janice Gallinger, College Librarian; Maynard Dow, Director-Editor, Distinguished Geographer Film Interview Series

General information: 1970. Budget: $3000 (for geography film series only). Tapes: 20 hours tape + 9 hours film, partially transcribed. Transcriptions: edited.

Accessibility: No catalog. Partially indexed by name only. Interlibrary loan possible. Permission required.

Major collections:
1. General collection. Very limited to date, this collection is oriented to folk tradition of northern New England and also includes recollections pertinent to social and intellectual history.
2. Distinguished Geographer Film Interview Series. An experiment in the oral history of North American geography. Its purpose is to produce films of leading scholars in order to preserve a record for contemporary and future generations of geographers.

NEW JERSEY

BERGEN COMMUNITY COLLEGE
400 Paramus Road
Paramus, New Jersey 07652
(201) 447-1500
Richard W. Lenk

General information: 1956. Budget: Funded by Richard W. Lenk.

Accessibility: Available to scholars who apply in person and agree to the regulations established by Dr. Lenk or the interviewee.

Purpose of the program: To record interviews with local residents who have special skills or unusual backgrounds and to preserve local history.

BURLINGTON COUNTY LIBRARY
Woodland Road
Mt. Holly, New Jersey 08060
(609) 267-9660
Catherine W. Wetterling

General information: 1932. Budget: none. Tapes: not transcribed.

Accessibility: No catalog. Indexed. No interlibrary loan. For use in the library only.

Purpose of the program: To preserve on tape recollections and research of local historians and old residents of Burlington County.

CRANFORD HISTORICAL SOCIETY
124 North Union Avenue
Cranford, New Jersey 07016
(201) 276-0082
Kenneth C. Mackay

General information: 1965. Tapes: 50 hours, not transcribed.

Accessibility: No catalog. List of interviewees only. No interlibrary loan. No restrictions.

Purpose of the program: Preservation of knowledge of Cranford's history through interviews with past mayors, public officials, government employees, civic leaders, long time residents, clergy, teachers, businessmen, and others.

PRINCETON UNIVERSITY LIBRARY
The Dulles Oral History Collection
Princeton, New Jersey 08540
(609) 452-3164; 452-3184
Alexander P. Clark, Curator of Manuscripts

General information: Program completed. Budget: produced by gifts. Tapes: 279 interviews, transcribed, preserved. Transcriptions: 12,000 pages, edited to make sense of tape, no deletions of statements or changes of text.

Accessibility: Catalog. ($2). Not indexed. No interlibrary loan, only through positive microfilm or copyflo. Restrictions are noted for each individual interview.

Purpose of the program: The Dulles oral history project centers on the life of John Foster Dulles and the historical events in which he participated.

NEW MEXICO

NEW MEXICO STATE LIBRARY
Santa Fe, New Mexico 87501
(505) 827-2103
Jerome Dean Simpson

General information: 1967. Tapes: 15 interviews, 22 hours, partially transcribed, fully preserved. Transcriptions: partial.

Accessibility: Indexed. Interlibrary loan. Research and reproduction services can be arranged for persons unable to come to the institution. Also available to persons applying in person and agreeing to the regulations established by the institution.

Purpose of the program: To collect the personal history of early pioneers, state history, and accounts of early state organizations and events.

UNIVERSITY OF NEW MEXICO
Doris Duke Indian Oral History Project
Albuquerque, New Mexico 57105
(505) 277-0111
Lewis Binford, Department of Anthropology

Note: Other institutions cooperating in the Doris Duke Indian Oral History Project are the Arizona State Museum, and the Universities of Florida, Illinois, Oklahoma, South Dakota and Utah.

UNIVERSITY OF NEW MEXICO
The Pioneers Foundation, Inc. Oral History Collection
Zimmerman Library
Albuquerque, New Mexico 87131
(505) 277-4241

General information: 1951, completed. Tapes: 500 hours, in process of transcription, preserved. Transcriptions: 9500 completed for 340 tapes, not edited.

Accessibility: Catalog. Indexed. No interlibrary loan. Restriction rights are retained by the University of New Mexico. A duplicate set of tapes is on deposit at the Arizona State Museum.

Purpose of the program: To document early New Mexico history.

NEW YORK

ALUMNI ASSOCIATION OF THE CITY COLLEGE OF THE CITY UNIVERSITY OF NEW YORK
Finley Center
New York, New York 10027
(212) 234-3000
Bertrand I. Klein, Director

General information: Tapes: preserved and transcribed. Transcriptions: edited.

Accessibility: Available to scholars applying in person and agreeing to the regulations established by the institution.

Purpose of the program: To collect memoirs of alumni educators, including Morris Meister, formerly principal of the Bronx High School of Science, Professor Ephraim Cross, and Gabriel Mason, New York City educator.

AMERICAN INSTITUTE OF PHYSICS
Center for History and Philosophy of Physics
335 East 45th Street
New York, New York 10017
(212) 685-1940
Charles Weiner, Director

General information: 1964. Tapes: 70 interviews, 300+ hours, transcribed, preserved. Transcriptions: 7500 pages, edited.

Accessibility: Indexed. Available to scholars applying in person and agreeing to the regulations established by the institution.

Purpose of the program: The oral history program is closely integrated with research and archival activities to document the history of contemporary physics.

AMERICAN JEWISH COMMITTEE
William E. Weiner Oral History Library
165 East 56th Street
New York, New York 10022
Milton E. Krents, Coordinator

General information: 1969.

Accessibility: Available to scholars applying in person and agreeing to the regulations established by the institution.

Purpose of the program: To trace the American Jewish experience in the twentieth century.

AMERICAN SOCIETY OF CIVIL ENGINEERS
345 East 47th Street
New York, New York 10017
(212) PL2-6800
Chairman, History & Heritage Committee (Present incumbent, Neal FitzSimons)

General information: 1963. Budget: volunteer system. Tapes: 50 hours, not transcribed.

Accessibility: No catalog. Not indexed. No interlibrary loan. Subject to clearance of the History and Heritage Committee of the American Society of Civil Engineers.

Purpose of the program: Preservation of the thoughts, impressions, and technical evaluations of prominent members of the civil engineering profession.

ARCHIVES OF AMERICAN ART—SMITHSONIAN INSTITUTION
41 East 65th Street
New York, New York 10021
(212) 628-1251
William E. Woolfenden, Director; Paul Cummings, Director, Oral History Program

General information: 1959. Budget: varies. Tapes: 1200 interviews of varying length, partially transcribed, fully preserved. Transcriptions: edited.

Accessibility: Catalog in preparation. Not indexed. No interlibrary loan. Permission of interviewee required; transcripts may only be used in office of Archives of American Art.

Purpose of the program: To supplement the manuscript program of the archives. Interviews attempt to follow chronologically the interviewee's recollections and reminiscences in relationship to art in America. Most major figures in art in America have been interviewed: painters, sculptors, collectors, curators, critics, museum directors, printmakers, craftsmen, photographers, designers, and dealers.

BROOKLYN COLLEGE
Bedford Avenue and Avenue H
Brooklyn, New York 11228
(212) 780-5346
Madeline C. Yourman, Acting Chairman, Library Department; Antoinette Ciolli, Chief, Special Collections Division

General information: 1966, on-going. Budget: not set. Tapes: 20 hours, not transcribed.

Accessibility: No catalog. Not indexed. No interlibrary loan. Restricted to use in the library by individuals engaged in scholarly research.

Purpose of the program: To preserve on tape the vital recollections of prominent people connected with Brooklyn College, who have seen the development of the college for thirty years or longer, thus getting a history of a municipal college in action and an insight into Brooklyn history.

BUFFALO & ERIE COUNTY HISTORICAL SOCIETY
25 Nottingham Court
Buffalo, New York 14216
(716) 873-9644
Wilbur H. Glover, Curator of Manuscripts

General information: 1970. Tapes: transcribed. Transcriptions: edited.

Accessibility: Indexed. Research and reproduction services can be arranged for persons unable to come to the institution. Available also to scholars applying in person and agreeing to the regulations established by the institution.

Purpose of the program: The accumulation of historical data, with politics the major topic.

CHEMUNG COUNTY HISTORICAL CENTER
Chemung County Historical Society, Inc.
Elmira, New York 14901
(607) 737-2900
Paul W. Ivory

General information: 1969. Tapes: 7 interviews, 9 hours, partially transcribed, fully preserved. Transcriptions: not edited.

Accessibility: Index planned. Research and reproduction services can be arranged for persons unable to come to the institution. Available to scholars applying in person and agreeing to the regulations established by the institution.

Purpose of the program: To record interviews with those people whose lives and knowledge represent important sources of local history.

CITY COLLEGE OF NEW YORK
See Alumni Association of The City College of the City University of New York

COLUMBIA UNIVERSITY
The Oral History Collection
Box 20
Butler Library
New York, New York 10027
(212) 280-2273
Louis M. Starr, Director; Elizabeth B. Mason, Associate Director

General information: 1948. Tapes: 2870 persons interviewed. Many memoirs, in general those done since 1962, may be heard on tape, restrictions permitting. Transcriptions: 374,525 pages, generally edited for accuracy by the oral author.

Accessibility: Catalog. Each memoir carries its own biographical index. The office maintains a master biographical card index to the entire collection and will search it in response to inquiries and report without charge. For those unable to visit its premises, Columbia arranges for research in the collection itself in response to precise instructions, a nominal sum being charged per hour. Many memoirs are available in microform from the *New York Times* Oral History Program, c/o Microfilming Corporation of America, Glen Rock, New Jersey 07452. In the name and subject index these memoirs are designated "also microfiche," and researchers interested in them should check the nearest major library to see if it has this series. If not, such memoirs may be ordered individually from the address given. Restrictions vary with each interviewee or project, and provisions regarding access are noted in the listings for each. Since these restrictions change with the passage of time, it is wise to inquire.

Purpose of the program: To provide source material on a broad scale in any phase of American history from the 1880s to the present.

Publications based on collection research:
Over 200 books include the following:
Hanby, Alonzo. *Beyond the New Deal.* New York: Columbia University Press, 1973.
Harbaugh, William H. *Lawyer's Lawyer: The Life of John W. Davis.* New York: Oxford University Press, 1973.
Lash, Joseph P. *Eleanor and Franklin.* New York: Norton, 1972.
Williams, T. Harry. *Huey Long.* New York: Knopf, 1969.
Major collections:
1. Air Force Academy project. In 1968, the faculty of the USAF Academy initiated a series of oral history interviews with significant figures in military aviation. The major topics discussed include strategy and tactics in World Wars I and II and Korea, the establishment of the Air Force Academy, and interservice relationships (on-going, 2288 pages, subject to individual restrictions). See *U.S. Air Force* in name and subject index for participants and pages.

2. Alaskan pioneers. This project gathers the reminiscences of pioneer settlers in Alaska, providing accounts of gold prospecting, mining, cattle driving, homesteading, and travel by trail and river. Included are descriptions of the pioneers, as well as accounts of the depression of 1893 and the Klondike strike (1959–1962, 394 pages, open). See *Alaska* in name and subject index for participants and pages.

3. American Association of Physics Teachers. Founding members discuss the formation of the American Association of Physics Teachers in 1930 and describe its relations with the American Physical Society and the American Institute of Physics. Discussions of efforts to improve teaching methods and to achieve a balance between teaching and research, anecdotes and appraisals of leading American physicists, including Karl Compton, Arthur Compton, and F. K. Richtmyer (1963, 193 pages, permission required to cite or quote). See *American Association of Physics Teachers* in name and subject index for participants and pages.

4. American Cultural Leaders. This series of interviews was conducted by Joan Simpson Burns to provide material for a study of patterns in American cultural life. Mrs. Burns' interest centered on her subjects' family backgrounds and early exposure to the arts as well as on their later contributions to American culture. Her interviewing method, frankly experimental, encouraged free association and frequent digressions. The principals' memoirs are supplemented by conversations with their professional associates (1968, 1510 pages, closed pending publication of a study). See *Culture* in name and subject index for participants and pages.

5. American historians. A series of interviews with leading historians, conducted by Prof. John Garraty, dealing with such topics as westward expansion and economic change to 1860; slavery in the U.S.; American nationalism, social and cultural changes in the U.S. between the Civil War and World War I; Reconstruction period; the U.S. in world affairs from 1918 to 1945; and problems of interpretation of history (1968–1969, 2660 pages, permission required to cite or quote). See *Historians, American* in name and subject index for participants and pages.

6. Argentina in the 1930s. This series of interviews provides a broad general view of Argentina at a critical period in that country's development. A joint effort of the Instituto Torcuato Di Tella in Buenos Aires and the Oral History Research Office of Columbia University, the project began in 1970 with a grant from the Tinker Foundation. While the memoirs focus primarily on the 1930s, there is much background information from prior years, and a number of the memoirists deal with events in the succeeding two decades. The institute plans to continue the project, concentrating next on the 1940s and the rise to power of Juan D. Peron. Taken together, the memoirs offer a richly detailed panorama of political, sociological, and economic developments unobtainable elsewhere. A group of labor leaders highlight the transition from craft to industrial unions, the factional and partisan conflicts within the labor movement, and attitudes toward ethnic and regional concentrations. Argentine industrial and manufacturing figures describe technological changes, relationships with foreign enterprises, and attitudes toward organized labor. Political leaders discuss internal organization and practices of political groups, with examples from municipal and national cam-

COLUMBIA UNIVERSITY (cont.)

paigns. The interviews, conducted by staff members of the institute, are in Spanish. The project is a continuing one (1971–   , 3349 pages, open except as noted). See *Argentina* in name and subject index for participants and pages.

7. Henry H. Arnold project. The life of the late Gen. Henry H. Arnold (1886–1950), first commander of the Army Air Forces, as related by his associates. Included are interviews with veteran Air Force officers in Great Britain who worked with retired RAF officers throughout the country and with Gen. Arnold during World War II. Primary emphasis is upon Arnold's role in the Air Forces, his relations with his associates, the types of problems he met, and his contributions to the development of military aviation, including a wealth of material of value to Air Force historians. The material deals with Arnold as a student at West Point, as infantry officer in the Philippines, as a close associate of Gen. William Mitchell, as chief of the Air Forces and member of the Combined Chiefs of Staff during World War II (1959–1960, 1726 pages, permission required). See *Henry H. Arnold* in name and subject index for participants and pages.

8. Association for the Aid of Crippled Children. Until its reorganization in 1948, the association had provided a variety of services to handicapped children in metropolitan New York for 50 years. Interviews with members of the association's board and staff focus on the transition from service agency to foundation made possible by the bequests of Milo Belding. The association's grants have supported research and conferences on prenatal and perinatal problems, genetics, and embryology. Studies of learning disabilities, mental retardation, and accident prevention are detailed. The association's international collaborative studies with the University of Aberdeen, the Karolinska Institute, and the University of Kyoto are described. Staff cooperation with NIH and the background of President Kennedy's panel on mental retardation are recalled. Memoirs include personal recollections of Drs. Howard Rusk, John Lind, Dugald Baird, and Clement Reid; and of William McPeak and Laurance Rockefeller (1972, 575 pages, permission required). See *Association for the Aid of Crippled Children* in the name and subject index for participants and pages.

9. Aviation. A broad survey of the development of aviation, beginning with accounts by associates of the Wright brothers and other pioneers in the U.S. and abroad. Those interviewed include designers, engineers, pilots and executives, stunt flyers, and barnstormers; their recitations are informal and seasoned with anecdotes. Veterans of World War I describe the development of aerial warfare in that conflict. Scores of recollections trace the rapid progress of aviation between the two World Wars; commercial aviation, air mail development, record flights, technological improvements, air races and polar flights, gliders, and lighter-than-air craft. Gen. William Mitchell's campaign for strengthening military aviation and Charles Lindbergh's solo flight to Paris provide focal points for many accounts of this period. Eyewitness stories of episodes in World War II deal with exploits of the RAF, the Luftwaffe, and the U.S. Air Force, and range from the Battle of Britain to Hiroshima. Research and production problems and achievements are detailed from the outset to the jet era and the beginnings of rockets and missiles. The material includes descriptions of the breaking of the sound barrier, stories of test pilots for supersonic planes and accounts of aerial warfare in Korea (1961, 5264 pages, permission of individual contributors required to cite or quote, except as otherwise noted). See *Aeronautics* in name and subject index for participants and pages.

10. Benedum and the oil industry. A record of the oil industry from 1890 to 1950 as shown in the development of the Benedum oil interests and the experiences of Michael Late Benedum (1869–1959) and his associates, notably Joseph Clifton Trees (1869–1943). Interviews with people having special knowledge of leasing, financing, geology, oil and gas production, legal and tax problems. The memoirs contain several accounts of Benedum and Trees as wildcatters, going into virgin territory and finding new sources of oil and gas in the U.S. (Illinois, 1905; Caddo, Louisiana, 1908; Central Texas, 1918; Big Lake and Yates fields in West Texas, 1923–1926); problems of oil exploration outside the U.S. (Mexico, 1911–1916; Colombia, 1915; Rumania, 1918–1919; the Philippines, 1920; and China, 1936; development of companies and corporate holdings including Transcontinental Oil Company, 1919; Plymouth Oil Company, 1923; Hiawatha Oil and Gas Company, 1926; and Bentex Oil Corporation, 1936; storage, transportation, marketing, and refining; conservation and proration practices leading to Interstate Oil Compact Commission, 1933; U.S. income tax claim against M. L. Benedum and Foster B. Parriott for $79 million in 1925, the Supreme Court decision in their favor in 1937; extensive biographical material on M.L. Benedum, including early life and political activities. Incidental material of interest includes: impressions of Woodrow Wilson at Princeton (McClintock memoir), E. L. Doheny, Senator Joseph Cuffey, John Archbold (M. L. Benedum memoir); John W. Davis (Johnson memoir); Texas General Land Office (Giles memoir); and Slick Research Foundation (Slick memoir) (1951, 1085 pages, open). See *Petroleum Industry and Trade* in name and subject index for participants and pages.

11. Book-of-the-Month Club. The founding and development of the Book-of-the-Month Club from 1926 to 1955. The material consists of interviews with the founders, members of the selection committee, executive and technical personnel. In the most detailed of these memoirs, Harry Scherman, founder and board chairman, describes his own background, gives the origins of the idea of selling current books by mail to subscribers, tells of the first judges and later additions to the selection committee, discusses problems of editorial policy and the preferences of various judges, and recalls many of the selections and their reception. Mr. Scherman and other participants also deal with: the reader system for culling books submitted by publishers, attempts of outsiders to influence selection, relationships with publishers, membership and sales through the years, characteristics of subscribers, the book dividend system, the use of premiums, the preparation and testing of advertisements, distribution of art reproductions and musical recordings, book design and calligraphy, the Literary Guild and other book clubs, opposition of the book sellers, book manufacture, corporate structure of the company, problems of servicing subscribers, personnel and employee relations. Students of the literary scene in these years will find the Canby, Fadiman, Fisher, Higher, Loveman, Marquand, Scherman and Wood memoirs of particular interest (1955, 1124 pages, open). See *Book-of-the-Month Club* in name and subject index for participants and pages.

12. Carnegie Corporation. This project traces the first 58 years of Andrew Carnegie's central philanthropic organization. Officers, staff members, and grant recipients discuss its work in adult education, area studies, art education, cognitive research, education testing, library science, music education, national security, social science research, teacher education, and other areas. The corporation's relations

with other Carnegie institutions are delineated in many memoirs. Other detail its own administrative history, as well as its relations with other major foundations and with the federal government. Still others trace the work of independent agencies which originally received all or part of their funds from the foundation. In general, the design was to provide comprehensive and candid information about the foundation, its work, and those who have served its end, "to promote the advancement and diffusion of knowledge and understanding." The material is rich in personal recollections of grantees and members of the corporation's board and staff. There is a comprehensive index (1966–1970, 9948 pages, permission required). See *Carnegie Corporation* in name and subject index for participants and pages.

13. Children's Television Workshop. This series of interviews traces the development of the Children's Television Workshop and the creation of "Sesame Street" in the words of some of those principally responsible. They recall 1966 discussions of how television might be made to serve preschool children, preliminary studies, the roles of the Carnegie Corporation, of Harold Howe II as U.S. Commissioner of Education, and of the Ford Foundation in advancing the concept and helping to finance it, the founding of the workshop and its staffing, and the emergence of the Sesame Street format, as well as the changing relationship of the workshop with National Educational Television, from which it became independent (1972, 134 pages, open). See *Television in Education* in name and subject index for participants and pages.

14. China missionaries. The oral history program at Claremont Graduate School, Claremont, California launched a project to assess the influence of the China missionary movement, 1900–1950. Christian workers of various denominations give their recollections of conditions and experiences in China; they include educators, medical administrators, teachers, ministers, authors, and translators. The accounts deal with local conditions in urban and rural China and interaction between American residents and Chinese communities (1969–1971, 1268 pages, open). See *Missions and Missionaries* in name and subject index for participants and pages.

15. Chinese oral history. In 1958 Professors Franklin L. Ho and C. Martin Wilbur formulated a project within the East Asian Institute of Columbia University to record the oral recollections of prominent Chinese leaders of the Republican era (1911–1949). In the ensuing decade 18 outstanding figures have compiled oral records of their careers. These have been transcribed, translated, researched, and edited to produce memoirs for use by scholars interested in this half-century of Chinese history. Many are accompanied by private papers. The memoirs represent the lives of men who played major roles in Republican China. Many attended American universities and returned to China bringing modern attitudes to the still traditional society. Their detailed reminiscences help clarify hitherto confused areas of scholarly inquiry: the historian, sociologist, literary historian, economist, and political scientist will find a wealth of material for research (4198 pages, open, except as noted, descriptions of individual memoirs available on request). See *China* in name and subject index for participants and pages.

16. Civil rights in Alabama. Leaders and participants in the movement at Tuscaloosa, Alabama in 1964 describe clashes with local law enforcement personnel, culminating in the tear gassing of the First Baptist Church. Included are the transcripts of two mass meetings and interviews with residents expressing widely varying attitudes toward the

movement (1964, 259 pages, open). See *Blacks—Civil Rights* in name and subject index for participants and pages.

17. Civil War Centennial. Civil War scholars at the final centennial meeting in Springfield, Illinois discuss sources, problems in historiography, and research experiences in the field (1965, 143 pages, permission required to cite or quote). See *U.S.—History—Civil War* in name and subject index for participants and pages.

18. Columbia Crisis of 1968. In this series of interviews, almost all conducted on campus in May 1968, participants and observers of every hue—student activists (conservative, independent, and radical), junior and senior faculty, administrators, supporting staff, and parents describe and discuss the many phases of the crisis that resulted in the occupation of five Columbia buildings by students April 23 and 24, the suspension of classes, fruitless negotiations, police intervention on April 30, a campus-wide strike, a lesser eruption May 21–22, and the eventual restructuring of the university. Factors behind the crisis are examined and weighed in tones ranging from analytical detachment to passionate concern. The project was conducted independently by the Oral History office (1968, 2426 pages, permission required, supporting papers). See *Columbia University* in name and subject index for participants and pages.

19. Columbia television lectures. Lectures on current world issues by Columbia scholars (1962–1963, 217 pages, open). See *Television in Education* in name and subject index for participants and pages.

20. Columbiana. From time to time the Oral History Research Office has interviewed persons who have made significant contributions to the development of Columbia University, or observed various phases of its development over the years. A few were asked specifically for their recollections of President Nicholas Murray Butler and his administration (1902–1945). In addition, a number of individual memoirs provide information of special interest on the university and on President Butler (1955–1971, 186 pages, open). See *Columbia University* in name and subject index for participants and pages.

21. James B. Duke project. Through a series of interviews, the origins and subsequent activities of the Duke Endowment are set forth, with particular focus upon the personality and career of the founder. Associates of James B. Duke (1857–1925) and persons active in his manifold interests provide personal reminiscences, anecdotes, and comments on the Duke family, the career of Duke, the development of the Duke Power Company and various other business ventures designed to advance the Piedmont region of North Carolina, his early interest in southern education, in particular Trinity College (now Duke University), and developments since his death. A number of the memoirs also contain first-hand material on life in the Piedmont in the early years of the century and the economic and social changes brought by industrialization, which followed hard upon the provision of dependable power. Others discuss the establishment of Duke University, with much material on the faculty and presidents during the Trinity College era. Recent efforts of the endowment in education, religion, and hospital work in the South are considered (1966, 2907 pages, permission required). See *James B. Duke* in name and subject index for participants and pages.

22. Thomas Alva Edison project. Interviews with family members and associates of Thomas Alva Edison (1847–1931) illuminate his character, personality and motivation. The appearance of and arrangement of the family home and the laboratory in West Orange, New Jersey, are described, and specific projects carried on in the laboratory are recalled. Earlier recordings prepared by the Edison National His-

COLUMBIA UNIVERSITY (cont.)

toric Site will be included (1972, 119 pages, permission required pending completion of project). See *Thomas Alva Edison* in name and subject index for participants and pages.

23. Eisenhower Administration. This project has gathered first-hand testimony from those who played major roles in the Eisenhower Administration (1953–1961), as well as the recollections of observers and of those knowledgeable about special aspects. In addition to Gen. Dwight D. Eisenhower and members of his family, the list of participants includes members of the White House staff, cabinet members, political advisers, members of Congress, administrators, scientists, journalists, ambassadors, military and civilian specialists, and others in a position to testify about trends and events of the period. Among topics well documented in material presently available are the Republican conventions and campaigns and staff, the functioning of White House advisers and staff, the president's relations with his cabinet, the functioning of the Bureau of the Budget and various independent agencies, relations with the press, scientific developments, and other special aspects too numerous to mention, the whole interlaced with anecdotes about major and minor episodes in public life in the 1950s. A series of interviews done in Little Rock, Arkansas on the school integration crisis there is of particular interest. Memoirs are on deposit at the Eisenhower Library in Abilene, Kansas as well as at Columbia under identical stipulations (1962–1972, 27,729 pages, papers). See *Dwight David Eisenhower* in name and subject index for participants and pages.

24. Farm Holiday Association. Farm Holiday Association pressure on the New Deal, 1933–1934, as recalled by participants, with descriptions of riots and violence, threats of a farm strike, demands for mortgage relief, and impressions of Milo Reno. The memoirs also include material dealing with the United Farmers League and other Communist-sponsored rivals of the Farm Holiday Association (1960–1961, 194 pages, open). See *Farm Holiday Association* in name and subject index for participants and pages.

25. Federated Department Stores. This project comprises a series of interviews with those who built the largest department store organization in the U.S., Federated Department Stores. Changes over the years in Federated's policies, methods, and objectives, changes in consumer tastes and buying habits, and the evolution of the organization are traced. There are also interviews with the family and friends of Fred Lazarus, Jr., founder and board chairman (1965, 291 pages, permission required). See *Federated Department Stores* in name and subject index for participants and pages.

26. James Lawrence Fly project. Friends and associates recall James L. Fly (1898–1966), particularly his chairmanship of the FCC, 1939–1944 (1967, 655 pages, closed until January 1, 1982). See *James Lawrence Fly* in name and subject index for participants and pages.

27. Flying Tigers. At the Flying Tiger reunion at Ojai, California, in 1962, pilots, mechanics, radiomen, administrative, and ground crew personnel reminisced of their experiences with Chennault's American Volunteer Group in Burma and China, and with the China National Aviation Corps, during and after World War II. They detail adventurous days in Rangoon, Toungoo, and Kunming, retreating over the Burma Road, flying P-40's against Japanese bombers and Zeros, and operating the Mukden shuttle before the fall of Shanghai in 1949. The natural focus of those days was Claire Chennault, and these men and women recount anecdotes and impressions of him. While informal and unstruc-

tured, these interviews provide source material on a thinly documented phase of World War II, and the lore that has grown around it (1962, 583 pages, permission required to cite or quote). See *Flying Tigers* in name and subject index for participants and pages.

28. Forest History Society. These interviews on forestry and logging contain material on conservation, woods safety, fire-fighting and the development of protective associations, old Minnesota logging camps, logging methods and machinery, and the development of the Paul Bunyan legends. Impressions of H. L. Mencken are included, as are impressions of George S. Long and other lumbermen (1957, 237 pages, permission required to quote). See Charles S. Cowan, George W. Dulany, Inman F. Eldredge, Royal S. Kellogg, Donald MacKenzie, Maggie Orr O'Neill, P. J. Rutledge, and James Stevens in name and subject index.

29. Friends of the Columbia Libraries. Selected speakers at dinner meetings of the Friends of the Columbia Libraries, generally on literary topics (95 pages, permission required to cite or quote). See *Friends of the Columbia Libraries* in name and subject index for participants and pages.

30. John Robert Gregg project. This is a compilation of interviews with friends and associates of John Robert Gregg (1867–1948), the man who developed the Gregg shorthand system (1956, 168 pages, permission required). See *John Robert Gregg* in name and subject index for participants and pages.

31. Dag Hammarskjold project. Colleagues recall their association with Dag Hammarskjold, his personal qualities, his training and experience in Sweden and elsewhere in Europe, his abilities and interests, and his approach to the administrative and executive challenges of the post of Secretary General of the UN, particularly staffing the Secretariat, the Congo crisis, and the Russian troika proposal (1962, 181 pages, permission required to cite or quote). See *Dag Hammarskjold* in name and subject index for participants and pages.

32. Health science. This project is laying the foundations for a study of the growth of the biological and medical sciences in the U.S., of the changing role of the federal government in relation to research and training in the health field, and of changing public attitudes toward such activities. Interviews have been conducted with persons closely associated with the National Institutes of Health (NIH) and its predecessors, upon which the study is primarily focused, but others prominent as researchers, administrators, and philanthropists in the field are included (1962–1967, 2905 pages, permission required). See *Public Health* in name and subject index for participants and pages.

33. Richard Hofstadter project. This project brings together the recollections of students, faculty colleagues, and others who knew Richard Hofstadter, for the most part during his years at Columbia (1946–1970), where he became DeWitt Clinton Professor of American History. Contributors recall him as teacher, social observer, writer, and friend, tracing the intellectual development of a major scholar. Specifics include comment on *Social Darwinism in American Thought*, *The American Political Tradition*, *The Age of Reform*, *Anti-Intellectualism in American Life*, and other works, as well as insights into the mind and character of the man (1972, 238 pages, permission required to cite or quote). See *Richard Hofstadter* in name and subject index for participants and pages.

34. Independence National Historical Park. The story of the Independence Hall Association from 1942 and the development of the Independence National Historical Park are recounted by those who played major parts, in particular Judge Edwin O. Lewis. Accounts of the ensuing urban redevelopment, of historic preservation, and restoration in

Philadelphia explore the legal, financial, architectural, and procedural problems and how they were surmounted. Park historians and superintendents describe the role of the National Park Service (1970, 574 pages, permission required). See *Independence National Historical Park* in name and subject index for participants and pages.

35. International negotiations. Edward W. Barrett, director of the Communications Institute of the Academy for Educational Development, conducted a series of interviews with practitioners in the field of international negotiations and mediation of disputes. The interviews are preserved and will be drawn on in delineating guidelines that may be useful to those mediating and negotiating international differences in the future. The work is part of a continuing study of international negotiation and meditation conducted by the academy under a grant from Dr. and Mrs. John S. Schweppe of Chicago (1970–1972, 704 pages, permission required).

    The academy has also canvassed academic and journalistic specialists for their views on future relations between countries, particularly in the Far East, in interviews by Prof. Frederick T. C. Yu of Columbia (1970, 426 pages, permission required). See *International Relations* in the name and subject index for participants and pages.

36. Jackson Hole Preserve. This project relates the history of Jackson Hole Preserve, describing the Rockefeller family's interest in preserving and protecting the area and problems encountered in acquiring the land which was eventually added to the National Park System. Included are memoirs of people who knew Jackson Hole as their home and who have experienced the transformation of the area since it became part of the National Park System in the 1940s (1966, 1080 pages, permission required). See *Jackson Hole Preserve* in the name and subject index for participants and pages.

37. Journalism Lectures. Guest lecturers at the Graduate School of Journalism of Columbia University occasionally provide firsthand accounts of pivotal events. Benjamin Fine's account of the integration crisis of Central High School in Little Rock, Harrison Salisbury's description of Nikita Khrushchev's visit to the U.S. and the "Battle of Coon Rapids," and Tom Wicker's recitation of the aftermath of the assassination of John F. Kennedy are examples. Other lectures grouped under this heading range from Watson Berry's on New York City journalism in the 1890s to discussions of the role of the news media from the 1950s on (1037 pages, permission required to cite or quote). See *Journalism* in name and subject index for participants and pages for all sections of this project.

    A. Basic issues in the news. In these lectures, given at the Graduate School of Journalism (1959–1963) each scholar has undertaken to tell newsmen something of what they need to know in various areas of specialization (429 pages, permission required).

    B. Consumer reporting. Two conferences at the Graduate School of Journalism examined problems facing journalists in covering the consumer movement. Aspects of reporting product analysis, consumer research, and ecological questions are discussed (1971–1972, 982 pages, permission required to cite or quote).

    C. Forums. Two Columbia forums assess American journalism in the 1960s—the first from the vantage points of learned observers, the second from those of professionals in the field (1963, 105 pages, permission required to cite or quote).

38. La Follette Civil Liberties Committee. These interviews deal with labor and civil liberties during the New Deal, with discussion of the roles of the NLRB and the CIO, anti-union practices in industry and agriculture, functioning of the committee, and recollections of Senator Robert M. La Follette, Jr. (1963, 163 pages, permission required to cite or quote). See *La Follette Civil Liberties Committee* in name and subject index for participants and pages.

39. League of Nations. The recollections of a number of officials of the League of Nations have been recorded through the cooperation of the Carnegie Endowment for International Peace. The interviews, obtained in Geneva, describe the early days of organizing the League Secretariat and record many international problems and negotiations. The memoirs are in French (1966–1969, 866 pages, individual restrictions apply). See *League of Nations* in name and subject index for participants and pages.

40. Herbert H. Lehman project. Herbert Lehman's own memoir is supplemented by a series of interviews with persons who were closely associated with him through various stages of his career (1959, 1184 pages, permission required to cite or quote). See *Herbert H. Lehman* in name and subject index for participants and pages.

41. McGraw-Hill. The development of McGraw-Hill, Inc. and its part in educational, industrial, and technical development in the U.S. and abroad, 1886–1964, are traced in a series of interviews beginning with the lives of James H. McGraw (1860–1948) and John A. Hill (1858–1912). Associates recall the career of each as a publisher of trade and technical magazines. Others deal with the merger of the book publishing activities of the two companies as the McGraw-Hill Book Company, 1909, and the purchase of the Hill interest in trade magazines by McGraw to form the McGraw-Hill Publishing Company in 1916. Interviews continue the story of the company's expansion through the acquisition of the F.W. Dodge Corporation in 1961, which brought the firm into the field of information services, the purchase of such periodicals as *House & Home* and *Modern Packaging*, and the acquisition of the Webster Publishing Company. Editors of McGraw-Hill trade, educational, and business publications discuss editorial and circulation policy, standards of responsibility in dealing with readers and advertisers, and new functions and fields for the company's publications and instructional materials. The construction of the McGraw-Hill building (1931) is described, together with data on production operations. Special phases include: changes in the writing and publishing of college textbooks, textbooks for courses in vocational education; elementary and high school materials, visual education aids, programmed books, and text films; Whittlesey House and trade book publishing, paperback books, technical writing, training manuals for the U.S. armed forces, and international aspects of book publishing such as translation, licensing, and international editions of textbooks. Interviewees give background on such McGraw publications as the *Catholic Encyclopedia*, the *Encyclopedia of World Art*, and *Science and Technology* (1956, 4170 pages; 1964, 420 pages, permission required). See *McGraw-Hill* in name and subject index for participants and pages.

42. Marine Corps. This series of memoirs by retired marines, begun in 1966, is a continuing program of the historical branch of the U.S. Marine Corps. Together the interviews provide a picture of the development of the Marine Corps in the twentieth century. Personal experiences and anecdotes highlight events of World War I, duty in China and the Caribbean, the development of amphibious warfare in World War II, marine aviation, the postwar unification struggle, and Korea. Also a series of interviews with marine Navajo code talkers conducted in 1971 in Window Rock, Arizona (1966– , 16,585 pages, individual restrictions). See *U.S. Marine Corps* in name and subject index for participants and pages.

COLUMBIA UNIVERSITY (cont.)

43. Marshall Plan. This group of memoirs gathers together material on the genesis and development of the Marshall Plan in the Department of State, and describes in particular the role played by Will Clayton (1947–1961, 103 pages, permission required to cite or quote). See *Economic Assistance* in name and subject index for participants and pages.

44. Mining engineers. Brief interviews with notable mining engineers on salient phases of their careers. Consultants and executives of companies in widely scattered areas from Alaska to South Africa, they also provide information on the discovery and exploration of new mines (1961, 518 pages, permission required to cite or quote). See *Mining Engineering* in name and subject index for participants and pages.

45. Mount Sinai Hospital. A history of Mount Sinai Hospital, New York City, with emphasis on staff contributions to medical knowledge, growth and development of specialized departments within the hospital, and comparison of modern medical training with earlier practices; brief description of establishment of Mount Sinai Medical School. Transcripts of certain faculty meetings, investitures, and seminars are included (1965–1969, 1212 pages, permission required) *See Mount Sinai Medical Center* in name and subject index for participants and pages.

46. Naval History. This project, conducted with the cooperation of the director of naval history (Navy department), covers many phases of modern naval history, among them training, procurement, logistics ordnance, naval aviation, submarines, scientific development, salvage, and intelligence. Operational strategy and tactics during World War I and in particular World War II are analyzed in detail; also material on Korea. Many political and military figures, American and foreign, appear along with fresh material on major battles. Unification of the armed services and relationships in the Department of Defense are discussed (1960–1969, 17,912 pages, individual restrictions apply). See *U.S.—History, Naval* in name and subject index for participants and pages.

47. Allan Nevins project. Associates of Allan Nevins during his long career at Columbia (1928–1958), and later at the Huntington Library, recall the historian and the man. Many of the first interviews, contributed by Mort Lewis, deal largely with his last years. Subsequent interviews will cover the Columbia years and other phases of the historian's life (1969–, 599 pages, closed until March 5, 1976, papers). See *Allan Nevins* in name and subject index for participants and pages.

48. New School lectures. Two lectures from the Wisdom of Life series delivered at the New School, dealing primarily with the management of human resources (1959, 58 pages, open). See *New School for Social Research* in name and subject index for participants and pages.

49. New York political studies. From earliest days the oral history research office has maintained an interest in gathering the recollections of those intimately connected with political developments in New York City and State. More than 100 memoirs illuminate varied aspects and events of New York City political life extending back to the Draft Riots of 1863. Includes a host of civic and political figures ranging from mayors, district attorneys, judges and reformers to precinct politicians, social workers, criminals, and members of street gangs. In addition, the three special projects described below focus directly upon particular aspects of the New York political scene. See *New York State* in name and subject index for participants and pages for all sections of this project.

    A. Brooklyn politics, 1930–1950. Selected individuals recount their experiences in the Brooklyn political arena

during these two decades. Journalists, lawyers, and politicians describe the problems and achievements of the borough and its relationship to the mayor and the city and state administrations. The office of the district attorney receives special attention, centering on William O'Dwyer and his incumbency: Mayors James Walker and Fiorello LaGuardia, John McCooey, Frank Kelly, John Cashmore, Rudolph Halley and other local leaders appear in these pages. Accounts of police procedure, political club practices, and court room incidents about (2723 pages, permission required).

    B. Citizens Budget Commission. Ten years after the establishment in New York City of the office of deputy mayor, a group of civic organizations undertook to sponsor a scholarly study of this office in its first decade. Participating organizations included the Citizens Budget Commission, the Citizens Union, the New York Chamber of Commerce, the Women's City Club, and the Commerce and Industry Association. Transcripts of these interviews became a basis for the report (1966, 379 pages, permission required except as noted).

    C. New York elections of 1949. A series of interviews and speeches on the New York City and state elections of 1949 in an attempt to record history as it transpired and to cover all candidates and parties. Discussion of the issues of the campaign, including federal aid to education, communism, municipal corruption, and minority problems is combined with analyses of political organization and techniques, voting of religious and nationality groups, and the effect of labor union support and newspaper coverage upon the election (1949, 292 pages, permission required to cite or quote).

50. Nobel laureates on scientific research. An intensive study of Nobel laureates in science with particular emphasis on their relations with co-workers. The interviews include information on their associations with Nobel prize winners and other eminent scientists who have played important roles in the discoveries for which they were awarded the prize. Each laureate was asked to describe the sequence of events leading to his discovery, and the parts played by others in this process. This project was supported by the National Science Foundation (1964, 1525 pages, permission required). See *Scientists* in name and subject index for participants and pages.

51. Occupation of Japan. This project embraces the memoirs of various participants in the occupation of Japan and in the formulation of its Constitution. Within the overall discussions of occupation programs and policies are specific accounts of social, economic, agricultural, educational, and cultural developments together with material on the purges and problems of civil rights; there are vivid descriptions of the drafting of the new Constitution and steps leading to the change in the role of the Emperor of Japan. Leading figures of SCAP and the Far Eastern Commission are portrayed in action, notably Generals Douglas McArthur, Courtney Whitney, Charles Willoughby, and Colonels Charles Kades and Richard Nugent (1960–1961, 1317 pages, permission required to cite or quote). See *Japan* in name and subject index for participants and pages.

52. Robert P. Patterson project. Interviews on the life of Judge Robert Porter Patterson (1891–1952) as related by his associates covering his career as a lawyer, U.S. district and circuit judge, assistant secretary of war, under secretary of war and secretary of war (1960–1961, 585 pages, closed until Jan. 1, 1980). See *Robert P. Patterson* in name and subject index for participants and pages.

53. Poets on their poetry. Discussions with modern American poets on the nature, technique, and qualities of their work

(1972, 202 pages, permission required). See *Poetry* in name and subject index for participants and pages.

54. Popular arts project. Material on the development of the performing arts in this century is provided through interviews with producers, directors, writers, playwrights, scenarists, composers, lyricists, orchestra conductors, designers, cinematographers, film cutters, actors, dancers, advertising and promotion men, distributors, music publishers, song "pluggers," journalists, columnists, critics, and "fan" magazine editors. The development of the motion picture is described from early nickelodeon days to the present: accounts of the early studios and equipment in New York and New Jersey and acting, directing, and distributing techniques; the Hollywood mythology from the time the industry moved to California until the coming of sound; recollections of the emergence of slapstick comedy, the Mack Sennett Studios and others; the beginnings of many Hollywood careers; scandals and provocative films; state censorship; pressure groups and the origin of the Motion Picture Code and the artistic problems created by the silent films; the effects on the introduction of sound; mechanical and technical innovations; the making of *The Jazz Singer*, new ideas in acting, writing, and producing; the casualties of sound.

The Hollywood of the 1930s is portrayed in comments on its social structure; the California election of 1934, artistic problems, and block booking. Problems of the postwar period, in particular the impact of television and of charges of communism upon the entertainment industry, are detailed together with other major changes. Some of the films discussed are: *The Great Train Robbery, Intolerance, Sunrise, Safety Last, The Jazz Singer, A Day at the Races, San Francisco, Gone with the Wind, How Green Was My Valley, The Southerner, The Best Years of Our Lives, Marty, Twelve Angry Men, Mr. Roberts*, and *The Three Faces of Eve*. Personalities discussed include D. W. Griffith, Douglas Fairbanks, John Gilbert, Rudolph Valentino, Carl Laemmle, Irving Thalberg, Louis B. Mayer, Frederic Murnau, Ernst Lubitsch, Harry Langdon, and W. C. Fields.

Interviews in the field of popular music cover Tin Pan Alley and the vaudeville circuits, effects of the player piano, phonograph and radio, music and the movies, the era of the big bands, and more recent trends in popular music. Interviews on the stage cover the theater of Victor Herbert, Jerome Kern, and George Gershwin, the stock company as training ground, the road, the Group Theatre, the Stanislavsky method, new methods of acting and directing, Actors' Studio, changes in business methods, the role of the legitimate theater in contemporary life, artistic freedom, comparisons of stage with screen techniques, concentration of theater in New York City (1958–1960, 7819 pages, open except as noted). See *Popular Culture* in name and subject index of participants and pages.

55. Joseph M. Proskauer project. Anecdotes and recollections from family, friends, and associates have been added to Judge Proskauer's own reminiscences, with a view to preparing a biography (1966, 299 pages, permission required). See *Joseph M. Proskauer* in name and subject index for participants and pages.

56. Psychoanalytic movement. The early history of psychoanalysis and its subsequent ramifications, as discussed by psychoanalysts and others closely associated with the movement. Interviews with associates of Sigmund Freud and leading representatives of major schools of psychoanalytic theory. The project aims to provide anecdotal, subjective material that will shed new light on the pioneers of the psychoanalytic movement and its influence on contemporary society (1963–1969, 1802 pages, individual restrictions apply). See *Psychoanalysis* in name and subject index for participants and pages.

57. Radio Liberty. In anticipation of the 50th anniversary of the Russian Revolution, Radio Liberty and the Institute for the Study of the Union of the Soviet Socialist Republics in Munich collected memoirs of participants in the events of 1917. The material presents a broad political, social, economic, and cultural panorama of Russia at that time. The 75 interviews, conducted in Europe, 1964–1965, are in Russian; a list is available from Columbia on request (1965, 824 pages, permission required). See *Russia* in name and subject index.

58. Radio pioneers. A comprehensive record of the early history of radio contributed by engineers, station and network executives, government officials, writers, directors, and performers. Scientific matters discussed include types of sending apparatus, early experiments with wireless, radio antennas, wireless and radio transmitters, the Alexanderson alternator, early experiments with television, transmitters for radio stations, mobile radio units, problems of engineering in network broadcasts, manufacturers' laboratory research, and the effects of World War II on radio engineering.

The growth of the radio business from the days of amateurs is described in accounts of manufacturing apparatus for the radio market (Westinghouse Electric Company, General Electric Corporation, and the Radio Corporation of America), wireless telegraphy and telephony on the Great Lakes, operating methods in early radio stations, establishing and financing a radio station in the 1920s, persuading advertisers to buy radio time, responses of and to the radio audience, broadcast ethics, and the impact of television with its new business and performing methods.

The growth of networks and network competition with local stations is detailed in accounts of the development of the National Broadcasting Company, the Red and Blue networks and the outgrowth of the American Broadcasting Company from them, Columbia Broadcasting Company, Mutual Broadcasting System, American Telephone & Telegraph Company, and the stations of General Electric and Westinghouse.

Radio's relations with government are dealt with in accounts of the Washington Conference assigning international wavelengths, 1927; Federal Radio Commission; FCC, radio law and legislation; government regulation and comparisons of radio in the U.S., Great Britain, and Canada; the British Broadcasting Corporation; patent-licensing and the Department of Justice, 1932; U.S. censorship in World War II and postwar problems.

The problems of programing and the evolution of types of radio programs are described, particularly musical programs, the use of music on the radio, early radio acting, talent scouting, audience participation programs, children's programs, and information and public service programs. News reporting is discussed, including matters such as news analysis, sports reporting, rivalry between the press and radio, radio columns and columnists, Association of Radio News analysts, and an account of reporting the Spanish Civil War by H. V. Kaltenborn.

Specific details are provided on the history of Stations WWJ, Detroit, and WBEN, Buffalo, the development of a classical music station (WQXR—NY) and a municipal station (WNYC—NY), and on such programs as "Amos n' Andy," "Information Please," "Town Meeting of the Air," and "The Voice of Firestone." Impressions are given of Walter Damrosch, David Sarnoff, Bertha Brainerd, Frank

COLUMBIA UNIVERSITY (cont.)

Conrad, Al Jolson, Owen D. Young, Henry Ford, Fred Waring, William S. Paley, George F. McClelland, Merlin H. Aylesworth, and others. Erik Barnouw, Professor of Film at Columbia University, has added to the original series a number of interviews conducted in connection with his three-volume history of broadcasting in the U.S. (1950– , 4789 pages, open except as noted). See *Radio* in name and subject index for participants and pages.

59. Rockefeller Foundation. The memoirs in this series all are about significant careers—in public health, plant pathology, foundation administration, and other areas—with the Rockefeller Foundation. Beyond this, the memoirs vary widely in subject, scope, and style, and there are comparatively few interconnections, each memoirist having been invited to respond in his own way. Copies are on deposit also at the Rockefeller Foundation Archives. See *J. Curtis Dixon, John B. Grant, Alan Gregg, J. George Harrar, Flora Rhind, E. C. Stakman, Benjamin Washburn, Robert Briggs Watson, and Warren Weaver* in name and subject index.

60. Theodore Roosevelt Association. Friends and associates reminisce about Theodore Roosevelt and the Roosevelt family and circle, with reappraisals of Theodore Roosevelt's impact upon American life. Some new light is thrown on the Bull Moose campaign (515 pages, permission required to cite or quote). See *Theodore Roosevelt* in name and subject index for participants and pages.

61. Scientist as citizen. The common denominator for thee interviews is the experience of scientists whose work has thrust them into national and world affairs. Among the subjects discussed are: problems of communication with scientists in other fields and with non-scientists, civil rights and freedom of speech, relationships with government and industry, the changing role of the scientist, control and direction of research, and influence of foundations. The memoirs reflect the education and background of the twentieth century scientists and the accelerated pace of scientific thought. There are evocations of some memorable moments in scientific research in such fields as nuclear physics, chemistry, plant pathology, meteorology, and genetics. See *Scientists* in name and subject index for participants and pages.

62. Social Security. This project has the dual aim of presenting personal recollections about the origins and early years of Social Security in the U.S., and of exploring the legislative history of Medicare. Pioneers in the social insurance movements tell about many who were prominent in its early years, including John B. Andrews, John R. Commons, and Frances Perkins. There are descriptions of the activities and personnel of the American Association for Labor Legislation and the American Association for Social Security. Special emphasis is given to experiences with the Committee on Economic Security and the growth and organization of Social Security Board. Recollections of early attempts to enact government health insurance, the work on the Committee on Costs of Medical Care and the Committee on Economic Security, the National Health Conference of 1938, the Wagner Bill, 1939, the Wagner-Murray-Dingell Bill, and the Forand Bill, 1957, provide background about the precursors of the Medicare program. The bulk of the Medicare recollections focus on the period 1960-1965. Included are memoirs of members of the Social Security Administration, the Kennedy entourage, organized labor, the National Council of Senior Citizens, the U.S. Senate, the insurance industry, Blue Cross, the House Ways and Means Committee, the American Hospital Association, and AMA (1965-1968, 10,649 pages, open except as noted,

papers). See *Insurance, Social* in name and subject index for participants and pages.

63. Socialist movement. This project describes the genesis and development of the Socialist Party, primarily in the words of those actively involved in the party, past and present. It deals with the relationship of the Socialist Party to unions, the American Labor Party, the Trotskyist movement, the Communist Party, and other groups. Included are analyses of failure of the Socialist Party to thrive in this country, and of the impact of Franklin Roosevelt and the New Deal on the party. Memoirists also describe the role socialists have played in civil rights activities. There are recollections about Eugene V. Debs, Samuel Gompers, Upton Sinclair, Norman Thomas, and others (1965, 1141 pages, permission required to cite or quote). See *Socialism* in name and subject index for participants and pages.

64. Southern intellectual leaders. This project consists of interviews with intellectual leaders in the south whose work fell predominantly in the period between the two World Wars and who were responsible for bringing a vigorous and modern intellectual life to their region (1970-1972, 1350 pages, closed pending publication of a study). See *Culture* in name and subject index for participants and pages.

65. Adlai E. Stevenson project. Friends and associates describe Governor Adlai Stevenson's life and career from a number of vantage points. Personal reminiscences and anecdotes recall his wit and contribute fresh material for a study of his personality. Political associates analyze and illuminate his career, particularly as governor of Illinois (1949-1953), as Democratic nominee for the presidency (1952 and 1956), and as ambassador to the UN (1961-1965) (1966-1970, 5326 pages, permission required). See *Adlai E. Stevenson* in name and subject index for participants and pages.

66. Robert A. Taft. The life and career of Senator Robert A. Taft (1889-1953) are recounted by colleagues, friends, and family. Interviews describe his legal development and political growth, as a Republican, his activities in Ohio and in Washington, and his family relationships (1967-1970, 1471 pages, permission required). See *Robert A. Taft* in name and subject index for participants and pages.

67. Weyerhaeuser Timber Company. Materials on the development of the lumbering industry and the lumber regions based upon the recollections of executives and employees of the Weyerhaeuser Timber Company and of others in the industry. Descriptions of lumbering practices include: labor problems; immigrants; fire-fighting in camp, mill and forest; CCC; reforestation, homesteading and land claims in Idaho about 1900; timber speculation; cooperation in the development of white and ponderosa pine stands in Idaho, Oregon, and Washington; and methods of forest transportation. Corporate developments are described in accounts of early days of the Weyerhaeuser Timber Company and the Weyerhaeuser Sales Company, the Potlatch Lumber Company, and other related or competing firms. There are impressions of members of the Weyerhaeuser and Denkmann families, George S. Long, William Deary, and others prominent in lumbering (1956, 2981 pages, permission required). See *Weyerhaeuser Timber Company* in name and subject index for participants and pages.

68. World Bank. Interviews with officers of the International Bank for Reconstruction and Development detail its history and operations from the 1944 Bretton Woods Conference. Organization, development of policies, management practices, personnel, and the relationship of directors and staff during the presidencies of Eugene Meyer, John McCloy, and Eugene Black are described. The functions of the World Bank are analyzed, including policy formulation

and supervision of end-use of funds, project appraisal, credit worthiness, administration and significance of loans, government banks, equity investment and venture capital, bond issues and corollary legislation, and foreign and domestic bond marketing. The relationship of the Bank to the International Monetary Fund and to other financing institutions is explored. There are descriptions of individual projects, particularly flood protection, railway rehabilitation, the Indus Basin Settlement Plan, the Mekong River Survey, and the Suez Canal (1961, 1392 pages, permission of individual contributors required to cite or quote, except as noted). See *World Bank* in name and subject index for participants and pages.

CORNELL UNIVERSITY

Department of Manuscripts and University Archives
101 Olin Library
Ithaca, New York 14850
(607) 256-3530
Gould P. Colman, Department Chairman

General information: 1962. Tapes: many hours, transcribed, preserved. Transcriptions: verbatim transcriptions, all changes made by respondent.

Accessibility: No separate catalog for oral history material. Indexed. Restrictions vary for each interview. All material can be obtained at either the Department of Manuscripts and University Archives or at the Labor Management Documentation Center.

Purpose of the program: To collect data of significance for the present and future understanding of our society by means of recorded interviews with shapers of events and witnesses to change.

Cornell is interested in recording the experiences and observations of people who have occupied key points in decision making, or who have been instrumental in setting taste or opinion, or who have been witnesses to significant events by chance or position. The program is not oriented toward interviewing people of top reputation who may have already recorded their ideas in print at considerable length. Cornell's principal concern has been with persons less well known in their own time.

This emphasis has not precluded a limited number of interviews with individuals who have occupied leadership positions, particularly when such interviews can advance the research of faculty members or graduate students or supplement manuscript collections located in the Department of Manuscripts and University Archives or in the Labor Management Documentation Center at Cornell.

Major collections:

1. Agricultural leaders project. See *Agriculture* in the name and subject index for participants.
2. *Alumni news* project. John Marcham interview. See *Cornell University* in the name and subject index for participants.
3. Daniel Berrigan Weekend project. See *Cornell University* in the name and subject index for participants.
4. Black studies project. A project to study the history and evolution of a black studies program at Cornell. See *Cornell University* in the name and subject index for participants.
5. Challenges to governance by students project. See *Cornell University* in the name and subject index for participants.
6. Challenges to governance by students project: Open House Ithaca. See *Cornell University* in the name and subject index for participants.
7. Challenges to governance by students project: Pentagon March (1967). Eighteen Cornell students who participated in the demonstration at the Pentagon in opposition to the Vietnam war were interviewed as part of a project undertaken in cooperation with Prof. Jay Schulman of the School of Industrial and Labor Relations. The project is designed to: 1) obtain information from 100 Cornell students who participated in the march concerning their previous participation in organizations, their motives and expectations at the time, what they did and observed in Washington, their post-march reactions and their current thinking about mechanisms for social change and 2) to compare the content and susceptibility to analysis of the information obtained by means of the 18 oral history interviews and by 82 interviews designed to obtain the same information by a structured questionnaire. See *Cornell University* in the name and subject index for participants.
8. Challenges to governance by students project: School of the Ozarks. See *School of the Ozarks* in the name and subject index for participants.
9. Challenges to governance by students project: Student activism. See *Cornell University* in the name and subject index for participants.
10. Challenges to governance by students project: Student activism—Jackson State College. An unhappy incident in May 1969, at Jackson State College, where two students were killed by the Mississippi State Highway Patrol, provided a challenge to oral history units to document the incident and reactions while memories were still fresh and before the witnesses had scattered. Twelve persons were interviewed between July 7 and 14, eight weeks after the initial incident and several weeks after a boycott of local stores. Eight of the respondents were students at Jackson State College; one was a student in a local high school. See *Jackson State College* in name and subject index for participants.
11. Challenges to governance by students project: *Trojan Horse* incident. See *Cornell University* in the name and subject index for participants.
12. John Lyon Collyer project (10 hours, 1973).
13. Cornell University Libraries project. See *Cornell University* in the name and subject index for participants.
14. Development of artificial insemination project. Artificial insemination (AI) is rapidly becoming the most common method of initiating the reproduction process in dairy cattle in the United States. In addition to its commercial importance, the widespread use of the technique has made possible complex statistical studies involving selective breeding. Early research on AI techniques, efforts toward breed improvement through genetic manipulation, and the development of organizations to make AI available to dairymen are subjects of a series of interviews with animal scientists and personnel of AI breeding organizations throughout the United States. See *Artificial Insemination* in the name and subject index for participants.
15. Dorothy Straight Elmhirst biography project. See *Dorothy Straight Elmhirst* in name and subject index for participants.
16. Farm families project. Some 20 farm families are interviewed at two-year intervals in an effort to study the process of decision making on a farm in New York State.
17. Food processing project. See *Food Industry and Trade* in name and subject index for participants.
18. George Junior Republic project. See *Alvord V. Baker, Georgia Fellows, Malcolm Freeborn, Mrs. Albert B. Genung, and John J. Kinance* in name and subject index.
19. Industrial and labor relations project. See *William B. Groat and Mary H. Donlon* in name and subject index.

CORNELL UNIVERSITY (cont.)

20. Ithaca Festival (Center for the Arts at Ithaca) project. A study of the development of a repertory theater in Ithaca. See *Ithaca, New York* in name and subject index for participants.

21. Perception of change in the Ithaca school district project. Conducted between 1966 and the present; interviews with people in leadership positions, and with a random sampling of parents and their children stratified by school. See *Ithaca, New York* in name and subject index for participants.

22. Law Enforcement Assistance Administration project. Cornell engaged in indirect cooperation with LEAA through Prof. Jack Holl, visiting fellow at the Institute. LEAA got a comparative study of English and American penal reform written by Professor Holl; Cornell received source material on penal reform generated by an appropriate interviewer. See *Law Enforcement Assistance Administration* in the name and subject index for participants.

23. Eugene McCarthy project. A study of the effort to organize support for McCarthy in the 1968 election. See *Eugene McCarthy* in name and subject index for participants.

24. Joseph McCarthy project. See *Joseph McCarthy* in name and subject index for participants.

25. Milk marketing in the New York State metropolitan area project. See *Milk* in name and subject index for participants.

26. Historic preservation in Nantucket. Six residents of Nantucket Island, Massachusetts, were interviewed in an exploratory project designed to determine the most appropriate set of documents for the work of the Historic American Buildings Survey of the National Park Service. This work involved determining the physical and social context in which the buildings were constructed and used, as well as the physical characteristics of the buildings. Information was obtained concerning the installation and operation of the water system in Nantucket, air transportation facilities on the island, the construction and operation of the wharves and local industries. In addition to the interviews a gam session (an occasion for telling traditional stories of the community) was recorded at a private party. See *Nantucket, Massachusetts* in name and subject index for participants.

27. National Farmers Organization project. Interviews with Mr. and Mrs. George Demeree treat the organization of NFO in New York State, Mr. Demeree's experiences as a farmer and as president of the Herkimer County Unit, and the procedures and objectives of the NFO in New York State. See *Mr. and Mrs. George Demeree*, and *Edward and Dorothy Geraty* in name and subject index for length and restrictions.

28. National Labor Relations Board. James A. Gross, associate professor in the School of Industrial and Labor Relations, has been preparing a history of the National Labor Relations Board up to Taft-Hartley. In this connection, this program has generated documentation to the extent of 45 interviews.

The documentation process began in the National Archives. Following this research in organizational records, Prof. Gross identified information potentially available through interviews which he needed either to fill gaps in his research, test tentative conclusions, or test reliability of information already known.

According to Prof. Gross, source material from these oral history interviews has been critical to his research. It provided a personal dimension not found in documents, often suggested connections between events which would otherwise have been unknown, and contributed to the development of interpretation. See *National Labor Relations Board* in name and subject index for participants.

29. New York City blackout (1965). See *Electric Power Failures* in name and subject index for participants.

30. New York State College of Human Ecology project. See *New York State College of Human Ecology* in name and subject index for participants.

31. Peace Corps project. Returned Peace Corps volunteers were interviewed. See *Peace Corps* in name and subject index for participants.

32. Collective bargaining at State University of New York project. See *State University of New York, Cortland* in the name and subject index for participants.

33. Sugar beet industry in New York State. In 1965 sugar beets were grown in New York State on a commercial basis for the first time since 1909. Six persons were interviewed who knew how an acreage allotment was obtained from the U.S. Department of Agriculture for New York State, and other matters associated with bringing the industry to the state. See *Beets and Beet Sugar* in name and subject index for participants, pages, length and restrictions.

34. United Transportation Union project. This was a joint effort by the United Transportation Union (formed by four railroad operating Brotherhoods) and the School of Industrial and Labor Relations at Cornell. The oral history project was designed to produce source material appropriate for a description and evaluation of the merger which formed the union. See *United Transportation Union* in name and subject index for participants and pages.

During the course of 34 interviews associated with this project, Cornell learned of the existence of two collections of records relating to the development of the industry. They eventually came to the Collection of Regional History at Cornell. These collections, together with the interviews, provided documentation for a narrative history of the industry, plus three chapters of analysis concerning the diffusion of ideas and technology. Neither the interviews nor the collection of organizational records was adequate documentation for the narrative history; being complementary was the source of their value. See *United Transportation Union* in name and subject index for participants and pages.

HARTWICK COLLEGE

Oneonta, New York 13820
(607) 432-4200, ext. 268
Gary G. Roth, Administrative Assistant, Office of Institutional Research

General information: 1971, on-going. Tapes: 20 hours, transcribed, partially preserved. Transcriptions: 148 pages, edited.

Accessibility: No catalog. Not indexed. Interlibrary loan. No restrictions.

Purpose of the program: The program was established to explore the history of Hartwick College, Hartwick Seminary, and the Pine Lake campus property.

HISPANIC SOCIETY OF AMERICA

613 West 155th Street
New York, New York 10032
(212) 690-0743; WA6-2234
Shirley A. Victor, Assistant Curator of Library

General information: 1963. Tapes: 15 interviews, 15 hours, partially transcribed, fully preserved. Transcriptions: edited.

Accessibility: Permission required from interviewee and interviewer.

Purpose of the program: To collect personal recollections on certain topics from society members. Major topics include Hispanic art, literature, and history.

INTERNATIONAL BUSINESS MACHINES CORPORATION

IBM Technological History & IBM Business History
Armonk, New York 10504
(914) 765-1900
L. M. Saphire and W. L. Rofes, Directors

General information: 1962. Tapes: 200 interviews, 485 hours, partially transcribed, partially preserved. Transcriptions: 190 interviews, 9000 pages, edited.

Accessibility: Indexed. No provisions for scholarly use at present.

Purpose of the program: To study IBM technology and the history of IBM.

Major collections:
1. IBM technology (tapes preserved, biographical and topical index).
2. IBM history (tapes transcribed and erased).

LEVITTOWN PUBLIC LIBRARY

Levittown, Long Island, New York
(516) PE1-5728
Robert N. Sheridan, Director, Oral History Program

General information: 1969. Tapes: 5 interviews, 10 hours, partially transcribed, fully preserved. Transcriptions: partial, edited.

Accessibility: Not indexed. Interlibrary loan for transcripts.

Purpose of the program: A history of the world's first mass-produced town, Levittown.

LIBRARY AND MUSEUM OF THE PERFORMING ARTS

See New York Public Library at Lincoln Center

MOUNT SINAI MEDICAL CENTER

Fifth Avenue and 100 Street
New York, New York 10029
(212) 534-4433
Albert S. Lyons, M.D., Archivist

General information: 1966. Budget: Varies with needs—about $4,000; archivist unpaid. Tapes: about 90 hour tapes, transcribed, preserved. Transcriptions: edited.

Accessibility: No catalog. See Columbia University entry for description and list of participants. No interlibrary loan. Copies on deposit at Columbia University, New York. Virtually all tapes and transcriptions are open with permission of archivist.

Purpose of the program: To recapture events and personalities of the past in the history of Mount Sinai Hospital and Medical School; to preserve and fix the events and personalities of the present for use of historians in the future.

NEW YORK OFFICE OF STATE HISTORY

55 Elk Street
Albany, New York 12224
W. K. McNeil, Director

General information: 1968. Tapes: 20 interviews, 20 hours, transcribed, preserved. Transcriptions: edited.

Accessibility: Available to scholars applying in person and agreeing to the regulations established by the institution.

Purpose of the program: To preserve details of New York State's 1967 Constitutional Convention.

NEW YORK PSYCHOANALYTIC INSTITUTE

247 East 82 Street
New York, New York 10028
(212) 879-6900
Robert S. Grayson, M.D., Chairman, Oral History Committee

General information: 1971. Budget: none. Tapes: 17 hours, preserved. Transcriptions: partially transcribed and edited.

Accessibility: No catalog. Not indexed. No interlibrary loan. Users must sign statement containing Library Manuscript Rules; some of the interviews are restricted.

Purpose of the collection: To document the history of psychoanalysis by obtaining recollections concerning the early events in the development of psychoanalysis in Europe and in the United States. The first priority goes to those who have made scientific contributions to psychoanalysis or were intimately connected with the origins of analysis.

Major collections:
1. Edith Jacobson, psychoanalysis history (3 hours, 80 pages).
2. Rudolph M. Loewenstein, psychoanalysis, history (3 hours).
3. Marianne Kris (4 hours).
4. Dora Hartman (4 hours).
5. Jeanne Lampl-de Groot (3 hours).

THE NEW YORK PUBLIC LIBRARY AT LINCOLN CENTER

Theatre Collection
111 Amsterdam Avenue
New York, New York 10023
(212) 799-2200, ext. 271
Betty L. Corwin, Project Director, Theatre on Film and Tape

General information: 1971. Budget: none. Tapes: 36 hours, not transcribed (videotape).

Accessibility: No catalog. Index to overall collection: a finding list. No interlibrary loan. The tapes and films will be located only at the Theatre Collection of the library and cannot be removed from the premises. Tapes cannot be loaned, copied, or used for commercial purposes. They can be viewed only by special request of bona fide professionals and serious students.

Purpose of the program: To establish a permanent visual record for research and study purposes of plays and musicals in their ultimate creative form, alive and on stage. Collection consists of videotapes of 18 theatrical productions and six dialogues between renowned persons of the theatre.

THE NEW YORK TIMES COMPANY, INC.

229 West 43 Street
New York, New York 10036
(212) 556-1555
Chester M. Lewis, Director of Archives

General information: 1969. Budget: Varies according to number of interviews annually. Tapes: 205 hours, transcribed, preserved. Transcriptions: 3561 pages, edited by interviewee.

Accessibility: No catalog. Indexed. No interlibrary loan. Closed—restricted to internal use.

Purpose of the program: To obtain pertinent current and historic data regarding the *New York Times* and its operations.

NORTHPORT PUBLIC LIBRARY

151 Laurel Avenue
Northport, New York 11768
(516) 261-6930
Victoria Wallace, Director

NORTHPORT PUBLIC LIBRARY (cont.)

General information: 1962. Budget: nothing allocated. Tapes: 7 hours, transcribed, preserved (tapes have been transposed to 33 1/3 rpm discs). Transcriptions: 71 pages, edited.

Accessibility: Card catalog. No interlibrary loan. Records may be borrowed by Northport Library patrons only. Listening equipment available in the library.

Purpose of the program: Local history, including a taped discussion between Jack Kerouac, author, and Stanley Twardowicz, artist.

Accessibility: Restrictions not determined.

ORANGE COUNTY COMMUNITY COLLEGE
Middletown, New York 10940
(914) 343-1121
Harold J. Jonas, Director, Oral History Project

General information: 1964. Tapes: 12 interviews, 30 hours, transcribed, preserved. Transcriptions: not edited.

Accessibility: Restrictions not determined.

Purpose of the program: To record the founding and early history of the college and of the community.

PLATTSBURGH STATE UNIVERSITY COLLEGE
Plattsburgh, New York 12901
(518) 564-2000
Betty J. Baldwin, Director of Oral History

General information: 1972. Budget: $1,500. Tapes: 30 hours, transcribed, preserved. Transcriptions: 500 pages, edited.

Accessibility: No catalog. Index in process. Possible interlibrary loan, policy not yet set. No restrictions.

Purpose of the program: To investigate Plattsburgh and surrounding communities during the 1920s and early 1930s through taped interviews with area residents who were active in the community during those years before the federal government became such an integral force in all our lives.

RIVERHEAD FREE LIBRARY
330 Court Street
Riverhead, New York 11901
(516) 727-3228
Elizabeth Overton, Library Director

General information: Budget: none. Tapes: 12 interviews of local citizens.

Purpose of the program: Local history.

ST. JOHN'S UNIVERSITY
Grand Central and Utopia Parkways
Jamaica, New York 11432
(212) 969-8000
Wilater L. Willigan, Director, Oral History Research Project

General information: 1967. Tapes: 5 interviews, transcribed, sample portions preserved. Transcriptions: partial, edited.

Accessibility: Available to persons applying in person and agreeing to the regulations established by the institution.

Purpose of the program: To collect material on the history of New York State and on African affairs.

SCOTT E. WEBBER COLLECTION
17 Sunrise Drive
Stony Point, New York 10980
(914) 786-2254
Scott E. Webber, Private Collector

General information: Tapes: 15 hours, not transcribed.

Accessibility: No catalog. Indexed. No interlibrary loan. No restrictions.

Purpose of the program: To study World War II and the postwar era, the G.I. in postwar era going to school, James A. Farley recollections (1900–1968), and local history of the Rockland County area.

SHIRLEY CAMPER SOMAN COLLECTION
40 West 77 Street
New York, New York 10024
(212) 787-8722
Shirley Camper Soman, Private Collector

General information: Tapes: 1000 hours, transcribed, preserved. Transcriptions: 50,000 pages, edited.

Accessibility: No catalog. Indexed. No interlibrary loan. Some releases not yet obtained. Material is private. Further use requires additional funding.

Purpose of the program: Collector is writing a book on social welfare history.

STATE UNIVERSITY OF NEW YORK COLLEGE OF ARTS & SCIENCES AT PLATTSBURGH
See Plattsburgh State University College

UNITED STATES MILITARY ACADEMY
Room 170, Thayer Hall
Building 601
West Point, New York 10996
(914) 938-3300
Colonel Thomas E. Griess, Professor of History

General information: 1968, ongoing. Budget: less than $500. Tapes: 25 hours, transcribed, preserved. Transcriptions: 20 pages, edited.

Accessibility: No catalog. Not indexed. No interlibrary loan. At present the collection is available to resident cadets, staff, faculty, visiting military personnel, and acknowledged visiting scholars. For a very small portion of the collection a security clearance for access to secret information is required.

Purpose of the program: To ultimately develop a reservoir of oral history tapes and transcripts in the field of military and modern history, particularly history relating to the organization and operation of the academy and its role in the national security of the United States throughout the years of its existence. Currently one area of special interest is to obtain the personal accounts of prominent military figures concerning strategical and tactical operations of all United States wars since 1940. The program is now in its formative stages.

WEBBER, SCOTT E., COLLECTION
See Scott E. Webber Collection

VIVO INSTITUTE FOR JEWISH RESEARCH, INC.
1048 Fifth Avenue
New York, New York 10028
(212) 535-6700
Josua A. Fishman, Director

General information: 1961. Tapes: 58 interviews, 280 hours, partially transcribed, fully preserved. Transcriptions: 900 pages, not edited.

Accessibility: Not indexed. Available to scholars applying in person and agreeing to the regulations established by the institution.

Purpose of the program: The history of the Jewish Labor Movement and Yiddish and Hebrew culture since the beginning of the century.

NORTH CAROLINA

APPALACHIAN STATE UNIVERSITY

Boone, North Carolina 28607
(704) 262-2186
Charlotte T. Ross, Curator, Appalachian Collection

General information: 1972. Budget: $1,029 grant received, no annual budget. Tapes: 40 hours, transcribed, preserved. Transcriptions: 300 pages, not edited.

Accessibility: Catalog in process. Not indexed. No interlibrary loan. Materials may not be used without permission of curator.

Purpose of the program: To collect materials from areas of disappearing folklore and to maintain a permanent place to house it.

See also Alice Lloyd College, Appalachian Oral History Project, Kentucky.

DUKE UNIVERSITY

Duke University Library
Durham, North Carolina 27706
(919) 684-8111
Mattie Russell, Curator of Manuscripts

General information: Tapes: 45 interviews, 89 hours, partially transcribed, fully preserved. Transcriptions: 40 interviews, 2907 pages, edited.

Accessibility: Indexed. Available to scholars applying in person and agreeing to the regulations established by the institution. Transcript of this collection is also on deposit at Columbia University. A full description of the collection appears under the entry for Columbia University, New York, in this section and a list of participants and pages appears under the entry for James B. Duke in the name and subject index.

GUILFORD COLLEGE LIBRARY

Greensboro, North Carolina 27410
(919) 292-5511
Herbert Poole, Director of Libraries; Treva W. Mathis, Curator, The Quaker Collection

General information: 1970, on-going. Budget: within the library budget.

Accessibility: No catalog. Card indexed within the collection. No interlibrary loan. Must be used in the Quaker Collection at the library.

Purpose of the program: To collect statements from elderly Friends (Quakers) within the North Carolina Yearly Meeting, emphasizing recollections of other persons and events among Friends, and noteworthy persons and events of local history in general. Some major topics include slavery, agriculture, transportation, Guilford College, social life and customs of settlers, family history, communities and the various changes that have taken place, economics of the various times, mills, education, and mining.

UNIVERSITY OF NORTH CAROLINA AT CHAPEL HILL

Chapel Hill, North Carolina 27514
(919) 933-2211
William S. Powell, Director, North Carolina Collection

General information: 1960. Tapes: 270 recordings, not transcribed.

Accessibility: Indexed. Available to scholars applying in person and agreeing to the regulations established by the institution.

Purpose of the program: To record North Carolinians and events in North Carolina. Interviews are mixed in with public addresses, sermons, and lectures.

UNIVERSITY OF NORTH CAROLINA AT CHARLOTTE

UNCC Station
Highway 49 North
Charlotte, North Carolina 28213
(704) 597-2221
Joseph F. Boykin, Jr., Librarian

General information: 1972. Budget: $3,500. Tapes: 70 hours, partially transcribed, fully preserved. Transcriptions: 150 pages to date, edited.

Accessibility: No catalog. Not indexed. Interlibrary loan. Until final legal questions are determined, the entire collection is closed. After these questions are settled, portions of various interviews may be closed at the desire of the interviewee.

Purpose of the program: To obtain information on the changing role of the Charlotte-Piedmont region of North Carolina from a rural area to an urban one. Emphasis is given to projects most directly related to the overall theme.

Major collections:
1. Leadership of Piedmont area of North Carolina (60 hours).
2. Founders and supporters of the University of North Carolina at Charlotte (10 hours).

WAKE FOREST UNIVERSITY

Reynolds Station
Winston-Salem, North Carolina 27109
(919) 725-9711, ext. 477
A. Lewis Aycock, Director

General information: 1971. Budget: $1,000, exclusive of salary. Tapes: 25 hours, not transcribed.

Accessibility: No catalog. Card index. No interlibrary loan. No regulations for use have been adopted. To date no interviewee has put any restriction on the use the university may make of the tape.

Purpose of the program: To secure tape recordings of the voices of retired faculty members and other persons significant to Wake Forest.

NORTH DAKOTA

CARNEGIE-BOOKMOBILE

Seventh & Griggs
Grafton, North Dakota 58237
(701) 352-2754

General information: 1970. Budget: none. Tapes: 10 hours, transcribed, preserved. Transcriptions: not edited.

Accessibility: No catalog. Not indexed. No interlibrary loan. No restrictions.

Purpose of the program: To collect tapes on the history of Walsh County, North Dakota.

OHIO

AMERICAN JEWISH ARCHIVES

3101 Clifton Avenue
Cincinnati, Ohio 45220
(513) 221-1875
Stanley F. Chyet

AMERICAN JEWISH ARCHIVES (cont.)

General information: 1960. Tapes: 82 interviews, 160 hours, partially transcribed, fully preserved. Transcriptions: partial, not edited.

Accessibility: Indexed. Research and reproduction services can be arranged for persons unable to visit the institution. Available to scholars applying in person and agreeing to the regulations established by the institution. Some tapes are restricted.

Purpose of the program: Research material on Jewish experience in the Western hemisphere.

ARCHIVES OF THE HISTORY OF AMERICAN PSYCHOLOGY

University of Akron
Akron, Ohio 44325
(216) 762-2441; 666-9030
John A. Popplestone, Director

General information: 1965.

Accessibility: No catalog. Name and institution index. Restrictions vary with individual tapes. Available only to scholars who display a bona fide interest in the history of psychology.

Purpose of the program: To serve the needs of scholars by collecting, cataloging, preserving, and in other ways maintaining the materials which provide the sources for the history of psychology. Among the deposits are tape recorded biographical reports by professional persons about their lives with emphasis on the men and events which influenced them, the work accomplished as well as the reasons for it.

CLEVELAND STATE UNIVERSITY LIBRARY

Euclid & 24 Streets
Cleveland, Ohio 44115
(216) 687-2477
John P. Herling, Director

General information: 1972. Budget: none. Tapes: 200 hours, not transcribed.

Accessibility: No catalog. Indexed. Interlibrary loan. No restrictions.

Purpose of the program: Since 1912, the City Club of Cleveland has provided a forum for leading municipal, state and national politicians, policy makers, and other public figures. The City Club Forum has become a major platform for airing views on current topics (especially if controversial); the City Club Debates are nationally noted for their pre-election debates of political opponents. Through arrangements with the City Club, the Cleveland State University Library has become the depository for audio tapes of all City Club Forums and Debates from 1965 on.

OHIO HISTORICAL SOCIETY

Interstate 71 and Seventeenth Avenue
Columbus, Ohio 43211
(614) 469-2060
David J. Rosenblatt, Oral History Specialist

General information: 1968. Budget: $15,000. Tapes: 340 hours, transcribed, preserved. Transcriptions: 3400 pages, edited.

Accessibility: No catalog. Not indexed. Interlibrary loan. Individual tapes may have restrictions; restricted to qualified researchers.

Purpose of the program: To augment archives and library collections. Special areas of study include state and city government.

Major collections:

1. Social welfare in Franklin County (1932-1970) (80 hours, 800 pages, mostly open).
2. Life of Kingsley A. Taft, Ohio Supreme Court Chief Justice (55 hours, 780 pages, mostly written permission required).
3. Black history in Columbus (60 hours, 550 pages, mostly open).
4. The governor's office (20 hours, 500 pages, written permission required).
5. The arts in Columbus, 1960-1970 (60 hours, 450 pages, mostly open).
6. Ohio political parties since 1945 (40 hours, 375 pages, mostly closed).
7. Ohio League of Women Voters (20 hours, not transcribed, mostly open).

OHIO STATE UNIVERSITY LIBRARIES

Columbus, Ohio 43210
(614) 422-5938
Robert A. Tibbetts, Curator of Special Collections

General information: Tapes: 92 seven-inch tapes, transcribed, preserved. Transcriptions: Not edited; being prepared for publication by James W. Wilkie. Some published.

Accessibility: No catalog. Checklist only. No interlibrary loan. Open to qualified scholars with written permission of James W. Wilkie, Department of History, UCLA.

Purpose of the program: Interviews with Latin American figures.

PUBLIC LIBRARY OF YOUNGSTOWN AND MAHONING COUNTY

305 Wick Avenue
Youngstown, Ohio 44503
(216) 744-8636
Elfreda Chatman, Director of Project Outreach

General information: 1973.

Accessibility: No catalog. Not indexed. No interlibrary loan. Restrictions not formulated yet.

Purpose of the program: To aid local history, beginning with the black community and later to include every group represented in Youngstown.

UNIVERSITY HOSPITALS OF CLEVELAND

Lowman House, Room 330
2065 Adelbert Road
Cleveland, Ohio 44106
(216) 791-7300
Eugenia Kucherenko, Archivist

General information: 1969. Tapes: 16 interviews, preserved, transcribed. Transcriptions: edited.

Accessibility: Available to scholars applying in person and agreeing to the regulations of the institution.

Purpose of the program: To fill the gaps in existing historical material and for the preservation of important information about the local history of medicine.

UNIVERSITY OF AKRON

See Archives of the History of American Psychology

OKLAHOMA

NORTHEASTERN STATE COLLEGE
Tahlequah, Oklahoma 74464
(405) 456-5511, ext. 3671
Billy Joe Davis, Director, Oral History Program

General information: 1971, on-going. Budget: no separate budget. Tapes: 60-80 hours, not transcribed.

Accessibility: No catalog. Partially indexed. No interlibrary loan, but arrangements possibly could be made. No restrictions.

Purpose of the program: To record information valuable for research purposes about local history and to encourage students to become familiar with oral history techniques and uses. The collection is of local history and contains no material on major individuals. The largest collection pertains to the history of Northeastern State College.

OKLAHOMA CHRISTIAN COLLEGE
North Eastern & Memorial
Oklahoma City, Oklahoma 73111
(405) 478-1661
Pendleton Woods, Director, Oklahoma Living Legends

General information: 1965. Budget: $20,000.

Accessibility: No catalog. Indexed. No restrictions.

Purpose of the program: To collect general reminiscences of state and local history in Oklahoma. Included are land runs, petroleum industry, Indian reminiscences, etc. Of great interest is the voice and sound of the people involved, and a major part of the effort is in the development of audiovisual programs using voices from Oklahoma's past.

Publications based on collection research: Three books are being researched or written using the oral history program: one deals with the life of Robert A. Hefner, one with the history of Oklahoma City, and one with the life of Hicks Epton.

TULSA COUNTY HISTORICAL SOCIETY
400 Civic Center
Tulsa, Oklahoma 74103
(918) 581-5232
Mrs. J. Leighton Avery, Audiovisual Historian

General information: 1971, on-going. Budget: $500. Tapes: not transcribed.

Accessibility: No catalog. Indexed. No interlibrary loan. Available to researchers at office of society on 4 track 7" taped reels for supervised research and special programs.

Purpose of the program: To focus on Tulsa area history: water, cattle, transportation, culture, beginnings of oil firms, schools, churches, industrial development, hospitals, roads, Tulsa race war (1921), human relations, and life in frontier of Indian territory.

UNIVERSITY OF OKLAHOMA
Doris Duke Indian Oral History Project
Norman, Oklahoma 73069
(405) 325-5408
B.D. Timmons

General information: 1967. Budget: project completed. Tapes: 1,200 hours, transcribed, preserved. Transcriptions: 15,000 pages, not edited.

Accessibility: No catalog. Indexed. Interlibrary loan. Permission required.

Purpose of the program: To focus on Indian history and culture. 460 Indians from 27 Oklahoma tribes were interviewed.

Publications based on collected works:

Jones, David E. "The Medicine Kit of a Comanche Eagle Doctor." *Bulletin of the Oklahoma Anthropological Society 18:* 1-12. 1969.

Sanapia: Comanche Medicine Woman. New York: Holt, Rinehart and Winston, Case Studies in Anthropology. 1972.

UNIVERSITY OF OKLAHOMA MEDICAL CENTER
800 North East Thirteenth Street
Oklahoma City, Oklahoma 73104
R. Palmer Howard

General information: 1967. Tapes: 7 interviews, 12 hours, preserved, transcribed. Transcriptions: edited.

Accessibility: No restrictions.

Purpose of the program: To record the experiences of early physicians in Oklahoma and the contributions of contemporary physicians.

OREGON

OREGON HISTORICAL SOCIETY
1230 SW Park Avenue
Portland, Oregon 97205
(503) 222-1741
Lawrence C. Skoog

General information: 1970. Budget: not yet determined.

Purpose of the program: Labor history, early recollections, and local performing arts will be the focus of the collection.

PENNSYLVANIA

ALLIANCE COLLEGE
Cambridge Springs, Pennsylvania 16403
(814) 398-4611
Robert D. Ilisevich

General information: 1971, on-going. Budget: not budgeted. Tapes: 50 hours, partially transcribed, partially preserved. Transcriptions: not edited.

Accessibility: No catalog. Not indexed. No interlibrary loan. Alliance is still developing a policy governing use of materials.

Purpose of the program: Emphasis is on the Polish Americans and the history of the college.

Publications based on collection research:

Robert D. Ilisevich, "Oral History in Undergraduate Research," *The History Teacher,* November 1972.

AMERICAN PHILOSOPHICAL SOCIETY LIBRARY
105 South Fifth Street
Philadelphia, Pennsylvania 19106
(215) WA5-9545
Murphy D. Smith, Assistant Librarian

General information: Tapes: 100 reels in quantum physics program transcribed, 500 in American Indians program not transcribed, fully preserved. Transcriptions: edited.

Accessibility: Research and reproduction services can be arranged for persons unable to come to the institution. Collection available to scholars applying in person and agreeing to the regulations established by the institution.

AMERICAN PHILOSOPHICAL SOCIETY LIBRARY (cont.)

Major collections:
1. American Indians.
2. Quantum physics.

BRYN MAWR COLLEGE ALUMNAE ASSOCIATION

Bryn Mawr, Pennsylvania 19010
(215) LA5-1000
Anne L. Nicholson, Archivist, Alumnae Association

General information: 1968. Tapes: 20 interviews, 30 hours, preserved, not transcribed.

Purpose of the program: To provide bases for future history of the college and of the achievements of alumnae of Bryn Mawr.

Accessibility: Index planned. No provision for scholarly use at this time.

CARNEGIE-MELLON UNIVERSITY

See Hunt Institute for Botanical Documentation

HAVERFORD COLLEGE

Haverford, Pennsylvania 19041
(215) 649-9600, ext. 281
Barbara L. Curtis, Acting Curator, Quaker Collection

General information: 1968. Budget: no special allotment. Tapes: 6 hours, not transcribed.

Purpose of the program: To tape interviews and speeches with notable Quaker leaders, or with persons with close associations with Haverford College, who also happen to be Quakers in most cases. Peace, Quakerism, Haverford College reminiscences are areas currently included.

Accessibility: No catalog. Not indexed. No interlibrary loan. To be used only at Haverford College.

HUNT INSTITUTE FOR BOTANICAL DOCUMENTATION

Oral Histories in the Plant Sciences
Hunt Library
Carnegie-Mellon University
Pittsburgh, Pennsylvania 15213
(412) 621-2600, ext. 552
Abby Levine, Archivist

General information: 1963, most interviews done in 1969. Budget: Although the collection is on-going, there is no current budget. Tapes: 150 hours, partially transcribed, fully preserved. Transcriptions: 224 pages, not edited.

Accessibility: No catalog. Not indexed. Interlibrary loan. Interviews with living persons restricted; permission of interviewee required.

Purpose of the program: To provide primary documentation relevant to the history of botany, horticulture, and other plant sciences. Included are lectures, seminars, and colloquia by plant scientists.

KING'S COLLEGE

D. Leonard Corgan Library
14 West Jackson Street
Wilkes-Barre, Pennsylvania 18701
(717) 824-9931, ext. 253
Margaret May Fischer, Director, Oral History Program

General information: 1968, on-going. Budget: included in general budget. Tapes: 12 hours plus 107 reels, transcribed, preserved. Transcriptions: edited.

Accessibility: Catalog in process. Index to overall collection in process. No interlibrary loan. Collection available to scholars applying in person and agreeing to the regulations established by the institution.

Purpose of the program: To collect information on various ethnic groups in Luzerne County, their folk customs and acculturation.

Major collections:
1. George Korson folklore archive (107 reels, transcribed, completed).
2. Oral history (12 hours, 300 pages, on-going).

KUTZTOWN STATE COLLEGE

See Pennsylvania Historical and Museum Commission

MONTGOMERY COUNTY—NORRISTOWN PUBLIC LIBRARY

542 DeKalb Street
Norristown, Pennsylvania 19401
(215) 277-3355
Pearl Frankenfield, Executive Director

General information: 1951–1952. Budget: none. Tapes: 78 rpm recordings only, not transcribed.

Purpose of the program: Recordings of radio interviews by Pearl Frankenfield with prominent authors, artists, teachers, librarians, ministers, and individuals in Montgomery County.

Accessibility: No catalog. Author and subject entries in main card catalog. No interlibrary loan. For use within the library.

NEW CASTLE PUBLIC LIBRARY

106 East North Street
New Castle, Pennsylvania 16101
(412) 658-6659
Helen M. Roux, Director

General information: 1973. Budget: none.

Accessibility: No catalog. Not indexed.

Purpose of the program: The emphasis of the program will be on material of local historical value.

PENNSYLVANIA HISTORICAL AND MUSEUM COMMISSION

Box 1026
Harrisburg, Pennsylvania 17108
(717) 787-3115
Edward Tracy, Director, Oral History Program

General information: 1969. Tapes: 25 interviews, 14 hours, preserved (one video tape is also being made of each interviewee and will be available with the tapes and transcripts). The program is jointly sponsored by the commission and the history department of Kutztown State College.

Accessibility: Available to scholars applying in person and agreeing to the regulations established by the institution.

Purpose of the program: To record the administration of the governors of Pennsylvania in the twentieth century beginning with Governor Janes, functions and effects of state governmental activities as viewed by state employees and elected officials.

PENNSYLVANIA STATE UNIVERSITY

Pattee Library
University Park, Pennsylvania 16802
(814) 865-1793
Alice M. Hoffman, Coordinator of Oral History Project

General information: 1969, on-going. Budget: approx. $10,000. Tapes: 400 hours, transcribed, preserved. Transcriptions: 4,000 pages, edited.

Accessibility: Catalog. Proper name index. No interlibrary loan. No interview may be quoted from or cited during the lifetime of the interviewee without his specific permission. Upon the donor's death there are no restrictions upon use of any of the interviews except in those few cases where the interviewee may have closed access for a specified number of years.

Purpose of the program: To collect and preserve the history of the American labor movement with a particular emphasis on the history of unionism in the metals industries and the graphic arts industries.

PRESBYTERIAN HISTORICAL SOCIETY
425 Lombard Street
Philadelphia, Pennsylvania 19147
(215) PE 5-4433
William B. Miller

General information: 1969.

Accessibility: No catalog. Not indexed. Restricted for research purposes.

Purpose of the program: To record outstanding personalities and events relating to the American Presbyterian tradition.

SOCIETY OF THE HOLY CHILD JESUS
1341 Montgomery Avenue
Rosemont, Pennsylvania 19010
(215) 525-9900
Sister Mary Roberta Dougherty, Director, the American SHCJ Oral History Program

General information: 1971, on-going. Budget: $100. Tapes: 45 hours, transcribed, mostly preserved. Transcriptions: 261 pages, not edited.

Accessibility: No catalog, a listing only. Index in process. Interlibrary loan. No restrictions, but borrower must supply tape and postage.

Purpose of the program: To preserve details of foundations and persons which otherwise might be lost. The major subject is the early days of the SHCJ in America.

TEMPLE UNIVERSITY
Samuel Paley Library
Thirteenth and Berks Streets
Philadelphia, Pennsylvania 19122
(215) 787-8840

General information: 1965, completed. Budget: none. Tapes: 25 hours, transcribed, preserved. Transcriptions: 374 pages, not edited.

Accessibility: No catalog. Index for internal use. No interlibrary loan. Restricted to internal university use, and occasional public use at the discretion of the curator.

Purpose of the program: To prepare for a history of Temple University. The interviews were recorded from 1965 to 1967 by the late Arthur N. Cook, then professor emeritus of history, and deal with various aspects of university history.

UNITED STATES ARMY MILITARY RESEARCH COLLECTION
Carlisle Barracks, Pennsylvania 17013
(717) 245-4113
Colonel George S. Pappas, Director

General information: 1970–1971, on-going. Tapes: 381 hours, transcribed, preserved. Transcriptions: 8000 pages, edited.

Accessibility: No catalog. Not indexed. No interlibrary loan. The tapes and transcripts are considered as personal manuscripts provided by the interviewee and certain proprietary rights have been retained by the individuals concerned. The U.S. Army Military History Research Collection is the sole repository for these tapes and transcripts. Transcripts are available for research use under the restrictions specified by individual interviewees.

Purpose of the program: To provide insight into command and management techniques used by senior officers who held key positions in the United States Army. The results of this program will be used to further scholarly research of army military history.

RHODE ISLAND

NAVAL WAR COLLEGE
See United States Naval War College

RHODE ISLAND DEPARTMENT OF STATE LIBRARY SERVICES
95 Davis Street
Providence, Rhode Island 02908
(401) 277-2726
Elizabeth G. Myer, Director, Department of State Library Services

General information: 1971. Budget: no separate budget. Tapes: 55 hours, partially transcribed, fully preserved. Transcriptions: edited.

Accessibility: No catalog. Not indexed. Interlibrary loan. Tapes are made available to scholars on request.

Major collections:
1. Mill life in Rhode Island (1890–) (45 hours, now transferred to Oral History Project of Rhode Island, see University of Rhode Island).
2. Cape Verdean oral history (on-going, 10 hours, restricted at present).

UNITED STATES NAVAL WAR COLLEGE
Newport, Rhode Island 02840
(401) 841-4052
Anthony S. Nicolosi, Curator, Naval Historical Collection

General information: 1971. Budget: Currently funded by the Naval War College Foundation. Tapes: 22 hours, 473 pages, transcribed, preserved. Transcriptions: 473 pages, edited.

Accessibility: No catalog. Not indexed. Interlibrary loan requests will be honored. No firm policy has been established at this time. Open to Naval War College faculty and students. Non-Naval War College scholars are required to secure permission from the president, Naval War College.

Purpose of the program: The program focuses on the history of the Naval War College and significant developments and events in naval warfare (i.e., strategy and tactics). A pilot project currently underway concerns the life and career of Admiral Raymond Ames Spruance. Copies of relevant oral histories done at other depositories are acquired whenever possible.

UNIVERSITY OF RHODE ISLAND
Oral History Project of the State of Rhode Island
Kingston, Rhode Island 02881
(401) 792-2528
Harvey A. Kantor, Director

UNIVERSITY OF RHODE ISLAND (cont.)

General information: 1973. Budget: $5,000. Tapes: transcribed, preserved. Transcriptions: edited.

Accessibility: No catalog. Not indexed. Interlibrary loan. No restrictions.

Purpose of the program: To coordinate oral history activities throughout the state and initiate interviews on topics of state and regional concern. Major areas include mill life and ethnic history.

SOUTH CAROLINA

THE CITADEL ARCHIVES—MUSEUM

The Citadel
Charleston, South Carolina 29409
(803) 723-0611, ext. 324
Lt. Commander Malachy Collet, Director

General information: 1960. Budget: $4,000. Tapes: 50 hours, not transcribed, preserved.

Accessibility: No catalog. Indexed. No interlibrary loan. No tapes allowed outside the archives.

Purpose of the program: The Citadel Archives—Museum is primarily a military museum. Its tapes are mostly the recollections of former Citadel graduates and/or Citadel presidents about their experiences during the war.

Major collections:

1. J. F. Kennedy assassination (8 hours, completed).
2. The General Hugh P. Harris collection (30 hours, completed).

WOFFORD COLLEGE

Archives
Spartanburg, South Carolina 29301
(803) 585-3821
Herbert Hucks, Jr., Archivist

General information: 1947. Budget: None—included in archives. Tapes: 45 hours, not transcribed.

Accessibility: No catalog. Not indexed. No interlibrary loan. Must be used in archives.

Purpose of the program: To gather any program connected with the history of Wofford College, such as addresses and/or speeches, inaugurations of presidents, and special events. Two appearances by Robert Frost are among those treasured, including one when Carl Sandburg was present.

SOUTH DAKOTA

AUGUSTANA COLLEGE

Center for Western Studies
28th & Summit Avenue
Sioux Falls, South Dakota
(605) 336-5329
Gary D. Olson, Executive Secretary, Center for Western Studies

General information: 1966. Budget: No on-going program exists. Tapes: 100 hours, preserved, transcribed. Transcriptions: edited.

Accessibility: No catalog. Not indexed. Interlibrary loan. No restrictions.

Purpose of the program: This project interviewed persons from three generations in Minnehaha and Lyman Counties in South Dakota. The same questions regarding certain social values and attitudes were asked of persons of all three generations to attempt to determine if significant changes had occurred since the period of original frontier settlement. For the first generation of original homesteaders the interviews tell much about life on the frontier.

SOUTH DAKOTA SCHOOL OF MINES & TECHNOLOGY

Devereaux Library
Rapid City, South Dakota 57701
(605) 394-2418
Estella Helgeson, Associate Librarian, Special Collection

General information: 1972. Budget: No specific budget; $250 per year for interviewer. Tapes: 6 hours, transcribed, preserved. Transcriptions: not yet edited.

Accessibility: No catalog. Not indexed. No interlibrary loan. For the present, tapes are not loaned out or reproduced.

Purpose of the program: Primarily, the collection has been set up to record reminiscences, etc. of people connected with the college—directly or indirectly. Secondarily, plans are in the works to include tapes from elsewhere in the state of South Dakota relating to events connected with the Black Hills and Western South Dakota.

UNIVERSITY OF SOUTH DAKOTA

American Indian Research Project
Vermillion, South Dakota 57069
(605) 677-5208
Joseph H. Cash, Director

General information: 1966. Budget: $50,500.

Accessibility: Catalog. Index forthcoming. The collection, until published by the *New York Times*, may not be used elsewhere than on the campus of the University of South Dakota. Access to the collection is given to serious scholars by the director. Direct quotations from the collection by permission of the director, although some individual tapes have other specific restrictions.

Note: Other institutions cooperating in the Doris Duke Indian Oral History Project are the Arizona State Museum and the Universities of Florida, Illinois, New Mexico, Oklahoma and Utah.

UNIVERSITY OF SOUTH DAKOTA

South Dakota Oral History Project
Vermillion, South Dakota 57069
(605) 677-5208
Joseph H. Cash, Director

General information: 1970. Budget: $23,400 (FY 1974). Tapes: 550 hours, partially transcribed, preserved. Transcriptions: 5500 pages, not edited.

Accessibility: Catalog. Indexed. No interlibrary loan. Material may not be directly quoted without written permission from the director of the South Dakota Oral History Project and the interviewee.

Purpose of the program: The major emphasis is on recollections of early statehood, homesteading, and frontier experience. There is extensive additional information covering rural life, development of towns, ethnic groups, ranching, the Depression, and politics.

Purpose of the program: To obtain history from the Indian point of view. Various collections include music, legend, religion, tribal politics, and discrimination.

Publications based on collection research:

The South Dakota Experience: An Oral History Collection of its People, Vol. I. Vermillion and Pierre, 1972.

Ward, Stephen R. "An Early Assessment of the South Dakota Oral History Project." *South Dakota History*, I (December 1970).

Ward, Stephen R. "The Flood in the Black Hills: An Application of Oral History," Oral History Association *Newsletter* (June 1973).

Major collections:
1. Black Hills flood of 1972 (200 interviews, 150 hours, 4000 pages, permission required to quote).
2. General historical collection: The South Dakota experience (400 hours, 1500 pages, permission required to quote).

TENNESSEE

CHATTANOOGA AREA HISTORICAL ASSOCIATION
University of Chattanooga
Chattanooga, Tennessee 37401
(615) 755-4011
Culver H. Smith, Oral History Project

General information: 1965. Tapes: 6 interviews, transcribed, preserved. Transcripts: edited.

Accessibility: Available to scholars applying in person and agreeing to the regulations established by the institution.

Purpose of the program: The acquisition of memoirs that may contribute to local history.

EAST TENNESSEE STATE UNIVERSITY
Johnson City, Tennessee 37601
(615) 929-4112
Thomas G. Burton, Director, Oral History Archives

General information: 1966. Budget: fluctuates. Tapes: 300 hours, transcribed, preserved. Transcriptions: 1600 pages, edited.

Accessibility: No catalog. Not indexed. No interlibrary loan. No reproduction of material is permitted.

Purpose of the program: Areas of special collection emphasis include folk tales, superstitions, customs, and recollections of the past from natives of the southern Appalachians.

FISK UNIVERSITY
Seventeeth & Jackson Street
Nashville, Tennessee 37203
(615) 329-9111
Ann Allen Shockley, Associate Librarian and Head of Special Collections

General information: 1970, on-going. Budget: National Endowment for the Humanities grant: $86,377 for one year. No university budget. Tapes: 212 hours, transcribed, preserved. Transcriptions: 657 pages, not edited.

Accessibility: No catalog. Indexed. No interlibrary loan. For use by students and bona fide scholars under the library's rules and regulations. Tapes and transcripts are to be used in the library and cannot be duplicated without permission from the interviewees or library if so designated.

Purpose of the program: The project is designated to tape persons from all walks of life who have contributed to black history and culture, and those who have been eyewitnesses or participants. Emphasis is placed on literature, music, and history which complements and supplements the archival and manuscript collections in the library. A special series is being done on black women in all areas of endeavor to document the black woman's history in America.

MEMPHIS PUBLIC LIBRARY AND INFORMATION CENTER
1850 Peabody Avenue
Memphis, Tennessee 38104
(901) 534-9686
Nathan A. Josel, Head, History and Travel Department

General information: 1964. Budget: Funded from personnel and book budget of history and travel department. Tapes: 230 hours, transcribed or in process of transcription, preserved. Transcriptions: 1100 pages, mostly edited, indexed.

Accessibility: No catalog. Not indexed. Some interlibrary loan; see individual collections below. For transcriptions: Open except for first collection below. For tapes: To be used only by qualified researchers.

Purpose of the program: In general support of the local history (Memphis and Shelby counties), the collection will focus on the development of the region politically, economically, culturally, and socially.

Publications based on collection research:

Grider, George, and Sims, Lydel. *War Fish*. Boston: Little, Brown & Co., 1958.

"The Once and Always Mr. Crump"—a television documentary.

Major collections:
1. Memphis blues—development and history (40 hours anticipated, an on-going project, indexed and transcribed, restricted until project has been published as a book).
2. Edward Hull Crump and his regime (44 hours, 246 pages, available through interlibrary loan, open).
3. George Grider *War Fish* memoir (42 hours, 240 pages, available through interlibrary loan, open).
4. Brigadier General Everett R. Cook memoir (44 hours, available through interlibrary loan, open).
5. Prentice Cooper, Governor of Tennessee (4 hours, 10 pages, available through interlibrary loan, open).
6. Admiral Harold M. Martin (27 hours, 165 pages, available through interlibrary loan, open).
7. Gordon R. Browning, Governor of Tennessee (36 hours, 144 pages, also at Columbia University NY, open).

MEMPHIS STATE UNIVERSITY
Memphis, Tennessee 38152
(901) 321-1524
Charles W. Crawford, Director, Oral History Research Office; Dewey Pruett, Curator, Special Collections, John Willard Brister Library

General information: 1967. Tapes: 700 hours, partially transcribed. Transcriptions: edited.

Accessibility: No catalog. Indexed. Interlibrary loan. No restrictions except for a few individually restricted tapes.

Purpose of the program: To collect oral materials on regional topics.

Major collections:
1. Oral history of the Tennessee Valley Authority.
2. Folk culture of the central Ozarks.
3. A study of Memphis Jewish community.
4. A history of the organization of labor in Memphis.
5. Documenting Memphis jazz and blues.
6. Memphis events of 1968: garbage strike, boycott, demonstrations, riots, and Martin Luther King's assassination.
7. Interviews with southern writers.

RACE RELATIONS INFORMATION CENTER LIBRARY
1109 Nineteenth Avenue South
Nashville, Tennessee 37212
(615) 327-1361
Mrs. Mal James Harris, Director

General information: 1970.

Purpose of the program: To record reminiscences of black political leaders in Davidson County.

TREVECCA NAZARENE COLLEGE
Mackey Library
333 Murfreesboro Road
Nashville, Tennessee
(615) 244-6000
Johnny J. Wheelbarger, Director of Learning Resources

General information: 1972. Budget: No special budget at this time. Tapes: Less than 50 hours, not transcribed.

Accessibility: No catalog. Not indexed. No interlibrary loan. Student and faculty use only.

Purpose of the program: To study the history of the college and of the Church of the Nazarene in the local area.

UNIVERSITY OF CHATTANOOGA
See Chattanooga Area Historical Association

TEXAS

BAYLOR UNIVERSITY
Box 228, Student Union Building
Waco, Texas 76703
(817) 755-3437
Thomas L. Charlton, Director, Baylor University Program for Oral History

General information: 1970. Budget: approx. $35,000. Tapes: 620 hours, transcribed, preserved. Transcriptions: 10,400 pages, edited.

Accessibility: No catalog. Indexed in the catalog of the archives of the Texas Collection, Baylor University. No interlibrary loan. Subject to the restrictions of the Archives of the Texas Collection, Baylor University. Individual memoirs may be open or closed at any given time.

Purpose of the program: The gathering and preservation of oral memoirs of persons who have made significant contributions to Texas society in recent times.

Publication based on collection research:
Jones, Eugene W., et al. *Practicing Texas Politics.* Boston: Houghton-Mifflin Co., 1971.

Major collection:
1. Religion and culture project (179 hours, 3202 pages).
2. Baylor University project (78 hours, 1386 pages).
3. Dallas Indian urbanization project (20 hours, 479 pages).
4. Texas judicial systems project (7 hours, 242 pages).
5. Texas economic history project (46 hours, 1072 pages).
6. Mexican American project (55 hours, 702 pages).
7. Special projects (87 hours, 2093 pages).
8. Curriculum project (141 hours, 1295 pages).

DALLAS PUBLIC LIBRARY
See Lakewood Branch, Dallas Public Library

EAST TEXAS STATE UNIVERSITY
Oral History Program, Department of History
East Texas Station
Commerce, Texas 75428
(214) 468-2981; 468-6107
Corrinne Crow, Coordinator; Joe Fred Cox, Director

General information: 1972, on-going. Budget: $10,000 FY 1972-1973 with an anticipated increase of about 40 percent for FY 1973-1974. Tapes: Most programs in preliminary states, will be transcribed and preserved. Transcriptions: will be edited.

Accessibility: No catalog. Not indexed. No interlibrary loan. Each interviewee is given the option of placing any restriction as to time or use on either the tape or the transcript. No restrictions have been made to date.

Purpose of the program: Presently, the programs at East Texas State University are directed along a local and regional line of research.

Major collections:
1. The great depression in east Texas.
2. Impact of Camp Maxey on Lamar County (12 hours, nearing completion).
3. History of blacks in east Texas (one 3 hour interview, ongoing).
4. Autobiography of Fletcher Warren, United States ambassador.
5. History of medicine in east Texas.
6. History of cotton in east Texas.
7. History of the railroad in east Texas.

FORT WORTH PUBLIC LIBRARY
Ninth and Throckmorton
Fort Worth, Texas 76102
(817) 335-4781
Patricia Chadwell, Head of the Southwest and Genealogy Department

General information: 1972. Budget: $642 (equipment and supplies only; personnel costs separately budgeted). Tapes: 31 hours, not transcribed (transcription planned).

Accessibility: No catalog. Index in preparation. Interlibrary loan. No restrictions.

Purpose of the program: The oral history project was conceived as part of a library outreach project for senior citizens, funded by a federal grant. Since the period of time shared by all members of this population was the Depression, the collection is limited in subject to everyday life in the southwest during the 1930s.

LYNDON B. JOHNSON SPACE CENTER
Houston, Texas

LAKEWOOD BRANCH, DALLAS PUBLIC LIBRARY
6121 Worth Street
Dallas, Texas 75214
(214) 821-5128
Dorothy Anderson, Branch Head, Lakewood Branch

General information: 1972. Budget: none. Tapes: 20 hours, not transcribed.

Accessibility: No catalog. Index in process. No interlibrary loan at present. Selective circulation. Policy not established.

Purpose of the program: Longtime residents of Lakewood are interviewed for their memories of early days in the neighborhood. Each person describes incidents that the era brings to his mind. The project's purpose is to capture the mood and flavor of early Dallas as well as collecting historical data.

NORTH TEXAS STATE UNIVERSITY ORAL HISTORY COLLECTION

Post Office Box 13734, University Station
Denton, Texas 76203
(817) 788-2558
Ronald E. Marcello, Coordinator

General information: 1963. Budget: $22,000. Tapes: 1450 hours, transcribed, preserved. Transcriptions: 14,500 pages, edited.

Accessibility: Catalog. No interlibrary loan. To be used at the university by bona fide scholars in accordance with the restrictions, if any, designated by the memoirist.

Purpose of the program: To preserve, in tape recorded interviews, the memoirs of Texans who have made significant contributions to society in recent times. The researchers are interested in gathering the experiences of people who have occupied key points of decision making, who have been instrumental in setting taste or opinion, or who have been witnesses to significant events by chance or position. The program also records memoirs and observations of persons closely associated with top echelon leaders while in such capacities as administrative assistants, speechwriters, and confidants.

Major collections:

1. Ex-governor's project. The oral memoirs of former governors of Texas. Wives, children and other close relatives are sometimes interviewed. Recollections are also gathered from speechwriters, administrative assistants, and intimate advisors of the ex-governors (200 hours, 2000 pages).

2. Legislative project. Members of the Texas state legislature are interviewed after each session. In selecting interviewees attempts are made to achieve a balance on the basis of region, party affiliation, political ideology, experience and likelihood to continue in the legislature for some time. Emphasizing the inner workings of government, personal relationships and other matters not a part of the public record, these files will provide scholars with better insights into the operation of state government (600 hours, 6000 pages, ongoing).

3. The New Deal project. Texans who played prominent roles in the FDR administration are interviewed, and special emphasis is placed upon the relief, recovery, and reform measures undertaken in Texas under the auspices of the New Deal (50 hours, 500 pages, ongoing).

4. Prisoner-of-war project. Memoirs are obtained from Texans who survived internment in German and Japanese POW camps during World War II (600 hours, 6000 pages, ongoing).

5. Miscellaneous. Land speculation in Texas, banking and finance, insurance irregularities of the mid-1950s, the controversy involving the dismissal of Homer P. Rainey as president of the University of Texas, and Mexican-American social action activities. Also biographical interviews.

RICE UNIVERSITY

Fondren Library, Oral History Project
Houston, Texas 77001
(713) 528-4141

General information: 1969. Tapes: 64 interviews, 120 hours, partially transcribed, fully preserved. Transcriptions: edited.

Accessibility: Open.

Purpose of the program: To document the university presidential appointment crisis of 1969.

SOUTHWEST TEXAS STATE UNIVERSITY

San Marcos, Texas 78666
(512) 245-2111
James W. Pohl, Director, Oral History Program, Department of History

General information: 1970. Tapes: 15 interviews, 60 hours.

Accessibility: Restricted for ten years.

Purpose of the program: To collect military history source material.

TEXAS A & I UNIVERSITY

Kingsville, Texas 78363
(512) 595-2111
Leslie G. Hunter, Assistant Professor of History

General information: 1971. Budget: none. Tapes: 125 hours, transcribed, preserved. Transcriptions: not edited.

Accessibility: No catalog. Not indexed. No interlibrary loan. Permission must be obtained from two members of the history department for access to the interviews.

Purpose of the program: South Texas oral history and folklore collection.

TEXAS A & M UNIVERSITY

College Station, Texas 77843
(713) 845-1951
Mary Lee Nolan, Associate Archivist

General information: 1973, on-going. Budget: undecided. Tapes: 15 at present, in process of being transcribed, preserved. Transcriptions: edited.

Accessibility: No catalog. Not indexed. No interlibrary loan. The collection is available to scholars applying to the university library.

Purpose of the program: The pilot project involves preservation for the historical record the experiences of individuals who came to Texas between 1910 and 1920 as refugees from the Mexican revolution. All but two of the persons interviewed to date were refugees or children of refugees.

TEXAS TECH UNIVERSITY

Southwest Collection
Box 4090, Tech Station
Lubbock, Texas 79409
(806) 743-3203
Roy Sylvan Dunn, Director

General information: 1955. Budget: No separate funds for oral history. Tapes: 800 hours, transcribed in selected cases, fully preserved. Transcriptions: 4000 pages, not edited.

Accessibility: No catalog. Indexed. No interlibrary loan. Abstracts only are circulated—no original tapes leave the premises. No restrictions.

Purpose of the program: To preserve on tape reminiscences of notable persons and events in the Southwestern United States and to supplement manuscript collections held by the Southwest Collection.

Publications based on collection research:

Dunn, Roy Sylvan. "Buffalo Bill's Bronc Fighter," (Biography) *Montana, the Magazine of Western History* (Spring 1957), 2-11.

Graves, Lawrence Lester (ed.). *A History of Lubbock.* Lubbock: West Texas Museum Association, 1962.

TEXAS TECH UNIVERSITY (cont.)

Major collections:

1. Athletic boom in West Texas (80 hours, 600 pages).
2. The "Big Band" era (20 hours, 2400 pages).
3. Biographical (132 hours, 400 pages).
4. Cotton industry (30 hours, 800 pages).
5. Lubbock, Texas: history (60 hours, 900 pages).
6. Lubbock, Texas: medical history (25 hours, 25 pages).
7. Lubbock, Texas: negro population (23 hours, 23 pages).
8. Cattle shoot of 1934–1935 (27 hours, 810 pages).
9. Lubbock, Texas: tornado, May 11, 1970 (60 hours, 1800 pages).
10. The Man-land confrontation in the arid and semi-arid southwest (110 hours, 2000 pages).
11. Oil industry (15 hours, 210 pages).
12. Ranching (160 hours, 2400 pages).
13. Rodeos and rodeo performers (20 hours, 50 pages).
14. Texas Crime Investigating Committee (26 hours, 26 pages).
15. Texas Tech University (40 hours, 850 pages).

UNIVERSITY OF TEXAS AT ARLINGTON LIBRARY

Division of Archives and Manuscripts
Arlington, Texas 76010
(817) 273-3391
Robert A. Gamble, Director, Division of Archives and Manuscripts

General information: 1967, on-going. Budget: Included in library budget. Tapes: 30 hours, transcribed, preserved. Transcriptions: 1383 pages, not edited.

Accessibility: Catalog. Indexed. No interlibrary loan. Oral history materials are available for scholarly research only. Transcripts and tapes may not be removed from the library. Photo-reproduction is not allowed except with the permission of the donor. Some transcripts are restricted in access by the wishes of the donor. All prospective researchers are interviewed and must register with the archives.

Purpose of the program: The oral history collection was established to preserve the memoirs of men and women who have made significant contributions to the growth of organized labor in Texas, along with the impact of related socioeconomic reform movements in the state. It is the purpose of this program to acquire candid recollections of these individuals so that scholars may gain new insight into previously unstudied areas and events.

UNIVERSITY OF TEXAS AT AUSTIN

Oral Business History Project
Department of Management, BEB-500
Austin, Texas 78712
(512) 471-4292
Floyd S. Brandt, Director of Oral Business History Project

General information: 1969. Budget: Funded by a Moody Foundation Challenge grant and by the College of Business Foundation. Tapes: 170 hours, transcribed, preserved. Transcriptions: 3000 pages, edited.

Accessibility: Catalog. Annual report. Not indexed. Interlibrary loan could be arranged. All publications are under the copyright of the Board of Regents of the University of Texas at Austin.

Purpose of the program: To record the individual recollections concerning the economic development of the southwest and Texas for the benefit of business historians and students of business.

UNIVERSITY OF TEXAS AT AUSTIN

Oral History Project
Box 8900
Austin, Texas 78712
(512) 471-1017
Joe B. Frantz, Director

General information: 1968. Budget: variable. Tapes: 634 persons interviewed, approx. 1600 hours, partially transcribed, fully preserved. Transcriptions: approx. 50,000 pages, partially edited.

Accessibility: No catalog. Not indexed. No interlibrary loan at this time. Restrictions vary.

Purpose of the program: To record the experience and observations of those persons whose careers have touched that of President Lyndon B. Johnson; to supplement the written record and provide future scholars with insights and information not otherwise available. The project focuses upon Lyndon Johnson and his personal relationships, but the project interprets its scope to include his "times" broadly defined.

UNIVERSITY OF TEXAS AT AUSTIN

University Archives
University Station
Austin, Texas 78712
(512) 471-3434
Chester V. Kielman, Director, Oral History of the Texas Oil Industry

General information: 1952. Tapes: 218 interviews, 200 hours, transcribed, preserved. Transcriptions: edited.

Accessibility: Indexed.

Purpose of the program: To preserve the history of the Texas oil industry from exploration through production.

UNIVERSITY OF TEXAS AT EL PASO

Institute of Oral History
El Paso, Texas 79968
(915) 747-5488
John H. McNeely, Director; David Salazar, Associate Director

General information: 1972. Budget: $31,500. Tapes: partially transcribed, partially preserved. Transcriptions: edited.

Accessibility: Card index. Interlibrary loan. Subject to restrictions placed by individual interviewees; these are noted in subject index.

Purpose of the program: Local history of the southwest area is the focus of this program. It includes West Texas, New Mexico, Arizona, the revolutionary era in Mexico, and the development of El Paso, Texas and Juarez, Mexico, both politically and militarily.

Publications based on collection research: Many articles by S. H. Newman for "Archives" column in the quarterly magazine called *Password* put out by the El Paso Historical Society Sonnichsen collection used by Dale Walker in UTEP magazine, *Nova*.

UTAH

BRIGHAM YOUNG UNIVERSITY

University Archives
112 J. Reuben Clark Library
Provo, Utah 84602
(801) 374-1211, ext. 2984

General information: 1961. Budget: none. Tapes: 310 hours, transcribed, preserved. Transcriptions: 7650 pages, edited.

Accessibility: No catalog. Index to overall collection: Table of contents (subject and name). Interlibrary loan. Transcripts may be purchased at the cost of duplication. Open to any serious researcher.

Purpose of the program: To collect reminiscences of alumni of Brigham Young University concerning Utah history (mining, banking, railroads, industry, etc.) and Mormon Church history.

THE GENEALOGICAL SOCIETY OF THE CHURCH OF JESUS CHRIST OF LATTER-DAY SAINTS

50 East North Temple Street
Salt Lake City, Utah 84150
(801) 364-2511, ext. 2323
John C. Laing, Director, Oral History Program-Pacific

General information: 1967. Tapes: 75 hours, transcribed, preserved. Transcriptions: 2500 pages, not edited.

Accessibility: No catalog. Not indexed. No interlibrary loan. The entire collection is restricted from public scrutiny for the time being as it contains confidential information relating to the land holdings of the various Polynesian families interviewed. This policy may change in the future.

Purpose of the program: The oral history program centers around the individual identification and historical and biographical background of persons who have lived in the Polynesian Islands of the South Pacific. These are arranged in the form of a pedigree, and the basis of the information collected originates from the memorized pedigrees of the native people, mostly chiefs and land-title holders. In addition to recording their memorized recitations, further interviews are conducted to more fully identify the ancestors discussed. The program provides research material for genealogical research in the Polynesian Islands. There are collections from Western Samoa, the Society Islands (Tahiti), the Austral Islands, and the Cook Islands, New Zealand.

SOUTHERN UTAH STATE COLLEGE LIBRARY

Special Collections Division
Cedar City, Utah 84720
(801) 586-6297
Inez S. Cooper, Director, Special Collections

General information: 1961. Budget: from general library budget. Tapes: 84 persons interviewed, 75 hours, preserved. Transcriptions: 1500 pages, edited.

Accessibility: No catalog. Not indexed. Permission to quote must be obtained by the author from interviewee or his survivors as well as from the special collections librarian. Tapes can only be used in the special collections room.

Purpose of the program: The oral history project was begun to supplement the few remaining primary records regarding the foundation of the college. Subsequently, it was enlarged to include the gathering of the memories of descendants of the southern Utah pioneers with a view to enrichment of the library's holdings in southern Utah history.

UNIVERSITY OF UTAH

Doris Duke Indian Oral History Collection
Salt Lake City, Utah 84112
(801) 581-7611
C. Gregory Crampton, Duke Research Professor

General information: 1967. Budget: Program in operation 1967–1972, now complete. Tapes: 2500 hours, transcribed, preserved. Transcriptions: 20,000 pages, edited.

Accessibility: Catalog incomplete. Card index. No interlibrary loan. Serious researchers may use the collection, housed in the Western Americana division, Marriott Library, Salt Lake City. Very few documents are actually restricted. Copies of documents not permitted. A few tapes were done by the Southern Utah State College Library and are also available there.

Purpose of the program: To obtain from the American Indian his views on Indian and American history.

Major collections:

1. Zuñi collection: creation myth, folkways, mores, myths, relations with Spaniards.
2. Navajo land claims collection: occupancy patterns, genealogical data.
3. Urban Indian collection: urban lifestyles, economic conditions, educational opportunities.
4. Navajo code-talkers: World War II activities.
5. Navajo oral history of Canyon de Chelly: ethnohistory, Lorenzo Hubbell, early Navajo trader.
6. Fort Lewis collection: Indian education, boarding schools, Indian militancy.
7. Random sampling: agriculture, anthropologists, art, BIA, burial customs, Catholic Church, dances, discrimination, foods, games, hunting, language, legends, medicine men, peyote, mining, songs, trade and traders, tribal law, and witchcraft.

Note: Other institutions cooperating in the Doris Duke Indian Oral History Project are the Arizona State Museum, and the Universities of Florida, Illinois, New Mexico, Oklahoma and South Dakota.

UTAH STATE HISTORICAL SOCIETY

603 East South Temple
Salt Lake City, Utah 84102
(801) 328-5755
Jay M. Haymond

General information: 1970. Budget: $10,000. Tapes: 1100 hours, partially transcribed, fully preserved. Transcriptions: 24,000 pages, edited.

Accessibility: Catalog in preparation. Not indexed. No interlibrary loan. Reproduction of whole manuscripts is restricted to scholarly and educational use. Some reproduction is available through California State University at Fullerton.

Purpose of the program: The Utah State Historical Society's oral history program is part of the society's library collection effort. Its collection priorities are: Utah history, Mormon history, western history.

VERMONT

UNIVERSITY OF VERMONT

University Archives
Burlington, Vermont 05401
(802) 656-3235
T. D. Seymour Bassett, University Archivist

General information: 1967. Budget: none. Tapes: 117 hours, not preserved. Transcriptions: estimated at 2500 pages, edited.

Accessibility: No catalog. Not indexed. Interlibrary loan available in some cases. No restrictions.

Purpose of the program: Areas of emphasis are the state of Vermont and the University of Vermont. Special topics have been pursued by individuals.

VIRGINIA

COLONIAL WILLIAMSBURG FOUNDATION

Goodwin Building
Williamsburg, Virginia 23185
(804) 229-1000, ext. 6243

General information: 1955. Budget: $9,000. Tapes: 500 hours, partially preserved. Transcriptions: 2400 pages, edited.

Accessibility: No catalog. Indexed. No interlibrary loan. The collection is restricted to use by qualified researchers in accordance with accepted archival and scholarly practice.

Purpose of the program: The program seeks memoirs pertaining to Williamsburg and the development of the Colonial Williamsburg Foundation, with special interest in the town before the restoration, the process of restoration, and the formulation and implementation of important policies and projects of the foundation.

Major collections:

1. Colonial Williamsburg foundation oral history program (500 hours, 2400 pages).

EMORY AND HENRY COLLEGE

Emory, Virginia 24327
(703) 944-3121
George Stevenson, Campus Director, Appalachian Oral History Project

General information: On-going. Tapes: 40 hours, partially transcribed, fully preserved. Transcriptions: edited.

Accessibility: Index in process (name and subject). Interlibrary loan. For non-commercial research.

See also Alice Lloyd College, Appalachian Oral History Project, Kentucky.

GEORGE C. MARSHALL RESEARCH LIBRARY

Box 920
Lexington, Virginia 24450
(703) 463-4242
Forrest C. Pogue, Director

General information: 1956. Tapes: 40 hours, transcribed, preserved. Transcriptions: edited.

Accessibility: No catalog. Indexed. No interlibrary loan at present. Closed until biography is finished.

Purpose of the program: Interviews with Gen. George Marshall and 325 contemporaries.

Publications based on collection research: Three volumes on Gen. Marshall by Forrest C. Pogue.

MADISON COLLEGE

Shenandoah Valley Folk Culture
Post Office Box 268
Harrisonburg, Virginia 22801
(703) 433-6211
Elmer L. Smith

General information: Tapes: 125 interviews, partially transcribed. Transcriptions: 80 interviews, not edited.

Purpose of the program: To preserve the folk culture of the past in an Appalachian Valley region undergoing change. The major topic is folklore with emphasis on the German heritage of the region.

WORLD TAPES FOR EDUCATION

2010 Leonard Road
Falls Church, Virginia 22043
William J. Weaver

General information: 1963. Tapes: 250 hours, preserved.

Accessibility: Indexed. Available to scholars applying in person and agreeing to the regulations established by the institution.

Purpose of the program: To preserve the spoken word in connection with various military topics. Major topics include the Philippine Campaign (December 8, 1941 to May 1942) and prison experiences, Pershing Expedition and the Columbus Raid by Pancho Villa, environmental oral history of the southwest including western life and Pueblo Indians, various military topics, the Boxer Rebellion and the Mexican Revolution.

WASHINGTON

BONNER COUNTY HISTORICAL SOCIETY

Box 730
Spokane, Washington 99201
Peter E. Holzemer

Purpose of the program: To study the history of Bonner County.

CENTRAL WASHINGTON STATE COLLEGE

Ellensburg, Washington 98926
(509) 963-2861
Jerome K. Miller, Coordinator of Audiovisual Library Services

Accessibility: No catalog. Indexed in card catalog; photocopy of cards is available at cost. Permission required to copy the tapes, but anyone may listen to them and make notes.

Purpose of the program: To study the history of Kittitas Valley County and the history of Central Washington State College.

ELLENSBURG PUBLIC LIBRARY

Third & Ruby Streets
Ellensburg, Washington 98926
(509) 925-6141
Carolyn S. Willberg

General information: 1971. Tapes: 30 hours, not transcribed.

Accessibility: No catalog. Partially indexed. Tapes may be listened to in the library. When cassettes are made, these will be able to circulate.

Purpose of the program: To tape longtime residents of Kittitas County who have knowledge on topics of local historical interest.

PEND OREILLE COUNTY HISTORICAL SOCIETY

Box 355
Newport, Washington 99156
E. E. Hupp

General information: 1966. Tapes: 10 interviews, 50 written stories, preserved. Transcriptions: partial.

Accessibility: Restriction policy not fully developed.

Purpose of the program: To preserve stories of the life of area pioneers.

SPOKANE PUBLIC LIBRARY
West 906 Main Avenue
Spokane, Washington 99201
(509) TE 3-3361
Janet Miller, Fine Arts Head

General information: 1954, temporarily arrested. Budget: Financed by Friends of the Spokane Public Library. Tapes: 40 hours, transcribed, preserved. Transcriptions: not edited.

Accessibility: Catalog. Not indexed. Interlibrary loan possibly. May be borrowed for one week.

Purpose of the program: To record the history of the early days in Spokane, and the immediate area around the city, first-hand from pioneers.

TACOMA PUBLIC LIBRARY
1102 Tacoma Avenue South
Tacoma, Washington 98402
(206) 383-1574
Mary Frances Borden, Director

General information: 1970. Budget: irregular gifts.

Accessibility: No catalog. Not indexed.

General information: 1958, on-going. Budget: Included in departmental budget. Tapes: 30 hours, not transcribed.

Accessibility: No catalog. Author and subject index only. Individual releases have not been signed with the subjects.

Major collections:
1. Pacific Northwest Americana.
2. Artists and writers of the Pacific Northwest.

UNIVERSITY OF WASHINGTON
Henry Art Gallery
Seattle, Washington 98195
(206) 543-2280
LaMar Harrington, Director, Oral History Program and Archives of Northwest Art

General information: 1970. Budget: irregular gifts.

Accessibility: No catalog. Not indexed.

Purpose of the program: The Archives of Northwest Art contains documents, photographs, color slides, and taped interviews on artifacts of Washington, Oregon, Montana, Idaho, and Alaska.

Publications based on collection research:

Kingsbury, Martha. *Art of the Thirties: The Pacific Northwest.* Seattle: University of Washington Press, 1972.

UNIVERSITY OF WASHINGTON LIBRARIES
Manuscripts and Archives Division, Suzallo Library
Seattle, Washington 98195
(206) 543-1879
Richard C. Berner, University Archivist

General information: No formal program, simply oral holdings. First taped interview took place in 1959. Budget: No separate budget.

Accessibility: No catalog. Name list of interviewees. No interlibrary loan. Serious researchers may use most tapes. Unless literary rights have been assigned to the library, extended quotation may be done only with permission of interviewee or his heirs.

Purpose of the program: Taped interviews are arranged whenever it is felt the informant or donor of any manuscript or archival accession can add anything to which there is or might not be sufficient documentation otherwise. Apart from interviews with key persons, most interviews have been in relation to three ethnic history projects: Afro-American, Japanese-American and Jewish-American.

WALLA WALLA COLLEGE
Department of Sociology
College Place, Washington 99324
(509) 527-2273
Dan S. Harris, Jr., Director, Local History in the Social Studies Program

General information: 1969. Budget: varies. Tapes: 50 hours, not transcribed.

Accessibility: No catalog. File card index. No interlibrary loan. No restrictions to date.

Purpose of the program: To develop materials on local history using junior high school and senior high school students and teachers as well as student teachers to integrate the various disciplines in the social studies. The program emphasizes oral history as a teaching technique. Major topic areas include agriculture (e.g. brands of cattle, freezing foods, etc.) and Indian culture.

WEST VIRGINIA

KANAWHA COUNTY PUBLIC LIBRARY
123 Capitol Street
Charleston, West Virginia 25301
(304) 343-4646
June R. Martin, Reference Librarian

General information: 1970. Budget: none. Tapes: 23 hours, not transcribed.

Accessibility: No catalog. Indexed. No interlibrary loan. Anyone can listen to the tapes in the local history room of the library.

Purpose of the program: To discuss Charleston, on its 175th anniversary, with local persons who had lived there a long time.

NATIONAL PARK SERVICE ARCHIVES
Harpers Ferry Center
Harpers Ferry, West Virginia 25425
(304) 535-6371
Richard W. Russell, Curator of Archives

General information: 1962. Tapes: 600 hours, transcribed, preserved. Transcriptions: edited.

Accessibility: No catalog. Not indexed. No interlibrary loan. Permission to quote any of the interviews must be obtained from the director, Harpers Ferry Center.

Purpose of the program: The program originated in 1962–1963 in an effort to record the recollections of participants in the emergency relief programs administered by the National Park Service during the 1930s. The oral history project was revived in 1971 and broadened to include more recent activities of the service. In all interviews, even the few with non-service people, the focus is on the developmental history of the National Parks System and the varied activities of the National Park Service.

WEST VIRGINIA UNIVERSITY
West Virginia Collection, University Library
Morgantown, West Virginia 26506
(304) 292-3240
George Parkinson, Curator

General information: 1956. Tapes: 120 interviews, 143 hours, partially transcribed, fully preserved. Transcriptions: not edited.

WEST VIRGINIA UNIVERSITY (cont.)

Accessibility: Available to scholars applying in person and agreeing to the regulations established by the institution.

Purpose of the program: To record the history and culture of the state and of the university.

WISCONSIN

MARQUETTE UNIVERSITY ARCHIVES

Memorial Library Archives
1415 West Wisconsin Avenue
Milwaukee, Wisconsin 53233
R. N. Hamilton, Oral History Program

General information: 1964. Tapes: 7 interviews, 14 hours, partially transcribed, fully preserved. Transcriptions: edited.

Accessibility: Not open for scholarly use at present.

Purpose of the program: A history of the institution. The major topic is the Northwestern Mutual Life Insurance Company.

ROCK COUNTY HISTORICAL SOCIETY

Post Office Box 896
440 North Jackson
Janesville, Wisconsin 53545
(608) 752-4519

General information: 1971. Budget: none.

Accessibility: No catalog. Not indexed. No restrictions.

Purpose of the program: A very small collection of oral history tapes on local history; a black history project is underway.

STATE HISTORICAL SOCIETY OF WISCONSIN

816 State Street
Madison, Wisconsin 53706
(608) 262-3421
James Morton Smith, Director; George Talbot, Curator of Iconographic Film and Recorded Sound

General information: Program inactive.

Accessibility: Catalog in process.

Purpose of the program: A collection of over 7000 disc recordings, a great many for radio transcriptions and events participated in by public personalities. The largest portion consists of the NBC collection of over 4000 processed discs. There are over 2000 tapes which deal with a broad range of subject matter, including the student movement, the development of the new left, civil rights, and Wisconsin. The Mass Communications History Center collection concentrates largely on news commentators and other news personalities. Within these collections there are interviews and informal reminiscences of personal experiences.

UNIVERSITY OF WISCONSIN—LA CROSSE

Murphy Library
1631 Pine Street
La Crosse, Wisconsin 54601
(608) 785-1800, ext. 237
Edwin Hill, Special Collections Librarian

General information: 1968. Budget: unspecified. Tapes: transcribed, preserved. Transcriptions: 2500 pages, edited.

Accessibility: No catalog. Indexed. No interlibrary loan. Materials must be used in the library. Most interviews are unrestricted.

Purpose of the program: Emphasis is on local history and the history of the university. Immigration, city history, social life around 1900, politics, education, the Depression, and the medical profession are included.

UNIVERSITY OF WISCONSIN—MADISON

University Archives, 443F Memorial Library
Madison, Wisconsin 53706
(608) 262-2277
Donna S. Taylor, Director

General information: 1972. Budget: $17,600. Tapes: 112 hours, preserved. Transcriptions: 1407 pages, edited.

Accessibility: No catalog. Indexed. No interlibrary loan. There are no general restrictions. Restrictions may be placed on the use of individual interviews at the discretion of the interviewee.

Purpose of the program: To record the recollections of faculty and administrators regarding the growth and development of the university.

UNIVERSITY OF WISCONSIN—RIVER FALLS

Area Research Center
Chalmer Davee Library
River Falls, Wisconsin 54022
(715) 452-6701, ext. 312
Patrick B. Nolan, Director of the Oral History Project and Archivist of the Area Research Center

General information: 1967. Budget: $1,000. Tapes: 146 hours, transcribed, preserved. Transcriptions: 2500 pages (incomplete), not edited.

Accessibility: Catalog. Indexed. Interlibrary loan. No general restrictions. Some specific interviews require permission of interviewee before use.

Purpose of the program: The project concentrates on the history of the St. Croix Valley and western Wisconsin. Pioneer farming, railroading, steamboating, logging, newspapers, early medicine, education, and other aspects of regional history available are covered. Contemporary affairs covered include political events, business and labor history, academic history at the university and the environmental crisis in the region.

SACRED HEART MONASTERY

Priests and Brothers of the Sacred Heart
Provincial History Archives
Hales Corners, Wisconsin 53130
(414) 425-6910
Rev. Frank Wittouck

General information: 1960. Budget: open. Tapes: 30 hours, partially transcribed, fully preserved. Transcriptions: not edited.

WYOMING

JOHNSON COUNTY LIBRARY

90 North Main
Buffalo, Wyoming 82834
(307) 684-7423

General information: 1971. Budget: $100.

Accessibility: No catalog. Not indexed. Cassettes may be checked out for two weeks.

Purpose of the program: To collect verbal records of the setting of the community, military use of the area, and reports of the Cattle War.

Accessibility: No catalog. Not indexed. Interlibrary loan. Approval of provincial administration is required. Individual tapes have specific restrictions.

Purpose of the program: This archive deals with the foundation of the American Province of the Priests and Brothers of the Sacred Heart. It consists of interviews with key people involved in the development of this province from 1925 to 1965. Some material deals with historical developments in the Congregation's Indian missions in South Dakota and northern Mississippi (1945–   ).

UNIVERSITY OF WYOMING

Western History Research Center
The Library
Laramie, Wyoming 82070
(307) 766-4114
Gene M. Gressley, Director, Western History Research Center

General information: 1950. This is not an "oral history program" but simply some oral interviews that have been conducted in connection with a manuscript collection pertaining to the economic and social development of the American West. Tapes: some transcribed, all preserved. Transcriptions: edited.

WYOMING STATE ARCHIVES AND HISTORICAL DEPARTMENT

State Office Building
Cheyenne, Wyoming 82001
(307) 777-7281
Katherine Halverson, Chief, Historical Research and Publications Division

General information: 1972. Budget: indefinite; currently dependent upon legislature. Greatest progress to date was made under a $5,650 grant from the Wyoming Committee for the Humanities for the period September–November 1972.

Accessibility: No catalog. Not indexed. Restrictions not yet determined.

Purpose of the program: To organize and train groups throughout the state in the use of tape recording equipment and effective techniques of interviewing. To establish a cataloged library of taped material in both cassette and manuscript form for research, and to obtain all possible information from pioneers, contemporary leaders in all the industries, and specialized activities in Wyoming and from political and educational leaders.

Foreign Oral History Centers

CANADA

CENTENNIAL MUSEUM
1100 Chestnut Street
Vancouver, British Columbia
Mrs. Kerry McPhedran, Acting Historian

General information: Tapes: 8 tapes.

Purpose of the program: Oral history of the Klondike Gold Rush of 1897 and early Vancouver history.

IMBERT ORCHARD—CBC RADIO
747 Bute Street
Vancouver, British Columbia
Imbert Orchard, Director

General information: Tapes: 1200 interviews, not transcribed.

Purpose of the program: An archive of personalities in the British Columbia area.

McMASTER UNIVERSITY
Division of Archives
Mills Memorial Library
Hamilton, Ontario
Susan Bellingham, Special Collections Librarian

Purpose of the program: Modern Canadian poetry as well as tapes of Irving Layton reading his own works and a large number of tapes dealing with the Canadian National Archives.

MANITOBA MUSEUM OF MAN AND NATURE
190 Rupert Avenue
Winnipeg, Manitoba
James B. Stanton, Chief, Human History Division

General information: Tapes: 500 tapes, not transcribed.

Purpose of the program: Collection deals with Hong Kong veterans, Ukranian pioneers, Ontario British and Jewish pioneers.

NATIONAL MUSEUM OF MAN
Canadian Centre for Folk Culture Studies
Ottawa, Ontario
Carmen Roy, Director

Purpose of the program: Oral history interviews about folklore of all ethnic groups in Canada.

PROVINCIAL ARCHIVES OF BRITISH COLUMBIA
Victoria, British Columbia
W. E. Ireland, Archivist

Purpose of the program: Oral history interviews about the East Kootenay region.

PROVINCIAL ARCHIVES OF NEW BRUNSWICK
Centennial Building
Box 39
Fredricton, New Brunswick
Michael Swift, Archivist

General information: Tapes: 15 tapes, not transcribed.

Purpose of the program: Interviews with University of New Brunswick presidents and interviews covering the dying mining industry in the community of Minto.

PROVINCIAL LIBRARY AND ARCHIVES OF MANITOBA
275 Legislature Building
Winnipeg, Manitoba
John A. Bovey, Archivist

General information: Tapes: 20 interviews, transcribed.

Purpose of the program: Oral history about Manitoba politics and pioneer settlements.

PROVINCIAL MUSEUM
British Columbia Indian Language Project
Victoria, British Columbia
Randy Bouchard, Director

General information: Tapes: 250 tapes, transcribed, transcribed, translated.

Purpose of the program: Legends, stories, and historical narratives of native Indian tribes.

PROVINCIAL MUSEUM AND ARCHIVES OF ALBERTA
12845–102 Avenue
Edmonton, Alberta
Alan D. Page, Provincial Archivist

General information: Tapes: 500 tapes have been recorded, 400 transcribed, translated.

Purpose of the program: Interviews in the Blackfoot and Cree languages.

PUBLIC ARCHIVES OF CANADA
395 Wellington
Ottawa, Ontario
Leo La Clare, Archivist

General information: Tapes: 3000 hours, mostly transcribed.

Purpose of the program: Oral history interviews about Canadian history.

QUEEN'S UNIVERSITY
History Department
Kingston, Ontario
Richard A. Pierce, History Department

General information: Tapes: 25 interviews, transcribed.

Purpose of the program: Individuals with particular backgrounds in the Russian Revolutionary Movement.

REYNOLDS RESEARCH AND STUDIES
Box 6225, Postal Station G
3760 West Tenth Avenue
Vancouver 8, British Columbia
W. J. Langlois, Chairman

General information: Tapes: 800 hours, about 500 hours have been transcribed.

Purpose of the program: Areas of research include: Japanese-Canadians, French-Canadians, the Depression years, labor movements in British Columbia, Vancouver pioneers, and the role of women in British Columbia.

ROYAL CANADIAN MOUNTED POLICE
Historian Liaison Branch
1200 Alta Vista Drive
Ottawa, Ontario
Stan W. Horrall, Historian

Purpose of the program: Oral history of the Royal Canadian Mounted Police.

THUNDER BAY HISTORICAL SOCIETY
48 Oak Avenue
Postal Station P
Thunder Bay, Ontario
K. Denis, Director

Purpose of the program: Oral history interviews about Thunder Bay history and pioneer radio broadcasting.

UNIVERSITY OF ALBERTA
Rutherford Library
University Archives
Edmonton, Alberta
James M. Parker, Archivist

Purpose of the program: Oral history interviews with faculty and staff about university history.

UNIVERSITY OF BRITISH COLUMBIA LIBRARY
Special Collections Division
Vancouver 8, British Columbia
B. Stuart-Stubbs, University Librarian

Purpose of the program: Oral history interviews with old timers about labor history.

UNIVERSITY OF CALGARY
Department of History
Calgary, Alberta
D. J. Bercuson, Director

Purpose of the program: Oral history documenting labor in Winnipeg 1900-1920.

UNIVERSITY OF GUELPH
Department of History
Guelph, Ontario

Margaret Evans, Director

Purpose of the program: Oral history project to investigate local history.

UNIVERSITY OF MANITOBA
History Department
Winnipeg, Manitoba
J. E. Rea, Director

General information: Tapes: 12 interviews, transcribed.

Purpose of the program: Oral history interviews about Manitoba history with emphasis on Winnipeg.

UNIVERSITY OF NEW BRUNSWICK
Department of History
Fredricton, New Brunswick
Dominick Graham, Department of History

General information: Tapes: 25 hours, not transcribed.

Purpose of the program: Oral history of the Boer War and World War I.

UNIVERSITY OF NEW BRUNSWICK
Irving Library
Archives and Special Collections
Fredricton, New Brunswick
Joan Boone, Archivist

Purpose of the program: Oral history about the University of New Brunswick's scientific and literary activities.

UNIVERSITY OF PRINCE EDWARD ISLAND
c/o Extension Department
Charlottetown, Prince Edward Island
Sharon E. Cregier, Director

General information: Tapes: 18 tapes, not transcribed.

Purpose of the program: Oral history of songs, folklore, family, and local histories of the region.

UNIVERSITY OF SASKATCHEWAN
Saskatchewan Archives Board
Regina Campus
Regina, Saskatchewan
Allan R. Taylor, Archivist

General information: Tapes: 112 interviews, partially transcribed.

Purpose of the program: Oral history interviews with pioneers and notable citizens of Saskatchewan.

UNIVERSITY OF SASKATCHEWAN
Department of Anthropology and Archaeology
69 Arts Building
Saskatoon, Saskatchewan
Georgian C. Short, Director

Purpose of the program: Primarily concerned with oral history for its importance to ethnography and linguistics (interests are research and teaching).

UNIVERSITY OF VICTORIA
Department of History
Victoria, British Columbia
J. E. Hendrickson, Director

Purpose of the program: Oral history interviews about Canadian history.

UNIVERSITY OF VICTORIA

Department of Military History and Strategic Studies
Victoria, British Columbia
Reginald Roy, Director

General information: Tapes: 100 hours, partially transcribed.

Purpose of the program: Interviews with participants in World Wars I and II.

UNIVERSITY OF WESTERN ONTARIO

Althouse College of Education
London, Ontario
Pat McKeon, Chairman

General information: Tapes: 10 tapes.

Purpose of the program: Collection deals with Canadian education.

YORK UNIVERSITY

Department of History
Downsview, Ontario
J. Granatstein, History Department

Purpose of the program: Canadian politicians and the Conservative Party, 1956–1967.

YORK UNIVERSITY

Political Science Department
Downsview, Ontario
T. Hickin, Department of Political Science

General information: Tapes: 3 interviews.

Purpose of the program: Canada's role in the formation of NATO.

ISRAEL

THE HEBREW UNIVERSITY OF JERUSALEM

Institute of Contemporary Jewry
Giv'at Ram
Jerusalem, Israel
02/30211, ext. 256/7
G. Wigoder, Director; Aharon Kedar, Scientific Director

General information: 1960. Budget: $20,000. Tapes: Approx. 5000 hours, transcribed, preserved. Transcriptions: Approx. 100,000 pages, not edited. The interviewee may enter corrections on the final copy (he is encouraged to correct and not to rewrite).

Accessibility: Catalog. A detailed card catalog is kept in the archive in which persons, places, organizations, etc. mentioned in the interviews are card-indexed. Copies of transcribed tapes may be obtained through the *New York Times* microfilm collection (c/o Microfilming Corporation of America, Glen Rock, New Jersey 07452). If the nearest major library does not hold this series, researchers may order individual memoirs from the above address. For restrictions see individual listings under subjects.

Purpose of the program: The program concentrates on all aspects of the world Jewry and Israeli history.

Publications based on collection research:

Bauer, Yehda. *Flight and Rescue. Brichah.* New York: Random House, 1970.

Cohen, H. *Zionist Activity in Iraq.* Jerusalem, 1969.

Frisel, E. *The Zionist Movement in the U.S. 1891–1914.* Tel-Aviv, 1970.

Sagi, Nana. *"Illegal" Immigration—1945–1948, The Epic of Aliyah Bet.* Midstream, 1971.

Major collections:

JEWISH COMMUNITIES

1. The stand of German Jewry in the face of Nazi Persecution, 1933–1935. This project examines the anti-Jewish policy of the Third Reich and the relationship between the anti-Semitic decrees and the reaction of the German Jewry. The organizational and legal aspects, the political orientation of the Jewish organizations, and mutual aid are among the subjects touched upon (14 interviews, approx. 430 pages).

2. Participation of Jews in the Spanish Civil War. The project examines the reasons for the participation of Jews in the war and the organization of the International Brigades (4 interviews, approx. 100 pages).

3. Lithuanian Jewry between the two world wars. This project traces a number of aspects in the process of integration of the Jews in the independent state of Lithuania (1918–1940). These aspects influenced the attitudes and behavior of the Jews of Lithuania during the Holocaust period (15 interviews, approx. 500 pages).

4. The Zionist movement in the USSR 1917–1935. At the time of the February Revolution in Russia, the Zionist Movement emerged and began to act openly in the organization of the political parties, youth movements and activities connected with Palestine. Under the Bolsheviks, the movement began to go underground again as a result of the authorities' objection to most of its forms of organization (43 interviews, approx. 1000 pages).

5. Jewish nationalism and Israel in the Reform Movement in the United States. These interviews form a part of a comprehensive study on the attitude of the Reform Movement in America toward Zionism and a national solution of the Jewish problem (12 interviews, approx. 170 pages).

6. American Jewry (12 interviews, approx. 680 pages).

7. Jewish life in Latin America. The project includes a series of interviews on a number of aspects of Jewish life in Argentina and Brazil. Special attention is paid to Jewish settlement, Jewish communal life and Jewish education (8 interviews, approx. 180 pages).

8. The Izmir community. A description of the Izmir community, its organizations, institutions and community life; the changes which have come about during the past thirty years (2 interviews, approx. 80 pages).

9. The Jewish community in Egypt. The aim of this project is to provide a basis for research into the history of the Jewish community in Egypt in the twentieth century. The social and educational aspects have been stressed (6 interviews, approx. 400 pages).

10. Jewish life in Iraq. The aim of the project is to examine the political situation of Iraqi Jewry, the educational and cultural life, the status of women, attitudes to religion, Zionist activities, and immigration to Israel. In Iraq the Jews lived in a number of towns and villages; interviews, therefore, were held with persons from two large cities (Baghdad and Basra), from two small communities in the South (Amarah and Hilla), and from two towns in the North (Arbil and Zakko in Kurdistan and Kirkuk) (77 interviews, approx. 1410 pages).

11. The Jewish community of Iran; immigrants from Iran in Israel. Differences can be found in the political, economic

THE HEBREW UNIVERSITY OF JERUSALEM (cont.)

and cultural standards of the various Jewish communities in the countries of the Orient. The Jews of Iran differ from the Jews of other countries of the Orient and it was important to examine how they had integrated into Israel. This is the first in a series of research projects examining how Jews from the Oriental countries have settled in Israel (14 interviews, approx. 400 pages).

12. Changes in the communal life of the Jews of Bukhara 1900-1935. The project examines the changes within the Jewish communities of Central Asia during the years between the two World Wars. The changes relate to the legal, economic, and social status of the Jews during this period. Special attention is paid to Jewish education, the place of the Hebrew language in the educational system and public affairs, political organization, Zionist activities, and accounts of escapes and immigration to Palestine (13 interviews, approx. 200 pages).

13. Jews in the Far East (6 interviews, approx. 180 pages).

14. Individual interviews.

WORLD WAR II: THE HOLOCAUST: RESISTANCE AND RESCUE

1. The Joint (American Jewish Joint Distribution Committee). This project was undertaken as a part of a research project on the history of the A.J.D.C. 1929-1951 (in cooperation with the A.J.D.C.). It relates to the different aspects of the history of the A.J.D.C. in the U.S., in Europe and the Near and Middle East, its organizational and financial aspects, rescue and rehabilitation, and reconstructive projects. Special attention is devoted to the role of the A.J.D.C. during and after World War II (25 interviews, approx. 500 pages).

2. The rescue of Jews via Spain and Portugal during World War II. This project is concerned with the part played by the countries of the Iberian peninsula in the rescue of Jews during World War II. The project examines the objective possibilities of Spain and Portugal to rescue Jews and the extent to which the countries of the Iberian peninsula, encouraged by the Allies, utilized these possibilities or attempted to increase them. It deals also with the activities of the Jewish organizations in Spain and Portugal and with the organized activities of the relevant Jewish underground movements in France and Holland (48 interviews, approx. 800 pages).

3. The Jewish underground movement in wartime France. This project deals with the underground activities conducted by the various French-Jewish organizations including attempts to save Jews during World War II (16 interviews, approx. 500 pages).

4. Jews in the underground in Belgium, 1940-1944. A number of persons who had been active in the Belgian underground movement in World War II were interviewed within the framework of this project. The stress was laid on personal contacts with the underground movement, the activities of the Jewish Council in Belgium (A.J.B.), setting up of the Comité de Défense des Juifs; financing of activities, underground press and propaganda, contacts with other Jewish groups, the Jewish armed underground, contacts with the authorities' attitude of the church to the persecution of Jews (20 interviews, approx. 600 pages).

5. Hiding children in Belgium during World War II (4 interviews, 80 pages).

6. The rescue of children and youth from Germany, Czechoslovakia and Austria to (or through) the countries of Western Europe 1933-1940. A study of the ways in which Jewish children and youth were rescued from Germany, Czechoslovakia, and Austria and transferred to the countries of Western Europe (Belgium, Holland, France, Denmark, Sweden and Norway) in the years 1933-1940. Special attention was paid to persons who organized the rescue operations. The project also deals with the settlement of the children in the various countries to which they were brought (34 interviews, approx. 550 pages).

7. Polish-Jewish refugees in Russian-occupied Poland 1939-1941. When the Germans occupied Western Poland in September 1939, many of the Jews from that area fled to Eastern Poland which was under Russian occupation from that period until the German invasion of Russia in June 1941. These six interviews are concerned with the experiences of Jewish refugees in Western Poland during those years. They deal inter alia with Jewish life in Eastern Poland, the initial relief after escaping from the Germans, attitudes of the local Jews and of the local population toward the refugees, difficulties in adaptation and absorption, Jewish education in these areas, the economic position of the Jews, the life of the intelligentsia (6 interviews).

8. Cultural life and education activities in the Theresienstadt ghetto (1941-1945) and in the special ("family") camp for Theresienstadt Jews at Auschwitz (1943-1944). The project examines the work of teachers, youth leaders, and artists in the Theresienstadt ghetto and in the family camp in Auschwitz, the activities carried out in the children's block, and the variegated cultural life developed in the ghetto. One of the important aspects of this project is the conception of the purpose of this education as seen by those who taught the children in Theresienstadt and in Auschwitz (22 interviews, approx. 1450 pages).

9. Resistance to the "final solution" in Auschwitz. This project deals with the underground activities in the Auschwitz-Birkenau camps, reports of escapes and their effect and the vain efforts to achieve diplomatic and military operations for destroying the annihilation installations and the railway line to the camps (15 interviews, approx. 300 pages).

10. Belorussian Jewry during the Holocaust period. This project describes the life of the Jews of Belorussia during the period of conquest: the attitude of the population to them; the Jewish community of Minsk before and during the war; the underground in the Minsk ghetto and outside; methods of rescuing Jews; the partisan camps; the attitude of the partisans to the Jews among them. The interviews include the evaluation of the role of the Jews in the war against the Nazis (20 interviews, approx. 1000 pages).

11. Jewish resistance in Slovakia during World War II. The project collects information on Jewish underground activities in Slovakia during World War II. The persons interviewed include members of the Jewish underground movements and officials of the Slovakian Jewish community (45 interviews, approx. 1600 pages).

12. Migration of Jews from the Baltic countries during World War II to Central Asia and other regions of the U.S.S.R. In 1941 many Jews from Lithuania and Latvia were transferred to the U.S.S.R. as "disloyal citizens" just prior to the Nazi invasion, while others became refugees fleeing from the Nazis. Those who were not conscripted into the army were concentrated in Central Asia. The 15 interviews in this project examine activities carried out among the refugees, their attitude to recruitment into the army, and their contacts with Jews in other countries including Palestine. This project and the next two projects are part of a research on the participation of Lithuanian Jews in World War II (15 interviews).

13. Underground activities in the ghettos and partisan activities of the Lithuanian Jews during World War II. This is part of a research project examining the problems of resistance as experienced by the Jews of the Baltic countries during World War II. The project describes the underground activities in Saulyai, Vilna and other ghettos. The

interviews also reveal acts of resistance and partisan activities on the part of the "ordinary" Jews who were not organized. Their problems and those of the "organized" Jews in the forests of Lithuania and Belorussia are discussed in connection with their struggle to exist and to fight despite the powerful political factors which impeded them (62 interviews, approx. 2400 pages).

14. Jews in the Baltic units of the Red Army during World War II. During World War II a number of national units were set up within the Red Army consisting of refugees from countries conquered by the Germans with the purpose of participating in the struggle to liberate their countries. The Latvian Corps and especially the Lithuanian Division included a high percentage of Jewish soldiers (over 50 percent). The interviews are part of an extended research project on the position of the Jews of the Baltic countries during the Holocaust period. They concentrate mainly on Jewish life in these units, the social and formal status of the Jewish soldiers, their part in the fighting and other duties and their contacts with Jews in other countries including Palestine (79 interviews, approx. 3500 pages).

15. Contacts between the Yishuv (Palestinian Jewry) and the U.S.S.R. during World War II. These interviews were collected in connection with a research paper dealing with various aspects of wartime contacts between Palestinian Jewry and the U.S.S.R. and their emissaries (7 interviews, approx. 100 pages).

16. Contacts between the Yishuv (Palestinian Jewry) and the U.S.S.R. up to the establishment of the State of Israel. With the entry of the U.S.S.R. into the war in 1941, contacts were established between representatives of the Yishuv and Soviet representatives, in connection with current problems and with the role that the U.S.S.R. would play in international settlements after the war (3 interviews, approx. 150 pages).

17. Forced labor camps under the Nazi occupation in Tunisia. During the six months of Nazi occupation in Tunisia (November 1942–May 1943) every Tunisian Jew from 18 to 28 years old was sent to forced labor camps. The project describes the life in these camps (9 interviews, 560 pages).

18. Individual interviews.

THE ANTECEDENTS TO THE STATE OF ISRAEL

1. The Jewish Agency executive in London 1938-1948. The Jewish Agency in London during the decade starting 1938 was a nerve center at a crucial period in Jewish history. Relations with British statesmen played an important role both in the work on behalf of the establishment of the Jewish State and in the various attempts to rescue Jews from Europe. This period incorporates the MacDonald White Paper era, World War II, and the period of the struggle with the Labor Government culminating in the establishment of the State of Israel (8 interviews, approx. 400 pages).

2. The "Brichah" (organized escape) and the camps in Germany 1944-1948. Research project dealing with the mass movement of Jews out of eastern Europe to central and southern Europe, and its political consequences. The organization of the underground routes, through which large numbers of Jews were brought into Displaced Persons Centers in Europe, constitutes one of the most significant episodes in modern Jewish history (100 interviews, approx. 3650 pages).

3. The "Ha'apalah" ("illegal" immigration) from Italy 1945-1948. After World War II, when immigration to Palestine was virtually forbidden, the organization of the so called "illegal" immigration was undertaken in various European centers, of which one of the most important was Italy. The project traces the setting up and development of the group of active workers who laid the foundation of the Ha'apalah from Italy. It describes the organization of the work in Italy and in Palestine, the activities of the Palestinian emissaries, the assistance afforded by non-Jews and the experiences of a number of "illegal" immigrant ships (32 interviews, approx. 1000 pages).

THE HISTORY OF THE YISHUV (PALESTINIAN JEWRY)

1. Second Aliyah pioneers of the kibbutz and the formation of the kibbutz system. This project (which was undertaken in cooperation with the Union of the Kvutzot and the Kibbutzim-Ihud Ha-Kvutzot Veha-Kibbutzim) describes the role of Second Aliyah pioneers in the formation of several kibbutzim. Special attention was paid to social and cultural problems in the kibbutzim (7 interviews, approx. 350 pages).

2. The organization of the private sector in Palestine from the Balfour Declaration to the establishment of the State of Israel. These interviews follow the attempts at organization of the Jewish private sector in Palestine, in both the political and economic spheres. The subject covers local private sector organization in the moshavot, local councils, and the cities. The general object is to reconstruct the attempts at political organization on a national level of these circles (18 interviews, approx. 600 pages).

3. The organization of the Sephardim in Palestine (3 interviews, approx. 100 pages).

4. Extreme Orthodox Jewry in Palestine during the period of British rule. This research deals with that section of Orthodox Jewry which opposed Zionism for religious reasons. During the period of the British Mandate various approaches were developed by these circles toward the social and political development of Jewish society in Palestine. These varied from cooperation and integration into the Jewish community's political structure to complete isolationism from the community. The interviews show the development of the various approaches, in particular as they were expressed through formal organizations such as the Naturei Karta, Agudat Yisrael and Poalei Agudat Yisrael (10 interviews, approx. 250 pages).

5. Gedud Ha-Avoda (The Labor Brigade) 1920-1926. The project deals with the history of Gedud Ha-Avoda named after Joseph Trumpeldor, founded in 1920 by Third Aliyah settlers. The Gedud worked as a unit until the end of 1926. Special attention was paid to the political and social developments and the internal structure of the Gedud (12 interviews, approx. 500 pages).

6. The beginnings of the Ha-Poel Ha-Mizrachi movement in Palestine 1921-1928. The Ha-Poel Ha-Mizrachi Movement was established in Palestine after World War I as a movement for religious laborers and pioneer settlers within the framework of the Mizrachi World Center. Ha-Poel Ha-Mizrachi played an important role in the development of the Yishuv during that period. The interviews with leaders of the various trends in the movement at that time reflect the general line of its development and organization (11 interviews, approx. 1100 pages).

7. The Irgun Tzevai Leumi (Etzel) and Lohamei Herut Israel (Lehi) organizations 1929-1948. The role played by the underground movements in the struggle for statehood in the years up to 1948 is still today the subject of bitter controversy and difference of opinion. This series of interviews has gathered material from the leaders of these movements. They have described how they saw the series of events in those critical years, with special emphasis on the internal history of two underground movements—the Etzel and the Lehi (16 interviews, approx. 2300 pages).

8. Revisionist "Ha'apalah" ("illegal" immigration) 1934-1939. The project describes the Revisionist "illegal" immi-

THE HEBREW UNIVERSITY OF JERUSALEM (cont.)

gration up to the outbreak of World War II on land and on sea. Stress is laid on the development of the idea of "illegal" immigration and the internal struggles around the idea (12 interviews, approx. 400 pages).

YOUTH MOVEMENTS

1. Jewish youth movements in Czechoslovakia between the two World Wars. Jewish youth movements constituted one of the most active and vital elements in Europe between the two World Wars. This project concentrates on the ideological development of the movements in Czechoslovakia from their origins through the interwar period. Due to the many activities of members of these movements in various spheres of Jewish life, information has also been obtained on different aspects of Jewish life in Czechoslovakia and on settlement in Palestine (28 interviews, approx. 1650 pages).

2. The Netzach (Zionist pioneering youth) movement in Latvia between the two World Wars. "Netzach" was one of the many Jewish youth movements between the two World Wars. This project reconstructs the history of the movement in Latvia (and also in Estonia). Many former members were interviewed both individually and in groups (36 interviews, approx. 750 pages).

3. The He-Haluz movement and agricultural training in Poland between the two World Wars. This project (which was undertaken in cooperation with Yivo U.S.A.) contains interviews with persons who spent some time in the agricultural training farms (Hachsharah) in Poland between 1937–1939. This subject will serve as part of a research project on the struggle of the Jews of Poland as a national minority living under pressure from the majority (9 interviews, approx. 50 pages).

CULTURE AND EDUCATION

1. Authors and their work (4 interviews, approx. 100 pages).
2. Higher education among Iraqi Jews. While carrying out the research project on the history of the Jews of Iraq (described earlier), the need became apparent to study higher education separately. Questionnaires were sent to hundreds of Jews born in Iraq who hold academic degrees, asking for details of their studies. The project was rounded out by interviews with a number of persons holding academic degrees on aspects of the subject which could not have been covered in a short questionnaire (12 interviews, approx. 120 pages).
3. The Greenberg Seminary for Teachers of the Diaspora. The Greenberg Seminary for Teachers of the Diaspora was established in 1952. The aims of the Seminary are: to give higher Jewish education to candidates for teaching in the Diaspora, and to create a young Jewish intelligentsia (3 interviews, approx. 90 pages).
4. Jewish schools in Transylvania between the two World Wars. With the annexation of Transylvania to Rumania in 1918, the Jewish schools were given a new status within the general education system. High schools were set up and a wide network of Jewish elementary schools established. This project deals with the struggle to establish the language of instruction (Hungarian, Rumanian or Hebrew), the ties between the school and the community, internal education problems, the attitude of the authorities to the schools, and the political struggle to obtain rights (5 interviews, approx. 90 pages).

BIOGRAPHICAL INTERVIEWS (9 interviews, approx. 550 pages).

PROJECTS IN PROGRESS 1969/1970 (available from Hebrew University).

REPUBLIC OF IRELAND

UNIVERSITY COLLEGE
Department of Irish Folklore
Belfield
Dublin 4, Ireland
Bo Almqvist

Purpose of the program: Emphasis on oral material relating to all aspects of Irish folk tradition.

UNITED KINGDOM

ABBOT HALL ART GALLERY
Kendal, England
E. M. Burkett, Director

General information: Five interviews have been recorded with rural craftsmen of the Lake District.

CARDIGANSHIRE JOINT LIBRARY
Aberystwyth, Wales
Alun Edwards, Director

General information: 1968. Tapes: 170 hours, edited.

Purpose of the program: To record local history material, including public lectures and addresses.

CASTLE MUSEUM
Department of Social History
Norwich, England
Bridget Yates, Director

General information: Tapes: 30 hours, partially indexed, transcribed.

Purpose of the program: A project has been set up to record information about craftsmen and agriculture workers in the Norwich area. There is also a special interest in the history of the Norfolk iron foundries.

CENTRE OF ASIAN STUDIES
Laundress Lane
Cambridge CB2 1SD, England
(0223) 65621, ext. 202
T. M. Thatcher, Bibliographer and Archivist

General information: 1968. Tapes: approx. 120 hours, preserved but not edited. No interlibrary loan. Restricted for scholarly use by bona fide scholars only or written application, with references and assurance of acknowledgement.

Purpose of the program: The program forms part of the archive collection at the Centre of Asian Studies. It is not distinct from the collection. The area is South Asia, particularly India, Pakistan, Bangladesh, and Sri Lanka. The topics are related to the period of British rule in India.

ESSEX UNIVERSITY
Department of Sociology
Colchester CO4 3SQ, England
(0206) 44144
Paul Thompson, Director

General information: 1968. Budget: £18,000 over 5 years. Tapes: 1500 hours, preserved but not edited. Transcriptions: 20,000 pages.

Accessibility: Permission of director required.

Purpose of the program: Interviews about family life and work experience in Britain before 1918.

HIGH WYCOMBE PUBLIC LIBRARY
Queen Victoria Road
High Wycombe, Bucks, England
(High Wycombe) 23981
I. G. Sparkes, Librarian and Curator

General information: 1955. Budget: £150. Tapes: 35 hours, preserved, edited.

Accessibility: Catalog in progress. Index to overall collection in progress. No interlibrary loan. Original tapes not loaned, but reel to reel tapes available.

Purpose of the program: Collection of reminiscences of workers in the chair industry and lectures on local history; also dialect (Bucks) associated with a small slide and film collection.

Major collections:
1. Furniture collection (35 hours, preserved and edited).

HULL UNIVERSITY
Department of Economic and Social History
Hull, England
John Saville, Director

Purpose of the program: Recording of personalities connected with the labor movement.

IMPERIAL WAR MUSEUM
Department of Sound Records
Lambeth Road
London SE 1, England
(01) 735-8922
David Lance, Director

General information: 1972. Tapes: 900 hours, in process of being cataloged and indexed.

Purpose of the program: To record the memoirs of people who have been associated with warfare in the twentieth century.

INSTITUTE OF COMMONWEALTH STUDIES
Rhodes House Library
Colonial Records Project
20-21 St. Giles
Oxford, England

General information: 1967. Tapes: 50 interviews.

Purpose of the program: Recollections of distinguished Colonial civil servants and politicians.

INSTITUTE OF CORNISH STUDIES
Trevenson House
Poole, Redruth
Cornwall, England
Charles Thomas, Director

General information: 1973.

Purpose of the program: To promote studies of man in the regional setting of Cornwall and the Scilly Isles.

KENT UNIVERSITY
Faculty of Social Science
Canterbury, Kent, England
Theo Barker, Director

Purpose of the program: Interviewing for memories of before 1900, with particular reference to food, clothes, the home, school, shopping, health, leisure, and parental attitudes.

LANCASTER UNIVERSITY
Department of History
Bailrigg, Lancaster, England
(Lancaster) 65201
J. D. Marshall, Director

General information: 1972. Budget: £670. Tapes: Several hundred hours, partially preserved and edited. Transcriptions: 1500 pages.

Accessibility: Index in preparation. No restrictions.

Purpose of the program: To study domestic life in the towns of Barrow and Lancaster within the period of living memory; the leadership of labor movements in the same towns and period.

LANCASTER POLYTECHNIC
Department of Social and Economic History
Priory Street
Coventry, England
Kenneth Richardson, Director

General information: Tapes: 60 hours.

Purpose of the program: Emphasis is on the twentieth century history of Coventry. Topics covered include local industry, apprenticeship, and economic development.

LYMM AND DISTRICT LOCAL HISTORY SOCIETY
72 Mill Lane
Heat Ley, Lymm, Cheshire, England
(Lymm) 3621

General information: 1966. Tapes: 40 interviews. Transcriptions: 120 pages.

Accessibility: Index to overall collection: brief synopsis.

Purpose of the program: General selection of living and working conditions in local rural community.

MUSEUM OF ENGLISH RURAL LIFE
University of Reading
Whitenights, Reading, England
Andrew Jewell, Director

Purpose of the program: Interviews to obtain information associated with the objects and records which it has acquired; also interviews in connection with field work on rural crafts.

NATIONAL MARITIME MUSEUM
Greenwich, London SE 10, England
(01) 858-4422
Campbell MacMurray, Program Director

General information: 1970. Tapes: 450 hours.

Accessibility: No catalog. Indexed. The material is at present restricted to the collector.

Purpose of the program: A labor, social, and industrial history of life and "living" at the workplace—the merchant ship. The years covered are from 1890 to 1939.

NATIONAL MUSEUM OF ANTIQUITIES OF SCOTLAND
Scottish Country Life Section
Queen Street
Edinburgh, Scotland
Alexander Fenton, Director

General information: 1960. Tapes: 8 interviews.

Purpose of the program: Emphasis is on the field of Scottish rural life and work.

NEWCASTLE UNIVERSITY
Department of Economics
Newcastle-Upon-Tyne, England
Norman McCord, Director

Purpose of the program: Interviews relating to the labor movement in the north east of England.

ROYAL AIR FORCE
Air Historical Branch
Queen Annes Chambers
3 Dean Farrar Street
London SW 1 England
(01) 930-7022, ext. 7032
Group Captain E. B. Haslam, Director

General information: 1972.

Accessibility: No catalog. Indexed. National (UK) Security gradings may be given to some interviews and narrations.

Purpose of the program: Interviews with prominent and usually senior officers and officials of the Royal Air Force and Air Force Department, mainly on or after retirement from active duty.

RUSKIN COLLEGE
Oxford University
Oxford, England
Raphael Samuel, Director

General information: Tapes: 35 interviews.

Purpose of the program: Interviews with old inhabitants of Headington Quarry giving a picture of social life in this laboring community.

SHEFFIELD UNIVERSITY
Archives of Cultural Tradition
Sheffield S10 2TN, England
(Sheffield) 78555, ext. 211
J. A. Widdowson, Director

General information: 1964. Budget: £450. Tapes: 180 hours, preserved, partially edited.

Accessibility: No restrictions.

Purpose of the program: A general survey of language and cultural tradition.

SUNDERLAND POLYTECHNIC
Education Department
Chester Road
Sunderland, England
(0783) 76191
Peter Liddle, Director

General information: 1967. Tapes: 1000 hours, preserved but not edited.

Accessibility: Catalog. Indexed. No restrictions.

Purpose of the program: Covers various personal experiences during the period 1914–1918.

UNIVERSITY COLLEGE OF SWANSEA
South Wales Miners Library
50 Sketty Rd.
Swansea, Glamorgan, Wales
(0792) 57366
R. Merfyn Jones, Senior Research Worker

General information: 1972. Budget: £11,000 for three years. Tapes: 230 hours, preserved but not edited.

Accessibility: Indexed.

Purpose of the program: To collect oral evidence relating to the history of the social, economic, and political life of the South Wales coalfield.

UNIVERSITY OF EDINBURGH
Department of History
Edinburgh, Scotland

Purpose of the program: Emphasis on the social history of coal mining since 1890.

Purpose of the program: Recordings have been made with senior military officers and civil servants who worked in India between the two World Wars. Recollections of the suffragette movement, domestic service and the European "colony" in Morocco before 1912 have also been recorded.

UNIVERSITY OF EDINBURGH
School of Scottish Studies
27 George Square
Edinburgh EH8 9LD, Scotland
(031) 667-1011, ext. 6674.
John MacQueen, Director

General information: 1951. Budget: £10,000. Tapes: 3000 hours, preserved but not edited. Transcriptions: 12,000 pages.

Accessibility: No catalog. Indexed. Access to all collections is restricted, but every effort is made to satisfy individual inquiries.

Purpose of the program: Collection and analysis of Scottish oral tradition. Much emphasis is laid on Gaelic Scotland, but there are considerable collections for other areas.

UNIVERSITY OF EDINBURGH
Science Studies Unit
34 Buccleuch Place
Edinburgh EH8 9JT, Scotland
(031) 667-1011, ext. 6245
D. O. Edge, Director Science Studies Unit

General information: 1969. Tapes: 30 hours, preserved, edited. Transcriptions: 600 pages. Prior agreement of interviewees required before access to tapes or transcripts can be allowed.

Accessibility: No catalog. Not indexed. No interlibrary loan.

Purpose of the program: Interviews with scientists involved with the growth of radio astronomy.

Major collection:
1. Pioneer radio astronomers. Those interviewed include Sir Bernard Lovell. (30 hours, 600 pages, edited).

UNIVERSITY OF LEEDS
Institute of Dialect and Folk Life Studies
School of English
Leeds, Yorkshire, England
(0532) 681109, ext. 6285
Stewart F. Sanderson, Director

General information: 1953. Tapes: 280 hours, preserved, edited.

Accessibility: No catalog. Indexed. No interlibrary loan. Bona fide students are allowed access and use by arrangement in each individual case.

WELSH FOLK MUSEUM
Department of Oral Traditions and Dialects
St. Fagans
Cardiff, Wales
Vincent Phillips, Director

General information: 1957. Tapes: 4500 tapes.

Purpose of the program: Emphasis on the whole field of folk life research; special attention is given to agriculture, crafts, domestic life, folklore, and dialect vocabularies.

YORK UNIVERSITY
Department of Economics and Related Studies
Heslington, York, England
Christopher Storm-Clark, Director

General information: 1969. Tapes: 150 hours, indexed.

Purpose of the program: Emphasis on the social history of